DICTIONARY

OF

INDUSTRIAL

ARCHAEOLOGY

To Sheila

DICTIONARY
OF
INDUSTRIAL
ARCHAEOLOGY

WILLIAM JONES

FOREWORD BY MARILYN PALMER

SUTTON PUBLISHING LIMITED

First published in the United Kingdom in 1996 by
Sutton Publishing Ltd · Phoenix Mill · Far Thrupp · Stroud · Gloucestershire

British Library Cataloguing in Publication Data

Jones, W.R.
 Dictionary of Industrial Archaeology
 I. Title
 609.41

ISBN 0-7509-1021-6

Typeset in 9/10 pt Times.
Typesetting and origination by
Sutton Publishing Limited.
Printed in Great Britain by
Butler & Tanner, Frome, Somerset.

CONTENTS

LIST OF FIGURES

FOREWORD

Industrial archaeology is a relatively new branch of archaeology, dating back to the 1960s when the world significance of Britain's industrial heritage first began to be appreciated. Its study was conducted mainly on an amateur basis, with numbers of county groups being established which compiled gazetteers of sites in their areas and campaigned for the preservation of the most outstanding examples. At the national level, similar activity was carried out by the Industrial Monuments survey, who succeeded in getting statutory protection for various important industrial monuments although many were needlessly demolished. This enthusiasm, however, was not followed by the introduction of systematic training in the subject. No university departments of Archaeology embraced the new discipline, but the Centre for the Study of the History of Technology at the University of Bath did so after the National Record of Industrial Monuments was transferred there in 1965. Industrial archaeology flourished in WEA and evening classes, but the first formal training in the subject at postgraduate level was provided by the Ironbridge Institute in collaboration with the University of Birmingham. Even now, undergraduate courses are rare, although there is now a focus in the East Midlands at the University of Leicester and Nene College, Northamptonshire. Trained industrial archaeologists are therefore few and far between.

Yet the study of Britain's industrial heritage is now recognized as of prime importance. English Heritage's policy statement on industrial archaeology (September 1995) states that it 'recognizes the unique significance of the country's industrial heritage and will complete theme studies of industrial buildings and monuments under the Monuments Protection Programme and List Review in order to identify important sites and structures which deserve to be retained and recorded'. The three Royal Commissions on Historical Monuments in England, Scotland and Wales also carry out both emergency recording and thematic surveys of industrial sites, such as textile mills, railway workshops, collieries and, more recently, defence structures, while Cadw and Historic Scotland have been faced with the particular problems of the closure and demolition of collieries and the rehabilitation of derelict land, with consequent loss of archaeology. Yet few of their fieldworkers have any previous knowledge of the subject, and one can only admire their ability to come to terms with whole new areas of study very rapidly indeed. Within RCHME, for example, archaeologists and architectural historians have become acquainted with the processes of textile manufacture, the working of collieries, the development of farm buildings and the manufacture of explosives, yet have to move on from one area of expertise to another as the nature of their work changes. This means they have to keep increasing their vocabulary to include a new range of technical terms.

Every branch of archaeology – indeed, of academic study – has its own jargon. The 'new archaeology' of the 1960s has been particularly prone to jargon, a trend satirized in *Bluff your Way in Archaeology*, in which the authors suggest that the way to appear knowledgeable is to learn a few key words and string them together with appropriate jargon, which no one else understands either! Unfortunately, accurate description and interpretation of industrial sites does demand understanding of a great range of technical terminology, a fact recognized by English Heritage who have instructed their consultants for their Industrial Monuments Protection Programme to include definitions of terms used in the industries on which they are reporting. What archaeologists need is a quick reference guide to the terms they are likely to come across, and a clear definition of what they mean. A momentous step in this direction was taken by the publication of *The Blackwell Encyclopaedia of Industrial Archaeology*, edited by Barrie Trinder (1992). This is a guide to the monuments, settlements, landscape and museums holding artefacts of the industrial societies which evolved in the West from the mid-eighteenth century, but it does include some definitions of terms in its descriptions of types of structures. The present *Dictionary of Industrial Archaeology* does not have the geographical spread of an encyclopaedia but is concerned to explain the terminology used in extractive, construction and manufacturing industries, and the development of transport, mainly of the eighteenth and nineteenth centuries in Britain. Bill Jones is an engineer by training and was involved for many years providing technical advice to overseas factories for the company for which he worked. It is perhaps this which has enabled him to present the reader with clear definitions which are mercifully jargon-free. Many of the entries provide references to books or articles from a wide variety of journals which amplify the subject under discussion, a most valuable feature of the book. Textual figures further clarify some of the complex technical detail. This *Dictionary* will be invaluable, for example, to the contract archaeologist suddenly faced with the remains of a lime kiln or ore calciner on a site on which he has to write a report in a short space of time. It will also assist the county society engaged in listing sites for Sites and Monuments Records, and can usefully be employed in conjunction with the IRIS Handbook, *Recording the Industrial Heritage* (AIA, 1993) which lists, but does not define, terms for sites and components of sites. Bill Jones has put a lifetime of experience at the service of every industrial archaeologist and deserves our gratitude for his monumental work.

Dr Marilyn Palmer
University of Leicester

INTRODUCTION

Industrial archaeology has been defined by the Association for Industrial Archaeology as 'a period study embracing the tangible evidence of technological, economic, and social development from the onset of industrialization to the recent past'. It is therefore an ongoing subject, since the technology and industries of today will become the industrial archaeology of the future.

The onset of industrialization in Britain is generally accepted to have happened in the early 18th century. But how recent is 'the recent past'? Is it, for example, thirty years ago, the rolling cut-off date for listing monuments of national importance used by the heritage bodies? Or should it be an earlier date? Thirty years ago is too near the present day to attract the attention of industrial archaeologists. For the purpose of compiling this dictionary, 'the recent past' has been interpreted in an archaeological sense, and a cut-off date chosen of around the late Victorian era. The period covered thus includes that known as the Industrial Revolution, a period of only four generations during which many seminal inventions and developments took place which changed Britain from a rural, domestic-based, hand-crafted economy, into an urban, factory-based, power using one. It is also that period which is studied most by the majority of industrial archaeologists, and may be regarded as the 'classical' period of the subject.

This dictionary attempts to provide industrial archaeologists and other interested readers with an easy-to-use reference guide, explaining the terminology of the subject. The principal terms used in the extractive, construction and manufacturing industries of the 18th and 19th centuries are covered in some depth, together with those of contemporary modes of transport by road, rail and inland water. The impact industrialization had on the working and living conditions of ordinary, wage-earning people is included. Machines of the time are described and their operation explained, in some cases accompanied by line diagrams, while short historical backgrounds of the more important machines and processes are given. Patent numbers and dates of many inventions have been included, so that the more serious student of the history of technology may obtain more details from a Patents Library. The cross-referencing system and the mini-bibliographies appended to many of the entries are intended to guide the reader to further sources of information.

A dictionary such as this cannot hope to be fully comprehensive when dealing with a wide ranging subject such as industrial archaeology. Some industries which are important today were only beginning to emerge near the end of the 19th century: the heavy chemicals industry and electricity generation and distribution are examples. The chemicals industry has left few monuments of merit from its early days: firms demolished and replaced outdated plants as the technology and complexity of the industry rapidly changed; and those early sites that do remain lack the romantic and nostalgic appeal of windmills, steam and canals, and so in general are not studied by industrial archaeologists unless they have a particular interest in that industry. (Those readers seeking explanations of the terminology of the chemicals industry may wish to consult J. Daintith (ed.), *The Concise Dictionary of Chemistry*, Oxford University Press, 1985; electricity terms are dealt with in K.G. Jackson, *Dictionary of Electrical Engineering*, Butterworth, 1981.

No claims are made for originality in the data here presented. Information and facts have been gathered together from many scattered sources too numerous to acknowledge here. Much has come from the books listed in the bibliographies. In particular, however, I would like to record my appreciation of the resources which I used extensively at Bolton Central Library and Manchester Patents Library, and the publications of the Association for Industrial Archaeology from which much information was culled. Workers' Educational Association tutors at the adult evening classes and weekend study courses that I attended over many years were also sources of inspiration. Finally I am indebted to the editorial staff at Sutton Publishing Limited for much helpful advice.

If there are any errors of fact or omissions in the following pages, they are entirely my responsibility, and it is hoped they are not too serious.

Bill Jones

HOW TO USE THIS DICTIONARY

ALPHABETIZATION

All entries are arranged in alphabetical sequence, letter by letter, not word by word, including acronyms and single-letter compound entries. Most entries are in the singular unless the plural is the form most used (e.g. rails). Where there are alternative spellings, which may indicate an older usage likely to be met in the literature of the 18th and early 19th centuries, or a regional variant, these are included either after the headword or in the text. Some common words have special industrial or technical meanings, in which case only the narrower meaning is described here: for example, the noun 'back' is used to describe a large vat used in the brewing and other industries.

NUMBERING OF SENSES

Where a headword has more than one sense, the different meanings are given separately and the definitions numbered, to avoid confusion.

DERIVATIONS

Derivations of words are given where they are of interest, or aid the understanding of a word; for example, this particularly applies to names of fabrics, which are often Anglicized versions of the placename where the cloth was first made or copied from. Some words used in the mining industry are of German origin, and some iron-making terms can be traced back to the Flemish language.

CROSS REFERENCES

SMALL CAPITALS are used in the text to indicate a cross-reference; '*see*' and '*see also*' are used to indicate other relevant entries or Figures.

UNITS OF MEASUREMENT

Imperial Units have been used throughout, since they are contemporary with the period this book covers. Metric or SI conversion factors will be found on page xvi, together with a table for converting £ *s d* to decimal coinage.

COUNTIES

The names of the old counties or shires in use before reorganization in 1974 have been used.

PERSONAL NAMES

It was common practice years ago for sons to be given the same forenames as their father. This can lead to historical confusion, and where father, son and in some cases grandson all have the same names, the eldest is indicated by (I) placed after his name, the son by (II), and so on. Where possible, the actual dates of birth and death are given. The Darby dynasty of iron masters is a case in point: there were four successive Abraham Darbys connected with the family Coalbrookdale enterprise.

PATENT NUMBERS AND DATES

All patents quoted up to the year 1852 relate to England and Wales only, since before that date if protection was required in Scotland and Ireland also, separate patents had to be filed in those countries. Scottish and Irish patent numbers are not quoted here. The Patent Law Amendment Act 1852 consolidated the separate patents into one, so patents quoted after 1852 apply to all four countries.

DATING OF ENTRIES

In general, the use of the present tense to describe machines, processes etc., indicates that they (or in some cases modern developments from them) are still in use. However, in many instances it is impossible to give a first or last date of use with any accuracy.

ABBREVIATIONS

AC	alternating current		**km**	kilometre(s)
b.	born		**l**	litre(s)
B.Th.U.	British Thermal Unit(s)		**£**	(libra) pound(s) money
C	Centigrade or Celsius		**lb**	(libra) pound weight
cap.	(caputitis) chapter		**lbs**	pounds weight
cc	cubic centimetres		**m**	metre(s)
cfm	cubic feet per minute		**min.**	minute(s)
C.I.	cast iron		**mm**	millimetre(s)
cm	centimetre		**mph**	miles per hour
cu.	cubic		**NTS**	not to scale
cwt	hundredweight (112 lb)		**OS**	Ordnance Survey
d.	died		**p**	penny, pence
d	(denarii) penny or pence (pre 1971)		**p.a.**	(per annum) per year
DC	direct current		**Proc.**	Proceedings
F	Fahrenheit		**psi**	pounds per square inch
fl.	flourished (was active)		**rpm**	revolutions per minute
fpm	feet per minute		*s*	shilling(s) (pre 1971)
ft	foot, feet		**sec.**	second(s)
GR	grid reference		**SI**	Système International
HMSO	Her Majesty's Stationery Office		**Soc.**	Society
hp	horsepower		**sq.**	square
hr	hour(s)		**tpsi**	tons per square inch
IA	industrial archaeology		**Trans.**	Transactions
in	inch(es)		**vol.**	volume
Inst.	Institute, Institution		**W**	watt(s)
kg	kilogramme(s)		**W.I.**	wrought iron

Units of Measurement and Conversion Factors

IMPERIAL UNITS				**METRIC/SI UNITS**
Linear measure				
1 in			=	25.40 mm
1 ft	=	12 in	=	0.3048 m
1 yd	=	3 ft	=	0.9144 m
1 fathom	=	6 ft	=	approx. 1.829 m
1 chain	=	66 ft	=	approx. 20.12 m
1 mile	=	5280 ft	=	approx. 1.609 km
Square measure				
1 sq.in			=	approx. 6.451 sq. cm
1 sq.ft	=	144 sq. in	=	approx. 0.0929 sq. m
Cubic measure				
1 cu.in			=	approx. 16.39 cc
Capacity measure				
1 pint			=	approx. 0.568 l
1 gallon	=	8 pints	=	approx. 4.546 l
1 bushel	=	64 pints	=	approx. 36.37 l
Weight				
1 lb			=	approx. 0.4536 kg
1 stone	=	14 lb	=	approx. 6.35 kg
1 hundredweight (cwt)	=	112 lb	=	approx. 50.80 kg
1 ton	=	2240 lb	=	approx. 1016 kg or 1.016 tonnes

Pressure/stress

1 inch water gauge (in.w.g.)	=	approx. 0.0362 psi	=	approx. 249.6 newtons/sq. m (N/sq. m)
1 foot head (water)	=	approx. 0.434 psi	=	approx. 2.995 kilo-newtons/sq. m (kN/sq. m)
1 pound per square in (psi)	=	approx. 2.3 ft head (water)	=	approx. 6895 N/sq. m
1 ton per square in (tpsi)	=	2240 psi	=	approx. 15.445 mega-newtons/sq. m (MN/sq. m)
1 bar	=	approx. 14.51 psi	=	100,000 N/sq. m
1 atmosphere (atm) (at sea level)	=	approx. 14.7 psi	=	101,325 N/sq. m

Note: A newton/sq. m is also known as a pascal.

Energy and power

1 foot-pound (ft lb)		=	approx. 1.356 joules (J)
1 horsepower (hp)	= 550 ft lb/sec	=	approx. 746 joules/sec (J/s) or 746 watts (W)

Temperature

To convert °F to °C, subtract 32 and multiply by 0.5555.

Heat

1 British Thermal Unit (B.Th.U)　　　=　　　approx. 1.055 kilo-joules (kJ)

Money before decimalization (pre 1971)

				Today's money
* 1 farthing	=	$^1/_4 d$	=	approx. 0.104 penny (p)
1 penny (*d*)			=	approx. 0.416p
* 1 shilling (*s* or 1/-)	=	12*d*	=	5p
* 1 florin	=	2*s*	=	10p
* 1 half crown	=	30*d* (2*s* 6*d*)	=	12.5p
1 pound (£)	=	20*s*	=	100p or £1
* 1 sovereign (sov.)	=	20*s* or £1	=	100p or £1
1 guinea (g.)	=	21*s* (£1/1/-)	=	£1.05

* no longer in use today.

A

abb an old name for the WEFT in woven cloth, although it has also been used for the WARP. It is probably a derivation of WEB, another old word for the weave of a cloth, and is a dialect word once used mainly in the West Country.

accommodation bridge a bridge across a canal carrying minor roads and farm tracks. Most such bridges are single arched, and to keep their cost down the canal is usually reduced to one boat width under the bridge. A sloping access from the towpath up onto the roadway is normally provided, and the towpath usually continues under the bridge, although in some instances it stops short of it. Cantilever-built bridges have a central narrow gap left at the top of the arch through which a tow rope can be passed to save unhitching the horse where the towpath does not pass under the bridge. Canal companies each had their own particular design of accommodation bridge, and bridges were usually numbered consecutively from the start of the canal. *See also* ROVING BRIDGE.

accumulator 1. a pressure-maintaining device in a HYDRAULIC POWER system. A dead-weight accumulator comprises a large vertical hollow cylinder in which a heavily weighted sliding ram or piston presses down onto the water below it. The lower end of the cylinder is in direct communication with the water in the hydraulic main and pumping system. When the pressure in the main reaches its maximum, the sliding ram is at the top of its stroke, and trip gear either bypasses water if the pumps are kept running, or the pumps are stopped. As water is used somewhere in the system, the ram gradually descends, maintaining the pressure on the water until at a certain point before it reaches the bottom of its stroke, either the bypass valve is closed and the pumps take over, or the pumps start up and commence applying pressure to the system. Usually a deadweight accumulator and its guides, etc., are contained in a tall brick tower. An accumulator therefore relieves the hydraulic pumps of a constant load, and provides a small reservoir of water under pressure for the system, i.e. it 'accumulates' pressure energy for later use in the system.

The invention of the hydraulic accumulator is attributed to William George Armstrong (1810–1900) of Newcastle in about 1851. It was first used at New Holland on the Humber estuary to operate cranes and to raise and lower platforms connecting the railway station to a floating ferry landing stage. A hydraulic pressure of 600 p.s.i. was used.

2. the old name for a rechargeable battery which stores electricity. The early secondary lead-acid cells owe their origin to the discovery in 1859 by a Frenchman, Gaston Planté (1834–89), of a reversible electrochemical cell, which after discharge could have its original chemical composition regained by passing an electric current in the opposite direction, i.e. it could be charged, or 'accumulate' electricity. The word came into use about 1880 at the same time that the accumulator industry started in Britain. It is sometimes loosely called a BATTERY, although strictly that term should be applied only to a primary, non-rechargeable electrical energy source.

acid chamber process, *see* LEAD CHAMBER PROCESS

acid egg an egg-shaped pressure vessel from which acids and corrosive liquids may be pumped up to a higher level by compressed air. It comprises a corrosion-resistant vessel (e.g. lead-lined cast iron) into which the liquid is emptied from large glass vessels or carboys, etc.; when the lid is fastened on, compressed air is admitted through a permanently attached connection to blow the contents out through a corrosion-resistant pipeline. Harrison Blair (1810–70) of Kearsley, near Manchester, is usually credited with its invention; acid eggs are used in the chemical industry, and by other users of acid such as bleachers.

acid lining a type of refractory lining used in an acid steel-making furnace and early BESSEMER converters for resisting high temperatures and attack by acidic SLAGS. Acid linings are obtained from oxides of siliceous materials such as GANNISTER. An acid lining is built up from such materials in brick form, frequently known as silica bricks.

A refractory lining with opposite chemical characteristics for use in furnaces employing the basic process of steel-making uses BASIC LININGS (*see* STEEL MANUFACTURE).

acid steel the first type of cheap steel produced by Henry Bessemer (1813–98) in 1856. It was so called because the CONVERTER in which it was made, had an acid silica refractory lining. Only high-grade iron, with no phosphorous content, could be used successfully. Eventually, a change in the lining to a basic variety enabled phosphoric ores to be used, the steel made by the later process being known as BASIC STEEL. *See also* ACID LINING, BASIC LINING, BASIC STEEL, BESSEMER STEEL.

Acts of Parliament important documentary sources of information for industrial archaeologists. For example, canals and railways had to have an Act empowering compulsory purchase of land over which they were to be built, and plans showing the route are included in the Act; while the regulation of industry by the State was through a number of Acts stipulating working conditions. After a Bill has passed both Houses of Parliament, it becomes law on receipt of the Royal Assent, and is added to the Statute Book. It remains in force until it is amended or repealed. An Act has a title, and until 1962 was dated with reference to the regnal year of the sovereign when it was passed, and to the Parliamentary session concerned. After 1962 the system of dating was changed to that of the historical or calendar year.

Titles. Some Acts have long, cumbersome titles, and are generally known by short versions, or in some cases by the name of the sponsor. For example, a well-known Act passed in 1802 affecting the textile industry, has the title 'An Act for the Preservation of the Health and Morals of Apprentices and Others, employed in Cotton and other Mills, and Cotton and other Factories'. This is known briefly as the Health and Morals of Apprentices Act, or as the First Factory Act.

Dating. An Act might be quoted in a reference as 42, Geo. III, cap. 87. This means that the Act was passed in the 42nd year of the reign of George III, and that it has a Parliamentary session or chapter number 87. Each regnal year commences on the anniversary of the day of accession of the sovereign; if the anniversary date occurs during a Parliamentary session, then two years are quoted, for example 8 and 9, Vict. c.118.

A complication affects Acts passed between 1 January and 24 March for all years prior to 1752. Until then, two calendar years were in use in England: the Civil or Legal Year (to which Acts properly belong), and the Historical Year. The Legal Year began on 25 March (Lady Day), and the Historical Year on 1 January. Thus a Legal date of, say, 2 March 1720, was 2 March 1721 in the Historical Year. This can account for the discrepancy of one year for the same pre-1752 Act as quoted by different authors, depending whether the Legal or the Historical Year is being used for Acts which were passed between 1 January and 24 March. The use of the Historical Year for all Acts enables them to be correctly related to other events. Although the regnal system is not used in this book, the following table gives the accession dates for each sovereign from Elizabeth I to Edward VII – the period most likely to be of interest to industrial archaeologists – so that the Historical Year may be worked out. Thus, the historical years for the two examples quoted earlier are: 42 Geo. III. cap 87 is 1760 plus 42 (1802); and 8 & 9 Vict. cap. 118 is 1837 plus 8 (1845) and plus 9 (1846), the Queen's accession anniversary having occurred during the Parliamentary session.

Sovereign's name and occasional abbreviation	Accession date (Historical year)
Elizabeth I. (Eliz.)	17 Nov. 1558
James I. (Jac.)	23 Mar. 1603
Charles I. (Car.: Chas.)	27 Mar. 1625
(The Commonwealth, 1649–59)	
* Charles II (Car.: Chas.)	30 Jan. 1649
(restored)	29 May 1660
James II (Jac.)	6 Feb. 1685
(deposed)	11 Dec. 1688
(The Glorious Revolution, 1688–9)	
William III & Mary II (Will: Wm)	11 Apr. 1689
Anne.	19 Mar. 1702
George I. (Geo.)	1 Aug. 1714
George II "	11 June 1727
George III "	25 Oct. 1760
George IV "	29 Jan. 1820
William IV (Will.: Wm.)	26 June 1830
Victoria (Vict.)	20 June 1837
Edward VII (Edw.)	22 Jan. 1901

*The regnal numbering of Acts passed during the reign of Charles II start at 11 in 1660 to allow for the 11 years elapsed since his father's death, during which time there was no sovereign.

adhesive force in railway parlance, the frictional grip between the driving wheels of a locomotive and the rails. It is the product of the weight on the wheels and the frictional co-efficient between the two metals of the wheels and rails.

In the first days of steam traction, there was a fallacy that a locomotive with smooth wheels could not haul heavy trucks on smooth rails. It was thought the driving wheels would merely spin round. Because of this belief, John

Blenkinsop (1783–1831) patented his rack railway (patent no. 3431, 1811) which commenced working in 1812 at Middleton Colliery, near Leeds, Yorks. Around the same time, Christopher Blackett and William Hedley (1779–1843) conducted experiments at Wylam Colliery, near Newcastle upon Tyne, using a weighted, smooth-wheeled truck, manually driven, to pull loaded trucks successfully, and thus demonstrated conclusively that sufficient adhesion could be generated.

The weight of early locomotives on their two driving wheels provided all the necessary adhesion, but as locomotives grew larger and heavier, the load on one pair of driving wheels became excessive. To protect the rails from damage, extra driving wheels became necessary to spread the weight more evenly and eliminate wheel slip. To distribute the driving effort over all the wheels, they were connected together by outside COUPLING RODS.

Climbing a gradient reduces the effective weight on the driving wheels, increasing the tendency for wheel slip. The inability to climb gradients greater than about 1 in 20 is the biggest drawback of steam locomotives. To operate over hilly country, expensive civil engineering work constructing cuttings and embankments is necessary, to keep the track as level as possible. Rack railways are still used on mountains where the gradients are too steep for adhesive working. *See also* RACK, TRACTIVE EFFORT.

adit a nearly level tunnel driven into the side of a hill or slope to give access to an underground MINE, or in some cases for draining a mine. When providing an entrance to a mine, and for removing material from the underground workings, adits usually slope downwards from the surface. When acting as drainage, adits slope down from the workings into a valley, or to a lower stream. Early coal mines were frequently adit mines, also known as drift mines; this method of entering a mine predates vertical shaft mines, although some modern mines are adit mines. The term comes from the Latin *aditus*, meaning to go. Adits were also used in ore exploration, so evidence of old adits does not necessarily indicate a once active mine.

Some drainage adits were of considerable length. For instance, the County Adit in Cornwall, begun in 1748, eventually totalled 31 miles underground including its side branches, and drained several mines into the river Carnon. *See also* SOUGH.

Adrianople red, *see* TURKEY RED

adventurer early name given to a shareholder

or speculator in a mining enterprise. A less common alternative name was 'intermeddler', used for someone concerned with Cornish tin mines. 'Adventurer' dates from the days of Henry VII when there was a Society of MERCHANT ADVENTURERS.

aeolipyle an instrument for showing the force of a jet of steam escaping from a small outlet into the surrounding air. It comprises a vessel holding steam with two diametrically positioned tangential outlet pipes facing in opposite directions. The vessel is mounted on an axle, and as the steam escapes it turns the vessel about the axle. It resembles a BARKER'S MILL and acts like a lawn sprinkler. The name comes from the Greek *Aeolus*, the god of winds. The toy aeolipyle made by Hero of Alexander (in the second century BC) may be regarded as the first REACTION STEAM TURBINE, but the aeolipyle has no industrial use.

aerial ropeway, *see* BLONDIN

A-frame roof truss a simple frame, usually of timber, in the shape of the letter A, and used to support narrow span roofs in early mills, warehouses, etc. It was copied from the old crucks used in medieval houses and barns. (*See* Fig. 57.)

A-frame steam engine a simple, single cylinder, vertical steam engine with its cylinder mounted directly on a baseplate, driving an overhead crankshaft which is supported by two A-shaped frames, hence its name (*see* Fig. 1). Such engines were once common in the earlier days of steam power for winding duties in the north-east coalfields, and also in the woollen and worsted industries of Yorkshire. The main disadvantage of the design is that the heavy rotating flywheel has to be supported in its overhead position, and for this reason, A-frame engines rarely exceeded 200 horsepower in size.

after blow the continuation of the BLOW in a basic-lined BESSEMER CONVERTER indicating that the LIME is combining with the phosphorous in the PIG IRON and forming a discard SLAG. That is shown by a low bluish flame leaving the top of the converter.

after damp, *see* BLACK DAMP

agent person appointed by a colliery or metal mine owner to look after his interests and manage the operation of the enterprise.

agistment grounds an *en route* resting place for beef cattle. In the 17th and early 18th centuries, grazing fields were maintained near to cattle fairs or railheads, where cattle which had been driven in herds, often over long distances involving several weeks, were allowed to rest and fatten before being sold or

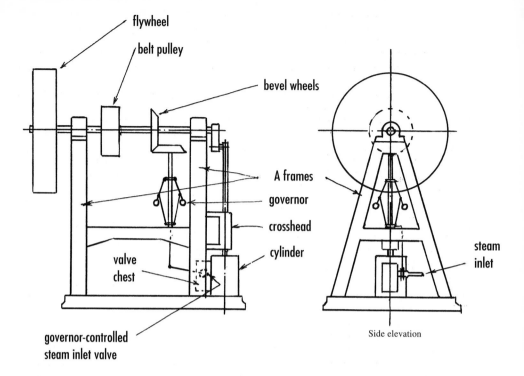

flywheel

belt pulley

bevel wheels

A frames

governor

crosshead

cylinder

valve chest

steam inlet

governor-controlled steam inlet valve

Side elevation

Fig. 1. Vertical A-frame steam engine

slaughtered. This mass movement of cattle 'on the hoof' became necessary to provide food for the growing population in Britain, particularly as concentration in the industrial areas increased. Cattle were driven over regularly used routes known as DROVERS' ROADS to the agistment grounds. The coming of the railways made agistment unnecessary since cattle began to be transported direct from the nearest railway to the slaughterhouses in towns and cities.

agrarian revolution the gradual improvements in the 18th and 19th centuries in the cultivation of land. The rise in industrialization in Britain, which quickened in the 18th century, was accompanied by increased activity in farming and the raising of livestock to feed the rising population of the manufacturing towns. Farms were extended over previously common land by enforced enclosure (*see* ENCLOSURE OF LAND) to increase the area available for cultivation and the grazing of animals; and agricultural productivity was raised by applying scientific principles to the growing of crops and the breeding of animals, and by the use of machinery to replace manual labour. Farmers and farm workers, forced off the land by the

enclosures, drifted into the industrial towns seeking employment, a population swing increased as the use of agricultural machinery spread.

The development of farming machinery and the application of steam power to agriculture is the main interest for industrial archaeologists in agrarian matters. Attempts at mechanizing agricultural work were made in the 18th century by inventions such as Jethro Tull's seed drill of 1733, which replaced hand broadcasting, and Andrew Meikle's threshing machine of 1788, which replaced hand methods. However, mainly because of the conservative nature of farmers and landowners, it was not until the mid-19th century that agricultural machines began being used in numbers. In the early 19th century, most market towns had small foundries supplying iron and brass castings to local blacksmiths and millwrights, who made and repaired farm implements and simple machines such as mowers and reapers; agricultural machinery-making developed slowly, and was stimulated by the showing of newly invented farming machinery at the GREAT EXHIBITION OF 1851. The manufacture of agricultural machinery became a specialized branch of the engineering industry and the use of steam power to drive farm machines, using portable steam engines and self-propelled traction engines, soon followed. Much agricultural engineering was centred in East Anglia where several inventions in ploughing, threshing and other machines were made and manufactured by firms such as Burrells (founded in 1770 in Thetford) and Ransomes (founded in the 1780s in Norwich). Steam ploughing of large fields was in use soon after the mid-19th century following its invention by John Fowler (1826–64) in 1854.

Alderton, D. and Booker, J. *The Batsford Guide to the Industrial Archaeology of East Anglia*, Batsford, 1980
Finberg, H.P.R. (ed.). *The Agrarian History of England and Wales*, Cambridge University Press, 1967
Fussell, G.E. *The Farmer's Tools*, Melrose, 1952
Harvey, N. *The Industrial Archaeology of Farming in England and Wales*, Batsford, 1980
Orwin, C.S. *A History of English Farming*, Nelson, 1949
Partridge, M. *Early Agricultural Machinery*, 1969

air furnace, *see* REVERBERATORY FURNACE

air pump a pump for removing condensed steam from the CONDENSER of a steam raising plant. A condensing steam engine exhausts its spent steam into a condenser, inside which a high vacuum is maintained by cold water turning the steam back into hot water. The hot water has to be continually removed without any air entering the condenser which would impair the vacuum. This is achieved by a pump, usually driven from the engine itself. The removed hot water is sent back to the HOTWELL for re-use as boiler feedwater. This pump is called an air pump, which is rather a misnomer since it extracts mainly water from the condenser, although the water it handles may contain a small amount of dissolved air.

air shaft term which often appears on larger scale Ordnance Survey maps, indicating an old coal mine. The shafts are usually ringed with stone at ground level, and may have been used to ventilate shallow mines, or for access to the underground workings. They are usually found in remote, moorland areas.

alamode a thin, lightweight, glossy black silk, dating from the mid-17th century and originally made in Lyon, France. It possibly takes its name from the French *à la mode* meaning 'fashionable'.

alder tree from which the bark was used for making a strong red cloth dye. Alders were also COPPICED frequently and the debarked poles used either for bobbin and spindle-making or for CHARCOAL, the latter being particularly used in gunpowder.

ale the forerunner of true beer in Britain. It comprised a fermented malt beverage without the addition of HOPS, which were not introduced into Britain until the 16th century. In time the word ale became synonymous with beer, which does contain hops.

An ale conner was an inspector usually appointed by a local authority to test the quality of ale being made for sale, and to check the measures being used. The quality was judged by drinking a sample! An ale wife, also known as a brewster, was a landlady of a tavern which brewed its own beer or ale. *See also* BREWING.

alkanet a red dye, dating from ancient times, made from the roots of the plant *Alkanna tinctoria*, also known as orchanet, or Spanish bugloss. Alkanet was imported from France and Spain; the term comes from the Arabic *al-henna*.

Allan straight link motion a mechanism for reversing the rotation of steam engines and varying the expansion ratio by altering the point of cut off. Invented and patented by Alexander Allan (1809–91) (patent no. 1747, 1855), it is similar in many respects to STEPHENSON'S LINK MOTION except that the EXPANSION LINK is straight and not curved. This makes it easier to manufacture, and it can also be accommodated in a shorter vertical height.

Two eccentric rods *ac* and *bd* join the ends of the straight expansion link at *c* and *d* respectively, as shown in Fig. 68b. The eccentrics are set with equal ANGLE OF ADVANCE to the engine crank, one for rotation in one direction, the other for reverse rotation. The expansion link *cd* is supported from below by link *fe*, and a block *j* can slide up and down the slot in the expansion link. The assembly *fgh*, pivoted at a fixed fulcrum *g*, can be tilted by the reversing linkages *gi* and the reversing rod. Another link *hk* is joined to link *jl* at *k*, whilst *l* is joined to the valve rod. When the gear is in the position shown in the diagram, the valve receives its motion from eccentric rod *ac*, and eccentric rod *bd* merely oscillates the end *d* of the expansion link without affecting the valve travel. If the reversing rod is operated to bring *j* to the top of the expansion link by lowering it, the valve is shifted to a new position and receives motion now from eccentric rod *bd* with no influence from *ac*. Steam is now admitted to the other side of the piston and the rotation of the engine is reversed. As with other link motions, positions of *j* either side of centre alter the travel of the valve, the effect of one eccentric cancelling out more or less that of the other, dependent on the position of *j* on the expansion link. The effect is to vary the point of cut off and the expansion ratio. With *j* at the central position, the valve travel is practically nil, and the engine will not be driven in either direction since no steam is admitted to the cylinder in this circumstance.

The Allan gear was first used on locomotives *c.* 1854, and has been used also on reversing stationary engines such as colliery winders.

Allen valve, *see* TRICK VALVE

all mine iron PIG IRON made entirely from iron ore, i.e. without the addition of scrap iron, etc.

alnager (or ulnager, alner, aulnager) a sworn Government or Crown official whose job was to inspect woollen cloth for quality and to measure its length and width in ELLS, an old unit now obsolete. If found satisfactory, a lead seal was affixed to the piece of cloth, the inspection usually taking place at a FULLING mill. The presence of the lead seal was a guarantee that the cloth had not been overstretched on the TENTER FRAME, that its weave was satisfactory, etc. A fee had to be paid by the cloth owner for this inspection and certification, the charge being called alnage. The office was instituted in the mid-14th century. It was abolished in 1724, but for many years before this the practice had not been properly administered, although the fee was still levied. It was allowed to die out after strong protests against its continuation by clothiers who found it burdensome and a hindrance to their trade.

Less commonly, an alnager was known as a stampmaster or lapper, although this terminology more properly belongs to the Irish linen industry of the 18th century. The same function was performed, i.e. certification of the cloth, which was lapped or folded ready for sale.

Alnager probably comes from the Greek *ulna* meaning forearm; measuring against parts of the body was common at one time.

alpaca (formerly spelt alpaco) cloth made from the long woolly hair of the Peruvian llama which has a staple length of about 10 in. It was first introduced into Britain by the Earl of Derby in 1836, and was being woven in the mill of Titus Salt (1803–76) in Bradford, Yorks., in 1850. Alpaca cannot be bleached satisfactorily so is only dyed in dark shades – black or dark browns. It has a silky crispness and became popular as ladies' dress material.

Althorp's Act, *see* FACTORY ACT 1833

alum a hydrous sulphate or salt combined with alumina, usually found naturally as aluminous grey shales. Large deposits were mined or quarried in north-east Yorkshire from the early 17th century. Alum was used as a MORDANT in the dyeing of cloth, and by calico printers. It was also used in tanning leather, by glass-makers and papermakers, and as a colour brightener when used with a dye. An old spelling was 'allome'.

Alum was made by extracting the shale by hand pick, layering it alternately with layers of brushwood to a depth of several feet, and setting it alight to calcine the shale to a rust-red colour. This operation was carried out close to the quarry or mine, and the burning was carried on for several months. The burnt shale was then put into large tanks or pits and water added. After about three days the solution was transferred into lead evaporating pans and boiled to make alum crystals. Some 50 tons of shale were needed to make one ton of alum, and some 6 tons of coal were used per ton of alum in the boiling operation. A final treatment with chemicals followed, and human urine was once used in this process. Spent shale was abandoned in large waste tips which are almost the only remains of this industry today. The price of alum rose and fell historically, causing periods of active industry followed by virtual abandonment of sites until prices rose again. By the mid-19th century work had ceased at the Yorkshire sites.

Pickles, R.L. 'A brief history of the Alum Industry in North Yorkshire, 1600–1875', *Cleveland Industrial Archaeologist* 2 (1975)
Singer, Charles, *The Earliest Chemical Industry: the Alum Industry*, 1948

amalgamation of railways the creation of a national railway system. Originally, railways were independent of one another, and there was no unified national system. The idea of a national system was first associated with the schemes of George Hudson (1800–97) of York, the RAILWAY KING who cherished the idea of one railway connecting York to London. Amalgamations of a number of small railways commenced in 1844 when the Midland Railway was formed. The benefits of amalgamation soon became apparent, and in 1846 the important London and North Western Railway came into being. This was followed by the Lancashire and Yorkshire Railway in 1847, and the North Eastern in 1854. In 1862 the Great Eastern Railway was formed, but there were still many small rival railways in existence.

In 1921, 123 separate railways were amalgamated into four main companies – the London Midland and Scottish Railway, the London and North Eastern Railway, the Great Western Railway, and the Southern Railway. Under the Transport Act of 1947, all British railways were nationalized from 1 January 1948. The idea of nationalization was not new, however, having been proposed as early as 1844.

The history of railway amalgamation by mergers, takeovers, etc. is very complex; many histories of individual railways have been published, and the main amalgamations are covered by the works listed below.

MacDermot, E.T. *History of the Great Western Railway*, 2 vols, 1927, 1931
Marshall, C.F.D. *History of the Southern Railway*, 1936
Marshall, J. *History of the Lancashire and Yorkshire Railway*, 3 vols, David and Charles, 1969–72
Nock, O.S. *The London and North Western Railway*, 1960
Robertson, W.A. *Combination among Railway Companies*, 1912
Stretton, C.E. *History of the Midland Railway*, 1901

American water turbine a mixed-flow water turbine of the REACTION type, favoured in the USA. The RUNNER vanes are curved in such a manner that they are acted on by the water as it flows radially inwards, and also acted on as it leaves axially (vertically downwards). This gives the turbine a high efficiency. A diagram of a mixed-flow runner appears in Fig. 83.

ancony an iron BLOOM which has been subjected to a second heating in a FINERY HEARTH and forged under a water-powered hammer into an elongated bar with an unfinished knob at each end. Forging the central portion drove most of the slag to the ends, the larger of which was called the MOCKET HEAD. The term comes from the French *encrenée*, meaning indented; it dates from the late 17th century, and was in use in the Sussex and Staffordshire ironworking districts in particular.

angle bob, *see* BELL CRANK

angle of advance an angular measure of how much an ECCENTRIC radius arm working a valve on a steam engine is in advance to displace the valve from its mid position. This ensures an adequate opening of the steam admission port at the commencement of the piston stroke and reduces throttling the steam. The exact angle of advance is determined by the combined lengths of the steam LAP and LEAD.

Angus Smith solution an anti-corrosion solution comprising coal, oil, pitch, and other ingredients which was painted on cast-iron sanitary pipes, piling for piers and jetties, etc. to protect against corrosion and prolong the life of metal parts, particularly those which were not accessible for regular painting. Invented by Dr Robert Angus Smith (1817–84), it was patented in 1848 (no. 12291). Smith was the first Chief Alkali Inspector, appointed under the Alkali Works Act 1863.

anil (anile), *see* INDIGO

aniline dyes the general name given to synthetic dyes made from aniline, a colourless, transparent, oily liquid obtained from coal-tar, a by-product of gas making. William Henry Perkin (1838–1907) discovered the first aniline dye, mauvine, and patented it in 1856 (patent no. 1984). Other important aniline dyes soon followed from discoveries by other industrial chemists, including magenta or fuchsine in 1859, by E. Verguin in France; aniline black in 1863, by John Lightfoot in England; Manchester or Bismarck brown in 1863, by Martius, in England; and methylene blue in 1876, by Heinrich Caro in Germany.

Aniline dyes were the first of many other synthetic dyes which replaced the older dyes of vegetable and animal origin. They were much more resistant to light and laundering than the natural dyestuffs, and gave more brilliant colours. Aniline dyes were also known as gas colours. *See also* DYES AND DYEING.

animal power the use of animal muscle to provide power, which has a long history. The European ox (*bos taurus*) was one of the first animals domesticated by humans and used for draught purposes – ploughing and pulling waggons. The horse (*equus caballus*) became the main alternative source of animal power, particularly after the horse collar was invented in the 10th century, permitting the animal to push instead of pull. By the mid-17th century the use of oxen in Western Europe had declined, and the horse was used wherever more than human effort was needed. Besides agricultural work, horses were used for carrying and pulling. A PACKHORSE could carry loads of up to about 280 lb slung across its back. When roads were improved, the horse pulled wheeled traffic, and when canals were built horses began towing barges of some 80 tons burden. Winding devices at early mines were horse operated (*see* HORSE WHIM). Machinery was also operated in a similar manner in the 18th century, for example Arkwright's first mill in Nottingham was powered by six horses in 1769. The basis for calculating mechanical power, devised in 1783 by James Watt, was related to the average pulling power of a horse (*see* HORSEPOWER). Horses were not the only source of animal power; it is recorded that in 1793, James Lewis Robertson ran two primitive looms in Glasgow powered by a Newfoundland dog. Light loads were often pulled by dogs, and dog-carts were not made illegal in Britain until 1885.

After the invention of the steam engine in the 18th century, horses were gradually replaced where industrial power was needed; similarly they were replaced for transport when steam locomotives were developed in the early 19th century. However, horses were still used on farms and roads well after the Victorian era, until the internal combustion engine was established.

Atkinson, F. 'The horse as a source of rotary power', *Newcomen Society Transactions* 33 (1960–61)
Major, Kenneth, *Animal Powered Machines*, Shire Publications, Album No. 128, 1985

annealing reducing internal residual stresses in metals or glassware by heating followed by slow cooling at a controlled rate. Some metals are hardened by cold working, e.g. by being hammered or rolled, and lose their malleability. This can be restored and the metal softened by heating to a certain temperature and allowing it to cool slowly; internal stresses are also relieved. This process is done in an annealing oven fitted with temperature control. Glassware becomes brittle and unusable if cooled rapidly after casting: subsequent annealing is an essential stage in its manufacture, and is usually performed in ovens or LEHRS arranged as side arches attached to the glass melting furnace or cone. Alternatively, tunnel lehrs may be used, through which the glass articles slowly pass in zones of decreasing temperature.

annotta (or anatto) possibly a native name for the plant *Bixa orellana* grown in the West Indies; the pulp surrounding the seeds of the plant is used to make an orange-red dye for cloth. Another name is roucou, which is taken from the French.

antherine (or anterne) an old East Anglian name for a kind of coloured poplin cloth, dating back to the 17th century, made from a silk warp and a worsted weft, or later from mohair and cotton.

anthracite a non-bituminous, hard, black coal, found in the south Wales coalfield. Anthracite is the oldest coal of the Carboniferous Age, is almost all carbon, and burns slowly with an intense heat yielding very little ash or smoke. Its cost is high because of its comparative rarity. Its lack of smoke made it a useful fuel for naval warships during the coal burning years, and for the same reason it is used in malting. Between 1837 and about 1860, it was used in south Wales BLAST FURNACES instead of coke. Powdered anthracite was used for colouring glass yellow in the early 19th century.

Anti-Corn Law League formed in September 1838 by two FREE TRADERS in the Manchester cotton industry, Richard Cobden (1804–65) and John Bright (1811–89). The League was set up to oppose the duties on imported corn which had been in existence since 1815. It was thought that cheaper food would allow a reduction in wages which, by reducing manufacturing costs, would promote the sale of British goods overseas. The League petitioned parliament for many years and symbolized the rising importance of the manufacturing industry brought about by the Industrial Revolution, challenging the old agricultural interest which wanted to maintain its hold on the economy of the country. In June 1846 the CORN LAWS were repealed, although a small import duty was retained. The repeal of the Laws was largely brought about by the Irish potato famine which commenced in 1845, and revealed the need for alternative sources of cheap food. In 1869 corn was admitted into Britain free of duty.

McCord, N. *The Anti-Corn Law League, 1838–1846,* 1958
Prentice, A. *History of the Anti-Corn Law Association,* 1853

anti-priming pipe a horizontal pipe, perforated by small diameter holes, lying high in the STEAM space of a steam-raising boiler. The steam leaves the boiler via this pipe, its purpose being to reduce as much as possible the carry over of moisture droplets into the steam flow so that the steam is dry. Dry steam is important if it is to drive a steam engine.

apprentice a young person legally bound to a master for an agreed period, for the purpose of learning the master's trade or craft. The word comes from the French *apprendre* meaning to learn, and an apprenticeship became a principal feature of the GUILD system of medieval crafts and industries. The STATUTE OF ARTIFICERS of 1563 laid down that an apprenticeship should last seven years, providing the apprentice was under 21 at entry. In those days an apprentice lived in his master's house and received only a very low wage, if any. He was bound by an indenture, a document containing articles of apprenticeship. The indenture, signed by both parties, was divided into two parts by an irregular zigzag cut, and each party held one piece.

An apprentice became a JOURNEYMAN after seven years, and could eventually become a master himself, and take on his own apprentices. The practice arose of sometimes paying a premium to the master or firm in exchange for being taught the trade or craft. An indentured apprenticeship became the accepted proof of a skilled workman in the engineering and manufacturing trades. A man who had gone through a proper apprenticeship was, and still is, known as a time-served craftsman.

Another kind of apprenticeship was that of the parish apprentice. This resulted from the Poor Law Act of 1601, which ordered that pauper children, both boys and girls, should be apprenticed to a trade so that they could later support themselves and not be a liability on the parish rates. Such pauper children were employed in large numbers, mostly in rural textile mills from the late 1700s to about the mid-1800s. Mill owners undertook to house, clothe, and feed the children, and a small wage was paid. They lived in APPRENTICE HOUSES, and received a rudimentary education. With some notable exceptions, the system was abused, and parish apprentices were overworked and badly housed. Eventually public social conscience was aroused, mainly through the efforts of Robert Peel I (1750–1830), himself a mill owner, and the Health and Morals of Apprentices Act was passed in 1802. The Act was, however, not very effective, and it was the FACTORY ACT 1833 (Althorp's Act) which brought about improvements. Employment of parish apprentices virtually ceased about 1850. By then, steam power meant that mills were now being built in or near towns, and children living nearby with their parents were a ready source of labour.

Dunlop, D.J. *English Apprenticeship and Child Labour*, 1912

apprentice house a building, usually close to a textile mill, in which parish APPRENTICES were accommodated by the mill owner who employed them. Many early textile mills had to be sited in rural areas where water power was available, and this made labour recruitment difficult. The problem was overcome by mill owners importing juvenile labour from distant areas, and housing them, dormitory fashion, in buildings normally placed close to the mill. Usually these children, boys and girls, were paupers or orphans, who were apprenticed to the mill for seven years. Large numbers of such children came from the south of England to work in northern mills. Formal indentures (agreements) were drawn up, signed by local Justices of the Peace, and the apprentice was bound to the mill for this period; unlike free labour, apprentices could not be dismissed when trade was slack. The mill owner had to provide food, clothing, accommodation, and some form of education.

The provision of apprentice houses was almost invariably from economic necessity rather than from philanthropy, and although some employers were more benevolent and paternalistic than others, many maintained a harsh regime and exploited their charges, working them long hours in bad conditions. Apprentice houses were introduced in the late 18th century, but had mostly disappeared by the mid-19th century, when the need for them declined and the system of apprenticing parish children fell into disuse. By then, steam-powered mills were being built close to towns and a supply of labour within walking distance became available; and many rural mill owners built houses for their workers when the apprentice system ceased. A few apprentice houses still exist, a good example being that at Quarry Bank Mill, Styal, Ches., owned by the National Trust.

aqua-thruster pump a type of water pump used in the Wigan coalfields in the late 18th and early 19th centuries, which worked on Savery's principle (*see* SAVERY ENGINE).

aqueduct a bridge-like structure, usually of several arches, that carries a man-made level waterway across a river valley, road, railway, or canal. Aqueducts are important features of the canal system. They were built to avoid either a flight of locks down one side of a valley and up the other, which would slow the passage of boats, or the expense of constructing large embankments to keep the canal level. The first aqueduct of note in Britain was built by James Brindley (1716–72), which carried the Bridgewater Canal across the river Irwell at Barton, near Worsley, Lancs. It was a stone structure on three semicircular arches, and the canal was made watertight by using PUDDLED CLAY. The first coal barge from the Worsley mines passed over the aqueduct on 17 July 1761. The structure was demolished in 1893 to make way for the Manchester Ship Canal.

To avoid the weight of puddled clay, cast-iron troughs, bolted together in sections, have been used to hold the water. Most aqueducts are constructed of stone or brick, but an all-iron one comprising a cast-iron trough supported on iron legs was designed by Thomas Telford (1757–1834) and erected at Longdon-on-Tern, near Wellington, Salop, in 1796.

An unusual aqueduct is the swinging one, also at Barton, designed by Sir E. Leader Williams (1828–1910). First used on 21 August 1893, it carries the Bridgewater Canal across the Manchester Ship Canal. It was built to replace Brindley's aqueduct, and is an all-steel structure supported on a central pier. It can be turned through 90° by hydraulic power, full of water, to permit large sea-going vessels pass into and out of Manchester's docks. Today very few large vessels use the Ship Canal and the aqueduct is seldom turned.

Elevated aqueducts were built by the Romans on mainland Europe for supplying water to cities. In Britain water supplies from distant reservoirs are brought by underground pipelines, which confusingly are misnamed aqueducts. Occasionally a LEAT is also wrongly called an aqueduct. *See also* PUBLIC UTILITIES.

arched bridge Structures spanning a river, or supporting a floor, etc., with clear openings curved at the top, are believed to date from 4000 BC. Such arched bridges began to be built in number in Britain during the Industrial Revolution due to the increase in all forms of

The Causey Arch of 1727 on the Tanfield Waggonway, Co. Durham

transport, first by road, then by canal, and later by railway. An arched bridge may have one or many arches; when there are many arches joined together, the structure may, more properly, be called a VIADUCT. Arched bridges were first built of stone, followed later by brick, iron or steel, and more recently of reinforced concrete. The theory of the arch is that the weight of the bridge plus the load it carries is transmitted to each side abutment by compressive stresses acting along the curved line of the arch, the abutments taking the sideways thrust. An arch shape may be semicircular, semi-elliptical, or some other mathematical curve. Some arches are pointed at their centre. Elliptical arches are flatter, which reduces the amount of rise needed by approach roads. A wide river spanned by a multiple-arched bridge may not need the road it carries to be raised at all. To lighten the weight of a bridge on its foundations, the spandrels were sometimes pierced by holes. Underwater foundations of multi-arched bridges were usually protected from erosion by tapered 'islands' called starlings.

As the need for improved communications and shorter routes developed in the 18th century, larger span bridges were required to cross rivers which had been considered too wide for the technology of the day. Large-span bridge theory and design originated in France, and influenced bridge building in Britain. By 1828, Thomas Telford (1757–1834) had built a single arch sandstone bridge of 150 ft span at Over, near Gloucester. Brick arches were extensively used in railway building, including some massively long viaducts. The world's first iron bridge is the well-known one at Ironbridge, Salop. Built in 1777–9, it carries a road across the river Severn on five semicircular cast-iron ribs of 110 ft span (*see* IRON BRIDGES). By the end of the 19th century wrought iron and steel began to replace cast iron for bridge building, but the arched form in these materials was rarely used, BEAM BRIDGES being preferred. The arched form in reinforced concrete dates from about the 1890s.

Ruddock, T. *Arch Bridges and their Builders, 1735–1835*, Cambridge University Press, 1979

archil (or orchil, orchilla) an ancient dye known to the Romans, producing a violet or purple shade from several kinds of lichens of the species *roccella*. The lichens grow on cliff faces and rocky seashores, and were imported into Britain from Spain and the Azores. The dye was used to dye silk and wool, and was also known as jarecork, or simply cork. Its use declined with the introduction of synthetic dyes in the mid-19th century.

argol a tartar from fermented wines which was formerly used as a colour brightener in the early days of textile dyeing. Dyed articles were boiled in it, and it also aided fixation of the dye. Argol was imported from Italy.

ark northern dialect term for a wooden bin for holding meal, etc. The word comes from the Latin *arca* meaning chest or box. Arks are also used in the pottery industry. Large settling arks hold some 20 to 30 tons of liquid, in bone and flint mills.

Arkwright-type mills the first generation of cotton spinning mills, modelled on Richard Arkwright's (1732–92) first mill at Cromford, Derbys., built in 1771. His mill measured 97 ft by 31 ft and had five storeys housing his WATER FRAME spinning machines, patented in 1769. Following the success of this improved method of spinning cotton, and the factory system he pioneered, the use of water frames spread rapidly. During the twenty years from 1771 to 1791, some sixty mills with common, recognizable features and approximately similar dimensions were built in various parts of the country. They stretched from Nottinghamshire to Perthshire, and from West Yorkshire to Flintshire, with a large number sited in Lancashire. Most have now disappeared, but all have been identified, either from documentary evidence or fieldwork, and show a common origin in design.

Most of these mills had an approximate 2:1 length to width ratio; on average they were 70 ft long and 30 ft wide, and three or four storeys high, the width being governed by the maximum allowable span for unsupported timber beams. They mostly operated 1,000 spindles which needed about 10 horsepower to drive them. Constructed in stone or brick with load-bearing walls, timber beams and floors and wooden roof trusses, they were water powered, the wheel being either placed internally (if the building spanned the stream or leat) or positioned at one end. Power to the machinery was by a vertical shaft and bevel gears to horizontal lineshafting on each floor. When the rotative beam engine became available in the 1780s, some of the later mills were built for steam power.

Arkwright actually licensed mill designs for 1,000 spindles to some mill owners, notably Robinson's of Nottingham who built mills of Arkwright type in the 1780s, but a large number of mills were copied from other early mills, both in building and power system.

Chapman, S.D. 'The Arkwright mills – Colquhoun's Census of 1788 and archaeological evidence', *Industrial Archaeology Review* VI (1981–2), 5–27

arras a rich tapestry fabric with figures and scenes woven in colour. It takes its name from the town of Arras in northern France which was famous for this type of textile, and was principally used as wall hangings. Sometimes spelt arays, it is also known as cloth of arras.

arsenic semi-metal element, which increases corrosion resistance of copper, and hardens lead; it is added to lead for making lead shot. It also has a use in making enamels, and there are medicinal applications. In the 19th century arsenic was mostly processed in Devon and Cornwall by roasting arsenical ores of iron (e.g. mispickel, a sulphide of iron and arsenic) and copper (e.g. tennantite, a sulphide of copper and arsenic). The ores were crushed to pea-sized pieces and calcined in rotating kilns, the fumes being led into long brick or stone flues and chambers known locally as lambreths, where they precipitated and condensed. The flues were emptied periodically and the arsenic refined in a refining furnace. Since arsenic is poisonous, the flues etc. were sited in remote places and their long length was designed to reduce the escape of arsenic particles into the atmosphere to a minimum.

Earl, B. 'Arsenic winning and refining methods in the West of England', *Journal of the Trevithick Society* 10 (1983), 9–29

arsenopyrite, *see* MISPICKLE.

Artificers, Statute of, 1563 an important piece of legislation which attempted to establish a uniform industrial system throughout the country. Its two main features were that apprenticeships to all existing crafts were to last seven years, and that local Justices of the Peace were to fix wages and review them annually. This law regularized anomalies which had crept in under the previous GUILD system of controlling industry, and laid a sound foundation for future British industrial skill and craftsmanship. It was generally followed for a century and a half, but by about the mid-18th century it was being largely ignored, particularly since it did not apply to the new industrial crafts. This was to the detriment of the workers who had lost the protection it gave. A growing anachronism, it was repealed in 1814.

The law is sometimes called the Statute of Apprentices, but it was in fact wider in scope; artificer is an old English word for a craftsman. *See also* APPRENTICE.

ashes, *see* PEARL ASH

assistant cylinder a small steam cylinder placed on top of the main slide valve on a large vertical steam engine and connected to a tail rod protruding from the valve chest of the main cylinder. Its purpose is to carry the weight of the main valve and to assist its vertical movements.

Association for Industrial Archaeology a voluntary-run association, established in September 1973, to promote the study of industrial archaeology and to represent the subject at national level. The Association maintains contact with traditional archaeological and other organizations concerned with the recording, preservation and funding of Britain's historic monuments. It supports individuals and groups involved in industrial archaeology, holds annual conferences, and since 1976 has published the results of research, recording, and conservation in its twice-yearly journal, the *Industrial Archaeology Review*. A Bulletin is sent quarterly to members and affiliated societies with details of projects and news.

The Association monitors threats to listed buildings and other important industrial sites which are reported to it, and is usually represented at public inquiries concerning the fate of such sites in an endeavour to prevent the destruction of Britain's industrial heritage. It also presents awards to encourage voluntary conservation work on sites and artefacts of historical industrial importance, and to encourage high standards of fieldwork and publication. It publishes regional gazetteers of industrial archaeological sites from time to time. The headquarters of the Association is at the Ironbridge Gorge Museum Trust, Ironbridge, Telford, Salop; most of its members are British, although some are from overseas. *See also* INDUSTRIAL ARCHAEOLOGY.

atmospheric bleaching, *see* GRASSING

atmospheric engine a pioneering engine worked by atmospheric pressure. The very earliest steam-using engines were the beam engines of Thomas Newcomen (1663–1729), whose first recorded engine was pumping water out of a coal mine in Dudley, Staffs., in 1712 (*see* NEWCOMEN ATMOSPHERE ENGINE). Atmospheric engines were single-acting, non-rotative, slow, and inefficient, but pioneered the design for later true steam-pressure using BEAM ENGINES.

atmospheric railway mid-19th century system in which trains were to be drawn along a track by suction. The idea was first proposed by George Medlock in the 1820s; a patent (no. 7920) was taken out by Samuel Clegg (1814–56) in 1839, and another by Jacob and Joseph Samuda (no. 10167, 1844). Great interest was shown in the concept, the main advantages claimed being quietness in operation and absence of smoke. Experiments on the Dublin and Kingstown Railway, Ireland, in 1844–45 appeared promising, although the great authority of the day, George Stephenson (1781–1848) and stated: 'It won't do'. I.K. Brunel (1806–59) took up the idea and experimented at great cost on the South Devon railway in 1847–8. The system comprised a 15 inch diameter pipeline laid between the rails, with a continuous slot running along the top, sealed by leather strips or flaps. The front carriage of the train was connected to a piston inside the pipe by an arm which passed down the slot. The pipeline in front of the piston was exhausted by a series of stationary pumping engines positioned every few miles along the track. The vacuum produced sucked the train along, the leather flaps maintaining a seal but allowing the arm to pass as the train moved. The system could not be made to work: the seals were the weakness, and a vacuum could not be properly maintained. It was abandoned in 1848 after much money had been spent on it.
Hadfield, C. *Atmospheric Railways*, David and Charles, 1967

automatic control mechanical or other devices to enable a machine to operate continuously without human intervention. An early example was the automatic opening and closing of the valves controlling the cycle of a NEWCOMEN ATMOSPHERIC ENGINE. The rocking action of the overhead beam was used to raise and lower the PLUG RODS upon which pegs tripped levers which operated the valves. It is said that Newcomen derived this idea from an ingenious boy engine minder, one Henry Potter, who rigged up a system of strings and levers to make the engine work itself, and relieve him of his monotonous job working the valves by hand. Other devices of the same period were the CATARACT and the BUOY CONTROLLER.

In 1750 Andrew Meikle fitted a FANTAIL to a WINDMILL which automatically swung the main sails into the wind when it changed direction. In about 1788 James Watt adapted the simple CENTRIFUGAL GOVERNOR, first used on corn mills, to regulate the speed of steam engines, and many more complex governors were developed from this. On textile machinery, the punched card system for automatically controlling the weaving of complex patterns was perfected in *c*.1804 by Joseph Marie JACQUARD. The spinning MULE was made automatic by Richard Roberts in 1824.

automatic loom a cloth weaving machine that works by itself. An automatic loom differs from the LANCASHIRE LOOM in that PIRNS full of weft thread are held in a magazine or battery attached to the loom, waiting to be used. When the shuttle needs replenishing the empty pirn is ejected and a full one fed into place in the shuttle during the short pause when the shuttle reverses direction at the end of its pass across the cloth. The loom therefore does not stop, and in fact runs for 90–95 per cent of its time weaving cloth. The NORTHROP LOOM is an example of an automatic loom.

Automatic looms are known as underpick looms because the PICKING mechanism is an arm moving in a vertical plane from a pivot at the base of the machine, one at each side of the loom, to project the shuttle across the width of the cloth being woven. This arrangement differs from the Lancashire loom which has its picking arms moving horizontally.

B

Babbit metal a low friction metal alloy, also known as white metal, comprising a large amount of tin with smaller equal amounts of copper and antimony, which is used for JOURNAL bearings etc. in machines. It was invented by Isaac Babbit (1799–1862) in 1839. Lead is also often added.

back a vat or large vessel for holding liquid. The term is used in the brewing, soap making and dyeing industries, and comes from the Dutch *bak* meaning tub. In brewing, for example, there are hopbacks which are vessels in which hops are removed from the WORT; liquorbacks for holding water (called liquor by brewers); underbacks which are vessels placed below the MASH TUN for collecting the wort, and so on.

backing off the motion of a spinning MULE or similar machine when the carriage moves outwards away from the CREEL, uncoiling slack yarn from the SPINDLE. This takes place between spinning and WINDING ON. The action is necessary in order to bring the yarn up onto the free end of the spindle so that spinning can recommence.

back pressure the pressure opposing a piston during, or near the end of, its power stroke. In a single-cylinder non-condensing steam engine

the back pressure equals the atmospheric pressure plus the pressure created during CUSHIONING in the cylinder clearance. This usually amounts to around 18 psi in total. In a single-cylinder condensing engine, the back pressure depends on the perfection of the vacuum maintained in the CONDENSER and the resistance to steam flow through the exhaust passages. Usually, with a good vacuum the back pressure amounts to some 4 psi. In the case of compound engines (*see* COMPOUNDING) the back pressure of the high pressure cylinder equals the inlet pressure of the low pressure cylinder plus the pressure needed to overcome the resistance of the connecting pipe or receiver and exhaust passage. For locomotives, the back pressure is increased by the pressure needed to force the exhaust steam through the blast pipe.

back-shot wheel, *see* PITCHBACK WHEEL

back-to-back houses cheap industrial housing built to a high density. This type of housing became common in the late 18th and early 19th centuries as large mills began to be built in towns. Sometimes built by speculative builders, sometimes by mill owners for their workers, the houses were crowded in to get the maximum rent from the land. Back-to-back houses had no rear exits, and only one door at the front of each. They were built either in double terraced rows, or sometimes in clusters of four with a space between each cluster. Narrow alleyways separated them, in which outside privies were sited. Some long terraces incorporated passageways at intervals to give access to the rear row, a design known as tunnel back-to-back. Some houses had only two rooms, one up, one down; more elaborate ones had four rooms, two up, two down. Living conditions were insanitary and overcrowded, and such houses soon became slums. The Borough Act of 1844 prohibited further building of back-to-back houses in Manchester, but they continued to be built in other industrial towns, particularly in Yorkshire, as late as the early 20th century. They died out through a combination of legislation and public demand for better housing. Many back-to-back houses still exist, but have been converted into through houses by knocking two into one, thereby providing rear exits.

A variation is top-to-bottom or dual houses, built in the narrow Pennine and Welsh valleys where level ground is limited. They appear to be four-storey rows built straight into the hillside, but actually are a bottom row of two-storey terraced houses accessed from the front only, with another row of two-storey houses built directly on top. The upper row may be accessed from a roadway higher up the hillside, or from a verandah running along their lower storey, reached by steps at one end from the lower roadway.

Caffyn, Lucy. *Workers Housing in West Yorkshire, 1750–1929*, HMSO, 1986
Chapman, S.D. (ed.) *The History of Working Class Housing*, 1971
Gauldie, Enid. *Cruel Habitations*, 1974
Lowe, J.B. *Welsh Industrial Workers' Housing: 1795–1875*, 1977
Morgan, N. *Vanished Dwellings*, Mullion Books, 1991

backwashing machine a machine used in the WORSTED industry for cleaning woollen SLIVERS after GILLING or CARDING. It comprises wash tanks containing soapy water, followed by a steam-heated drying chamber and a gill-box to restore the openness of the sliver and freedom from clinging. Sometimes a blue solution is drip-fed into the wash tank to improve the whiteness of the wool. Besides cleaning the wool, backwashing improves the condition of the sliver before it is combed by stretching the fibres and giving a temporary 'set'.

backwatering problem which occurs on a waterwheel installation when the river or stream is in flood. The normal water level is raised and water backs up the TAILRACE to immerse the lower part of the wheel, introducing a drag which slows down the wheel, of which in extreme cases can stop its rotation since discharge of water is prevented. Backwatering may be prevented or reduced either by a steeply falling tailrace, or arranging for the final discharge back into the river well downstream at a lower level.

badger itinerant dealer who carried corn and provisions, needles and thread, etc. about the countryside by packhorse or jagger pony to sell to outlying villages and farms. The name of badger, or bodger as it is also erroneously known, dates from the 1500s, and the word is a dialect one of unknown origin, but still in use in the mid 1800s; alternative dialect names were swailer and swealer. Badgers were not very popular since they were middlemen between the producers, farmers, fishermen, etc., and the purchasers, thus adding to the cost of the articles they sold, although they did provide a service to remote areas. The trade disappeared when roads were improved, canals made distribution of commodities easier, and shops became more common in villages.

Another meaning of the word badger is to barter or haggle over a bargain, whilst another relates to the Settlement Act of 1697 when paupers were required to wear a badge in the shape of a letter P, and were known as badgers.

bagman 1. a name often given to early commercial travellers, so called from the bag of samples carried on horseback in outsize saddlebags or in the large boot of a horse-drawn gig. The coming of the railways took the bagman off the road. 2. a middleman in the hosiery trade who bought yarn and put it out to domestic frame knitters, collecting their output, and selling it at a profit for himself. Some bagmen also rented KNITTING FRAMES from people such as shopkeepers and publicans who had bought the frames as investments, and sublet them to knitters at a further profit. By the 1880s some bagmen had become prosperous enough to build small knitting factories, and were known as bag hosiers.

bal a word from the old Cornish language for a mine, or the surface of a mine. It dates from about 1600, and was sometimes spelt ball. An example of its use is in the name Godolphin Bal. However, another Cornish word – wheal – is more commonly used in the names of Cornish mines.

balance arm a massive arm or beam projecting horizontally about waist high from a lock gate on a canal. Its purpose is to balance the gate itself about its vertical hinges and to enable the gate to be opened or closed once the water level either side of it is equalized. This is done by pushing the balance arm through 90°. A series of ridges in the paving on a radius is usually provided to assist the pusher gain purchase with his feet. The winding gear for operating the paddles in the lock gates is often fitted on the balance arm. Most balance arms are timber, but some are metal.

balance bob an auxiliary pivoted beam, usually placed at ground level, to balance the weight of long PUMP RODS on a BEAM STEAM ENGINE sited at a mine. The balance bob was often constructed in a similar way to the main beam of the engine, but was of smaller dimensions. One end terminated with a BEAM ARCH and was connected to the top pump rod, while the other end comprised a large box into which stones etc. were placed to balance the weight of the rods. Acting like a seesaw as the pump rods rose up and down, the downwards pull of the balance weight partly cancelled out the weight of the pump rods to reduce the strain on the main beam, and relieve the engine of some of its load. The beam of the balance bob was often at 90° to the main engine beam in plan, and a shallow pit was often positioned under the weighted end, into which it dipped as the pump rods rose.

Balance bobs were occasionally placed underground in deep mines to counteract the weight of the massive pump rods.

balasore a fine, muslin-like cotton fabric woven in Lancashire in the late 18th century, and used mainly for handkerchiefs. It was named after the port of Balasore on the east coast of India near Calcutta, where a similar fabric was woven.

bale a bound package of a raw material. After raw cotton has been cleaned in a COTTON GIN, the loose fibres (lint) are compressed into blocks for the purposes of transport. These blocks are called bales. The compression is performed either by steam presses or by hydraulic presses. After compression, the lint is wrapped in coarse jute bagging and banded with iron bands for protection during the journey and to prevent the contents spilling out. The size of cotton bales varies according to their place of origin: American bales can vary from 54 to 80 in long, 24 to 40 in wide, and 18 to 27 in thick, with a weight of around 480 lb. Indian bales measure approximately 48 by 20 by 18 in and weigh 396 lb. On arrival at the mill, bales are opened and the cotton usually requires some further cleaning to remove entrapped dirt and sand. The contents of different bales are mixed to secure an even cotton quality, the main considerations being length of STAPLE, spinning qualities, colour, and price.

Raw RUBBER from a plantation is also shipped in bales which are formed by compressing several thin sheets of smoked rubber into one block. The bale is chopped into small pieces before it is masticated either in a BANBURY MIXER, or between the rolls of a RUBBER MILL at the rubber processing factory.

baling press a machine in which finished cloth is squeezed into rectangular sacks or bundles ready for despatch. It is also the term for the press in which raw cotton is compressed to reduce its bulk before shipment.

ball the hot lump of wrought iron drawn from a PUDDLING FURNACE before being hammered to remove impurities in a SHINGLING HAMMER. *See also* BALL FURNACE.

ball clay a special kind of clay, also known as potter's clay, found in certain clay beds in Devon and Dorset. It is similar to china clay, being a feldspathic mineral (a silicate of aluminium) formed from decomposed granite, but it is more plastic than china clay. It is used as a stiffening agent in porcelain, and when fired produces a near-white pottery. It was first quarried in the 1760s, especially from the rich deposits around Bovey Tracey in south Devon, and later mined extensively. Originally it was dug out by spade in lumps known as balls, hence its name.

Rolt, L.T.C. *The Potters' Field: A History of the South Devon Ball Clay Industry*, David and Charles, 1974

ball furnace a furnace for reheating short, cut-up lengths of wrought-iron billets after their first rolling so that they can be rolled again to give a finished product. The bars are piled on top of one another in alternate directions inside the furnace so that when rolled hot, the grain of the metal runs at right angles to give greater strength. Placing the bars in this manner is known as cross piling.

balloon boiler, *see* HAYSTACK BOILER

ball winding machine a hand-operated machine for winding cotton and linen thread into balls, invented by Mark Isambard Brunel (1769–1849) in 1802. Thread was previously only available in skeins.

bal-maiden Cornish word for a young woman who works at a tin mine, BAL being an old Cornish word for mine. A typical job of a bal-maiden was to operate KIEVES at the surface of a tin-streaming works.

Banbury mixer a RUBBER processing internal mixer, named after its inventor Fernley H. Banbury. It comprises a fully enclosed mixing chamber inside which specially shaped spiral rotors rotate at slightly different speeds. The rotors and chamber walls can be heated or cooled. The raw rubber and other ingredients are fed in at the top, and a ram is lowered to keep pressure on whilst mixing takes place. The dough is discharged through a discharge door at the bottom of the chamber onto a pair of metal rolls, and rolled into sheet form. The Banbury mixer is faster than mixing rolls, and is still used in the rubber industry. *See also* RUBBER MILL.

band clutch, *see* SLACK BELT DRIVE

band saw a sawing machine comprising a band or belt of flexible metal saw-blading driven at speed around a pair of vertical pulleys placed one above the other. The saw band passes through a slot in a horizontal metal table on which the object to be sawn is held, and pressed against the moving band. A band saw is used for cutting wood or metal to intricate shapes by moving the workpiece about as desired. The idea of a band saw came from William Newberry in 1808, but band saws did not become popular until after the mid-19th century when better steel for the bands became available. Before this frequent breakages were common.

banking the transactions of a financial company investing deposited money, and lending it out at interest. The Industrial Revolution could not have taken place without banks to provide capital and credit for the factory system as it built up; the building of turnpikes, canals, and railways was also financed by banks. Goldsmiths were the first source of capital, emerging as informal bankers during the Civil War (1642–49) in London. The Bank of England was founded in 1694 in London as a joint-stock concern: it owes its origin to the financial difficulties of the government of the day, which borrowed extensively from it. The Bank gave interest to encourage private depositors, and by gathering people's savings together, large sums were made available as loans to finance industrial undertakings. Later, many private individuals founded their own banks in the provinces to service local requirements, and had the right to issue their own banknotes as well as the Bank of England. By 1821 there were some 800 small private banks, but between 1815 and 1830 over 200 of them failed, and their banknotes became worthless. In 1844, the issue of banknotes by provincial banks was limited and eventually Bank of England notes became the only legal notes in England and Wales, although two northern banks – the Bank of Scotland, and the Royal Bank of Scotland – continued to issue their own notes, as they still do today. *See also* BLACK FRIDAY, TRADE TOKENS, TRUCK SYSTEM.

Clapham, J.H. *The Bank of England: A History, 1694–1914*, Cambridge University Press, 1944
Cottrell, P.L. *Industrial Finance: 1830–1914*, 1980
Pressnall, L.S. *Country Banking in the Industrial Revolution*, 1954

banksman a man who oversees the loading and unloading of coal mine cages at the top of a shaft.

barberry a dye made from the roots and bark of the tree *Barberis vulgaris*, used to dye silk yellow, before the introduction of synthetic dyes in the mid-19th century.

bargain an agreement made between miners and a mine owner or his agent for a certain amount of lead mining to be undertaken for a fixed payment. Bargain day, or setting day, was a meeting held every six to eight weeks, to award tasks at a lead mine to teams of men known as pares or copers who bid for the jobs. The tasks could be to win ore, drive a level, sink a shaft, etc.

barilla a form of alkali or soda, obtained by burning Spanish salt marsh reeds of the genus *salsola soda*. Barilla was imported for hard soap, glass making, and copper refining as early as the mid-16th century. During the 18th century, various wars severely curtailed the import of barilla from Spain, and indigenous KELP was used instead until imports were resumed in the early 19th century.

bar iron long pieces of wrought iron, square or rectangular in cross-section, produced in a BAR MILL or ROLLING MILL from BLOOMS. Bar iron was the raw material from which engineers and blacksmiths fabricated structures, machinery, or articles. Until Henry Cort (1740–1800) patented his PUDDLING process in 1783, large amounts of bar iron were imported from Sweden and Russia (*see* DANNEMORA IRON). Cort's process enabled British PIG IRON to be used to produce cheap bar iron as good as the Swedish.

Barker's mill an early type of reaction water turbine invented *c*.1743 by Dr Robert Barker of Massachusetts, USA. It worked on a jet propulsion method, comprising two diametrically opposite arms through which water under pressure flows and escapes via a nozzle at the extremity of each arm, the nozzles pointing in opposite directions. The lawn sprinkler is based on the same principle. It was used for small power outputs. A steam version was tried out by Richard Trevithick in 1815 which he called his WHIRLING ENGINE, but it was proved unsuccessful and was abandoned. Barker's mill is also known as a Scotch mill or turbine, because of the improvements made in 1839 by James Whitelaw of Paisley.

bark peelers itinerant, self-employed workmen who peeled bark from oak COPPICE wood in early summer when the rising sap made its removal easier. They mostly sold the bark to tanners. Manual peeling of bark was a woodland industry of the 17th and 18th centuries: bark peelers usually worked in conjunction with men felling coppice wood for CHARCOAL burning, and they lived rough, 'camping' out in the coppice woods, moving from place to place as supplies of bark were exhausted. Another use of oak bark was for the curing of fish, and many fishing villages often had a building known as a bark house in which fish were cured in the smoke from burning oak bark.

Barmaster the chief person who presided over the 'jury' or BARMOTE COURT which administered lead mining laws in Derbyshire, Yorkshire and other mining areas. The Barmaster, a Crown official, kept the standard brass gauge or dish, called the 'freeing dish', which was used for measuring lead ore. He was also responsible for measuring out MEERS on lead veins. Besides acting as judge in disputes between miners, one of his duties was to allocate mining rights to miners and landowners or owners of the mineral rights when a new lead vein was discovered. Barmaster is sometimes spelt Barghmaster and Bermer. The name comes from the *Bergmeister* of German miners who performed similar functions in medieval times.

bar mill a ROLLING MILL with grooved rollers for producing round, square, flat, or similar shaped bars of iron from BLOOMS. The matching pair of rolls has grooves cut in each circumference side by side; each matched pair of grooves increases in depth across the width of the rolls, the profile of the space between them gradually approaching that of the finished cross-section of the bar required. The red-hot bloom is rolled between the rolls, passing from front to back at each pass through the machine, being guided through each groove in turn from the first which roughly shapes it until it reaches the final groove. The length of the bloom increases at each pass until it emerges as a bar of the required shape. Water-powered bar mills date from the 17th century and possibly earlier.

Barmote a kind of court controlling the activities of lead miners. Derbyshire lead miners had their own customs and privileges governing their system of working dating back to 1288, and the 'laws' of this were administered by the Barmote court. The Barmote (or Barmoot) was presided over by the BARMASTER and a 'jury' of miners (once twenty-four, later reduced to twelve) who settled disputes, gave out punishments, and so on. Every miner had the right to prospect for lead, and when a vein was found, it had to be 'freed' from the owner of the mineral rights by giving him two 'freeing' dishes of ore. This was done through the Barmaster who allocated certain lengths of the vein (called MEERS) to the miner and to the owner of the mineral rights. The Barmote performed several other duties, and any miner breaking the 'laws' could be tried by the court and an appropriate punishment handed out. After nearly 600 years the system was regularized and made statutory by Acts of 1851 and 1852. Similar courts were held in other lead mining areas, such as the West Riding of Yorkshire. The word Barmote, once spelt Bargmoot, probably came from the German *Berg* meaning a mine, and the Old English 'moot' meaning an assembly or court.

Rieuwerts, J.H. *The History of the Laws and Customs of Derbyshire Lead Mines*, Peak District Mining Museum, 1988

barring engine a small auxiliary engine to help start up a large steam engine, invented in 1866 in Bolton, Lancs., by William Knowles and William Nash. Should a large single

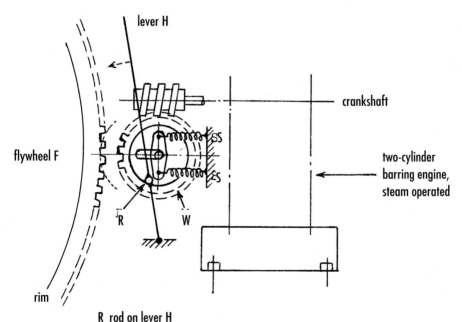

R rod on lever H
W wormwheel which slides in horizontal slot
S spring for pulling W back along slot

Fig. 2. Action of a barring engine

cylinder steam engine stop on DEAD CENTRE, it could only be restarted by manually levering the FLYWHEEL round a few degrees, using an iron bar against notches cast in the periphery of the flywheel for this purpose. Also, the piston might have to be moved slightly during repair work whilst there was no steam on the engine, and this was again done by manual levering, known as barring. Barring could be heavy work if it had to turn a very large engine together with the mill LINESHAFTING attached to it via the rope drives. Small ancillary steam engines, called barring engines, were therefore added to large installations for this purpose, and they were also used to help start up the main engine.

Fig. 2 shows the principal features of a two-cylinder barring engine. To start up the main engine from rest, the worm attached to the extended crankshaft is rotated by the barring engine and engages with the wormwheel W which is held back in its slot by the two springs SS. To turn the main engine flywheel F, the lever H is pushed in towards the flywheel causing rod R to press against the rim of W stopping it from rotating. The rotating worm causes W to move along the slot towards the flywheel until its teeth engage with the notches or teeth on the flywheel. Pressure between the meshing teeth keeps the flywheel and wormwheel in contact, allowing the lever H to be released. The barring engine now begins to turn the flywheel, and as it picks up speed, aided by the steam entering its own cylinder(s), it reaches a speed of rotation faster than that of the barring engine, and the pressure between the meshing teeth is released. At this point W is automatically drawn back by the springs SS, and the mechanism is disengaged. The barring engine can then be stopped. Without steam on the main engine, the flywheel can be turned a few degrees by repeating the above, but pulling lever H away from the flywheel after it has turned the required amount.

barwood a redwood imported from Gaboon, west Africa, in bars, and ground down to a powder to make a brown dye. The bars came from the tree *Baphia nitida*.

barytes (barium sulphate) a GANGUE mineral usually associated with galena (lead) ore, used in paint, as a filler in paper, as a FLUX in copper smelting, and in the manufacture of plate glass. It is also known as heavy spar, and as cawk in Derbyshire.

bascule bridge a bridge which is hinged at one end, or at both ends if in two parts, so that it may be raised into a vertical position to allow the passage of shipping taller than the clear height beneath the bridge when lowered. The

rising parts of the bridge are counterbalanced. Large bridges are power operated: a well-known example of a 2-part bascule which opens in the middle is the hydraulically operated Tower Bridge, London, 1894. Smaller examples exist over canals.

base, *see* MORDANT

baseplate, *see* BEDPLATE

basic lining a refractory lining used in metallurgical furnaces and BESSEMER converters for resisting attack by basic SLAGS, and to withstand high temperatures. Basic linings, introduced in 1878 by Sidney Gilchrist Thomas (1850–85), are derived from oxides of metallic substances such as DOLOMITE and magnesite. They enabled phosphorus-containing iron ores to be handled in Bessemer converters by allowing lime to be added to remove the phosphorus, thus producing a basic slag. Before the introduction of basic linings, any phosphorus-bearing ores which had lime added produced a slag which rapidly attacked the ACID LININGS which were previously used.

basic steel steel made in a furnace lined with a basic refractory material. Sidney G. Thomas (1850–85) and Percy Gilchrist (1851–1935) patented this steel making process in 1879 (patent no. 1019) by substituting a basic lining of DOLOMITE in a BESSEMER CONVERTER and using a lime flux to remove phosphorus from the PIG IRON. The steel produced was called basic steel to differentiate it from the earlier Bessemer, or ACID STEEL.

basin a loading and unloading place on a canal, usually at a canal terminus, or at an intermediate town. The canal would be widened or have several short branches to provide mooring places for the barges and room for manoeuvring. Wharves, cranes, warehouses, etc. were built alongside the canal, and the basin was usually surrounded by a wall for security with a gate leading to the outside road system. A wharfinger (manager) would be in charge of the basin, with his house located inside the wall or adjacent to the basin.

basset old word for an outcrop of coal or metallic ore such as lead.

bast fibres the collective name for fibres which lie in the inner bark (or bast) of stems of plants such as flax, hemp, jute, and ramie. Such fibres are used in the manufacture of specific textiles; linen, for example, uses flax fibres.

batiste, *see* CAMBRIC

batten another name for a SLEY on a loom. It possibly comes from the French *battre* meaning to strike or beat, since one function of a batten is BEATING UP the WEFT against the cloth just woven.

battery 1. an electrochemical device for producing or storing electricity. A battery is a collection of cells, each cell comprising an electrochemical couple which will give a voltage dependent on the materials involved. The current which can be taken from a battery is direct current. The total voltage a battery can give depends on the manner in which the cells are connected together, either in parallel or series.

There are two types of battery, primary and secondary. Primary batteries are non-reversible, i.e. they cannot be recharged, and are used only once. The first person to discover how to produce electricity by electrochemical means was Alessandro Volta (1745–1827) in Italy in 1799. Other types of cell were developed in Britain by John Fredrick Daniell (1790–1845) in 1836, followed by William Robert Grove (1811–96) in 1839, but the basis of modern primary batteries was the work of Georges Leclanché (1839–82), a French railway engineer, in 1868.

Secondary batteries are the invention of R.L. Gaston Planté (1834–89) who produced the first practical secondary cell in France in 1859. This is the lead-acid cell, improved in 1881 by Camille Faure (*fl.*1880s). The secondary battery can be recharged i.e. is reversible, and is therefore known as an accumulator. The lead-acid cell produces 2.0 volts. In 1899, the alkaline cell, with a nickel-cadmium couple, was developed: this produces 1.5 volts per cell.

The early uses of batteries included supplying electricity for telegraphs, lighting, spark ignition for gas engines, small power units, etc. Battery lighting on passenger trains was introduced in 1881; an electrically propelled tricycle by Ayrton and Perry in 1882; and battery driven river launches in *c.*1883. In 1899 a battery driven car, *La Jamais Contente*, actually held the world land speed record of 65.7 mph. Electric cars powered by secondary batteries were popular until the arrival of the petrol engine.

2. the name given to the manufacture of sheets and plates in iron, copper and brass, etc., alternatively known as plating. Iron sheets, plates and hoop iron were made in the late 17th and early 18th centuries by flattening bars etc. with water-powered hammers in a Battery mill. From the sheets, smiths made hollow-ware, such as bowls, pans, etc. and items such as shovels. Later, ROLLING MILLS were introduced to replace the hammering method. The word battery in this case comes from the French *battre*, meaning to strike.

batting (or picking) cleaning raw cotton by manually beating it against a wire sieve, the dirt and impurities falling through the mesh. The hand process was superseded by the SCUTCHING MACHINE. Batting was often carried out by women working in their own homes for a nearby spinning mill in the early days of the textile industry.

bay 1. a subdivision of the long side of a mill, warehouse, or similar building. Usually a bay is the distance between successive columns and contains one or sometimes two windows. A textile mill is often measured in bays. A bay varies in width according to the design of the building, but is usually between 10 and 16 ft; the line of columns across the building's width, supporting the main beams, effectively divides up the internal space into bays. The spacing of the bays is designed to suit both the construction of the building and the dimensions of machinery such as looms, etc., so that the internal columns do not interfere too much with machinery layout or storage aisles. The spacing of columns also provides suitable means for supporting LINESHAFTING. **2.** on the Sussex weald, the name for a dam forming a HAMMER POND, the water from which drove iron forging hammers. The word was also used in Somerset and Devon.

bayes (or baise, baize, bays) a coarse woollen cloth with a long nap used for coverings, curtains, and warm clothing. The name possibly comes from the colour bay, a reddish-brown or chestnut to which the cloth was often dyed, although it is said that the cloth originated in Baiae, near Naples, Italy. The cloth was being made in Colchester, Essex in 1660, usually of narrow width, some 18–27 in, and frequently it had a worsted WARP and a woollen WEFT. Double bayes were woven 36 in wide.

beam 1. in a BEAM STEAM ENGINE, the means of transmitting power from the steam cylinder to the point where it was required. The up–down movement of the end of the beam opposite the cylinder produced either a reciprocating motion, or a rotary motion according to the design of the engine. Engine beams were also known as bobs or great levers, and the engines known as lever engines.

The beams of the first beam engines were massive timbers with iron wearing parts. Later, single beams of cast iron were substituted, and on the larger engines twin cast-iron beams. Sometimes these were strengthened by adding a central king post and bridles of wrought iron to the top of the beam to take the tensile stresses, cast iron being weak in this respect. Beams weighing as much as 100 tons were made in the 19th century for very large engines. Usually a beam was pivoted at or near its centre, but in a

GRASSHOPPER or half-beam engine the beam is pivoted at one end.

To prevent overstroking of reciprocating engines, side projections at each end of the beam were fitted which would just touch the engine frame as the beam reached the extremity of its movement. Such devices are unnecessary on rotating beam engines since the revolution of the crank limits the movement of the overhead beam.

2. in the textile industry, a wooden roller or metal tube onto which either WARP or woven cloth is wound. Usually beams have large flanges at each end to guide the warp threads or cloth onto the central part of the beam. Different kinds of beam include warper's beams, onto which warp threads are wound before sizing; weaver's beams – let-off beams fitted at the rear of a loom to hold the sized warps (also known as yarn beams, or simply beams); and take-up beams, onto which woven cloth is slowly wound at the front of the loom as weaving proceeds.

beam arch the arc at each end of early single-acting BEAM STEAM ENGINES, whose centre lay at the pivot of the beam. Chains were wrapped round the arcs or arches and fastened to them at their highest points. One chain was connected to the PISTON ROD, the other to PUMP RODS hanging down a mine shaft. As the piston moved downwards during its power stroke, its chain pulled down the overhead beam, and due to the arch, the chain remained in the same vertical plane. Similarly, at the other end of the beam the chain pulled the pump rods up in the same vertical plane. Beam arches were dispensed with when DOUBLE-ACTING was introduced in 1782; chains were no longer suitable for joining the piston rod to the beam as a rigid rod was necessary to push the beam up on the return power stroke. In the absence of crosshead guides, the movement of the piston rod still had to be maintained in a true vertical line, and this was achieved by Watt's PARALLEL MOTION.

The beam arch is also known as the arch head or sector. To operate injection water pumps and condenser air pumps, smaller arches were positioned on the beam closer to the pivot to give the shorter strokes needed by these auxiliaries. Such arches were known as little arches.

beam bridge bridge in the form of a horizontal structure, either of solid or lattice construction. A beam bridge puts its top half into compression, and its bottom half into tension, as opposed to ARCHED BRIDGES which have compressive stresses only. Since stone and brick and their joints are too weak in tension,

metals – cast iron, wrought iron and later, steel – are used for beam bridges. Simple beam bridges of short span were made of cast iron 'I' cross-section, the lower flange made larger than the top one to resist the tensile bending stresses, cast iron being weaker in tension than in compression. The flanges may be parallel, or the lower one FISHBELLIED. When wrought-iron plates and structural sections became available in quantity and suitable sizes, solid plate girders were used, the component parts riveted together to form the bridge. Hundreds of bridges of this type were used by railways. Solid plate girders are only suitable for modest spans since they deflect under their own weight when the span gets excessive. Lighter constructions, more economical of metal and permitting wider spans, were developed in the early 19th century by using a lattice or truss type construction built up of rolled sections riveted together. Two well-known lattice girders are the PRATT TRUSS and the WARREN GIRDER. The Pratt truss, sometimes known as the Linville truss, was patented by Thomas Willis Pratt (1812–75) and his father Caleb in 1844, and was used extensively on American railways. The Warren girder was patented by James Warren and Willoughby Theobald Monzani (no. 12242, 1848) in Britain. The Pratt truss comprises a series of 'N'-shaped modules, the Warren a series of triangles. Both are designed so that all members of the lattice are either in compression (struts) or in tension (ties) (*see* Figs 11 and 12 for diagrams of various lattices). In some cases the road surface or railway track runs along the top – a deck bridge – or along the bottom between the girders – a through bridge. Another type of beam bridge is the TUBULAR BRIDGE designed by Robert Stephenson (1803–59). Beam bridges are built today in reinforced concrete. *See also* BRIDGE GIRDER, TRUSS.

de Maré, Eric. *The Bridges of Britain*, Batsford, 1954
Richards, J.M. *National Trust Book of Bridges*, Jonathan Cape, 1984

beam engine, *see* BEAM STEAM ENGINE

beam loft the top access floor or platform built round the massive, early BEAM STEAM ENGINES at a level where the rocking beam and its TRUNNIONS could be reached; it was also known as a bob loft. Other floors were the DRIVING FLOOR and the PACKING FLOOR.

beam roller (or warp beam, weaver's beam) a large roller which fits horizontally across the back of a loom on which WARP threads have previously been wound. As weaving proceeds, the beam roller slowly turns, unwinding the warp.

beam steam engine a steam engine which operates machinery via a rocking beam. The first steam engines were of this design. A vertical cylinder containing a piston was mounted below one end of a horizontal beam, and connected to it. The beam was pivoted at or near its centre, and the other end worked reciprocating pumps as it rocked like a child's seesaw under the action of the piston. A beam engine is said to be an indirect acting engine, since the beam is interposed between the piston and the work to be done by the other end of the beam. A variation was the inverted design, with the steam cylinder arranged above the beam.

Beam engines date from 1712 when the first primitive engines were built by Thomas Newcomen (1663–1729) for dewatering Cornish mines. Improvements were made by later engineers such as James Watt (1736–1819) and others, and the beam engine reached its peak in the type known as the CORNISH ENGINE. The earliest beam engines provided vertical reciprocating motion only, but by 1779 rotative designs became available which greatly increased their use since they could now drive machinery. Some beam engines were paired, arranged side-by-side and working a single flywheel positioned between them. Beam engines were the first source of mechanical power to be independent of the vagaries of the weather, which affected the working of waterwheels and windmills. For a long time beam engines were the main prime movers in industry and transport. They began to be superseded from around the mid-19th century by direct acting HORIZONTAL STEAM ENGINES, although beam engines were still being installed as late as 1900 by municipal authorities for pumping water and sewage. Beam engines have long lives, and although thousands have been scrapped, some are still in operation today, and many have been preserved as monuments to the early days of steam power. *See also* NEWCOMEN ATMOSPHERIC ENGINE.

Principal developments of the beam steam engine

1712	Newcomen atmospheric engine (single-acting, non-rotative)
c.1760	Smeaton improvements to Newcomen engine
1769	Watt engine with separate condenser
1779	Watt rotative engine
1782	Watt expansive working, and double-acting
1784	Watt parallel motion
1795	Heslop rotative compound engine
1799	Murdock slide valve
c.1800	side lever engine (low height)
1803	half-beam or grasshopper engine
1804	Woolf compound engine
c.1830	design of Cornish engine established
1841	Sims tandem compound engine
1845	McNaught compound engine

Barton, D.B. *The Cornish Beam Engine*, Cornwall Books, 1989
Dickinson, H.W. *James Watt: Craftsman and Engineer*, Cambridge University Press, 1935
Dickinson, H.W. and Jenkins, R. *Watt and the Steam Engine*, Moorland, 1927; reprinted by Moorland, 1981
Rolt, L.T.C. and Allen, J.S. *The Steam Engine of Thomas Newcomen*, Moorland, 1979

bearded needle a hooked needle made of spring steel, first used on the KNITTING FRAME of William Lee in 1589. The normally open hook or beard is closed by the PRESSER pushing the point into a groove in the straight part of the needle at the appropriate time in the knitting sequence, so that the loop of thread previously made passes over the beard and is not caught by it. *See* Fig. 72(A).

beat used in connection with steam or water flow control valves, a seating against which the moving part of the valve closes. The word conveys the idea of a moving part striking or beating against a stationary part, and is used in describing two designs of control valves – the single-beat valve, and the double-beat valve (*see* Fig. 3).

A simple single-beat valve comprises a circular disk with a conical edge, which fits tightly against a similar edge or seating, in the fixed valve body. The disk can be moved away from the seating to allow a fluid to pass, and this is done by moving a stem attached to the back of the disk which passes through the valve body in a gland which allows this movement without leakage of the fluid being controlled. Thus, when the disk is pressed against the seating in the valve body, all fluid flow is stopped, and when moved clear of the seating, flow commences. The disadvantage of the single-beat valve, particularly where high fluid pressures are involved, is that since the full pressure acts over the valve area, a large force is required to open the valve. The double-beat valve largely eliminated this difficulty: it was first invented by Nicholas Harvey and William West for reducing shock in water pumps, and patented by them in 1839 (patent no. 8103). This design has two seatings in the valve body on which sits a hollow cylindrical moving valve with two corresponding seats. When the valve is shut, very little of the valve area is subjected to unbalanced fluid pressure since it is almost

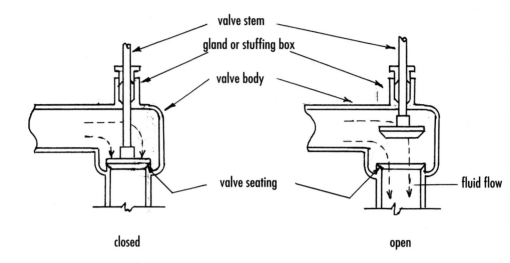

Single-beat valve

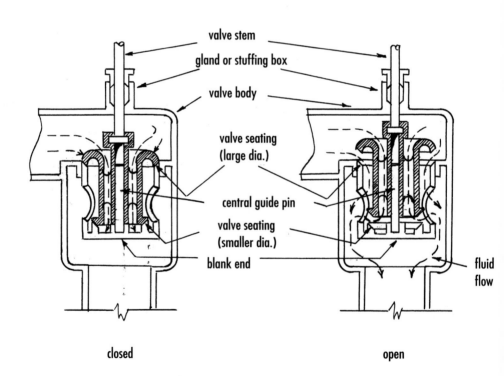

Double-beat valve

Fig. 3. Cross-sections of single- and double-beat valves

balanced by pressure against the slightly smaller blank end, reached through the hollow centre of the cylinder; only a small force is thus needed to open the valve. Another advantage is that only half the lift of a similar sized single-beat valve is necessary because there are two through passages. Double-beat valves are used on high pressures. They are also known as drop valves, Cornish valves, or equilibrium valves.

beating engine, *see* HOLLANDER

beating up in weaving, the movement of the REED which pushes each thread or pass of the WEFT through the SHED against the previously woven fabric to consolidate it. The edge of the consolidated woven fabric is called the FELL of the cloth.

bedplate (or baseplate) a horizontal base of cast iron or steel onto which a machine or engine is bolted. In the early days, steam engines such as Newcomen's were not provided with bedplates, but were fastened directly onto the ground or into the building which housed them – house-built as it was known. A bedplate improves the rigidity, ensures greater accuracy, and simplifies the erection of a machine. It enables it to be erected and tested in the workshop before being dismantled and transferred to site, and spreads the weight better.

Bedplate construction was introduced about 1802 by Matthew Murray (1765–1826). BEAM ENGINES with the overhead rocking beam supported on A-frames carried on a bedplate were developed in the 1850s, and versions with six columns (often fancifully decorated) appeared about the same time until the 1880s, when the design disappeared. As engines increased in size, bedplates were often made in sections and bolted together on site before the machine was erected on them.

bedstone the bottom, stationary stone of a pair of millstones, also known as a nether stone.

beehive boiler, *see* HAYSTACK BOILER

beehive kiln a brick kiln for firing pottery. It has straight vertical sides, and is circular in plan with a domed roof, taking its name from its similarity to a beehive.

beehive mine, *see* BELL PIT

beehive oven a coke-making oven, shaped like a domed beehive. Old, primitive, coke-making ovens, built of rough stones and earth covered, may still be found near coal BELL PITS, where coke was made on the spot. More sophisticated designs, dome-shaped in brick, were built later, often at collieries, or alongside canals. A

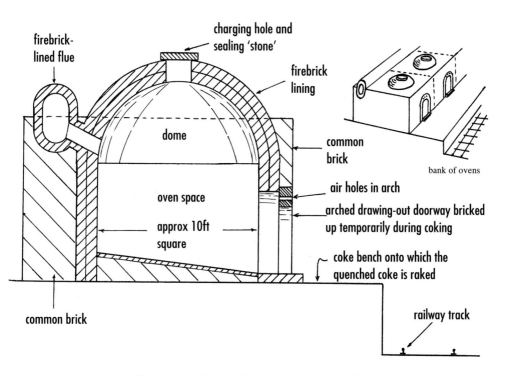

Fig. 4. Cross-section through a beehive coke oven, *c.* 1860

number of ovens were normally arranged side by side in banks; each oven held about 5 tons. Thomas Ramsay patented an oven (no. 81, 1862) for making coke from powdered coal. Fig. 4 shows a typical oven. Crushed coal is fed in at the top, and raked level through the ground-level door. Both doors are sealed while carbonization takes place, and air flow is controlled by plugging or opening the small holes in the door arch. After between 72 and 96 hours, the coke is drawn out through the unbricked door, and quenched on the bench or platform in front of the oven. The domed roof retained enough heat from a previous charge to ignite the gases rising from a fresh charge. Beehive ovens were replaced by patent COKE OVENS in the 19th century.

beetling a finishing process in linen and cotton manufacture in which slowly rotating cloth is pounded by a row of wooden mallets or beetles some 4–8 in square, to close up the weave and put a sheen on the cloth surface. The first beetling 'engines' were water-powered and said to have been invented in 1725 by Hamilton Maxwell of Drumbridge, County Down, Ireland. Beetling can also be arranged to give a 'watered' effect to a cloth surface.

Belfast truss a timber bowstring roof truss with twin curved rafters and twin horizontal ties, rafters and ties connected together by a lattice of diagonal members sandwiched between the pairs of rafters and ties (see Fig. 57). It was used for fairly large spans. This type of truss originated in Belfast, Northern Ireland, around the end of the 19th century. If the diagonals fan out from two imaginary centres below the truss, it is known as a Ritchie girder.
Gould, M.H., Jennings, A. and Montgomery, R. 'The Belfast Truss', *The Structural Engineer*, 70 (1992)

Belgian train, *see* WIRE

bellanding the poisoning of animals caused by contamination of their grazing pastures by emissions from lead smelting operations. The loss of cattle during early lead mining activities led to litigation, and attempts to prevent the emission of lead fumes from smelting furnaces were introduced in the mid-19th century. These took the form of very long flues, usually built into the ground, leading to a distant chimney; the fumes and products of combustion passed along the flue. A high percentage of lead fumes condensed and settled out in the flue: this was removed periodically and resmelted, and the settling flue reduced the poisonous emissions. To improve the condensing of the hot fume, primitive chambers called STOKOE CONDENSERS were introduced in the mid-19th century.

In Derbyshire, powdery lead ore – created by crushing the ore before smelting it – is called belland.

bell casting a craft which dates from the 8th century in Britain, where a bronze alloy of around 76 per cent copper and 24 per cent tin was used. For centuries, small church bells were cast by itinerant bell founders who carried their bell metal with them on packhorses. The bells were cast in loam moulds made from a mixture of sand, chopped hay and horse manure, often sited in the churchyard or a nearby field, a temporary furnace being built for melting the metal and a BELL PIT (2) dug for holding the mould. Remains of such activity can sometimes still be traced in rural areas. Fields near churches and cathedrals, and corners of graveyards can still be found called Bell Pit.

Eventually, static firms emerged who were able to cast much larger bells as well as other objects when the demand for bells was low. Today, only two old established bell foundries remain in Britain, one in Loughborough, Leics., the other in Whitechapel, London. After being cast, a bell is turned upside down on a turntable and rotated against a fixed lathe which machines the inside surface to tune the bell. The insignia of the bell maker, man or company, is cast somewhere on the bell itself, and often an inscription is also cast in the rim of the bell. Besides casting the bell or chime of bells, the bell foundry provides the framework in which the bells are assembled in the church tower. The early name for a bell founder was a belzettar, or belsetter.

bell crank an L-shaped lever, pivoted where the two arms join, the arms being at right angles to each other and lying in the same plane. Usually the arms are of equal length, but not necessarily so. A bell crank is used to convert motion from one direction to another at 90° to it, e.g. from horizontal to vertical. It is also known as an angle bob, especially when one arm is weighted to balance the weight of parts attached to the other, e.g. PUMP RODS hanging down a mine shaft.

bellows a device for forcing air into a furnace to increase the rate of burning and raise the temperature. Bellows comprise a pair of flat boards joined by a flexible leather skirt, with an outlet pipe through which air under pressure is forced when the boards are brought together. A one-way air inlet valve flap allows air to enter the space between the boards when the bellows are open, and closes as the boards come together, trapping the air inside which is pressurized by the closing movement of the boards.

Early bellows in forges, etc., were usually operated by waterwheels. Cams on the shaft, which was turned by the wheel, opened the bellows, and weights closed them. Two bellows working alternately were necessary to give a continuous blast of air to the furnace. This simple type of bellows was replaced by cast-iron blowing cylinders or engines which gave a more powerful blast. The first such blowing engine was introduced by John Smeaton (1724–92) at the Carron Ironworks, near Falkirk, Scotland, around 1760.

bell pit 1. an early form of mining for metallic ores and coal. Shallow shafts up to about 20 ft deep were dug to reach the coal seam or metal vein lying just below the surface. The unwanted soil and rock was spread out around the shaft in a ring. After the wanted material had been dug out and raised to the surface, either by a simple windlass, or carried up ladders in baskets, the base of the shaft was widened out to extract more coal or ore. This undercutting was extended outwards in a circular fashion without any roof supports until it became unsafe to go further for fear of a roof collapse. The resulting shape of the excavation in a vertical section was therefore like the outline of a hand bell, with the vertical access shaft as the bell handle. Another bell pit would then be dug a short distance away so that the 'caves' nearly touched. Mining proceeded in this manner, and the soil etc. from the second pit would be partly backfilled into the first shaft to close it up for safety.

There are many remains of bell pits in old mining areas in open country. They can be readily detected by a sunken depression surrounded by a raised, circular mound, usually overgrown. Sometimes traces of the material mined can be found in the raised mound, where it was thrown away or dropped. Coal and iron ore bell pits are usually scattered about the area mined, whereas lead ore bell pits are usually in lines as the course of the vein was followed. Bell pits date from the 16th through to the early 18th centuries. Not many were dug after the latter date since by that time the easiest reached seams had been worked out, and deeper mining techniques were necessary to reach lower deposits. Bell pits are sometimes called a beehive mine, again because of the shape of the underground cavity.

2. the name, sometimes seen marked on maps or plans, on a field or other point close to a church or cathedral, given to a pit used for BELL CASTING in medieval times.

Belpaire firebox   a locomotive firebox invented in 1860 by the Belgian, Alfred Belpaire (1820–93), which he later modified in shape and details. It was adopted in Britain in 1891 and became more or less the standard firebox in British locomotives because of its high efficiency.

belt drive   endless leather belts also known as straps, were extensively used to drive machinery from overhead LINESHAFTING in the 18th and 19th centuries. The belts, made in various widths and thicknesses, were flat, and the power which could be transmitted depended on their dimensions, the linear speed of the belt, and the amount of frictional lap round the connected pulleys, i.e. the arc of contact between belt and pulley. Linear speeds of up to 3,000 ft per minute were used, and a 4:1 ratio between the pulley diameters was about the maximum difference in practice, although this could be increased by using a JOCKEY PULLEY. The wide rims of the pulleys were slightly crowned outwards to keep the belt central whilst running. It was possible to disconnect a machine from the constantly running lineshaft when required, by use of FAST AND LOOSE PULLEYS and BELT STRIKING GEAR. Open, unprotected belt drives were a source of accidents in their early days until legislation forced them to be guarded or boxed in. The coming of electric motors around the 1890s to drive each machine eventually eliminated the forest of belt drives once common in textile mills and engineering workshops.

belt striking gear   a simple mechanism, also known as a strap fork, by which a belt driving a machine could be moved sideways from a fast (driving) pulley onto a loose (non-driving) pulley, or vice versa. It comprised a metal fork through which the moving belt passed, and a lever within reach of the machine operator, which when moved slid the belt sideways. Operating the belt striking gear enabled the machine to be stopped or put into motion. *See also* BELT DRIVE, FAST AND LOOSE PULLEYS.

bent   a mining term used to describe the point where a vein of metallic ore suddenly deviates from its normal direction.

Berlin Decree, *see* CONTINENTAL SYSTEM (2)

Berlin wool, *see* ZEPHYR

Berthollet process   the method for making the first chemical bleaching agent, discovered by the French chemist Claude Louis Berthollet (1748–1822) in 1785. His process involved passing chlorine through potash to make a bleaching liquid called *Eau de Javelle* (named after a district near Paris). Berthollet's process was the base from which Charles Tennant (1768–1838) and Charles Macintosh (1766–1843) developed their bleaching powder thirteen years later.

Bessemer steel name given to the first cheap, mass-produced variety of steel, made by blowing air through molten iron in a vessel called a CONVERTER until all the carbon present in the iron is burnt off, no additional fuel being needed. A known quantity of carbon and manganese, in the form of SPIEGELEISEN is then added to produce a mild steel. It is named after Henry Bessemer (1813–98) who discovered the process in 1856.

Bessemer steel actually ran through two stages of development. The original process required high-grade non-phosphoric haematite iron ores from Cumberland and the Forest of Dean, or imported pure iron ore from Sweden and Spain. The refractory lining of the converter was an acid silica material which was severely attacked during the melting if other irons were used, thus precluding most of Britain's iron ores which contained phosphorus; the first Bessemer steel was thus called ACID STEEL. Goran Fredrik Goransson, working in Edsken, Sweden, under licence from Bessemer, developed the process further in 1858. In 1878, Sidney Gilchrist Thomas (1850–85) developed the second variety known as BASIC STEEL, by substituting a basic dolomite lining which allowed less pure iron ores, including the bulk of British and other phosphoric ores, to be used. On the Continent, the basic process is known as the Thomas process. In a further development, Robert Forester Mushet (1811–91) found that adding ferro-alloys in the form of special pigs rich in carbon, silicon, and manganese (his 'triple compound') removed the oxygen from Bessemer steel, the process being known as deoxidation.

For a number of years both acid and basic Bessemer steels were made, but gradually the Bessemer process was superseded by the OPEN HEARTH method; it is now obsolete, with the last steel produced by the old method (an acid steel) in 1974.

Barraclough, K.C. *Steelmaking 1850–1900*, Institute of Metals, 1990
Gale, W.K.V. *Iron and Steel*, Ch. 6, Longmans, 1969
Mushet, R. *The Bessemer–Mushet Process for the Manufacture of Cheap Steel*, 1883

bevel gears toothed gearwheels designed to transmit power or motion from a driving shaft to a following or driven shaft which lies at an angle to the driving shaft. Most bevels work at 90° to each other, but the angle between the intersecting shafts need not be at right angles. As with other gears, there may be a difference in the speed of rotation between driver and driven depending on the number of teeth on each bevel. Bevels thus perform the same function as SPUR WHEELS on parallel shafts, but their gear teeth, instead of being parallel to each other as in spurs, diminish in thickness and pitch across their face as the apex of an imaginary cone connecting the bevels is approached. If a pair of bevels have the same number of teeth, and join two intersecting shafts at right angles to each other, they are properly called mitre wheels.

Bevel gears were commonly used in early textile mills where the horizontal driving shaft of the prime mover – a WATERWHEEL or BEAM STEAM ENGINE – transmitted power to LINESHAFTING on each mill floor via a vertical shaft which ran up through the floors. A pair of bevels connected the driving shaft to the vertical shaft, and more pairs of bevels drove each lineshaft in turn. By employing smaller bevels on each lineshaft, a more useful speed of revolution to drive the machinery was obtained from the slow moving vertical shaft. Bevel gearing used in this way was superseded in time by rope drives off the engine flywheel. Bevel gears have, of course, innumerable other uses in machinery where a change in direction of transmitted power is required. The first use of cast-iron bevels for mill work is attributed to William Murdock (1754–1839) who had them cast by the Carron Ironworks in the 1760s.

bi-cylindro-conical drum a WINDING DRUM with a special profile across its width, used especially at deep coal mine shafts. As the rope is wound onto the drum, the radius of the profile varies, first to reduce the starting torque on the engine, then to assist the acceleration of the cage, and finally to help slow it down as the end of the wind is reached.

'Big Ben' the nickname given to Edmund Cartwright's (1743–1823) improved wool COMBING machine of 1792 (patent no. 1876). It was named after a prize fighter of the day on account of its flailing action. Although not a success, the machine was naturally unpopular with hand combers who saw in it the beginnings of the mechanization of their trade. The hand wool combers of Doncaster expressed their opposition in a doggerel song, the first verse of which ran:

Come, all ye Master Combers, and hear of
new Big Ben,
He'll comb more wool in one day than fifty
of your men
With their hand-combs and comb-pots and
such old fashioned ways,
There'll be no more occasion for old Bishop
Blaize.

Bishop Blaize was the patron saint of wool combers.

Big Ben had a circular revolving comb, an idea which was followed successfully by later inventors of wool combers, such as the NOBLE and LISTER machines of the 1850s. Cartwright's wool combing patent was infringed during its lifetime and, despite securing an extension in 1801 to the life of his patent, he made no money from it.

billet another name for a bloom, or lump of iron or steel. It is also an intermediate product in the rolling of a steel ingot, being smaller than an ingot but larger than a bar, usually of a cross-section no bigger than about 5 in square.

billy a machine for making ROVINGS. In the days of the hand spinning JENNY in the woollen industry, wool which had been carded through the early Arkwright-type rotary carder came off in strips of fibre the width of the machine. This was because the last roller on the carder was covered by card cloth in strips across the roller, usually about 36 in wide. The strips of sliver or slubbing had to be pieced together and drawn out before they were suitable for spinning in the jenny, and this operation was performed on a wooden, hand-worked machine called a billy. A billy was a jenny or kind of mule modified to take the strips of slubbing instead of the ROVINGS normally fed to it. Billies, sometimes called slubbing billies or roving billies, remained in use in the woollen industry until about 1850, by which time they had become power driven and had entered spinning mills. They became unnecessary as carding machines were improved and delivered single slivers. Billies were also used in the cotton industry, and the machine was possibly invented by John Swindells of Stockport, Ches., some time in the 1780s.

The origin of the word billy is obscure. It possibly comes from an old Northern dialect word meaning mate or friend, indicating that the machine was of assistance in the preparation of the roving for the jenny.

bing 1. lumps of galena, or top quality lead ore, not needing much cleaning off of unwanted rock. A bingstead is a place where bing ore was stored. **2.** an old mining measure of 8 cwt (896 lb) of lead. **3.** in Scotland, a slag heap, or waste from a coal mine.

biscuit 1. pottery after its first firing, in a kiln, known as a biscuit oven or a biscuit kiln. If GLAZING or decorating is required, it is added to the biscuit and hardened on by a second firing in a glost oven. **2.** a lump of smoked RUBBER on a flat stick. In the early days of rubber harvesting, native tappers in Brazilian jungles coagulated the latex over a wood fire by pouring the liquid onto a flat stick which was rapidly rotated in the smoke until a lump about 2 ft long and 1 ft in diameter had built up. These lumps or biscuit rubbers were floated down river on a raft to traders near the coast.

bit-gatherer in the hand manufacture of glass articles, a man who takes lumps of molten glass from the furnace and hands them to the SERVITOR.

bituminous coal coals containing a high proportion of volatile hydrocarbons. Most British coals are bituminous, although there are variations in their chemical composition. Carbon contents can range from 75 per cent to as high as 97 per cent, and hydrogen from 1.5 to 5.7 per cent by weight. The coals can be subdivided into caking and non-caking varieties: the softer caking coals are used for making town or coal gas and coke, and for steam raising in boilers; non-caking coals, once known as splint coals, are harder and more compact, and are mostly used as domestic fuel. Most bituminous coals burn with a long flame.

Blackburn loom, *see* LANCASHIRE LOOM

black-cawke, *see* GRAPHITE

black damp a mining term for non-inflammable carbon dioxide or air in which the oxygen has been replaced by carbon dioxide as the result of an explosion or combustion. Black damp is invisible, and heavier than air: the word damp comes from the German *Dampf*, meaning smoke, gas or steam. It is also known as after damp and choke damp, because it causes choking and suffocation.

Black Friday the name given to Friday 11 May 1866, which saw the collapse of the railway boom. This brought an end to the reckless speculation which was current in the late 1850s, encouraged by the investment finance companies of the day who provided capital to industrial entrepreneurs, by borrowing it themselves. Injudicious dealings led to liquidity problems, which caused a loss of confidence among depositors who became worried by rumours of over-commitment. There was a panic run on money, causing the greatest finance company in Britain, Overend, Gurney and Co., in London, to collapse and stop payments on Friday 11 May 1866. This brought ruin to many investors and railway companies, not only in Britain, but in Europe and elsewhere.

black jack, *see* BLENDE

blacklead, *see* GRAPHITE

blackleg, *see* KNOBSTICK

black oak, *see* QUERCITRON

black powder, *see* GUNPOWDER MANUFACTURE

black seed cotton, *see* SEA ISLAND COTTON

blackstone, *see* TOADSTONE

black tin, *see* CASSITERITE

black walnut, *see* BUTTERNUT

blackwood, *see* LOGWOOD

Blanketeers hundreds of starving handloom weavers and spinners who met in St Peter's Field, Manchester on 10 March 1817, each carrying a blanket, for their intended march to London to present a petition about their plight to the Prince Regent. Although to some extent the Blanketeers' demands were political, the underlying reason for the unrest was the economic depression which followed the cessation of the Napoleonic Wars two years earlier. There was high industrial unemployment, particularly in the cotton trade, exacerbated by the demobilization of some 400,000 ex-soldiers seeking work.

The march itself was a failure, for 167 Blanketeers were arrested before they reached Stockport, Ches., and although a few hundred more struggled as far as Derbyshire, only one man is known to have reached London. He handed in the petition on 18 March. However, unrest continued, culminating in the PETERLOO MASSACRE in 1819.

White, R.J. *Waterloo to Peterloo*, Mercury Books, 1963

blast furnace a vertical furnace for smelting metallic ores, using an air blast to attain high temperatures. The common use of blast furnaces is for smelting iron ore to produce PIG IRON, but similar furnaces are used for smelting other metals such as copper and lead. Primitive blast furnaces for smelting iron originated in Belgium, and were introduced into Britain in the early 16th century. Charcoal was used for fuel, with the air blast provided by water-powered bellows. Furnaces were therefore sited near water supplies in wooded areas where a ready supply of CHARCOAL could be obtained, rather than near ore deposits. This reduced the amount of transport needed. Often, early furnaces were built into hillsides to facilitate top charging (*see* Figs 5 and 8). Production of pig iron expanded rapidly in the 17th and 18th centuries. Denuding of forests for charcoal making became a big problem, which fortunately was alleviated in 1709 when Abraham Darby I (1667–1717) succeeded in using coke instead of charcoal in his blast furnace at Coalbrookdale, Salop. Coke was made by slow, air-starved combustion of local coal in clamps: limestone FLUX assisted SLAG formation in the furnace. However, the use of coke spread only slowly in Britain, and did not become widespread until the late 18th century. Charcoal-fired furnaces were still operated in

Backbarrow blast furnace, Cumbria. Built in 1711, this was the last furnace to change from charcoal to coke during the 1920s

decreasing numbers until the last one ceased using charcoal as late as the 1920s at Backbarrow, Cumbria.

Various improvements to blast furnaces were made by a number of engineers and inventors. The introduction of steam driven blowers in 1775 enabled furnaces to become independent of water power; HOT BLAST, introduced in 1828, whereby the air was heated in a separate coal-fired chamber, reduced coke consumption; and the regenerative heat exchanger, first used in 1857, used the heat in the waste gases to preheat the blast air (*see* COWPER STOVE).

Essentially, a blast furnace comprises a vertical, large diameter metal tube, refractory lined, which narrows at its base, and sits on top of a refractory hearth. Some early furnaces were square in cross-section. The air is forced into the furnace just above the hearth, through metal nozzles called TUYÈRES, to ensure rapid combustion and a high temperature. When smelting iron, the ore and coke are fed in at the top together with limestone, and as the charge descends, the coke burns in intimate contact with the ore, melting out the iron which collects in the bottom hearth. The products of combustion leave from the top of the furnace, and the molten iron is run out from time to time through a TAP HOLE in the hearth, into moulds made in a sand floor as pigs. The limestone flux combines with impurities in the ore to form a molten slag which floats on top of the molten iron, and is removed through another tap hole in a similar manner to the iron. The iron picks up carbon from the coke, and normally contains from 2.5 to 4.5 per cent depending on the ore smelted. The pigs of iron are the raw material from which WROUGHT IRON or STEEL may be made in subsequent processes. Alternatively, the pigs may be re-melted in a CUPOLA FURNACE to make iron castings.

Palmer, M. and D. 'Moira Furnace', *Industrial Archaeology Review* I (1976), 63–9
Raistrick, A. 'The Old Furnace at Coalbrookdale, Shropshire', *Industrial Archaeology Review* IV (1980), 117–34
Riden, P. *A Gazetteer of Charcoal-fired Blast Furnaces in Great Britain in use since 1660*, Merton Priory Press, 1993
Survivals of 17th and 18th Century Blast Furnaces, Historical Metallurgy Group of the Iron and Steel Institute, 1973

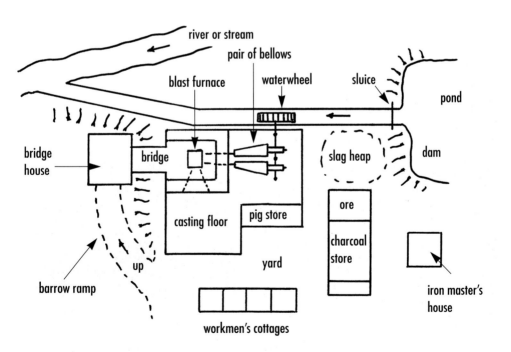

Fig. 5. Typical layout of a charcoal blast furnace for producing cast-iron pigs for the indirect process of iron making (mid-18th century)

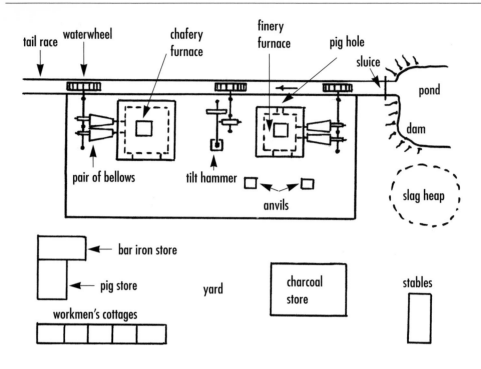

Fig. 6. Typical layout for a refinery forge for making wrought-iron bars from cast-iron pigs (mid-18th century)

blast lamp, *see* CLANNY LAMP

blast pipe **1.** pipe which conveys exhaust steam from the cylinders of a locomotive to an upwards-pointing nozzle placed in the chimney. As each jet of exhaust steam is emitted, a partial vacuum is created in the chimney which induces a greater amount of air to enter the firegrate than would occur under natural draught. This considerably raises the rate of burning of the fuel, enabling higher and sustained steam pressures to be maintained. A primitive blast pipe was used by Richard Trevithick (1771–1833) in his steam driven road vehicle, the 'Travelling Engine' in 1802, to increase boiler draught, and again on the Penydarran locomotive in 1804. George Stephenson (1781–1848) used one *c.*1815 on his Killingworth steam locomotives. A few years later, he tried to create a blast with two bellows worked by eccentrics under the locomotive. A variable blast pipe comprising a movable cone inside the pipe, controlled by a lever from the cab, was introduced by Peter Rothwell (1792–1849) of Bolton, Lancs., in 1839 for use on locomotives. **2.** pipe through which air under pressure is forced from a blower to the TUYÈRES in a blast furnace or to

a BESSEMER converter. The blast or bustle pipe encircles the furnace with branch pipes leading to each tuyère.

bleach croft a field over which freshly woven 'grey' cloth was spread out and regularly washed and turned to be bleached white by the prolonged action of sunlight; sometimes called a bleach green, a whitening field, or simply a croft. Such fields surrounded early bleach and dye works but were eventually dispensed with when chemical BLEACHING was introduced at the beginning of the 19th century, although the building in which chemical bleaching takes place is still called a croft today.

An early 18th-century method of operating a bleach croft was to boil up the grey cloth, adding sour milk or some other easily obtained acidic liquor, and then to lay out the pieces to dry and bleach in the sun. Boiling sheds were sited to one side on large bleach crofts. The turning and regular washing of the pieces was frequently performed by women. Nightwatchmen and, often hidden, mantraps or spring guns were used to guard the cloth against theft, which was a penal offence (*see* CROFT BREAKING).

Bleach crofts needed an ample supply of clean water for washing the cloth, so were sited on meadows alongside a suitable stream or river. Bolton, Lancs., became the bleaching centre for cotton cloth in England in the 18th century, carrying out bleaching on a commission basis for the nearby mills. The water in the area was particularly suitable, being soft and clean. In Ireland, the Trustees of the Linen and Hempen Manufacturers of Ireland specified the requirements of bleach greens in 1724. They had to be sited on suitable streams and comprise water channels for sprinkling the 'brown' (i.e. unbleached) linen cloth during bleaching, together with a buck, or boiling house with boilers and kiers for steeping and boiling the cloth, and vats for lyes and sours.

bleaching removal of the natural colour of cloth and any impurities by an oxidation process. The word comes from the Anglo-Saxon *blaecan* meaning 'to be pale'. Raw cloth needs bleaching or whitening before it can be dyed or colour printed. Long before the Industrial Revolution, bleaching was done by prolonged exposure of cloth to the oxidizing action of sunlight. Woollen cloth was stretched out on TENTER FRAMES, and cotton pegged out flat on grass in BLEACH CROFTS. The process was very slow, and only possible in the summer months. It was hastened by first scouring the cloth in a lye containing plant ashes (*see* BOWKING), then treating it with dilute acid (*see* SOURING). Frequent washing and turning of the pieces was all done by hand. One method, not dependent on sunlight, was to hang wet cloth in a sulphur house, a brick- or stone-built large room, inside which fumes from burning pots of sulphur whitened the pieces.

Faster methods were sought and a breakthrough came with the discovery of chemical bleaching in 1785, when Claude Louis Berthollet (1746–1822) demonstrated the action of chlorine on fabrics in France. The method came to Britain within a couple of years, and by 1799 the partners Charles Tennant (1768–1838) and Charles Macintosh (1766–1843) were making a chlorine-based bleaching powder in Glasgow, Scotland. Chemical bleaching rapidly spread, revolutionizing the textile industry by removing the bottleneck of traditional slow bleaching. It could now be carried out under cover in a few days, all the year round. This encouraged a large increase in cloth manufacture, matching the introduction of the POWER LOOM. The cost of making bleaching powder rapidly fell at Tennant and Macintosh's works. In 1800, only 59 tons were made, sold at £140 per ton – a very high price at that time. In 1850, 5,719 tons were made, and sold at £14

per ton, a price reduction reflected in the price of cloth.

Since bleachworks need large quantities of clean water, they were sited in river valleys in the textile producing areas. Many firms developed from the old crofting days by adopting chemical methods, usually in association with dyeing and printing and other cloth finishing processes. By the early 19th century, machinery began to replace manual methods for handling the individual pieces of cloth. Continuous bleaching was introduced by temporarily sewing the pieces together to form a long 'ribbon' of cloth which was drawn through the various processes by powered winches. The cloth snaked through overhead porcelain 'eyes' between vats and kiers to keep it clear of the factory floor.

A bleaching process is also used in the PAPER MAKING business, for whitening paper.

Higgins, S.H. *A History of Bleaching*, Longmans Green, 1924

McTear, J. 'The growth of the alkali and bleaching powder manufacture of the Glasgow district', *Chemical News* XXXV (1877)

Musson, A.E. and Robinson, E. *Science and Technology in the Industrial Revolution* (Chapter 8), Manchester University Press, 1969

blende sulphide of zinc, the common ore from which zinc is obtained; often associated with lead deposits. It is also called sphalerite, mock lead, or black jack. The name blende comes from the German *blenden* meaning to deceive, since zinc-blende resembles GALENA (lead ore), but yields no lead. The ore is found in Derbyshire, Cumberland, and Cornwall. Other blendes include manganese-blende and antimony-blende.

bleu foncé a navy blue hempen, linen, or woollen cloth popular in the mid-19th century for garments.

blister steel wrought iron which has had its surface converted into steel by the CEMENTATION PROCESS. Before about 1740 this was the only 'steel' available. It was produced by prolonged heating of wrought-iron bars in contact with charcoal inside airtight chests. Carbon was absorbed, and resulted in a rough, blistery surface, hence the name. It was in effect a wrought-iron core with a steel outer skin. Blister steel was used for making edge-cutting tools, its flexible, low carbon inner core combined with its hard outer skin – capable of maintaining a cutting edge – making it very suitable for this purpose. It was also the starting point for the manufacture of CRUCIBLE STEEL developed by Benjamin Huntsman (1704–76) in 1740. Production of blister steel ceased around 1860, when better ways of making cheaper steel had been invented.

block short name for a pulley block for manually lifting heavy weights. A pulley block comprises two sets of freely rotating grooved pulleys or sheaves, each set held in a frame or cage. One set of sheaves is hooked onto an overhead support and the load to be lifted is hooked onto the cage of the other set. A long rope or chain is wound over pairs of sheaves in sequence, connecting the two sets together. One end of the rope is permanently secured to the upper cage, the other end hangs loose. By pulling on the loose end, a load may be raised, a mechanical advantage existing depending on the number of connected pairs of sheaves. Thus, a small pulling force acting through a certain distance will lift a greater load through a smaller distance.

Blocks have many uses. They may be permanently located, say in a warehouse or workshop, or be portable, for example when used to help erect heavy machine parts on site. Wooden blocks were very important on sailing ships for raising and lowering sails, loading and unloading, etc. and thousands were needed every year in the early 19th century by the navy. Marc Isambard Brunel (1769–1849) designed forty-four machines for mass production of wooden blocks for Portsmouth Naval Dockyard in 1808. Some of his machinery was in use for 140 years.

Cooper, C.C. 'The production line at Portsmouth Block Mill', *Industrial Archaeology Review* VI (1981–82), 28–44

Gilbert, K.R. *The Portsmouth Block-making Machinery*, HMSO, 1965

block printing a method of printing coloured patterns and designs by hand on silk and cotton fabrics etc., and on wallpapers, using carved wooden blocks. Blocks measuring about 12 by 7 in area, made in hard, fine-grained woods, or softer woods faced with sycamore, were engraved in relief, i.e. with the background cut away, to leave a raised flat design on the surface. Where fine lines were required, shaped thin metal strips were let into the wood block, the strips offering greater resistance to wear than if fine ribs were left on the wood itself. Metal pins were placed in the corners of the blocks to leave dots on the material being printed to act as registers to aid the accurate placing of adjoining or superimposed blocks. Felt was let into the printing surface wherever an area of solid colour was required.

Moist colouring matter was placed in a shallow tray and the printing block lightly dipped into it so that the colour was smeared on its surface, and carefully transferred to the fabric or paper stretched across a printing table by pressing the block onto the material. A different block was used for each colour, and several blocks might be required to build up a large design. The pattern was repeated by sequential applications as desired.

Block printing was extensively carried out in London in the late 17th century, dyed cloth being sent there from the textile districts for printing and finishing. Later, the industry moved to the northern textile towns and usually became part of a bleaching and dyeing concern. The craft of block printing was a specialized one, and there was once a block printer's trade union.

This hand method of printing designs on textiles persisted well into the 19th century, although it was beginning to be replaced in the 1770s by machines using engraved rollers which printed continuously repeating patterns onto rolls of cloth. The continuous printing of wallpaper was introduced in 1839. *See also* CALICO PRINTING.

block tin tin smelted and cast into blocks of about 3 cwt (336 lb) and stamped while still in a soft state with the mark or design of the smelter.

blondin an alternative name for an aerial ropeway or cableway for transporting materials across a quarry or similar opening. It comprises a system of cables stretching over the quarry from supports on either side, so that a skip can travel along the cables and be raised or lowered at any point along them. Devised in the 1870s, it takes its name from Charles Blondin (1824–97), the famous French tightrope walker.

bloodstone, *see* HAEMATITE ORE

bloom 1. a mass or lump of malleable or wrought iron which, after undergoing its first hammering or SHINGLING, is formed into a piece about 2 ft long with a square cross-section, weighing around 120 lb. The bloom was made in a PUDDLING FURNACE or BLOOMERY. The name comes from the old Saxon *bloma*, meaning a lump of metal. Often the bloom was fashioned with an enlarged square knob at each end, of different sizes: the larger end was called the mocket head, and the smaller the ancony. The bloom needed shingling to expel the SLAG impurities entrapped in it. 2. a steel ingot which has been rolled to about 7.25 in square in cross-section in a blooming or COGGING MILL.

bloomery a simple furnace for smelting iron ore to produce a wrought-iron bloom. Primitive bloomeries consisted of a stone hearth with a domed baked clay top. Iron ore was smelted on the hearth using charcoal as fuel, and the clay top was broken open to extract the BLOOM and remade at each smelt. This was the direct

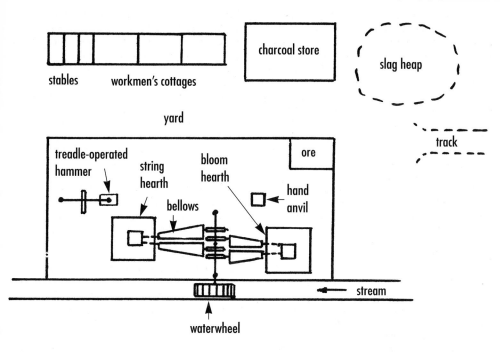

Fig. 7. Typical layout of an early two-hearth bloomery with treadle-operated hammer

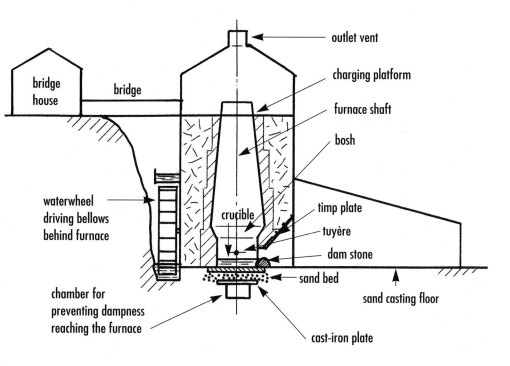

Fig. 8. An 18th-century charcoal-fired blast furnace

method of making iron. Since one ton of iron would consume about 20 acres of woodland, bloomeries were sited in forested areas rather than near the source of the ore, to reduce transport costs. When the surrounding fuel was exhausted, a bloomery would be abandoned, and a fresh site started elsewhere. Bloomeries were in use for many centuries, from the Middle Ages until BLAST FURNACES began to be built in numbers in the 17th century. Although the yield of iron from a bloomery was very low compared with that from a blast furnace, bloomeries continued in use for many years in remote places contemporaneously with blast furnaces, until they could no longer compete.

Iron blooms need hammering to expel entrained SLAG to make them suitable for subsequent use. At first this was done under treadle operated hammers, and later by water-powered hammers. Some bloomeries had only one hearth in which the initial smelting, and any reheating required for the hammering operation, took place; such a bloomery is called a bloomhearth or bloomsmithy. Other larger bloomeries with two hearths – one for smelting, one for reheating – are known as STRINGHEARTHS. Water-powered bellows provided the air streams for the furnaces. A bloomhearth was worked by a bloomer, a stringhearth by a smith. Fig. 7 shows a typical layout of an early bloomery equipped with two hearths.

blow the descriptive name given to the cycle of operations in a BESSEMER CONVERTER when air is blown in to remove the carbon and impurities from the molten pig iron. In an acid-lined converter, the blow lasts about 15 minutes; a large yellowish flame leaves the top of the vessel, and as it dies down the man in charge, the blower, tells by experience when the metal is ready to be poured into a ladle. In the case of a basic-lined converter, an AFTERBLOW occurs before the sequence is completed.

blowing engine a steam engine driving a reciprocating air pump to provide air for a BLAST FURNACE. A typical blowing engine of the mid-18th century was a BEAM ENGINE with the steam cylinder working one end of the overhead beam in the usual manner, and a large diameter blowing cylinder, or tub as it was known, at the other. Tubs of 80–100 in diameter were made, to force large quantities of air at around 5 psi to blast furnaces. In the 1750–60s, tubs were single-acting, but by the 1770–80s they were double-acting. Blowing engines were sometimes arranged in pairs, discharging air into a common main which served several

furnaces at a large ironworks. The air blast was often maintained at a steady pressure by a water regulator interposed between the blower(s) and the furnace(s). A water regulator comprised a water-filled brick pit holding an inverted iron box, which had an open side below the water surface forming a sealed air space above the water. The air pipe from the blowing engine led into the sealed air space, and another pipe led from it to the furnace. Any fluctuation in air pressure was smoothed out by the rise and fall of the water level inside the box. Beam engines were later replaced by more modern engines, and the use of blowers as described began to decline around the 1870s when improved types of air blower became available.

Arnott, A.T. and Sayer, M. 'Beam engines in blast furnace blowing', *Industrial Archaeology Review* III pp. 29–44 (1978)
David and Sampson, a Pair of Blast Furnace Blowing Engines, booklet 4.03, Ironbridge Gorge Museum Trust, 1973.

blowing house name given to the 17th- and 18th-century tin smelting BLAST FURNACES which used charcoal as fuel. The bellows providing the blast were driven by small waterwheels, and the molten tin was frequently cast into moulds made from granite.

blowing room department in a cotton spinning mill which houses the cotton opening and cleansing machinery, i.e. bale openers or breakers, SCUTCHERS and WILLOWS. The name is descriptive: air streams are important in assisting the removal of the lighter impurities found in the bales, such as sand and dust. All the machines are connected to exhaust fans to convey such impurities away from the cotton as it is processed in the department, which is isolated from the main spinning rooms and usually placed on the ground floor. After extraction of the airborne dust etc. via ducting, the dirty air passes through a filtering device which separates the dust for disposal.

blow valve, *see* SNIFTING VALVE

bluewood, *see* LOGWOOD

blunger a machine used in the pottery industry for mixing clay, flint powder, etc. in water in a cylindrical vessel by revolving knives. The mixing action is called blunging, a word which is possibly a combination of 'bludgeoning' and 'plunging' since the process of mixing the clay resembles these two motions, especially in hand mixing.

boardgate wooden boards laid on the floor of a mine gallery to form a smoother passageway along which trucks and barrows can be pushed, similar to the wheelbarrow runs used on construction sites. The word 'gate' means a way or road.

boat lift a structure for vertically raising or lowering canal boats for direct transfer from lower water courses to higher ones and vice versa; also known as a canal lift. Several such structures have been built in situations where locks were not practical: there are some well-known boat lifts in Belgium and France, although lifts were probably first installed in Britain. An early design for a boat lift was that patented in Britain by James Fussell in 1798 (patent no. 2284) and intended for the Dorset and Somerset Canal, but never completed. Seven lifts were used by James Green on the Grand Western Canal near Taunton, Som., in 1838, with lifts varying from 16 ft to 46 ft. These were simple balance locks, comprising two tanks containing water connected by cables passing over pulleys on a framework. When a boat needed lifting from the lower level, extra water was run into the upper tank until it outweighed the lower tank containing the boat, its descent being controlled by a brake on the pulleys. These lifts ran for 30 years.

A well-known boat lift, originally hydraulically operated, is the Anderton Lift, near Northwich, Ches., connecting the Trent and Mersey Canal with the river Weaver some 50 ft below. This was built in 1875, designed by Edwin Clark (1814–1894) following an earlier proposal by Edward Leader Williams (1828–1910), the engineer of the Manchester Ship Canal. It comprises two long tanks side-by-side, each capable of holding 70 ft long canal boats which are floated into them. The tanks can then be raised or lowered as required between the two water levels. In 1908 the hydraulic system was changed to electric power. The lift replaced a steep inclined plane which had been in operation since 1799.

Similar lifts are called boat railways in the USA; the Morris Canal near New York had 23 lifts along its length.

Tew, David. *Canal Inclines and Lifts*, Alan Sutton Publishing, 1984

bobbin a spool for holding yarn or thread which is wound onto it, and from which it is unwound as required. There are various sorts of bobbins. In weaving most bobbins were made from wood: those for holding WARP yarn have flanges, whilst those for holding WEFT do not. In hand-made pillow or BOBBIN LACE, bobbins are small diameter rods some 4 in long with a recess turned at one end, in which 7 to 8 yd of thread are wound. Many bobbins are employed in producing the patterned lace. Attached to the opposite end of the bobbin is a circle of beads, the spangle, whose purpose is to give weight to tension the thread. The beads are either cubes or flat sided, so that the bobbin will not roll about on the pillow when not in use, and get in the way of the lace-maker. LACE MAKING bobbins were made from wood (often from apple, cherry or plum trees, or spindlewood) or sometimes from pewter, glass, or bone, and frequently highly decorated. In the bobbinet lace making machine invented by John Heathcoat in 1808, flat, disk-like bobbins were used which could pass between the vertical warp threads and twist the weft round them (*see* OLD LOUGHBOROUGH).

The bobbin on a spinning wheel has a WHARF or whorl integral with it at one end. The wharf is made slightly smaller in diameter than the wharf fixed on the spindle on which the bobbin is loosely mounted. This is so that the bobbin rotates faster than the flyer which is fixed on the spindle, thus winding the spun yarn onto the bobbin.

bobbing John Scottish name for a WATER-BALANCE ENGINE

bobbin lace type of LACE introduced into Britain by Flemish refugees in the 16th century as a hand craft. The pattern is drawn on parchment which is stretched over a straw-filled pillow or cushion: pins are stuck into the pillow to reproduce the pattern. Silk or linen cotton threads are twisted, looped or plaited round the pins, the threads being wound from small BOBBINS. When the area being worked on is complete, the pins are removed, the lace moved on, and the process repeated after refixing the pins. Bobbin lace is also known as pillow lace, cushion lace, and bone lace, the latter because some bobbins were made from bone.

Bobbin lace making was mechanized in 1808 by John Heathcoat (1783–1861) of Loughborough, Leics. (*see* OLD LOUGHBOROUGH). Lace net made by machine was much wider than that made by hand.

bobbin mill mill which supplied wooden BOBBINS, reels, PIRNS, etc. for the textile industry. A reasonably sized cotton spinning mill would need several million bobbins of various sizes and constant replacements. The bobbins were made from COPPICE wood and the bobbin mills were sited near a source of such timber, there being many in the Lake District. The bobbins were turned in lathes to different designs and sizes to suit the requirements of the customers. Other cylindrical wooden items such as tool handles and cotton reels were frequently also made in bobbin mills.

A mill would comprise large, airy storage and drying sheds for the coppice wood, wood-turning machinery (either water- or steam-powered), and a wax polishing section for finishing the bobbins. The shavings from the lathes were usually used to fire the boiler which provided steam for drying, or for driving a steam engine in the case of a steam-powered mill. As the textile industry declined, there was less demand for wooden bobbins, and with the appearance of cheap bobbins made from compressed paper, the mills closed. Their buildings still remain in some cases, but turned over to other uses. Open-sided drying sheds often indicate what was once a bobbin mill. Stott Park Bobbin Mill, near Newby Bridge, Cumbria, has been turned into a working museum.

bobbin winding winding WEFT onto shuttle BOBBINS. In the days of the handloom weaver, a winding wheel usually stood at the side of the loom, and empty shuttle bobbins were pushed onto the slightly tapered spindle of the winder and yarn wound onto them from a hank or skein holder. Such machines were usually operated by boys or the women of the family to keep the weaver supplied with full bobbins for his shuttle. Winding wheels are very similar in appearance to spinning wheels and are sometimes mistaken for them.

As the textile industry developed, bobbin winding became mechanized and machines known as winders came into existence. These speeded up the preparation of PIRNS for weaving and became specialized, automatic machines.

bob wall the massive wall in the engine house of a BEAM ENGINE which supports the overhead beam or bob. The beam protrudes through a slot in the bob wall with the engine inside the house, and PUMP RODS suspended from the outer end of the beam to operate pumps situated down the mine shaft.

bocking a coarse woollen drugget or BAYES; it takes its name from the village in Essex where it was once made.

bodger a wood-turning craftsman who worked in a clearing in a wood under a simple shelter, making legs and spindles for Windsor type chairs. He used COPPICE wood, or pieces of timber which he first shaved roughly to a circular cross-section, before turning them on a primitive pole lathe to their finished dimensions. In addition to making components for chairs, other items such as tool handles etc. would be made. When the supply of timber from the immediate surrounding area was exhausted, the bodger would move on to another site in the forest. It is not clear how the name originated: it may have come from BADGER, a travelling salesman.

bogging, *see* RETTING

bogie a low, short, undercarriage with usually two pairs of wheels which supports the ends of a railway coach, or helps distribute the weight on some locomotives. The frame of a bogie is pivoted below the main frame of the coach or locomotive so that it can swivel through a small angle, thus enabling the long rigid body of the coach or locomotive to negotiate tight curves which would be impossible with fixed wheels. The bogie was patented by William (1749–1832) and Edward Walton Chapman of Durham in 1812 (patent no. 3632). It was part of their system in which an engine hauled itself along a chain laid between the rails, the engine being supported on two bogies. The chain haulage idea was a failure, but the bogie became extensively used. The first conventional locomotive to use a bogie was in 1833 on the Dundee and Newtyle Railway, Scotland. A bogie engine, or articulated locomotive, is carried on one or two steam powered swivelling bogies for use on tracks with severe curves: well-known examples are the locomotives running on the Ffestiniog Railway, north Wales, designed and patented by Robert F. Fairlie (1831–85) in 1863.

boil name given to the critical stage in the PUDDLING of wrought iron when all the carbon has been burned out and PUDDLER'S CANDLES appear at the surface of the molten metal.

boiler a steam generator comprising a pressure vessel, and/or rows of tubes arranged to receive heat from a firegrate. There are two main types of steam boiler: the shell type, externally or internally fired; and the tubular boiler in which the heating medium may be external to water tubes, or passes through them. Boilers provide steam under pressure to drive steam engines or turbines, and locomotives, or to provide a heating medium for process work in factories, or for space heating. The main developments in boiler design over the years have been to generate steam at higher and higher pressures, and to provide larger outputs from a single unit.

Shell boilers. In Newcomen's day, steam boilers were very primitive, and capable of producing only low pressures, not much higher than that of the atmosphere. Such boilers were externally fired from below with brick flues surrounding them. One design, known as a HAYSTACK BOILER on account of its shape, is shown in Fig. 61a. Later, the WAGGON BOILER was evolved, which could be externally or internally fired; this is shown in Fig. 61b. The horizontal shell boiler with one internal firetube, developed by Richard Trevithick (1771–1833) in 1808, became known as the CORNISH BOILER, and this permitted steam pressures of around 50 psi (*see* Fig. 61d). In

1844, the ubiquitous, twin firetube, LANCASHIRE BOILER was patented by William Fairbairn (1789–1874) and John Hetherington (pat. no. 10166) which became the mainstay of textile mills, collieries, etc. (*see* Fig. 61c). Thousands of coal-fired Lancashire boilers were made. Where large quantities of steam were needed, Lancashire boilers were arranged in banks, hand-fired at first, and later equipped with MECHANICAL STOKERS. By the late 19th century steam pressures of the order of 200 psi were possible. Several variations of the horizontal shell boiler were invented. Two unusual designs which enjoyed a short period of popularity are shown in Figs 9 and 10. For small steam outputs, vertical shell boilers were built, needing much less floor space than horizontal types. A well-known vertical boiler was the Cochran (*see* Fig. 61e), patented by Edward Crompton and J.T. Cochran in 1878 (pat. no. 770).

Tubular boilers. Tubular boilers were developed quite early. Stephenson's (1803–59)

Rocket (1829) had horizontal firetubes, setting the pattern for all later locomotives. Watertube boilers became necessary as higher and higher steam pressures were demanded, it being easier and safer to contain a high pressure in tubes and small diameter drums than in the large shell of a Lancashire boiler. During the 19th century many attempts were made to construct reliable watertube boilers, but most failed due to the primitive methods of construction then available, poor materials, and defective water circulation. One of the early successful watertube boilers (*see* Fig. 82a) was designed by George Herman Babcock (1832–93) and Stephen Wilcox (1830–93) in the USA in 1867. Many other designs followed, such as the Stirling boiler (Fig. 82b).

Coal was the principal fuel used for steam raising, but alternative heat sources were investigated as early as 1827 when John Urpath Raistrick (1780–1856) raised steam by waste gases from four iron puddling furnaces. Boilers were once rated in terms of horsepower, but this

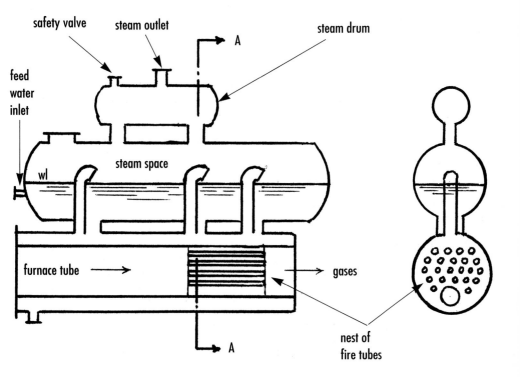

Longitudinal section

Cross-section A–A

Fig. 9. Fairbairn–Beeley steam boiler, *c.* 1895 (brickwork setting and firegrate omitted)

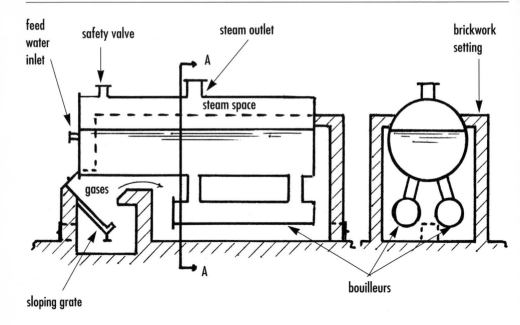

feed water inlet

safety valve

steam outlet

A

brickwork setting

steam space

gases

bouilleurs

sloping grate

Longitudinal section

Cross section A–A

A

Fig. 10. An 'Elephant' steam boiler, *c.* 1820

was an inaccurate measure, and was superseded by expressing boiler capacity in terms of pounds of steam generated per hour at the design pressure.

Burgh, N.P. *A Practical Treatise on Boilers and Boilermaking*, 1873
Dryden, I.G.C. *The Efficient Use of Energy* (Chapter 10), 2nd edn, Butterworth, 1982
Gunn, D. and Horton, R. *Industrial Boilers*, Longman, 1989
Kershaw, J.B.C. *Boilers and Boiler Control*, Davis Brothers, 1911
Powles, H.H.P. *Steam Boilers, Their History and Development*, 1905

boite (or boit) old name for the supporting block, usually of cast iron, on which the circular journal of the axletree (*see* TREE) of a WATERWHEEL revolved; it was sometimes fitted with a low friction metal. The word comes from the French *boîte* meaning 'box' or 'case'.

bole (or bolehill, bail, bale) an early metal smelter which comprised a shallow bowl cut into the ground a few feet across, with a low circular retaining wall of stones. Usually a bole was sited on a remote windy hillside with an opening in the stone wall facing the prevailing wind which provided a natural draught. Wood or charcoal was used as fuel, with crushed ore placed on top for smelting. Lead is believed to have been smelted in this way in the 15th and 16th centuries. Later, foot-operated bellows were probably added to increase the draught. Bolehills are also known as tag bails and bolestids. The introduction of ore hearths with water-powered blast, sited in river valleys, caused the demise of bole smelting.

Although the word bole sometimes appears as a place name, careful archaeological search and excavation are required to find evidence of former smelting. The word bole is of northern origin.

Willies, L. and Cranstone, D. (eds) *Boles and Smeltmills*, Historical Metallurgy Society, 1992

boll 1. an old dry measure for the weight of coal and meal, now obsolete, which varied from place to place and with time, not being standard. On Tyneside a boll of coal was generally around 2.33 cwt (approximately 260 lb). The word is thought to come from 'bowl'. Two bolls of meal were said to be a load. 2. the fruit or seed pod of the cotton plant (*see* COTTON BOLL).

Bollman truss a timber bridge truss comprising a top horizontal stringer and a number of vertical members projecting downwards from it at regular intervals (*see* Fig. 11). Two inclined members run from the lower extremity of each vertical, one either side of it, to the end supports, thus forming a series of triangles which brace the top stringer. The Bollman is a deck bridge and was used in the USA and on the Continent.

bolt a roll of woven fabric of a definite length, which varied from place to place and was usually between 30 and 40 ft.

bolter (or boulter, bowter) a shaking or rotating device in a corn mill for sieving the ground meal or flour; to bolt means to sift. A boultel is a cloth used for sieving, usually made of silk.

bombasine (or bombazeen, bombazine) a twilled dress material originally made of silk and worsted, but later also made from cotton and worsted, or worsted alone. The name comes from bombast, the thread of the bombyx or silkworm; bombast was the old name for cotton wool, and was used as padding in medieval clothes. Bombasine dates from the mid-18th century, and when dyed black was used for mourning clothes in Victorian times.

bone china a fine POTTERY similar to porcelain, made from clay and bone ash, which was developed in the early 19th century by the Spode family, father and son. Josiah Spode I (1733–97) experimented in the manufacture of porcelain but was prevented from using KAOLIN by Cookworthy's patent (*see* PORCELAIN). When the patent expired, Spode combined kaolin and china stone with white ashes added from the burnt bones of slaughtered cattle, to produce the material which became known as bone china. After his father's death, Josiah Spode II (1754–1827) continued developing the material, adding FELDSPAR to make it harder.

Bone china is non-porous, and is in effect a compromise between the true hard porcelain and the softer varieties. In 1833 the Spode factory at Stoke-on-Trent was acquired by the Copeland family, but still operates under the name Spode; bone china was once known as Stoke porcelain.

Whiter, L. *Spode: A History of the Family, Factory, and Wares, 1733–1833*, Barrie and Jenkins, 1978

bone lace, *see* BOBBIN LACE

book muslin a fine muslin, so named because it was folded like a book when sold in the piece.

boon the woody core and bark of flax removed by SCUTCHING, sometimes known as shire or shove. Boon was used as a fuel.

bord and pillar (or board and pillar), *see* PILLAR AND STALL

boring machine a machine tool for boring out large cylindrical holes in items such as steam engine cylinders, pump barrels, etc. There are two types: horizontal borers and vertical borers.

A boring machine or boring mill comprises a robust frame carrying a drive head from which projects a boring bar. The boring tools or cutters are held in the boring bar which, in the case of horizontal borers, is rotated inside the item to be machined, cutting away surplus metal. The work piece is held stationary and the revolving boring bar is slowly advanced through until the bore is completed. In the case of vertical borers the workpiece is clamped onto a large horizontal circular table or faceplate which is rotated: the boring tools remain stationary whilst they are gradually fed vertically along the axis of the bore.

An early use of metal borers was to smooth the rough bore of cast-iron cannons. John Wilkinson (1728–1808), the Shropshire ironmaster, developed a horizontal machine in 1774 for this job, and when Watt's steam engine cylinders required boring, he adapted his machine in 1775 for this purpose. It was driven by a waterwheel and comprised a substantial hollow boring bar which was rotated by gears, and supported at both ends in bearings. The bearing remote from the drive end could be dismantled to allow the steam engine cylinder to be placed in position, and then reassembled. A sleeved disk encircling the hollow boring bar and holding several radially cutting tools was drawn along the bar by a rod which passed down the centre of the bar. The tool disk was rotated by a projection from it running along a longitudinal slot in the revolving hollow boring bar, and its movement along the item it was boring was manually operated by turning a pinion engaging in a rack which formed an extension to the central rod. Wilkinson's machine was so successful that he obtained orders for supplying, and boring, many of Watt's early steam engine cylinders. A vertical boring machine was installed in Boulton and Watt's Soho foundry, Birmingham, some twenty years later for cylinder boring.

Vertical borers have many advantages over horizontal machines, although the latter were still in use in railway workshops for many years, boring locomotive cylinders. The basic design of boring machines remained unchanged for about a hundred years, although several improvements were made to details, increasing accuracy and speed.

Barker, R. (ed.) *Wilkinson Studies*, vol. 1, Merton Priory Press, 1991

bosh 1. the lower part of a blast furnace tapering down from its widest part to the hearth. Early blast furnace boshes were usually square in cross-section but became circular later. The word possibly comes from the German *böschen*, meaning to slope. **2.** the water trough used by a smith for quenching tools, etc. and for breaking off scale from steel bars etc. by plunging them into the cold water and instantly removing them.

Botany wool originally, wool from the area around Botany Bay in Australia; today, the term is used for any wool of 60s COUNT and upwards, i.e. fine quality. Such wool is used in worsted manufacture: botany twill is a twilled worsted cloth. *See also* MERINO WOOL.

bounding, *see* MEER

Bourdon gauge a pressure gauge invented in 1849 by the Frenchman Eugène Bourdon (1808–84). It comprises a flattened tube bent to a particular curve, housed within a circular casing, and connected by a small bore pipe to the vessel whose pressure it indicates. The curved tube tends to straighten a little under the internal pressure, and by a suitable magnifying mechanism, moves a pointer over a circular scale which is graduated in appropriate pressure units. Bourdon gauges are used to indicate the pressures of all manner of fluids, steam, water, compressed air, and so on. They are calibrated against master gauges for accuracy. The safe working pressure of a boiler etc. is marked by a red line on the gauge scale.

bouse (or boose) that part of a metal vein in which ore is mixed up with loose rock as mined. Bouse has to be dressed (*see* DRESSING OF ORE) to separate the ore from the unwanted rock before the ore goes to a smelter. The material is stored in a bunker or hopper to await dressing; in northern mining areas such storage places are called bouse teems or teams, in Cornwall as hutches, and in Derbyshire as kilns. A bouse is also known as a fell.

bow hauler (or haler) man employed to tow boats along river navigations prior to the use of horses. Halers were also often needed to draw a boat upstream against the rush of water when a FLASH LOCK was opened. On some rivers, haling rents had to be paid to the landowner for crossing his riverside property. Bow haulers were also known as trackers in some parts of the country.

bowk 1. a tub in which Staffordshire miners descended and ascended a coal mine. **2.** a container in which debris and waste is brought to the surface when a mine shaft is being sunk. **3.** *see* LYE.

bowking (or bucking) the scouring of cloth to remove impurities and waxes prior to BLEACHING. The cloth was soaked in a warm ash LYE (or bowk, buck) for about twelve hours, then boiled in a KIER for about three hours. Bowking was an alkaline process, and

was followed by washing and SOURING the cloth. The word is believed to come from the Anglo-Saxon *bui* meaning 'pitcher', probably because a pitcher-like vessel was used in early days for the soaking and boiling. A bowker is a man who prepares the alkaline liquors and supervises the boiling.

bowl a large heavy roller, of which there are several on a calender as used in the textile and paper-making industries. Originally made from wood with metal shafts, they were later made entirely from metal. The name comes from the bole or trunk of a tree.

box girder a form of metal girder used in bridge work (*see* Fig. 11). There are two kinds: a one-piece cast-iron girder of hollow rectangular cross-section, and a fabricated girder built up from either wrought iron or steel plates and angle irons. The latter is properly known as a box plate-girder and comprises two plate webs riveted to plate flanges and enclosing a rectangular space between them, angle irons making the joints between flange and web.

box of tricks name for the device on a spinning machine which ensures that a ROVING is built up correctly by regulating the speed of the BOBBIN and reversing the traverse of the lifting rail and controlling its movement. It is also known as the escape motion.

Bradford system a method of WORSTED manufacture which uses British invented machines, generally comprising NOBLE COMBERS and THROSTLE SPINNING to make worsted yarn. Medium to long fibred wools are used. It is sometimes called the English system as opposed to the CONTINENTAL SYSTEM (1), which can accommodate shorter fibres of wool.

brakesman the engineman controlling the winding gear at a colliery, or the rope hauling equipment on a SELF-ACTING INCLINE. Such equipment is stopped, or its speed controlled, by the application of a brake onto the wheel round which the rope passes. George Stephenson (1781–1848) was brakesman at West Moor colliery, near Killingworth, Newcastle upon Tyne in 1804, and began his engineering career there.

brake wheel the primary gear wheel in a WINDMILL mounted on the windshaft and on which a brake acts to control or stop the machinery.

Brama or Bramah process, *see* DISCHARGE BLEACHING

brass a common alloy of copper and zinc, made in several varieties. Queen Elizabeth I founded the MINERAL AND BATTERY WORKS in 1568 for making sheet brass, and in the 17th century a brass casting industry developed in the Bristol area based on zinc ore calamine mined in the Mendips. The calamine, copper and charcoal were roasted together in a crucible to produce the brass which had, and still has, many uses as wire, sheet, and castings. An early example is that of the first steam engine cylinders which were cast in brass before cheaper cast iron superseded brass *c.* 1718. Brass was once used for renewable low friction bearing surfaces in machinery, and although other materials replaced it later, the bearings were still called brasses.

Day, J. *Bristol Brass*, David and Charles, 1973
Hamilton, H. *The English Brass and Copper Industries*, Cass, 1967

brasses, *see* STEPS

brattice (or brattish, bartice) a divider placed in an underground gallery or in a mine shaft. When placed in a gallery its purpose was to direct air currents to improve the ventilation of the mine. The framework was covered with brattice cloth, which was heavy tarred canvas or a similar cloth, and which could be moved aside at certain places to allow the passage of men and tubs to and from various parts of the mine. The introduction of brattices is attributed to Carlisle Spedding (1696–1755) of Whitehaven, Cumberland, in the 1750s.

In a mine shaft, a brattice is a continuous vertical timber partition which divides the shaft into two. The winding of materials and men took place on one side of the brattice, and pumping out of mine water on the other.

brayer that part of the compound lever system which supports the BRIDGE TREE in a water- or windmill, the vertical movement of which alters the grinding gap between the millstones (*see* Fig. 74). The origin of the word is unknown.

brays a dialect variation of breeze, small coke or coal.

brazen dish a standard measure used in Derbyshire lead mines, chained in a special place under the charge of the BARMASTER.

brazil wood (or brassil wood) a redwood tree (*caesalpinia echinata*) originally imported from the East Indies and India to make a dyestuff. If used alone it made pink and peach shades, and if used with a tin salt, it produced a brilliant red, although prone to fading. The origin of the word brazil is unknown. When South America was discovered it was found that the same redwood trees were growing there, and the Portuguese named their former colony 'Brazil' after the tree, meaning literally 'red dye-wood land'. Logs from the Brazilian tree became an additional source of supply. The wood was also known as pernambuco after the Brazilian port.

A brassil or brazil mill was a factory or workshop, usually water-powered, which ground the pieces of this type of tree to a fine powder for the dyeing trade.

break rolls in a ROLLER MILL, enclosed machines containing fluted rolls which open the wheat grains by a tearing and shearing action. The rolls rotate at different speeds, and the fluting is cut at a slight angle. After passing through the break rolls, the stock is carried by scoop conveyors to PLANSIFTERS for grading into sizes.

breast wheel a WATERWHEEL in which the incoming water is directed onto the periphery at, or about the same level, as the wheel axle. A high breast wheel is where the water enters above the axle, whereas a low breastshot wheel is where the water enters below the axle. Breast wheels are used where there is only a modest fall available in the water supply. If the wheel is fitted with FLOATBOARDS the incoming water merely imparts an impulse on them, but if buckets are fitted they fill, and the weight of the water assists in the turning force on the wheel. A breast wheel with the water inlet level with the axle is sometimes described as a 3 o'clock wheel for obvious reasons; high breast wheels may be known as 2 o'clock wheels, etc. If the water enters the wheel almost at the top, i.e. a very high breast wheel, it is known as a pitchback wheel. Various types of waterwheel are shown in Fig. 84.

brewing industry ALE was being brewed in Britain before Roman days for consumption in the home, usually by the women in the household (called brewsters). Medieval monasteries also brewed ale, and by the 13th century alehouses were in existence selling ale to travellers, the ale being brewed on the premises. As demand increased over the years, the idea of a common or commercial brewer supplying ale from a central brewery to nearby taverns and inns gradually evolved.

Ale was a fermented malt drink: when, in the 16th century, hops began to be added, introduced by Flemish brewers settling in England, true beer began to be brewed. Hops added flavour to ale and extended its life. Beer was the universal drink of men, women and children at that time, and remained so until tea began to be cheap enough to make inroads into beer consumption. Every town and village had its own brewery, the larger ones supporting several. Beer was brewed by commercial brewers, and in outhouses of inns, and many regional varieties developed. A survey of taverns and inns in England and Wales in 1577 produced a total of 19,759; by 1840 the number of breweries in the United Kingdom totalled almost 50,000. Forty years later the figure had halved, as brewers joined forces and the number of innkeeper brewers diminished. It was during the Industrial Revolution that many of the large brewery firms of today were founded. To ensure a market for their product, brewers began buying and building their own inns in the late 18th century, and the concept of the tied house arose, making brewers publicans also. The number of small breweries attached to pubs rapidly fell. Beer has always been a target for taxation: the first beer tax was as early as 1188, and it has been taxed, one way or another, ever since.

Beer is made by a fermentation process from barley, sugar, hops, yeast and water (called liquor in the industry). Barley is allowed to partially germinate under controlled conditions, and dried to prevent further growth. It is then called malt; certain changes have taken place during the malting which prepare its starch for subsequent conversion to sugar. The malt is then ground in a malt mill, and the resulting end product (the grist) is passed into a MASH TUN and mixed with hot water, where the starch is converted into sugar. A sweet liquid known as WORT is drawn out of the mash tun and passed into a boiling copper where more sugar and dried hops are added. After boiling in the copper, the wort is cooled in a cooler, and passed to a fermenting vessel where yeast is added. The yeast feeds on the sugar in the wort as fermentation proceeds, converting it to alcohol, and after a few days, excess yeast is removed; the beer then requires maturing before it is either put into casks or bottled.

Mathias, P. *The Brewing Industry of England, 1700–1830*, Cambridge University Press, 1959
Richmond, L. and Turton, A. (eds) *The Brewing Industry: A Guide to Historical Records*, Manchester University Press, 1990

brick a building block, usually rectangular in shape, made from clay mixed with sand, etc., and shaped in a mould; used as a substitute for stone in building. Bricks were made in Roman days, and the dimensions have varied somewhat with time, but they were always of a size which could comfortably be handled. Brick making involves the winning of clay, crushing processes, pugging (stirring), moulding to shape, and drying in a kiln. Early bricks were hand made, mostly by children and women, and their dimensions therefore varied slightly before machinery was employed. A typical brick size is 9 x 4.5 x 3 in thick; special shapes are also made for certain uses, such as tapers for arches. Bricks are made in various qualities and from various basic materials: besides the common

building brick there are hard-wearing facing bricks, and bricks made from fire-resistant clays used in refractory work.

The shortage of timber in the early 18th century, led to more extensive use of bricks. The development of canals and railways aided the cheap transport of clay and coal for the kilns. The growing output of bricks attracted an excise tax in 1784 which was not repealed until 1850. Records of brick output were kept from 1784 for tax purposes. A tax was also imposed on tiles in 1803, and repealed in 1833. Working conditions for women and children employed in brickworks, were greatly improved by the passing of the Brickfield Act of 1871.

Wirecutting of bricks was invented by William Irving in 1841 (patent no. 9165) and extruded bricks in 1875. Bricks and tiles were dried by batches in kilns until the continuous drying kiln was patented by Friedrich Hoffmann in Germany in 1858. The Hoffmann kiln was not adopted in Britain for many years.

In construction, bricks are fitted together and joined by a thin layer of mortar in such a way that they mutually support each other, the vertical joints staggered so that there is no continuous weak line. Various configurations have been used over the years to create the bonding, such as the Flemish bond and Old English bond; each produces a distinctive pattern of joints and brick surfaces (sides or ends) on the visible surface. Bricks placed longitudinally in a wall are called stretchers, whilst bricks placed transversely showing only their ends are called headers.

Bricks and Brickmaking, Shire Publications, album no. 75, 1979
Brunskill, R.W. *Brick Building in Britain*, Gollancz, 1990
Hammond, M.D.P. 'Brick kilns: an illustrated survey', *Industrial Archaeology Review* I (1977), 171–92
Hudson, K. *Building Materials*, Longman, 1972

bridge 1. a structure to carry a road or railway across a river, another road, etc. The design of a bridge depends on a number of factors such as the topography of the site, the materials from which it is to be constructed, the span required, and the load to be carried; various types have developed over the years. For the main ones, *see* ACCOMMODATION BRIDGE; AQUEDUCT; ARCHED BRIDGE; BASCULE BRIDGE; BEAM BRIDGE; BRIDGE GIRDERS AND TRUSSES; CANTILEVER BRIDGE; CHAIN BRIDGE; IRON BRIDGE; LIFTING BRIDGE; PACKHORSE BRIDGE; SUSPENSION BRIDGE; SWING BRIDGE; TRANSPORTER BRIDGE; TUBULAR BRIDGE; VIADUCT.

de Maré, Eric. *The Bridges of Britain*, Batsford, 1954
Hopkins, H.J. *A Span of Bridges*, David and Charles, 1970

2. a low firebrick wall across the end of the firegrate in a SHELL-TYPE STEAM BOILER or a REVERBERATORY FURNACE; it is called a bridge because the gases from the fire pass over it on their way to a chimney.

bridge girders and trusses timber, iron or steel structures which form load-bearing bridges. Timber bridge trusses are made from straight lengths of timber, joined to form an open framework of triangles, so that individual members are in simple tension or compression without any bending. Since bridges carry rolling loads, stresses may be reversed in some members as the load crosses, and they have to be designed to accommodate the change. This applies also to iron and steel bridges and trusses. Figs 11 and 12 illustrate various types of bridge girders and trusses.

Timber bridges were particularly used in the pioneering days of railways in the USA, when they were being built far from foundries and rolling mills. The Bollman timber truss is a typical American example. Isambard Kingdom Brunel (1806–59) built timber railway bridges and viaducts in the late 1840s to cross the valleys of Devon and Cornwall.

Solid metal girder bridges were first made in cast iron for small spans, but later, when large wrought-iron plates became available, fabricated plate girders with either single vertical webs, or double webs in box form (*see* BOX GIRDER), enabled greater distances to be spanned. Solid girders are subjected to bending and shear stresses, so extra top and bottom flange plates of varying lengths are added for additional strength to resist central bending stresses. Vertical stiffeners are added to prevent the web(s) buckling under heavy loads (*see* Fig. 11). Metal lattice girders or trusses (from the old German *Latta* meaning lath) are similar to timber trusses, and comprise top and bottom longitudinal members called stringers, braced together by diagonally crossing bars – the latticework giving a lightweight construction offering little resistance to side wind pressure.

A large number of lattice girders were patented in the 19th century by engineers and named after them. The better known ones are: the Warren girder (by James Warren and Willoughby Theobald Monzani, pat. no. 12242, 1848); the Pratt truss, and the Linville girder in the USA; and the Whipple–Murphy truss (by Squire Whipple and John W. Murphy, in 1847). There are variations on each design. Sometimes the top stringer has a convex curve upwards, in which case it is called a hog back truss, to give a uniform strength across the span. On very large spans, the individual members may themselves be made as lattice girders.

The first metal used for bridge construction was wrought iron. In 1877 the Board of Trade authorized the use of steel for bridge work, and metal bridges built since then are of steel.

bridge house a roofed building placed either on the hill alongside a charcoal BLAST FURNACE, or on the bridge leading from the hill onto the charging platform. It was used to store raw materials to keep them dry just before they were fed into the furnace.

bridge tree the horizontal beam, usually wooden, which supports the vertical stone spindle in a wind- or watermill. It is capable of a small vertical adjustment so that the gap between the grinding stones may be varied, a movement known as TENTERING.

brine salt water. It has many uses: for instance, an early form of food preservation was to pickle in brine, particularly fish. Brine is the source of common salt: natural or 'wild' brine is pumped up from underground 'lakes', usually some 200–400 ft below the surface, as a solution of rock salt, or halite (sodium chloride). The salt is obtained by evaporating in a brine pan, a shallow iron vessel, heated from below. The extraction of brine from underground in the 19th century often led to subsidence at the surface, creating water-filled hollows known as flashes; such depressions are fairly common around Northwich in Cheshire, which is a salt manufacturing area.

Chilled brine is used as the cooling medium in refrigerated chambers, being pumped through cooling coils arranged round the chamber. Its low freezing temperature makes it particularly suitable for this purpose.

British Association for the Advancement of Science founded in 1831 by the Scottish philosopher Sir David Brewster (1781–1868), a multi-disciplinary association of scientists to encourage scientific research and the diffusion of scientific knowledge. It holds an annual meeting in different provincial towns and cities, where the latest ideas and advancements in all branches of science and technology are presented and published by leading authorities. Many important advances have been made public in this manner: for example, Henry Bessemer (1813–98) announced his process for making cheap steel at the 1856 meeting. The Association was granted a royal charter in 1928 and has charitable status; it has its headquarters in London.

broadcloth originally a woollen cloth of PLAIN WEAVE, finished with a dress face, and 2 yd in width (or greater than 54 in in some cases). It

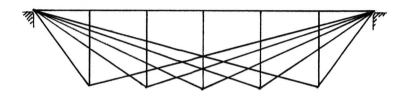

Bollman timber bridge truss

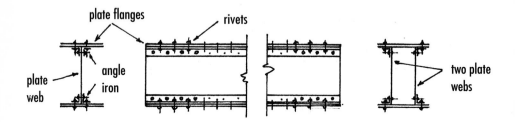

plate flanges   rivets

plate web   angle iron   two plate webs

Cross-section
through plate girder
(iron or steel)

Cross-section through
box plate girder
(iron or steel)

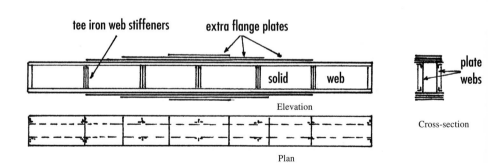

tee iron web stiffeners   extra flange plates

solid   web

plate webs

Elevation

Plan

Cross-section

Fabricated iron or steel solid bridge girder (uniform strength)

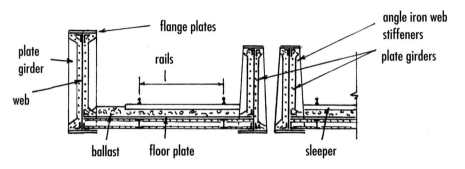

flange plates

angle iron web
stiffeners

plate girder

rails

plate girders

web

ballast   floor plate   sleeper

Cross-section through typical plate girder railway through bridge

Fig. 11. Some bridge girders

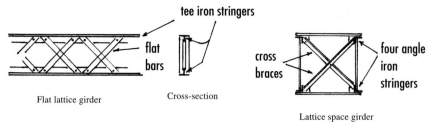

tee iron stringers

flat
bars

Flat lattice girder

Cross-section

cross
braces

four angle
iron
stringers

Lattice space girder

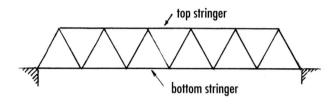

top stringer

bottom stringer

Warren girder (1848)

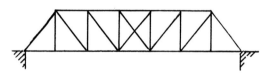

Pratt truss (1844)

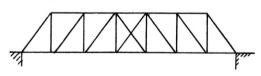

Linville girder or N truss

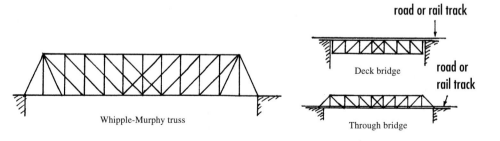

Whipple-Murphy truss

road or rail track

Deck bridge

road or
rail track

Through bridge

Fig. 12. Lattice bridge trusses or girders

45

was usually dyed black and used for men's garments. An Act in 1482 reserved the term to describe quality rather than width, whereas a Clothing Statute of 1552 stated that a broadcloth piece must be 63 in finished width after FULLING, 26–28 yd long and 44 lb in weight. The size of broadcloth varied however with time and place. By the 19th century broadcloths were 50 yd long and took some three weeks to weave. Undyed broadcloth was exported to the Low Countries for dyeing, the Flemish dyers being more skilled than their English counterparts at that time; it was cheaper for them to import English cloth than to buy locally made cloth. Broadcloth was a particular product of the West Country.

In the days of handloom weavers, broadcloths were woven by a weaver and an assistant or apprentice, working together on the same loom: the width was too great for one man to pass the shuttle comfortably from side to side, so the weaver and his assistant would pass the shuttle across to each other. Cloths which could be woven by one man alone were known as NARROW CLOTHS or KERSEYS.

When the FLYING SHUTTLE was invented by John Kay in 1733, broadcloths could be woven by one man alone, and at a faster rate; by c.1760 broadcloths had ousted kerseys. Yorkshire became the main producer of woollen broadcloth by the 18th century: the growth in output in the West Riding is shown below.

year	no. of pieces × 1000	yards × 1000
1727	29.0	–
1740	41.4	–
1750	60.5	–
1760	49.4	–
1770	93.1	2,717
1779	110.9	3,427
1790	172.6	5,152
1800	285.8	9,264

Source: Heaton, H. *The Yorkshire Woollen and Worsted Industries*, 1965

broad gate (or broad alley) the wide passageway at right angles to lines of looms in a weaving shed. It has to be wide enough to allow BEAMS to be brought to and from the looms, and turned to line up with them.

broad gauge, *see* GAUGE

brocade originally, a woven fabric with raised patterns or figures in gold or silver thread; later, the term came to describe any richly patterned silk cloth which had raised or embossed figures. It is used for hangings etc.

brocatelle an imitation brocade, usually made in silk or wool. The word comes from the French *brocatel* meaning tinsel, or thin cloth of gold or silver.

brogger (or bragger) a trader, common in the 16th and 17th centuries, who collected wool from a wool farmer and sold it to domestic weavers, CLOTHIERS, or at wool markets; he carried his supplies on packhorses. Although providing a service to weavers and clothiers, saving them the trouble of gathering wool themselves, broggers – as middlemen – were not popular and were often accused of sharp trading practices, of cornering the wool market and forcing up the price of wool. The name came to be associated with corruption. As clothiers became more wealthy they were able to buy direct from the wool farmers and broggers died out. The name is possibly a dialect corruption of broker, and originates from Yorkshire.

broken-weft stopping motion a device for stopping a POWER LOOM immediately a WEFT thread is broken. Before a power loom could be called fully automatic, it had to be capable of stopping immediately a weft thread broke so that faulty cloth was not woven. This problem exercised the minds of many inventors including Edmund Cartwright and Richard Roberts, both of whom incorporated a weft stopping motion in their looms of 1786 and 1822 respectively. Cartwright's device was a hinged 'buckle-like' component on the shuttle which was held flat whilst the weft was intact, but opened out when the weft broke, and by catching against a suitable mechanism, brought the loom to a stop.

Most later inventions involved devices attached to the loom itself rather than to the shuttle. John Ramsbottom and Richard Holt's Todmorden patent (no. 6644, 1834) comprised what they called a 'hands and fingers' system of levers, whilst Moses Poole's 1839 patent (no. 8270) used what is described as a weft fork. A forked sensing device of some kind formed the basis of most later inventions, such as James Bullough and William Kenworthy's Blackburn patent 'weft watcher' (1841). John Osbaldston of Blackburn, Lancs., patented his weft fork in 1842 (no. 9257), which comprised a pair of small sensing prongs placed in the centre of the SHUTTLE RACE and which rested lightly on the weft at each PICK, but fell into a recess when the weft was missing and stopped the loom via a system of levers.

bronze properly an alloy of around 90 per cent copper and 10 per cent tin; however, there are other 'bronzes' with alloying metals other than in or with additional metals, e.g. manganese bronze and bell metal. Zinc and lead are added to bronze to increase fluidity when molten and reduce brittleness when cold. Bronze was known before Roman times, and was probably an accidental discovery by early metal workers. Some early cannon were cast in bronze before cast iron took over. The alloy was used extensively as bearing metal for rotating shafts in the form of renewable sleeves which were known as 'brasses'.

brown linen unbleached linen cloth.

Brunton buddle a machine for continuously separating lead slimes (small lead particles) from waste material by means of a water washed, inclined moving belt. It was patented by William Brunton II (1817–81) whilst he was living in Pool, Cornwall (patent no. 10378, 1844) and comprised a wide, painted canvas endless belt with rope edges to form a shallow flexible trough. The belt ran over rollers spaced apart, the top driven roller being set at a higher level than the bottom one so that the belt ran up an incline. The return loop of the belt dipped into a water tank. The driving roller had a number of axial wooden slats or bars spaced out on its periphery which engaged in similarly spaced slats attached to the underside of the belt, thus forming a toothed driving system. Clean water was trickled onto the belt near the top roller and ran down the belt, and the lead slimes fed onto the belt a short distance below the water feed. The belt slowly moved up the incline, and waste material with densities less than that of lead was washed off the belt at the lower roller. The heavier lead particles were not dislodged by the opposing trickle of water and were carried to the top of the belt where they were discharged into the water tank below as the belt went over the top roller. Brunton buddles were particularly favoured in northern lead mining districts where they were in use for several decades. *See also* BUDDLE.

Brunton calciner an ore roasting or CALCINING furnace, invented by William Brunton I around 1835. It comprised a circular iron base set in a firebrick chamber, the base being slightly convex when viewed from above. It was covered by firebricks to form a circular hearth, and could be slowly rotated from below. Two diametrically opposite furnaces heated the hearth. Ore was fed onto the hearth at its centre, and was calcined as it gradually worked its way to the outside edges of the hearth under the actions of circular motion and gravity. Stationary iron rods hanging from above stirred the ore pieces as they passed between them.

Brussels point lace, *see* NEEDLEPOINT LACE

buck 1. the body of a POST MILL which contains the millstone driving machinery. **2.** a boiling house with BOILERS and KIERS for steeping and boiling cloth at a BLEACH CROFT. **3.** the LYE used in bleaching (also called bowk); to 'lay the buck' meant to lay the cloth in lye.

bucking 1. the breaking up of lumps of metallic ore into small pieces prior to separating the unwanted rock waste from the metal bearing pieces, usually in a BUDDLE. In the early days of lead and tin mining, this operation was usually carried out by women or children (mostly boys), by manually hammering the lumps with a bucker or bucking hammer on a bucking stone (or knock stone) or iron plate. The bucking stone was usually located close to the buddle, and the bucking hammer was usually an iron plate as big as a man's open hand with a wooden handle. Bucking was known as cobbing in Cornwall. The place where bucking took place was known as a SPALLING floor, or dressing floor. **2.** an alternative name for BOWKING.

buckram (also spelt bokeram) linen cloth stiffened with gum or paste to make a strong binding for books. The origin of the word is unknown. Sometimes cotton or jute fabrics were used.

buddle (or buddel) an ore-cleaning device for separating metallic ore from waste material by washing the dirty ore in a continuous flow of water. A buddle uses the difference in density between the metal and the waste material as its means of effecting the separation. Lead and tin ores are treated in buddles.

There are many varieties of buddles; all are set into, or on the ground of, the dressing floor of a smelter. They may be rectangular, square, or circular in plan, the latter shape being introduced in the mid-19th century. Rectangular buddles are known as common or running buddles, or trough buddles, and were the first types to be used. Primitive rectangular buddles were usually sited close to BELL PITS (1) or shallow shafts, and were roughly constructed from stones with paved floors and stone sides to form shallow troughs in the ground. They were built with a slight slope along their length and could be up to 20 ft long. Ore lumps were first broken into small pieces by hand hammering (*see* BUCKING) and gradually fed into the highest end of the buddle. A continuous trickle of water was directed into the top end of the buddle from a nearby stream or artificial water course brought to it, and as it flowed down the buddle slope, impurities with densities less than the ore being treated, were washed away. At the same time, the metallic pieces were roughly graded by size, the largest and heaviest pieces settling at the top end of the buddle floor, and the lightest and finest particles at the low end. The feed stock of dirty ore was gently stirred to aid separation, and the waste material, called tailings, removed and dumped nearby. The cleaned ore pieces were removed from the buddle from time to time, and sent to the smelter. Such buddles therefore operated as a batch process.

More sophisticated designs followed with wooden or masonry floor and sides, operating on the same principle. Later, circular buddles with concave and convex floors were developed, complete with revolving sweeps or paddles to agitate the material, driven by horse or by waterwheel. Buddles with concave floors were fed at the edge, and the heaviest material settled at the rim, whilst convex buddles were fed at the centre where the heaviest material collected. Sometimes a smaller round depression or shallow tank called a dumb buddle was sited close by, in which the dirty ore was mixed before it was fed into a true buddle. Dumb buddles were without sweeps. The BRUNTON BUDDLE enabled continuous operation by use of a moving belt.

Buddles were known by different names in some mining areas: in mid-Wales they were called ore slides, and wash kiln was another name. The origin of the word is obscure, but it might have come from old German *butteln*, meaning to shake or agitate.

buffin(e) a coarse woollen cloth used in Elizabethan times for ladies' gowns.

bulldogger the curious job title of the man who stands at the back or return side of a two-high ROLLING MILL to pass the red-hot billet over the top roll to the front of the machine so that it may be rolled again. He grips the billet with long-handled tongs suspended on a chain from an overhead girder as it leaves the rolls. The chain takes most of the weight and the revolving top roller assists the return of the billet which he rests on it. Bulldogging is a dangerous and arduous job.

Bull engine an early design of steam engine contrived by Edward Bull (*fl.*1790–6), a former employee of Boulton and Watt. It operated like a CORNISH ENGINE, but was inverted over a mine shaft with the piston rod directly connected to pump rods, and dispensed with an overhead beam (*see* Fig. 13). Bull's engine infringed Watt's condenser patent, and Watt obtained an injunction stopping Bull from building any more such engines after 1794. Nevertheless, many Bull engines had been built, and some remained in use until the mid-19th

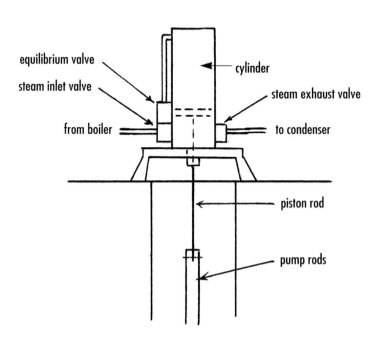

Fig. 13. A Bull engine for pumping duty

century. They were compact and cheaper than the conventional BEAM ENGINE, but the main drawbacks were the difficulty of reaching the stuffing box for repacking the piston rod gland, and the engine's position over the mine shaft, which prevented the raising of ore, etc.; they could therefore only be used for dewatering. They were also difficult to regulate. Similarly positioned, hydraulically operated engines were made later.

bunning a horizontal temporary platform onto which ore may be thrown as it is mined. A series of bunnings placed one above the other, each within the reach of a man shovelling the ore upwards, enables the mined material to be raised to another level by successive throwings. Another use of a bunning is when mining proceeds by stoping (*see* STOPE): the material brought down onto it from above is carted away in the level in which the bunning forms a temporary roof. More rarely, a bunning is

known as a bunyan, both words being dialect versions of the word bunding.

buoy controller a device invented by Thomas Newcomen (1663–1729) to control the speed of his beam engines. The primitive steam boilers available in his day were not able to raise steam sufficiently rapidly to replenish the cylinders of the engines each cycle. The cylinders consumed large amounts of steam, temporarily draining the steam reserve in the boilers. As the piston rose under the action of the unbalanced weight of the PUMP RODS, steam was sucked out of the boiler; it took time for the boiler to recover and accumulate enough steam for the next upwards stroke. To allow enough time for the boiler to fill its steam space, Newcomen devised the controller which became known as the buoy.

Fig. 14 shows the essential parts of the device. It comprised a small buoy floating on the surface of the water in the boiler, inside a vertical tube, which projected through the boiler

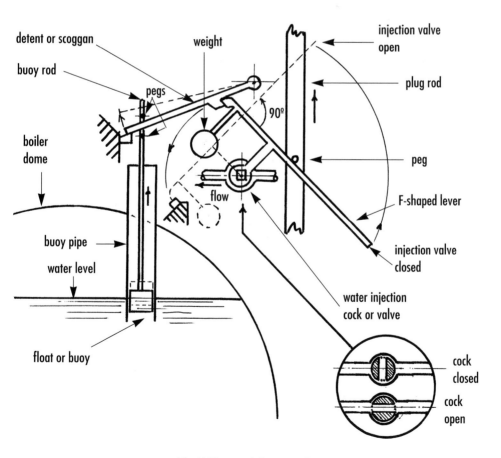

Fig. 14. Newcomen's buoy controller

dome. A rod extended upwards from the buoy and was arranged so that it could push up a pivoted detent arm (called a scoggan in Cornwall) to release a weighted and pivoted lever (called the *F* arm from its shape). The *F* lever could turn through 90° under gravity, and open the injection cock or valve to admit cooling water into the engine cylinder, creating a vacuum under the piston and initiating the power stroke. As the PLUG ROD descended with the power stroke, a peg on it struck the end of the *F* lever, depressing it until it was turned back to its original position, at the same time closing the injection valve. By now the detent arm had fallen back to its original position against a stop, and this held the *F* lever up ready for the cycle of events to recommence.

To commence the cycle, the buoy had to rise a little inside its tube to lift up the detent arm sufficiently to release the *F* lever. The weight attached to the *F* lever ensured that it opened the injection valve quickly, once the lever was free of the detent arm. The buoy was forced a little up its tube by the steam pressure acting on the water surface which could only occur when sufficient steam had been raised by the boiler after being exhausted by the previous steam stroke of the engine. The opening and closing of the steam inlet valve to the cylinder was synchronized by the movement of the plug rod, the piston remaining at the top of its stroke until sufficient steam had accumulated in the boiler steam space and low pressure built up to lift the buoy, and hence set in motion the opening of the injection valve. Fig. 14 shows two configurations of the system: the full lines show the injection valve closed, and the dotted lines show it open. Thus, the steaming capacity of the boiler controlled the working of the engine; when more rapidly steaming boilers were developed, the busy controller was dispensed with (*see* CATARACT CONTROLLER).

burden in mining or quarrying, the mass of unwanted rock or deposit which lies above the sought-after ore or other material such as slate, which has to be removed before the desired material can be reached.

burial in wool a practice made compulsory by an Act of 1666, in an attempt to protect the woollen industry. The legislation stated: 'No corpse of any person (except those who shall die of the plague) shall be buried in any shift, shirt, sheet, or shroud, or anything whatever made or mingled with flax, hemp, silk, hair, gold, or silver or in any stuff or thing, other than what is made of sheep's wool only.' A fine of £5 was made on those who disobeyed the law, and clergymen were obliged to carry out an inspection of the body in the coffin at the lychgate before the lid was fastened down. Largely ignored, the Act of 1666 was reinforced by an Act of 1680 which stipulated that an affidavit by relatives of the deceased had to state that everything about the corpse was made in sheep's wool only; a register of these affidavits had to be kept in every parish. This Act was repealed in 1814.

Burying baise, the material used for shrouds, was made from poor quality wools, or a low quality worsted warp and inferior weft. Another example of a law to benefit the woollen trade was an Act of 1571 which stipulated that all males over the age of six had to possess a woollen cap (known as a Statute cap) which had to be worn on holidays. Non-compliance incurred a heavy fine. The Act was repealed in 1597.

burling (or birling) the final removal of irregularities in woven woollen cloth. In the early days of the woollen industry, burling was frequently carried out by women in their own homes after the cloth had been woven in a nearby factory; later, the operation was carried out under supervision in the factory itself. *See* PERCHING AND BURLING.

burning house a Cornish name for a REVERBERATORY FURNACE in which tin ores were roasted; also known as a tin kiln or hand calciner (*see* CALCINING). Arsenic ores were roasted in similar furnaces.

burrow, *see* SPOIL HEAP

burr 1. seed from one of various plants adhering to raw wool, embedded in the fleece of the sheep. Burrs have to be removed at a preliminary cleaning operation. **2.** a particular type of millstone; *see* FRENCH BURR.

bush a metal lining of a hole through which a shaft passes. The lining may be to strengthen the surrounding material and prevent excessive wear, for example a metal sleeve inserted in the centre of a wooden cartwheel, or to provide a bearing surface of low friction metal; in fact a bush nearly always serves this purpose. Bushes are also used to repair a worn hole, or to make one smaller. Bush-metal is an alloy of copper and tin frequently used as a bearing surface for a rotating shaft, and is fixed in the surrounding housing so that it cannot itself rotate. When it becomes worn, a fresh bush can be inserted. The word possibly comes from the French *bouche* meaning mouth, or from the verb 'box', i.e. to surround. It is sometimes spelt bushel, and occasionally the word coak was used.

bushel a dry measure of approximately 8 gallons capacity. There was some variation in the volume of a bushel in different parts of the country: a Winchester bushel had 2,150 cubic in, whereas an Imperial bushel contains 2,218 cubic in. Mined coal was often measured in bushels. A bushel contained from 84 to 94 lb coal according to district. In 1824 an Act of Parliament fixed the Imperial bushel (also the Winchester) at 84 lb. The sale of coal by volume was made illegal in 1834.

bustle pipe large pipe or main carrying the blast air which encircles a BLAST FURNACE, connected to the TUYÈRES by a quick release pipe called the GOOSENECK.

butterfly hook, *see* MINE SAFETY HOOK

butterfly valve **1.** a non-return valve comprising two semicircular plates hinged on a central spindle, placed diametrically across a pipe and arranged so that they swing open to flow in one direction, but close to a reverse flow. The name obviously comes from the similarity of the moving parts to a butterfly, with the central spindle the body and the two half disks the wings. **2.** a simple throttle or flow control valve comprising a disk which turns on a diametrical spindle in a circular pipe or chamber. When the disk lies at right angles to the axis of the pipe any flow is stopped, while positions between this and maximum flow position, when it lies along the axis, regulate the flow. Such valves have a long history: James Watt (1736–1819) used butterfly valves to regulate the flow of steam to engines, the valves being under the control of GOVERNORS.

buttermilk the liquid left after churning milk; as it is slightly acidic, it was used in the early days of BLEACHING to neutralize cloth after it had been treated with an alkaline LYE, before dilute sulphuric acid was introduced.

butternut the North American tree *Juglans cinerea* from which a black dye was made, used particularly for linen cloth; also known as white, or black walnut.

butty **1.** a man who contracted with the proprietors of a mine to work a section of it, whether coal or ore, and led a butty-gang who worked for him and shared the contract price with him on an agreed basis; used particularly in Staffordshire. A butty-gang was also a method used by the early railway constructors, such as Thomas Brassey (1805–70), for navvying. Prior to 1842, a butty working in a coal mine often 'employed' his wife and children. **2.** a butty-boat is the name given to an engineless narrowboat on a canal towed by a powered boat. The use of the word dates from about the 1850s when engine driven boats were taking over from horse drawn. **3.** a mate or assistant; a usage of uncertain origin.

bye-wash a spillway or bypass to convey water past a lock on a canal. Bye-washes are used where a canal is fed from a flowing river, to prevent the canal and locks overfilling; they can be open channels or underground culverts.

'by house', *see* 'COME INTO THE HOUSE'

C

cabbling (or scabbling) the breaking up of flattened, refined iron blooms into small pieces preparatory to reheating them for making into bar iron.

cadger, *see* HUCKSTER

Cadw (Welsh Historic Monuments) a body for the protection, preservation and conservation of historic monuments in Wales. Cadw operates in a similar manner to ENGLISH HERITAGE, being partly funded from government sources and partly from the annual subscriptions of members of its Heritage in Wales scheme. It awards multi-million pound grants annually for the repair and conservation of the historic monuments in its care, some of which are of industrial importance. The headquarters of Cadw are in Cardiff. *See also* HISTORIC SCOTLAND.

caisson a large diameter, watertight vertical cylinder, open at its base, which is used in the construction of underwater foundations. The caisson is sealed at its top or partway down its length, to provide a working space below the seal. It is lowered into the water onto the river bed, and water is prevented from entering the working space by pumping in compressed air. Men and materials enter and leave the working space via air locks. The idea of caissons dates from the early 18th century. Isambard Kingdom Brunel (1806–59) used caissons for constructing the foundations of the Royal Albert Bridge over the Tamar in 1859, enabling some 80 ft of sand and mud to be removed from the river bed until solid rock was reached.

At some docks, hollow rectangular caissons or pontoons with solid bottoms are used in place of hinged lock gates. They can be filled with water when in position at the entrance to a dock or basin, and some of the water can be pumped out so that they can be floated out of the way when required. The advantage of caisson gates is that water leakage past them is less than with large hinged gates, and a roadway can be made across their top surface to improve access around the dock. Samuel Bentham (1757–1831) patented such a caisson gate (patent no. 3544, 1812).

calamanco (or callimanco) originally a cloth woven in Flanders, but later woven in Lancashire. It was made from wool and silk, woven with a satin TWILL to give a check on the silken side only, and was very popular in the 18th century for garments, particularly men's waistcoats.

calamine an oxide form of silicate of zinc, mined from veins, usually found in close association with lead ore. Calamine was used in the 19th century to make a kind of BRASS before ZINC became available, and the brass was used for making gilt items such as cheap buttons. It is also known as dry-bone to lead miners. A cream coloured mineral, it results from the weathering of BLENDE. The name calamine comes from the Latin *calamaris* meaning a reed, and is so called because of the reed-like mass which forms in the bottom of the furnace during smelting. An old spelling was callamy.

calcar a small oven or REVERBERATORY FURNACE in which sand and potash are roasted to make FRIT in glass making. *See also* CALCINING.

calcining the prolonged heating or roasting of materials to drive off water, volatiles and sulphur so that they may be reduced to a powder. Calcining is often a preliminary process. Limestone is calcined in LIME KILNS to produce powdered lime; ores are often calcined before actual smelting, and other materials such as alum are also calcined.

Before kilns or calcining furnaces were introduced, roasting was carried out on the open ground. The material to be calcined was laid in layers interspersed with layers of fuel (wood, charcoal, peat or coal) and burned for a day, or more, as required. Mechanical calciners, such as the BRUNTON CALCINER and the OXLAND AND HOCKING, were invented to speed up the preliminary processing of ores.

calcite (or calespar) a GANGUE material usually associated with the lead ore galena; a crystalline form of calcium carbonate. It is used in the manufacture of white paint.

calender a machine comprising a number of horizontal rollers through which a material is passed, under pressure from pairs of rollers, to impart a desired surface finish, ensure a constant thickness, or combine two materials together. Calenders are used for various purposes in the paper, rubber, and textile industries. For example, paper is given a gloss or glazed surface in a calender, the degree of gloss depending on the pressure applied. In the 18th century cloth calenders were simple, like a pair of mangle rollers, across which a long, flat-bottomed box containing weights was drawn by a horse or men to provide the pressure. The cloth, which had previously been immersed in hot water, was fed in between the rollers, and ran out on a flat table.

In the rubber trade, Edwin M. Chaffee of Roxbury, Mass., USA, invented a three-roll calender in 1835 for making rubberized waterproof fabric. The rolls were mounted one above the other, and COMPOUNDED rubber was fed into the nip between the top and the middle rollers. Here it was masticated until it formed a thin sheet of soft plastic rubber which clung round the middle roller by virtue of the middle roller's slower speed. The gap between the middle and the bottom rollers was set slightly wider than the thickness of the thin rubber sheet, so that a continuous length of fabric could be fed in between these rollers. The thin sheet of rubber was therefore pressed onto one surface of the fabric with a wiping action which forced the soft rubber into the interstices of the fabric, there being a speed differential between the rollers. The rubberized fabric was then VULCANIZED by heat.

caliche soda nitre imported from Chile in the mid-19th century and used in the manufacture of sulphuric acid; also known as Chile saltpetre.

calico a plain woven cloth (*see* PLAIN WEAVE) either grey (unbleached), or white (bleached) in its undyed and unprinted state, and made of cotton. It is coarser than MUSLIN in texture. The name comes from Calicut, a city on the Malabar coast, western India, from where cotton cloth was first imported into England in the late 16th and early 17th centuries by the East India Company; it was known then as Calicut-cloth. Calico is one of the most common of cotton fabrics, and is woven in different qualities.

calico printing printing coloured patterns on cotton cloth. The process was introduced into Britain c.1700, and the industry became concentrated mostly in the north-west textile manufacturing districts of England. At first, printing of patterns onto cloth was by the BLOCK PRINTING hand method, using engraved wooden blocks in a similar manner to reproducing book illustrations by woodcuts. Frequently, such printing formed part of a bleaching and dyeing concern, providing a cloth finishing service to the textile trade. A large works would employ a few hundred hand block printers, each man with his own printing table or bench. Many firms also had their own block making department. Although it began to be replaced around the 1770s–80s by machine printing, hand block printing lasted well past the mid-1800s, after machine printing had been introduced.

Machine printing of cloth by roller or cylinder was invented in the 1770s. A patent (no. 1007) was granted to Charles Taylor, Thomas Walker, and Joseph Adkin, all of Manchester, in 1772 for printing by engraved wooden rollers. Thomas Bell, of Walton-le-Dale, Lancs., took out a patent in 1783 (no. 1378) for a copper-covered roller engraved on its curved surface, which worked in the reverse manner to hand blocks, i.e. the engraved lines were the printing area, and smooth areas were kept clear of colour. Cloth was passed continuously from an overhead roller through the nip between the engraved roller and a plain roller. The lower part of the engraved roller dipped into a colour trough, and as it revolved its surface was wiped clean by a doctor knife before the cloth reached it. Colour was thus left only in the engraved lines, which transferred the pattern onto the cloth. The pattern was printed full width, and repeated itself in the distance equal to the circumference of the copper roller. At first, single colours only were printed, but soon multicolour machines were invented with several rollers, each carrying part of the pattern and fitted with its own colour trough and doctor knife. The cloth passed each roller in sequence, building up the final multicoloured design.

In 1702 a tax of 3*d* per yard was imposed on all calicoes printed, painted, dyed, or stained; this was increased to 6*d* per yard in 1714, and was not finally repealed until 1831.

Graham, J. *History of Print Works in Manchester and District, 1760–1846*, 1846
Robinson, S. *A History of Printed Textiles*, Studio Vista, 1969
Turnbull, G. *A History of the Calico Printing Industry of Great Britain*, 1951

calico weave, *see* PLAIN WEAVE

Calicut-cloth, *see* CALICO

caloric an old name for heat. The caloric theory was that heat consisted of a weightless fluid called caloric, which flowed from hotter to colder bodies. The theory was abandoned by the mid-19th century as scientific knowledge increased. A caloric engine was the name once given to a HOT AIR ENGINE.

cam a raised portion of a shaft, or a plate with a periphery shaped to a particular profile, which when rotated causes a FOLLOWER which is pressed up against it to describe a particular motion. This may be irregular or regular according to the movement desired. Cams are used to operate various mechanisms in machinery or engines. In some cases the follower is held in contact with the cam continuously; in other instances the cam raises the follower until a point is reached during the revolution when the follower falls away rapidly (sometimes spring assisted) to impart a rapid action to some other part of the mechanism. Such cams are called trips. FULLING STOCKS and HELVE HAMMERS, for instance, are operated by trips.

cambric originally a white linen fabric made in Cambrai, northern France (formerly in Flanders), mostly used for handkerchiefs, napkins, etc. A hard-spun cotton imitation later also became known as cambric. Cambric is known as batiste in France.

camel-hair a strong fabric made from the Bactrian camel of Central Asia, with fibres 1.5–2.5 in long of soft and fine texture. As Camel hair cannot be bleached, it is used in its natural yellow-brown colour to make the fabric of the same name.

camlets a plain weave cloth, originally worsted but also copied in silk, wool and a combination of materials. Worsted camlets were being woven in Norfolk in the 16th century, and were still being made in the 18th century. There were two varieties woven – single camlets, which had warps thicker than wefts, and double camlets, which had thick warps and wefts. Sometimes camlets were 'watered' after weaving by being sprinkled with water and hot pressed to give a kind of moiré finish. Camlets were used for garments and upholstery, and were often lined with silk for bedcurtains and hangings.

campaign the working period between starting up (blowing in) of a BLAST FURNACE and its shutting down (blowing out). Early blast furnaces were run continuously round the clock over many months. This was usually in the winter months, or as long as there was water to operate the bellows. Periods of thirty to forty weeks were normal, and a system of water reservoirs was necessary to ensure an uninterrupted operation. The summer weeks would be used to carry out repairs to the furnace, and collect stocks of wood for charcoal ready for the next campaign. The later, coke-fired blast furnaces employing steam power, being independent of a continuous water supply, ran for much longer campaigns.

camwood a hard red wood from the tree *Baphia nitida* which was imported from West Africa to make a red vegetable DYE; it is similar to BARWOOD. The wood is white when first cut, but turns red on exposure to the atmosphere; it was ground to a powder before use. The tree is also found in Brazil. Camwood was in use until the invention of synthetic dyes in the mid-19th century.

canal man-made inland waterway for transporting goods and passengers. Canals date from Roman times, and 17th-century France had many canals. The first true canal in Britain is usually accepted to be the Newry Canal in Co. Down, Ireland: started in 1730 and finished in 1744, it carried coal to Dublin. The Sankey Navigation, near St Helen's, Lancs., cut in 1755, is regarded as England's first, closely followed by the Bridgewater Canal at Worsley, Lancs., started in 1759, and opened for coal traffic to Manchester in 1765. The success of this canal led to the establishment of the canal network over the less hilly parts of Britain.

Canal construction needed Parliamentary authority to buy land on the route, and planning and supervision of the work was by the civil engineers of the day, men such as James Brindley (1716–72), Benjamin Outram (1764–1805), and John Rennie (1761–1821). Excavation was mainly carried out by manual labour provided by itinerant gangs of men known as navigators, a name shortened to 'navvy' around the 1830s. Two main problems had to be overcome – the terrain the canal was to cross, and the provision of a constant supply of water. The natural contours of the land were followed where possible to keep the canal level, resulting in winding routes; unavoidable slopes were crossed by LOCKS, while AQUEDUCTS or embankments were built to cross steep valleys. Hills were passed by cuttings or tunnels. Water supply reservoirs were built at summit levels to feed the canals, and at difficult places the water had to be recirculated by pumping.

Individual canals were built in isolation, with the result that when they were eventually joined up, there was no standard width or lock size, which hindered through traffic considerably. There are roughly four sizes of canals: tub boat canals for small boats carrying about 5 tons; narrow canals for boats up to 72 ft long by 7 ft wide carrying 25–30 tons; broad canals for barges up to 80 ft long by up to 21 ft wide, for 50 tons upwards; and ship canals for sea-going vessels with large locks, some up to 600 ft long.

Originally, canal companies were not themselves carriers, but took tolls from users, until the Canal Carriers Act of 1845 permitted them to act as carriers as well. Boats were pulled by horses walking along a towpath, and tolls were paid at canalside toll houses.

Wharves and warehouses were built alongside canals, and many factories and mills in industrial towns were also built to ease the transport of raw materials and finished goods. Canals were particularly suitable for carrying heavy, bulky goods such as coal, where speed was not essential.

At their peak in 1858, there were some 4,250 miles of canal linking all the important industrial centres in England. With the coming of railways canals could not compete, particularly for speed, and one by one they declined or were bought up by railway companies and closed down. In the three years 1845–7 railways bought and closed some 900 miles of canal, almost one-fifth of the system then existing. Today, many canals lie derelict and neglected, relics of a transport age now gone, but many have been or are being restored by enthusiastic members of canal societies, and are enjoyed both by boating enthusiasts and by holidaymakers. *See also* CANAL BOAT, CANAL MANIA.

Boucher, C.T.G. *James Brindley Engineer, 1716–72*, Goose, 1968
Boucher, C.T.G. *John Rennie, 1761–1821: Life and Work of a Great Engineer*, Manchester University Press, 1963
Burton, A. *The Canal Builders*, Eyre Methuen
de Maré, E. *The Canals of England*, Architectural Press, 1961
Hadfield, C. *British Canals: An Illustrated History*, 2nd edn, David and Charles, 1966
Hadfield, C. (ed.) *The Canals of the British Isles* (series of regional titles), David and Charles, 1967–70
Ransom, P.J.G. *The Archaeology of Canals*, World's Work, 1979
Russell, R. *Lost Canals and Waterways of Britain*, David and Charles

canal boat boat for conveying goods or passengers on inland waterways. Several sizes of boats or barges were used as a result of the non-standard dimensions of British canals and locks (*see* CANAL). Freight-carrying canal boats were horse drawn and could cover up to about 25 miles per day, at 2–3 mph. Horses could be changed at staging points if required, where stabling was available. In early days, a canal boat was manned by a steersman and a boy, the boatman's family living in a canal-side cottage somewhere along the canal he normally worked. The freight carried was subject to tolls, the loading being checked against gauge marks on the side of the boat (*see* GAUGING DOCK). Experiments with steam-powered canal boats were first made before the end of the 18th century, and in the mid-19th century steam-powered boats, which could also act as tugs, became more common. By the 1870s, the employment of towing horses was being seriously challenged by powered boats.

Passenger traffic was carried in specially built PACKET boats or flyboats pulled at about 8–10 mph by two horses, regularly changed. Packets enjoyed some popularity in the early 19th century until superseded by the railways, with their greater speed. In the declining years of the canals when they were faced with competition from the railways, the wages of boatmen were reduced to cut costs. The men were forced to economize by giving up their cottages, and bringing their families on board to live in tiny cabins. This saved rent, and their wives and children could help work the boat, eliminating the need for any paid help. By the 1870s, family boats – particularly the brightly decorated narrow boats – became a common feature on canals. Life on board was generally squalid, with children missing education as a result of constant travelling. Improvements came with the 1877 and 1884 Canal Boats Acts, largely brought about by the efforts of George Smith (1831–95) of Coalville, Leics. In 1875, it was estimated there were some 25,000 boats working the canals.

Canal boats often had local names: for instance, on the Yorkshire and Humber Canal they were known as keels, Weaver and Mersey boats were called flats, and Norfolk had its wherries. *See also* STARVATIONER.

Hanson, H. *The Canal Boatmen, 1760–1914*, Alan Sutton Publishing, 1984
Lewerey, A.J. *Narrow Boat Painting*, David and Charles,
Pee, R. 'The first iron boat', *Journal of the Wilkinson Society*, no. 14, 1986
Rolt, L.T.C. *Narrow Boat*, 1944; reprinted by Alan Sutton Publishing, 1994
Smith, G. *Our Canal Population*, 1878: reprinted by EP Publishing, 1974
Weaver, C.R. and C.P. *Steam on Canals*, David and Charles,

canal mania the rush in speculation in canal shares in the 1790s. Encouraged by the financial success of the Bridgewater Canal of 1765 and the obvious advantages to be gained by better transport of goods by inland waterway, more canals began to be built, funded by joint stock companies. The rush to get new canals authorized by Act of Parliament reached a crescendo in the years 1789–97, the period of canal mania. The table below indicates the number of canals authorized during this period:

Year	No. of new canals authorized	Capital authorized £ x 1,000
1789	2	131
1790	1	90
1791	7	743
1792	7	1,056
1793	20	2,825
1794	10	2,038
1795	4	395
1796	3	585
1797	1	18
	—	
	55	7,881

By the 1830s, nearly £20 million had been spent. There was an earlier period of lower activity in the 1760s and 1770s, followed by a slowing during the period of trade recession which followed the American War of Independence (1775–83). Although 165 Canal Acts were passed between 1758 and 1802, a number of speculative and worthless schemes were floated which brought ruin to many investors and led to a waste of capital and labour.

Ward, J.R. *The Finance of Canal Building in Eighteenth-Century England*, 1974

candles blocks or sticks of tallow or wax with a central textile wick which gives light when the wick is burning. The commonplace candle dates to pre-Biblical times, and candle making became a separate trade of its own in Europe by the 15th century or earlier. The first candles were made from tallow (cattle and sheep fat), and later ones from whale spermaceti (a white wax obtained from the head of a sperm whale). Paraffin wax was introduced in the middle of the 19th century, and West African palm oil began reaching Britain in 1772, and this too was used in making candles. The wicks were made of braided cotton or linen, and some small mills specialized in making material for candle wicks.

Before the introduction of gas lighting in the early 19th century candles and oil lamps were the only form of artificial lighting in textile mills. This was a big fire hazard, and many mills were burnt down in fires started by candles. Candles were also the cause of explosions in 18th and 19th century coal mines.

Although candles today are only used decoratively or in emergencies, the word candle is still in use as the scientific measurement of the intensity of artificial light. The first standard was the light emitted by a sperm wax candle, weighing ⅙ lb, and burning at the rate of 120 gms per hour. This was called one English Standard or Parliamentary Candle, and other light sources were compared against this and expressed in candle powers. Today's standard is the International Candle which is the more reliable light emitted from a specially constructed electric lamp. One International Candle equals 0.98 of the old English unit.

The word candle comes from the Latin *candere*, meaning to shine.

candy an Indian measure of weight used for cotton; in Bombay, one candy weighs 560 lb.

cannel a type of coal with a high ash and volatiles content, which burns with a clear, bright flame. It has been known since the 16th century, and is found among seams of ordinary coal, particularly in the Wigan, Lancs., coalfield, and also in Scotland. It is possible that the word is a dialect variation of 'candle' because the flame it produces, like a candle's, burns without smoke. Cannel coal has a jet-like appearance, and does not soil the hands when handled. It will take a polish, and can be carved into ornaments, etc. In some areas it is known as parrot coal. Cannel coal was highly prized for gas manufacture during the 19th century, until scarcity raised prices too high. Kannell and kennel were 18th-century spellings.

cantilever bridge bridge comprising a pair of cantilevers arranged back-to-back, from a common central support, each cantilever balancing its opposite number: a cantilever is a beam fixed at one end only, projecting outwards like a bracket or arm. In multi-span cantilever bridges, a simple short beam joins the otherwise free ends of two cantilevers pointing towards each other. Not many cantilever bridges have been built, the most famous one (and the first in Britain) being the Forth railway bridge in Scotland. Built in 1883–90, it comprises three towers 361 ft high, with two main spans of 1710 ft carrying twin railway tracks 156 ft above high water. Of lattice girder construction, it was the first bridge built in Britain of steel rather than iron, some 54,000 tons of steel being used. Designed by Benjamin Baker (1840–1907) and John Fowler (1817–98), it was built by William Arrol (1839–1913).
Paxton, R.A. (ed.), *100 Years of the Forth Bridge*, Thomas Telford Publications, 1990

canvas a strong, unbleached cloth made from linen or hemp and used for ships' and windmill sails, tents, and other heavy duty applications. It is the base cloth which when tarred to make waterproof is known as tarpaulin. The word canvas comes from the Greek *kannabis*, meaning hemp.

cap name frequently given to the top part of a machine: in windmills, for instance, the cap is the separate top of a TOWER or SMOCK MILL, which rotates to keep the sails facing into the wind.

cap spinning frame a variation of the THROSTLE FRAME, invented by Charles Danforth (1797–1876) and John Thorp (1784–1848) in the USA about 1828. It gained some popularity for a while until it was superseded by RING SPINNING, also an American invention. The FLYER of the throstle was replaced by a stationary cap, from which the machine got its name. In the cap spinning frame, a wooden BOBBIN is placed over a brass tube and engages with raised nibs on the tube. The tube has an integral WHORL and the tube and bobbin are placed over a stationary vertical spindle. A metal cap with a circular skirt slightly larger than the diameter of the bobbin flange is fitted over the protruding end of the spindle, above the bobbin. Yarn from the overhead drafting rollers is wound round the bobbin and rests against the edge of the cap skirt. When the tube and bobbin are rotated at high speed, the yarn runs round the edge of the stationary cap imparting twist to the yarn. At the same time it 'balloons' outwards due to centrifugal force, and the air resistance opposing it causes it to lag behind the speed of the bobbin. The bobbin therefore winds yarn onto itself, the edge of the cap skirt guiding the yarn onto the bobbin. DRAFTING, twisting, and winding on are therefore performed simultaneously. The bobbin is arranged to move up and down the stationary spindle for even winding.

Cap spinning was used in the cotton and worsted industries. Its main problems were that the yarn SNARLED when the machine was stopped to change bobbins, and the degree of TWIST varied with the diameter of the yarn as it wound onto the bobbin.

captain old name for an experienced mining engineer who directed and oversaw the miners and managed the business for the owners; it was a courtesy title, used frequently in Cornwall, and had nothing to do with any military or naval rank. Like so many mining terms, the title is believed to have originated in Germany in the 16th century, where it meant a foreman in a mine.

car, *see* TRAM (2)

carbon a common, non-metallic element naturally present in many compounds such as diamond, COAL and COKE, CHARCOAL, petroleum, etc. Carbon is an important element and forms the basis of organic chemistry. Carbon itself has a high calorific value, being the main source of heat in coal, coke, and charcoal. Besides its value as a fuel, carbon's great affinity for oxygen is used in reducing ores of the oxide type to their metallic state, by chemical combination. The complete combustion of carbon produces the harmless gas carbon dioxide, but incomplete combustion gives the poisonous gas carbon monoxide. The latter has uses as a reducing agent in some industrial processes.

carbonizing a process for destroying non-wool fibres from shredded material in the SHODDY and MUNGO industries. There are two methods: wet carbonizing, where the shredded material is soaked in acid baths, and dry carbonizing where the material is rotated in finely perforated drums, usually hexagonal, in a hot acidic gas, the gas being made in heated retorts. The resulting all-wool product is called extract.

card cloth fabric similar to a wire brush for roughly paralleling cotton or wool fibres (*see* CARDING). The cloth has a 'brush-like' construction of short, slightly bent, metal pins or wires, set closely together in rows, with their pointed ends of a uniform height. The wires are held in a leather or similar backing, and the density of wires per square inch and their diameter vary according to the purpose for which the card is intended. Card cloth is defined by the number of wires per square inch. The wires are bent into a slight 'V' so that their points are directed away from the vertical, as shown:

card cloth

With constant use in a carding machine, the points become blunt and require sharpening with emery rollers; the process of re-pointing, adjusting the gap between the opposing cards, and cleaning the cards is performed by a skilled workman known as a stripper and grinder.

In 1750, William Pennington patented a machine for making holes in the leather backing through which the wires were inserted (patent no. 657); soon afterwards Robert Kay (*fl.*1760) developed a machine for cutting, bending, and inserting the wires through the leather. Card cloth manufacture became a specialized service to the textile industry.

carding preparing raw wool or cotton for subsequent spinning by separating, and paralleling the fibres of the tangled mass to form a SLIVER. Carding is performed between the wires of CARD CLOTH which removes short fibres, untangles the mass of material, and brings the fibres more or less parallel with each other in a loose sliver or web, without any twist. The word carding comes from the Latin

carduus meaning a thistle – thistles were used for this purpose in ancient times.

When spinning and weaving were cottage industries, carding was done by hand, frequently by children helping their mother and older sisters to prepare raw wool or cotton ready for spinning on a wheel. Hand carding used a pair of cards resembling square table-tennis bats covered in card cloth. A thin layer of tangled wool or cotton was laid on one card, and the other card drawn across several times, with the wires point-to-point, until the fibres were straightened out. By reversing the direction of movement of the top card so that the wires were point-to-back, the carded material could be stripped off as a soft, loose roll, called a rolag. It was now ready for hand spinning. When demand for cloth outstripped domestic carding, STOCK CARDS were used, although this was still a manual operation.

Carding became a serious bottleneck when spinning machines were invented, holding up yarn production. Several attempts were made to mechanize the process: Daniel Bourn's early attempt (patent no. 628, 1748) was not very successful, but set the pattern for later designs. The most notable carding machine or engine, as they were called, was invented by Richard Arkwright (1732–92) and patented in 1775 (no. 1111). His machine used a rotary principle, feeding the material to be carded between a series of card cloth covered rollers spaced round a large drum also covered in card cloth. Several later improvements to the basic design were made, one being to substitute flat bars covered in card cloth for the rollers to give an increased area for carding.

A cross-section through a typical carding engine is shown in Fig. 15; the two alternative methods, roller or flats, are shown. The raw cotton in a continuous lap or roll is picked up by the licker-in which attenuates it and feeds it onto the periphery of the SWIFT: this conveys it to the first pair of rollers. The carding roller rotates at a slower surface speed than the swift, and the fibres are laid upon it, causing them to be condensed (shortened). Next to the carding roller, a clearer roller running at a faster surface speed takes the fibres off the carding roller, attenuates them, and returns them to the swift. The swift conveys the fibres on to the next pair, and the action is repeated in subsequent pairs of rollers round the swift until the DOFFER is reached. The direction of the wire points on the various rollers is arranged to suit each action required. The doffer takes off the fibres, which are now made parallel and drawn out into a thinner sliver than the original lap. The machine delivers the sliver into a revolving can, ready for the next stage of manufacture. Carding by flats differs from roller carding, since the fibres stay on the swift as they pass round to the doffer, and are continuously carded as they pass under the flats. A later improvement consisted of putting the flats on a slowly moving conveyor chain which took them away from the swift after they had been in contact with it for some time, so that they could be cleared of short fibres and rubbish before returning to it. This enabled the machine to be kept in continuous operation.

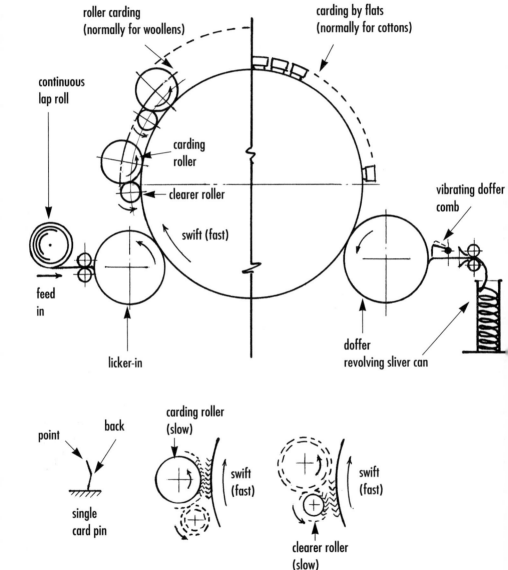

Fig. 15. Cross-section of a carding engine

carding and jenny mill a small workshop, employing up to about ten men, working on hand-operated CARDING engines and hand JENNIES, spinning yarn for HANDLOOM WEAVERS. Such small enterprises were the forerunners of later water- and steam-powered spinning mills.

Carmichael valve gear, see GAB VALVE GEAR

Carnot cycle the cycle of operations in an imaginary perfect heat engine with maximum thermal efficiency, in which the expansion and subsequent compression of the working fluid operates at constant temperature. It is the theoretical ultimate standard of comparison for all heat engines, but not attainable in practice. Propounded in 1824 by Nicolas Léonhard Sadi Carnot (1796–1832) in France, it laid the foundation for the study of thermodynamics.

carpet a floor covering made from various textile materials and woven in several constructions, the main ones being Axminster, Brussels, Chenille, Kidderminster, and Wilton. Carpets originated in the East, and their manufacture in Britain did not commence until the 16th century when they could only be afforded by the rich. Turkish techniques were copied at first by hand-tying tufts of coloured wool in vertical looms. Weaving of carpets commenced around the mid-18th century and within a short period the main types were being made: Kidderminster carpets were being woven in 1735, Wiltons in 1745, Brussels in 1750, and Axminsters in 1755. All these types of carpet take their names from the places where they were first woven.

The Kidderminster is a flat woven patterned carpet, developed originally by Pearsall and John Brown c.1735, and was once known as a Kidder or ingrain carpet. Wilton carpets have a warp pile surface: the yarn is woven over sharp wires which cut the loop when lifted out of the loom, and the surface is later made level by shearing. Cheaper substitutes for Wilton carpets, known as tapestry carpets, were introduced in the 1830s: these were woven with yarn which was dyed different colours along its length to produce the coloured pattern effect. Brussels carpets have looped pile which is left uncut; the loop is made by weaving over round wires which are later slid out. Axminsters have small tufts of worsted or wool fastened under the warp and brought to the surface by a combing action.

Hand weaving of carpets was heavy work. Some looms needed up to four men to handle the width, passing the SHUTTLE from one to another. The JACQUARD was applied to carpet weaving in the 1830s, and shortly afterwards power looms were introduced, a successful one being that invented and patented by George Collier in 1851 (patent no. 13888). This machine increased output twelvefold over previous methods. A technique for weaving CHENILLE carpets was developed by James Templeton in Glasgow in the 1840s, and much inventive work was carried out in the USA during the next decade or so. This resulted in power loom inventions for Brussels and Wilton carpets by Erastus B. Bigelow (1814–79) in Massachusetts in the 1850s to 60s, and the power tufting loom for Axminsters by Halcyon Skinner (1824–1900) of New York in the 1860s. John Crossley (1722–1837) established a large carpet factory in Halifax, Yorks.: the firm bought the patent rights of Bigelow's power loom and by the 1870s had built up the largest carpet manufacturing concern in the world. The patent rights of Skinner's loom were purchased by Michael Tomkinson, who renamed the carpets it made 'Royal' Axminster.

Several materials have been used in carpets – WORSTED, WOOL for the surface, LINEN and JUTE for the backings. Powered carpet looms became extremely complicated and intricate due to the many yarns of different colours needed to reproduce the patterns.

Bradbury, F. *Carpet Manufacture*, Lord and Nagle, 1904

cart gate an underground tunnel in a lead mine large enough to permit transporting ore by trucks running on rails.

Carvés oven, see COKE OVENS

cashmere a soft, much prized fabric made from the coat of the Kashmir (India) or Tibetan goat, popular for shawls. Woollen imitations are also made: cashmere wool is brown to greyish-white, with a staple length of 1.5–3 in.

cassimere a superfine twilled woollen fabric named after the cashmere cloth made in Kashmir, India.

Cassimere cloth was invented by Francis Yerbury (1707–87) of Bradford-on-Avon, Wiltshire, and patented in 1766, pat. No. 858 of 26th August. It was given a name similar to cashmere which it resembled, and became an important West Country cloth. It was sometimes wrongly called KERSEYMERE.

cassiterite an oxide of TIN, or tin ore; a dark brown mineral found in near-vertical veins or lodes and in alluvial gravels. It can contain up to about 60 per cent tin. Tin was once extensively mined in Cornwall, either by deep lode mining or streaming – separating the ore pieces by washing in water. Cassiterite is also known as black tin.

cast iron The material obtained direct from the iron ore in a BLAST FURNACE which is cast into

PIG form; it is sometimes called pig iron. It contains 2.5–4.5 per cent carbon and is therefore an iron-carbon alloy. One of the most useful metals, it has been known since very early times, and was the basic constructional material on which the development of the Industrial Revolution relied. Depending on the proportions of charge fed into the blast furnace, different grades of cast iron may be produced. About six different grades may be differentiated. The 'whitest' and hardest cast irons have all the carbon content combined with the iron, whilst 'grey', softer irons have only a part of the carbon in combination, the remainder being in the form of graphite particles intimately mixed in the material. Iron has a high melting point of 1535°C.

Hard, 'white' cast iron was exclusively used for the manufacture of WROUGHT IRON; today, the softer grades are used for foundry work by being remelted in a CUPOLA and cast into moulds. The moulds comprise cavities previously formed in clayey sand (loam) by wooden patterns which have been made to the shape of the article required to be cast in iron. The pattern is made slightly larger than the finished article to allow for contraction of the iron as it cools. The molten iron is carefully poured into the mould, and when it is cold and solidified, the sand is knocked away. Cast-iron articles made in this way in foundries include cannon (in the days when they were used), machine parts, building columns, pipes, railings and gates, and small domestic items such as pots and smoothing irons.

Cast iron is strong under compression, but weak under tension (only about one-third as strong). It is a hard, brittle material which cannot be bent or worked, and is not suitable for impact loads unless only very lightly loaded. Cast iron began replacing the wooden frames of early machines such as looms in the early 19th century. Its advantages over wood are its durability, strength, and ability to be cast into intricate shapes not easily achieved in wood. Furthermore, its ability to withstand high temperature is an essential quality for engineering parts such as the cylinders of steam engines and locomotives. Output rose rapidly in the 19th century, the age of iron, from 30,000 tons of pig iron in 1760 to 3,600,000 tons in 1860. *See also* IRON ORE.

cast steel literally, steel which has been cast to a desired shape in a mould and not shaped by machining. The name was originally given to steel made by the CRUCIBLE PROCESS and not by the CEMENTATION PROCESS. Cast steel was first developed by Benjamin Huntsman (1704–76) in the UK in 1740. He was a Doncaster clockmaker and he produced his steel by melting broken-up BLISTER STEEL by COKE, in heat resisting clay crucibles, and pouring it as cast steel. The process was costly and Huntsman used his small output for making improved clock springs and pendulums. Later, it was used by the CUTLERY trade in Sheffield and for edge cutting tools. No notable improvement in the quantity produced, or any cheapening of the process, was made for a century until a cheap method of steel manufacture was introduced by Henry Bessemer with his CONVERTER, and Frederick Siemens with his OPEN HEARTH process.

Catalan furnace, *see* TROMPE

cataract controller a device developed in Cornwall for controlling the stroke frequency of BEAM ENGINES by varying the time at which the cooling water injection valve was opened to create the vacuum in the steam cylinder. Fig. 16 shows the essentials of the device. It comprised a wooden box supported on pivots and counterbalanced: a stream of water was directed into the box, and when a certain amount had entered, the weight of the water caused the box to tip over, discharging the water to waste. The action of the tipping box activated a lever system which opened the injection valve, admitting cold water into the engine cylinder and initiating the power stroke of the engine. A tumbling bob-weight ensured rapid opening of the valve. When the box had emptied itself of water, the counterbalance swung it back to its original position, closing the injection valve via the lever system, and the box commenced filling again with water. Fig. 16 shows two configurations of the system, the full lines when the injection valve is shut, and the dotted lines when it is open. By regulating the rate of flow of water into the box, the time-dwell between successive engine cycles could be infinitely varied, since the power stroke could not commence until the injection valve was opened. The cataract therefore controlled the time interval between strokes.

It is not known who invented the cataract. Newcomen used it on his engines, and James Watt used it on some of his early engines in the 1770s. Several variations in design were developed over the years, and an air version using circular bellows was also developed. The water cataract is virtually a form of water clock. It was also known as a Jack-in-the-Box. *See also* BUOY CONTROLLER.

catchpit, *see* SLIME PIT

Catchpole brake a device fitted to the sails of a WINDMILL, invented by Catchpole in 1860. It

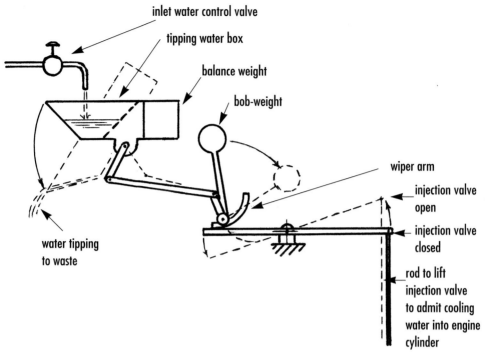

inlet water control valve

tipping water box

balance weight

bob-weight

water tipping
to waste

wiper arm

injection valve
open

injection valve
closed

rod to lift
injection valve
to admit cooling
water into engine
cylinder

Fig. 16. Cataract controller, 1779

comprised two longitudinal shutters added to one side of each sail. In light winds the shutters remained closed and added to the surface area of the sail; in high winds they were opened and in this position disturbed the air flow and acted as a brake, assisting the main brake on the brakewheel inside the mill, thus preventing overspeed.

catchwing a cantilever buffer made from a springy wood, fastened to an engine house or supporting beam, and projecting over the end of the engine beam or bob. Two such buffers are provided, one at each end of the bob: their purpose is to prevent overstroking, since their positions are such that the bob strikes against them at the end of each stroke, thus preventing damage to the piston and/or the cylinder. A catchwing is also called a spring beam.

cat dirt, *see* CHANNEL

catechu, *see* CUTCH

cat head a small capstan, crane, or projecting beam positioned above a LOADING SLOT in a warehouse, on which pulleys etc. are placed for lifting and lowering goods into and out of the building. The name is borrowed from a similar device used on board ships; a cat head is also known as a LUCAM.

caul, *see* WEIR

causeway a path or road, normally paved, raised above the surrounding land, which is usually soft or marshy, to provide a hard surface for wheeled or horse traffic such as packhorses. A causeway is known as a sarn in Wales.

causey stones Large flat stones or flags laid to form a raised packway or causeway over soft ground, for use by packhorses. Causey stones are also known as SETTS, or in some old documents as eases (because they make for easier passage across difficult ground).

cawk (or cauk, calk) a Derbyshire miners' term for BARYTES or barium sulphate. The word is possibly a dialect version of 'chalk', and so named because the rock is generally of an opaque creamy colour not unlike chalk.

cement a calcinated mixture of lime and clay ground into a powder which, when the correct amount of water is added, is used for joining building materials together, or for making CONCRETE. It is applied as a stiff paste between stones or bricks, and when set (i.e. hardened) it has an adhesive power bonding the items together. Hard cement is strong in compression, but weak in tension, hence its usefulness in foundation work.

Cement was known in Roman times. An underwater cement was devised by John Smeaton for the Eddystone lighthouse in 1756. James Parker was granted a patent (no. 2120) in 1796 for 'Roman' cement. Joseph Aspdin (1779–1855) of Leeds, Yorks., made the first artificial cement and called it Portland cement after its likeness to the natural building stone of that name; he patented the formula (patent no. 5022) in 1824. Louis Vicat of France determined the chemical formula for cement containing natural limestone in 1839. In 1844, Isaac Johnson discovered the modern high-temperature method of making Portland cement, and the use of concrete as a structural material stemmed from this date; ten years later, reinforced concrete was developed to overcome the inherent tensile weakness of cement.

Francis, A.J. *The Cement Industry 1796–1914: A History*, David and Charles, 1977
Halstead, P.E. 'The early history of Portland Cement', *Newcomen Society Transactions* 34 (1961–2), 37

cementation process   an early method of making steel from iron by subjecting the iron to prolonged heating in contact with a carbon-rich substance, so that the iron absorbed carbon at its surface and thus converted into steel. This way of adding carbon to wrought iron was devised by William Ellyot and Mathias Meysey as early as 1614, using a REVERBERATORY FURNACE in the Forest of Dean area. The method was introduced into Yorkshire c.1650, where it was further developed. Bars of imported Swedish pure iron ore were packed into containers in layers, with intervening layers of charcoal, and the whole covered by a layer of sand to make it airtight. The containers were then placed inside a cementation or converting furnace and held at a high heat for several days. When the cool bars were removed, their surfaces were found to be very rough and lumpy, earning the material the name of BLISTER STEEL. The big problem with the cementation process was controlling the carbon content absorbed, so quality was variable. Blister steel began to be replaced by CRUCIBLE STEEL in 1740.

Cementation furnaces were tall conical structures in stone or brick, and were usually coal fired.

central exhaust engine, *see* UNIFLOW STEAM ENGINE

centre-pick loom   a design of loom in which a central arm flicked the shuttle across from side to side, imitating the action of a weaver using the FLYING SHUTTLE. The centre-pick loom was not in use for many years before it was replaced by looms with two cam-operated picking sticks or arms, one at each side.

centre valve steam engine, *see* WILLANS CENTRE VALVE STEAM ENGINE

centrifugal governor   a device for automatically controlling the speed of an engine, using centrifugal force. The basic principle is that two diametrically opposite revolving weights will move outwards under the action of centrifugal force if their speed increases, and move inwards if the speed decreases. The radial movement of the weights is linked by a system of levers to the engine's steam or fuel inlet valve. The valve is slightly closed when the speed increases, and slightly opens when the speed decreases, the effect being that the engine speed returns to a mean value. Since the governor is driven by the engine itself, the speed regulation is automatic.

In steam engines, the control is achieved either by slightly closing or opening the steam inlet valve, called THROTTLE GOVERNING, or by varying the point of CUT-OFF in the stroke. HIT-AND-MISS GOVERNING is used for gas engines, and SPILL CONTROL for oil engines.

Centrifugal governors date from the 18th century when they were first used on corn mills, not to regulate their speed, but to control the gap between the millstones and adjust the rate of feed to them. Thomas Mead patented a mill governor in 1787 (patent no. 1628), and Stephen Hooper patented another in 1789 (patent no. 1706). James Watt (1736–1819) applied the principle to control engine speeds in 1788, using throttle valves. The simple Watt governor (Fig. 17) is known as a flyball, or centrifugal pendulum.

Simple governors tend to oscillate widely or hunt around their mean speed setting; to provide a more constant speed, damping by added weights or springs was introduced on several patented governors, many of which are shown in Figs 17 and 18.

Hall, H.H. *Governors and Governing Mechanism*, 1903
Porter, C.T. 'Of the Allen engine and governor', *Proceedings of the Institution of Mechanical Engineers* 22 (1868)

centrifugal pendulum, *see* CENTRIFUGAL GOVERNOR

cerussite   a lead carbonate ore, which is a source of metallic lead; it contains about 83 per cent oxide of lead and 17 per cent carbonic acid. It usually occurs in association with GALENA, and is sometimes known as white lead.

chafery   a kind of blacksmith's hearth used for reheating iron from a FINERY to remove any residual carbon in the lump of iron, or ANCONY. The refined iron from the chafery was then forged under a hammer into wrought-iron bars. The chafery hearth was situated next to

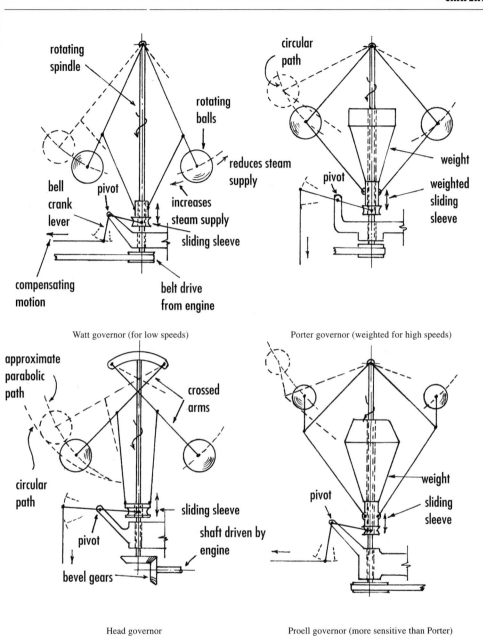

Watt governor (for low speeds)

Porter governor (weighted for high speeds)

Head governor

Proell governor (more sensitive than Porter)

Fig. 17. Examples of centrifugal governors

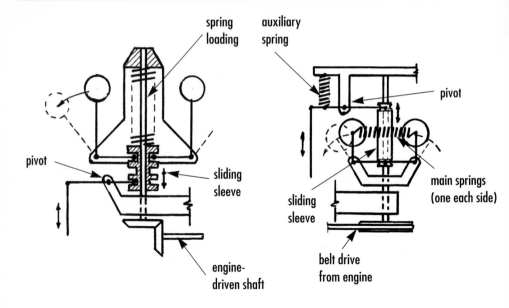

Hartnell governor (can be modified to work with spindle horizontal)

Hartnell governor (cross spring model)

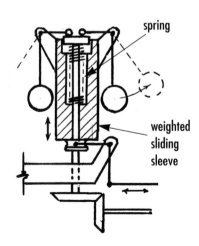

Governor with combined dead weight and spring load

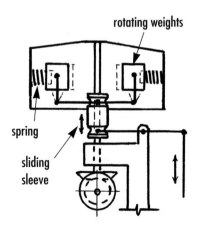

Governor with enclosed spring loaded weights

Fig. 18. More centrifugal governors

the finery hearth, the pair constituting a forge. Chafery comes from the old French word *échauffer* meaning 'to heat up'. Fig. 6 shows the layout of a typical 18th-century finery and chafery forge.

chain 1. an obsolete linear measure, equal to 22 yd (66 ft), in use when the canals and railways were being built in the 18th and 19th centuries. When canals and railways were being surveyed, Gunter's chain was used for measuring purposes: named after an English mathematician, Edmund Gunter (1581–1626), this comprised 100 links (iron or steel wires 7.92 in long) looped end-to-end to form a chain whose overall length was 66 ft. Every tenth link had a small brass tag attached bearing a number to show how many links it was from one end. An Engineer's chain, made up of 100 links each one foot long, is also used in survey and construction work. **2.** One of several alternative names for WARP.

chain bridge a suspension bridge where the deck is hung from chains spanning the distance between towers at opposite ends of the bridge. Chains made from wrought-iron flat plate links were invented by Samuel Brown (1774–1852) and patented in 1817 (patent no. 4137); they were extensively used in the 19th century. Telford's Conway suspension bridge (1826) is a good example of a chain bridge. *See also* SUSPENSION BRIDGE.

Day, T. 'Samuel Brown in North-east Scotland', *Industrial Archaeology Review* VII (1985), 154–70

chain making the making of small iron chains was a hand domestic industry from the 17th century onwards, centred on the Black Country, e.g. Cradley Heath, etc. The work was carried out in outhouses attached to dwellings which contained small forges, anvils, etc. A considerable number of female workers were involved in the industry, the chains being made from small diameter iron rod, cut and bent to shape, and the ends hammer welded, either by a hand-held hammer, or by a small pedal-operated, bench-mounted hammer called a Tommy hammer. Sometimes the work was combined with nail making, which was a similar occupation. Larger chains, such as ships' chains and industrial chains, were made in factories which often had their own PUDDLING FURNACES, OLIVERS, and so on. Chain proving houses were set up where the strength of chains was tested and certified. Chain making by hand persisted in some places until the beginning of the 20th century.

chain pump an early design of pump dating from the 16th century, used for raising water from mines. A primitive design comprised a circular or square vertical barrel through which an endless chain passed. Fastened to the chain at regular intervals were 'pistons' or tight bundles of rags, of the same shape as the bore of the barrel through which they passed. One end of the barrel was immersed in the water and as the chain moved upwards, dragging the 'pistons' through the barrel, water was trapped above each 'piston', lifted to the top, discharged into a channel and led to waste. The chain passed over pulleys at the top and bottom of the barrel to provide a continuous action, the top pulley being the driver (*see* Fig. 53a).

A similar arrangement had buckets fastened to the outer side of the chain loop. As they rounded the bottom pulley, which was immersed in the water, they scooped water up and conveyed it to the top pulley where it was flung out to waste as they turned through 180° to commence their downward journey again.

chair 1. the support under a plateway or edge rail lying between it and the sleeper on a railway track. The rail 'sits' on it, hence its name. **2.** a team of glass workers, usually of four men, each performing a separate task; the name is taken from the special working chair used by the team leader or GAFFER. He sits in a glass maker's chair which has long arms projecting in front of him, along the tops of which he rolls the blowpipe when fashioning an article. Next comes the SERVITOR, who blows out the bowl when making a wineglass, and hands it to the gaffer. The FOOTMAKER brings a small lump of molten glass to the gaffer who shapes the stem and foot from it, and attaches them to the bowl. The gaffer then attaches a solid rod called a pontil to the base of the foot and removes the blowpipe from the bowl. When the wineglass is finished, the fourth member of the chair, called the TAKER-IN, takes it by the PONTIL to the ANNEALING furnace. Glass makers once served a seven year apprenticeship, and were paid by piecework, the gaffer earning the highest pay, the servitor next, followed by the footmaker. The taker-in was often a child apprentice in the 19th century.

chalcopyrite a sulphide of copper and iron found in veins or lodes as a brassy coloured mineral which usually contains 6–12 per cent copper. It is the commonest copper ore, and was extensively mined in deep lode mines in Cornwall from about the end of the 16th century. By the mid-19th century Cornwall was the world's largest producer of copper, but as foreign competition began to gain the world markets the industry rapidly declined in Cornwall. Chalcopyrite is also known as copper pyrite.

Reconstructed chaldron wagon at Tanfield, Co. Durham

chaldron 1. a dry measure of capacity or weight, mostly used in the early days of coal mining. The exact weight of a chaldron varied from place to place, and with time: the London chaldron was about 28 cwt, whereas the Newcastle chaldron was fixed by statute at 53 cwt in the 18th century, although it had been less than that in earlier times. The word chaldron comes from the Latin *calidus* via old French *chauderon*, meaning a large pot. **2.** the name used on Tyneside for the large, originally wooden, horse-drawn coal waggons which ran on plateways. Chaldron waggons were constructed with sloping sides and were emptied via a large trapdoor in the base. Their wheels were also made from wood at first until cast-iron ones were introduced in the mid-18th century. By the first quarter of the 19th century, chaldron waggons had sheet iron sides on wooden frames, and had flanged wheels running on edge rails. A brake could be applied via a long lever onto one of the wheels to control the waggon on downhill slopes. Some chaldron waggons remained in colliery use as late as the early 20th century.

chalon a worsted cloth used for blankets and bedcovers etc., possibly taking its name from the town Châlons-sur-Marne in France where it was made.

chamber dye a euphemistic name for urine. Stale human urine was sometimes used with alum as a MORDANT for dyeing woollens in the 17th and 18th centuries. *See also* LANT.

chamber lye, *see* LANT

chambray a kind of GINGHAM cloth with a LINEN finish.

changeline bridge, *see* ROVING BRIDGE

channel a lead mining term for decomposed TOADSTONE, a basaltic rock of volcanic origin which has weathered to a crumbly clay-like material or ash; also known as cat dirt.

chapman an old word for a small trader. The word comes from the Latin *caupo*, a proprietor of a wine tavern who also traded in local wares. A chapman was usually an itinerant pedlar or hawker who carried his goods around from place to place, or attended fairs as a stall holder. Some chapmen specialized in selling cloth or arranging for its manufacture by delivering wool to spinners and weavers on credit, and paying for their work when collecting the finished cloth. The term dates back to medieval times, and probably died out during the 19th century.

charcoal a carbon-rich form of wood, obtained by a distillation process involving controlled burning or charring of lengths of small diameter wood with the virtual exclusion of air. Wood is mainly composed of carbon, oxygen, hydrogen and some oils: in charcoal production, oxygen, hydrogen and oils are liberated, leaving behind mainly carbon, although any sulphur and phosphorus originally present remain.

Charcoal was the main fuel for all industrial heating processes from the time of Elizabeth I well into the Industrial Revolution. Being mostly carbon with all moisture removed, charcoal is capable of producing higher temperatures than untreated wood, and temperatures in excess of 1,000°C may be reached. It was therefore used for iron production, non-ferrous metal smelting and refining, the manufacture of glass and salt, and for brewing, dyeing, etc.

Hardwoods were used to make charcoal: ash, birch, hazel, alder, willow, sycamore and oak. The trees are COPPICED and 'poles' are cut in the winter, then burned during the summer months. Charcoal burners were usually self-employed itinerant workers, working in pairs and paid by their output. They would cut the timber (or cordwood as it is also known), strip off the bark to enable moisture to escape, and stack the 'poles' to dry in piles known as windrows. Sometimes the stripping operation was carried out by separate workers called BARK PEELERS. The poles were then carefully piled in a circular stack leaving a central chimney, and finished off in a beehive shape by a covering of soil or turf. Slow combustion was maintained for up to five days and nights, controlled by movable windshields made from hurdles of twigs, and by opening or closing draughtholes as required. Constant watch was necessary, the men sharing the duty between them, sleeping in rough shelters nearby. Clearings in forests where charcoal burning took place are known as pitsteads, and may still be traced today in some areas. As the timber around a pitstead was used up, a new pitstead would be made in a fresh site.

All early iron manufacture was based on charcoal. Enormous quantities of timber were consumed by early iron furnaces: it took about an acre of timber to produce 2 tons of iron. It was therefore more economic to site iron furnaces in forests than close to iron mines, to reduce transport costs. Deforestation by iron works became a serious threat to timber resources, and Acts of Parliament were passed in the 16th century restricting the felling of timber. Fortunately, in 1709 Abraham Darby I (1677–1717) introduced the smelting of iron by coke, and the demand for charcoal diminished; by 1806 there were only eleven charcoal-using BLAST FURNACES still operating in Britain.

By the beginning of the 19th century charcoal production by the old stack method had been largely replaced by the use of cast-iron retorts at fixed sites to which the stripped wood was brought, and charred by fires underneath the retorts. The gases driven off were collected and condensed since they contained valuable by-products which were lost by the old method.

Another important use for charcoal was in the manufacture of gunpowder: here, superior grades of charcoal were required, usually carefully made from juniper, silver birch, willow, and alder.

Charcoal could also be made from peat.

Armstrong, L. *Woodcolliers and Charcoal Burning*, Coach Publishing, 1978
Kelley, D.W. *Charcoal and Charcoal Burning*, Shire Publications Album, no. 159, 1986
Linnard, W. 'Sooty bands from tents of turf: woodcolliers and charcoal-burning in Wales', *Folk Life* 25 (1986/7)

charking (or cherking, chirking) an early 18th-century method for making COKE in open heaps in a manner similar to the making of CHARCOAL. Piles of coal were kept smouldering with restricted air supply until all the volatiles had been driven off, leaving coke which was used in BLAST FURNACES for iron production. The process was also known as torrefying, from the Latin *torrere* (meaning to parch with heat).

charre (or char) an old measure for lead. One charre of lead comprised 30 pigs each weighing 70 lb, making a total of 2,100 lb. The word was also used for a cartload. It was in use in Scotland as early as the 14th century. In some literature, the term charge of lead was wrongly used instead of charre of lead.

chartermaster a master coal or iron miner who worked by charter or written contract. The term was used in Staffordshire and Shropshire coal and iron mines, and meant a skilled miner who hired other men to work for him and was paid by the mine owner according to the tonnage got under the contract. Sometimes the mine worked was known by the name of the chartermaster rather than that of the mine owner. The system of working died out by the end of the 19th century. A chartermaster was also known as a BUTTY.

Brown, I.J. 'The chartermaster system of mine management in Shropshire', *Peak District Mines Historical Society Bulletin* 11 (1992), 277–80

Chartist a supporter of the 1838 'People's Charter' for parliamentary reform. Economic depression in the early 19th century resulted in high unemployment, low wages, and dear bread for the labouring poor. This, coupled with poor housing, squalid conditions, and a sense of injustice, fuelled great discontent, and it was felt that better representation in parliament would improve matters and lead to a better life.

A movement arose, particularly among industrial workers, to support a People's Charter which had six demands for reform: universal suffrage for every man; electoral districts with equal numbers of voters; voting by secret ballot; annually elected parliaments; payment to members of parliament; and abolition of property qualifications, so that every voter was eligible for election.

A petition was got up, and in 1838 the Charter was presented to parliament, which promptly rejected it. This caused frustration among the more militant Chartists, leading to strikes and rioting in some parts of the country. Some textile mills were burnt down, and in others machinery such as looms, stocking frames, and so on, were destroyed by gangs (see PLUG RIOTS). Two more petitions were presented. The second in 1842 had over 3 million signatures, but was again rejected. By now the Chartists had adopted a more peaceful policy. The third petition in 1848 had fewer signatures, since the economic situation had eased, and Chartism was losing its impetus. Parliament still took no action, and allowed things to gradually die out, and by 1855 Chartism was virtually dead with none of its aims achieved. However, by 1918, all the Chartists' objectives had become law, except for annual parliaments.

Schoyen, A.R. *The Chartist Challenge*, 1958
Ward, J.T. *Chartism*, Batsford, 1973

Cheap Trains Act, *see* PARLIAMENTARY FARE

checkers refractory bricks arranged in crisscross fashion with gaps in between to allow the passage of air or waste gases in a COWPER STOVE or the regenerator of an OPEN HEARTH FURNACE. The bricks are heated up when the hot waste gases from the furnace are passed through, and give up their heat to the incoming cold combustion air when that is directed through. The checkers are therefore a heat storage medium and act as a heat exchanger, reducing fuel consumption and raising the thermal efficiency of the equipment they serve.

check valve, *see* CLACK VALVE

chemick a solution of chloride of lime, used in BLEACHING.

chenille 1. a type of upholstery cloth, or flat-woven CARPET, popular in the 1840s and made from a furry yarn to give a kind of pile surface. Chenille carpet manufacture was patented by James Templeton and William Quigley (patent no. 8169, 1839) and later by Templeton alone in 1850 (patent no. 12954). The word chenille is the French for caterpillar. **2.** the description of a furry cotton or silk thread used in hand embroidery.

child labour the use of children for industrial employment. Before the Industrial Revolution, HANDLOOM WEAVERS employed their children, hand-CARDING wool to assist the women of the family at their spinning wheels. Long hours were worked under this domestic system. When the factory system developed in the late 18th century, children, often parish APPRENTICES, were employed in textile mills, commonly for up to fourteen hours per day under conditions amounting to slavery. Poor families living in industrial areas sent their children into the mills to supplement the family income. Girls as well as boys were employed underground, filling and pulling coal tubs. It is recorded that a boy as young as three was found employed in a coal mine as a TRAPPER, in complete darkness.

Eventually, the inhuman conditions in which children were exploited were brought to public notice through the campaigns of several 18th- and 19th-century philanthropists. In 1784 Manchester magistrates refused to sign indentures for parish apprentices if they were to work at night, or more than ten hours a day in textile mills. Sir Robert Peel (1750–1830), himself a mill owner in Bury, Lancs., introduced the Health and Morals of Apprentices Act in 1802 to control the condition of work for pauper children. Other reforms followed, notably the FACTORY ACT 1833 which related to textile mills, and the 1842 Coal Mines Regulation Act which prohibited the employment of girls (and women) in mines and collieries, and made unlawful the employment of boys under ten. This Act was promoted by Anthony Ashley Cooper (1801–85) who became the 7th Earl of Shaftesbury. Another factory reformer was Richard Oastler (1789–1861) of Bradford, Yorks., whose name is associated with the TEN HOURS ACT of 1847, which included a measure reducing the hours of work of children in the textile industry. Although the initial legislation on children's employment related to textiles and mining only, gradually all other types of employment became subject to control, and eventually child labour ceased.

Cruickshank, M. *Children and Industry*, Manchester University Press, 1981
Dunlop, D.J. *English Apprenticeship and Child Labour*, 1912
Walvin, J. *A Child's World*, Penguin, 1982

Children's Charter, *see* FACTORY ACT 1833

Chile saltpetre, *see* CALICHE

chimney a free-standing, vertical flue, for discharging high into the atmosphere chemical fumes or the hot products of combustion from furnaces and steam raising plant. A chimney also provides a natural draught at the level of the fire, created by the difference in density of the hot gases inside the chimney and the density of the outside air at a lower temperature, the hot gases rising up the chimney and sucking in fresh air at the furnace. The strength of the draught is directly proportional to the height of the chimney. Chimneys for discharging chemical fumes do not as a rule create much draught since the fumes are often too cool, and a fan is normally used to blow them up the chimney.

Early factory chimneys were usually built of stone, and were mostly square in cross-section, sometimes round, and seldom taller than about 40–50 ft. Later, brick construction was introduced, and as more and larger steam boilers became necessary to power bigger mills, chimneys became larger in girth and taller to provide increased draught. Circular cross-sections became popular in the 1860s, being cheaper to build than square and better able to withstand high winds, important as their height increased. Octagonal cross-sections were also used. Chimneys taper towards their top since the thickness of their walls is increased in the lower lengths to support the weight above. The outside top of most chimneys was enlarged in an attempt to provide a scientific shape which would assist unimpeded discharge of the smoke plume into the surrounding air stream. This projecting enlargement, called the oversailer, gave scope for decoration, and some chimney builders or mill architects had their own favourite design. Apart from some decoration at the oversailer, most chimneys were purely functional in appearance, but a few were highly decorated, such as the well-known (still standing) chimney at India Mill, Darwen, Lancs., built in 1868 and modelled, it is said, on the campanile in St Mark's Square, Venice, complete with windows! There is a similar Venetian-style chimney at Listers' Mill, Bradford, Yorks., and Marshall's Mill in Leeds once had a chimney shaped like Cleopatra's Needle! Because of their prominence, textile mill chimneys often advertised the name of the mill high on their side.

Factory chimneys are usually built very close to the boiler house, often in the mill yard, separated from the building by a short underground flue. Some chimneys have, however, been built a considerable distance away, often sited on a nearby hill and connected to the factory or furnace by a long underground flue. Many of the old lead smelting furnaces on the Yorkshire moors had their chimney a long way off, the connecting flue acting as a settling chamber to collect most of the lead fume before

it was discharged into the atmosphere. The short stone chimneys with brick tops of the 18th-century Cornish tin mines were usually integral with the engine house, being built in one corner. Local by-laws specified minimum heights of chimneys in towns to reduce smoke nuisance. In Victorian times, literally hundreds of mill chimneys dominated the skyline of northern textile towns, but today very many have been felled. The spread of electric power made mill chimneys redundant, but processes using heat, such as metal furnaces, dyeworks, etc. still need chimneys to discharge waste gases safely, as do many chemical works where very often the fumes are filtered to remove almost all dangerous and noxious pollutants before the chimney is reached. In more recent years metal chimneys have appeared; these may be of free-standing design, or require guy ropes to hold them against overturning side pressures from high winds.

The stack or shaft of a chimney is also known as its stalk.

Douet, James. *Going up in Smoke: The History of the Industrial Chimney*, Victorian Society, 1989
Pickles, W. *Our Grimy Heritage*, Centaur Press, 1971
Warburton, R. 'The factory chimney: some technical aspects', *Industrial Archaeology Review* IX (1987), 195–8

china clay a feldspathic (silicate of aluminium) mineral or decomposed granite found in conjunction with its parent granite, and extensively extracted in the West of England, particularly around St Austell, Cornwall. Its principal use is in the POTTERY and PAPER-MAKING industries. China clay was first discovered in Cornwall in 1746 by a Plymouth chemist, William Cooksworthy (1705–80) who made the first hard porcelain in England in 1768. Pottery firms like Wedgwood and Spode commenced mining the Cornish clay soon afterwards until about the mid-19th century when their mining leases ran out. Many small local Cornish firms supplied the market after this until mergers and takeovers substantially reduced the number of concerns operating. The use of china clay in paper making commenced around the late 1800s and the paper industry became the principal user of the material: china clay production in Cornwall rose from 2,000 tons in 1800 to 65,800 tons in 1858.

Originally china clay was dug out by pick and shovel, by the mid-19th century washing it out as a slurry started. A shaft is sunk below the clay level and the clay washed out by a water jet through pipes and allowed to settle in large tanks. The waste quartz and mica is discarded, making the huge white pyramids of spoil characteristic of the area. The clay is dried in a

pan kiln and stored in open fronted buildings called LINHAYS. China clay is also known as kaolin (from the district in China where it was found centuries ago) or as porcelain clay.
Hudson, K. *The History of English China Clay*, David and Charles, 1966

chlorine a non-metallic element which is a greenish-yellow poisonous gas at ordinary pressures, and is a powerful oxydizing agent. It was first discovered by Karl Wilhelm Scheele (1742–86) in Sweden in 1774, and its bleaching action on cloth was demonstrated by Claude Louis Bertholet (1748–1822) in France in 1785. Chlorine was then obtained by the action of oxydizing agents on hydrochloric acid. In 1799, Charles Tennant (1768–1838) of Glasgow patented (no. 2312) a solid compound of chlorine and lime, known as chloride of lime or bleaching powder, which revolutionized the bleaching of cloth, replacing the long and slow method of sun bleaching by a quick chemical process.

choke damp, *see* BLACK DAMP

chopwood specially selected wood, with its bark removed, and all sap removed by drying in specially built kilns, which was used as fuel on ORE HEARTHS at lead mining and smelting sites. *See also* ELLING HEARTH.

cinder another name for metal SLAG. The name was sometimes used in the early 18th century for COKE.

cinder pig pig iron made in a BLAST FURNACE from a mixture of iron ore and PUDDLING FURNACE slag or cinder.

circular saw a steel disk with sawteeth on its periphery, which is rotated at speed in a vertical plane to cut various materials continuously. A circular saw was patented in the name of Elizabeth Taylor, the widow of Walter, in 1762 (patent no. 782). Walter, an ex-ship's carpenter, and his son, ran a small family business in Southampton, making wooden ships' blocks for the Navy. They were among the first to manufacture interchangeable parts, the circular saw playing an important part in their factory.
Pannell, J.P.M. 'The Taylors of Southampton', *Proceedings of the Institute of Mechanical Engineers* 169 (1955), 924–31

clack valve a simple type of valve in a PUMP or similar piece of equipment, which permits flow in one direction only, i.e. a non-return valve; it is also known as a check valve, or retaining valve.

There are different types of clacks. The simplest comprises a disk made from metal, leather, gutta-percha or India rubber, hinged at one side, which lifts to permit flow in one direction, and falls back on its seating to prevent a back flow. Most clacks operate in a vertical pipe or passage, and if made from a

non-metallic material are strengthened and weighted by metal plates so that they will close quickly when the fluid pressure below them ceases. When hinged at one side, they are also called flap valves. Another design is a disk in two halves, hinged in the centre, each half lifting to allow flow, and closing to stop reverse flow; this is known as a BUTTERFLY VALVE. A third design is the ball clack. This comprises a ball which seats over the orifice, is lifted off when flow takes place, and falls back to seal against reverse flow. The ball is restrained within a cage to limit its travel. Balls are made from gunmetal, or rubber-covered metal balls which must have a greater specific gravity than the fluid they work in so as to close rapidly and not 'dance' if too light.

Clanny lamp an early miners' safety lamp invented by Dr William Reid Clanny (1776–1850), a physician of Sunderland, Co. Durham, in 1813. However, it was too unwieldy and did not come into general use; George Stephenson (1781–1848) and Sir Humphry Davy (1778–1829) both invented more practical safety lamps soon afterwards. The Clanny lamp was also known as a blast lamp, since bellows attached to its base were used to supply it with air, which was pumped through water on its way to the flame; the products of combustion also returned to the outside air through water. It needed someone constantly to operate the bellows. *See also* SAFETY LAMP.

clapper box the tool holder on a PLANING MACHINE.

clasp, *see* CLOVE

clasp arm wheel a type of construction for a wooden WATERWHEEL where the arms or 'spokes' form a square clamped round the central square axle (*see* Fig. 85). This design, introduced in the first quarter of the 18th century, is superior to the older COMPASS ARM design, since it does not weaken the axle at the point where the torque is transmitted from the wheel to the axle. Clasp construction was also used on other large wooden wheels such as brakewheels on windmills.

cleading narrow strips of polished timber fastened to the surface of a boiler or steam cylinder to reduce heat loss by radiation; an early form of thermal insulation. The cleading was in strips so that it could follow the curvature of the vessels it enclosed.

clearance the small space left at each end of the stroke in a steam engine, by virtue of the fact that the interior length of the cylinder is made slightly longer than the stroke plus the thickness of the piston. This prevents the cylinder covers being knocked off should water accumulate in the bore, and allows a small amount of steam to be trapped in the space at the end of each stroke to CUSHION the piston.

clew, *see* YARN

clicking cutting out leather uppers, linings, etc. for boots and shoes. This work is done on a clicker press, which cuts out several shapes at once from piled sheets of material.

clicks, *see* RATCHET

cliff name given on Tyneside to a French limestone used in the manufacture of BLEACHING powder. It was a particularly pure calcium carbonate and was burnt in kilns preparatory to being spread in the bleaching chambers. Cliff was brought back from the Seine as ballast in colliers which had taken coal across to France.

clip general term used for the total quantity of sheared wool obtained from a source such as a wool-producing farm, a geographical area, etc. in a given period of time.

clipper a fast, wooden-hulled sailing ship, first built in Baltimore, USA, in 1833. They were designed with a narrow hull, a forward-raking bow, and aft-raking masts. Mostly used for shipping tea from China and wool from Australia, the American vessels at first outsailed the then-existing British sailing vessels and stole the East Indian trade, causing the tonnage of the British merchant fleet to decline. The design was so successful that it was soon copied by British ship builders. The most famous British-built clipper was the *Cutty Sark*, built in Dumbarton, Clydeside, Scotland, in 1869, and named from a Burns poem. The ship is preserved in dry dock at Greenwich. Britain regained merchant vessel superiority when she introduced iron-hulled ships powered by steam-driven propellors, ending the days of the clipper.

MacGregor, D.R. *The Tea Clippers*, Marshall, 1952

clockmaker the making of early clocks originally was undertaken by blacksmiths, the moving parts being made from iron. As increasing precision was attained, gradually clockmaking became a separate, more highly skilled trade, and clockmakers were employed by pioneer makers of textile machinery for the supply of gearwheels, etc. The mechanics in early cotton mills were frequently known as clockmakers. Machinery and small equipment which is operated by a system of mechanical gears, such as mechanically operated toys, are still said to work by clockwork.

WATCHMAKING grew out of clockmaking and became a separate industry in its own right.

cloth hall a kind of warehouse where cloth was sold. Many large commercial buildings were erected, particularly in the West Riding of Yorkshire, as markets, where locally made woollens and worsteds were sold. Such buildings were known as cloth or piece halls (piece because the cloth was woven in pieces), and buyers would visit to view samples and buy. These halls were more permanent than the old open-air street markets, since a clothier would rent space, or a room, and store unsold cloth under lock and key until the next market or selling day. Heptonstall had a small hall as early as 1545, but the main period of building cloth halls was in the 18th century. Wakefield had one in 1710 for selling undyed broadcloth; Leeds had one in 1711, and a larger one built in 1755; Wakefield had another in 1766 for its worsted tammies; Bradford's was built in 1773, and the most famous of all, in Halifax, in 1779. Cloth halls were not, however, only found in the north of England. There was a centre for selling woollen cloth in London at Blackwell Hall (also known as Bakewell Hall) in Cheapside, in 1396. Cloth from the west of England, East Anglia, and Yorkshire was sent by packhorse or by sea for purchase by London merchants, either for local consumption or export to the Continent. Witney, in Oxfordshire, built its Blanket Hall in 1721 (still in existence), and there was a Flannel Exchange in Newtown, mid-Wales, in 1832. There were once several small cloth halls in south-east England, associated with the Flemish weavers who settled there in the 15th century.

Increasing use of steam power for cloth manufacture made cloth halls too small to cope with the large output. Firms began building their own private warehouses and sale rooms where their cloth could be displayed. As the railway system developed, it enabled representatives to take samples to prospective customers more easily, instead of the latter having to visit a sale room. Cloth halls therefore became redundant in the 19th century and closed. Piece Hall, Halifax, still exists as an outstanding example, though no longer performing its original function.

Dunn, J.B. *Piece Hall, Halifax*, Amenities and Recreation Dept, Calderdale, 1981

Murtagh, Maria. *Handlooms and Cloth Halls*, Pennine Heritage, 1982

clothier a merchant who dealt in cloth, often as a kind of middleman. Clothiers were frequently owners of FULLING MILLS which became centres of domestic spinning and weaving areas. The clothier would buy wool from sheep farmers and send it out to domestic spinners. On receiving the yarn back he would pass it out to HANDLOOM WEAVERS who would return it to him as cloth for fulling and TENTERING before the clothier sold it to a city merchant. The clothier therefore acted as a middleman relieving the merchant of the need to deal with large numbers of individual spinners and weavers for purchasing cloth. Sometimes a clothier would be acting for the merchant on a commission basis, not actually owning the raw materials or finished cloth. In other cases, particularly in the woollen areas of Yorkshire, clothiers owned the raw wool and the woven cloth, and employed workers to spin and weave, or used their own families to manufacture the cloth.

Besides handling yarn and cloth, a clothier would own HEALDS and REEDS which he would loan to weavers so that they could weave different cloths. Often he would also have a warping frame and yarn-winding machinery for preparing yarn for weavers.

clothing and footwear industry the mass manufacture of clothing using power machinery did not commence until c.1850; before this clothes were hand-made, every town having its own tailor and dressmaker. Bespoke tailoring is still available today for individual requirements, and numerous small workshops and outworking still exist, a residue of the old domestic system.

The clothing industry was concentrated in and around Leeds, close to the wool and worsted industries of Yorkshire and the cotton industry of Lancashire. As factories came into being, one of the first power machines to be used was the band knife, similar to the band saw, which cut out garment pieces in bulk against templates for ready-made clothes. This machine was invented by Frederick Osbourne in 1853 (patent no. 1955). Isaac Merrill Singer (1811–75) produced his first practical domestic sewing machine in Boston, USA, in the early 1850s, which was soon adopted in Britain. Heavier industrial machines came later for factory use, and even heavier machines followed for use in the footwear industry for sewing uppers to soles. Sewing thread for stitching garments was obtained from cotton doubling mills in Lancashire. Button making was one of the staple trades of the Birmingham area. Matthew Boulton (1728–1809) made metal buttons in his factory before he went into partnership with Watt to make steam engines. Military uniforms were another type of clothing made in quantity in the 19th century. Benjamin Gott (1762–1840) of Leeds supplied the armies of Prussia, Russia and Sweden as well as Britain with their uniforms, whilst Titus Salt (1803–76) of Bradford introduced ALPACA into the clothing industry in 1850. The Scottish

chemist Charles MacIntosh (1766–1843) invented a waterproof cloth (patent no. 4804, 1823) which bears his name. It comprised two layers of cloth bonded by a varnish of rubber dissolved in naphtha, and was made in his Manchester factory.

The boot and shoe industry was also originally a domestic craft industry with shoemakers working in their own homes or outhouses for local markets. Shoemaking slowly became a factory industry, mass producing for larger markets, in the late 19th century. At first, mainly imported American machinery was used. Leather was obtained from old established tanneries which tended to be located near market towns, operating processes which gave little scope for mechanization.

Some early machinery used in the clothing industry is preserved in museums such as Armley Mills Museum, Leeds, where an old clothing factory has been reconstructed. Some shoemaking firms have collections of their old machinery. *See also* HAT MAKING.

Hudson, K. *Towards Precision Shoemaking*, David and Charles, 1968
Lyons, L., Allen, T.W. and Vincent, W.D.F. *The Sewing Machine*, Williamson, 1924
Mounfield, P.R. 'Early technological innovation in the British footwear industry', *Industrial Archaeology Review* II (1978), 129–42
Peacock, P. *Buttons for the Collector*, David and Charles, 1972
Schmiecken, J.A. *Sweated Industries and Sweated Labour. The London Clothing Trades, 1860–1914*, Croom Helm, 1984
Willet, C. and Cunnington, P. *The History of Underclothes*, Faber and Faber, 1981

cloth names a bewildering number of names have been given to the different kinds of cloth that have been, or still are, woven. Some refer to the construction of the fabric, e.g. TWILL and SATIN. Others may have been taken from the place name where that particular type of cloth originated in early times, e.g. CALICO and FUSTIAN. The English name is often a distorted Anglicized or shortened version of the original native word. BROADCLOTH takes its name from the width of the cloth. Some fabrics were made from different, often cheaper, materials at later dates than the original materials, but retained the same name, e.g. BOMBASINE. Many names are now obsolete, newer materials having replaced them in the course of time.

There are seven basic weaves in cloth construction – plain, twill, satin, spot, flush, cross-warp, and double cloth. Combinations give an almost infinite variety. The different kinds of cloth are obtained by a variation in the order in which warp threads are lifted or depressed for receiving the weft, called the shedding process, the use of multiple shuttle boxes, and the mixing of materials for warp and weft; all these variations give rise to different names.

clough, *see* CLOW

clove **1.** the pair of clasp bars through which the ROVINGS pass on a SPINNING JENNY (*see* Fig. 41). The top bar is grooved on its underside to receive the rovings, and there are matching projections on the top side of the bottom bar. The two bars are carried on a carriage which is moved along the frame of the machine on rails. After allowing a certain length of roving to pass through the clove with the bars opened slightly, they are clamped together to grasp the rovings, the projections on the bottom bar fitting into the grooves on the top bar to prevent any further delivery of the rovings. The clove is then drawn away from the spindles whilst twist is applied to the clamped length of yarn. The word clove comes from an old meaning of the word cleave, meaning to adhere. **2.** an instrument for removing flax BOON.

clow (or clough) a sluice or floodgate across a river or large open drain, etc. by which the water flow can be regulated or, for example, a reservoir emptied. It may also control the flow of water to a WATERWHEEL. The alternative spelling clough is also used as a synonym for a paddle, the opening in a canal lock gate.

club houses houses or cottages built by a workers' building club for their members. Such building clubs were first established in the late 18th century when a group of workers would form the club to buy land and build an agreed number of houses. Regular, often weekly, payments were made by the members into a central fund and when sufficient money had accumulated one or two houses were built. A lottery was then held and the winners moved into the houses. Everyone continued with their payments and when more houses were completed, another lottery was held, and so on until all the houses had been built and every member was housed; the club then dissolved. This type of building club was in effect a terminating building society, whereas today's building societies are permanent societies issuing mortgages and paying interest to investors, with a constantly changing membership.

If the houses built by the building club were terraced, they can often be identified by vertical joints between adjoining sets of houses showing where additions were made at later dates.

Price, S.J. *Building Societies, Their Origin and History,* 1958

clutch a mechanical device by which two coaxial shafts or machine parts may be connected or disconnected at will so that rotary motion may be transmitted from a driving member to a driven member, or not, whilst rotation takes place. There are many instances where a machine or piece of equipment needs to be brought to a standstill by disconnecting it from a constantly rotating power source, or alternatively started up from rest by connecting it to a rotating system. Examples are machine tools, spinning mules, etc., driven from lineshafting, and warehouse cranes, sack hoists in corn mills, etc., driven from waterwheels, wind sails, etc. This facility has been solved in many ways, the most important of which are described below.

FAST AND LOOSE PULLEYS were commonly used to connect machinery to lineshafts in textile mills, machine tool workshops, and so on, and may be regarded as a type of clutch where motion is transmitted or stopped by moving the driving belt sideways from one pair of pulleys onto another.

Band clutches were used in water- and windmills for operating sack hoists as and when required from constantly rotating systems, and in warehouses for working cranes. A flat rimmed pulley which drove the hoist or crane was arranged to be vertically above a similar pulley driven from the constantly rotating power source. A flat endless belt hung over the top pulley and passed round the lower half of the bottom pulley but did not touch it when the hoist or crane were at rest, i.e. it hung slack, the bottom pulley rotating within the loop. The top pulley was mounted on a pivoted lever which could be raised at one free end so that the centre distance between the two pulleys could be increased. When this was done the bottom pulley began to drive the top pulley as the slack in the belt was taken up. Disconnection was done by reducing the centre distance again so that the belt hung slack. Sometimes metal chains were used instead of flat leather belts. The band clutch was also known as a slack belt drive. In the case of pulleys mounted at fixed centres, a jockey pulley could be swung against the belt to take up the slack until driving commenced.

Friction clutches rely on the frictional resistance between two surfaces pressed together being greater than the turning resistance of the driven machine, so that rotary motion is transmitted from the driving member to the driven without slip occurring at the clutch surfaces. The surface belonging to the driven member can be slid axially along a feather key or splines so that it lies at rest when disengaged from the driving member. Various designs of friction clutch have been developed. The simplest is the disk or plate clutch in which two flat circular or annular friction surfaces are pressed together, each disk keyed to its respective shaft. They are disengaged by sliding them apart. Another design uses conical surfaces, where an external cone is moved axially in and out of a mating internal cone to engage or disengage the drive as required. A compact disk type clutch of smaller diameter is the Weston or multiplate clutch in which several disks are used to increase the surface area. The moving members of friction clutches were often operated by levers, sometimes by springs.

Centrifugal clutches had friction surfaces which were engaged automatically at a pre-arranged speed and maintained in contact by the centrifugal force created by revolving weights. Dog clutches, also known as claw couplings, comprised a pair of flanges (one to each coaxial shaft) which could be brought together or moved apart. Projections (the dogs or claws) on one flange fitted into recesses on the other and rotary motion was transmitted by the shear resistance of the projections. Dog clutches could only be engaged when both flanges were stationary, or turning only slowly.

Coade stone a superior and durable type of clay, fired with other ingredients and resembling TERRACOTTA. It was made from the late 18th century until near the middle of the 19th century by G. and E. Coade of Lambeth, London, mainly under the direction of Mrs Eleanor Coade (d.1821). It was used for decorative architectural details on important buildings, e.g. coats of arms, etc., fancy chimneypots, and for statues and smaller figurines. A well-known example of Coade stone is the large lion on the South Bank of the Thames in London, put there in 1837. Being contemporary with Josiah Wedgwood, it was for a while in competition with his pottery. The firm closed c.1840, and there are several hundred surviving examples of Coade stone in the country.

Kelly, Alison. *Mrs Coade's Stone*, Self Publishing Association, 1990

coak, *see* BUSH

coal the principal fuel and energy source of the Industrial Revolution. It was mined in several areas in Britain, and industry tended to concentrate on or near coalfields as earlier water power was gradually superseded. Coal occurs in seams averaging 4–6 ft in thickness and is the fossilized remains of prehistoric plants and trees (*see* COAL MEASURES). The principal content of coal is CARBON, but coals from different seams vary somewhat in their make-up. In some cases coal from the same seam can change its properties in different locations. Besides carbon, coal usually contains hydrogen, sulphur, and a certain percentage of moisture. Its calorific (heating) value therefore varies according to its content.

The extraction of coal commenced in the 13th and 14th centuries from outcrops by what are known as drift mines, the miners following the coal seam into a hillside until the workings became unsafe for the primitive methods used. Then BELL PITS (1) were dug to reach seams lying just below the surface. As these deposits became worked out, deeper, ladder shafts were developed, and when power winding and pumping became available in the early 18th century deep shaft mining became possible.

Different coals are used for different purposes. For example, some coals are used only as fuel for steam raising in industry, while others are used for domestic purposes, coke making, or gas making. Transport, railways and steamships were other big users of coal. An idea of how coal production increased over the centuries is given by the following summary:

Estimated annual coal production

decade	production in tons
1551–60	210,000
1681–90	2,982,000
1781–90	10,295,000
1901–10	241,910,000

Source: Nef, J.U. (1932)

Adams, P.J. *The Origin and Evolution of Coal*, HMSO, 1960
Church, R., Hall, A. and Kanefsky, J. *The History of the British Coal Industry, Vol. 3, 1830–1913*, Clarendon Press, 1986
Duckham, B. *A History of the Scottish Coal Industry, 1700–1815*, David and Charles, 1970
Flinn, M.W. and Stoker, D. *The History of the British Coal Industry, Vol. 2, 1700–1830*, Clarendon Press, 1984
Galloway, R.L. *A History of Coal Mining in Great Britain*, David and Charles, 1969
Nef, J.U. *The Rise of the British Coal Industry*, 2 vols, 1932; reprinted by Cass, 1966

coal and wine tax posts posts marking London's city limits for tax purposes. A number of these still exist around the boundary of the City of London on roadsides and alongside railways. They refer to the days when a duty was payable on coal and wine when they entered the City. They mostly date from 1861, and take the form of standard cast-iron posts or stone pillars with cast-iron plates affixed. The idea of levying a duty on coal as it entered

London dates from after the Great Fire of 1666 when it was introduced to raise money for the rebuilding of the city. The duty finally elapsed in 1889.

coal bearer an old Scottish term for the underground worker whose job was to convey coal from the working face to the pit bottom. Up until the 1840s this was often done by boys, girls and women, physically carrying large pieces of coal or small pieces in a basket or CREEL. Such workers were bound in a state of bondage to the colliery they worked for, until the Emancipation Acts of 1775 and 1799, which applied to Scotland, freed them; in 1842 the employment of all women and boys under ten years of age was prohibited.

coal brass, *see* PYRITES

coal drop a large structure for lowering coal trucks from a wharf directly into the hold of a waiting ship. The drop comprised a pair of counterbalanced pivoted arms which bodily lowered a truck under the control of a drum brake and returned it onto the rail track when empty. Its main advantages were to avoid breaking up the coal into small pieces, which occurs if it is tipped down a long chute from a height, and to avoid double handling by keel boats. Domestic coal in particular had to be kept in large lumps to keep its value. The coal drop was invented by William Chapman (1749–1832) in 1807 (patent no. 3030) and introduced at the north-east coal ports and riverside STAITHES. Coal drops replaced the use of KEELS which had previously been used to transport coal from the land out to ships.
Preece, G.P.J. 'Railway and canal coal drops at Sharpness Docks', *Industrial Archaeology Review* II (1977), 78–84

coal gas, *see* TOWN GAS

coal measures the geological name for the layers of fossilized organic remains of plants and trees which were laid down in the Carboniferous period some 300 million years ago. The layers, or seams, comprise COAL, of which CARBON is the main constituent. In Britain, the coal measures may reach some 8,000 ft in total thickness, and contain many comparatively thin seams spaced apart in other rock. The seams of economic value vary from about 2 ft up to about 10 ft in thickness, with an average of 4–6 ft. Most seams lie approximately horizontally, but continuity is sometimes interrupted by geological faults which can displace a seam vertically by up to several hundred feet. The main coalfields in Britain are in Fifeshire, Durham, Yorkshire, Lancashire, south Wales, Staffordshire, Leicestershire, Nottinghamshire, and Derbyshire. A small field lies in Kent. Often associated with coal are other useful materials such as ironstone, ganister, fireclay, and alum shales.

There is evidence that coal as a fuel was known to the Romans, probably discovered by accident where a seam outcrops to the surface. By the 13th and 14th centuries extraction of coal was beginning to take place, particularly in Tyneside, where coal was sent to London and other places by sea (*see* SEA COAL). As easily reached supplies were exhausted, deeper mining became necessary, and by the beginning of the 17th century coal was being mined in several localities in increasing quantities; as the Industrial Revolution developed, different techniques of working were necessary. Deeper mines introduced flooding and ventilation problems, and the invention of NEWCOMEN's ATMOSPHERE ENGINE early in the 18th century enabled water to be pumped out of deep mines, and large power-driven fans had to be built to provide adequate ventilation.
Trueman, A. *The Coalfields of Great Britain*, Arnold, 1954

coal tip a structure for transferring coal from railway trucks into canal boats or coastal ships. Several canal companies and railways built coal tips which were designed to elevate and tip a truck so that the coal ran down a chute into the waiting vessel. The chute could be raised and lowered to suit, and the tipping gear was often counterbalanced so that the truck would automatically return to a level position when empty. The disadvantage of a coal tip was that the more valuable large coal pieces could be broken up as they cascaded down the chute, and to avoid this, COAL DROPS were used, which considerably reduced the falling distance. Coal tips were also known as spouts, particularly on the north-east coal STAITHES.

coal whipper one of a gang of men (usually numbering eight) who unloads (or whips) coal from a ship's hold at a port. A WHIP gin is used to raise a large basket full of coal, which is tipped into a barge or dockside cart. Three of the gang would work in the ship's hold filling the basket, and four whippers on deck hauled it up. The eighth man swung the basket over a chute and tipped the coal out. Manual unloading of coal ships by whippers continued until the end of the 19th century, when mechanized methods were introduced.
Mayhew, Henry. *London Labour and the London Poor*, ed. V. Neuberg, Penguin, 1985 (first published 1861–2)

coatings a coarse woollen cloth much used for making coats, such as KENDAL CLOTH. The material was also known as 'cottons', a corruption of the word coatings. Cottons was a name used on the Continent for certain types of material made there.

cobbing, *see* BUCKING (1)

cobble a ball of hot iron which has been withdrawn from a furnace before it has been sufficiently PUDDLED.

Cobden-Chevalier Treaty, 1860 a trading treaty between Britain and France which allowed French woven silk into Britain duty-free, while British silks exported to France had to pay a 30 per cent duty. It resulted in a decline in the British silk industry.

cochineal dried bodies of the female insect *coccus cacti* cultivated on cactus in Mexico, etc. and used to make a scarlet DYE. It was introduced into Britain *c*.1640. Cochineal often had powdered pewter added to it. The Dutchman Cornelius Drebbel (1572–1633) is usually credited with the discovery of this dyestuff, which can also be used to colour certain foods. When used for dyeing, a tin MORDANT is needed.

cock a valve for controlling the flow of a liquid, etc. Usually a cock is a quick-acting valve comprising a central cylinder which can be turned in a surrounding body. The body has two diametrically opposite bored holes, and a similar sized hole passes through the cylinder. When the holes line up, fluid can pass through the cock. A half turn of the cylinder blocks off the through passage, thereby stopping all flow. Some regulation of flow is possible by partly opening the cock, but normally a cock is used either fully open or fully closed, and is sometimes known as a stopcock because of this open–shut function. Another name is a plug.

The origin of the word is obscure, but curiously, equivalent words are used in some other languages for the same type of valve, e.g. *Hahn* (cockerel) in German, and *robinet* (cock robin) in French.

Cockayne project a shortlived 17th-century policy to dye and finish woollen broadcloth in England instead of sending it undyed to Holland, which resulted in a serious loss in the cloth trade after the project had been abandoned. It was a long-established practice for the MERCHANT ADVENTURERS to send English undyed cloth to Holland for finishing, since Dutch dyers were more skilled at that time than English dyers. William Cockayne, a wealthy alderman, proposed to the king and parliament that the monopoly of the Merchant Adventurers be broken, and the work be carried out in England on cloth intended for export. It was expected that the Crown would gain income from increased customs duties on imported dyes, that the value of the cloth would be raised, and employment would increase in England among those engaged in cloth finishing

operations. The Merchant Adventurers declined to handle English dyed cloth, and a new company, the King's Merchant Adventurers, was formed in 1614 to export the finished cloth. However, the Dutch refused to buy finished cloth from England, and found other sources for undyed material. The new company lacked the contacts and expertise of the old Merchant Adventurers and failed to prosper. It was wound up in 1617 after only three years. The Merchant Adventurers were reinstated, but it took many years to build the cloth export trade up again. The West Country cloth industry in particular suffered heavily from the loss of business.

Friis, Astrid. *Alderman Cockayne's Project and the Cloth Trade*, Oxford University Press, 1927

cock horses an extra pair of horses hitched to the front of a stagecoach to assist the vehicle up a steep hill. It is from this practice that the children's nursery rhyme 'Ride a cock horse to Banbury Cross' possibly arose. On some turnpikes, noticeboards were placed at the foot of a hill, stating its length, and extra horses were added to ascending coaches at this point. In Yorkshire, the practice of hiring extra horses to help pull a carriage up a steep hill was called snigging.

cockle (or coakle) an 18th-century iron chamber in which a fire was maintained to heat air by contact. It is attributed to William Strutt (1756–1830), and in cotton and silk mills, the warm air was conducted in brick flues to the working spaces to minimize breakages of the fibres or filaments during cold weather. It is also known as a Belper stove. Similar stoves were used for heating hop and malt kilns.

coe a small building, usually of stone, built over an early lead mine shaft, or near to it, to protect the shaft, serve as a tool store, sometimes to store ore, and act as a clothes changing room for the miners. Sometimes the climbing shaft lay under a trap door in the floor. The word probably comes from an old German word *Kove* for a hut or cage, and was in use in Derbyshire from the early days of lead mining. In Scotland the word cow is used.

cog a wooden tooth on a composite material gearwheel. Cogs were hand shaped from a hard wood such as appletree or hornbeam, and morticed into the rim of a cast-iron pinion or gearwheel. Usually they meshed with iron teeth on their mating wheel, to give quiet running and freedom from the possibility of making sparks. For this latter reason they were particularly used in dusty flour mills. Cogs could easily be replaced when they broke, and hornbeam trees were sometimes grown near to wind- or watermills to provide a ready source of wood.

A cog wheel therefore has wooden teeth, but the word is often used in everyday speech for an all-metal gearwheel, although possibly reserved for gears with cast teeth as opposed to those with machine-cut teeth.

cog and rung gin an early 18th-century winding gear used to raise materials from a mine shaft, used fairly widely but particularly at Tyneside coal mines (*see* Fig. 28). It comprised a large horizontal cogwheel geared by a pinion to a roller placed directly over the shaft opening. A rope wound onto the roller as loads were raised from the shaft bottom when the cogwheel was rotated. This was achieved by a horse harnessed to a long horizontal arm which turned the cogwheel as the animal walked round the shaft opening in a circle. The disadvantage of the cog and rung gin was that the wooden teeth on the wheel and pinion were prone to break, and that the roller was vulnerable to damage by explosion from the mine shaft, a not uncommon happening in those days. By the mid to late 18th century, cog and rung gins were being replaced by HORSE WHIMS, in which the winding was direct without the intervention of gearing and the horse path was to one side of the shaft opening.

cogging mill a rolling mill for reducing a steel ingot down to a BILLET. It is also known as a slabbing or blooming mill, although strictly speaking a slabbing mill is for rolling plates, and a blooming mill is for producing rounds and sections.

cog railway an early experimental railway in which one of the cast-iron rails had a RACK cast on one side. A toothed cog wheel on the locomotive engaged in the teeth of the rack to drive the locomotive along. The first cog railway was that of John Blenkinsop (1783–1831) in 1812 for the Middleton Colliery Railway, Leeds, Yorks. A similar railway was constructed at Orrell Colliery in Lancashire in the same year by Robert Daglish (Senior) (1777–1865) which was two miles long, and on which the locomotive *Yorkshire Horse* operated. The cog wheel drive was used because it was thought a smooth wheel could not grip a smooth rail enough to propel a locomotive along. This was found to be fallacious and cog wheel drives were soon abandoned. However, early cog railways were the forerunners of the rack railways used on steep mountain slopes.

cog ring a large metal circular ring, usually made in sections and bolted together, with gear teeth formed on its inner edge, and fastened to a waterwheel. The drive from the wheel is taken off the cog ring by a pinion which meshes with

it. Cog rings are usually fastened to SUSPENSION WHEELS.

cogware a cheap, coarse cloth made from very inferior wool. It was mostly made in the north of England and the Lake District. A better variety was known as KENDAL CLOTH. Because of its poor quality cogware was not subject to ALNAGE, and was not normally handled by reputable cloth merchants.

coinage the old practice of weighing and stamping tin blocks before they were sold, carried out at certain STANNARY towns in Cornwall. Each block was weighed to determine the duty to be paid to the Duke of Cornwall, and a coign or corner cut off for assaying to ascertain the purity of the tin. An official seal was then stamped into the block. Coinage ceased in 1838.

coke the solid residue left after heating coal in a closed RETORT in the absence of air, to drive off inherent volatiles in the coal. Coke is a lightweight, sponge-like, and brittle material comprised of at least 75 per cent carbon, plus some nitrogenous compounds and the mineral impurities of the original coal. Coke has many uses as a fuel or in metallurgical processes. The distillation process produces TOWN GAS which is used as a fuel, and until the early 20th century was used for lighting purposes. Coke is a by-product when the main purpose of using the coal is to make town gas, and the coke is afterwards used as a domestic or industrial fuel; but it is also deliberately made for metallurgical purposes, and the gas drawn off is then the by-product.

Before retorts or coke ovens were introduced, coke (or coak) was made by controlled slow smouldering of heaps of coal in the open air in the mid-18th century, a method known as torrefying (from the Latin *torrere* meaning to parch with heat), and also as charking. Dampened fine coal slack was spread over the smouldering heap, and portable hurdles used as wind shields to control the rate of burning by restricting the air supply. Later, primitive stone-built ovens, often sited close to BELL PITS (1), were built to manufacture coke on the spot where the coal was mined. These ovens were something like limekilns in construction, and due to their shape are known as BEEHIVE coke ovens. No attempt was made to capture the escaping gases. Later still, vertical coke ovens comprising tall, narrow vertical chambers, firebrick-lined and arranged in banks, side-by-side, were built with arrangements to draw off and purify the gas, which was stored in large gasholders.

Coke was used as the fuel in GLASS making, malting for BREWING, and in DYEING processes in the 17th century. In these processes, the fuel was kept separate from the raw materials it was heating, being burned in self-contained furnaces. In 1709, Abraham Darby I (1667–1717) of Coalbrookdale, Salop., successfully used coke to smelt iron, replacing CHARCOAL which was the former fuel. The discovery heralded an important use of coke in the iron, and later the steel, industries. Coal by itself could not be used for smelting iron because the impurities present (sulphur and phosphorus mainly) disastrously affect the quality of iron made; in iron manufacture, the coke is in intimate contact with the ore, serving both as fuel and a reacting agent. The metallurgical use of coke created a large increase in coal mining.

There are different qualities of coke dependent on the grade of coal from which it is made. Coke intended for metallurgical use has to be strong to withstand the weight of the ore it supports whilst in the BLAST FURNACE. Other types of coke are mainly used as fuels. Coke burns almost without creating smoke, and was the sole fuel for early locomotives since they were obliged by law not to make smoke. Coal was not burned on locomotive grates until the invention of the firebox with brick arch in 1860. In the 17th century coke was called charked coal.

Mott, R.A. *History of Coke Making*, Cambridge University Press, 1936

coke ovens ovens or retorts for converting COAL into COKE by heat. Coke is made by high temperature carbonization of caking coals out of contact with air, and an early way of doing this was burning coal in BEEHIVE OVENS. By the beginning of the 19th century patent coke ovens or retorts were invented, such as the Coppée oven, and the similar Carvés oven. The Coppée oven comprised long horizontal coking chambers arranged in rows, each chamber tapered to assist coke removal from the back by hydraulic rams. Between each two chambers, vertical flues led the volatile products from the top of the chambers to a horizontal flue, which passed under the retorts to join a main flue. This often led the gases under a steam boiler before being discharged up a chimney stack. The Carvés system was similar to the Coppée, but the gases were first passed through a water-cooled condenser and scrubber before going to the retorts. In coke making, the by-product gas produced was often piped to a nearby local gasworks for purification.

cold blast the smelting of iron by blowing combustion air at ambient temperature into the furnace. The earliest BLAST FURNACE used

unheated air in this manner. Thermal efficiency of the furnace was greatly increased by the use of HOT BLAST introduced in 1827, and all blast furnaces adopted pre-heated air soon after this date.

cold short iron which is brittle (or 'short', as in shortcake) when cold, i.e. at atmospheric temperature. Iron can also be brittle when hot, a condition called HOT SHORT. Cold shortness is caused by an excess of phosphorus in the composition of the iron.

collar beam truss a timber roof truss in which the two rafters are tied together by a horizontal beam (the collar) which joins them at their mid point; it is used only for moderate spans (*see* Fig. 57).

collier 1. originally, someone who made or marketed wood charcoal, dating from the 15th century; an early spelling was cholyer. Later the name came to be applied to coal, and a coal miner became known as a collier. **2.** a ship used for the carrying of coal. Coal was brought to London in wooden sailing ships down the east coast from the north-east coalfields as early as the 14th century. Coal so brought was known as sea-coal. In the year 1861, when larger iron-hulled ships were carrying on the trade, it was estimated that some 2,700 colliers had carried 3.4 million tons of coal to London. This coastal trade lasted until 1980, when the last Thames-side coal-fired power station was closed.

collier's lung, *see* PHTHISIS

'Colossus of Roads' the punning nickname given to Thomas Telford (1757–1834) by his friend Robert Southey the poet, on account of Telford's extensive road and bridge building activities.

Rolt, L.T.C. *Thomas Telford*, 1958, reprinted by Penguin, 1979

comberboard a perforated horizontal board in a JACQUARD loom positioned above the WARPS to prevent the harness cords becoming entangled as they move up and down. It has as many holes as there are hooks and cords, a cord passing through each hole, and 'combs' the cords into order, hence its name.

Combination Laws 18th-century Acts forbidding associations of masters and workers. The uprising of the common people in the French Revolution of 1789–95 alarmed the ruling classes in Britain in case the same should happen in Britain. They were therefore conditioned against any form of combined action by the masses, or groups of people. When the possibility of organized opposition to employers arose, to attempt an improvement in the lot of workers, the Combination Laws of 1799 and 1800, were passed. In theory these pplied equally to combinations by employers, ut in practice they were not enforced against hem. Thus, any association of workers in the orm of a craft or trade union was made illegal. Breaking the law incurred a prison sentence. These measures were effective until 1824 when it was thought a relaxation would be beneficial to industry and they were repealed. The Repeal of the Combination Act of 1824 permitted bargaining with employers on wages and hours of work, and was immediately followed by an outburst of strikes, sometimes accompanied by violent disorder. This created fresh alarm among employers and it was felt the Combination Laws should be reintroduced. Accordingly, the 1824 Act was replaced by another Act in 1825, which, whilst repealing the Combination Laws, did legalize well-conducted strikes on matters of wages and hours and in addition made the use of violence and intimidation illegal. The later Act did not give trade unionism a secure legal basis, and combinations of workers were always vulnerable to attack on the grounds that they were seditious, but the Act did last almost 50 years.

In 1834 six agricultural labourers, the TOLPUDDLE MARTYRS were prosecuted under an old law of 1797 for taking an oath of combination, and were transported. In spite of this, combinations of workmen were still formed in secret, but the practice of taking oaths on joining was abolished. Legalized friendly societies were introduced to provide benefits to members during sickness and unemployment. A less aggressive and more conciliatory attitude to disputes gradually arose on the part of worker's associations, and the embryonic trade unions eventually gained employers tolerance and respect. Unions came more into the open and laid the foundations of the British trade union movement. In 1868 most of the existing trade unions formed the Trades Union Congress, and in 1871 trade unions were given full legal status in the Trade Union Act of that year. By 1875, contracts between employer and worker were made a civil contract, and collective bargaining together with peaceful picketing became legal.

combing the process of parallelizing long fibres of wool, known as TOPS, in preparation for spinning into WORSTED yarn, and removing the short ones or noils, which are sent to woollen spinners. Combing was originally performed by hand, using combs with long steel teeth arranged in up to nine rows. The work was usually carried out by four men working together as a team, moving from place to place and giving a service to worsted spinners and merchants. Wool combers washed and scoured the raw wool, oiled it, and combed it, warming the combs on charcoal stoves (*see* COMB POT). It was arduous work, and a guild craft. Wool combers were highly organized, and held a powerful hold over worsted manufacturers. Wool combing was the last process to be mechanized in the trade, and some hand combing was still being done as late as the 1850s. The Reverend Edmund Cartwright (1743–1823) patented his first primitive machine comber in 1790 (patent no. 1747), but although he improved it in a later patent, it was not a success (*see* 'BIG BEN'). It was some fifty years before successful machines were invented. Then, four were invented during a ten-year period: HEILMANN's in 1846, LISTER's in 1851, NOBLE's in 1853, and HOLDEN's in 1856 (*see also* Figs 34, 35 and 43).

There are subtle differences between the combing and CARDING of raw wool. Carding is performed by CARD CLOTH which has hundreds of short, closely pitched wire pins: these align the wool fibres without removing short ones, to give a bouncy, hairy, woollen yarn. Combing is performed by long toothed combs, much wider spaced than card cloth, and short fibres are separated out, so that a worsted yarn is compact, flat, with a smooth surface. Some cottons are also combed.

Burnley, J. *The History of Wool and Wool Combing*, 1889; reprinted by Kelley, 1969

comb pot a charcoal-fired stove used by hand combers producing wool for worsted spinning. Their hand combs were warmed on the stove to aid combing the wool. Charcoal was used instead of coal to avoid sulphurous fumes which could damage the wool, besides creating an unpleasant atmosphere for the combers to work in. A comb pot was known as a 'pot of four', possibly from the French *pot au feu* (pot of fire), or because hand combers usually worked in teams of four men sharing one pot between them.

'come into the house' a phrase used by the enginemen of Newcomen or Cornish BEAM ENGINES when the overhead beam came down inside the engine house. When the beam 'came into the house', the engine was making its power stroke, i.e. the piston was descending inside the cylinder, raising the other end of the beam to operate the mine pumps. 'By house' or 'indoor stroke' meant the same thing. The converse upward movement of the beam was termed 'going out of the house'.

'coming to grain', *see* 'COMING TO NATURE'

'coming to nature' (or 'coming to grain') the expression used by the men operating a

PUDDLING FURNACE manufacturing wrought iron. It described the critical state of the iron in the bath of the furnace when it was ready to be gathered into a ball by RABBLING, prior to its extraction by tongs. The iron never actually melts, and remains in a pasty condition but 'boils' whilst the carbon content of the pig iron is reduced. When all the carbon has been oxidized, the bath becomes calm and its melting point rises. At the same time particles of solid iron begin to form which can be worked into balls by the operator, a process called balling up.

commission system, *see* DOMESTIC SYSTEM

common beam in the 19th century cast-iron beams of inverted T cross-section were referred to as beams of common shape, or common beams. This shape is necessary because more material is needed on the underside of the beam to resist the tensile stress due to the load carried, cast iron being weak in tension.

common engine name generally used for the Newcomen ATMOSPHERIC ENGINE in the late 18th century. SAVERY ENGINES have also been called common engines on occasion.

common sails windmill sails comprising canvas cloth set on a wooden lattice frame.

compass arm wheel a type of wooden WATERWHEEL construction where the arms or 'spokes' radiate from the central axle, and are secured to it by mortice and tenon joints (*see* Fig. 85). The possible origin of the name is that the wheel arms resemble a compass chart in as much that they radiate from a central point, as opposed to the alternative CLASP ARM construction. The compass arm construction weakens the axle at the very point where maximum strength is needed to transmit torque from the action of the water at the wheel circumference.

compensating motion the system of levers, gears, etc. which transmits the action of a CENTRIFUGAL GOVERNOR to the VALVE GEAR on a steam engine so as to control its speed at a constant value.

compensation water water which had to be passed continuously from a dam or reservoir to supply downstream users, who took water directly from the stream before the reservoir was constructed. This is a legal requirement, still in force today, to comply with the RIPARIAN RIGHTS of the downstream users.

compounding 1. a term introduced in the mid-19th century, describing a steam engine with more than one cylinder. Provision of a second cylinder (or more) enables steam to be progressively expanded through cylinders of increasing volume. Jonathan Carter Hornblower (1753–1815) built a few BEAM ENGINES in Cornwall with two cylinders based on his patent no. 1298 of 1781 to increase power (*see* Fig. 19a). Arthur Woolf (1766–1837) continued the idea a couple of decades later by taking out patent no. 2772 in 1804 (*see* Fig. 19b). A Scottish engineer, William McNaught (1818–81), working in Rochdale, Lancs. patented a method of compounding (no. 11001, 1845), for increasing the power from existing beam engines by adding a short stroke, high pressure cylinder under the beam, and turning the existing cylinder into a low pressure one. This saved the cost of buying a new bigger engine, and the practice was known as McNaughting an engine (*see* Fig. 19c).

Pressure compounding enables high pressure steam to be used expansively. Since it is not possible to expand steam too much within one cylinder without condensation troubles, the problem is overcome by restricting the volumetric expansion to about three times the entry volume. Thus, high pressure steam is allowed to expand to this maximum in a first cylinder, and is exhausted at lower pressure into a second, larger cylinder, where it expands again to about three times its entry volume. This process may be repeated in a third, or even a fourth cylinder, as required. The volumes of the cylinders have to be in the correct ratio, and the power produced in each more or less equal. In direct-acting engines, the stroke is the same for each cylinder, so the larger volumes are by increased diameters.

The different configurations for compound engines of the horizontal mill type are shown in Fig. 20. In the *single tandem compound* (a) high pressure and low pressure cylinders in line, one behind the other, driving one crank (two steam expansions). The *cross compound engine* (b) has high pressure and low pressure cylinders side by side, each cylinder acting on its own crank with the flywheel between the cranks (two steam expansions). In the *twin* (or double) *tandem compound engine (c)* two single tandem compounds work side by side, each tandem driving its own crank, with a central flywheel (two steam expansions in four cylinders). Finally, the *triple expansion engine (d)* has intermediate pressure cylinder in tandem with one of two low pressure cylinders, and the high pressure cylinder is in tandem with the other low pressure cylinder. Each tandem drives its own crank, with a central flywheel (three steam expansions in four cylinders).

In vertical engines, compound cylinders are side by side, each driving onto one crankshaft. A hybrid design of compound engine is the MANHATTAN, which comprised a vertical high

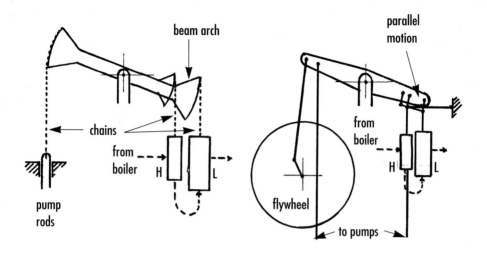

(a) Hornblower pumping compound beam engine, *c.* 1781/2

(b) Woolf compound beam engine arranged to work two pumps, *c.* 1820

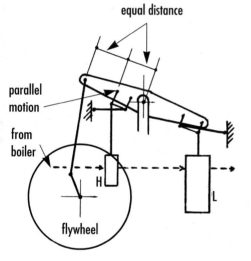

The path of steam through the cylinders is shown by a dotted line

H high pressure cylinder
L low pressure cylinder

(c) McNaught rotary compound beam engine, *c.* 1850

Fig. 19. Early compound beam engines

81

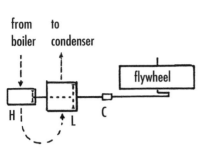

Typical ratios of cylinder volumes
2 expansions: L (2.5 to 3.5) x H
3 expansions: I (2.25 to 2.5) x H
L (6 to 6.5) x H

(a) Single tandem compound engine (two steam expansions)

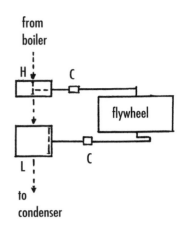

(b) Cross compound engine (two steam expansions)

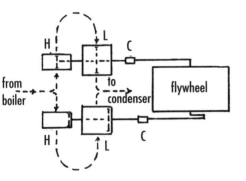

(c) Twin tandem compound engine (two steam expansions)

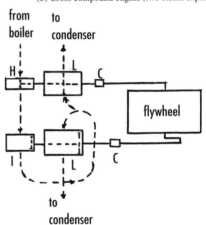

(d) Triple expansion engine (three steam expansions)

Path of steam through
the cylinders is shown
by a dotted line

C crosshead
H high pressure cylinder

I intermediate pressure cylinder
L low pressure cylinder

Fig. 20. Cylinder configurations for horizontal compound steam engines

82

pressure cylinder, and a horizontal low pressure, each driving on one crank (*see* Fig. 44).

Compounding was applied rather late on steam locomotives. In 1884, Francis W. Webb (1836–1906) designed a three-cylinder compound locomotive with two outside high pressure cylinders, and one large low pressure cylinder between frames.

Watkins, G. *Textile Mill Engines*, 2 vols., David and Charles, 1970–1

2. Mixing of plasticized raw rubber with sulphur and other ingredients. Thorough mixing of plasticized raw rubber with sulphur, fillers, accelerators, pigment, etc., is necessary before the mixture is moulded or extruded into its final shape, and vulcanized. Compounding may be done in a RUBBER MILL, BANBURY MIXER, or a MASTICATOR.

compressed air air, compressed to a pressure significantly above atmospheric, stored in a pressure receiver, and conveyed by pipelines to points of usage. Compressed air is a convenient form of energy and power, and works by virtue of a pressure drop and expansion, just as steam does. A problem can arise as the air expands since the accompanying temperature drop may freeze the inherent moisture, but this can be overcome by pre-heating the compressed air just prior to its point of use. Unlike steam, air needs no special arrangement to receive it when it is exhausted back into the atmosphere.

Early use of this medium was in mining and tunnelling, to power compressed air tools and operate underground haulage systems. A public compressed air system was in operation in Paris in 1881, and an Act of Parliament in 1886 permitted a similar public system in Birmingham. There, some 23 miles of pipeline supplied small factories, where it was used to drive small steam engines by air instead of steam (eliminating the need for steam raising equipment), and to operate air tools. Air was distributed at 45 psi from a central, steam-powered air compressing station.

Another use of compressed air is in the pneumatic braking system on railway trains developed in the USA by George Westinghouse (1846–1914) *c.*1866, and first used on British trains in 1871.

compression ignition engine (or diesel engine) an internal combustion engine invented by Rudolf Diesel (1858–1913) of Germany in the 1890s. The temperature necessary to ignite the air-oil mixture inside the cylinder comes from compressing air to a high pressure and spraying in the oil at the correct moment in the cycle. The engine works on a modified Carnot cycle, and can be of the two-stroke (one

revolution per cycle), or four-stroke (two revolutions per cycle) variety. No spark or hot spot is required to ignite the fuel mixture. Diesel commenced work on his engine *c.*1893, and by 1897 had a successful prototype. The diesel rapidly superseded oil engines and became the main PRIME MOVER for heavier and more powerful applications, such as ship propulsion.

concentrate metallic ore with a high mineral content which has been separated from the useless portion (the gangue) by various methods such as crushing, washing and flotation. It is thus the valuable mineral content of the mined ore ready for further treatment or smelting. The separation depends on a physical difference between the wanted and unwanted materials, the gangue being discarded and the concentrate processed further.

concentrating table a device for separating waste rock from metallic rock by means of shaking the broken-down mixture on a slightly inclined flat surface. This separation is achieved by the acceleration and deceleration imparted to the individual heavier metal grains and the lighter waste material respectively.

concrete a building material composed of CEMENT, sand and gravel mixed with water. The word comes from the Latin *concretus* meaning to grow. Modern concrete dates from the late 1830s, although similar material was being used centuries earlier from Roman times. Concrete is strong in compression but weak in tension, so steel reinforcement is added where tensile stresses occur. William Boutland Wilkinson patented reinforced concrete beams in 1854 using old steel wire colliery ropes (patent no. 2293). Mass concrete is very useful for foundation work where the main stress is compressive. Concrete can be formed into almost any shape by being cast inside temporary wooden or steel shutters or formers which support it while it sets. It will also set and harden under water. Concrete roads first appeared in Britain in 1865.

condensate condensed steam, i.e. hot water. Condensate may come from a steam CONDENSER (1) attached to a steam engine, or drained from steam mains via steam traps. It is returned to a steam boiler as feedwater to conserve its own heat, and thereby raise the thermal efficiency of the system.

condenser 1. a vessel for condensing exhaust steam from a steam engine or turbine back into hot water, which is then known as CONDENSATE. A condenser raises the overall efficiency of the steam plant, since the condensation of the steam creates a partial vacuum in the vessel, increasing the pressure drop across the engine and thus making the BACK PRESSURE lower than atmospheric. A condenser is a separate vessel closely connected to the exhaust outlet of the engine, the condensing action being obtained by cold water. The degree of vacuum obtained is measured in inches of mercury by a gauge (*see* PRESSURE). The first condenser was that invented by James Watt (patent no. 913, 1769) which he added to a NEWCOMEN STEAM ENGINE. It was a separate vessel into which spent steam from the engine cylinder was exhausted and condensed by a cold water spray. This removal of condensation from inside the engine cylinder to an outside vessel kept the engine cylinder hot and raised the efficiency.

There are two types of steam condenser, the jet condenser and the surface condenser. In the jet condenser, cold water is sprayed directly into the exhaust steam, the resulting flow from the condenser being a mixture of condensed steam and the condensing water. In the surface condenser, the steam is condensed by passing over the cold surfaces of a nest of tubes through which cold water flows, the steam and water being kept separate. Here, the outflow from the condenser is condensed steam only. AIR PUMPS continuously remove the condensate from the condenser together with dissolved air which is usually present in the original steam, and maintain a high vacuum in the vessel. The condensate is pumped back into the boiler as hot feed water. The degree of vacuum that can be obtained in a condenser is affected by the barometric pressure. When it is high, a slightly better vacuum can be maintained, so seasonal and daily variations in the atmospheric pressure slightly affect the overall efficiency.

Law, R.J. *James Watt and the Separate Condenser*, 1969

2. an enlarged chamber, of brick or stone construction, in a SETTLING FLUE from a lead smelter. Its purpose was to filter out lead particles from the lead fume as it passed through on its way to the chimney. Sometimes known as Stokoe condensers, these chambers were introduced in the mid-19th century and were usually filled with small twigs or brushwood, loosely packed to provide a large surface area on which the lead fume could condense. Water was sometimes sprayed into the chamber to assist in trapping the lead particles, and collected in a settling pit. Steam jets have also been used. Periodically the dirty brushwood would be removed and sent to the smelter to recover the lead adhering to it. Joseph Dickinson Stagg patented a lead fume condenser (patent no. 9920, 1843).

3. a mechanism added at the end of a CARDING ENGINE to produce a number of lightly twisted ROVINGS. The first condensing patent was by Thomas Wood in 1776 (patent no. 1130), and improved designs were later developed. Typically, a condenser comprises a means of cutting the web of cotton after it leaves the DOFFER into a number of narrow strips. These are carried forward between bands of wide leather belts, which also have a transverse reciprocating motion. This action rolls each strip into a small-section roving with a light twist, sufficient to hold the material together, so that the cotton is ready for further processing. (*See also* CONDENSER SPINNING.)

4. equipment for cooling hot coal gas to remove valuable volatile tars and ammoniacal liquors by condensation; if not removed, the tars would block pipes when they cooled to viscous liquids. The tars and liquors removed are sold as by-products. The earliest condensers comprised a number of inverted U-tubes through which the hot gases passed, drawn through by the EXHAUSTER. Devised by John Perks of London in 1817, the tubes were cooled by the atmospheric air surrounding them, the tars and liquors being syphoned off from a tank or sump into which they drained. By the 1870s, more efficient annular condensers were in use, using air or water as the cooling medium.

condenser spinning the spinning of poor quality or short-fibred cotton waste, much of the waste arising from normal CARDING processes or, for example, from HEILMANN COMBERS; condenser spinning is also known as waste spinning. The staple (i.e. fibre length) of cotton waste is too variable and too short to be made into yarn by roller drafting, as on a standard MULE (*see* Fig. 64) so spinning is done by spindle drafting, as on the JENNY (*see* Fig. 41). The waste is carded on a carder fitted with a CONDENSER (3), which delivers the material as lightly twisted, small section ROVINGS. The rovings are wound onto large flanged condenser bobbins, usually 24–30 in long, and these are held in a CREEL on a spinning mule specially adapted for condenser spinning. Such mules do not have a roller drafting system, and are therefore similar to woollen spinning mules. The rovings are fed between only one pair of rollers which deliver them at the same speed as the mule carriage's outward run until, at a certain point in the carriage travel, the rollers disengage, and draft is applied by the rotating spindles during the completion of the carriage travel.

This specialized section of the cotton spinning industry first developed in the mid-

19th century. The yarns made from waste were used in the manufacture of fabrics not subjected to excessive wear and tear when in use, such as blankets, curtains, and WINCEYETTES.

condensing of wool the process by which, after being CARDED into a flat, flossy mat, wool is condensed into a series of soft 'ropes' about 0.125 in diameter called ROVINGS, prior to being stretched out and twisted in a SPINNING MULE to make yarn.

condensing steam engine a STEAM ENGINE in which the spent steam leaving the cylinder passes to a CONDENSER (1) instead of being exhausted to the atmosphere. The condenser creates a partial vacuum which increases the pressure drop across the engine, so raising its efficiency.

conditioning the application of moisture to spun yarn by artificial means to bring the moisture content up to a recognized standard. This improves the behaviour of the yarn in subsequent working.

cone pulley drive a drive method which comprises a pair of parallel cones of considerable width compared to their diameters, arranged so that the smaller diameter of one pulley was opposite the larger diameter of the other. A flat driving belt connected the two, the gradual increase in diameter of one corresponding with the gradual reduction in diameter of the other so that the length of the belt was constant at all positions along the length of the cones. By moving the belt along the pulleys, an infinite variation in the speed ratio could be obtained between driver and driven shaft, within the limitations of the diameters, which was usually from half to twice the driving pulley speed, i.e. an overall variation of 4:1. Such drives were used particularly on STOCKING FRAMES.

conjuror an old word used to describe an inventor or improver of textile machinery in the mid- to late 18th century; it was generally used pejoratively.

connecting rod that part of an engine mechanism which transfers the reciprocating motion of the piston to the rotating motion of the crank. In a conventional steam engine, a connecting rod is usually between three and six times as long as the crank, and one end – called the little end – is pivoted on the crosshead, whilst the other – the big end – is pivoted to the crankpin.

On rotative beam engines, the connecting rod joining the rocking beam to the crank was known as the sweep rod, while on timber sawing machines, the connecting rod is sometimes known as a pitman. This is because it gives the same motion to the reciprocating saw as the sawyer, known as the pitman, did who stood in the bottom of the old type sawpit.

constant volume cycle, *see* OTTO CYCLE

contact process the method of making SULPHURIC ACID developed in the second half of the 19th century, in which sulphur dioxide is combined with oxygen in the presence of an iron oxide catalyst to make sulphur trioxide which is dissolved in water to make a strong acid. The contact process superseded the older LEAD CHAMBER PROCESS. Peregrine Phillips II pioneered the process in Bristol as early as 1831, but progress was slow because of difficulties with the catalyst he was using (platinum) becoming poisoned. It was when iron oxide was found to be a more satisfactory catalyst that the process took off, largely thanks to work in Germany by Clemens Winkler in the 1870s and Rudolph Messel (1847–1920) in Silvertown, London. Because of their pioneering work, the contact process was also known as the German process.

Continental comb, *see* HEILMANN COMBER

Continental drawing, *see* PORCUPINE DRAWING

Continental system 1. a method of WORSTED manufacture which developed using machines of Continental invention such as the French HEILMANN COMBER, the French or porcupine method of drawing, and MULE spinning. The advantage of the Continental system is that it can use shorter fibres than the BRADFORD SYSTEM. **2.** When Britain was at war with France, Napoleon I tried to bring the country to its knees by attempting to blockade Europe, preventing the importation of British goods and thus ruining its export trade. He introduced this in 1806–7, the ban on British goods being known variously as the Berlin Decree of 1806, the Milan Decree of 1807, or collectively as the Continental system. Besides banning British ships, any neutral ship which had visited a British port was liable to be seized as a prize by the French or their allies. In fact, Napoleon's control of the European coastline was inadequate, and British goods were smuggled in at several places. Britain retaliated by a counter-blockade of French ports by diverting any neutral ship approaching one to a British port. Partly shut out from European markets, Britain developed new ones in India and South America during this period. The Continental system collapsed in 1815 with the defeat of Napoleon at Waterloo, but British industry went through a difficult time with much unemployment, and it took a long time for the economy of the country fully to recover.

contour canal a type of CANAL which winds about the countryside keeping to the same height contour to avoid the construction of locks and expensive earthworks or aqueducts. James Brindley (1716–72) favoured this construction. Although cheaper in initial cost, it adds to the travelling time of boats.

contra-flow steam engine the common design of steam engine, where steam enters the cylinder at one end, and after it has pushed the piston to the other end, its direction of flow is reversed as the piston returns, the steam leaving the cylinder through the exhaust ports. This occurs whether the engine is single- or double-acting. The design in which the steam flow through the cylinder is not reversed is called the UNIFLOW STEAM ENGINE.

conversion, *see* WEAVING

converter a vessel for holding molten pig iron while it is converted into steel in the BESSEMER process. Invented by Henry Bessemer (1813–98) in 1856, it enabled cheap steel to be made in quantity for the first time. A converter comprises a specially shaped steel vessel, firebrick-lined, mounted on TRUNNIONS and open at the top. One trunnion is hollow and a pipe leads from it to a chamber below the firebrick base. The firebricks forming the base are perforated, making a number of TUYÈRES. In operation, the converter is tilted so that previously melted iron can be poured into it from a large ladle. It is then righted, with an air blast blowing up through the bottom tuyères via the hollow trunnion to oxidize all the carbon, manganese, and silicon present in the iron, the flames and gases leaving at the open top. When the process is judged to be completed, the force of the blast is reduced, alloying elements added to the pure iron to give the desired composition of steel, and the converter is tilted again to pour the melted steel into another large ladle. The steel is then cast into billet moulds. The original firebrick lining of Bessemer's converter was composed of ACID firebricks, but because these could only process low phosphorus ores, BASIC LININGS were introduced in 1879, allowing a larger variety of ores to be used. A phosphate of lime slag is formed, and this is removed from the converter and sold to be ground up for use as a fertilizer.

Converters used in steel works are large and bottom blown. Small converters, side blown, are used in foundries to make small amounts of steel from iron melted in a CUPOLA FURNACE.

Bessemer, Sir H. 'Sir Henry Bessemer FRS – An autobiography with a concluding chapter', *Engineering* (1905)

convoy a Tyneside name for the simple brake on a horse-drawn coal waggon of the 18th century. It comprised a curved wooden lever at one side of the truck which could be moved so that one end acted as a brake on the rim of one wheel to control the speed of the waggon when going downhill. The waggon-man usually sat on the free end of the lever and varied the pressure on the brake accordingly, the towing horse trotting behind on a hitch. The word probably comes from the old French *convoier*, which meant to conduct or guide. A convoy was also known as a jig in Shropshire.

cop the package of wound yarn produced on a spinning MULE. The yarn is wound directly onto a bare spindle in a special manner which aids its subsequent unwinding when shuttle PIRNS are being prepared for weaving. The way in which the cop is built up is controlled by the COPPING MOTION of the mule mechanism. The completed cop is firm enough to stand on its own without collapsing when lifted off the spindle (i.e. doffed). When the yarn is unwound from a cop it is drawn off the tapered end and in an axial direction without having to be rotated. The origin of the word cop as applied to such a yarn package is obscure, but it possibly comes from the word 'cope' meaning a covering.

cope 1. a duty or royalty paid by a lead miner to the owner of the mineral rights of the land he is mining. Payment of cope allowed the miner to extract and sell the ore to whom he pleased, although the Crown had first claim to purchase. The word was used in Derbyshire and probably comes from an old German word *kopen* meaning to buy or barter. A cope-bargain was an agreement for miners to mine the lead at their own cost at an agreed price. 2. in foundry work, the upper part of a mould, or the outer mould for a bell. The word probably comes from the Latin *cappa*, meaning a cap or cape. The lower part of a mould is called a drag.

coper a term used particularly in the Derbyshire lead mining area to describe a worker. Teams of copers made bargains with the mine owner or his agent to work a section of the mine. They therefore acted rather as contractors than as employees of the mining company. *See also* COPE (1).

Coppee oven, *see* COKE OVEN

copper 1. a non-ferrous, reddish-brown metal with a high melting point (1084°C) which corrodes only slowly and is a good conductor of heat. It is also very ductile. Its main ores are copper pyrites (chalcopyrite), copper glance, and cuprite. The ore is found in veins or lodes, and after extraction by mining the metal content is separated from the rock by roasting the ore to form an oxide, then refined, and reduced to a very pure copper by mixing in CHARCOAL or COAL and stirring with a green oak or birch pole. This causes a slag to form on the surface containing the impurities as the charcoal or coal deoxidizes the copper; the slag can be cast into blocks or pigs and used again in the initial roasting stage.

Copper was mined in several places in Britain, particularly Cornwall and Devon, near Coniston in the Lake District, Flintshire in north Wales, and on Anglesey. Extensive mining of copper took place in Cornwall and Devon in the 18th and 19th centuries. Between 1750 and 1800 Cornwall was the main supplier of copper in the world: the ores from this area were mainly smelted in south Wales, around Swansea where coal was readily available. More copper was extracted by a combination of mining and quarrying on the island of Anglesey at Parys Mountain, particularly after the rich Golden Venture vein was discovered in 1768. Output from Britain declined as the important copper mines of Rio Tinto in southern Spain were exploited, and by the 1870s British copper mining had virtually ceased, as easily reached veins were exhausted and imported copper became cheaper.

Copper is used extensively where its heat conductivity is particularly useful such as heating and cooling tubes in heat exchangers, and its slow corrosion rate is useful where water is in contact with it. It is also an important alloying component, e.g. in brass (copper and zinc) and bronze (copper, zinc, tin, and usually some lead). TIN is found in the same vein as copper, but at a much greater depth.

Barton, D.B. *A History of Copper Mining in Cornwall and Devon*, 2nd edn, Truro, Barton, 1968
Hamilton, H. *The English Brass and Copper Industries*, Cass, 1967
Holland, E.G. *Coniston Copper: A History*, Cicerone Press, 1987

2. a large pan, such as the pans used to boil soap, or large vessel in which WORT is boiled with the addition of sugar and hops in the BREWING industry. Originally these vessels were made from riveted copper sheets, but although other materials such as stainless steel are used today, the old name is still used.

copperas iron sulphate, which results from atmospheric oxidation and decomposition of iron pyrites found in coal measures. When it is heated, the oily liquid known as oil of vitriol or green vitriol is produced by absorbing the gas given off in water: this is concentrated SULPHURIC ACID, which was used as a MORDANT in the DYEING industry in the 18th century, and for making ink. Copperas was important also from the mid-18th to the late

19th centuries in the LEBLANC PROCESS for making soda. Its use declined when better ways of making sulphuric acid were discovered (*see* LEAD CHAMBER PROCESS), when synthetic dyes were introduced, and later when the SOLVAY PROCESS superseded the Leblanc. Copperas burning continued in use near Whitehaven, Cumberland, until 1856.

'Copper King' name by which Thomas Williams (1737–1802) became known as owner of the important copper quarry at Parys Mountain on Anglesey, north Wales.
Harris, J.R. *The Copper King*, Liverpool University Press, 1964

coppice trees periodically cut to permit growth of small poles. Coppicing, a form of arboriculture, was developed in the 17th century to provide a renewable source of wood for CHARCOAL production, charcoal being an early fuel for iron making etc. A coppice tree would be cut just above the bole, and from this base, or stool, some 10 to 20 'poles' tapering from about 4 to 2 in diameter and some 15 ft long, would be allowed to grow. When this length was reached, the 'poles' would be cut off and used either for making charcoal or for BOBBINS for the textile industry. Coppice wood was also used for firewood and hurdle making. About 8,000 'poles' per acre could be grown, and this was renewable every 14 to 16 years. Woods were managed so that a continuous supply of coppice was available by cutting the trees in rotation year by year. Coppice wood was also called cordwood. Fast-growing hardwood trees such as ash, birch, alder, willow and sycamore were mostly grown for coppicing; oaks were also grown, and the bark stripped off and sold to the tanning industry. The cutting of coppice wood was done by itinerant gangs.

All early iron furnaces were fired by charcoal until COKE was introduced as fuel by Abraham Darby I (1677–1717) in 1709, although many furnaces continued to use charcoal long after this; even up to the commencement of the 19th century there were still a few charcoal furnaces in operation. It is estimated that in 1770 about 1 acre of timber in the form of charcoal was consumed daily to produce 2 tons of iron. Although coppice woods were renewable if properly managed, overall the supply of timber was a diminishing resource. Since timber was an important material for building and ship construction, as early as Tudor times, Acts restricting the use of timber had been passed, particularly because of the fear of deforestation depriving the country of timber for naval construction. A large wooden man-of-war could require up to 50 acres of oak woodland for its construction, a quantity of timber not renewable for a century. There was a shortage of timber by George III's reign (1760–1820) largely brought about by the use of timber as a fuel, but fortunately coal and coke relieved the situation.

copping motion the mechanism invented by William Eaton of Wiln, Derbyshire, in 1818 (patent no. 4272), which automatically winds the thread into COP form on a spinning MULE. The thread is wound on in a certain manner to facilitate its subsequent unwinding when shuttle bobbins are prepared for weaving.

cord a measure of cut COPPICE wood comprising a piled heap 4 ft high by 4 ft wide by 8 ft long, i.e. 128 cubic ft in volume. Cordwood was a name for cut lengths of coppice from which either CHARCOAL or WHITE COAL were made; or lengths of cut wood (usually 4 ft) intended as fuel.

corduroy (or cord) a ribbed cotton fabric, used for hard wearing outer garments; corduroy trousers are often known simply as cords. The fabric construction dates from a British patent of 1776, and the origin of its name is obscure. A popular misbelief is that it comes from the French *corde du roi* (cord of the king), but this type of fabric has a different name there – *velours côtelé*. It is possible that corduroy is a corruption of an old English surname. In its earlier days it became known as the poor man's velvet.

cordwood or chopwood, *see* WHITE COAL

corf (plural corves) a northern name for a large, strong wicker basket, usually made of hazel twigs, used for bringing coal or ore up from a mine and transporting material underground from the working face. There was no standard size of corf: they varied in capacity from 2.5 up to 7.5 BUSHELS. Sometimes their capacity was measured in pecks, where 4 pecks equalled 1 bushel. Corves were used in the early days of mining and were replaced by wooden or iron tubs in later periods, although these were often still called corves. They were also used to distribute coal to houses by coal merchants. The word possibly comes from the Latin *corbis*, meaning a basket.

A corf-bitter was a person who picked out stones and unwanted rubbish from a corf. An ore corf was called a WISKET in Derbyshire lead mines.

corkir (or korkir) a lichen, *Lecanora tartarea*, from which a red dye was once made; the word is of Gaelic origin.

Corliss valve a type of quick acting steam valve used on stationary steam engines (*see* Fig. 21). Named after its inventor, George Henry Corliss (1817–88) of Rhode Island, USA,

whose second patented design was in 1851, it comprises a small valve which is partially rotated inside a chamber or port in communication with the main cylinder of a steam engine, to control the flow of steam. The engine cylinder has four such valves: two control the steam admission, the other two the exhaust outlet. The valves are actuated by rocking a WRIST PLATE b which oscillates through arcs to the left and right about its centre by the rod h moved by an eccentric on the engine shaft. When the steam inlet port is being opened, the catch plates c and part d move as one as the wrist plate rotates. This compresses spring a. At the point of cut-off, cam e has changed its position relative to the catch plate, i.e. its angle of inclination is different causing it to prize open the arms of c. This allows the spring a to snap shut the inlet port, the final closure being slowed by the DASHPOT or damper in its housing, and the part d slides along the catch plates past the step. The wrist plate then rotates in the opposite direction, the arms of c closing to catch hold of d as the new position is taken up. The exhaust port opens and closes without a snap action by the movement of link g. The point of cut-off is under the control of the governor which alters the angle of cam e by movement of rod f.

Corliss valves were introduced into Britain about 1863, and were superior to the earlier D VALVES and PISTON VALVES, particularly for high speed engines; since the low temperature exhaust steam does not cool the inlet ports, a higher thermal efficiency is maintained. The point of CUT-OFF can also be varied on some Corliss type valves under automatic governor control. Variations on the original design were made, such as that by William Inglis (1835–90), patented in 1863 (no. 652). *See also* Fig. 79.

Inglis, W. 'On the Corliss expansion valve-gear for stationary engines', *Proceedings of the Institution of Mechanical Engineers* 22 (1868)
Wood, J.L. 'The introduction of the Corliss engine to Britain', *Newcomen Society Transactions* 52 (1980–1)

corning the granulating of gunpowder by forcing it through sieves of punched parchment to form 'corn' powder. This was done on a corning machine, which comprised a shaking frame holding two sieves, inside which *lignum vitae* disks broke up the gunpowder by sliding about, the sieve material retaining the required size of powder grain, and unwanted dust falling through. Different mesh sizes were used to produce powders of different grain size. Gunpowder for use in cannons had larger grain sizes than that for use in muskets, the former being between 8 and 16 meshes per inch, the latter 16–36. The process was so named

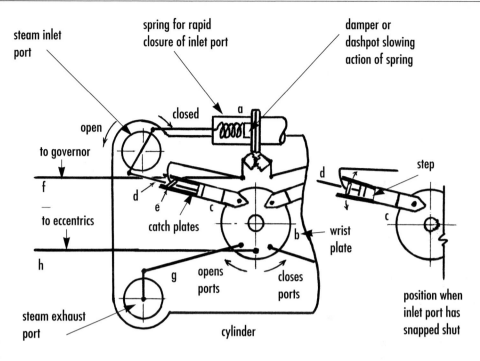

Fig. 21. Corliss valve gear for stationary steam engine

because the resulting pellets of powder resembled grains of corn. Corning consolidated and compacted the grains and reduced their tendency to separate into their ingredients which could happen during transport in barrels. *See also* GUNPOWDER MANUFACTURE.

Cornish boiler a horizontal SHELL TYPE BOILER with one firetube (*see* Fig. 61). Attributed to Richard Trevithick (1771–1833) and dating from c.1803, the boiler was developed originally for raising steam for the early steam engines at the Cornish tin and copper mines; it superseded the earlier, primitive HAYSTACK and WAGGON BOILERS, being designed to provide higher steam pressures. The Cornish boiler comprised a large diameter cylindrical shell arranged horizontally with one firetube running from front to back in the lower part of the shell (the LANCASHIRE BOILER, developed some forty years later, had two firetubes). Within the front portion of the firetube, a grate is positioned with a space below into which ashes may fall from the fire. A firebrick wall is built across the firetube at the end of the grate with space left above it for the products of combustion to pass over and continue along the inside of the firetube. Water surrounds the firetube to a depth of approximately two-thirds of the diameter of the outer shell, the space above being that in which the steam is formed. The boiler is set in brickwork which forms return side flues and there is another flue underneath, the products of combustion therefore making three passes along the length of the boiler: once inside the firetube from the grate to the rear, then splitting to return to the front via side flues, then rejoining and returning through the bottom flue to pass to the chimney.

The Cornish boiler was made in sizes up to about 30 ft long and 6 ft diameter, with steam pressures up to about 50 psi. It had two disadvantages: first, since the internal firetube was the hottest part of the boiler, its greater expansion tended to bulge out the shell ends, aggravated by the changes in temperature due to the state of the fire burning brightly or low. Secondly, when fresh fuel was thrown onto the fire, there was a tendency towards heavy smoke emission and loss of heat by the escape of unburnt volatiles. The Lancashire boiler was intended to overcome this latter disadvantage.

Cornish engine (or whim) a beam steam engine developed from NEWCOMEN'S ATMOSPHERIC ENGINE. Originating in Cornwall, this type of engine was first used for raising water from mines. The engine resembles a Newcomen or a Watt engine, but it is a true steam engine using steam under pressure to move its piston in a closed cylinder, whereas the cylinder of an atmospheric engine was open to the air at the top. Reciprocating (pumping) and rotative (winding) engines were built, single- and double-acting, the earliest ones designed by Cornish engineers such as Richard Trevithick (1771–1833) and Arthur Woolf (1776–1837). Many were made at the famous Cornish engine works and foundries of Harvey and Co., Copperhouse Foundry and Perran Foundry, whilst others were made by engine builders from Cornwall to Scotland. The Cornish engine became the workhorse of mines and collieries from 1800, and of municipal waterworks, some of whose engines worked for around one hundred years. The size of a Cornish engine is normally denoted by its cylinder diameter in inches: sometimes its stroke in feet is added, but the term horsepower is not used.

Fig. 22 shows a typical layout of a pair of Cornish engines at a tin mine, with one engine for winding, and the other for pumping. Sometimes only one engine was used for both duties, pumping at night and winding during the day.

Barton, D.B. *The Cornish Beam Engine*, Cornwall Books, 1989
Hassis, T.R. *Arthur Woolf: The Cornish Engineer 1766–1837*, Barton, 1966
Hills, R.L. 'The Cruquius Engine, Heemsteds, Holland', *Journal of Industrial Archaeology* 3 (1966) (describes a giant 1845 engine built from parts supplied by Harveys of Hayle)

Cornish valve a double BEAT steam valve used on Cornish beam engines. The housing containing the valve was called a nozzle in Cornwall.

Cornish type engine house at a lead mine, Minera, Clwyd

Corn Laws various 17th–19th-century laws regulating the export and import of corn. At the beginning of the Industrial Revolution, Britain was an exporter of grain, but by some fifty years later, population growth, and the rise in industrialization which attracted labour away from agricultural areas into the manufacturing towns, meant that home produced corn could not meet the demand for more food. This shortfall raised the price of corn to an excessively high level. Attempts at stabilizing prices had been made by a number of successive Acts since the 1689 Corn Bounty Act, and culminated in the Corn Law of 1815 which stipulated that no foreign wheat could be sold in Britain until the price of home-grown wheat reached 80s per quarter (28 lb). This was the price calculated to give farmers and landowners a fair return on their invested capital and interest rates they had to pay. Lower ceiling prices were fixed for other grains, such as barley and oats.

The resulting high cost of bread was extremely unpopular with the working classes, and civil unrest followed for a number of years. In 1830–33, hungry agricultural labourers rioted in southern England (*see* SWING RIOTS). The well-being of the country depended largely on the export of manufactured goods such as textiles in return for the importation of cheap food. Many industrialists were also opposed to the 1815 Act, and in 1838 the ANTI-CORN LAW LEAGUE was founded, with the aim of bringing about the repeal of the Act. This it succeeded in doing when the Act was repealed on 26 June 1846, with a token duty of 1s per quarter on wheat; in 1869 this duty was abolished and corn was admitted free.

Whilst the 1815 Corn Law was in force, the area under cultivation was increased to try to satisfy the increasing demand for food. Farmers had predicted that if cheap corn were imported, British agriculture would collapse. In fact, the opposite occurred, and the thirty years or so after 1846 are known as the Golden Age of English agriculture. Industrialization was thus an important factor in bringing this about.

Crosby, T.L. *English Farmers and the Politics of Protection, 1815–52*, David and Charles, 1976

corn milling grinding corn (wheat) into flour. There are two ways of grinding corn into flour, either between traditional MILLSTONES, or between steel rollers. The former is the older method: stoneground flour was made in water-powered mills or in WINDMILLS, the grinding taking place between a top rotating millstone, the runner, and a bottom stationary stone, the bedstone. Mills were sited on rivers and tidal inlets, or in windy places. A typical

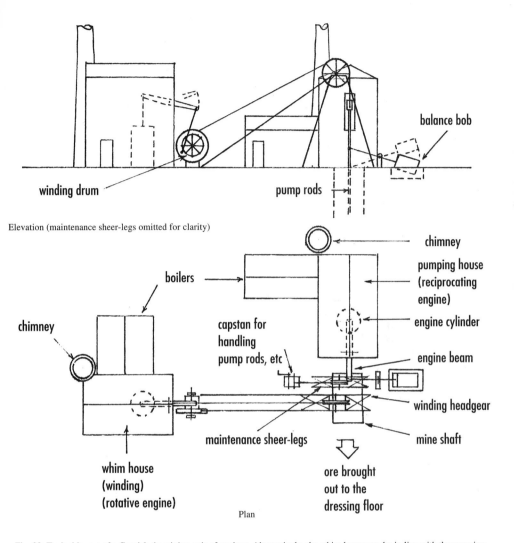

Elevation (maintenance sheer-legs omitted for clarity)

winding drum

pump rods

balance bob

chimney

boilers

pumping house
(reciprocating
engine)

engine cylinder

capstan for
handling
pump rods, etc

engine beam

winding headgear

maintenance sheer-legs

mine shaft

whim house
(winding)
(rotative engine)

Plan

ore brought
out to the
dressing floor

Fig. 22. Typical layout of a Cornish tin mining pair of engines. Alternatively, the whim house can be in line with the pumping house on the other side of the mine shaft, and the ore brought out to one side of the shaft

arrangement of a water-powered flour mill is shown in Fig. 23. A small mill would have one pair of stones, and large mills up to four. Water- and windmills are dependent on the vagaries of nature, so after the invention of the steam engine some mills were converted to steam operation, though still using millstones for grinding (*see also* WATERMILL).

The newer, alternative method of grinding between a pair of rotating steel rollers was first developed in Hungary in the 1840s; by 1862, steam-powered ROLLER MILLING was introduced into Britain. Large roller mills were built at ports, handling imported grain direct from ships. Such mills were capable of much larger outputs than the old fashioned wind- and watermills, which rapidly became obsolete, with a corresponding decline in the demand for millstones.

costeaning Cornish mining term for digging pits into the rock to ascertain the direction of a tin LODE. The word comes from 'stean', the Cornish for tin; a costeen is a pit.

cottage wheel, *see* SPINNING WHEEL

91

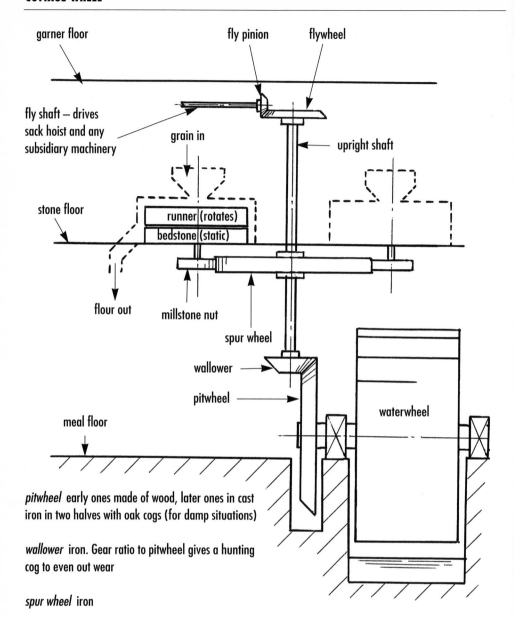

garner floor

fly pinion

flywheel

fly shaft – drives
sack hoist and any
subsidiary machinery

grain in

upright shaft

stone floor

runner (rotates)

bedstone (static)

flour out

millstone nut

spur wheel

wallower

pitwheel

waterwheel

meal floor

pitwheel early ones made of wood, later ones in cast
iron in two halves with oak cogs (for damp situations)

wallower iron. Gear ratio to pitwheel gives a hunting
cog to even out wear

spur wheel iron

millstone nut hornbeam or applewood cogs for
quietness and non-sparking. Cogs easily replaced
when worn

millstones a 48 in diameter pair would grind about
180 lb of flour per hour

Fig.23. Typical arrangement for a water-powered flour mill

cotton an important textile fibre obtained from the plant *Gossypium herbaceum*. Cotton fibres cover the seeds of the plant which are contained inside pods or bolls (*see* COTTON BOLL), which burst open when ripe to form fluffy tufts of fibres. Cotton grows naturally in damp, tropical and semi-tropical climates lying between about 40°N and 30°S, the main growing areas today being north and south America, the West Indies, India, the Levant, and Egypt. Cotton fibres are almost pure cellulose and lock together when brought parallel to each other, attenuated, and twisted or spun into a thread or yarn. The length of individual fibres is called the STAPLE and varies from about 1.9 in for best Sea Island cotton, to about 0.65 in for Surat cotton. After picking off the tufts, the bolls are cleaned in a COTTON GIN to remove seeds and other rubbish, and the fibres compressed into bales for shipment to a cloth manufacturing country.

It is thought that cotton was first cultivated in India, spun by hand, and woven into cloth on primitive looms. This was in pre-Christian days, and by c.1500 cotton fabrics were generally known throughout the civilized world. Although the origins of cotton manufacture in Britain are obscure, it is known that raw cotton was imported from the Levant and Cyprus in the 16th century. In these early days, raw cotton being a new and strange material in Britain and western Europe, it was often confusingly called wool, cotton-wool, and even tree-wool (the German for cotton is *Baumwolle*, literally meaning tree-wool). In 1783, the East India Company began sending supplies home from Bombay. Cotton plants from the Levant were grown under specially controlled conditions in the Chelsea Physic Garden, London (founded 1673) and seeds were sent from there to Georgia, USA, then a British colony, to start off the plantations which later were to be the main source of supply for the British cotton industry. It is somewhat remarkable that such an important industry was built up in Britain in the 18th and 19th centuries based on a raw material which had to be imported. The enormous rise in raw cotton imports is shown in the table, the largest proportion coming from north America.

Raw cotton imports, in millions of lb

year	quantity	year	quantity
1679	1.97	1825	199.27
1764	3.87	1835	364.00
1774	4.76	1854	750.00
1780	6.77	1856	895.11
1784	11.48	1879	1275.00
1789	32.29	1881	1479.00
1815	83.00	1895	1514.00

Increasing amounts of home produced cotton fabrics and yarns were exported, and by 1830, the total value of exported cotton goods exceeded that of woollens for the first time. Between 1786 and 1807, the price of cotton yarn fell in Britain from 38*s* per lb to 6*s* 9*d* per lb, mainly as a result of the mechanization of cotton ginning in America, and the use of bigger, faster spinning machinery in Britain.

When cotton fibres are spun into a yarn or thread, its size is denoted by a number derived from the number of hanks of yarn per lb, the number (or COUNT) indicating the coarseness or fineness of the yarn. *See also* COTTON PICKING.

Baines, E. *History of the Cotton Manufacture in Great Britain*, 1835; reprinted by Cass, 1966
Chapman, S.D. *The Cotton Industry in the Industrial Revolution*, Macmillan, 1967, reprinted 1984
Farnie, D.A. *The English Cotton Industry and the World Market, 1815–1896*, Clarendon Press, 1979
Nasmith, J. *The Students' Cotton Spinning*, 3rd edn, Nasmith and Heywood, 1896
Wadsworth, A.P. and Mann, J. de L. *The Cotton Trade and Industrial Lancashire, 1600–1780*, Manchester University Press, 1931

cotton boll the fruit or seed pod of the cotton plant, from which raw cotton is obtained. The surrounding pod contains the cotton seeds from which the fluffy fibres grow. When the fibres within the pod grow sufficiently, they burst open the pod and form the tuft when ripe. At this stage the boll is ready for picking. The fibres are mixed with and attached to the seeds, which must be removed by 'ginning'. In the early days of cotton cultivation this was done by hand, but the process was greatly speeded up by the invention in 1793 of the COTTON GIN.

cotton exchange a building in which the buying and selling of raw cotton and finished goods took place. There were small exchanges in a number of cotton towns, e.g. Blackburn in 1862–5, but the largest and most important was established in Manchester as early as 1729. Built by Oswald Moseley, it was replaced by another building in 1790 and subsequently enlarged several times, quickly becoming the most important cotton market in the world. In 1851 the institution became the Royal Exchange, eventually closing in the late 1960s. There was also an important cotton market at Liverpool, the main port of entry for raw cotton, where large warehouses held stocks of cotton awaiting purchase. Glasgow was also an important importing centre with its own exchange.

Liverpool handled over 80 per cent of Britain's total raw cotton imports. Most Liverpool cotton merchants imported on a commission basis and relied on specialist cotton brokers to dispose of their cotton to manufacturers at the exchange. In 1820 there were some 600 importers, many only small concerns, and by 1840 they were reduced to around 340 more substantial firms, some of whom were agents for American cotton growers. Hundreds of mill owners and their buyers attended the exchange on market days to buy their supplies and sell their products. Cotton was bought either on the spot, or bought before it actually arrived in Liverpool by a complicated procedure called the 'futures' market, which attempted to compensate for anticipated rises and falls in prices.

As the quantity of imported cotton rose, the existing transport system of river navigation and canal between Liverpool and Manchester became hopelessly inadequate: it often took longer to pass goods from Liverpool to Manchester, than to bring cotton all the way from America! This unsatisfactory state of affairs resulted in the building of the Liverpool to Manchester railway in 1830, which reduced delays both in transporting raw cotton to the cotton towns of south-west Lancashire and north Cheshire, and in the exporting of finished goods via Liverpool. To facilitate the sale of finished cotton goods, and for the convenience of prospective buyers, hundreds of warehouses were built in Manchester for holding stocks. Because of the great importance of cotton to Manchester, it earned the sobriquet 'Cottonopolis'. In 1852 there were over 3,000 merchant members of the Royal Exchange trading in cotton.

Cotton Famine the interruption in raw cotton supplies to Britain in 1862–5 caused by the American Civil War. The Lancashire cotton industry in particular was disastrously affected by the Civil War of 1861–5. The northern States' navy blockaded the cotton exporting ports of the southern States to prevent the sale of their principal export, cotton. Britain had relied almost exclusively on American cotton, and by 1862 mills began closing or running part-time, causing great distress to large numbers of workers, and ruin to some mill owners. Unemployed cotton workers suffered their privations stoically, believing in the righteousness of the abolition of slavery over which the Civil War was being fought. A national relief fund was raised, and alternative employment created by building roads, parks and so on in the affected areas. Attempts to substitute Indian cotton were largely unsuccessful. Coal mines were also affected due to the closure of mills. The 'famine' completed the death knell of HANDLOOM WEAVERS. At the cessation of the Civil War, cotton supplies were rapidly restored. *See also* COTTON SUPPLY ASSOCIATION.

Longmate, N. *The Hungry Mills*, Temple Smith, 1978

cotton-flannel, *see* DOMETT

cotton gin a machine engine or 'gin' used for removing seeds from picked COTTON before it is packed for shipment. The first successful cotton gin was invented by Eli Whitney on a cotton plantation in Georgia, USA, in 1793, and patented in March 1794. Manually operated at first, it enabled short STAPLE cottons to be used in addition to the longer fibre variety. Later, the machine was horse driven and could clean as much cotton as formerly needed 50 men in the same time.

Whitney's gin used a clawing action. It comprised a wooden roller with wire teeth which protruded through narrow slits in a curved iron guard. The COTTON BOLLS were fed against the guard and the revolving wire teeth pulled the fibres through the slits. The seeds, being wider, could not pass through the slits and fell into a box. The cotton fibres were swept off the wire teeth by contra-rotating brushes. The loose cotton was then compressed into bales in a separate operation. The seeds were sent for oil extraction, and the remaining meal used for cattle feed. Whitney's gin was improved in 1796 by Hogden Holmes who replaced the wire teeth by circular saws.

The cotton gin steadily reduced the cost of raw cotton as its use spread over the southern States of America, by reducing the labour cost of seed removal and raising output. This was reflected in lower yarn costs and hence the lower cost of finished cloth, which in turn resulted in increased demand for cotton fabrics worldwide.

cottoning an old name to describe the raising of a down or nap on the surface of a cloth. Other names for the process were friezing, or rowing.

'Cotton is king' famous quotation taken from a speech made by Senator James Henry Hammond (1807–64) of South Carolina in the US Senate on 4 March 1858. The relevant passage runs: 'Sir, you dare not make war on cotton. No power on earth dares make war upon it. Cotton is king. Until lately the Bank of England was king, but she tried to put her screws as usual, the Fall before last, upon the cotton crop, and was utterly vanquished. The last power has been conquered.' The speaker probably took his quotation from a book published in Cincinnati in 1855 entitled *Cotton is King; or Slavery in the Light of Political Economy* by David Christy. 'Cotton is king' is also attributed to Governor Manning in a speech at Columbia, South Carolina, USA, also in 1858.

cotton mill usually a cotton spinning factory, although some mills have weaving sheds attached, in which case the end product is completed cloth, not yarn only. Cotton mills are found mainly in south Lancashire, neighbouring parts of Yorkshire, north Cheshire, parts of Derbyshire, and Lanarkshire in Scotland. In the early days of the Industrial Revolution, mills were sited on fast running streams and rivers from which power was obtained by WATERWHEELS. Early mills were usually built of stone with wooden floors, a few storeys high; they were narrow, and built long enough to house the number of machines to be accommodated. Since they were almost always sited away from towns where water power was available, mill owners frequently had to build houses nearby to attract labour. Examples of such industrial villages may be found at Cromford, Derbys., built in the 18th century by Richard Arkwright (1732–92), and at Styal, Ches., built by Samuel Greg (1758–1834) in the 1820s.

With the development of the steam engine, mills no longer had to depend on water power, and tended to be erected near coalfields for the economic supply of fuel. The high risk of fire suffered by early mills was overcome by the development of the fire-resistant design pioneered by William Strutt (1756–1830) of Belper, Derbys., at the end of the 18th century. Building construction improved, spans increased, and mills were now being erected in what became the textile towns of the Industrial Revolution, each mill surrounded by streets of terraced houses put up by speculative builders. Many mills in the early 19th century had their own gas-making plant to provide lighting during the hours of darkness.

By the mid-19th century spinning mills had reached large sizes and were the largest industrial buildings of that time, housing many thousands of spindles each, turning out enormous quantities of cotton yarn of various COUNTS for the home and export markets. Many mills were built in pairs with a common, centrally placed engine house. Often, only one mill and engine house were built at first, with space alongside for extension. If business prospered, the second (often identical) mill was built to complete the pair, and the engine capacity was increased to suit, space having been left in the original engine house for this eventuality. The mills were then known as mill no. 1 and mill no. 2. *See also* SPINNING MILL, WEAVING PROCESSES.

Holden, R.N. 'Structural engineering in the Lancashire cotton spinning mills 1850–1914: the example of Stott & Sons', *Industrial Archaeology Review* XV (1993), 160–76

Nasmith, J. and F. *Recent Cotton Mill Construction and Engineering*, 3rd edn, Nasmith and Heywood, 1909

Sington, T. *Cotton Mill Planning and Construction*, 1897

Williams, M. with Farnie, D.A. *Cotton Mills in Greater Manchester*, Carnegie, 1992

Cottonopolis sobriquet by which Manchester was known in the mid-19th century, reflecting its status as the centre of the British cotton industry and trade. Disraeli called the city the great metropolis of labour.

cotton picking removal of COTTON BOLLS from the cotton plant, a manual operation demanding great dexterity and keen eyesight until it was mechanized in the 1960s. It was repetitive and laborious, and until the end of the Civil War in America in 1865, was performed by slaves on the cotton plantations of the southern States. The crop had to be gathered in quickly after the bolls opened, otherwise they were spoiled by being over-dried in the hot sun. A picker had to grasp the whole of the cotton of each boll with his or her fingers and bring it away cleanly without also bringing any of the boll pod or leaves, which were difficult to remove subsequently, and which added to the unwanted rubbish in the crop.

A picker could pick about 100 lb of cotton in a day, although up to 1,000 lb per week were picked by slaves. After picking, the bolls were ginned in a COTTON GIN to remove the seeds etc., and then compressed into bales for transport, which, in the early days of the plantations, was by steam-driven paddle boats down nearby rivers to ports such as Savannah in Georgia or Charleston in South Carolina.

cottons in the 17th century and earlier, a word used for woollen cloth; later, it came to mean fabrics made from the cotton plant. The early meaning of cottons is probably a corruption of the word 'coatings', a collective word for woollen materials used for making coats. Later, cottons was properly applied to materials made from the fibres of the cotton plant. This change of meaning over time has been the cause of confusion in the reading of old documents.

Cotton Supply Association a 19th-century pressure group aiming to reduce Britain's dependence on American cotton. The Association was formed in 1857 by several Manchester cotton men, who were concerned at the country's dependence on America alone for cotton supplies. They advocated that the Indian colony should be developed as an alternative source of supply, and tried to force the Government to do so. Their efforts were unsuccessful, mainly because of the depressed state of the Indian economy, together with the fact that cotton growing in India was languishing because Indian hand spinners and weavers could not compete against the cheap, machine-made cotton goods that were flooding into the country from Britain – goods made almost exclusively from American cotton. The Association's fears were realized when the American Civil War broke out in 1861, and the interruption in raw cotton supplies led to the COTTON FAMINE in Britain. Great attempts were then made to import more cotton from India, particularly from Surat, but the quality was extremely poor and almost unworkable. Soon after American supplies were restored, the Association, realizing it was having no success in its aims, dissolved in 1872. The Association was also known as the Manchester Cotton Association.

Silver, A. *Manchester Men and Indian Cotton, 1847–1872*, Manchester University Press, 1966

cotton-wool the name first given to the fluffy woolly fibres of the COTTON BOLL. A report from a British agent of the Merchant Adventurers in Persia (now Iran) as early as the 1580s spoke of a 'little tree' which grew a substance 'like a fleece of wool'. Raw cotton was first imported into Britain from the Levant around the middle of the 17th century in small quantities. The name cotton-wool was therefore given to what was then a new and strange material, to differentiate it from indigenous sheep's wool with which people were then familiar, and which the new material resembled; in time, the material became known simply as cotton.

What is called cotton-wool today is a loose mat of bleached cotton lightly pressed into sheets. It has many medical, industrial and other uses.

coucher man who lays the wet, pulpy sheets of hand-made paper onto woollen felts before they are pressed; the name comes from the French *coucher*, meaning to lay down.

couching (or flooring) the spreading of steeped barley in a malting so that germination can take place. The barley is laid to a depth of 12–14 in, and is occasionally turned to ensure aeration. The term is also used in PAPER MAKING for the process of laying paper onto felt for pressing.

count in textiles, a way of denoting the size of a yarn or thread by a number. Usually a count is given by the number of units of length in a unit of weight, although for some materials the reverse method is adopted. The unit of length and weight vary in some districts, and also for the material being measured. The nomenclature

also depends on whether single ply yarn is being described, or multi-ply yarn.

The units used for single ply yarns are as follows:

(a) *Cotton.* The unit of length is the hank of 840 yards, and that of weight is one lb or 7,000 grains. (A reel used for measuring lengths of cotton in hanks of 840 yards, made by Richard Arkwright (1732–92), is in the Science Museum, London.) If one hank of cotton yarn weighs 1 lb its count is said to be No. 1. Similarly if 20 hanks weigh 1 lb, the yarn count is 20, known as 20s. A hank is subdivided into 7 leas, i.e. 1 lea is 120 yd long, and an alternative method to obtain the count of a yarn is to weigh 1 lea in grains and divide by 1,000. Low counts indicate coarse yarns, high counts indicate fine yarns. Roughly, coarse yarns have counts up to around 24s, medium counts lie between 25s and 50s, while counts above 50 are classed as fine. An incredibly fine thread of 800s was prepared by a Bolton firm for the Great Exhibition of 1851, but was unfortunately destroyed in a fire before being shown. The thread was respun but too late for the exhibition. Since that date even finer threads have been spun, up to 2,000s. Bolton mills specialized in fine spinning, and counts of 50s and above were once referred to as Bolton counts. An idea of the fineness of a high count is shown by the fact that 1 lb of cotton spun to 250s would stretch 119 miles! Early cotton spinning machines could only produce coarse yarns; finer yarns came with improvements in preparation processes and better spinning machinery. The source of raw cotton also controls the degree of fineness that can be spun.

(b) *Wool.* In Yorkshire, the unit of length is the skein which equals 256 yd, and the unit of weight is 1 lb. In the West of England woollen area, the unit of length is the snap of 20 yd and that of weight is 1 oz, i.e. there are 320 yd to the lb.

(c) *Worsted.* Counts are given by the number of hanks of 560 yd per lb.

(d) *Linen.* Counts are given by the number of leas of 300 yd per lb.

(e) *Silk.* Hanks of 840 yd and a unit weight of 1 lb are used.

(f) *Jute.* The count is obtained by dividing the number of yards of yarn which weigh 1 lb into 14,400, this latter figure being a length of 14,400 yd and called a spyndle.

(g) *Flax.* This is measured in leas, obtained by dividing the number of yards of yarn which weigh 1 lb by 300, i.e. if 900 yd of a flax yarn weigh 1 lb, then it has a lea count or number of 3.

(h) *Hemp*. The count or number is obtained by dividing the number of yards of hempen thread which weigh 1 lb by 4.5, i.e. if 90 yd of hemp weigh 1 lb, then it has a count or number of 20.

Where the yarn is multi-ply, an extra number is added to the count number. For cotton and wool, multi-ply yarn is indicated by prefixing the number of single component yarns in the build up, e.g. 2/10 indicates 2-ply or doubled yarn, each ply being of 10s count. Similarly, 3/20 indicates three components of 20s count, etc. For silk, the reverse nomenclature to cotton and wool is used for multi-filament threads, e.g. 30/2 means 2 components of 30s count twisted together.

counter-faller wire a horizontal wire which is positioned across the spindles of a MULE spinning machine to guide the yarn as it is wound onto the spindle to form a cop. It works in conjunction with a FALLER WIRE. Both wires are arranged to rise and fall to spread the yarn evenly along the length of the spindle. The faller wire guides the yarn down the spindle, and the counter-faller wire guides it up the spindle. *See also* QUADRANT.

countershaft an intermediate shaft interposed between the driving shaft and the driven shaft of a geared system or belt drive. It is used to obtain a larger speed ratio than would be possible without it, or in places where it is impossible or impractical to connect the driving and driven shafts directly. Here, the prefix 'counter' has the meaning of reciprocity, i.e. the countershaft takes the drive from the main shaft and transmits it on to other parts of the system. Is sometimes known as a lay shaft, or SECOND MOTION SHAFT.

counting house a room, or sometimes a separate building, which is part of a mill, warehouse or factory, for keeping commercial accounts of the business. Here, activities such as book-keeping, correspondence, and payment of wages were carried out. The manager's or mill-owner's private office usually adjoined the counting house.

country rock a lead mining term for the valueless rock forming the walls etc. of a mineral LODE or vein.

coupling usually, a pair of metal parts for joining together two rotating shafts to convey motion and power from one to the other. With the development of machinery during the Industrial Revolution, the need to join rotating parts arose. For instance, in the textile industry as factories grew in size, LINESHAFTING was introduced to drive rows of machines, and lengths of shafting had to be joined together to reach the end of the row. Several types of coupling were developed to suit different situations. For joining shafts which are exactly in line, rigid couplings are used; these may be either flanged, or box or muff type. Flanged couplings comprise a pair of circular disks, one of each secured to the ends of the shafts, and joined by a ring of bolts. The muff or box coupling comprises a sleeve covering the join between the shafts, and keyed to each. When the shafts are not exactly in line, or vibration may be present, flexible couplings are used which have an elastic member interposed between a pair of flanges, such as a rubber disk, which takes up the slight misalignment or absorbs the vibration.

For shafts which intersect at an angle, the universal coupling, or Hooke's Joint, is used. This type was invented as long ago as 1676 by Robert Hooke (1635–1703), and comprises fitting a Y-shaped piece or yoke to the end of each shaft. The arms of each yoke enclose a cruciform component which swivels between them, transmitting the motion across the inclination between the shafts. Some couplings need to be disengaged so that the drive from one shaft to another may be interrupted at will. This is achieved by arranging for one half of the coupling to slide axially away from the other. When engaged, a ring of protruding teeth on one half mate with a similar set of teeth on the other to transmit the motion. Such a coupling is called a claw coupling although it is better described as a CLUTCH. An OLDHAM COUPLING can join two shafts which are parallel but not in line.

coupling rod the metal bar or link which connects the driving wheels together on a steam locomotive so that they rotate in unison. The coupling rod is fastened to a projecting pin on each driving wheel on the same side of the locomotive, the pins being a short radial distance from the axle of each wheel. As the wheels rotate, the pins describe circular paths but the coupling rod maintains an oscillating horizontal line, the pins turning within the rod to allow this to happen. The purpose of the coupling rods is to spread the TRACTIVE EFFORT of the engine over all the driving wheels and so increase the adhesion to the smooth rails. The more wheels coupled together, the greater the effect and less chance of the wheels slipping on the rails.

The advantage of coupling the driving wheels together was soon realized when multi-wheeled locomotives were developed. George Stephenson's (1781–1848) *Locomotion No. 1* was built with coupling rods in 1825; before this chains or toothed gearing were used to connect the wheels together.

course a horizontal row of stitches across the width of a knitted fabric. It may be regarded as equivalent to the WEFT in a woven fabric, and like the weft is sometimes known as the filling. The opposite to a course is a WALE.

'Cousin Jack' collective name given to those Cornish miners who emigrated in the 18th and 19th centuries to places such as North America and Australia. The main reason for emigration was the decline in the Cornish mining industry. In the States they helped to set up early mining concerns, erected steam engines, and so on. The discovery of lead and copper in South Australia in the 1840s and gold in the 1850s attracted others, and it is said that almost every Cornish mining family had a 'cousin Jack' overseas by the 1880s.

Payton, P.J. *The Cornish Miner in Australia: Cousin Jack Down Under*, Dyllansow Truran, 1988

coutil a close-woven kind of canvas used for mattresses and pillows in the 1850s. The term comes from the French *coutelle*, meaning twill or drill.

cow, *see* COE

Cowper stove an air pre-heater used on iron BLAST FURNACES and glass melting furnaces, patented by Edward Alfred Cowper (1819–93) in 1857 (patent no. 1404), and based on Frederick Siemens' 1856 patent (no. 2861). It comprised a tall metal tower almost filled with brick CHECKERS but with a passageway down one side. Air on its way to the furnace was directed up through the checkers and down through the passageway, leaving the stove at the bottom. Valves controlled the air flow at inlet and outlet of the tower. The stoves worked in pairs, and hot exhaust gases from the furnace were directed through one stove, heating up the checkers. At the same time ambient temperature air was passed through the other stove which had previously been heated up by the exhaust gases as they passed through it. The fresh air picked up heat from the hot checkers, which were cooled in the process, and after a while, the air and gas flows were interchanged, so that the new incoming air was continually being heated by the residue heat left by the exhaust gases. Cowper stoves are regenerative heat exchangers, and their introduction enabled higher temperatures to be reached in the furnace, made use of waste heat raising the thermal efficiency of the system, and economized on fuel. Modern designs are still in use.

crab (or crabb) a small winch or capstan for lifting or hauling along heavy loads. Sometimes a crab takes the form of a three-legged tripod or

frame with a lifting block at its highest point. The mechanical advantage is obtained by a system of gearing, arranged so that a small effort acting through a long distance moves a large load through a short distance.

cranes and hoists mechanical devices for raising and lowering heavy loads. Cranes date from very early days, the first ones being powered by human or animal effort. Treadmill cranes, in which the mechanical advantage is obtained from the difference in diameter between the large wheel 'trod' by men or animals and the much smaller axle onto which the lifting rope or chain is wound, date from Roman times. A 17th-century crane of this type, dating from 1666, is preserved at Harwich, Essex, and comprises two 16 ft diameter wooden wheels mounted on a wooden axle, the lifting rope winding onto the latter between the two wheels. This crane was formerly sited at a naval harbour. Men trod inside the wheel to operate the crane, walking in one direction to raise the load, and in the other to control the lowering. Smaller treadmill cranes were often installed in early warehouses.

Leonardo da Vinci (1452–1519) designed cranes, and Georgius Agricola (Georg Bauer) (1494–1555) illustrated a crane driven by a 36 ft diameter overshot reversible waterwheel in his book *De Re Metallica*, published in 1556. Water-powered cranes were in common use in warehouses during the early 19th century, being brought into action by means of a band CLUTCH or slack belt drive from the constantly rotating waterwheel. Similar devices were used for sack hoists in corn mills, either water- or wind-powered.

Some 19th-century textile mills and warehouses used simple horse-operated cranes. These usually comprised a swivelling iron crane jib mounted above the highest access door, with a pulley mounted at or near ground level immediately below the crane. A pulley BLOCK was attached to the jib, and the rope brought down to the lower pulley, wrapped round it and attached to a horse. To raise goods, the horse was led away from the bottom pulley, and backed towards it for lowering. The mechanical advantage was obtained by the number of sheaves in the lifting block.

When reliable metal gearwheels became available, winches were added to hand cranes. This type of crane was to be found in workshops, on canal wharfs, in warehouses, etc. The winch was mounted at waist height on the vertical rotatable post of the crane, and the crane jib could sometimes be derricked or luffed to vary its radius of action, altering its inclination by lengthening or shortening the tie ropes. Ratchets in the winding mechanism of the winch prevented the load from descending accidentally during lifting, and a hand-operated hand brake controlled lowering. Cranes on board ships became known as derricks from their similarity to the hangman's gallows, taking their name from that of a notorious Tyburn executioner of c.1600.

Swivelling iron wall cranes or JIGGERS mounted outside warehouses date from the late 18th century. Hydraulic power was frequently used in the 19th century to operate them; portable hydraulic cranes were used in the construction of the Forth bridge in the 1890s. Steam cranes were first recommended by John Rennie (1791–1821) in 1808 for London Docks, and were introduced there a few years later, replacing the horse- and man-powered cranes formerly used.

The overhead travelling crane used in engineering workshops, storage yards, etc., is usually credited to Johann Georg Bodmer (1786–1864) a Swiss engineer working in England, who erected one in Bolton, Lancs. c.1816. Also known as a shop traveller, it comprised a winch running on rails along a transverse girder which itself could be moved longitudinally along the length of the workshop, running on rails supported by a row of columns along each long wall. The crane hook could thus be moved around the workshop floor.

Electrically powered cranes were introduced in the 1890s and electricity soon became the normal power source. In addition to cranes on fixed sites, there are mobile cranes, cranes temporarily erected on building and civil engineering sites, dockside cranes running on tracks, tracklaying and breakdown cranes for use on railways, and so on. Smaller lifting devices include travelling hoists suspended from overhead girders positioned over process plants, and CAT HEADS protruding from buildings, etc.

crank an arm attached at right angles to a shaft, which may be used to rotate the shaft or to convert a circular motion into a reciprocating one. A crank may be single, as in (a), when it is at the end of a shaft, or double, as in (b), when it is partway along a shaft or axle:

In a steam engine, a crank is turned by the motion of a connecting rod pivoting on a crankpin. Example (a) is typical for a crank on a stationary steam engine, whilst (b) is typical for that of a locomotive with inside cylinders, the connecting rod working in the space between the two crank arms. The turning effort produced by a crank varies from zero when it is

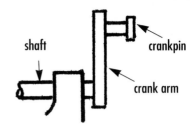

(a) *Single crank*

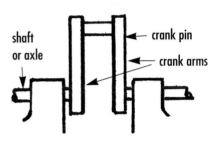

(b) *Double crank*

directly in line with the piston rod, to a maximum when it is at right angles to it. When crank and piston rod are in line, the crank is said to be on a DEAD CENTRE, and it is impossible to start a single cylinder engine from rest when this occurs. Engines with two cylinders have their cranks set at 90° to each other so that starting is always possible.

High speed engines may have a crank in the form of a solid disk instead of an arm, with the crankpin projecting at a radius from the centre; this is known as a disk crank. The disk is hollowed out around the crankpin so that the area diametrically opposite acts as a counter-balance weight for the pin and part of the connecting rod. A return crank is a short crank fixed at a backwards looking angle outside the main crank of a locomotive with outside cylinders, to act as an eccentric for WALSCHAERT VALVE GEAR.

It was James Pickard's patenting of a crank mechanism in 1780 that led James Watt to invent the SUN AND PLANET MOTION.

craunch, *see* RIDER (2)

crazing mill an early type of ore crushing machine resembling the horizontal stones of a corn mill: tinstone, for example, was crushed between the stones.

creel a framework for holding a large number of bobbins on a spinning frame or other textile machine. In particular, a creel holding several hundred bobbins is used when a WARP BEAM is built up, the individual threads being wound onto the beam to construct the warp pattern of the cloth to be woven. A creel is also known as a spool rack or a bank.

creel alley the access walkway between the backs of a pair of spinning MULES, which are always arranged back-to-back. This space allows the BOBBINS of ROVINGS to be replenished as required.

creosote a wood preservative, or an antiseptic. There are two kinds of creosote, one made from the distillation of wood-tar, the other from coal-tar. Creosote from wood-tar is a colourless oily liquid, mostly phenols, which has antiseptic properties; discovered by Reichenbach in 1832, it was once used extensively for medical purposes. The other, better known creosote from coal-tar is a dark brown oil, largely composed of hydrocarbons, and mainly used for preserving timber. One example is the impregnation of wooden railway sleepers which was introduced in the 1840s, replacing the KYANIZING process.

cretonne a type of cloth having a hemp WARP and a linen WEFT; it is named after the village of Creton in Normandy, France, which was famous for its linens.

croft, *see* BLEACH CROFT

croft breaking the stealing of cloth from the BLEACH CROFTS or fields, which was a penal offence in the days when bleaching was done by this method. The penalty for croft breaking was frequently death by hanging; a man was convicted and hanged at Newton Heath, Manchester, for stealing cloth as late as 1798. Bleach crofts were guarded by watchmen, and in some cases protected by hidden mantraps and spring guns.

crofter in textile districts, a person engaged in the bleaching of cloth by the old method of spreading it out on a field, or BLEACH CROFT, to be bleached naturally by long exposure to the sun.

crook string the cord used in a WINDMILL to adjust and set the angle and direction of the chute down which grain flows into the eye or centre of the grinding stones.

cropping frame a machine for cutting the raised nap on woollen cloth to a uniform length to give a smooth surface. The first powered cropping or shearing frame was invented in 1787 by Enoch and James Taylor, of Marsden, near Huddersfield, Yorks. It was in effect the mechanical operation of two pairs of hand shears mounted on a wooden frame side by side, and made to open and shut by arms moved by an underneath crankshaft, belt-driven from an overhead lineshaft. The woollen cloth was stretched out just below the shears over rollers at each end of the frame. One roller was slowly turned by belts driven off the crankshaft, pulling the cloth off the other roller which was held back by a simple friction brake. As the cloth passed under the shears, the nap was cropped by them.

Cropping frames were greatly resented by the hand croppers and many were destroyed in the Huddersfield district by LUDDITES in the riots of 1812. The Luddites had a 'Croppers' Song', which included the verses:

Come, cropper lads of high renoun,
Who love to drink good ale that's brown,
And strike each haughty tyrant down,
With hatchet, pike, and gun!

Oh, the cropper lads for me,
Who with lusty stroke,
The shear frames broke,
The cropper lads for me.

Great Enoch still shall lead the van,
Stop him who dare! Stop him who can!
Press forward every gallant man,
With hatchet, pike, and gun!

'Great Enoch' was a large sledgehammer carried by the Luddites in their raids for breaking up the frames, sardonically named after the principal inventor of the frame, Enoch Taylor.

crossbred wool wool from a class of sheep which gives fibres of medium fineness and length.

cross compound a steam engine which has two cylinders arranged side-by-side, rather than in line. One cylinder takes steam direct from the boiler at high pressure, and after expanding it to a lower pressure, passes it across to the other, low pressure cylinder. The cylinders are sized so that each does the same amount of work, which is transmitted to a crank in each case. The flywheel is centrally placed between the two cranks and is therefore balanced. Cross-compound engines were built for a range of powers, and were very reliable and steady in operation. The cranks were set at 90° to each other so that the engine could not stop on DEAD CENTRE, which eased restarting. Wide flywheels were possible because of the balanced running, which permitted a large number of driving ropes to be accommodated. *See also* COMPOUNDING (1), and Fig. 20b.

crossed belt a power transmission belt connecting two pulleys in such a way that it crosses over in the space between the two pulleys so as to reverse the direction of rotation of the second pulley with respect to the first. For flat driving belts, the belt turns through 180° as it crosses between the pulleys, so that the same side passes round each pulley in turn. The converse is an open belt which does not cross over, and hence both pulleys rotate in the same direction.

crosshead a sliding part which supports the outer end of a piston rod in a steam engine mechanism. It runs in a straight line on crosshead guides or slide bars, and the connecting rod is pivoted to it and free to swing through a small arc as the crank rotates. If the engine always rotates in the same direction, the crosshead may slide to and fro on a bottom guide only, but if the engine is a reversing type, guides top and bottom are needed since the vertical pressure exerted by the crosshead also reverses. Alternatively, the crosshead may slide on a rod instead of between bars. It is also known as a motion block.

cross-over bridge, *see* ROVING BRIDGE

cross-sticks, *see* LEASE

crotch spindle, *see* QUANT

crown glass a leadless GLASS made from small thin disks from the 16th century. Until about the mid-19th century, most window glass in Britain was of this kind. It was made by first blowing a hollow glass globe attached to a metal rod or a PONTIL, then reheating it and rapidly spinning the globe about the pontil until it collapsed into a flat disk under the influence of the centrifugal force induced. Panes of clear glass were cut from the disk: the blemish at the centre where the pontil was attached became the 'bull's-eye' pane often seen in the windows of old buildings. The clear panes were restricted in size (the maximum was about 24 x 15 in), which explains why window panes in old buildings are small if made from crown glass. The name crown glass came from the trade mark in the form of a crown which John Bowles, an early manufacturer of this kind of glass, embossed in the centre of each pane he made in his London glasshouse. An alternative name was Normandy glass.

In the mid-19th century crown glass began to be superseded by PLATE GLASS which enabled larger panes to be made. *See also* CYLINDER GLASS.

crown wheel 1. in a windmill, the geared wheel on the main vertical shaft from which drives to operate other parts of the machinery are taken. **2.** the larger geared wheel of a BEVEL pair.

crucible steel a CAST STEEL made by a process invented by Benjamin Huntsman (1704–76) about 1740–2 in Handsworth near Sheffield, Yorks. Huntsman made his steel in secret and did not patent the process. Originally a clockmaker in Doncaster, he developed the process since he was dissatisfied with the steel then available for making clock springs and pendulums. Crucible steel was made by melting pieces of BLISTER STEEL, previously made from Swedish BAR IRON, together with a FLUX, in sealed clay pots or crucibles, for three to four hours in coke fired crucible furnaces or 'holes'. The crucibles were made from fireclay, china clay, and coke dust, mixed with water and kneaded by prolonged treading in a floor tray similar to the way in which grapes are trodden. The clay 'dough' was then moulded into crucible shape and fired in an oven. A crucible only lasted for two or three heats, so a continuous supply was needed. The prolonged melting of the blister steel resulted in a more homogeneous metal structure and enabled it to be cast into an ingot by lifting the crucible out of the furnace by tongs, and hand teeming the molten metal into a vertical mould; the ingots were then reduced in cross-section under TILT HAMMERS to the required shape. Huntsman's process thus produced cast steel for the first time. At first, Huntsman's crucibles only held some 6–8 lb of steel, but later up to 60 lb were being melted in one crucible (the maximum weight a man could handle), and steel ingots weighing several tons were cast by teeming very many crucibles into one mould. The carbon content of crucible steel varied from around 0.8 per cent up to 1.5 per cent depending on its intended purpose.

Crucible steel became a speciality of Sheffield where it was used for making scythes, various edge cutting tools, clock and watch springs, razors, files, dies, and quality cutlery (although at first Sheffield cutlers refused to use Huntsman's steel!). The process was costly but for well over a century it remained the only way of making a high grade cast steel until other methods superseded it, and it is no longer used today. By the late 18th century cast steel was being made by others, both in England and on the Continent. John Marshall of Sheffield was another producer who enjoyed a high reputation almost equal to that of Huntsman and his successors. *See also* STEEL MANUFACTURE.

Barraclough, K.C. *Benjamin Huntsman (1706–1776)*, Sheffield City Libraries, 1976

Peatman, J. 'The Abbeydale Industrial Hamlet: history and restoration', *Industrial Archaeology Review* XI (1989), 141–54

crutch pole, *see* QUANT

Crystal Palace large hall designed by Joseph Paxton (1803–65) to house the GREAT EXHIBITION OF 1851 in London. It was an enormous iron and glass conservatory-type exhibition hall, 1848 ft long by 408 ft wide, with a central transept 72 ft wide by 108 ft high; Paxton's design, for which he was knighted, was chosen from 246 entries in the design competition for an exhibition hall. The Crystal Palace comprised 9,642 tons of cast iron columns and wrought iron girders, and about 25 acres of glass held in wooden glazing bars of Paxton's patented ridge and furrow design; its arches were also made from wood. The building cost £1.5 million, and was financed by private subscriptions and the Bank of England. It was rapidly erected as a temporary building in Hyde Park, London, by the Birmingham firm of Fox, Henderson, railway contractors, in a little over six months from prefabricated parts. The name Crystal Palace was conferred by the magazine *Punch*.

After the closure of the exhibition, the Crystal Palace was dismantled and re-erected with considerable extension in size with two extra transepts, on Sydenham Hill, south London. Extensive ornamental gardens and lakes were constructed around it, and water towers, 282 ft high, were built at each end to supply water for fountains in the grounds. Officially opened in 1854, it had many educational, leisure, and cultural uses until a disastrous fire destroyed it during the night of 30 November 1936; only the two towers survived, and they were later demolished in 1941.

Buchanan, A., Jones, S.K. and Kiss, K. 'Brunel and the Crystal Palace', *Industrial Archaeology Review* XVII (1994), 7–21
Chadwick, G.F. *The Works of Sir Joseph Paxton*, Architectural Press, 1961
Enefer, T. 'The great men and the gardener who built the Crystal Palace', *The Valuer*, October 1988
Hobhouse, C. *1851 and the Crystal Palace*, John Murray, 1950

Crystal Palace Exposition, *see* NEW YORK WORLD FAIR, 1853

Cuba wood, *see* FUSTIC

cubilow a rarely used old word for a ventilation shaft from underground workings, taken from the French for a cupola or shaft furnace.

cudbear a vegetable dye made from varieties of lichens of the *lecanora* species which grow on the west coasts of Scotland. The dye, which produces shades from blue to pink, was developed in Scotland in 1758 by George and Gordon Cuthbert; the name is a corruption of their surname.

cullet broken glass, which may be wastage from the blowing process, damaged items, or scrap glass; it is added to new raw materials to assist in manufacture of new glass. The word comes from the French *coulé*, meaning cast.

cullin stone a variety of solid millstone once imported from Germany, south of Köln (Cologne). It is a basaltic lava, blue in colour, and was quarried in the Eifel region. Cullin (or cullen) is an English corruption of Köln. Cullin millstones were used up until about 1800, when French BURRS became available in Britain.
Major, J. Kenneth. 'The manufacture of millstones in the Eifel region of Germany', *Industrial Archaeology Review* VI (1982), 194–204

culm (or calum) coal dust or slack, frequently used to fuel lime kilns and malt drying kilns.

cup bearing, *see* FOOTSTEP BEARING

cupellation a process used in silver recovery from lead. The argentiferous lead is melted in a shallow dish, called a cupel, and oxidized by an air blast; the silver is not oxidized and remains in the cupel.

cup leather a sealing component usually made from soft leather and shaped like a cup, secured on the end of a plunger or ram in hydraulic and pneumatic equipment. The back of the cup leather is held against the plunger by a JUNK RING, and the cup sides are pressed against the cylinder bore by the pressure of the working fluid thus preventing leakage past the cup, whilst permitting movement of the plunger in the cylinder. Cup leathers were in use in the early 18th century.

cupola furnace 1. a vertical, shaft-type metal-melting furnace, similar to a BLAST FURNACE but smaller. It is used for remelting cast-iron pigs sometimes with scrap iron added, for the production of iron castings, and is an essential part of an iron foundry. The word comes from the Latin *cupula* for a small cask or barrel. Cupola furnaces usually had cold air blast only. **2.** a low-arched REVERBERATORY lead smelting furnace introduced in Derbyshire *c.*1735.

cupola kiln a type of kiln used in the clay industry, circular in plan with a domed top and a central chimney. It works on the down-draught principle.

cushioning preventing shock as a piston completes its stroke. In a steam engine, the exhaust valve is closed just before the piston reaches the end of its stroke, leaving a small amount of steam trapped in the CLEARANCE. This steam is compressed as the stroke is completed, creating a BACK PRESSURE which helps to bring the piston gradually to rest before it commences its return stroke. This cushioning effect gives smoother running of the engine, hence its name. The raising of pressure is accompanied by a rise in temperature of the trapped steam, and this helps to heat up the cylinder walls which have just been cooled by the exhausting steam.

cushion lace, *see* BOBBIN LACE

cut 1. an old name, still sometimes used today, for a canal; canal workmen were once known as cutters. **2.** a standard length of linen equal to 300 yd. **3.** a piece or length, usually 20–30 yd long, of woven cloth cut from the CLOTH BEAM of a handloom and normally representing a week's work for the weaver. The yarn was often the property of the CLOTHIER. **4.** another name for a LEAT.

cutch the commercial name for the natural dye and tanning substance catechu. It is obtained from the tree *Acacia catechu* found in India and Malaya and was first imported from there into England in the 17th century. Early users wrongly thought it was an earth, and for a while it was known as *Terra Japonica*. The bark and fruit of the tree contain 40–55 per cent tannin, and it dyes cloth brown. Alternative old spellings of cutch are cotch and cacha, all derived from the Malayan *kacha*.

cutlery manufacture making metal knives and edge cutting tools. Table cutlery only became common in England during the 17th century, but edge cutting steel tools such as shears, scissors, scythes, etc. had been made for many years before this period. In Sheffield, a Cutlers Guild Company was founded in 1624, and by the 18th century the town had become the centre of the industry, although some cutlery was also made in Birmingham. Sheffield was a natural site for steel making with easy access to timber for charcoal making, water power for driving tilt hammers used in steel making, and millstone grit for making the grinding wheels needed to sharpen the cutting edges.

At first, the industry was a domestic one, with small workshops attached to the dwellings of self-employed master cutlers. Swedish and Russion irons were imported and brought to the town via the Humber, Ouse and Don rivers. The iron was converted into steel by the CEMENTATION PROCESS, and around 1740, Benjamin Huntsman (1704–76) was making CRUCIBLE STEEL in Sheffield. After some initial reluctance to change, cutlers began using the indigenous steel and foreign imports declined. Cutlery steel is iron with 0.35–1.00 per cent carbon added.

Knife handles were made from natural materials such as wood, horn, etc., but in the early 18th century hollow silver handles, stamped out in two halves, were being made,

the knife blade secured inside the handle with pitch. Less expensive handles made from SHEFFIELD PLATE were introduced in the mid-18th century. The large scale production of scissors began in the 1760s. Large items such as scythes were made with wrought iron blades with a steel strip welded on to give the cutting edge. Grinding the cutting edges was carried out in a workshop called a GRINDING HULL, which was water-powered.

The early 18th-century Abbeydale Industrial Hamlet, Sheffield, is an interesting museum containing a crucible steel furnace and a grinding hull for making scythes. *See also* SCYTHE GRINDING.

Smethurst, P. *The Cutlery Industry*, Shire Publications, Album No. 195, 1987

cut-off 1. point at which the admission of live steam to a steam engine cylinder is stopped by the action of the VALVE GEAR. This is at a fraction of the full stroke of the piston and allows the steam to work expansively for the rest of the stroke. The cut-off is usually expressed as a fraction or percentage of the stroke, and the higher the inlet steam pressure the earlier the cut-off as a rule. The speed of some engines is automatically governed by variation of the cut-off, and locomotives in particular can have their cut-off altered whilst running by means of a LINK MOTION. Cut-off allows the steam to work expansively inside the cylinder for part of the stroke and therefore gives economy of steam consumption. But if the cut-off is made too early, excessive and undesirable condensation of the steam occurs towards the end of the stroke: choice of the point of cut-off is therefore a balance between economy of steam and loss by condensation, and for a D VALVE the optimum point is around two-thirds of the stroke. High speed engines and superheated steam allow earlier cut-offs. The amount of LAP on the valve, and the angular position of the ECCENTRIC operating the valve, regulate the point of cut-off. The point of cut-off was once known as the point of suppression.

2. the shortening of an existing railway route.

cut-off governing a method of controlling the speed of a steam engine. The CUT-OFF point on some stationary steam engines was under the control of a GOVERNOR if the engine had the type of VALVE GEAR which permitted this. The governor could make the cut-off take place earlier or later in the stroke as the engine speed varied. Two examples of valve gear which allowed the cut-off to be varied whilst the engine was running are the MEYER EXPANSION GEAR and CORLISS VALVE. If the load on the engine fell, the speed would increase, the steam inlet pressure remaining constant. This would cause the governor to respond by operating the mechanism on the valve gear so that the inlet steam was cut off earlier, allowing the steam to act more expansively and slow the engine speed down. The reverse happened if the load increased, the governor delaying the cut-off point, and these two actions maintained the engine speed around a mean figure, the variation either side depending on the sensitivity of the governor.

cutting a man-made trough or valley cut through a hill, carrying at its base a railway, road, or canal. A cutting has a horizontal level base in the case of a canal, but may have a gradual gradient in the case of roads and railways. Cuttings are made to level out the passage of roads, railways and canals where hills present obstacles, thereby shortening the route. The opposite of a cutting is an EMBANKMENT.

There are several well-known large cuttings which were dug out in the early days by shovel and wheelbarrow. The Smethick cutting on the Birmingham Canal, completed in 1829 with Thomas Telford (1757–1834) as engineer in charge, is some 70 ft deep. It bypassed six locks on the old route of the canal, saving in distance and time. The Liverpool to Manchester railway entailed making a 70 ft deep cutting in sandstone at Olive Mount, the Liverpool end of the line; it was opened to traffic in 1830. The Sonning cutting in Berkshire, completed in 1840, carries the London to Bristol railway of I.K. Brunel's wide gauge, and is 2 miles long and up to 60 ft deep in parts. A large, hand-cut road cutting is that at Godley just north of Halifax, Yorks., which took three years to complete in the early 1830s. It was made to improve the road for horse-drawn coaches and waggons. Soil and rock 60 ft in depth were removed from a hill, and re-used to embank 0.75 mile in the Shibden valley.

cuttling the folding of finished cloth in a manner suitable for subsequent handling.

cut-ups name given to stockings or other garments made by cutting shapes out of knitted fabric and sewing them together to make the finished article. Cut-ups were first introduced when the thread carrier was invented at the end of the 18th century, which enabled wider fabrics to be knitted than formerly. Known as 'spurious articles' by the frame knitters of FULLY FASHIONED hose, stockings made from cut-ups were made and sold more cheaply. Resentment of cut-up production was one of the causes of the LUDDITE riots, when wide frames in particular were destroyed.

cutwater, *see* STARLING

cylinder 1. a closed chamber with a circular bore, in which a piston or plunger reciprocates. Steam engines and locomotives have cylinders in which power is generated. In pumps fluids are transferred. In a steam engine, one end of the cylinder is closed by a removable cap and the other end by a STUFFING BOX through which the piston rod passes. Steam ports are cast in one side of the cylinder, over which a steam chest is bolted enclosing the valves which admit or exhaust the steam either side of the piston during its stroke. The length of a cylinder bore is slightly more than the combined piston thickness and stroke, to give a small CLEARANCE each end for CUSHIONING the piston. Early cylinders were made in brass, but by *c.*1720 cast iron became the standard material.

The first steam engines had vertical cylinders (i.e. BEAM ENGINE), and for many years there was a prejudice against horizontal cylinders, it being thought that excessive wear on the lower surface of the bore would result from the weight and friction of the moving piston. Robert Stephenson (1803–59) used inclined cylinders in 1828 on locomotives, and by the mid-1800s horizontal cylinders were common. Since the expansion of steam within a cylinder is limited to about three times the inlet volume for technical reasons, large stationary steam engines have more than one cylinder, the steam passing through each cylinder in turn. *See also* COMPOUNDING (1).

2. a square section bar with each face having as many holes as there are NEEDLES in a JACQUARD loom (*see* Fig. 40). The cylinder makes a quarter turn at each pick, swinging away from the needles to allow a fresh punched card to be interposed between it and the rows of needles which it then presses up against. Each face of the cylinder has protruding pegs for accurately locating the cards. The needles enter those holes in the cylinder which coincide with holes in the card, resulting in certain WARP threads being raised. Where there are no holes in the card, the corresponding holes in the cylinder are blanked off, and those warps connected do not move.

cylinder glass flat window glass made by an old method (also known as the broad glass method) dating from *c.*1832, introduced into Britain from Europe. First, a hollow cylinder of glass was blown, then slit longitudinally whilst still molten and opened out and flattened on a table. Contact with the table dulled the surface, and after ANNEALING the glass was ground to make it flatter, and polished to remove the dullness and make it transparent. This method produced glass panes larger than could be made by the older CROWN GLASS method: sizes up to 48 by 36 in were possible. During the Victorian age, cylinder sheet glass making became highly developed, and enabled glass to be more extensively used in buildings: the CRYSTAL PALACE of 1851 used nearly 300,000 panes, all of a standard size, supplied by Chance Brothers of Birmingham. The removal of a tax on glass also encouraged more use of the material. Some fifty years after its introduction into Britain, a mechanical method for making the cylinders was invented. Eventually, cylinder glass was replaced by PLATE GLASS.

D

dabbing brush a component on a wool combing machine, such as the LISTER COMBER, which is positioned above the circular comb and forces the woollen fibres down into the pins of the comb by a rapid up and down motion. When the fibres are subsequently drawn out of the pins, they are combed.

Dacca muslin, see JAMDANI

dam a barrier built to hold back water to form a RESERVOIR. There are two types of dam, the gravity and the arched. The gravity dam is the earlier, and relies on its dead weight for stability. The first gravity dams were built of earth, and were usually straight, with sloping faces on both sides. The side against the water was faced with stone to prevent erosion, and normally a core of puddled clay made the dam watertight. High earth dams have a few level 'steps' formed on the grassed, air side, called berms (from the old Norse *bermr*, meaning a ledge) which lessen the risk of earth slips destroying the dam.

Small, simple earth dams forming hammer ponds were made in the 17th century on the Weald of Kent and Sussex to store water for the old iron making sites. Such dams are known in that area as bays. By the 18th century larger earth dams were being built in textile areas for powering waterwheels and for the cloth finishing industry. Later, gravity dams were made in stone with two outer skins and a rubble and mortar or concrete interior.

Arched masonry or concrete dams were introduced in Britain in the 1860s, originally based on French theory. An arched dam is curved, with the convex side facing the water to resist the water pressure. It acts like an arched bridge lying on its side, directing the compressive thrust onto the abutments at the side of the valley. Arched dams are slimmer than earth dams, although there is an element of gravity resistance to the water pressure also present. They are thicker at the base where the water pressure is greatest. A spillway is provided at one side of a dam to allow excess floodwater and COMPENSATION WATER to pass downstream into the dammed river.

After *c*.1835, local authorities were empowered to construct reservoirs for supplying domestic water to towns, and suitable nearby river valleys were dammed up. Thomas Hawksley (1807–93) was responsible for building many dams for public water supply and constructing water treatment plants.

Binnie, G.M. 'Masonry and concrete dams, 1880–1941', *Industrial Archaeology Review* X (1987), 41–58

Smith, N. *A History of Dams*, Peter Davies, 1971

damask a rich, highly patterned, coloured fabric, originally made in Damascus, Syria. Silk damask was imported in the 17th century and imitation fabrics in linen and cotton were woven in Britain in the 18th and 19th centuries using SATIN and SATEEN weaves so that the pattern contrasted well with the background. Damask was popular for furniture coverings, curtains, table linen, etc.

damper an iron plate which slides in vertical guides built into the flues of a steam BOILER. By adjusting the vertical position of the damper, the size of the flue opening below it regulates the draught at the boiler fire and hence the burning rate. Dampers are usually counterbalanced and may be adjusted by hand from the front of the boiler via a wire rope passing over pulleys. Other types of damper revolve about a central spindle, a design usually employed in circular flues or ducts, the damper blade being a metal disk. This type is also known as a butterfly damper or valve.

damsel a rotating device fastened to the top of the stone spindle in a CORN MILL which vibrates the feed chute to ensure an even flow of grain into the eye of the runner stone. A similar effect is obtained by a curved bar called a clapper which trails on the surface of the rotating runner stone. Damsel is a dialect word of uncertain origin; in some parts of the country, a damsel is called a rattler or a dolly.

dandy cart or waggon a truck for conveying a horse on a horse-worked railway. To increase the effectiveness of horse power in the early days of the Stockton and Darlington Railway, in 1828 George Stephenson introduced four-wheeled low platform trucks, called dandy carts. These were placed at the end of the line of waggons, and after a horse had pulled the train up an incline or on the level, it was trained to climb onto the dandy cart, where a load of hay awaited it, and ride on downhill gradients, resting. This increased the effectiveness of the horse by about one-third, by reducing its workload overall. The idea was soon copied on other railways, including the Ffestiniog, and also in the USA in Pennsylvania. A dandy cart was still in use on the Throckley waggonway, near Newcastle upon Tyne, as late as 1907. On the narrow gauge Ffestiniog Railway, Gwynedd, opened in 1836, loaded trains ran by gravity from the slate quarries at Blaenau Ffestiniog down to Portmadoc. Empties were pulled up by horses who rode down with the loaded trains until 1863, when steam locomotives were introduced.

The vehicle was also known as a horse dolly, and was used at some coal mines where loaded coal trucks could be run downhill towing the horse dolly on which a brakesman and the horse rode. The horse would then pull the empty trucks back up the gradient.

dandy loom a hand loom with a lightweight iron frame. This nickname was given to the newer hand looms introduced c.1820 on account of their neatness and compactness compared with the old heavy wooden framed looms. Dandy looms also incorporated an automatic cloth take-up mechanism, invented by William Radcliffe (1760–1841), which had a RATCHET and PAWL activated by the motion of the SLEY, the pawl moving the front roller a fraction of a turn at each BEATING UP.

A small loom for weaving handkerchiefs was also known as a dandy loom.

dandy roll a roller with a raised design for putting a WATERMARK in the paper made on a Fourdrinier machine, invented by John and Christopher Phipps (patent no. 5075, 1825).

Danish wheel, *see* NORSE WHEEL

Dannemora iron a famous, high quality Swedish iron from the Dannemora iron mine, Osterby, 30 miles north of Upsala. Iron was discovered there in 1448 in a low hill about 2 miles by 0.5 mile wide of almost solid iron ore. The ore was quarried rather than mined, and smelted by charcoal. Production was controlled by the Swedish government's College of Mines from 1740 onwards.

Dannemora iron was imported into Britain in the 18th and 19th centuries and was greatly prized for its purity. An alternative name was Oregrund iron, after the Swedish port from which the iron was exported.

danter a woman who oversaw children winding silk in early 19th century silk mills. The name seems to have been restricted to Cheshire.

Danzic iron, *see* OSMOND IRON

'dark Satanic mills' a line from the poem *Jerusalem* by William Blake (1757–1827), written between 1804 and 1820, and much quoted by later writers to describe industrial conditions in Victorian days. The full verse runs:

> And did the Countenance Divine
> Shine forth upon our clouded hills?
> And was Jerusalem builded here
> Among these dark Satanic mills?

Blake's poem was set to music in 1916 by Sir Hubert Parry (1848–1919).

dashpot a mechanical device for slowing the action of a mechanism. Several sorts have been used, all depending on the resistance offered to rapid motion through a fluid or gas by a piston inside a small cylinder or pot. Air, oil, or some viscous fluid is contained in a small static vessel, and a piston or plunger is attached by linkage to the part(s) which are to be prevented from moving too rapidly. As the piston moves inside the pot, the fluid in which it is placed transfers from one side to the other through a restricted passage, thus creating a resistance and preventing rapid movement of the piston, and hence the mechanism to which it is attached. Dashpots are attributed to James Watt (1736–1819), who used them to control the descent of a valve upon its seat. A dashpot is also called a hydraulic, or air buffer. Sometimes it is designed to operate slowly only in one direction, the reverse action being unimpeded.

dashwheel an early washing machine used in BLEACHING works for washing calico, etc. Some types of dashwheel comprised a wheel with compartments which was driven round, partly in a cistern of running water, with calico pieces placed in each compartment. As the wheel revolved, each piece was alternately dipped into the water and dashed from side to side in its compartment. This washed and rinsed the cloth prior to subsequent processing, which might be printing. Other designs used a jet of clean water which entered each compartment in turn as the wheel revolved. Dashwheels date from the 1730s. It is said that small apprentice boys had to climb inside the compartments to help load the machine in some bleachworks.

Dashwheels were used before and after CHEMICKING to wash the cloth; by the mid-19th century, they were being replaced by more modern washing processes.

dataller a day-wage labourer generally employed at a colliery on maintenance and repair work such as packing waste material into GOAFS, repairing underground roads, etc. It is also spelt day-taler, the word 'tale' having an old meaning of to reckon, i.e. (wage) reckoned by the day.

Davy lamp the miners' safety lamp invented in 1815–16 by Sir Humphry Davy (1778–1829). There was controversy at the time as to whether George Stephenson (1781–1848) had invented his 'GEORDIE' LAMP first, but eventually the Davy lamp became the standard lamp for use at the coal face, giving a superior light. Its success lay in the use of a fine wire gauze cylinder surrounding the naked flame which admitted air, but prevented heat from the flame reaching any FIREDAMP which might be present outside the lamp.

The Davy lamp reduced the number of accidents underground due to explosions, and enabled increased coal output to take place. Its importance led the poet Thomas Moore to allude to it in his poem 'Sylph's Ball', comparing its main feature to the wall which separated Thisbe from her lover Pyramis, who lived next door:

O for that lamp's metallic gauze
That curtain of protecting wire
Which Davy delicately draws
Around illicit, dangerous fire!

The wall he sets 'twixt Flame and Air
(Like that which barred young Thisbe's
      bliss)
Through whose small holes this
      dangerous pair
May see each other, but not kiss.

Davy altruistically did not patent his invention, but in 1817 was presented with a service of plate worth £2,500 by northern coal owners. Davy's lamp was improved in 1840 by Meuseler of Belgium, and was eventually replaced by electric battery lamps.

Griffin, A.R. 'Sir Humphry Davy: His life and work', *Industrial Archaeology Review* IV (1980), 202–13
Treneer, Anne. *The Mercurial Chemist*, 1963

day level, *see* SOUGH

day pit a coal mine which is entered from the surface via a DRIFT MINE and not a shaft. The entrance to the drift was known as a DAY'S EYE.

day's eye a north country dialect name used in mining circles for the exit opening from an ADIT. It is an apt description for the opening leading to the outside world when viewed from inside the adit, with the daylight streaming through. A drainage adit or SOUGH is called a day level in some mining areas, the name being a shortening of day's eye level.

dead centre occurs when a crank of an engine is directly in line with the piston rod. The turning effort of a crank in this position is zero. There are two dead centres in each revolution of a crank. On a horizontal engine, one is when the crank points towards the piston, called the inner dead centre, the other when the crank points away from it, called the outer dead centre. For inverted vertical engines the two positions are called top and bottom dead centres respectively. When an engine is running, the momentum of the flywheel carries it past the dead centres, but if a single-cylinder engine is allowed to stop on a dead centre, it cannot be restarted unless the crank is moved on slightly by some means (*see* BARRING ENGINE). It can, by mistake, be started in reverse, with disastrous results on driven machinery. By having the cranks set 90° from each other, twin-cylinder engines can always be started.

deads unwanted rock or stone sorted from BOUSE in mineral mining. Deads were dumped nearby to form surface spoil heaps, or stacked in the empty spaces underground from which ore had been taken.

deckle the loose wooden frame placed over the wire 'sieve' of a PAPER-MAKING mould to limit the size of the sheet of paper to be made in hand-made paper. The mould and deckle are dipped into the paper vat by the vatman and slowly withdrawn in the horizontal plane with slight shaking movements. The deckle is removed by his assistant and handed back to him for use on a second mould. The word comes from the German *Deckel*, meaning lid or cover.

delaine, *see* MOUSSELINE

delph (or delf) a mine or quarry, usually confined to mean a quarry in the north of England.

denim a coarse cotton DRILL much used for hard-wearing garments such as overalls, trousers, etc. The name is a shortened version of *serge de Nim*, which comes from Nîmes, the town in southern France where this type of fabric originated.

dent one of the thin wires which makes up a REED on a loom, although it can also mean the space between two successive wires in a reed. It has two functions. First, it spaces out the WARP threads or ends to maintain the number of threads per inch required in the cloth construction; thus, the pitch of the dents determines the warp construction. More than one end can be threaded through each dent if required. Secondly, the wire dents push each new pick of WEFT up against the woven cloth to consolidate it when the sley carrying the reed is swung against the cloth, the action being called BEATING UP.

dephlogisticated marine acid a bleaching term used in the 19th century for CHLORINE. Sometimes the word muriatic was used in place of marine.

dephlogistic system an old name given in the 1790s to the BERTHOLLET method of BLEACHING cloth using oxygenated muriatic acid. The name comes from the original name for oxygen given by Joseph Priestley in *c*.1775; he thought oxygen was air minus PHLOGISTON, the latter being a substance which was thought to be the 'principle' of fire, and which was absorbed in air when something was burnt.

deposited plans plans of proposed railways lodged with parliament at the time of applying for an Act to acquire the land and construct the line in accordance with the plans. Copies of the plans were also lodged with the county authorities through which the proposed railway was to run, and with the governing bodies of major towns affected. Such plans may be consulted today in the appropriate county and town archives. Besides showing the route of the railway, they often show nearby buildings etc. and are thus a useful information source for industrial archaeologists.

deputy, *see* FIREMAN

Derby grit, *see* PEAK STONE

Derby rib frame a STOCKING FRAME developed in 1758 by Jedediah Strutt (1726–97) of Derbyshire. It was patented (no. 722) in the names of Strutt and William Woollatt, its main feature being that it could produce ribs on the surface of knitted fabrics. Ribs are made by knitting a plain stocking stitch followed by a purl stitch in sequence, a purl stitch being a reversed or inverted plain stitch. Strutt attached an iron frame containing a row of extra vertical needles to the front of Lee's stocking frame; this acted in between the horizontal needles and reversed every other stitch or loop to create the ribbed effect. The attachment increases the versatility of the stocking frame, and enabled more decorative work to be knitted. The Derby rib frame produced flat work: Matthew Townsend of Leicester invented a circular rib frame in 1847 (patent no. 11899).

devil a 19th-century name for a machine used to recover COP bottoms in the hard cotton waste trade. To save using bobbins or tubes, mule yarns were often spun directly onto spindles, which were covered with a starch paste. The starch hardened, holding the core hole of the cop firm, but that part of the stiffened yarn could not be used for weaving, and was known as the cop bottom. To recover the hard cotton forming the cop bottom, the bottoms were fed into a devil which comprised revolving cylinders covered with teeth which tore up the bottoms into the original fibres. The fibres were then re-carded and re-spun into a coarse yarn. The operator of such a machine was known as a cotton deviller.

The name devil is often used for machines with a destructive action: another example is the flock-making machine used in the SHODDY trade, which grinds up old cloth.

dialing a mining term for surveying; a dial is a miner's magnetic compass.

diaper a woven fabric, usually in linen or cotton, which has small diamond-like or other geometrical patterns woven into it; it is mostly used for table linen. The name possibly comes from *d'Ypres* (or Ypres) – the town in west Flanders, Belgium, which was once famous for its woven linen.

dib hole a sump at the bottom of a mine shaft for collecting drainage water. It would be emptied by pumping the water up to the surface or to a suitable SOUGH.

Diesel engine an internal combustion engine of the COMPRESSION IGNITION type, named after its inventor, Rudolf Diesel (1858–1913) of Germany.

dilly a Northumberland collier's dialect name for a coal waggon. The word is probably an abbreviation of diligence, the name of a four-wheeled stage coach, and carries a sense of speed: the waggon 'speeds' the transport of the coal.

dilving the action of separating TIN particles from waste material by shaking the ore pieces in a canvas sieve in a tub of water. The waste flows over the rim of the sieve, leaving the tin behind. 'Dilleuing' is an alternative Cornish word.

dimity (or dimithy) a strong cotton fabric woven with raised stripes or fancy figures, and popular for quilts and other bedroom fabrics besides garments. The name possibly derives from Damietta, a town on the Nile, Egypt, where this type of cloth was originally made. Alternatively, dimity may indicate that the cloth is woven with two threads to make the stripes, coming from the Greek prefix *di-* or *dis*, meaning twice or double, and another Greek word *mitos*, meaning warp.

dip the inclination of a stratum of rock, coal seam, etc. from the horizontal (*see* Fig. 73). The dip is the complement of the HADE. The angle of dip is measured in the direction of the maximum slope and is indicated on geological maps by a small arrow, the dip arrow, with a figure alongside showing the inclination from the horizontal in degrees. The angle of the dip is the maximum angle between the plane of the seam and the horizontal plane; angles of apparent dip are less than this. In the case of most coal seams, the plane of the seam is near the horizontal, i.e. the angle of dip is small, while metallic ore veins usually lie almost vertically so that the angle of dip approaches 90°. A dip is reversed at a syncline or anticline. Dip is sometimes also given as a gradient.

dipper wheel a driven wheel in a vertical plane with buckets fastened on its periphery, used for lifting TIN-bearing slurry at tin streaming sites to higher levels for further processing of the slurry; it is sometimes called a scoop wheel.

direct-acting engine an engine in which the force from the piston is directed straight onto the crank without the interposing of a beam as in the early BEAM ENGINES. Direct-acting engines transmit their power either via a sliding crosshead and connecting rod, as in the conventional steam engine, or by a trunk piston (*see* TRUNK STEAM ENGINE) as used in most internal combustion engines.

direct process of iron making the old method of making WROUGHT IRON directly from the ore. This was done, for example, at BLOOMERY forges, using CHARCOAL as a fuel to provide the necessary heat for smelting the iron ore until it formed a bloom which was then hammered to expel entrained slag. The direct method generally fell into disuse around the end of the 15th century, but persisted for a while in remote areas; it was replaced by the INDIRECT PROCESS. The Catalan furnace (*see* TROMPE) is another method of obtaining iron by direct reduction. *See also* IRON MANUFACTURE.

discharge bleaching a method of producing a pattern on a coloured cloth by BLEACHING out (discharging) certain areas of colour; it is also known as the Brama method, or the Monteith process, and was invented around the end of the 18th century. The method involves placing a dyed cloth in smooth folds between two thick cast lead plates which are each perforated with the pattern to be produced, the two plates being precisely located so that the perforations are exactly opposite each other. The cloth and plates are then pressed together vertically in a screw or HYDRAULIC PRESS so that wetting of the cloth under the unperforated areas is effectively prevented. Discharging fluid (bleaching powder with an excess of free acid) is poured onto the top plate and filters through the perforations and the stack of cloth folds, bleaching out the colour. When all the colour has been discharged, clear water is passed through, the cloth removed, washed, and finished off. The edges of the bleached out pattern are blurred as a result of capillary action; the greater the pressure used, the less is this effect.

dish an old weight measure for lead ore, actually based on volume, but equal to around 65 lb. Nine dishes equalled one load of lead ore, and four loads equalled approximately one ton. *See also* FREEING DISH.

disk engine a HYDRAULIC ENGINE patented by the brothers Edward and James Dakeyne in 1830 (patent no. 5882). It comprised a large, specially shaped cast-iron outer casing enclosing a close fitting but separate solid globe. An annular flat disk encircled the globe about its equator, protruding into a chamber which surrounded it. A spindle at right angles to the disk extended through the casing from the globe and was connected to a crank fastened to a central vertical output shaft positioned above the casing. An entry pipe admitted water under head pressure to the chamber surrounding the disk, and another exit pipe conducted water out of the chamber. The water entering the chamber caused the disk to tilt rhythmically but without turning it, and this created a precessional movement of the spindle which in turn rotated the output shaft via the crank. Disk engines were used to operate pumps in lead mines in Derbyshire, and to drive flax spinning machinery, but not many were made; other types of hydraulic engine, which gave more positive action, were preferred.

Glover, S. *History and Gazetteer of the county of Derby*, Vol. 2 (1829), 387
The Mechanics Magazine (1833) no. 492

displacer the long top piston in a Stirling HOT AIR ENGINE which contains the REGENERATOR coils and moves the air from the top hot end of the cylinder via an annular space surrounding it to the lower cold end, and vice versa. The air is heated or cooled by the regenerator as it passes in the four-stroke cycle.

distaff the holder for a bundle of previously cleaned and CARDED fibres waiting to be spun into yarn. The word possibly comes from the obsolete verb 'dizen' meaning to dress up or deck out, plus 'staff', or from an old German word for a bundle of flax. In medieval and earlier times, distaffs were sticks or short poles about a yard long, often decoratively carved, or in the form of cleft sticks or cages. The fibres to be spun were loosely tied to the distaff, or placed in the cleft or cage, and the distaff either tucked under one arm, or into the belt of the spinner, its purpose being to leave the hands free for spinning the yarn by SPINDLE AND WHORL. Sometimes the fibres had been formed into a ROVING, in which case the roving was loosely wrapped round the distaff. With the introduction of spinning wheels, the distaff was fastened to the framework of the wheel near the spindle on a vertically protruding arm, and the bundle of fibres waiting to be spun was hung from it. The distaff is also known as a rock.

The distaff side of a family is the female branch, a name derived from the old domestic occupation for women and girls, of spinning wool or flax.

distance posts posts erected at equal distances either side of some canal locks. Their purpose was an attempt to prevent arguments between bargees travelling in opposite directions towards the lock as to who had priority at the lock; the boat passing the distance post first had the right to enter the lock first.

dobby (or dobbie) a mechanism attached to a loom for automatically controlling the SHED formation on machines which have many HEALDS, enabling patterned cloth to be woven. The dobby is usually fixed above the loom at the opposite end from the drive, and actuates linkages from which the healds are suspended.

There are various types of dobby. Some only raise the healds, which are returned by springs or weights; others perform each movement. One design comprises a number of strips of hardwood, known as LAGS, which are connected together to form an endless chain. Each lag is perforated by holes into which wooden or metal pegs may be inserted according to the pattern to be woven, some holes being left without pegs. Another type has pegs set in a revolving drum. After each pass of WEFT, a fresh lag is automatically moved into position, or the drum indexed one part-revolution. The pegs strike linkages which raise healds, whilst other healds remain down where there are no pegs. In this manner successive sheds are formed to reproduce a pattern in the cloth, the whole sequence repeating itself when the first lag again comes into the operative position, or the drum completes a full revolution.

Dobbies were developed from the JACQUARD mechanism. Their origin is obscure, as is their name. One, a peg and drum type, was patented by John Potter in 1824 (patent no. 4951), and another was introduced by S. Dean in 1830 for the silk industry. Punched cards could be substituted for lags if required. The drum witch loom was a hand loom fitted with a simple drum dobby which was activated by a foot treadle. Because a dobby raises warps in sets and produces geometric patterns in the cloth being woven, it is not as flexible as the Jacquard which could lift individual warps and make non-geometrical figures. A complicated, large repetitive pattern would require a large number of lags or cards for its execution, and to reduce the cost of these Messrs Robert Hall, of Bury, Lancs., obtained the manufacturing rights in the 1890s to a German dobby invention, which reduced the number needed by an ingenious reversing mechanism that repeated the pattern after each one was completed.

docks places of safe anchorage for sea-going ships where they may be loaded and unloaded, with facilities for storage of goods in transit and for repairing ships. Designed and built by civil engineers, their interest for industrial archaeologists lies in the early remaining wharves, cranes, warehouses, customs buildings, repair docks, sea locks, etc., all enclosed by high security walls.

The principal docks during the period of the Industrial Revolution were London, Bristol, Liverpool, and Glasgow. After London, Bristol was at first the most important dock in Britain, but this position was rapidly overtaken by Liverpool. Docks were of great importance to Britain during this period, since by the middle of the 19th century over 40 per cent of the world's manufactured goods came from Britain. The docks were connected to the inland manufacturing areas firstly by the CANAL system, then by the RAILWAYS. Besides the four docks mentioned, several smaller docks developed all round the coast.

Before the construction of such docking facilities for sea-going vessels, larger ships moored off-shore and loading and unloading were effected by lighters, flat bottomed boats which 'lightened' the larger ship because they could approach the wharves in shallow water. Such arrangements were vulnerable to smuggling and theft. In London there were in fact organized gangs of thieves operating on the Thames in the 1790s with names such as the River Pirates, the Night Plunderers, and the Mud Larks. Docks with built-in security became necessary to prevent losses. At first there were only private docks in London, such as the Greenland for whalers, and Mr Perry's for East India ships. The first true dock in Britain was probably the Old Dock, opened *c.*1728 in Liverpool, followed by Salterhouse

Dock in 1760, also in Liverpool. Before the last quarter of the 18th century about 450 acres of dock accommodation had been constructed in England. The first secure public docks in London were the West India Dock built by William Jessop in 1800–2, and London Docks by John Rennie, built in 1802–5. William Jessop also built Bristol's docks in 1803–8. By 1830 the total area of docks covered over 4,850 acres, financed both by government and public expenditure.

Coad, J. *The Royal Dockyards 1690–1850: Architecture and Engineering Works of the Sailing Navy*, Scolar Press, 1989
Pudney, J. *London's Docks*, Thames and Hudson, 1975
Ritchie-Noakes, N. *Liverpool's Historic Waterfront*, HMSO, 1984

doeskin a highly finished, closely cut, thick twilled woollen cloth, usually black in colour. It was dressed so as to show very little TWILL and it resembled the skin of a doe, hence its name. It was principally made in the west of England, and being hard wearing was used for garments such as riding breeches. Formerly, doe leather or the harsher buckskin were used for this purpose, but by the middle of the 19th century these leathers had become too expensive, and cloth substitutes were used. Doeskin is sometimes known as Venetian cloth.

doffer the small cylinder or roller at the delivery end of a CARDING engine which is covered over its circumference by CARD CLOTH and which takes the carded cotton off the main cylinder. The doffer passes the cotton round its periphery to the doffer comb which, by a rapid oscillating movement, removes the cotton from the doffer before it is condensed into a SLIVER (see Fig. 15). To doff means to take off, and probably comes from the Old English 'do off'. The action of removing full COPS from a spinning mule is called doffing. The word is mostly used in northern textile industries.

doffing stick, *see* NEEDLE STICK

dog belt the leather belt worn round the hips by a boy or woman 'drawer' working underground in early coal mines. It had a length of chain attached to it which was hooked onto the CORF or load being dragged towards the shaft. In low seams this meant crawling along on all fours, with the chain passing between the legs dragging the corf behind. This degrading form of labour was made illegal by the Coal Mines Regulation Act of 1842, which forbade the employment underground of women and boys under the age of ten years. A drawing harness of this kind was also known as a guss harness.

John, A.V. *By the Sweat of their Brow: Women Workers at Victorian Coal Mines*, Croom Helm, 1980

dog clutch a type of CLUTCH by which a ROLLING MILL may be connected to, or disengaged from, the engine which drives it. It comprises a pair of opposing flanges, one carrying a number of projections, the dogs, which engage in slots in the other flange; one flange slides axially on the engine shaft so that the pair may be disengaged, and the other is fixed to the rolling mill drive shaft. When engaged, the dogs transmit the torque from the engine to the mill.

dog-tooth roof, *see* NORTH LIGHT ROOF

dolly, *see* DAMSEL

dolly tub, *see* KIEVE

dolly waggon a truck used for conveying dirt from a mine.

dolly wheel wheel mounted on top of a post or stone pillar supporting FLAT RODS, which move to and fro as power is transmitted from the PRIME MOVER to the driven item.

dolomite a type of limestone used as a BASIC LINING for steel-making furnaces. It can withstand high temperatures and attack by basic slags, and contains calcium and magnesium in equal proportions. Whereas originally found in the Dolomite district of the eastern Alps, the name is also applied to other refractories made from magnesium limestone used in metallurgical furnaces.

domestic system the system for making cloth in cottages or farms, before the introduction of factories. From about the 15th century cloth making was carried out in workers' own homes. Raw wool would be purchased by a CLOTHIER who would distribute it to spinners and weavers: they worked it up into cloth at home, using their own hand-operated spinning wheels and looms. The domestic workers sometimes employed APPRENTICES and JOURNEYMEN to assist them, besides their own families. The clothier would pay the domestic workers for the work done, and arrange for the fulling, dyeing and eventual sale of the finished cloth.

The domestic worker was therefore self-employed, contracting a price and time of completion with the clothier, on whom he relied for continuation of employment. Usually he owned his own simple equipment, although sometimes the clothier would own it and charge a rent for its use. Normally, such workers had an alternative source of income or means of livelihood, such as a small-holding. The domestic system was superseded by the FACTORY SYSTEM. It is also known as the commission system, or the putting-out system.

domett a loosely woven mixed cloth, usually with a cotton WARP and a woollen WEFT; it was sometimes called cotton-flannel. Popular in the early 19th century, it was used as an inexpensive material for blankets, linings, etc., and was used for bandages in the First World War.

donkey engine a small steam engine used for crane work on board ships. It has two cranks, set at 90° to each other, and no flywheel, so that it can be easily stopped and started from any position, rapid stops and starts being essential when loads are being manoeuvred on the crane.

dormant timber, *see* SLEEPER (1)

dornick (or dornock) a union fabric, i.e. one made from a combination of different materials such as linen and wool, or wool and silk. The original material was made in the Flemish town of Doornijk (now Tournai), from which the English name came when manufacture of the fabric began in East Anglia in the 16th century. There is no connection with the Scottish town of Dornoch.

double-acting term used to describe an engine in which power is transmitted by a piston working inside a cylinder, in each direction of its travel, i.e. each stroke is a power stroke. This is obtained by admitting steam either side of the piston in turn, by means of automatically operated inlet valve gear working in conjunction with automatically operated exhaust valves.

James Watt (1736–1819) introduced double-acting in his steam engines (patent no. 1321, 1782); before this, all his earlier engines and those of Newcomen were SINGLE-ACTING, with the power stroke downwards only. By admitting steam under pressure (although only a few pounds per square inch above atmospheric at that time) on one side of the piston and creating a partial vacuum on the other, and reversing the sequence, double-acting was obtained, and both the downward and upward strokes became power strokes. This gave a smoother movement to the engine and increased its power output. It meant that chains connecting the piston rod end to the overhead beam had to be changed for a direct linkage capable of transmitting an upward thrust. This was achieved at first by the THREE BAR MOTION and shortly afterwards by the PARALLEL MOTION, both of which were necessary to guide the piston rod in a straight line.

double cloth two separate cloths woven at the same time on a loom, achieved by an arrangement of the SHEDDING MOTION. If the cloths are joined at the edges, they will open out into a circular large tube; if joined at intervals across the width, when cut down the centre of the joining strip they will make hose pipes, bags, etc.

double way a term originating on Tyneside to describe a single track wooden railway which has a second easily renewable layer of wooden rail pinned on top of the first. Probably dating from about 1750–60, it should not be confused with the twin track which was known as a double railway or waggonway, usually comprising a main load-bearing doubleway, and a return, or bye way for empty waggons. Bye ways did not normally have a second top rail, since there was less wear due to the lighter loading.

doubling the twisting together of two or more single yarns to provide stronger 'cords', or what is known as manifold yarn. Doubled yarn is used in sewing threads, and lace, crochet yarns, carpets, and industrial work where heavier and stronger yarns are needed. Doubled yarn is also known as folded yarn, and doubling is also used to describe combining SLIVERS in a DRAW FRAME. Doubling may be carried out in a separate department in a spinning mill, but more usually the process is done in a separate mill on machines which are modifications of spinning machines.

Doubled yarn is specified by the COUNT of its component threads and the number of them in the finished yarn. For example, a doubled cotton yarn made by twisting two single yarns of 12s count would be said to be a 2/12s yarn; similarly, a four-fold yarn of 16s single count, would be a 4/16s yarn, and so on. Several individual silk threads are doubled to make ORGANZINE, the number chosen depending on the type of organzine required.

douk a material resembling clay, usually light blue, found in mineral veins. It is either decomposed rock, or the result of friction between rock faces.

dowlas a kind of plain weave, coarse linen cloth, originating in Daoulas, Brittany, in the 17th century. A similar cloth, known as dowlas or douglas in Britain, was woven in cotton particularly in Scotland during the Victorian period, and used for towelling, etc.

downcast shaft the shaft down which fresh ventilation air is sucked or blown into a mine. The vitiated air leaves the underground workings via another shaft, the UPCAST SHAFT. Two shafts became necessary as mines became deeper and more extensive to provide adequate ventilation, and from 1862 two shafts became a legal requirement for safety reasons.

dozen 1. an old measure for the weight of coal used in Yorkshire, and often equal to a CHALDRON. **2.** a kind of coarse woollen kersey, possibly getting its name from being 12 yd long. **3.** a quantity of iron ore weighing 6.75 tons.

dozzle (or dozzler) a short fireclay collar placed on top of a vertical ingot mould in which CRUCIBLE STEEL was cast in the Huntsman process. The inner diameter of the dozzle was about half the cross dimension of the ingot. The dozzle was heated to a red heat before being placed in position, and its purpose was to provide a reservoir of molten metal to feed the ingot as it cooled and contracted so that cavities did not form down its centre. The pip of metal left by the dozzle was knocked off when the ingot was cold, and the fracture plane indicating the crystalline structure of the metal allowed the carbon content to be visually estimated. The dozzle, which is also known as a hot top, was invented by Robert Forester Mushet (1811–91) and patented in 1861 (patent no. 1310).

drafting (or drawing) the attenuation or drawing out of textile fibres to straighten and parallel them. It is difficult to separate drafting from the final drawing out into a spun yarn since drafting also takes place as twist is inserted. In the simple JENNY, draft and twist were applied simultaneously. Later spinning machines put draft in by methods depending on the material being handled: short fibred materials such as cotton use roller drafting, whereas long fibred materials such as worsted or jute use pins as well, since rollers alone are not practical.

Roller drafting was first attempted unsuccessfully by John Wyatt (1700–60) and Lewis Paul (d.1759), covered by two patents in Paul's name (no. 562, 1738; no. 724, 1758). Richard Arkwright successfully used four pairs of weighted rollers in his WATER FRAME, but his patent (no. 931, 1769) was later disallowed as it was alleged he had stolen the idea from Thomas Highs (or Hayes). Samuel Crompton (1753–1827) used roller drafting on his cotton MULE, with two pairs of rollers at first, later increased to three pairs. Woollen mules have only one pair of rollers. Fig.64 shows three pairs of drafting rollers.

Pin and roller drafting is combined in the gill box, which is used in worsted spinning. The gill box was invented (patent no. 6464) by Samuel Lawson and William King Westley in 1833 (*see* SCREW-GILL DRAW FRAME). In it, moving pins comb out the worsted fibres prior to feeding them between a pair of drafting rollers. The GOOD DOUBLE-CHAIN DRAFTER has a similar action in hemp and jute spinning.

In roller drafting, the rotational speed of each pair of rollers is slightly faster than the previous pair. Thus, as the material passes through the rollers some fibres are gripped in the roller nip and pulled forward at their leading ends at a faster speed than others which are still held back at their trailing ends by slower rollers, which attenuates or draws out the material. A similar thing happens in the gill box, the rollers draw out some fibres while others are held by the moving pins.

draft tube an exit tube from a WATER TURBINE which surrounds the moving vanes of the runner at the top and extends downwards, tapering out to a larger diameter. It conveys the exit water to the tailrace, and slightly increases the overall efficiency of the turbine. Its function is twofold: it permits a negative head to build up beneath the turbine runner, allowing the turbine to be set above the tailrace, and it enables a large proportion of the velocity energy in the leaving water to be converted to pressure energy, thus increasing the effective head. The draft tube, also known as a suction tube, was invented by Boyden in 1844. In some water turbine installations there is insufficient room below the turbine for a straight draft tube, and it is turned through 90° to discharge horizontally, with a slightly smaller efficiency gain.

drag 1. a non-passenger carrying steam-driven road vehicle of the early 1800s which acted as a tractor, towing a passenger carriage behind it. **2.** a shovel-like metal shoe or skid used as a brake by horse-drawn carriages and waggons when descending steep hills. The drag was attached to the framework by a chain and hung on a hook when not required. The coach stopped at the top of a steep hill, the drag placed in front of and under the nearside hind wheel which locked it as the hill was descended, relieving the horses of holding back the weight of the coach, the locked wheel acting as a brake. At the bottom of the hill the drag was hung back on the framework. Eventually, drags were replaced by foot-controlled rim brakes. **3.** the bottom part of a foundry moulding box or flask. The upper part of the mould is called a COPE.

drag link a rod for moving the linkage on a locomotive or steam engine to alter the cut-off point.

dramway the Welsh alternative for a TRAMWAY.

draperies various kinds of textile fabrics. Drapery is an alternative name for cloth, and once had a meaning of the place where cloth was made. The influx of Huguenot refugees in the latter half of the 16th century brought many weavers into Britain who introduced new varieties of cloth. New names were given to these, and collectively they became known as NEW DRAPERIES, to differentiate them from the old varieties, which were called the 'old draperies'. Old draperies were broadcloths, bays, kerseys, etc., and new draperies were perpetuanoes, serges, says, and (later) worsteds. The new draperies were lighter, finer cloths, and were popular in the reign of Elizabeth I (1558–1603).

draw-bar pull, see TRACTIVE EFFORT

drawer 1. a person whose job was to drag, or sometimes push, tubs of coal underground from the coal face to the winding shaft. In early coal mines, women and boys were employed on this laborious and degrading task; an alternative name was a putter. See also DOG BELT. **2.** a person who pulls the threads through the HEALD and REED assembly when preparing it before weaving commences (see DRAWING AND REACHING).

draw frame a machine for drawing out the SLIVERS produced by a CARDING machine, combining several together and attenuating them to the same cross-sectional area as one of the component slivers. The object is to improve a new sliver by making the fibres more parallel and evening out any defects or irregularities that might exist in individual slivers delivered from the carding machine. A draw frame is therefore a machine intermediate in the preparation of cotton for spinning into yarn. Drawing is achieved by feeding card slivers into a roller drafting system; up to six or eight such slivers may be combined at each set of rollers (see Fig. 24). The drawing action is done in successive stages as the slivers pass through the rollers; four pairs of rollers would generally be used, each pair rotating faster than the previous pair, causing the fibres to slide over each other and lock together to form an attenuated sliver. The speed of the final roller is arranged to be as many times faster than the first roller as the number of slivers from the carding engine being combined. The issuing sliver will thus have the same cross-sectional dimensions as one of the original slivers, but will be more uniform in composition.

Drawing was first introduced by Richard Arkwright (1732–92) when he combined two slivers to correct the irregularities in the slivers he was obtaining from his primitive carding machine. Putting two slivers together and drawing them into one was literally 'doubling', and the process was so called in the early days of machine spinning. Although drawing two slivers together was an improvement in the preparation of cotton before spinning, it was not long before three and more slivers were combined in draw frames, for better results, six to eight being the optimum. The delivered slivers are coiled into tall metal cans before passing to the SLUBBING operation, which further attenuates the slivers.

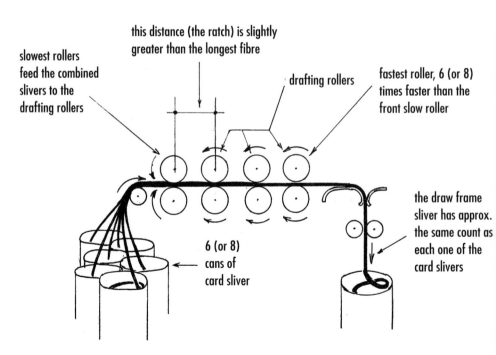

Fig. 24. Action of a draw frame

drawing, *see* DRAFTING

drawing and reaching (or entering and threading) the process of preparing the WARPS before fitting onto a weaving loom. Each warp thread has to be threaded through its appropriate HEALD eye and in its correct space in the REED. This is done away from the loom by hand by two workers (usually male) who work one on each side of the heald and reed assembly. One, called the drawer, pulls each thread through its correct path by means of a small hook from the reacher, who passes each thread through from the other side in the correct order according to the pattern of cloth to be woven. This clothing up of the loom mechanism is a painstaking operation lasting several hours and requires great concentration, particularly if the pattern to be woven is a complex one. If the next warp assembly is to be the same as a previous one, time and trouble is reduced by fastening the end of each new warp thread to its corresponding end of the old warp and pulling the new one through.

draw kiln, *see* LIME KILN

draw loom a hand-operated loom on which figured cloth could be woven, also known as a drawing engine. It was more complicated than the ordinary hand loom, costing about twice as

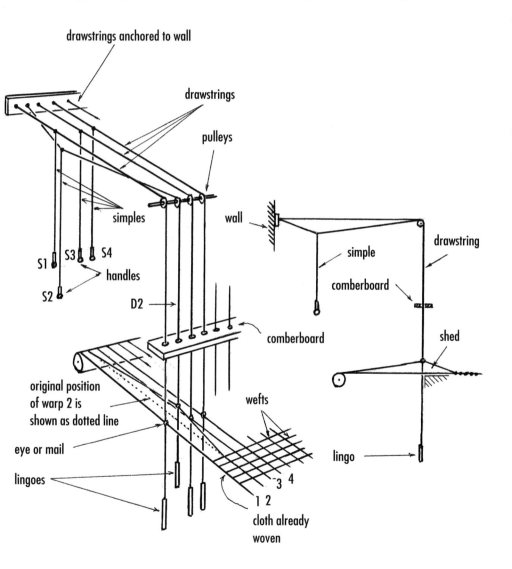

Fig. 25. Simplified diagram of a draw loom

much, and was introduced into Britain from Flanders in the mid-16th century. Joseph Mason patented a draw loom in Britain in 1687 (patent no. 257) although it is possible that such looms were in existence in the Middle East before then. The draw loom represented an important advance, since it enabled patterns to be woven that were not possible hitherto. It needed two to operate it – the weaver and a young assistant called the draw boy. A simplified diagram is shown in Fig. 25. The warps were raised in repetitive rotation by a system of looped strings, called a SIMPLE, to make various combinations of SHED to form the pattern. The draw boy stood at one side of the loom and pulled the strings of the simple in strict order. In the diagram, simple *S2* has been pulled down to raise drawstring *D2*, which lifts warp 2 to form the shed for the shuttle. On releasing simple *S2*, the weight of its lingo returns warp 2 to its original position. In practice, several drawstrings were joined together and were raised in turn to make the desired pattern in the finished cloth. Setting up the loom was skilled work, but the job of the draw boy was monotonous.

Patterned fabrics were more costly than plain due to the higher labour cost of the draw loom. The selection of the correct warps to raise was eventually made automatic by the invention of the JACQUARD loom in the 18th century, which eliminated the need for a draw boy. A mechanical drawboy loom (cam-operated) was introduced around 1800 but was soon replaced by the Jacquard device.

draw plate, *see* WORTLE

dressing frame another name for a WARP SIZER. Warps require sizing to protect them from the rubbing action they are subjected to in a loom, and the dressing frame was invented by Thomas Johnson and William Radcliffe of Stockport in 1803, to size and dry warps before they were wound onto a warp beam. The warps were passed under a roller immersed in a trough of adhesive size and dried by a fan. This allowed continuous weaving on power looms, and considerably increased output. Prior to this invention, looms had to be stopped after every yard or so of cloth had been woven to apply flour paste size to the unwoven part of the warp, and allow it to dry *in situ*. Johnson and Radcliffe's first patent (no. 2684, 1803) was later improved upon (patent no. 2771, 1804), and other improvements were made by later inventors. The dressing frame was eventually superseded by TAPE SIZING.

dressing of ore preparing metallic ores for further processing. Mineral ores, when brought up from the mine, contain unwanted rock, etc. which requires separating and discarding before the valuable ore is prepared for the smelter. The process of separation is called dressing, and different methods have been used over the centuries for achieving this. At first, sorting by hand was used, then separation by flowing water (e.g. in a BUDDLE), and later, as power became available, crushing by STAMPS or rollers. The place where this was carried out was known as the dressing floor, usually a level area on the surface close to the mine shaft and often cobbled or paved. The unwanted waste material was normally dumped nearby. In some mines, ore dressing was carried out underground in an enlarged 'cave' to reduce the amount of material which had to be wound up to the surface. Waste material separated underground was packed into old workings.

Truscott, S.J. *Textbook of Ore-dressing*, 1923

drift mine a mine where access from the surface is by a near-horizontal tunnel leading down to the vein or seam. Often these mines were driven into a hillside following an OUTCROP of the mineral being mined. Drift mines date back to the 15th century and were the early method of obtaining coal etc. before vertical shafts were employed. An old Shropshire word for a drift mine was an inset or insett, and another word still in use today is footrill, occasionally footrid. In some parts of the country a drift mine is known as a DELPH mine, or ADIT mine, and more rarely a slope shaft.

drill a coarse TWILLED linen or cotton fabric used for light clothing. The word drill is a shortening of drilling, which was its original form. It implies a cloth woven with three threads, since it comes from the Latin *trilecum* meaning three (*tri*) threads (*lecum*). Drill was being woven in Britain in the mid-18th century and is still in use today.

drilling machine a machine tool for making cylindrical holes in objects. There are three basic types of drilling machine: the pillar drill and the radial arm drill (which both drill one hole at a time), and the multi-spindle machine, which drills several holes at once.

Pillar drills comprise a substantial vertical pillar supporting an overhead HEADSTOCK which drives a vertical spindle terminating in a self-centring tool-holding chuck. The spindle may be raised or lowered by moving a lever or arm, and means are provided for rotating the spindle at various speeds to suit the job in hand. A table capable of vertical adjustment is arranged beneath the chuck on which the work piece is clamped. A drill bit made from tool steel and of appropriate diameter and length is held in the chuck and is brought down onto the work piece to drill one hole at each operation. The spindle is accurately guided in a vertical direction to ensure that a true circular and straight hole is made in the work piece. Radial arm drills enable drilling of work pieces too large to fit onto a pillar drill table. The headstock and spindle are carried on an arm which may be rotated radially about a robust vertical pedestal, and they may also be traversed along the arm to operate at different radii. On multi-spindle drills the spindles may be adjusted to different centres, there being of course a minimum dependent on the physical size of the spindles and chucks themselves.

Primitive drilling machines such as the bowstring drill for use on wood date from ancient times. Such drills were manually driven. Clockmakers in the 18th century had small drills capable of drilling metal. An important landmark in drilling machinery was in c.1844, when Joseph Whitworth (1803–87) made all-metal pillar drills of greater accuracy than hitherto. Radial arm drills were available by 1851, and multi-spindle drills were introduced in 1860, primarily for drilling rows of rivet and bolt holes in structural members. The drill bits themselves were of flattened arrowhead shape up until about 1860, when the helical twist drill was introduced. Sharpening machines were invented to service the drills to maintain their cutting edges. When holes too large in diameter for drilling machines are required, they are made on BORING MACHINES. The same basic types of drilling machines are still in use today, although they are faster, more powerful and more accurate.

driving bargain, *see* TUTWORK

driving floor the lowest of the access floors built round large, early BEAM STEAM ENGINES at different levels. From the driving floor the valve gear could be reached, and the engine man spent most of his time there. Other floors or platforms were the PACKING FLOOR and the BEAM LOFT.

drop box an arrangement on a hand loom which enabled a change in WEFT or colour to be made while weaving. Invented by Robert Kay (son of the inventor of the flying shuttle) in 1760, the drop box was not patented. The device (*see* Fig. 27) comprised a 'box' at each side of the loom with (usually) three compartments one above the other. Each box could be raised or lowered at will by the weaver moving a lever to bring a compartment level with the picking block. A shuttle rested in each compartment, and held either a different sort of weft (e.g. a different count) or a different colour, so that the weaver could select whatever he required as weaving proceeded.

Squire Diggle mechanized the drop box (patent no. 10462, 1845) by arranging an endless chain fitted with cams which hung at the side of a power loom, and brought the different compartments and shuttles into operation as the chain slowly moved round. A later improvement was made by Wright Shaw on his check loom (patent no. 2219, 1868). Revolving shuttle boxes were also developed.

drop forging a method for mass producing small articles in steel by forging them to shape whilst red hot and plastic. The operation is carried out on drop hammers which have a shaped cavity in the hammer block, and another shaped cavity sunk in the anvil. The mass of steel is hammered between the two cavities, and is passed successively through a series of dies which progressively shape the article until the final form is reached.

drop shaft, *see* WINZE

drop valve a hydraulically operated steam valve design used on high speed steam engines. Developed around 1900 to enable an increasing use of superheated steam which required fast moving valves, the drop valve was faster than the CORLISS VALVE, its pistons having little inertia. It was very economical in its use of steam, and its virtually instantaneous opening and closing prevented wear on the valve seats. It also assisted in tight governing of the speed of the engine, a necessary condition for the driving of textile machinery. Drop valves were also cam operated and therefore opened and closed faster than SLIDE VALVES, which were eccentric operated. The return action was usually by spring, giving a snap shut closure.

dross metallic oxides which rise and float on the surface of molten metals in metallurgical oxidation processes, and are skimmed off as impurities.

drovers' roads routes along which beef cattle were driven. From about the 17th century herds of cattle were driven south from Scotland, where they had been reared, to cattle markets and fairs in England for slaughter. Certain routes or unmetalled 'green tracks' were followed by the men who drove the herds along, using particular valleys where water was available, and avoiding ENCLOSURES. Drovers slept rough with their cattle en route, typically covering seven to nine miles a day, and at the end of the trek the cattle were allowed to rest and fatten in areas known as AGISTMENT GROUNDS before being sold for slaughter. The meat and hides were valuable for meeting the needs of the growing industrial population concentrated in the emerging industrial towns and cities in England. The drovers trade was ended by the coming of the railways, when cattle began to be transported in trucks direct from their rearing grounds to the slaughterhouses in the towns. PACKHORSES also used drovers' roads.

drugget (or droggitt) a coarse woollen material made in Somerset in the 18th century, used as table or floor coverings. The word possibly comes from an old German word *Droguett*, the name of a similar cloth. When made as a mixture of wool and silk, or wool and linen, it was used for clothing.

drum house a building housing a winding drum or broad faced wheel placed at the top of an incline down which loaded trucks ran on rails. The trucks were connected to a rope which coiled round the drum, and ran down the incline by gravity. Empty trucks were pulled up on another set of rails by the descending trucks and the speed of both was controlled by a brake attached to the winding drum, which was operated by a brakeman in the drum house who had a view down the incline. Such arrangements were used in mountainous mining areas where ore was lowered from highly placed mines to processing sites lower down.

drum witch a simple device added to a loom which enabled fancy cloths to be woven. It comprised a wooden drum which was partly rotated after each pass of the shuttle. Projecting from the surface of the drum were pegs which lifted groups of HEALDS as they moved round, the pegs being inserted in a definite order to produce the pattern in the cloth. The drum witch was the forerunner of the DOBBY.

dry-bone, *see* CALAMINE

dry dock an arm off a waterway (canal, river, or open to the sea) into which boats may pass for repair, or in which they may be built. The water can be drained or pumped out and the dock kept empty by a lock gate. The vessel rests on raised piers or keel blocks placed in the bottom of the dock so that access is possible to its underneath for inspection or repair. A dry dock is also called a graving dock: to grave a boat is to remove accretions from its underwater surfaces and repaint etc. Small dry docks such as those on canals usually have a roof built over them; dry docks for ship building and repair, being much larger, are usually uncovered.

dryhouse a building in which cloth was dried. There are two types of old dryhouses: air drying, and heated drying. Air dryhouses date from the late 18th century and comprise long

Dry dock at Lathom, Lancs., on the Liverpool to Leeds Canal

buildings with open sides in which woollen or linen cloth was hung on poles to dry by natural circulation. Sometimes they were built over the mill's steam boilers to use the rising heat. Heated dryhouses could have more than one storey, with wooden slatted or metal perforated floors, heated by steam pipes or by vertical iron flues from a ground-floor stove. These buildings were also known as stove houses or simply stoves, and were used particularly in the West Country.

dry hurry an INCLINED PLANE connecting two sections of a canal, used where the difference in levels between the canals is too great for locks. The term was used particularly in Ireland, where a dry hurry was built on the Tyrone Canal in the 1780s.

dry puddling a method of making wrought iron from cast-iron pigs invented by Henry Cort (patent no. 1351, 1783). It remained in use for some 50 years until superseded by the improved 'wet' method of Joseph Hall (1789–1862). *See also* PUDDLING FURNACE.

dry salter a dealer in dyes, gums, etc. and therefore related to the textile finishing industry and the chemical industry. A dry salter would procure the raw materials and mix the dyes as a specialist supplier to the textile industry.

ducape a plain woven strong silk cloth used for women's garments, introduced into Britain by French refugees of 1685. The word is of obscure origin. The popularity of the fabric had declined by the mid-19th century.

duck a strong untwilled linen or cotton fabric. Manufacturing commenced in Britain during the 17th century, and the material was often used for small sails, being finer than canvas. It was also used for sailors' outer clothing. In the first half of the 19th century it became popular for men's trousers, which were known as ducks, and were usually white.

duffel (or duffle) a cheap, thick woollen cloth with a pronounced nap used for warm outer garments and blankets. It takes its name from the town Duffel near Antwerp in Brabant, Belgium, where it was made. In early references, the name is sometimes spelt duffield. The weaving of duffel was brought into East Anglia in the 17th century by Dutch immigrants, and a little later into the West Country. An original outlet for the cloth was for bartering with Red Indians in the new colonies, and when intended for this, the cloth was usually dyed red or blue. Today's duffle coats come from naval attire.

Duke's Canal, The The Duke's Canal or cut was the name given to the Bridgewater Canal, financed by the Duke of Bridgewater (1736–1803) and engineered by James Brindley (1716–72). This canal was the first commercially successful canal in Britain, and was originally intended for the transport of coal from the Duke of Bridgewater's coal mines at Worsley, near Manchester. Construction started in 1759 and the first section of the canal partly opened for traffic on 17 July 1761. This first section was 10.25 miles in length, running from Worsley Delph where the Duke's mines were situated, to the Castlefield terminus in Manchester which was opened for traffic by 1765. This stretch included the famous aqueduct which carried the canal across the river Irwell at Barton. The Bridgewater Canal was later extended to Runcorn with a connection to the Mersey estuary, and a connection to the Trent and Mersey Canal at Runcorn, Ches. The Bridgewater Canal was of great benefit to the manufacturing districts of Manchester, and the extensions enabled cheaper transport between that city and Liverpool and the Potteries. Its success encouraged the construction of other canals throughout Britain.
Malet, H. *The Canal Duke*, Phoenix, 1961

Duke's watercourse, the a man-made watercourse system, also known as the Duke's level, comprising a High and Low system measuring some 6.5 miles on the Grassington Moors, in the West Riding of Yorkshire. It was laid out by John Taylor (1779–1863) who was appointed chief agent to the Duke of Devonshire in 1818 to manage his mineral rights on the lead mining activities in that area. The watercourses brought water to some eight waterwheels and several ore dressing sites from dams high up on the moors. The water operated wheels for winding ore from deep shafts and for pumping water from the mines, and enabled a big expansion of lead production in the area in the mid-19th century. The watercourses can still be traced on the moor today, together with the remains of many of the waterwheel pits and shafts. All underground mining ceased in 1877, although some reworking of waste tips took place afterwards.

dukey, *see* JOURNEY

dunter 1. a name in use in the mid-19th century for the main operator of a silk winding frame, usually a woman. The work comprised supervising the operation of several winding frames with the assistance of a young girl, keeping the machines supplied with bobbins and joining the filaments when they broke. 2. a compressed-air driven, hand-held tool used in quarries for dressing a flat surface on granite blocks. It operates by a rapid radial percussion action.

duplex pump a type of direct-acting, twin-cylinder, steam-driven water pump invented by Henry Rossiter Worthington (1817–80) in New York in the 1850s. The engine piston rod is directly connected to the pump ram, and the engine slide valve is operated by the motion of the other piston so that the pumps work alternately. Such pumps were first made in the UK by James Simpson under licence. Small sizes were very popular as boiler feed pumps, whilst large units with compound engines were used by municipal water undertakings. Duplex pumps are still in use.

durant a woollen cloth, also known as everlasting, and a variety of TAMIE. It dates from the mid-18th century.

Durham winder an early design of vertical WINDING ENGINE extensively used in the north-east coalfields, patented by Phineas Crowther of Newcastle upon Tyne (patent no. 2378, 1800). In place of an overhead beam, a WINDING DRUM was driven by a crank and connecting rod from a crosshead which was guided by a THREE BAR PARALLEL MOTION. The vertical steam cylinder had CORNISH VALVE gear, and the engine needed a tall engine house to accommodate it. Crowther's engine gave faster winding than BEAM ENGINES, and a flat rope was normally used, winding on itself on a narrow reel-type drum, although normal ropes were also used at some collieries. Often a counterweight was attached to a rope which led over a pulley down a staple or extra shaft, sited behind the engine to assist starting and stopping. Several engine makers made winders to this design and some were still being used in 1855. They were also used for hauling waggons up inclines.

Hill, A. *Single Cylinder Vertical Lever Type Winding Engines as Used in the North East of England*, De Archaeologische Pers., 1986

duroy (or deroy) a coarse woollen fabric formerly woven in the West of England, similar to TAMIE; it should not be confused with CORDUROY.

dust cage the slowly revolving drum with a fine wire mesh or perforated metal circumference in a SCUTCHING MACHINE (*see* Fig. 60). The interior of the drum is under suction from an exhaust fan, and cotton fibres are drawn onto the outer surface forming a thin sheet across the drum width. Any dust present in the fibres is drawn through the mesh by the air stream, thus cleansing the cotton. The cotton fibres are removed from the dust drum or cage by a pair of grooved rollers and consolidated into a lap.

duster a machine for cleaning paper making rags. It comprises a slowly rotating cylindrical wire cage, slightly inclined from the horizontal, into which the rags are tipped after sorting. Dust and loose dirt falls out through the wire mesh as the rags are tumbled about, assisted by a suction fan. The dusting machines were usually placed in a separate dusting house.

Dutch loom (or ribbon loom, inkle loom, swivel loom) a loom for weaving several narrow fabrics such as ribbons simultaneously. Looms for weaving several narrow items side-by-side such as silk ribbons, braids, tapes, etc., are believed to have originated in the Baltic region in the late 16th century. In Holland, improvements were made by William Direxz in 1603–4, and by the 18th century such looms were in use in Britain, hence the name by which they were known.

Several small shuttles were activated by the movement of a bar holding pegs which threw the shuttles across the loom by a swivelling action. Some looms had twenty or so shuttles with a warp beam to each. They replaced the older table-top narrow loom which wove only one ribbon at a time.

Dutch wheel an alternative name for a SAXONY WHEEL, used particularly in Ireland to describe this type of hand spinning wheel, because at one time it was believed to have been invented or at least originated in the Netherlands and Flanders.

duty the useful work done by a steam engine pumping water, at a Cornish tin mine for example. The term was devised by John Smeaton (1724–92) to mean the weight of water in pounds raised through one foot by the consumption of one BUSHEL of coal; later, one hundredweight was used. The measure enabled the efficiency of different engines to be compared.

James Watt (1736–1819) used the duty of an engine as a means of finding the fuel saved by one of his engines against that of the engine he was replacing (usually a Newcomen ATMOSPHERIC ENGINE). He charged an annual PREMIUM of one-third of the cost of the fuel saved for the same duty performed by both engines. Joel Lean of Crenver, Cornwall, began publishing monthly reports in 1810 of the duties of various CORNISH BEAM ENGINES, which by promoting rivalry between mines, gradually raised the efficiency of many engines in that county (*see also* ENGINE REPORTER). Duty money was a bonus paid to engine men in Cornwall to encourage efficient working.

D valve a simple type of valve gear to control the admission to and exhaust of steam from a steam engine (*see* SLIDE VALVE). It gets its name from the general shape of the moving part of the valve: the flat part of the letter D slides across the inlet and outlet (exhaust) ports (*see* Fig. 63a).

dyers' oak, *see* QUERCITRON

dyers' thistle, *see* SAFFLOWER

dyer's weed, *see* WELD

dyes and dyeing the substances and process used for colouring matter by staining or impregnating cloth, paper, leather, etc. in different hues depending on the properties of the dye itself and how it combines with the material being dyed. The dyeing of cloth originated in the East in ancient times. The art spread into Europe in the Middle Ages, and Florence, Italy, became renowned for its dyers in the early 14th century. By the 16th century the Dutch were enjoying a high reputation as expert dyers of cloth.

The earliest dyes were of vegetable or animal origin. Certain parts of suitable plants and trees were used to make dyes for different colours, e.g. roots, leaves, bark, etc. Large amounts were imported into Britain from foreign parts, although a small number of British plants were also used, such as WOAD (*Isatis tinctoria*) which had been used since ancient times for a blue dye. INDIGO, another dye with a long history, was obtained from the plant *Indigofara tinctoria* which was cultivated in India, and another important plant was MADDER (*Rubia tinctorum*) whose root yielded a red dye. Many dyestuffs were also made from the timber of a variety of tropical trees imported from the West Indies after discovery of their dyeing properties. Examples of animal dyes are the purple made from the shellfish *Murex purpura*, and the red from cultivated insects *Coccus cacti* (*see* COCHINEAL). There were a large number of such natural dyes, and information on them will be found under their individual names.

The dyeing processes were often closely kept secrets in the 17th and 18th centuries. Many dyers had their own formula or recipe and method of preparing the dye. Much was based on empirical knowledge and some unusual materials were sometimes used, such as urine. Many dyes required a MORDANT to fix the colour onto the fibres of the cloth: popular mordants were ALUM and COPPERAS. Vat dyes, such as indigo, which is insoluble, coloured the cloth by oxidation after exposure to air. Cotton, wool, and linen required BLEACHING first before dyeing, so dyeworks became intimately associated with bleachworks and were sited where there was a plentiful supply of clean water for both processes. Sometimes the yarn was dyed before weaving, especially when coloured patterns were to be woven. Dyeing

was never a cottage industry. Several auxiliary industries served dyers, including the cultivation of the natural raw materials, quarrying and mining of alum, and the commercial importation of foreign materials. A specialized dyestuff preparation industry arose, such as LOGWOOD mills, in which the imported woods were ground down to powders for the dyers' use.

Until an export prohibition law was passed in 1614, it was the practice to send most English cloth to Holland for dyeing and finishing since the Dutch dyers at that time had more expertise than their English counterparts. The MERCHANT ADVENTURERS held a monopoly on exporting undyed cloth, and the prohibition was introduced to try to break their monopoly and provide more employment for English dyers. Sir William Cockayne undertook to arrange for all English cloth to be dyed in England in 1615, but the project failed in 1617 since Holland retaliated by refusing to buy dyed cloth (*see* COCKAYNE PROJECT). It took many years for the export trade to recover, Holland having increased her own cloth manufacture in the meantime. The Dutch continued to lead the dyeing industry for many years, but British dyers gradually acquired expertise and became less dependent on foreign dyers.

Colours from natural dyes were somewhat muted and tended to fade with age. A big breakthrough resulting in brighter colours and better resistance to light and laundering came with the discovery of synthetic dyes. An early synthetic dye had been made by Peter Woulfe in 1771 when he made the yellow dye PICRIC ACID from indigo and nitric acid in small quantities. But the breakthrough came in 1856 when William Henry Perkin discovered mauvine, the first ANILINE dye, which he patented in 1856 (patent no. 1984). From it came rapid developments: aniline is made from coal-tar, which at that time was becoming readily available from the developing gas industry, and many more aniline dyes followed from chemists working in England, France and Germany. August Wilhelm von Hofmann, a German chemist working in England from 1845 till 1864, developed more synthetic dyes. As the result of the invention of these new dyestuffs, indigo growing in India declined, as did madder importation from European growers, releasing large areas of land to other uses. By the late 1870s Germany began to dominate the synthetics dyestuffs industry largely due to its superior expertise in industrial chemistry, and Britain became very dependent on Germany for dyes.

Dyeing cloth manually by the piece was speeded up in the early 1800s when semi-continuous dyeing was introduced by temporarily stitching several pieces together to make one long length, and winching it through the dyeing equipment in sequence. The cloth was drawn through 'cloth eyes', ceramic collars strategically positioned above each vessel to keep the cloth clear of the floor and any obstructions. Most dyeworks also finished the cloth after dyeing, TENTERING to restore its width, CALENDERING to give the cloth a sheen, and raising the nap (if required).

Dyes are also needed for wallpaper manufacture, and the production of printing inks is another branch of the dyestuffs industry.

Grierson, S. *Dyeing and Dyestuffs*, Shire Publications, Album No. 229

Hummel, J.J. *The Dyeing of Textile Fabrics*, 1885

Ponting, K.G. *A Dictionary of Dyes and Dyeing*, Mills and Boon, 1980

Ponting, K.G. 'Important natural dyes of history', *Industrial Archaeology Review* II (1978), 154–9

Robinson, S. *A History of Dyed Textiles*, Studio Vista, 1969

dye-woods general name given to various kinds of wood such as LOGWOOD from which textile dyes were made. Dye-woods were prepared in LOG MILLS where the pieces were chipped and ground to a powder.

dyke 1. a narrow intrusion of a different mineral into another; usually an igneous rock which has been forced into an existing fissure in an older sedimentary rock, and is usually more or less vertical. It was called an elvan by Cornish miners. 2. a name sometimes used for an EMBANKMENT. 3. a ditch or watercourse. 4. *see* TRAINING WALL.

E

earthenware a cheap form of POTTERY, and the earliest pottery material. The clay is fired at low temperatures (750–1,100° C) and is porous with a soft body. If the article is to be made impervious to liquids it has to be glazed (*see* GLAZING). Josiah Wedgwood (1730–95) made cheap, mass-produced earthenware articles in the 18th century, including his cream coloured 'Queensware', named after the royal patronage of Queen Charlotte.

Easterlings, *see* HANSEATIC LEAGUE

East India Company a joint-stock company, founded in 1600 by Elizabeth I, operating under royal charter to develop trade with India. It gradually brought large areas of India under British control and became the Government agent in India. The Company played an important part in introducing the cotton industry into Britain in its early days, erecting its first factories in Surat in 1612. It sent Indian cotton textiles home to Britain, which created a demand in Britain for the material as an alternative to indigenous wool. Later, raw cotton was sent from Bombay in 1783 for converting into cloth in Britain. The monopoly of the East India Company was dismantled by parliament in 1858 after the Indian Mutiny of 1857.

eau de Javelle the chlorine-based BLEACHING solution discovered by the French chemist Claude Louis Berthollet in 1785. It was named after a district near Paris where bleaching by traditional methods had been done. Eau de Javelle was obtained by dissolving chlorine in potash. A similar, less well known solution, using soda instead of potash, was named Eau de Labarraque after the Parisian apothecary who invented it. Eau de Javelle was the first chemical bleaching agent.

eccentric a mechanical device for converting rotational motion into reciprocating motion. An eccentric comprises a disk, called a sheave, which is larger than a shaft of which it forms a part, with its centre displaced a certain distance from the shaft axis. A circular ring, called a strap, encircles the sheave and is free to move round it. The strap is attached to a long link or eccentric rod which is restrained to move in a linear path at its remote end. As the sheave rotates with the shaft, the strap moves on it, and imparts a reciprocating motion to the eccentric rod. An eccentric therefore acts as a crank of small radius, but with frictional losses due to the sliding between sheave and strap. A common application is to operate SLIDE VALVES on steam engines. It is believed that the eccentric was first used for this purpose by William Murdock around 1800 at Boulton and Watt's Soho foundry. It was never patented. *See also* LOOSE ECCENTRIC VALVE GEAR.

ecliptic James Watt's (1736–1819) name for a SWASH PLATE.

economiser a steam boiler feedwater pre-heater. It comprises a bank of vertical tubes, usually of cast iron, installed in the brick flue which leads the hot gases from the boiler to the chimney. Feedwater on its way to the boiler is pumped upwards through the tubes and is heated by a heat exchange between the hot gases passing between the bank of tubes and the cold feedwater inside them. This improves the overall thermal efficiency of the steam raising system and economizes on fuel, hence its name. Collars encircling each tube, called scrapers, are arranged to slide up and down the tube to scrape off any soot which accumulates on the outer surface. This maintains a clean surface and therefore ensures a constant unimpaired heat exchange. The soot scraped off falls to a chamber below the bank of tubes and is removed periodically through doors provided for this purpose, a bypass flue being used whilst this is done. The economizer was invented by Edward Green (1799–1865) of Wakefield, Yorks. (patent no. 10986, 1845). The scraper mechanism was driven by a small auxiliary steam engine.

Fowler, W.H. (ed.) *Fifty Years' History of the Development of Green's Economiser*, 1895
Waste Not: The Story of Green's Economiser, E. Green and Son, 1956

edge mill a crushing machine comprising a heavy wheel mounted vertically on an arm which revolves round a central post. The wheel has a broad rim which runs in a circular path inside a horizontal trough or flat-bottomed bowl, the post carrying the horizontal arm being at the centre of the trough or bowl. The material to be crushed is spread in a layer in the bowl and is crushed under the weight of the heavy wheel as it passes over it. Early designs were horse-operated, the radial arm extended beyond the circumference of the bowl with a horse harnessed to it. As the animal walked round outside the bowl, the wheel performed its crushing job inside the bowl. Small edge mills were used in the TANNING industry for grinding oak bark, and in the DYEING industry for grinding LOGWOOD, etc. Larger mills were used for crushing lead ore, and these frequently had two wheels, one either side of the central post with the horse arm extending right across the bowl and driven by two horses, one at each end. Water-powered edge mills were introduced later. Edge mills were also used for mixing powdery materials, either dry or wet, a plough being fastened to the arm(s) carrying the wheel(s) to turn over and spread the material being mixed. The wheels were made of cast iron or stone, the latter being used in the case of gunpowder incorporating mills to avoid the possibility of sparks. The edge mill was also known as an edge runner, or in some industries as a pulping stone.

edge rails rails on which locomotives and rolling stock fitted with flanged wheels operate, the rim of the wheel running along the top edge of the rail and the wheel flanges running against the inner surfaces of the pair of rails to keep the train on the track. Edge rails superseded FLANGED RAILS around the 1790s and early 1800s when many designs of cast-iron edge rails were introduced, notably the short 'fish-bellied' rail of William Jessop (1745–1814). Malleable iron edge rails were first tried out in 1805 but were unsuccessful, and wrought iron was introduced in 1808. Edge rails belong to the period when steam locomotives were being developed by George Stephenson (1781–1848): his locomotive *Blucher* of 1814 was the first successful locomotive with flanged wheels at Killingworth colliery. John Birkinshaw, of Bedlington, Northd., patented a method of rolling wrought iron edge rails in 1820 (patent no. 4503). Steel edge rails were first introduced at Derby in 1857, made by R.F. Mushet (1811–91).

eduction pipe pipe through which warm CONDENSATE from the base of the cylinder of a NEWCOMEN ATMOSPHERIC ENGINE flowed and entered the HOTWELL via a leather non-return valve. Today, it would be called the exhaust pipe.

egg and eye a lead mining term for slots cut into opposite walls of a vein to hold STEMPLES or timber beams.

Egyptian wheel the chain and bucket pump introduced in the late 16th century for raising water from coal mines. Such a device was used *c.*1590 at Culrose colliery, Fifeshire, and at later sites. It comprised an endless iron chain with buckets attached at intervals. The lower end of the chain loop hung down a shallow mine shaft and dipped into a drainage sump. The upper end passed over a wheel which was rotated by a horse. As buckets entered the sump, they scooped water out and discharged it to waste as they turned over the top wheel, returning empty down the shaft to be refilled at the bottom. The device was probably used earlier in German mines, and was no doubt copied from the ancient irrigation devices used in Egypt and the Middle East, hence its name.

electricity a form of energy associated with an excess or deficiency of electrons on an atom. There are two kinds of electricity: static, and voltaic or current electricity. Static electricity is produced when certain materials are rubbed together, producing either negative or positive charges. The fossil resin amber becomes electrically charged by friction when rubbed, and it is from the Greek name for amber, *electron*, that the word electricity was coined some time in the 16th century. Voltaic electricity is named after Alessandro Volta

(1745–1827), an Italian physicist, who around 1800 caused an electric current to flow through a wire from a simple primary cell in which chemical energy was converted into electrical energy. An electric current can also be made to flow through a coil of wire when it is rotated in a magnetic field, and conversely a coil in a magnetic field can be made to rotate when a current is passed through it. The former arrangement is the principle of the electric generator, and the latter that of the electric motor.

Electricity as we know it today only began to make an impact at the end of the Industrial Revolution, although it was a scientific curiosity for many years before that. Its static form was known for centuries, and it was not until flowing currents could be produced that practical applications of this form of energy were investigated by a succession of scientists, physicists, and engineers, worldwide. Electric current was first obtained from primary batteries, and the first useful application was in the communications field, when William Fothergill Cooke (1806–79) and Charles Wheatstone (1802–75) took out their first patent (no. 7390) in 1837 for the electric telegraph. Their first trial comprised a battery-powered circuit of about two miles between Euston and Camden Town stations on the London North Western Railway: a signal could be sent from one end to the other which caused a magnetized needle to rotate and point to a letter on a board mounted behind it, allowing a message to be spelled out. BATTERIES provided the energy source for all early electric currents, and the next experimental applications were to drive various conveyances by devising an electrical means for obtaining rotation.

Michael Faraday (1791–1867) had produced an embryo electric motor experimentally in 1821 at the Royal Institution, London, when he succeeded in demonstrating the inter-relation between an electric current and a magnetic field. In 1831 he laid the foundations for the transformer, the direct current (DC) generator and the alternating current (AC) alternator. The first DC electric motor is usually credited to dal Negro of Padua, Italy, who in 1830 obtained rotary motion from an oscillating magnet maintained in continuous movement by the current flowing through a coil from a battery. One end of the magnet was connected to a pawl acting on a ratchet wheel whose axle received intermittent pulses from the magnet oscillations but was kept in constant rotation by a flywheel. Other improved motors were invented and generators or dynamos (from the Greek

dunamis meaning power) for producing direct current driven by PRIME MOVERS such as waterwheels and steam engines were developed to give bigger electric currents than could be obtained from batteries.

Electric power for industrial use was developed in the 1880s, and a number of small local power stations were built supplying power over limited areas. To drive the generating equipment, WILLANS compound vertical high speed steam engines were preferred for their smooth running. Around 1854 generation by STEAM TURBINE was introduced in a small way using Parsons machines. Electric power for traction from a non-battery source was first introduced in Britain in 1883 when Magnus Volk's beach railway of 2 ft gauge opened in August at Brighton, Sussex, drawing current from a 140 volt DC third rail. Power was provided from a Siemens dynamo driven by a 2 hp Crossley gas engine. Up till this date electric power was by direct current, but the advantages of alternating current were beginning to be realized and investigated. The first attempt to produce a rotating electromagnetic field without any physical rotation of parts was in 1879 by Walter Bailey, using two pulsating currents out of phase by 90°. Some ten years later, Nicola Tesla built the first two-phase induction AC motor in the USA. The squirrel-cage AC, three-phase induction motor, soon to be the workhorse of industry, was developed soon after, the USA taking the lead. By 1900 there were many factories in the USA using them, and Britain swiftly followed suit.

By the 1890s electric motors were beginning to replace steam engine driven LINESHAFTS and belt drives in mills and factories. In some instances, industrial concerns installed their own generating equipment driven by steam engines to supply current to motors driving the machinery in their plant, and large horsepower motors were installed to drive existing lineshafting. When public supplies became available from local power stations, the demise of the steam engine commenced, and metered power was taken from the public supply. In due course lineshafting and belt drives were dispensed with completely, and machinery was driven by individual AC electric motors. This arrangement allowed greater flexibility in siting machinery which was no longer constrained by the layout of lineshafting. Although AC is the main type of electric power in use today, DC machines still have their own particular uses. *See also* LIGHTING.

Appleyard, R. *History of the Institution of Electrical Engineers: 1871–1931*, IEE, 1939

Development of Power Cables, Hunter and Hazell, 1956
Dunsheath, P. *A History of Electrical Engineering*, Faber, 1962
Fleming, A. *Fifty Years of Electricity*, 1921
MacLaren, R. *The Rise of the Electrical Industry during the Nineteenth Century*, Princetown University Press, 1943
Parsons, R.H. *Early Days of the Power Station Industry*, Cambridge University Press, 1939
Randell, W.L. *S.Z. de Ferranti, and his Influence upon Electrical Development*, Longmans Green, 1943
Tucker, D.G. 'Refuse destructors and their use for generating electricity', *Industrial Archaeology Review* II (1977), 5–27

'elephant' boiler a pioneering design of WATERTUBE STEAM BOILER developed in the early 19th century, and used on the Continent and Britain for raising steam in mills etc. A typical design of around 1820 is shown in Fig. 10, and comprised a large wrought-iron horizontal shell or cylinder which was the main boiler, set in brickwork, with a hand-fired sloping grate beneath it. The hot gases from the fire passed under the boiler shell to the rear, where two long horizontal water drums or tubes round which the gases passed were slung below the main shell and connected to it. These two tubes, known as 'bouileurs', may be regarded as elementary water tubes, whose purpose was to increase the heating surface to raise the thermal efficiency of the unit.

Such boilers were popular during the years 1830–50, but were gradually superseded after about 1845 when the LANCASHIRE BOILER with its twin internal firetubes was introduced.

ell (or eln) a measure of length (from the Greek *ulna*, elbow) used among other things for measuring lengths of cloth (*see* ALNAGER). The actual length varied with time and place over the centuries: it was based on the length of the human arm, but different versions were used, as measurements were taken either from the elbow or shoulder to the wrist or finger-tips. An English ell was reckoned to be 45 in but a Scottish ell was 37.2 in, whereas a Flemish ell was 27 in. Double ells were also in use, the French ell of 54 in being double the Flemish. The unit is now obsolete, but was still in use in some remote parts until early in the 19th century. An ellwand or elwint was a yard measure. There are instances of mine depths being measured in ells in the 18th century.

elling hearth a drying kiln for producing WHITE COAL. It comprised a stone-lined bowl some 10 ft in diameter and of similar depth, with several large branches laid across about 2 ft above the base to form a staging with narrow spaces left between the branches. Small pieces of wood, stripped of its bark, were piled up on the staging and a slow fire of brushwood maintained in the space below. The heat and smoke rising through the piled wood dried out all the sap from the pieces of wood to form white coal, which was then used as a fuel for ORE HEARTHS.

elvan, *see* DYKE

embankment a man-made ridge to carry a road, canal, or railway across a declivity, or area subject to flooding, by a near-level surface (level in the case of canals of course) thus eliminating, or reducing unnecessary gradients, or skirting circuits. For a canal, an embankment would have a level top surface, but this is not always so for roads and railways. The opposite to an embankment is a CUTTING.

There are some well-known early embankments which were built mainly by shovel and wheelbarrow by the navvies of the first railways and canals. Among these may be mentioned the south approach to the famous Pontcysyllte aqueduct on the Llangollen Canal, opened in 1805, which comprises a 97 ft high embankment, 1,500 ft long. The Burnley embankment on the Leeds and Liverpool Canal carries the canal across the town for 0.75 of a mile. The Wolverton embankment in Buckinghamshire is 1.5 miles long and carries the London to Birmingham Railway, opened in 1838. The Stanley embankment on Anglesey, north Wales, completed in 1823 by Thomas Telford as part of the London-Holyhead (A5) road improvement, is 1,300 yd long by 16 ft above sea-level, and shortened the old circuitous road by 1.5 miles.

A reservoir DAM is sometimes called an embankment, as are the raised banks of rivers designed to prevent flooding. An embankment was often called a battery in the days of early wooden railways, and it is sometimes called a dyke (or dike).

enclosure of land (or intake) the conversion of common and waste land near towns and villages into areas for agricultural and grazing use. Voluntary private enclosure had gone on from Tudor times, but as the pressure to turn uncultivated land to agrarian uses increased, it became necessary to obtain parliamentary sanction for the change, and override minority opposition. A few Acts of Parliament were obtained during the reign of George II (1727–60), and they became numerous by the first decade of the 19th century. Separate Acts were necessary at first to enclose each parcel of land, but the General Enclosure Acts of 1801, 1836 and 1845 streamlined and cheapened the process. The rate of forceable parliamentary enclosure was nearly 53,000 acres per annum in the period 1802–15, and an increase occurred during the Napoleonic war because of pressure for home-grown food. By 1820 or so, old open-field type of agriculture was becoming a rarity: whereas 75,000 acres were enclosed in the period 1727–60, the years 1761–92 saw a further 478,000 acres enclosed and 1793–1815 over 1.0 million more acres. The legal enclosure of land ceased in 1876.

Enclosure increased agricultural productivity, and caused a population shift by displacing farmers and their labourers who were forced off the land into the towns: fortunately, the rise in industrial output at the same time meant that there was a demand for this displaced labour. Whereas 16th-century enclosures were intended primarily to provide sheep grazing for wool production to supply the expanding woollen cloth industry of that period, 18th- and 19th-century enclosures were driven by the need to provide more food more cheaply to feed the rapidly increasing industrial population in towns and cities.

In upland Britain, the Enclosure Acts resulted in the building of the majority of dry stone walling now seen on the fells and moors surrounding towns and villages. The Acts included the building of public and access roads in many cases: existing DROVERS ROADS were diverted from direct routes and made to skirt parcels of enclosed land, often with acute bends. A typical 'enclosure wall' measures 4 ft 6 in high, for which itinerant stone wallers were paid around 8*s* for a 7 yd stretch, involving some 10 tons of stone. When an enclosure took place, an accurate map or plan was made of the area involved, showing field boundaries and names, buildings and roads. These are useful sources of contemporary information for the industrial archaeologists: there are large numbers of maps for the years 1770 to 1876, and they are kept in county record offices.

end one WARP thread in a cloth.

engine a term commonly applied today to a machine for producing power, such as a steam engine, petrol engine, etc. In the early 17th century, however, it merely meant any 'device' or mechanical contrivance, whether hand- or horse-operated. Early spellings were ingyne, engin, often shortened to gin, or ginny, or jenny – hence HORSE GIN, COTTON GIN, etc. The word is related to the Latin *ingenium* meaning ingenious or clever, and a person who practised the building of engines began to be called an engineer. A distinction was made between a military engineer who built engines of war and one who made engines for civil purposes, and from the latter came the present-day designation

of a civil engineer who builds roads, dams, etc. Prior to the introduction of steam engines, waterwheels were described by some writers as engines. The first mechanized versions of CARDING MACHINES were known as carding engines, and are still known by the same name today.

engine clock, *see* MILL TIME

engineering industry the industry concerned with applying scientific principles to the design and construction of engines, buildings, roads, etc., brought into being by the INDUSTRIAL REVOLUTION. In medieval times the term engineer was used to describe a military man versed in the design and construction of fortifications and the cumbersome machines used in waging war such as siege catapults, and later, in the 16th century, the making of cannons.

In the 18th century, when peaceful works such as improving rivers for navigation and the cutting of canals began, the men engaged in this type of work were called civil engineers to differentiate them from military engineers. Civil engineering as a separate activity then developed. John Smeaton (1724–92) called himself a civil engineer, and during his lifetime was responsible for a variety of work such as improvements to the NEWCOMEN ATMOSPHERIC ENGINE, mathematical instrument making, the construction of the Eddystone lighthouse, and the building of canals, bridges and harbours. He was in fact a generalist without any speciality, as were other engineers of his day. In 1771 he founded the Society of Civil Engineers, also known as the Smeatonian Society, which became an important professional body for the infant civil engineering industry. This Society led to the formation of the Institution of Civil Engineers in 1818, with Thomas Telford (1757–1834) as its first president.

In 1847 a separate professional body was formed which specialized in mechanical engineering, calling itself the Institution of Mechanical Engineers, with George Stephenson (1781–1848) as its first president. The origin of mechanical engineering can be traced back to the invention of the rotative steam engine by James Watt (1736–1819) *c*.1782. The building of steam engines and other machinery, particularly for textiles, created an industry specializing in the manipulation of metals and the design of mechanisms. The coming of the railways added further stimulation to the growth and need for this branch of engineering.

Men engaged in mechanical engineering were known in its early days as mechanics or millwrights. Early steam engines were hand built on site by millwrights using traditional skills acquired from building water- and windmills. These men were used to working in timber and iron, combining the skills of both blacksmith and carpenter. They had limited scientific knowledge, designing empirically from experience and a certain amount of trial and error. Much of their work was overdesigned because of a lack of knowledge of the STRENGTH OF MATERIALS, and considering also their limited material resources and primitive tools, remarkable results were obtained to their credit. A Society of Millwrights was formed in 1805, and this together with the establishment of MECHANICS' INSTITUTES in 1827 spread technical knowledge among those engaged in engineering. The *Mechanics' Magazine*, begun in 1823, also helped in the interchange and spread of engineering information.

An important branch of mechanical engineering is the manufacture of MACHINE TOOLS. When the Institution of Mechanical Engineers was formed, only primitive machine tools were available for cutting and forming machine parts. Cast iron and wrought iron were the main materials for heavily stressed components; the main non-ferrous metals were brass and gunmetal. Wrought iron could only be made in comparatively small pieces and had to be welded or bolted together to make large items. Cheap, mild steel did not make its appearance in bulk until the 1860s. In the 1840s cutting tools, which have of necessity to be harder than the materials they are to cut, were confined to chilled cast iron and carburized wrought iron. Screw threads were only standardized in 1841 by Joseph Whitworth (1803–87), and prior to this nuts and bolts were hand-made in a variety of screw threads, each mating pair being almost unique making interchangeability virtually impossible. Gradually improvements were made to machine tools resulting in the ability to manufacture parts to a greater accuracy. Joseph Bramah (1748–1814) and his pupil Henry Maudslay (1771–1831), and others, were notable pioneers in the field. Better machine tools bred still better machine tools, enabling greater precision and interchangeability of machine parts to be realized. At the same time, a wider selection of metals became available as advances in metallurgy introduced alloy steels, heat treatment techniques, etc. Large engineering works came into being making engines, boilers, locomotives, and all kinds of manufacturing machinery, employing apprenticed tradesmen, designers and draughtsmen. Rolled steel sections began replacing cast iron and built-up wrought iron girders in the 1840s, extending the scope for structural engineering.

Civil engineering is a largely outdoor activity, and responsible for the creation of the contractor for carrying out work on site. One of the first civil engineering contractors was William Cubitt (1785–1861), who built canals and railways. The railway age brought to the fore a famous contractor, Thomas Brassey (1805–70), who built many railways in Britain and overseas, working for engineers such as Robert Stephenson (1803–59) and Joseph Locke (1805–60). The main materials of construction were timber, stone and brick at first, with all earth moving done by sheer muscle power. Brassey employed as many as 100,000 navvies (*see* NAVIGATION) at one time on occasions. Mechanical aids were not at their disposal until the 1880s. Civil engineering included construction of canals, railways, roads, bridges, docks, public water supplies etc. An early civil engineer was James Brindley (1716–72), constructor of the first British canals including the famous Harecastle tunnel near Stoke-on-Trent, in 1777. Industrial and commercial buildings such as warehouses were often included in contracts for docks and railways carried out by civil engineers, although here there is some impingement on the work of the architect.

Further specialization in the engineering industry took place when the use of ELECTRICITY spread. This more or less began with its application to signalling when the Electric Telegraph Company began operating railway telegraphs. This created another branch of engineering, and the Society of Telegraphic Engineers, founded in 1871, eventually changed its name in 1889 to the Institution of Electrical Engineers. By then electric LIGHTING was established and electric power just commencing, the first steam-driven power station in the world being built at Holborn Viaduct, London, in 1882. The civil, mechanical, and electrical institutions are the three senior engineering bodies. Many further subdivisions and specialities were to come later.

In the world of marine engineering and ship building, a change from wooden hulls to iron took place in the mid-19th century, and steam power was introduced about the same time. SHIP building became more closely allied to engineering than in former times, and the Institution of Naval Architects was founded in 1860.

The engineering industry was responsible for a large number of inventions and patents during the Industrial Revolution and succeeding years. By providing manufacturing machinery, power sources, and mechanized transport systems, the engineering industry was mainly responsible for Britain earning the title 'Workshop of the World' by the mid-19th century.

Armytage, W.H.G. *A Social History of Engineering*, Faber, 1970
Buchanan, R.A. *The Engineers: A History of the Engineering Profession in Britain 1750–1914*, Kingsley, 1989
Burstall, A.F. *A History of Mechanical Engineering*, Faber, 1963
Dunsheath, P. *A History of Electrical Engineering*, Faber, 1962
Lea, F.C. *Sir Joseph Whitworth: A Pioneer of Mechanical Engineering*, Longman, 1946
Rolt, L.T.C. *Victorian Engineering*, Penguin, 1970
Upton, N. *An Illustrated History of Civil Engineering*, Heinemann, 1975

engine indicator an instrument which can be attached to the cylinder of a working engine to draw a diagram showing the internal pressure and volume changes; from the diagram, the indicated horsepower of the engine may be calculated. The instrument can be used on both steam and internal combustion engines. *See also* INDICATOR DIAGRAM.

Engine Reporter a series of monthly reports first published in 1810 by Joel Lean of Crenver, Cornwall, giving the DUTY each month of various BEAM STEAM ENGINES dewatering mines in that county. The reports ran for nearly 100 years and were carried on by his sons Thomas and John after his death in 1812. By promoting rivalry between mines, duties were considerably raised, from 20.4 million ft–lb per cwt of coal in 1811 to 61.8 million in 1850, for Watt-type engines. By comparison, the best duty achieved by a Newcomen type engine in 1772 was about 12.6 million ft–lb per cwt of coal, giving a thermal efficiency of about 1 per cent. After *c*.1850, duties began to fall off, probably because of ageing engines, and the increased friction and weight of pump rods as mines got deeper, and shafts often more crooked.

Lean, T. and brother. *Historical Statement of the Improvements made in the Duty Performed by the Steam Engines in Cornwall*, 1839; reprinted Truro, 1969

English Heritage a government body responsible for the protection, preservation and conservation of historic buildings and monuments in England. Created in 1984, English Heritage is partly funded by the government, and partly from the annual subscriptions of its members. It manages over 350 historic buildings and monuments, including some of industrial interest, and works with the government and local authorities on the LISTING of buildings and scheduling of monuments. Its other responsibilities include the awarding of repair grants for major conservation projects, such as for the well-known Ribblehead railway viaduct in Yorkshire.

English Heritage has its headquarters in London. Similar bodies manage monuments in Scotland and Wales (*see* HISTORIC SCOTLAND, CADW).

Conserving the Inheritance of Industry: English Heritage Grants for Industrial Archaeology 1984–1993, English Heritage, 1995
Industrial Archaeology: A Policy Statement by English Heritage, English Heritage, 1995

English process, *see* LEAD CHAMBER PROCESS

entablature an upper structure supported by columns, and the name given to the overhead framework supporting the beam bearings etc. on a BEAM STEAM ENGINE carried on columns from the base. On later engines this was frequently highly decorative, as were the supporting columns. The entablature made beam engines self standing and independent of the engine house for support.

entering, *see* DRAWING AND REACHING

epicyclic gear two gearwheels in which the axis of rotation of one wheel is carried on a link which keeps them in mesh, and is free to revolve around the axis of rotation of the other wheel. The central wheel is known as a sun wheel, and the other as a planetary wheel. When used with a connecting rod attached to the planetary wheel, the system can convert linear to rotary motion. James Watt used this idea to avoid the CRANK patent of James Pickard (*see* SUN AND PLANET MOTION). Epicyclic gearing can be used for large speed reductions in limited spaces.

equal beam the beam of a BEAM STEAM ENGINE which is pivoted at the centre of its length. Not all engine beams were equal beams: the beams of CORNISH PUMPING ENGINES could be pivoted off-centre, making the piston stroke longer than the stroke of the pumps.

equilibrium ring a steam-tight ring which fits between the back of a large SLIDE VALVE and the inside of the valve chest. Exhaust steam acts inside the ring so that the pressure partially balances the pressures inside the valve and reduces the force necessary to move it.

equilibrium valve the valve in the steam passage of a Cornish BEAM ENGINE which connected the top of the cylinder to the bottom. When the piston reached almost to the bottom of its stroke, the steam admission above it was cut off and the equilibrium valve opened automatically by a linkage operated by the movement of the overhead beam. This allowed the steam pressure to equalize either side of the piston and exhaust to the atmosphere (or a CONDENSER). The piston then returned to the top of the cylinder under the action of the unbalanced weight of the heavy pump rods attached to the other end of the beam. The return movement of the beam closed the equilibrium valve so that the cycle could repeat itself.

everlasting, *see* DURANT

everlastings, *see* LASTINGS

exhauster in GAS MANUFACTURE, a low pressure vane pump which drew gas from the RETORTS, through the HYDRAULIC MAIN and CONDENSER, and pushed it on through the purification plant to the GASHOLDER. It increases the gas output from the retorts. Originally invented by Simeon Broadmeadow (patent no. 5146, 1825), it was later improved by John Grafton in 1841 and by John Beale in 1866 (patent no. 1402).

exhibitions expositions or fairs which showed progress in industrial expertise and technology. The first industrial exhibition in England was in 1761, organized by the Society for the Encouragement of Arts, Manufactures, and Commerce. Later important exhibitions were the GREAT EXHIBITION, CRYSTAL PALACE, London (1851); the NEW YORK WORLD FAIR, USA (1853); the PARIS EXHIBITION, France (1855); the International Exhibition, South Kensington, London (1862); the Centennial Exposition, Philadelphia, USA (1876); the Düsseldorf Exhibition, Germany (1880) and the Universal Exhibition, Paris, France (1889). The latest inventions and developments were often shown for the first time at such exhibitions, and the exhibition catalogues form a useful source of information for industrial archaeologists. The most famous exhibition was the 1851 one, and this spurred other industrially developing countries to follow suit, the USA and France being quick to stage their own.

Findling, J.E. *Historical Dictionary of World's Fairs and Expositions, 1851–1988*, Greenwood Press, 1990
The Great Exhibition Official Catalogue, 4 vols, 1851
The International Exhibition of 1862 Catalogue, 5 vols, 1862
(Copies of these two catalogues are usually in the archives of main libraries.)

expansion link that component of a linkage motion on a reversing steam engine which enables the CUT-OFF point to be altered by changing the position of a block sliding in a slot in the link. The sliding block imparts motion to the steam valve rod, and its location on the expansion link is altered either by lifting or lowering the link itself on some link motions, or by moving the block up or down on a stationary link on other designs. The expansion link also reverses the rotation of the engine.

expansive working refers to the method of using steam in a steam engine which conserves the amount used in each stroke, by using the expansive properties of steam under pressure. High pressure steam from the boiler is admitted to the cylinder at the commencement of each piston stroke, and after the piston has travelled part of its stroke, the admission of further live steam is stopped by the action of the valve gear. The steam trapped inside the cylinder then expands, and in so doing gives up some of its internal energy accompanied by a lowering of pressure and temperature as it forces the piston along for the remainder of the stroke until it is exhausted from the cylinder at a lower pressure. The point at which the admission of steam is stopped is called the CUT-OFF, usually expressed as a fraction of the full stroke. The ratio of expansion is then the reciprocal of the cut-off fraction, ignoring the CLEARANCE VOLUME.

Expansive working of steam was first thought of by James Watt in 1769, but he did not patent it until 1782 (patent no. 1321). Most stationary steam engines and locomotives were worked expansively after this date, and in some cases, particularly locomotives, the ratio of expansion can be altered whilst the engine is running by varying the point of cut-off. The degree of expansion possible is limited by the piston speed and cylinder dimensions, and the need to avoid condensation resulting from lowered temperature.

extraction engine a compound steam engine with provision for bleeding off some steam after it has passed through the high pressure cylinder and before it enters the low pressure cylinder, i.e. from the transfer pipe. Such extracted steam is used for some other purpose in the factory. *See also* COMPOUNDING (1).

F

factory a generic name for a building, or group of buildings, housing machinery or equipment for manufacturing. The word factory comes from the Latin *factorium* meaning 'place of making' and its first recorded use in Britain dates from 1582. There were elementary 'factories' in medieval monasteries, but the true, purpose-built factory dates from the beginning of the 18th century in Britain. It is believed that the first such factory was the three-storey silk throwing mill equipped with water-powered, primitive Dutch machinery erected in 1702 in Derby by Thomas Cotchett. His business failed after a few years, and nothing remains today of the mill. Other factories were built after this, but the father of the factory system as it is known today is regarded as Richard Arkwright (1732–92) because of the organizational skills he applied to his cotton factories around Cromford, also in Derbyshire.

The term factory has a very wide application, and is usually qualified by the addition of a description of the type of activity carried on in the premises, e.g. lace factory, furniture factory, food factory, etc. There are several synonyms, such as works (as in ironworks, gas works, etc.); mill (e.g. fulling mill, cotton mill, paper mill); and foundry, forge, brewery, etc. The buildings comprising a factory are normally specially designed to suit the requirements of the industry it houses, and therefore incorporate certain features peculiar to that industry. These, and the materials and type of construction used at different periods, together with the method of providing a power source, are of interest to industrial archaeologists. The history and development of factory buildings are outlined in more detail under INDUSTRIAL BUILDINGS. INDUSTRIAL SETTLEMENTS often grew up associated with some early factories, often built by the factory owner to attract a labour force.

Meakin, Bridget. *Model Factories and Villages: Ideal Conditions of Labour and Housing*, 1905
Sundstrom, E. *Work Places*, Cambridge University Press, 1986
Tann, Jennifer. *The Development of the Factory*, Cornmarket Press, 1970

Factory Act 1833 known as Althorp's Act after its sponsor Lord Althorp (John Charles Spencer, 1782–1845), the Act's full title was 'An Act to Regulate the Labour of Children and Young Persons in the Mills and Factories of the United Kingdom'. Also known as the Children's Charter, the Act came into force on 1 March 1834, and is regarded as the first really effective FACTORY ACT. It applied to all textile factories. No child under nine was to work in a mill (except silk mills); those under thirteen were restricted to a nine-hour day; and young persons between thirteen and eighteen were restricted to a twelve-hour day. Children from nine to thirteen were to receive two hours schooling per day. Salaried inspectors were introduced for the first time; at first there were only four, but the number increased later. The

Act marked the beginning of compulsory education on the part-time system (*see* HALF-TIMER) although it only applied to factory children. The 1833 Act was unpopular with many mill owners who thought the textile trade would be ruined by the restrictions imposed. Their opposition led to the forming of the FACTORY LAW AMENDMENT ASSOCIATION.

Factory Acts parliamentary Acts or laws passed during the 19th century to regulate the working hours and conditions of employment in factories. As factories developed in the previous century, scant attention was paid by most employers to the working conditions or length of time workers had to spend in the factories, although there were some exceptions. Young children were employed for long hours, and child paupers were a common source of labour, particularly in textile mills, where they were often exploited. The conditions under which the industrial workforce laboured was not widely known throughout the country, but eventually a few enlightened individuals created enough concern in the first half of the 19th century to force a series of Acts through Parliament to ease the situation. Among the philanthropists who succeeded in bringing these about, Anthony Ashley Cooper, the 7th Earl of Shaftesbury (1801–85), was prominent.

The first Factory Act, known as the Health and Morals of Apprentices Act, was passed in 1802. It limited the number of hours to be worked per day by apprentices to twelve, and applied to cotton mills only. This Act was not very effective, and led to the passing of the Cotton Factory Act in 1819 which again dealt with the abuse of child labour: it applied to apprentices and wage-earning children who lived with their parents, and stipulated that children under the age of nine could not be employed. Later Acts in 1820, 1825, and 1830 amended the 1819 Act in details, and all were repealed by the 1831 Act, which prohibited night work for young persons under twenty-one. This again proved ineffective, employers finding ways of evading the requirements. In its turn, it was repealed in 1833 and replaced by the FACTORY ACT 1833, known as Althorp's Act after the then-leader of the House of Commons. This may be considered to be the first effective Factory Act to bring about reform in factory conditions.

A later Act in 1844 extended the 1833 Act, introduced the guarding of dangerous machinery, and transferred the power of prosecution from the inspectors to local magistrates, a fairer manner of dealing with alleged cases of employers breaking the law. By now there was widespread agitation for shorter working hours in factories, and after several attempts, the TEN HOURS ACT was passed in 1847. This Act was amended in 1850 and again in 1853. Other industries than the textile industry were gradually covered by various Acts, such as the Coal Mines Regulation Act of 1842 which forbade the employment of girls and women underground. In 1867, the Workshops Regulation Act was introduced to cover places of employment other than factories, meaning places where a handicraft was carried on by under fifty young people or women, excluding domestic residences not under the direct control of an employer. All these various Acts were consolidated in one Act, the Factory and Workshop Act of 1878, which covered all types of industry. Further reforms continued: in 1891 a Factory and Workshop Act forbade the employment of children under eleven, and domestic outworkers were brought into its scope. The HALF-TIME schooling system was not finally abolished until the Education Act of 1918.

Whilst the main aims of the various Factory Acts were of a social nature, they are of interest to the industrial archaeologists in that they affected processes, methods of working, and machinery design, etc., as well as the design of industrial buildings. *See also* ACTS OF PARLIAMENT.

'Factory King' nickname given to Richard Oastler (1789–1861) of Bradford, Yorks., who spent most of his life trying to improve the lot of factory workers, particularly that of children. His activities brought about the TEN HOURS ACT of 1847. A bronze monument to Oastler by J.B. Philip stands in the centre of Bradford.
Driver, Cecil. *The Life of Richard Oastler*, 1946

Factory Law Amendment Association a 19th-century employers' association opposed to FACTORY ACTS. Opponents of the FACTORY ACT 1833 thought the cotton trade would be ruined by the loss of cheap child labour, leading to high yarn prices and consequent loss of foreign trade, and that the loss of children's income to families working in the textile industry would lead to poverty. The Association was founded by mill owners and supporters to try to amend the Act. In the event, their fears were unfounded; the Association was unsuccessful and eventually disbanded.

factory system the system of working in which a number of workers are employed under one roof for a wage, as opposed to the DOMESTIC SYSTEM of earlier times. The main features of the FACTORY system are the division of labour (leading to job specialization), direct supervision, regulation of hours of work, and the use and provision of power for machinery. To these may be added quality control, and concentration of materials in one place.

The transfer from domestic working to factory was a gradual process which accelerated during the INDUSTRIAL REVOLUTION. It was the direct result of the invention of machinery which needed space and capital, not available to the domestic worker, and brought about the entrepreneur who put up the money to finance the venture. Machinery required power to operate it, again not available to the domestic worker. The congregation of workers in one workplace led to the formation of trade unions to raise standards of employment. Factories were not popular with domestic textile workers in the early days, since they were forced to relinquish home working for working in the factory, thus giving up their independence for the rigid control of the factory, because they were unable to compete with the high output from power driven machinery. Conditions in factories were unsatisfactory at first: women and children were made to work long hours for pitiful wages. Eventually legislation to control conditions was introduced through a series of FACTORY ACTS.

Not all industries were absorbed into the factory system, particularly the craft industries, many of which remained largely domestic industries for a long time. However, there is evidence of isolated approaches to some kind of factory system prior to the onset of the Industrial Revolution: John Wynchcombe, a clothier of Newbury, Berks., employed several hundred workers in the 16th century. Stumpe purchased Malmesbury Abbey, Wilts., after the Dissolution (1536) and turned it into a textile 'factory'; and there were other instances in Kendal and Halifax. Early Cornish tin miners also worked for a wage.
Pinchbeck, Ivy. *Women Workers in the Industrial Revolution, 1650–1850*, 1930
Tann, Jennifer. *The Development of the Factory*, Cornmarket Press, 1970
Ward, J.T. *The Factory System; Vol. 1, Birth and Growth; Vol. 2, The Factory System and Society*, David and Charles, 1970

faggotting (or piling) bars of puddled iron placed upon each other and reheated in a furnace before being hammered together to form one piece, from which MERCHANT BARS were made after rolling. This tended to produce a more even composition in the finished bar.

faience another name for TERRACOTTA. The word comes from the name of the Italian town Faenza near Bologna, noted for its production of articles made in this material.

Fairbairn–Beeley boiler a steam raising boiler comprising three horizontal inter-connected drums mounted one above the other, and set in brick flues. It was popular in the 1890s. Fig. 9 shows a typical unit: it has a lower water drum 5 ft in diameter by 18 ft 6 in long, with three connections to a middle drum mounted above it, the latter being 21 ft long and of similar diameter. The lower drum has a large central tube running for part of its front length to take a mechanical stoker and firegrate, and this leads to a nest of small firetubes near the rear of the shell. The middle drum holds water in its lower half with a steam space above. The top drum, which has two connections to the steam space of the middle drum, is much smaller than the other two shells – only measuring 2 ft in diameter by 8 ft long – and acts as a steam reservoir from which the steam is drawn off. The hot gases from the furnace pass through the firetubes at the rear of the lower drum and split into two streams to return to the front of the boiler through passageways or side flues formed by the external brickwork (not shown) surrounding the lower drum. They then rise to return to the back of the middle drum in similar external brick flues before leaving towards the chimney. Such boilers were built with a typical working pressure of 150 psi and high thermal efficiencies were possible. Besides general steam raising duties in factories and mills, the design was popular for providing steam to drive hydraulic pumping gear in hydraulic power systems.

Fairbairn's lever a mechanical testing machine, built by William Fairbairn (1789–1874) and Eaton Hodgkinson (1789–1861) and used in Fairbairn and Lillie's Manchester engineering works. It was used to carry out important, pioneering tests on various materials particularly cast-iron beams, to determine practical information on their strength and other properties.

Fairbairn, Sir W. *The Life of Sir William Fairbairn, Bart*, edited and completed by W. Pole, 1877; reprinted by David and Charles, 1970

faller one of a number of bars with rows of upstanding COMBING pins which are moved along a horizontal path in a GILL BOX to feed fibrous materials such as wool into a machine. Each bar falls vertically at the end of its travel to return empty underneath to the start position where it rises to pick up fresh material. In this manner a continuous feed mechanism is obtained.

faller wire the wire stretching across the width of a spinning JENNY or MULE which, when lowered onto the spun yarn, directs the yarn perpendicularly onto the spindle so that WINDING ON can be done. Whilst spinning is taking place, the faller wire is positioned clear of the yarn. By traversing the wire in a small arc, a COP of yarn may be built up whilst winding on proceeds. This wire was originally called a presser wire by James Hargreaves in his 1770 patent specification.

false twist description given when the central portion of a strand of fibres held at each end is twisted to give an S-TWIST along one half from the centre, and a Z-TWIST over the other half. Fibre cohesion is provided along the length although the net twist between the extremities is zero. This has useful applications in wool COMBING machines and the spinning of waste cotton yarn. The twist is applied by passing the strand through a rotating tube where the friction between its inner surface and the strand gives the required rolling or twisting action.

fang a Derbyshire term for a pipe bringing fresh air into the underground workings of a lead mine.

fans and blowers mechanical means for moving large quantities of air for purposes such as ventilating mines, delivering combustion air to blast furnaces, steam boilers, etc. Primitive fans were described by Georg Bauer as early as 1556 for ventilating German mines. Attempts to ventilate mines mechanically in Britain were made in the late 18th century to replace the old method of maintaining a fire at the base of the UPCAST SHAFT so that the rising gases would draw fresh air through the workings from the DOWNCAST SHAFT. By the mid-19th century James Nasmyth (1808–90) had designed a centrifugal fan for mine ventilation, but real improvements were made a decade or so afterwards when the Guibal and Waddle fans were introduced. These were large, slow-running fans with impellors often up to 40–50 ft in diameter, drawing air through the galleries from the downcast shaft. They were mounted on top of the upcast shaft, and were driven by a steam engine. Two engines were provided, one in use and the other on standby in case of failure of the driving engine. The fan runner was often set in a large curved brick housing. The Guibal fan, developed *c*. 1859 by a Belgian engineer, was a large, paddle-bladed fan with eight to ten wooden paddles; the Waddle fans, made by two Welsh brothers, had twenty-four or so backwards-curving metal blades. Another well-known maker of mine ventilating fans and steam engines to drive them was Walker Brothers of Wigan, Lancs., who supplied large fans with double entry impellors (patent no. 17141, 1887).

Volute for the 36 ft diameter Guibal fan at Duke Pit, Whitehaven, Cumbria

Alternatives to fans with rotating impellors were reciprocating air pumps, such as the STRUVE VENTILATOR which was popular around the 1860s for mine work. Similar positive displacement blowing cylinders were used to force air into blast furnaces. The ROOTS' BLOWER, originally used for mine ventilation, was later used for blast furnaces since it is capable of producing higher air pressures than centrifugal fans. By 1890 ventilation of mines by underground furnaces had almost ceased, and large centrifugal fans became standard practice, improving safety underground and permitting deeper working. Later still, the more efficient axial flow or propellor fans were adopted. In 1911 all mine fans had to be made reversible so that galleries could be cleared of smoke and heat resulting from underground fires.

Chapman, N.A. 'Ventilation of mines', *Industrial Archaeology Review* XV (1992), 45–57

fantail a set of six or eight small windsails placed at right angles to the main sails of a TOWER MILL, and diametrically opposite to them, supported on a protruding arm attached to the cap of the mill. The function of the fantail is to keep the main sails continually facing into the wind to obtain maximum power to drive the mill mechanism. When the wind is blowing directly onto the main sails, the fantail does not revolve, since it is shielded from the wind by the mill cap. When the wind changes direction, it catches the fantail, causing it to revolve. The fantail is arranged to drive a system of gears which slowly turn the main sails back to face into the wind, the fantail ceasing to revolve once it is shielded from the wind again. Invented by Edmund Lee in 1745, the fantail is also known as a fly or Lee's Flier, in some parts of the country.

On a POST MILL, the fantail is carried on a fan stage or carriage which has wheels running on the ground in a circular path round the central post. The carriage is attached to the mill upper body, which can revolve on the post. In a manner similar to that described above, the fantail rotates the ground wheels via gearing to turn the mill body and hence the main sails into the wind.

fast and loose pulleys lineshaft-driven pulleys on a machine, permitting it to be started or stopped at will. Before individual electric driving was introduced, power was transmitted to machinery by overhead LINESHAFTING and flat leather belts. Lineshafts ran continuously, but some machines, such as machine tools, had to be stopped and started at will. Above each machine, a wide flat-faced pulley or fast pulley was keyed to the lineshaft, round which a flat belt was tensioned to drive down onto a pair of belt-wide pulleys side-by-side on the machine. One of the latter pulleys would be fast on the machine drive shaft, the other loose, i.e. not keyed to it, so capable of 'freewheeling' on the shaft. The belt passed between two metal prongs, called a strap fork or BELT STRIKING GEAR: when this was slid sideways, the constantly moving belt could be pushed onto the fast pulley to drive the machine, or slid back to put the belt onto the loose pulley to stop the machine.

If the machine always ran in the same direction, an OPEN BELT drive was used; if reversal from time to time was required, an additional CROSSED BELT was necessary, and three pulleys were needed on the machine – a fast one for each belt when it was driving, and a central loose pulley when it was idling. The lineshaft pulley had to be increased in width to accommodate the two belts.

fasteners small but important items for securing machine and structural parts to each other. Several types of fastener have been developed over the centuries, and made in a variety of materials. To some extent the type of fastener may be used as a rough dating aid to the age of a machine or structure if it is original, and has not been replaced at some time by a more modern fastener.

Early machine frames such as hand looms, roof trusses of 18th-century buildings etc., were almost invariably wooden. Joints between component parts were either made by traditional joiners' techniques – mortise and tenon, dovetails, etc – or by hardwood pegs (trenails) or wedges, driven through corresponding holes to pin the parts together.

The first metal fasteners for wood were hand made wrought-iron nails (*see* NAIL MAKING). Machine-made nails were introduced in the 1840s. Metal wood screws, hand-made particularly in the Birmingham area, were available *c*. 1780. At first these were simply hammered in – it is believed the head slot was only used for extraction. John Sutton Nettlefold's machine-made wood screws of superior design (patent no. 6223, 1832) permitted screws to be screwed in as well as screwed out.

The simplest method for joining metal plates together is by the age-old rivet, a permanent fastener only removable by cutting off one of the rivet heads. Plates of steam boilers, ships' hulls and structural sections were riveted together before modern welding superseded rivets. The strength of a rivet depends on its shear resistance. Rivets may be inserted cold or

hot: cold riveting relies on the nip between the rivet heads and the parts joined; pre-heating a rivet to red heat before insertion, and forming its second head by hammering the protruding shank to shape, increases the strength of the joint as the rivet cools, because of the contraction. Riveting was originally done by hand; multiple riveting by a steam operated riveter was invented by William Fairbairn (1789–1874) in 1837.

Re-usable fasteners tightened and untightened by a spanner are the ubiquitous bolt and nut. Early nuts and bolts such as those used in Newcomen's day (the early 18th century) were made in wrought iron; the screw threads were hand-made and not standard. Nuts and bolts were made in marked pairs, since the nut from one bolt would not necessarily fit any other bolt. Bolt heads and nuts were square at first: hexagonal shapes were not introduced until the mid- to late 19th century. Interchangeability of screwed items was made possible by standardizing the profile and pitch of the thread, as proposed by Joseph Whitworth (1803–87) in 1841, and adopted as the British Standard in the late 1850s (*see* SCREW THREADS).

When the first cast-iron bridge was erected at Ironbridge in 1779, there was no precedent to follow for fastening its large iron parts together, so carpentry practice was followed, and all joints were made with iron pegs or wedges. Later bridges used rivets and/or nuts and bolts.

A foundation bolt was often firmly held in a reverse tapered hole cut in the solid base by pouring in molten lead, which when solidified held the splayed out end of the bolt. The hinges of canal gates were often fastened in the stone wall of the lock compartment in this manner.

Wheels, pulleys, cranks, etc., were fastened onto their shafts by a KEY or keys; large wheels, such as waterwheels, were sometimes staked on. If the wooden axle was square, as many once were, as many as eight tapered wedges (stakes) would be driven in between the axle and the wheel boss, two per side. Staking on permitted a slight adjustment to the concentricity of the wheel on its axle to be made by driving some stakes farther in on one side, and slackening off other stakes elsewhere. This was a useful facility in the days when manufacturing accuracy was crude.

Another fastening device was the cotter, which was usually a tapered metal bar or round pin, driven into slots cut or cast in the parts to be joined together. Engine pistons and pump rods were often cottered. The segments of large metal flywheels were sometimes joined by cotters, perhaps with bolts also for additional strength.

As manufacturing accuracy improved, shrink fits were introduced. This method was used to secure engine cranks to their shafts in addition to using keys. The bore of the hole in the crank was expanded by heating the crank until it could be forced onto the cold shaft; as the crank cooled, it contracted onto the shaft, gripping it tightly to increase the strength of the joint. The ends of meeting cast-iron floor beams in textile mills were sometimes fastened together by shrinking a wrought-iron ring over projecting bosses cast on the sides of the beams for this purpose.

Father of the English cloth trade nickname for Edward III (1312–77) acknowledging his far-sighted policies protecting and developing the woollen industry in the 14th century. He encouraged immigration of foreign weavers from the Low Countries who had superior skills to the English weavers at that time. The Flemish weavers settled in England and greatly stimulated the woollen industry, introducing many new types of cloth and improved methods, and laid the foundation of later capitalism in the textile trade in Britain (*see* NEW DRAPERIES).

fathom a measurement of 6 ft. The word comes from the Old English word *faethm*, meaning outstretched arms. Depths of mines were measured in fathoms.

feeder, *see* LEAT

feigh name for metal dross, specifically the refuse from lead ore.

feighing (or faying) a primitive way of mining by removing the top surface soil, i.e. a kind of open-cast mining method.

feldspar (or felspar) a common rock, which forms about 51 per cent of the earth's crust. Feldspar is an aluminium silicate material which may contain potassium, sodium or calcium, and it occurs in all classes of rock. It is widely distributed in igneous rocks, showing that it was formed by the cooling and crystallization of the hot material below the earth's crust millions of years ago. Feldspar's principal industrial use is in the manufacture of GLASS and POTTERY: when added to pottery clay and heated to 1,100–1,450° C the mixture becomes translucent PORCELAIN. A feldspathic glaze used on pottery is also translucent.

fell 1. the edge of already woven cloth in a loom against which the next pass or pick of WEFT is pushed by the action of BEATING UP by the movement of the REED. 2. (or bouse) lead ore in its rough state, i.e. as mined and mixed with rock. 3. a sheepskin or other hairy animal's skin after slaughtering. A fellmonger is a dealer in hides and skins.

felloe (or fellie, felly) a segment of a rim of a coach or wooden waggon wheel. Felloes were made from ash, and usually each felloe was joined to the wheel hub or nave by two spokes. Each felloe was joined to its neighbours to make up the complete wheel rim, an iron tyre being heat shrunk onto the outer edge. Felloes were made in different widths, and turnpike tolls depended on the width of the rim: wide rims were charged less than narrow rims because it was considered that they caused less damage to the road surface. For example, early 19th-century charges at a toll house in Somerset read:

For any Waggon, Cart, Caravan or other such carriage, having fellies of less breadth than four and a half inches	6*d*
Ditto of breadth four and a half and less than six inches	5*d*
Ditto of six inches and less than nine inches	4*d*
Ditto, nine inches and upward	3*d*

felt a non-woven cloth or stuff made from wool, or wool and fur or hair, compacted into a mat by being rolled under pressure with LEES or size. The fibres lie in random directions, interlocking with each other to form a dense material. It is generally believed that the manufacture of felt was introduced into Britain in the 16th century by French and Flemish immigrants. A Feltmakers Company was formed in London in 1604. Felt made from SHODDY was first made in Batley, Yorks., in 1813. Originally, felt was mostly used for HAT MAKING; a later use was for manufacturing slippers. A felt works was started in the Rossendale district of Lancashire in 1854, and in 1875 slipper manufacture commenced and developed into a speciality of that area, which it still is today.

felting the closing up of WEFT and WARP and raising a nap on woven cloth, particularly in woollen fabrics.

ferret weaving ferret silk (from the Italian *fioretto* meaning floss-silk, or rough waste silk) was narrow-ware made in pennywidths – up to six pennywidths – in the form of tapes, ribbons, fringes, inkles, trimmings, hatbands, braids, laces, etc. It was also called parchmentry (from the French *passementerie*).

fester a Lancashire dialect word for an agent controlling domestic HANDLOOM WEAVERS. The word was in use in the 18th century and is possibly a corruption of fustian master, FUSTIAN being woven extensively at that period.

fettling in the context of puddling or open hearth furnaces, the lining of the furnace bath or hearth in which the metal is processed. In the WET PUDDLING furnace, the bath was lined with a mixture of iron oxides – rolling mill scale, hammer scale, etc., often with an addition of red haematite ore ground to a powder, to provide the reactive lining necessary for the decarburization of the pig iron. This lining had to be made good after each melting, the processing being known as fettling.

The word is also used to describe the action of cleaning off sand from iron castings after their removal from the mould, and in the POTTERY INDUSTRY it describes the cleaning up of a pottery article after removal from the mould, e.g. taking off burrs, etc.

fibre a single hair in wool, cotton, etc. There are about 100,000 fibres in one pound weight of sheep's wool and diameters vary from 1/600th to 1/1600th of an inch according to the breed of sheep. Fibres lengths vary from 3/8th of an inch for short cotton to 7 ft for jute. There are three types of fibre: vegetable in origin, from just under the outer bark or covering of the stem, e.g. flax, hemp, jute, or from the leaf, e.g. sisal, manila, or seed, e.g. cotton; animal in origin, e.g. wool, camel or goat's hair, mohair, alpaca; and silk, which strictly is a continuous filament from the silk worm, not fibrous.

Field boiler a vertical steam boiler which embodied a number of patented Field tubes hanging down in the combustion space, whose purpose was to increase the heat transfer to the water. Each Field heating element comprised a small bore tube held inside a larger bore tube, the latter being closed at its lowest end, whilst the smaller tube was open at each end, with its lowest end terminating a short distance from the closed end of the outer tube, and the other end reaching up into the water space. Water from the water space passed down the central tube, and picking up extra heat in the annular space, rose by convection back into the water space of the boiler. The element was patented by Edward Field and Francis Wise (patent no. 1694, 1866) and was used mainly on small vertical boilers providing steam for fire-engines, river launches, and road traction engines in Victorian times.

fieldwork in industrial archaeology since Industrial Archaeology is the study of the physical remains of the industrial past, fieldwork is essentially an outdoor activity. Fieldwork can comprise locating, inspection, interpreting, surveying and measuring, and photographing or sketching industrial sites and structures. It is complementary to documentary work which in some cases might precede fieldwork, or in other instances follow it.

An important point about fieldwork is the recording of sites and structures. In some circumstances recording may be vitally necessary before a site, building, etc., is lost due to impending development or demolition, an activity known as rescue archaeology or emergency recording. In other cases, perhaps following an accidental documentary discovery, or a deliberate archival search, fieldwork verifies whether there still are any physical remains. If so, an appropriate recording is made. There is a national facility for recording industrial sites which uses standard forms for input to computer records – *see* NATIONAL MONUMENTS RECORD, and IRIS. At local level, many Industrial Archaeology societies maintain records of sites situated in their area.

Fieldwork covers most aspects of Industrial Archaeology, ranging from tracing routes of old packhorse ways and turnpikes, or locating and recording sites of bloomeries, old furnaces, kilns, etc., to photographing and measuring up industrial buildings such as mills, factories, etc. Part of the attraction of fieldwork is the detective work often needed in interpreting and dating the technology formerly used in abandoned buildings and derelict sites. Buildings have sometimes been converted to other uses during their lifetime, which often results in alterations, additions, or deletions to original layouts. Robbing of abandoned sites for building stone, timber etc., or vandalism, are problems which can make deductions difficult. The inside walls and the floors of buildings are usually more interesting than their façades since they can give clues to what type of machinery and equipment was once installed. The pattern of holding down bolts, pits and plinths, wall fixtures, and so on, or stains and wear marks are often the only visible indications of what past technology has been there. Interpretation of these 'footprints' requires experience and some technical knowledge. Much remains to be done in building up a reference corpus of typical machine foundations to aid the Industrial Archaeologist in this work. The laboratory analysis of slags, tailings, and other discarded materials found during fieldwork, are further aids to help unravel the past history of sites.

Most fieldwork is carried out on above-ground sites but occasionally it may be necessary to resort to some kind of excavation to uncover buried features. It is essential that the techniques and methodology of classical archaeology be used otherwise important discoveries might be destroyed, and such work is best left to the professional archaeologist. Underground exploration might be needed in the case of mines, and it is stressed that all underground work is dangerous, and should only be attempted by those experienced in such matters.

The results of fieldwork should be written up with any documentary references appended, and scale drawings made showing plans, elevations and sections as appropriate. An annual award for the best fieldwork is presented by the ASSOCIATION FOR INDUSTRIAL ARCHAEOLOGY to those who submit their work to the Association. Both amateur and professional industrial archaeologists may enter the competition.

Finally, it must be borne in mind that not all industrial sites are on public or easily accessible land, and if they lie on private land, prior permission from the owner must be obtained before any fieldwork is undertaken.

Cranstone, D. 'Excavation: the role of archaeology', *Industrial Archaeology Review* XIV (1992), 119–25
Hudson, K. *Exploring our Industrial Past*, Hodder and Stoughton, 1975
Hudson, K. *Industrial History from the Air*, Cambridge University Press, 1984
Major, K.J. *Fieldwork in Industrial Archaeology*, Batsford, 1975
Pannell, J.P.M. *Techniques of Industrial Archaeology*, David and Charles, 1966
Royal Commission on Historical Monuments (England) and the Society of Architectural Historians of Great Britain, *Recording Historic Buildings* (Papers from a Joint Symposium), HMSO, 1990
White, P.R. 'The excavation of industrial archaeological sites', *Industrial Archaeology Review* II (1978), 160–7

file making the craft of making metal cutting hand files, which dates back to the early 17th century; by the 18th century Warrington, Lancs., had become the main centre for the industry, although files were also made in Sheffield and Wolverhampton. The industry was originally domestically based with workers cutting the teeth of files by chisel and hammer in their homes or small workshops, and their output collected by master file makers who provided them with the blanks. The outworkers or cutters were known as country hands, and they were paid on piecework rates for 'long dozens' of fourteen files but only paid for twelve. The trade was known in Lancashire as 'poverty knocking' on account of the poor pay for the constant hammering of the steel bars. Nevertheless, file making was a skilful job demanding precision and good eyesight.

Steel bar was bought from local forges and SLITTING MILLS by the master file maker, ANNEALED, and distributed to his outworkers for cutting the teeth. Different types of file were made in various cross-sections for the west Lancashire watch and clock makers, for nailers, millwrights, and sawyers, etc. The blanks were clamped on pewter or lead blocks by leather straps passing through holes in the bench top and held down by the feet. This left both hands free for the cutting. The soft metal block reduced the recoil from the hammer blows and prevented damage to a finished face when the file was turned over to cut the reverse face. After cutting, the finished files were collected and hardened by the master file maker in his own furnace where better control over the process could be maintained. By 1802 an important file-making factory was built in Warrington by Peter Stubs (1756–1806), which in a few years was employing about 100 workmen, although for a time the putting out of work to country hands still continued in parallel with factory production. Gradually outworking diminished and production was concentrated in factories.

Little remains of the old industry apart from a few outhouses which were once occupied by cutters. A collection of old tools and equipment may be seen in some museums in and around Warrington.

Surrey Dane, E. *Peter Stubs and the Lancashire Hand Tool Industry*, Sherratt and Sons, 1973

filling another name for WEFT, i.e. the cross yarn which 'fills' in the body of a cloth.

finery a furnace or hearth in which pig iron from a BLAST FURNACE is reheated to reduce its carbon content. Usually a finery was closely associated with a CHAFERY, the pair forming a forge; frequently there were two finery hearths to one chafery. The layout of a typical 18th-

Finery hearth with pig iron hole, Stony Hazel, Cumbria

century finery and chafery forge is shown in Fig. 6. A finery hearth was normally square in plan. Pig iron was melted slowly in the finery by being pushed into it in stages through a hole in the back of the furnace, and most of the carbon was burnt out. The resulting mass of iron was then ready for hammering into an ANCONY. Men working at a finery were called finers or hammermen. The word finery means, in effect, to refine, and comes from the old French *affinage* which has that meaning.

Thus, a finery made wrought iron by the indirect method from pig iron from a blast furnace. A typical layout of a contemporary blast furnace is shown in Fig. 5 and the similarity between the two layouts is apparent. Sometimes a finery forge site would include a blast furnace.

finishing works a textile finishing works is where previously woven cloth is bleached, dyed or printed, and given any other finishing process specified, before it is despatched to the user. Finishers work on a commission basis since they do not own the cloth they process.

A finishing works is almost invariably a collection of single storeyed buildings in which the various processes take place, with a warehouse and office block. Often the works presents a rambling appearance due to extensions and alterations which have taken place over the years. It is sited near a reliable supply of clean water since enormous quantities of water are used in the processes. Associated with the works is a water storage reservoir, and of course a large boiler-house for providing the steam needed in the DYEING and drying processes. A works will include a 'grey room', in which customers' cloth awaiting processing is stored. This is so called because of the grey colour of untreated cloth as received from the weaver. The department where the cloth is bleached prior to dyeing is called the bleach 'croft', a name carried over from the early days of cloth finishing when BLEACHING was done by long exposure of the cloth to the action of the sun in crofts or fields. Bleaching by chemical methods was introduced in the second half of the 18th century and the bleach croft will contain large, heated vessels in which the grey cloth is bleached, washed, and dried on steam-heated rollers. The dyeing department comprises more vessels of hot liquor, and the printing section will contain roller printing machines. These replaced the hand block method of printing by the end of the 18th century. Some finishing works contain specialized equipment for particular types of cloth finishing, e.g. MERCERIZING. All finishers

will include STENTERING machines for stretching wet cloth back to its original width. In the final processing there will be a cloth inspection room and a making up department where the finished cloth will be folded and batched to the customer's requirements. The more progressive finishers had small laboratories where tests and experiments on dyes etc. were made.

A problem in the early days of finishing works was the control of effluent from the processes, and pollution of rivers was a frequent cause of complaint against bleachers and dyers.

fireclay (or seat-earth) clays which are capable of withstanding high temperatures, and from which heat-resisting bricks and fire-resisting cements are made. The soils in which plants and trees of the Carboniferous period lived eventually changed their nature by the loss of certain chemical substances. Such clay, as it became, therefore underlies coal seams and was found to have the foregoing property. Often, when a coal seam had been worked out, the fireclay bed would be worked to advantage. Some clays are highly siliceous, others highly aluminous, the former making ACID LININGS, the latter BASIC LININGS.

firedamp Coal miner's name for carburetted hydrogen or methane gas found in mines. Firedamp is formed by the decomposition of vegetable matter dating from when coal seams were first laid down, and is usually found in fissures which, when broken open during the mining operation, are known as blowers. Firedamp is lighter than air, so rises into the roof space of galleries where it collects in pockets. It is highly explosive in concentrations of air between 5.6 and 13.0%, and has been the cause of many disastrous fires and explosions with loss of life.

Coal mines were lit mostly by candles until the DAVY safety oil lamp was invented in 1815/16. Before this, the presence of firedamp was detected by a candle flame turning blue, or extinguishing in high gas concentrations. Very gassy seams were sealed off and not worked, but in working seams the gas was either removed by deliberately exploding it (*see* FIREMAN) or, in shallow mines, by wafting it away with sacks, etc. Wafting was not successful as mines got deeper, so improved ventilation was the answer. Mechanical fans forced a greater volume of air along a specified underground route, known as coursing, and diluted the gas below its explosive level as it was driven out of the workings. To maintain the correct air route, trapping was very important *see* TRAPPER). Dilution by this method also reduced the danger from other gases such as BLACK DAMP.

Firedamp was once known as fulminating damp (fulminating means explosive) whilst damp comes from the German *Dampf* meaning vapour or steam. Another name is wild-fire.

fire engine an early name by which STATIONARY STEAM ENGINES were known.

fireman a supervisor who works underground in a coalmine, and is responsible for safety, particularly from fires and explosions.

Before the use of safety lamps in coalmines, the presence of gas was detected by a change in colour to blue, of the candle flame by which miners worked. Heavy concentrations of gas would extinguish the flame. It was the duty of the fireman in 17th and 18th century mines, to find and remove FIREDAMP pockets by actually exploding them before work commenced. To do this the fireman, wrapped in protective leather or wool, would lie flat on the floor of the gallery, or hide behind some shield, and ignite the gas by a burning torch or candle held on the end of a long pole which he thrust out before him. Hence his occupational name, which still persists today.

An old nickname for a fireman was penitent, owing to his monk-like attire and prone position when firing the gassy pockets. A fireman is also known as a deputy.

fire-resistant building a mill or warehouse, etc. constructed with the minimum amount of combustible materials. Early textile mills and warehouses used timber extensively in their construction: they were prone to catching fire since the textile materials themselves were flammable, and naked lights were used for illumination before safer means of lighting were introduced. Large numbers of mills were destroyed by fire, forcing up insurance premiums, and alternative materials of construction were sought to reduce the fire risk. Some protection was afforded by plastering or sheet-metal cladding all exposed timber surfaces such as beams, posts, ceilings, etc., this technique dating from about 1790.

William Strutt (1756–1830) and Charles Bage (1752–1822) were pioneers in designing fire-resistant buildings for the textile industry. Bage introduced cast-iron beams and columns in a flax mill at Shrewsbury in 1796, a building which is regarded as the first fire-resistant factory building in the world. The flooring comprised shallow brick arches spanning between the flanges of cast-iron inverted T-beams, with stone flagged flooring, eliminating timber entirely from this part of the mill

structure. Strutt built a cotton mill in Belper, Derbys., in 1803 on the same principles, and this type of construction soon became standard. John Rennie (1761–1821) used cast-iron columns to support the roof of a 29 ft 3 in span warehouse, 1,300 ft long, for the East and West India Dock Company in London in 1813. A problem with the initial use of cast-iron beams was insufficient knowledge of the strength of what was then a new construction material. Some mills collapsed from beam failure, but destruction by fire was considerably reduced. It was not until experimental work by Eaton Hodgkinson (1789–1861) was carried out in the 1830s (*see* STRENGTH OF MATERIALS) that cast-iron beams began to be scientifically designed, and the I-shaped beam was adopted. The ends of beams were supported over the columns; some were bolted together, others joined by shrinking a wrought iron ring over protruding bosses cast on the side of the beam for that purpose. The beam ends embraced the columns and were supported on collars cast on the columns. The columns were either solid cruciform in cross-section, or circular, the latter sometimes solid, more often hollow. Hollow columns were occasionally used to convey steam or hot water to the mill space heating system, but this practice was soon abandoned when it was discovered that thermal expansion caused structural problems. Gas from the mill's own gas plant has been conveyed through hollow columns. Circular columns became the standard.

Abraham Henthorn Stott (1822–1904) a well-known Oldham, Lancs., mill architect, patented a fire-resistant mill design in 1871 (patent no. 1881) using brick arches. Concrete floors were introduced in the late 1880s; and cast-iron beams fell into disfavour due to failures through faulty castings, and steel girders became the standard structural material for later mills. Reinforced concrete beams were patented by William Boutland Wilkinson (patent no. 2293, 1854).

Fire resistant construction had the added benefit of being stronger than previous designs, and therefore permitted heavier and more machines to be installed.

Fitzgerald, R. 'Albion Mill, Manchester', *Industrial Archaeology Review* X (1988), 204–30
Fitzgerald, R. 'The development of the cast iron frame in textile mills to 1850', *Industrial Archaeology Review* X (1988), 127–45
Johnson, H.R. and Skempton, A.W. 'William Strutt's cotton mills, 1793–1812', *Newcomen Society Transactions* XXX (1960), 179–205

fire-setting a primitive aid to extracting rock in a mining or quarrying operation. The rock was heated by building a fire against it, and when hot was rapidly cooled by throwing water against it causing it to crack. Tools could then be inserted in the cracks to lever material out.

firetube boiler a steam generator in which tubes convey the hot gases from the fire through a surrounding mass of water. The tubes may be large and few in number, such as the LANCASHIRE BOILER, or many and small in diameter, such as in a locomotive.

Fischer gear, *see* WALSCHAERT VALVE GEAR

fish bellied term applied to a beam or rail when its lower edge is curved downwards to give a greater depth at the centre than at each end. The design resembles the shape of a fish. The increased depth at the centre provides a greater resistance to the bending stresses which occur there because of the load being supported, or the passage of a wheel along the rail. Fish bellied rails came into use *c.*1789 at Loughborough, Leics.; they were made in cast iron, 3 ft long at first, and later increased to 15 or 18 ft, but bellied at 3 ft intervals to suit the pitch of the supporting sleepers. Fish bellied beams usually have a heavy bottom flange if in cast iron to provide enough material to resist the tensile stresses, cast iron being weak in tension. The opposite shape, i.e. with the top edge curving upwards, is called HOG BACK.

fishplate a rectangular metal plate used to join and strengthen the butt joint between adjacent rails of a railway track. Two fishplates are used, one either side of the rail, with bolts passing through rail and plates. The 1847 patent (no. 11,715) of William Bridges Adams and Robert Richardson refers to wood or iron fishes for joining rails together. The name fishplate is borrowed from nautical usage where a fish was a wooden strengthening piece on ships' masts. It possibly comes from the French *ficher*, meaning to fix. Cast-iron fishplates were used at first, but were found to be unsatisfactory, and were replaced by wrought iron.

fitter an old Tyneside term for a coal merchant, sometimes called a HOSTMAN.

fixed engine a stationary winding steam engine positioned at the top of a railway incline for hauling up trains and their locomotives. Early railways used fixed engines before locomotives were powerful enough to climb gradients unaided. The locomotives would haul the train along level or near level stretches of the track and would be attached to a cable to be pulled up a steeper incline by a fixed or stationary engine before continuing on the next level stretch. The Bolton to Leigh Railway of 1828, for example, had two fixed engines positioned at the top of inclines; the Cromford and High Peak Railway

had several; a good surviving example may be seen at Middleton, Derbys. The first use of a stationary steam engine to haul waggons up an incline was in about 1805 on one of the north-east colliery lines.

flanged rails, *see* PLATEWAY

flannel (or gladden) a soft, loosely woven woollen fabric, usually without a nap, and used for warm undergarments. It was being woven in Wales in the 16th century, and the word possibly comes from the Welsh *gwlanen*, meaning wool.

flannelette a cotton imitation of flannel. Unlike flannel, which usually has a smooth surface, flannelette has a soft fine nap on both sides, and is used in particular for nightwear.

flash a northern name for a water-filled hollow caused by subsidence resulting from some underground industrial activity. Coal mining in Lancashire has caused the creation of flashes, and salt extraction by pumping natural brine from the Cheshire salt fields has caused others. Rock salt was discovered in Cheshire *c.*1670 and extensively mined from that date, and the presence of a flash in Cheshire is often an indication that salt mining once took place in the area. Flashes are also known in some cases as meres.

flash boiler a design of steam boiler which enables steam to be raised very rapidly, i.e. the water is 'flashed' into steam almost instantly. It comprises in essence a long, coiled metal pipe through which water is pumped and heated by a high temperature source as it passes through. Jonathan Hornblower (1753–1815) tried one out in 1778, and it was later used on steam carriages where rapid availability of steam was very desirable. Its main disadvantage is its low steam reserve.

flash lock a removable barrier across a navigable river. A flash lock has several alternative names: water gate, navigation weir, staunch, beam and paddle weir, and half lock. Flash locks date from the Middle Ages, and were devised when rivers began to be used for navigation. Weirs for raising the water level for corn and fulling mills presented obstructions to the passage of boats, so openings with temporary barriers were made in them. There were two types: rimmer and paddle locks, and hinged gates. Rimmer and paddle locks consisted of a row of closely fitting, removable paddles, held upright against a horizontal bar (the rimmer) and a submerged sill on the river bed. When a boat wanted to pass, sufficient paddles were lifted out of the way, and the rimmer swung clear. A hinged gate lock comprised a pair of wooden gates arranged so that they formed a 'V' when closed, the point facing upstream so that water pressure forced it shut.

A boat passing downstream would shoot through an opened lock on the 'flash' of water which with luck would carry it over the shallows on the downstream side. A boat passing upstream waited until the initial surge of water had subsided on opening the lock, and was then worked through against the water flow, sometimes with the aid of a winch. There was an obvious clash of interests between mill operator and boatmen. The miller naturally wanted to conserve water, and sometimes would not allow a flash lock to be opened until a queue of boats had formed. The flash lock was a clumsy solution and very wasteful of water and time, and on canals was replaced by the POUND LOCK.

Lewis, M.J.T., Slatcher, W.N. and Jarvis, P.N. 'Flashlocks on English waterways – a survey', *Journal of Industrial Archaeology* 6 (1969)

flask, *see* MOULDING BOX

flat rods a length of solid links or rods joined together to transfer reciprocating motion from a waterwheel or engine to operate pumps at a distant mine. The rods crossed open ground, usually supported on rollers or dolly wheels placed on top of wooden posts or stone or brick pillars, and might be made of flat timber or iron bars arranged on their edge. Being rigid, they were capable of transmitting the push and pull motion, and rocked a bell crank or angle bob at the top of the mineshaft, which in turn operated a reciprocating pump down the mine to raise water to the surface. Considerable distances were covered by this method, an outstanding example being a mine near Tavistock in Devon, where power was transmitted nearly three miles by flat rods.

flats 1. on a CARDING engine, metal bars the same width as the main cylinder and covered on the side facing the cylinder with CARD CLOTH. Only a few thousandths of an inch separate the card cloth on the flats from that on the cylinder, and the wool or cotton is carded between the two, the cylinder revolving and the flats remaining stationary. In some designs the flats actually move slowly round on a continuous chain, and when they are on the return strand and not in contact with the material being carded, they are cleaned of any adhering short fibres and fluff by fast rotating brushes. Flats replaced earlier rollers, thereby increasing the periphery coverage of the cylinder to improve the carding action (*see* Fig. 15). **2.** name sometimes given to the floors in a spinning mill. **3.** wide barges or boats used on some navigational rivers and canals, particularly the rivers Mersey and Weaver and those canals connecting them. Flats were up to 72 ft long and generally 15 ft wide with a shallow draught and a carrying capacity of around 80 tons. Some flats had sails. When operating on a canal, the mast was lowered and the barge pulled along by gangs of men, and later by horses; later still, engines were added. Some flats were used for coastal work out of the river estuary.

Paget-Tomlinson, E. *Mersey and Weaver Flats*, Robert Wilson, 1974

flax the plant *linum usitatissimum*, cultivated for its fibres from which LINEN is made, and for its seeds (sometimes called lintseeds) from which linseed oil comes. Flax grows best on clay soils in lowland areas: Ireland and west Lancashire were big flax growing areas in the 17th and 18th centuries, and the plant is still cultivated in Ireland today although none is grown in Lancashire now. Besides Ireland, flax was imported from Russia. During the reign of George III (1760–1820) flax growing in Britain and its processing was encouraged by the imposition of duties on foreign linen, and bounties given to boost flax growing in Britain. In 1773 the total British grown flax was estimated at 8.96 million pounds.

The plant grows 3 to 4 ft tall, and has a purplish-blue flower which is followed by a seed pod. The stem of the plant provides the fibres from which linen yarn or thread is spun. The fibres, which lie in an annulus between the outer bark and a woody central core, run the full length of the plant stem in one piece and are smooth with slight bumps which catch onto each other during spinning, helping to consolidate the component fibres of the thread. The fibres are more or less non-elastic and make a stronger thread than cotton. Like all fibres of vegetable origin, flax is mainly cellulose in composition. When harvested, flax is pulled out of the ground rather than cut so as to obtain the maximum length of the fibres. Seeds are removed by passing the heads of the plants through a rippler, a coarse comb, and the fibres loosened in their stems by the RETTING PROCESS. After drying, the stems are first bruised before the fibres are extracted. In early days this was done by beating the stems with wooden mallets by hand, a process also known as BEETLING; by the 18th century fluted rollers were in use for this purpose. The fibres were then removed from their stems by a SCUTCHING operation which involved beating the fibres out of the outer stalk material using a revolving wheel which had between four and twelve wooden blades. Finally, the flax fibres were

drawn through steel combs called hackles to remove any remaining unwanted material and short fibres, and at the same time to align the long fibres parallel to each other. The long fibres are called line, and the short ones retained in the hackle are called tow. The flax fibres are tied up in bundles called stricks, and are then ready for delivering to the spinner.
Baines, Patricia. *Flax and Linen*, Shire Publications, Album no. 133, 1985

flax wheel, *see* SAXONY WHEEL

fleece the yield of wool obtained when a sheep is sheared. A typical weight of a fleece is about 12 lb, but depends on the breed of sheep. The fleece is sometimes called the clip, although clip is usually reserved for the total quantity of wool from a mass shearing.

Flemish mill a machine introduced *c*.1870 for SCUTCHING flax, superseding the old hand methods. It comprised a rotating shaft, power driven, on which a number of hardwood blades (usually twelve) are mounted: these beat a bundle of flax stems held in their path through a slot in a vertical board.

Flemish weavers weavers from medieval Flanders, now part of modern Belgium. In the Middle Ages, Flanders' cloth, made by weavers in Ghent, Ypres, and Bruges, was held in high regard throughout Europe, including Britain, which as that time had almost no worthwhile textile industry of its own. Since raw wool was not available in Flanders in sufficient quantities, Bruges bought up almost the entire English CLIP and converted it into cloth; most of the cloth used in England was imported from Flanders. In an attempt to encourage the home industry and reduce dependence on imported cloth, Edward III (1327–77) invited Flemish weavers to settle in England under royal protection. As there was unrest in Flanders at that time, many hundreds seized the opportunity to leave their native country and come to England. They settled in various areas, particularly around Norwich where they helped develop the worsted industry in that area. In addition to settling in East Anglia, the Flemish weavers settled in London, the West Country, Lancashire and Yorkshire, and were largely responsible for the development of the early woollen industries in those areas. Although resented by English weavers at first, there is no doubt that the injection of foreign skills into the economy was of lasting benefit. In addition to weaving, the Flemings introduced spinning by the GREAT WHEEL to Britain. The weaving of cloth became the staple industry of Britain and was its principal export at the commencement of the Industrial Revolution.

flight of locks a series of closely spaced locks on a canal which take it across a slope. There is a short POUND between each lock (not exceeding about 400 yd in length, otherwise the flight is broken), often widened to allow boats to wait in between locks. A flight can vary from a few locks to a large number if a big difference in levels is covered. The biggest flight of locks in Britain is at Tardebigge, Worcs., on the Worcester and Birmingham Canal, where 30 narrow locks raise the canal 217 ft in about 2 miles. If a steep slope is to be overcome, a STAIRCASE of locks is adopted.

flint mill 1. a grinding machine used in the pottery industry for grinding flints after they have been CALCINED into a fine powder. At first the flints were ground dry, which produced an injurious dust; an improvement, attributed to James Brindley (1716–72), which he introduced in his early mill working days, was to grind the calcined flints under water in an edge type runner. This was in 1758. An alternative method was to grind in a ball mill using heavy iron or steel balls tumbling about inside a rotating drum. The powdered flint is added to clay to lighten its colour and to harden it. **2.** the short name sometimes used for a STEEL AND FLINT MILL used to illuminate early mines.

flitched beam a composite beam of timber strengthened by an iron plate, or plates, used in the construction of 18th- and 19th-century timber framed mills and warehouses. Usually an iron plate was sandwiched between two timber beams, the whole being securely bolted together by a row of bolts. In a similar manner joints between two lengths of a timber beam were made by halving the meeting ends of each beam, overlapping them, placing an iron plate top and bottom of the joint, and bolting the assembly together. Also known as a scarf joint.

floatboard 1. a flat board fastened across the width of an undershot WATERWHEEL to form a paddle against which the incoming water strikes to rotate the wheel. The floatboards are mounted on the rim of the wheel by short posts called starts. **2.** the paddles of a paddleboat steamer which when rotated propel the vessel through the water. William Poole of Lincoln patented hinged floatboards which 'feathered' as they entered the water to reduce drag (patent no. 5793, 1829).

flood gate, *see* CLOW

flop-jack Cornish name for a WATER-BALANCE ENGINE.

floss silk rough silk strands taken from the outside of a cocoon, or broken off during winding, and used in WASTE SILK SPINNING.

flume a water channel or leat. The word comes from the Latin *flumen*, a river.

fluorspar a calcium fluoride mineral, often found associated with galena (lead). It occurs in several colours, mostly blue, green, and lilac, but can be colourless. It is of cubic construction. Fluorspar was once discarded by lead miners as of no value, but today is worth more than lead. Its main use is as a FLUX. Also known as fluorite, its name comes from the Latin *fluere* meaning 'to flow'. A particular variety was extensively mined in Derbyshire near Castleton in the 18th and 19th centuries for its decorative value: known as Blue John, it was made into semi-precious jewellery, vases, statuettes, etc. Only small quantities of Blue John are extracted today.

flushing a rough, thick woollen cloth made in Britain in the early 19th century. Similar cloth was first made in Flushing, Holland, hence its name.

flux a material added during metal smelting to aid the separation of the metal from other combining elements in the ore. The flux combines chemically with the unwanted impurities forming a SLAG, which is removed and usually discarded, leaving a more or less pure metal. For example, lime is added to pig iron during smelting to remove phosphorus. A flux aids the flow of metal, the word coming from the Latin *fluxus* meaning flow.

fly 1. (or fuzz) short, loose cotton fibres liberated during spinning and which float about in the air in the spinning room, settling on machinery and operatives alike. The machinery has to be continually cleaned otherwise the fly eventually interferes with its correct working. Accumulations of fly on ledges in the building also forms a fire hazard. 2. the large driving pulley on a spinning MULE, also known as a rim. 3. an alternative name for a windmill FANTAIL.

flyball, *see* CENTRIFUGAL GOVERNOR

flyboat fast, passenger-carrying canal boat, sometimes called a packet (or swift in Scotland). Flyboats were popular in the 19th century before the coming of the railways. They operated to a regular timetable, and comprised boats with covered cabins, usually pulled by two horses, one behind the other, the second one ridden, and frequently changed *en route*. An average speed of 8–10 miles per hour was maintained. Flyboats were very light and narrow, and had priority over the slow commercial barges which were expected to give way on hearing the horn blown by an approaching flyboat. A razor edge prow was fitted to flyboats which could cut the tow rope of any barge not complying in time. Flyboats also has preference over other canal users at locks. Besides passenger flyboats, some carriers operated similar fast boats for the rapid carriage of goods, using relays of horses.

flyer an attachment on the SPINDLE of a spinning wheel or machine to guide yarn onto a bobbin. The flyer is generally thought to have originated in Saxony, and a spinning wheel fitted with a flyer is known as a SAXONY WHEEL. Fig. 26 shows the typical wooden flyer and metal spindle of a Saxony wheel. Along each arm of the flyer are some small hooks or hecks, which guide the yarn being spun onto a bobbin. The flyer is attached to the spindle and rotates with it. The bobbin has an integral small pulley or whorl at one end, and is loose on the spindle. Another slightly larger whorl may be screwed onto one end of the spindle, which is hollowed out at the opposite end for a short distance up to a side hole or eye. Spindle and flyer are rotated at speed by a cord from the large wheel, and since the spindle whorl is slightly larger than the bobbin whorl, a differential speed between them is created. Thus, the bobbin rotates faster than the flyer.

A length of previously spun yarn is threaded through the hollow end of the spindle and out through the eye, hooked over the nearest heck, and wound round the bobbin. As spinning proceeds, the bobbin winds yarn onto itself due to its superior speed, and when sufficient yarn has been wound onto the bobbin opposite the heck, the wheel is stopped, and the yarn transferred onto the next heck so that more yarn can be wound onto a fresh space along the bobbin. In this manner, the full width of the bobbin can be covered in yarn. When it is full, spinning is stopped, the spindle whorl unscrewed, and an empty bobbin substituted for the full one.

Richard Arkwright's spinning machine (patent no. 931, 1769) had four spindles and flyers, vertically positioned, and the flyers and spindles only were driven by a belt from below. Differential speed between flyer and bobbin was achieved by the bobbin rotating on a flannel washer which provided frictional resistance. Coniah Wood patented the traverse rail (patent no. 1018, 1772), to give even winding on the bobbin by moving it up and down the spindle, dispensing with hecks.

Not all flyers were horseshoe shaped: S-shaped flyers were in use as early as 1607 in the Italian silk industry. Fig. 26 shows a spindle and flyer of this design. Bobbins were first wound with non-twisted silk filaments, and placed on the spindles of a twisting machine.

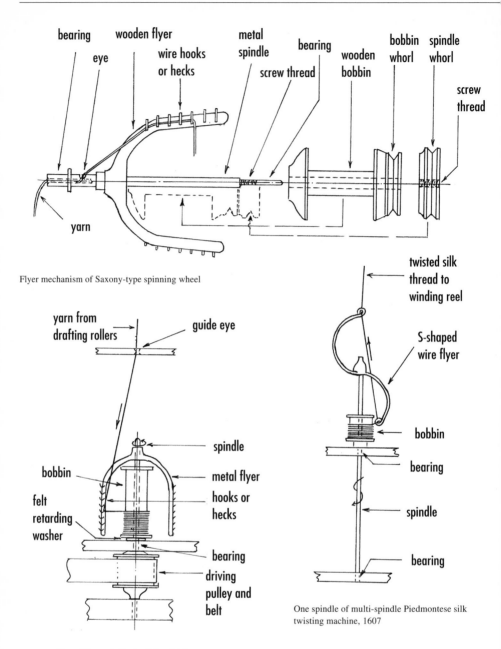

Flyer mechanism of Saxony-type spinning wheel

One of four spindles on Arkwright's
spinning frame, 1769

One spindle of multi-spindle Piedmontese silk
twisting machine, 1607

Fig. 26. Flyers for spinning textile fibres

As the bobbins rotated, the silk threads were unwound and given twist by passing through the two eyes of the flyer and wound onto a rotating reel positioned above the spindle, the flyer rotating slightly slower than the bobbin holding the untwisted filaments.

fly frame a machine used prior to final spinning of a yarn in which a loosely spun SLIVER is formed with a small strengthening twist. Such machines are SLUBBERS, ROVING FRAMES, JACK FRAMES, etc.

flying shuttle the device patented by John Kay (1704–64?) in 1733 (patent no. 542) for speeding up the weaving of cloth (*see* Fig. 27). Originally called the wheel shuttle, it comprised two open topped boxes, one at each side of the loom, connected by a board called the shuttle race placed below the warp threads. A shuttle carrying the weft had four small wheels and could be propelled across the raceboard from side to side, passing through the SHED by the weaver jerking a hand-held string. The string was attached to a hide-covered block which slid along a metal rod, giving the shuttle a smart blow to send it across to the other side of the loom. The action was then repeated from the other side after the shed had been reformed, there being another sliding block in the other box. Later, wheels on the shuttle were dispensed with.

The device was first introduced in Colchester, Essex, Kay having gone there from his native Bury, Lancs. He was assisted by a Colchester baizemaker named Solomon Smith. The invention was soon christened the flying shuttle and it greatly speeded up weaving and enabled much wider cloth to be woven than before, since the weaver was no longer restricted to the distance his arms could reach to throw the shuttle through the shed by hand. The increase in productivity of weaving brought about by the flying shuttle rapidly caused a bottleneck in spinning: between four and ten hand spinners were needed to keep one weaver going, depending on the yarn COUNT. This state of affairs concentrated attention on increasing the output of spinning and resulted in the first attempts at inventing spinning machinery soon afterwards. The flying shuttle was first used on wool, and on cotton about thirty years later. Its introduction was at first resented in East Anglia and Lancashire, and was slow in being adopted, although Kay was forced (unsuccessfully) to take legal action against weavers in Lancashire who pirated his invention. The device was not extensively used in Yorkshire until around 1760–70, where it was known in the early 19th century as a spring shuttle.

flypress a machine for punching holes in, pressing out, or bending small metal items. It comprises a bottom anvil, and a frame which incorporates a vertical square-threaded screw. A die is held in the anvil, and another die or punch is fastened to the bottom of the screw. When the screw is quickly rotated by spinning round a heavy overhead FLYWHEEL or weighted arm, the two dies are brought rapidly together, to deliver a blow on the work piece placed between them. The momentum of the revolving mass of the flywheel or arm overcomes the resistance of the work piece to produce the finished item. Small flypresses are worked by hand, large ones are power operated: Matthew Boulton patented a power flypress in 1790 (patent no. 1757).

flywheel a large diameter wheel, made of cast iron or cast steel, with a heavy rim which when rotating at speed stores kinetic (rotational) energy. There are two main uses for flywheels: to rotate constantly and reduce speed fluctuations in a reciprocating engine; and to provide short-term energy to overcome a resistance by slowing down rapidly, as in the case of a punch.

In reciprocating engines such as steam engines, the turning effort produced varies from a minimum to a maximum during each full cycle. When the turning effort is at a minimum, the rotating flywheel, which is fastened to the engine crankshaft, assists in maintaining the engine speed by giving up some of its stored energy due to the momentum of the revolving mass and slows down very slightly. Conversely, when the turning effort builds up to its maximum, the flywheel speeds up very slightly, storing excess energy which it gives out again as the next minimum is approached. Thus the uneven torque from the engine is smoothed out, and its rotational speed maintained more constantly than it would if there were no flywheel. The rotational speed only varies by a small percentage because of the action of a correctly designed flywheel, and since many machines driven by an engine need a constant speed, or can tolerate only a slight variation, flywheels are fitted as a matter of course. In the case of engines driving textile machinery, the flywheel is in effect the large rope drum which drives the LINESHAFTING on the various floors of the mill. Similarly, the winding drum in colliery and other mines acts as the flywheel. A flywheel smooths sudden speed fluctuations and assists a GOVERNOR.

The diameter of a flywheel is usually around four times the stroke of the engine, but it must be kept within safe limits dependent on speed,

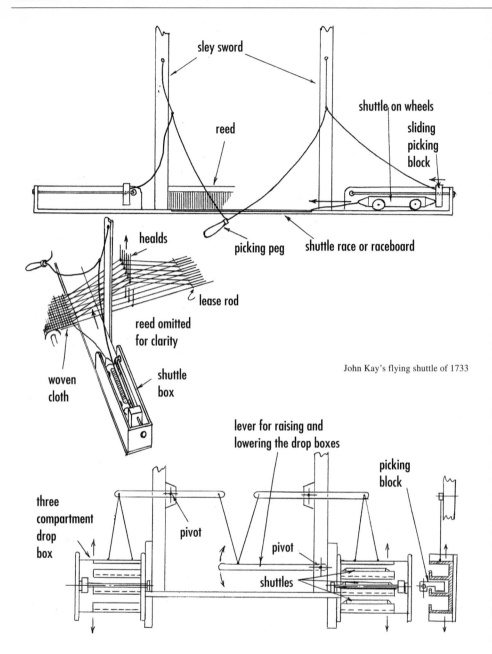

sley sword

reed

shuttle on wheels

sliding
picking
block

healds

picking peg

shuttle race or raceboard

lease rod

reed omitted
for clarity

woven
cloth

shuttle
box

John Kay's flying shuttle of 1733

lever for raising and
lowering the drop boxes

picking
block

three
compartment
drop
box

pivot

pivot

shuttles

Robert Kay's drop box of 1760 (picking peg omitted)

Fig. 27. Improvements to the hand loom

otherwise the centrifugal stresses created in the rim become excessive and the flywheel could burst, an event which has often occurred. It is believed a flywheel was first applied in 1779 to a rotative steam engine by Matthew Wasborough in Snow Hill, Birmingham.

The other use to which a flywheel is put is to store up energy in a punching or shearing machine, etc.: this energy is then utilized to assist overcoming the resistance of the metal being cut by rapidly slowing down and driving the cutting tool through the metal.

fogger a nailmaker's middleman who would supply domestic based nailmakers with materials, and buy the finished nails from them for sale to users. A similar name occurs in other European languages for a merchant or dealer, and it is thought they may be derived from the family name of Fugger, wealthy merchants in Augsburg in the 14th to 16th centuries.

folded yarn yarns composed of two or more single threads. Two fine threads twisted together into one is known as a two-fold yarn, and similarly three threads as three-fold etc. A two-fold yarn is stronger and more flexible than a single yarn of the same diameter as the combined threads, and would be used in more expensive and finer fabrics, such as top quality shirting. Folded yarn is also known as doubled yarn.

follower a machine component which receives its motion from a revolving CAM. A follower transmits its motion (often linear) to some other part of the machine or mechanism, and may be in constant contact with the profile of the cam, or make contact only during a part of the cam's revolution. Sometimes a follower is known as a tappet; on looms operated by tappets, followers are known as wipers.

fool's gold, *see* PYRITES

footmaker (or gatherer) the member of a team of glassblowers, who gathers a blob of molten glass from which the foot of a wineglass, or a handle, etc. is made by the team leader. *See also* CHAIR (2).

footrid (or footrill, footrail, futteril) a Staffordshire dialect mining term dating from the late 17th century, meaning a drift entrance to a shallow coal mine. It has the meaning of clearing coal away more or less from underfoot, i.e. the coal lying close to the surface.

footstep bearing (or cup bearing) a pedestal bearing which supports the weight of a vertical shaft and allows it to rotate. Such footstep bearings are required at the base of the vertical central shaft of a HORSE WHIM and at the base of the vertical shaft transmitting power by gearing to LINESHAFTING in early textile mills before the introduction of rope driving.

forefield the working face in a Derbyshire lead mine, usually that face which is farthest from the shaft.

forge (or hammer mill) a workshop where hot metal is shaped by hammering or rolling. Early forges usually comprised a FINERY HEARTH and a CHAFERY, each with its own air bellows, and TILT HAMMERS. Brittle cast-iron pigs were converted into malleable wrought iron and forged (i.e. shaped) into bars of various sizes suitable for use by blacksmiths etc. as the basic construction materials for iron structures, machines, and articles. WATERWHEELS provided the power for operating the bellows and tilt hammers. Later forges included reverberatory type metal melting furnaces, shingling and steam hammers, rolling mills, power shears, etc. *See also* SMITHY.

forge train the set of primary rolls for rolling a wrought iron billet immediately after SHINGLING into a muck bar. The rolls of a forge train are kept cool by cold water continually pouring over them, and the mill scale washed off the iron is collected in a pit below the rolls for subsequent re-use in the puddling furnace. A forge train is also known as a MUCK ROLLING MILL. Rolls of early design were two high (i.e. one pair), one part for roughing down, the other for finishing. After each pass through the rolls, the metal slab or bar had to be lifted onto the top roll which carried it back to the feeding side. To avoid this delay, some rolls could be reversed so that feeding in was possible from either side. Later rolls were three high so that they rotated continuously and were fed from either side.

forked pump rods mine pump rods with a side arm to each pump. The reciprocating pumps used to lift water from mines were limited in the distance each could raise the water by the vertical sweep of the rocking beam of the beam engine which operated them. Several pumps were therefore arranged in the shaft one above the other, the lowest pump lifting water from the shaft bottom and discharging into a receptacle or sump above, from which the next higher pump drew its water. This pump in turn raised the water to another sump, and so on, until the highest pump discharged the water at the ground surface to drain, or to an underground drainage sough. To operate each pump, the pump rod was forked just above each pump, one arm of the fork being attached to the pump piston, the other continuing down past the pump to the next lower fork to operate that pump (*see* Fig. 53c).

fossil alkali an old name, current in the 1780s, for soda made from salt. Another name for this was mineral alkali.

fote-cloth a flat-woven floor covering made on broadlooms from coarse wools, being woven in the mid-17th century.

fother (or fodder, stother) an old unit of weight in which lead and coal were measured. Its exact value varied somewhat from place to place and with time, but a common weight of a fother of lead was 19.5 cwt (2184 lb). It could vary from 15 to 22.5 cwt in Derbyshire, while in Durham and Northumberland, a fother of coal equalled one-third that of a CHALDRON, i.e. it weighed 1979 lb.

founder the foreman in charge of early BLAST FURNACES.

foundry a workshop where metal articles are made by casting molten material into moulds. Iron foundries are separate from places where iron is made, came into being in Britain around 1700. An iron foundry uses a CUPOLA FURNACE for re-melting pigs, and has a sand casting floor for making flat articles, a pattern making facility and pattern store, and a FETTLING shop for cleaning up castings. A place where glass articles are cast is also known as a foundry.

Fourdrinier machine a machine for making paper in a continuous length, developed by the brothers Henry (1766–1854) and Sealy (1766–1847) Fourdrinier, London stationers of HUGUENOT descent, who were assisted by John Gamble and Bryan Donkin (1768–1855), a London millwright. Their machine was based on a 1798 French invention by Nicholas-Louis Robert whose financial backer St Leger Didot approached his brother-in-law John Gamble c.1803 after a quarrel with Robert. The Fourdrinier machine was perfected in 1809, and was based on their patent no. 3068 of 1807. It was the first machine capable of making paper continuously from pulp fed in at one end and wound onto a reel at the other. Their early machine comprised a moving wire gauze belt onto which the pulp was fed, water draining away through the mesh as the web of pulp was carried along, the belt returning underneath to the feeding-in end in a continuous loop. The paper web then passed through a succession of squeezing rollers to extract more water before it was wound onto a drum, still wet. A further improvement was the addition of steam-heated drying cylinders and cutter, patented by Thomas Bonsor Crompton of Farnworth, Lancs. (patent no. 4509, 1820). There were several other later improvements and additions to the basic machine: a watermarking roller, called a DANDY ROLL was invented by John and Christopher Phipps in 1825, and water suction boxes for drawing out water through the wire

gauze belt faster and more efficiently were invented by James Brown of Edinburgh in 1836 (patent no. 7098). The Fourdrinier machine rapidly replaced hand methods of paper-making by single sheets: by 1830 about half of Britain's paper was machine made, and thirty years later around 95 per cent was machine made.

Fourneyron water turbine an outward radial-flow REACTION WATER TURBINE developed by Benoit Fourneyron in 1827. The first turbine, built at Pont sur l'Ognon in France, was one of the earliest reaction turbines, and ten turbines of a similar design were the first machines to be installed in the Niagara Falls, USA, electrical generating station each developing 5,000 hp running at 250 rpm. A diagrammatical cross-section of a Fourneyron turbine is shown in Fig. 83. This type of turbine was also known in its early days as a horizontal waterwheel.

four stroke cycle the common INTERNAL COMBUSTION heat engine cycle, often known as the OTTO CYCLE and also as the constant volume cycle, since heat is received and rejected at an almost constant volume of the cylinder.

foyboat a Tyneside word for a small rowing boat, in which foymen take provisions out to ships.

frame 1. the name frequently given to a complete machine, particularly in the textile industry. There are, for instance, stocking frames, draw frames, and slubbing frames. Richard Arkwright's (1732–92) spinning machine became known as the water frame, being a spinning machine for cotton driven by water power. The framework of early machines was wood, usually oak, beech or ash; screwed parts were sometimes made from elm, more frequently of iron. SLEYS on looms were first made from cane; parts subject to high stresses or wear were made from metal, iron or brass. Wooden frames were made by carpenters and wood-turners, with metal parts by blacksmiths. Precision components, such as gearwheels, were made by clockmakers and locksmiths. 2. a general term used in the 18th century for a WAGGONWAY track, comprising the wooden rails and sleepers.

framed building a building in which all loads are carried on a skeleton framework of iron or steel, the walls merely enclosing the space within. Early large industrial buildings such as textile mills and warehouses relied on the walls to support the building itself and all superimposed floor loadings such as machinery and stored goods. As spans between outer walls increased, intermediate posts, timber at first but later cast-iron columns, were used to support

oor beams, but the outer walls were still load-
earing. By the mid-19th century large
ructures were being designed where the loads
ere carried on self-standing metal frames; the
alls were virtually non-load-bearing, as their
eight was carried on horizontal girders
pported by the verticals to which they were
ttached. An early British example of a large
ingle-storey building using these principles
as the CRYSTAL PALACE which housed the
REAT EXHIBITION OF 1851 in London; an
xample of a large multi-storey framed
uilding, built seven years later and still
rviving, is the naval boat store at Sheerness,
ent, which used cast iron and wrought iron,
nd was designed by Godfrey T. Green
(807–86).

The principle of using a load-bearing frame
as not new: on the domestic front, houses,
rge halls, and barns, were being built as early
s the 12th century with timber frames and
attle and daub infill walls. But the first iron
amed building in the world is generally
cognized to be the flax mill for making linen
read built at Ditherington, Shrewsbury, by
harles Bage (1752–1822) in 1796. It
mprised a framework of cast-iron pillars and
eams with brick walls and arched brick
eilings, five storeys high, the loading being
rried on the iron members.

Much pioneering work on framed buildings
as done in the USA. In the early 1850s James
ogardus was building cast-iron framed
ructures in New York, and some thirty years
ter, William Le Baron Jenney had designed
nd built the ten-storey Home Insurance
uilding in Chicago. He used square cast-iron
all columns and circular internal columns with
uilt-up wrought-iron beams up to the sixth
oor and steel beams above, in what was a
rerunner of later skyscrapers. A well-known
arly framed building in France is the four-
orey Meunier chocolate factory, built in
871–2 at Noisiel-sur-Marne, and designed by
les Saulnier using wrought-iron framing and
n-load-bearing walls.

As cheap steel became available after the
ESSEMER PROCESS of 1858, rolled steel
ructural sections were increasingly used as
ad-bearing frames towards the end of the 19th
entury, replacing wrought and cast iron. By
908 structural engineering became a separate
rofessional branch of engineering with its own
stitution.

tzgerald, R.S. 'The development of the cast iron frame
    textile mills to 1850', *Industrial Archaeology Review*
    (1988), 127–45
empton, A.W. and Johnson, H.R. 'The first iron
ames', *Architectural Review* CXXXI (1962), 175–86

frame rent, *see* RACK RENT

frameshop a room containing several knitting
frames (*see* STOCKING FRAME).

framework knitting hand knitting garments
on simple hand frames. This was a domestic or
cottage industry which was mostly concentrated
in the East Midlands from the 16th to early 18th
century. The knitting frames are also known as
STOCKING FRAMES, since they were originally
used for making hosiery, and the men who
operated the frames were known as stockingers.
Henson, G. *History of the Framework Knitters*, 1867;
reprinted by David and Charles, 1970

Francis water turbine a mixed-flow
REACTION WATER TURBINE developed by
James Bicheno Francis in 1840 in the USA, and
based on an earlier patent by Samuel B. Howd.
The water enters the runner radially inwards
and leaves axially. A diagrammatic cross-
section of a Francis turbine is shown in Fig. 83.

Freehold Land Society a 19th-century scheme
to help people buy freehold land on which they
could build a house, which was founded in
Birmingham by John Taylor in the 1840s. Other
societies were formed, particularly in the
industrial towns, soon afterwards. Members
subscribing to a society for the purchase of a
plot of freehold land which was then divided
into smaller plots and distributed to the
members, often by ballot. Each member would
then build a house on his plot as and when his
finances allowed, or in some cases short
terraces typically of six houses, were built and
the estate gradually filled up. Popular street
names for such areas are Freehold Street, or
Freetown, which indicate the site of an original
plot of a Freehold Land Society. A further aim
of Freehold Land Societies was to enable
working men to vote by virtue of owning land.
Lovell, J. 'The Northamptonshire Freehold Land Society
and the origins of modern Far Cotton', *Northamptonshire
Past and Present* VIII (1992/3), 299–305

freeing dish a dish containing lead ore,
presented to the BARMASTER by a Derbyshire
lead miner for the right to work a newly found
lead vein. The amount of ore varied from
around 58 to 85 lb dependent on its quality, and
this was given to the owner of the mineral
rights of the land on which the vein had been
found. The Barmaster then marked out certain
lengths of the vein, called MEERS which the
miner could work, and a length which was to be
the exclusive property of the owner of the
mineral rights. The vein was then said to be
freed. There is a dish presented to Derbyshire
miners by Henry VIII in 1513 preserved in the
Moot Hall at Wirksworth, Derbys., which holds
about 65 lb of ore; this is known as a freeing
dish.

Freeminer a man who was born in the Hundred of St Briavels, Glos., and has the right to mine coal in the Forest of Dean, providing he has worked at the coalface for one year and a day. This is a very old privilege which was granted by Edward I (reigned 1272–1307). Coal mining by Freeminers has been a cottage-type industry, the mines being small and worked by hand; today, it is a dying industry, with very few mines actually working.

Free Traders industrialists who believed in the policy of non-protective trading by allowing foreign goods to be imported without imposed duty, and to compete freely with home produced goods. The idea was popular in Britain in the second half of the 19th century; it was first advocated by the economist Adam Smith (1723–90). The repeal of the Corn Laws in 1846 was in accordance with this policy. The Free Traders believed that the industrial interests of the country were best served by capital flowing into those industries the country was naturally best at. Exponents of Free Trade included Richard Cobden (1804–65) and John Bright (1811–89); they and many other supporters were connected with Manchester, and Free Traders were also known as the Manchester School.
McCord, N. *Free Trade*, David and Charles, 1970

French burr millstone a millstone made from pieces of quartz (flintstone) imported from the La Ferté quarries near Paris, France. Burrs or buhrs are irregularly shaped bricks or pieces of rock, and in the case of millstones, such pieces of rock are cemented together to form the circular shape required. Hot iron bands are shrunk round the circumference to prevent the millstone bursting under centrifugal force when in use. The milling surface is dressed level and the desired pattern of furrows cut into it. Monolithic stones made from La Ferté rock are rare; built up stones are common, since burrs are more readily quarried than pieces of rock large enough to make one-piece stones. The burrs are trimmed to shape and arranged in a segmental fashion on the stone. A plaster of Paris backing is provided.

Burrs began to be used in France as early as the late 15th century; they were exported elsewhere soon afterwards, and were in regular use in Britain by the early 19th century. French burrs were mainly used for grinding wheat and maize and were regarded as the best millstones since they kept their cutting edges a long time. Sometimes the central pieces of stone were made from cheaper, local rock (particularly in Scotland), and La Ferté burrs were used only for the outer surfaces where most of the grinding takes place.

Ward, Owen H. 'Millstones from La Ferté-sous-Jouarre, France', *Industrial Archaeology Review* VI (1982), 205–10

French comb, *see* HEILMANN COMBER

French drawing, *see* PORCUPINE DRAWING

French limestone, *see* CLIFF

French muslin, *see* MOUSSELINE

French truss a roof truss usually in iron c steel for large spans 40–60 ft, comprising a pa of internally braced isosceles triangles meetin at the top to form the roof ridge, and joined their apexes by a horizontal tie, their long side forming the rafters (*see* Fig. 57).

frieze a coarse woollen cloth, usually with nap on one side, copied from the cloth made i Friesland, Holland.

frit partly fused raw materials in glass makin; This preliminary heating was carried out in a oven called a CALCAR to remove any gases an burn off any impurities which might be presen Similar treatment is given to the raw materia of pottery, etc. The word comes from the Italia *fritta*, meaning to fry.

frizadoes (or frizes, friezes) coarse woolle cloths with a raised nap, usually on one sid only. They were mostly woven in the norther counties of England, particularly aroun Manchester and the West Riding of Yorkshir: although some were made in the souther woollen areas in the 16th century. Originall this kind of cloth was woven in Holland in th Friesland province, from which the name probably derived. It was copied in Englan when the FLEMISH WEAVERS brought the skills into East Anglia.

frizzing (or friezing, rowing) the old process (raising a NAP, usually curled, on woollen clot by use of teazels, hand held at first, and later t GIG MILLS and MOSING MILLS. Hand frizzir persisted until about 1850 in some areas.

frock mill, *see* SMOCK MILL

frog the V-shaped, grooved iron plate place where the inner rails intersect or cross eac other at switching or crossing points on railway or tramway. The origin of the word obscure.

frue vanner an ore dressing machir comprising a wide, slightly inclined, endle: moving rubber belt down which a stream (water flows and onto which finely crushed o is fed. As the belt passes over the lower pulle a sideways shake is imparted, which washe light minerals away from the heavier on which are gathered separately. The machine used, for example, to recover tin particles fro sands and slimes. The Frue vanner w; introduced from the USA, where it had bee invented in 1874.

fuller's earth a non-plastic soft clay of fine texture containing alumina, found principally in the chalk areas. It was used for FULLING woollen cloth, being mixed with water to form the liquor in which the cloth was pounded in FULLING STOCKS. It absorbed the natural fats and added oils present in the woollen fabric, thus cleansing it so that the cloth would take a dye. It was from this main application that the clay received its name. Sometimes it was called tucker's earth or clay, tucker being an alternative name for fulling. The most prolific sites in Britain were in Kent, Surrey, Somerset, and Bedfordshire where the material was dug out in BELL PITS. From *c*.1870 fuller's earth was also used for bleaching vegetable oil and paraffin wax. A slightly inferior clay with similar properties is known as walker's earth.

fulling pounding newly woven woollen cloth in an alkaline liquor, which absorbs natural greases and oils which were added during the weaving, and thickens up the fabric to give a stronger and denser material. In medieval times, fulling was done by treading the cloth under bare feet in water in a wooden trough, in a manner similar to the treading of grapes. This method was known as waulking, i.e. walking. Various alkaline substances were added to the water, like stale urine, a special clay called FULLER'S EARTH, and so on, to aid the cleansing action and help shrink the fabric. Fulling was the first textile process to be mechanized, and as early as the 13th century there were primitive fulling mills sited by rivers to drive their waterwheels. After the cloth had been fulled, it was stretched out on TENTER FRAMES to dry. Fulling mills are often known as tucking mills in the West Country and Ireland. Fulled cloth is shaggy and unattractive in appearance when dry, so it has to be raised to give it a nap, and then sheared or cropped to an even surface (*see* FULLING STOCKS, and

RAISING AND SHEARING). Fulling by pounding under heavy stocks was replaced by passing the cloth under rollers, a process called MILLING today.

fulling stocks large wooden machines for pounding woollen cloth to shrink it and tighten the weave. Water-powered fulling stocks were the first machines used in the textile industry. The earliest design comprised a massive wooden frame holding heavy wooden mallets, the stocks, which were lifted vertically by trips on a slowly revolving wooden shaft, and allowed to fall into a trough containing the cloth in water; the shaft was turned by a WATERWHEEL. This type is known as a falling stock or a wood faller. Later designs, called driving or swinging stocks, had an inclined arm pivoted at one end with a heavy stock at the other; the arm was raised up in a similar manner to that described above, and the stock freely swung down in an arc onto the cloth. Usually there were several such arms arranged in a row, all operated by one shaft running along the back. The beating face of the stock and the shape of the trough were made so that the bundle of cloth rolled over slowly under successive blows to expose fresh areas to the pounding action. A piece of cloth would be fulled for several days until all signs of the fabric weave had disappeared as shrinking and felting up took place.

The capital required to build a fulling mill was beyond the means of domestic weavers. They took their pieces to be fulled, just as farmers took their corn to be milled, the owner of the fulling mill charging for his services. In fact, some fulling mills were housed in the same building as a corn mill; such mills are known as double mills.

fully-fashioned in the hosiery industry, term used to describe knitted items which are shaped to fit some part of the human body, e.g. stockings. Early hand-operated knitting frames had to be adjusted by hand as work proceeded to widen or narrow the fabric when making fashioned hose. Several inventions in the mid-19th century attempted to make the width alteration automatic, the most successful being that of William Cotton of Loughborough (patent no. 70, 1860); his vertical needle machine was known as Cotton's Patent Rotary frame. Fashioning was done by transferring loops at the SELVEDGE and changing the number of needles in action.

fulminating damp, *see* FIRE DAMP

furnace pit, *see* VENTILATION FURNACE

furrow a groove cut in the surface of a millstone leading from the centre to the outer

Cheesden Lumb Mill, Lancs., a former fulling mill built in 1786

edge. The ground material finds its way along the furrow as the stone rotates within the enclosing casing until it leaves at the exit chute. Several furrows are cut in the surface in different patterns joining the grinding areas to the outer edge.

fusible plug a safety device to prevent explosion or excessive damage to a steam boiler resulting from low water. In shell-type boilers such as CORNISH or LANCASHIRE BOILERS, unless the water level is maintained above the tops of the firetube(s) the metal becomes overheated and can collapse, usually causing a disastrous explosion as the steam under high pressure ruptures the weakened tube and escapes to atmosphere. To counteract this, Richard Trevithick (1771–1833) placed a lead rivet in the highest point of the firetube in 1803. If the water level fell to a dangerous level, the lead rivet would melt, allowing the steam to dampen down the fire in a controlled manner and prevent damage to the boiler. Fusible plugs of this kind were soon fitted to all steam boilers after this, special alloys of bismuth, lead and tin being developed for the purpose.

fusoe an obsolete word for the spindle part of a ROCK hand-held spinning device. The word is the Anglicized spelling of the French *fuseau*, meaning spindle, and was used mostly in East Anglia.

fustian (or fustane, fostin) a heavy, hard-wearing cloth, originally with a linen WARP and a cotton WEFT. Linen was used as warp because in the early days of spinning, there was no spun yarn strong enough to resist the action of BEATING UP by the reeds during weaving. Later, when robust warp yarn could be produced, the description fustian continued to be used for any thick twilled all-cotton cloth with a short pile or nap. It was particularly used for hard-wearing clothing. The name comes from Fostat, an old suburb of Cairo, Egypt, where this type of cloth originated. Bolton, Lancs., is regarded as the originating centre for the manufacture of fustian in Britain, which commenced in the 17th century.

Fustian Tax, *see* MANCHESTER ACT 1736

fustic a natural dye of which there are two kinds, young fustic and old fustic. In spite of its name, young fustic was the earlier dye used and was made from the wood of the small tree *rhus cotinus* or sumach. It was imported from Greece, Turkey, and Jamaica, and when MORDANTED with alum gave a darkish orange, whilst with tin it made a bright reddish-yellow. Old fustic, also known as Cuba wood or Yellow brazilwood, came from the tree *morus tintoria* found in the Americas and the West Indies. It was mainly used to dye wool, producing a light yellow when used alone or, when mordanted with chrome, an olive-green to gold, or khaki colour.

fuzz, *see* FLY (1)

G

gabardine a TWILL fabric which can be made from a worsted surface warp and a cotton weft, or may be all cotton or in silk; it is often waterproofed for rain wear. The name is possibly a variation of the old German word *Wallevart* meaning pilgrimage: pilgrims often wore a long outer garment called a gaberdine (*sic*) made from a similar type of cloth.

gabart (or gabbard, gabbart, gabert) a Scottish word for a canal boat or sailing barge, particularly those sailing on the Clyde. The word comes from the old French *gabarot*.

gab valve gear (or Carmichael valve gear) a simple means of reversing stationary steam engines and locomotives and varying the CUT-OFF. The gab valve gear is one of the earliest ways of reversing the rotation of a steam engine, and was used on rotative beam engines where reversal was necessary, e.g. on mine winding engines and stationary rope haulage engines on railway inclines. It was applied to locomotives by Robert Stephenson in 1841 (patent no. 8998).

Fig. 68a shows a typical gab valve gear comprising two ECCENTRICS keyed on the engine crankshaft, one set for forward rotation, the other for reverse. Two eccentric rods *ac* and *bd* are joined together at *c* and *d* by a connecting link which has protruding pins at *c* and *d* for operating the gab. The gab is a component shaped like an X which is fastened at its centre onto the valve rod. As the eccentrics rotate, the pins at the ends of the eccentric rods move backwards and forwards within the V-shaped spaces of the gab. The connecting link *cd* may be raised or lowered by a system of levers comprising the bell-crank *efg*, pivoted at *f*, and the reversing rod, and a lifting link *ce*. When the link *cd* and its protruding pins is raised to its maximum position, the gab is pushed backwards and forwards by the pin at *c*. Thus, the valve receives motion from eccentric *ac*, and the other eccentric *bd* has no effect on the valve movement. Lowering *cd* brings eccentric *bd* into operation, and at the same time the position of the valve is shifted so that the engine runs in the reverse direction. With the link *cd* in its mid-position, there is virtually no valve movement, and since no steam is therefore admitted to the cylinder, the engine is stationary. Intermediate positions between maxima and centre alter the stroke of the valve due to the shape of the gab, and hence vary the cut-off point and expansion ratio.

The STEPHENSON LINK MOTION originally had gabs for controlling the valve gear, when it was known as Stephenson's Fork Motion, until 1842 when William Howe (1814–79) invented the curved link to replace the gabs or forks at the ends of the eccentric rods. The main difficulty with gabs was that the protruding pins frequently broke off making the valve motion inoperative.

gad **1.** (or gadd, gade) an old name for a bar or piece of iron, sometimes used instead of BLOOM. In Old English, a gad was a small bar or spike. Gad steel, also known as Flemish steel, was so called since it was imported from the Liège area in Belgium in the 16th and 17th centuries, noted for its early iron and steel manufacture. Gad steel was made by carburizing the outer skin of wrought-iron bars by prolonged heating in contact with charcoal. **2.** (or gadder) a short, pointed chisel or wedge used in mining.

gadding machine a rock drill used in quarrying. It drills horizontal holes under a block of stone to assist its removal from the quarry face.

gaffer the leading man or foreman in a glass making team or CHAIR. The word dates from the mid-17th century and is either a corruption and shortening of godfather with a vowel change or, as some believe, a corruption of grandfather.

gag up a means of stopping the action of a HELVE HAMMER by inserting a bar to hold the pivoted arm or helve in an open position so that the revolving CAMS are inoperative. A helve hammer is said to be gagged if a work piece too large for it is placed on the anvil so that an effective blow cannot be delivered.

gain the excess distance a mule carriage moves out away from the DRAFTING rollers over the length of yarn they deliver in the same time. The gain is therefore the amount of stretch or extra draft given to the yarn, and aids the production of a uniform thread by pulling out any untwisted or thick parts. The amount of gain given

depends on the STAPLE length of the cotton being spun. In a typical run of a mule carriage of say, 64 in, the gain would be about 2 in.

Gal a shortening of Galloway, a breed of small, hardy horses from Scotland, extensively used for haulage in underground mines and as packhorses.

gale either the royalty paid by a FREEMINER in the Forest of Dean for the right to mine ore, coal, etc. in a specified piece of land, or the plot of land itself.

galena sulphide of LEAD, the principal lead ore. It occurs in veins, mostly in the Carboniferous systems, and generally has limestone walls. Galena is a heavy ore, varying in colour from a steely grey to a bright blue, the lead content being usually around 85 per cent. It has been extensively mined in Britain and most deposits are now worked out; the surface remains of the industry are quite widespread. Pieces of galena may still be picked up from old waste heaps at former mining sites.

gallery the horizontal working passageway in a mine, also known as a level, road, roadway, or simply way.

galley beam, *see* STAUNCH

galley lane, *see* PACKWAY

galligu an obnoxious black waste material left over from the LEBLANC PROCESS for making soda ash.

gall nuts swellings found on trees due to insect attack. Gall nuts from oak trees in particular were used as a MORDANT in the early days of DYEING cloth to dye cloth black. Large amounts were imported from Italy and Turkey. Ink was also made from oak galls.

galloon narrow silk or cotton braid or ribbon used for trimming women's clothes; the word is of French origin.

Galloway horse or pony, *see* GAL

Galloway tube a slightly conical tube inserted across the firetube of some LANCASHIRE BOILERS behind the firegrate in the path of the gases, patented by John and William Galloway of Manchester (patent no. 13552, 1851). Usually some five or so such tubes were fitted, spaced out along the length of the firetube, some placed vertically, others inclined at a slight angle to the vertical. The tubes were open ended and therefore filled with water: they increased the heating surface area, improved water circulation within the boiler, and acted as strengthening stays to the firetube. Galloway tubes were also fitted to CORNISH BOILERS, and in some vertical boilers. They gradually fell into disfavour since they tended rapidly to become coated with scale on the water side, which reduced their thermal efficiency.

A Galloway boiler, covered by the same patent, had two firetubes at the front part of the boiler shell which joined into one large oval tube for the remaining length of the boiler; the cross tubes were placed in the large tube. However, the large oval tube could not withstand external pressure as well as a circular tube, as in a Lancashire boiler, and the design was discontinued after a while.

galvanizing an anti-corrosion coating of ZINC on iron and steel, which protects those surfaces against atmospheric corrosion (rusting) as a result of sacrificial corrosion of the zinc, which is preferentially attacked by the carbonic acid in the atmosphere and forms a protective layer of basic zinc carbonates. The most important use of galvanizing is probably the protection given to corrugated iron sheeting used extensively as roofing on small buildings.

There are two methods of galvanizing: dipping an article into molten zinc, and zinc coating an article by electro-plating. The hot dip method originated in France, and first began to be used in Britain in Wolverhampton in 1838 when thin rolled iron sheets were so treated. The sheets were thoroughly cleaned and treated with a flux (a zinc-ammonium chloride), before being dipped into molten zinc and cooled. Sheet steel was galvanized later, and in the 1880s wire was being galvanized. The electro-plating method was a later development and is a cold treatment using zinc sulphate solutions, which is reserved for smaller articles. The electro-deposited zinc has a better adhesion than that applied by hot dip.

The term galvanizing is derived from that of the 18th-century Italian scientist Luigi Galvani.

gangue (or gang) valueless material in an ore, i.e. the part which contains no metal. The word comes from the German *Gang*, meaning a vein of metal ore. It is also known as vein-stone.

gannister a siliceous sandstone found associated with coal in the coal measures. It was used for lining BESSEMER CONVERTERS during the manufacture of steel. Gannister is also used to make silica firebricks or acid refractories (*see* ACID LINING).

gantree the wooden supports above a loom which carry a JACQUARD mechanism.

gantry, *see* HURST

garnetting shredding woollen rags in a machine invented by Charles Garnett in 1859, for use in the SHODDY industry. The saw-like teeth on the LICKER-IN on a CARDING machine are called Garnett teeth.

gas a substance in the physical state in which the particles forming a substance have the least cohesion between them, which allows them to expand to fill completely any containing vessel or void. Gases are compressible, and may be liquified by cooling them below their critical temperature; they readily diffuse into each other, and are soluble in many liquids.

There are many types of gas, some occurring naturally e.g. FIREDAMP which occurs in coal mines, or manufactured gases such as PRODUCER GAS. The manufacture of gas as a fuel or lighting medium commenced in France in the 1790s and was developed in Britain shortly afterwards (*see* TOWN GAS). The word 'gas' was invented by a Dutch chemist, J.B. Van Helmont (1577–1644) and comes from the Greek word *khaos* meaning chaos. When first adopted in the English language it was spelt gaz.

Most gases are poisonous and/or explosive in certain conditions. Air is a mixture of gases, the main ones being nitrogen (75.5 per cent by weight) and oxygen (23.2 per cent), with small amounts of argon (1.3 per cent), carbon dioxide (0.03 per cent), and tiny amounts of some other gases. Nitrogen is an inert gas which will not support combustion.

gas colours, *see* ANILINE DYES

gas engine an internal combustion heat engine which uses a gas as its fuel, and acts as a PRIME MOVER or power source for driving other machinery, etc. Several attempts at inventing an engine powered by gas were made from the last decade of the 18th century onwards, but the first successful engine was that invented in 1860 by Jean Joseph Etienne Lenoir, a Belgian working in Paris. It used TOWN GAS and followed horizontal steam engine design and operation. It was DOUBLE-ACTING with two power strokes per revolution, an air–gas mixture being admitted at atmospheric pressure to either side of the piston in turn, and ignited at part stroke. Ignition was by an electric spark from a high tension trembler coil supplied from storage batteries. Admission and exhaust of the explosive mixture was controlled by simple SLIDE VALVES, the mixture expanding after ignition for the remainder of the stroke. Only small sizes of Lenoir's engines were made from fractional up to about 3 hp. The smallest engines were rated in 'manpower', and although inefficient, some 400 engines were built, some in Britain under licence.

Improvements to Lenoir's first engines were made by others, e.g. Pierre-Constant Hugon of France c.1865. In 1876 Nicholaus August Otto of Germany invented a SINGLE-ACTING FOUR-STROKE engine which had one power stroke every two revolutions. Its main advantage over Lenoir's engine was that it compressed the air–gas mixture before ignition took place, increasing the power output and efficiency. Ignition in Otto's engine was by a naked flame carried in a special slide valve which only exposed the flame to the mixture inside the cylinder at the correct moment. Since this action blew out the igniting flame, it was relit by a separate, continually burning pilot flame. At first Otto's engines ran on piped town gas, but by 1881, cheaper gases such as PRODUCER GAS began to be used, and the engine was modified to suit. Otto and his partner Eugene Langen went into production, and by 1889 over 40,000 gas engines had been made in sizes ranging from 1 to about 16 hp. Many were made in Britain under licence, particularly by the brothers Frank and William John Crossley in their Manchester works incorporating important modifications of their own. Larger engines were built, vertical as well as horizontal, and by the end of the 19th century gas engines were competitive with steam engines as prime movers; engines as large as 5,000 hp were being made. Their popularity was short lived, however, since electric power became available soon afterwards. The main advantages of gas engines over steam engines were that no boiler was needed: they therefore cost less, took up less floor space and started up instantly. The main disadvantage was that a piped gas supply was needed, although this was overcome in the 1880s when producer gas plants were directly coupled to gas engines. Such arrangements were known as suction gas plants since the gas engine sucked in its own supply of gas from the producer as it ran. Other alternative gases were used to drive gas engines, such as WATER GAS and waste gases from BLAST FURNACES and COKE OVENS.

In 1880, the TWO-STROKE cycle was invented by Dugald Clerk. This was first applied to gas engines, and required a blower or pump driven by the engine itself to push the air–gas mixture into the cylinder at the beginning of the compression stroke, whilst the exhaust was achieved by the piston uncovering ports in the cylinder wall at the end of the stroke. The two-stroke cycle gives a power stroke every revolution.

Clerk, D. *The Gas, Petrol, and Oil Engine*, 2 vols, Longmans Green, 1916

gasholder (or gasometer) a large vertical cylindrical storage vessel for holding TOWN GAS at a constant pressure prior to distribution to consumers. Gasholders are of variable volumetric capacity since they are made from a number of large cylinders (three is usual) whose diameters are arranged to telescope inside each

other to accommodate different volumes of gas. The oldest design of gasholder, made from wrought-iron plates, telescopes vertically and dates from an 1824 patent. The cylinders, which are usually of equal height, are guided by grooved wheels running up and down vertical guide rails fastened to vertical uprights spaced at intervals round the circumference. The uprights may be hollow cast-iron columns or of lattice girder construction, braced together by horizontal and diagonal cross-members to form a rigid ring round the holder.

Gas from the purification plant is pumped into the bottom cylinder at its base, and leaves from it to enter the distribution pipes. The top cylinder is closed by a slightly domed roof, and the whole assembly of cylinders floats in an annular, water-filled trough, held up by the internal gas pressure, which is low, acting on the underside of the roof. The water in the trough acts as a seal to prevent gas escaping round the base circumference. When the sections are telescoped together for lowest overall height, the holder contains the minimum volume of gas. If more gas is pumped in than is drawn off by consumers, the upper sections rise to provide extra internal volume until they are fully extended to their full height for maximum holding capacity. Seals are provided at the circumferences where the sections telescope inside each other. With a three-section holder, an extra capacity of nearly 200 per cent is thus available. Later designs of gasholder dispensed with the supporting ring of uprights: spiral guides are fitted outside each section of the holder, and expansion and contraction of the contained volume is made by the sections sliding inside each other with a twisting action, with appropriate seals to prevent gas escapes. This design was introduced by W. Gadd in 1890.

Gasholders iron out fluctuations in demand, providing a reserve of gas when full or near full to meet peaks by the sections descending as the above-average amount of gas is drawn off, and filling up again during drops in demand, thereby enabling the gas-making plant to run on a constant load. Small gasholders were used in factories and mills which had their own gas manufacturing plant for providing lighting. In the early 1800s, when gas lighting was commencing, factory gasholders were often rectangular and of fixed dimensions.

In the pioneering days of gas manufacture, gasholders had to be enclosed in a brick building by law, as this was believed to be safer against explosion. This fallacy was soon realized, and gasholders were left open to the atmosphere, so that if any explosion occurred the damage from flying bricks was averted.

gas manufacture the manufacture and use of coal gas owes its origin in Britain to the pioneering work of William Murdock (1754–1839), one of Boulton and Watt's engine erectors, who lit his house and an outside lamp in Redruth, Cornwall, by gas in 1792 whilst working there erecting a Watt steam engine. He later further developed gas making at his employers' Birmingham Soho works, which was gaslit by 1802, and shortly afterwards, Boulton and Watt began to sell gas-making equipment to private users. Phillips and Lee's cotton mill in Salford, Lancs., was lit by gas in 1806 from their own equipment. At first, mill owners installed gas plants for lighting their factories, replacing dangerous candles, but soon centralized stations came into being selling gas to the public and municipalities for lighting houses, streets and public buildings. The Gas Light and Coke Company of London was the first such public gas company, founded mainly by Samuel Clegg I (1781–1861), a former employee of Boulton and Watt, in 1812.

CANNEL coal was the preferred coal for gas making, giving a high gas yield. Gas is obtained by the destructive distillation of coal in externally fired RETORTS, leaving residual coke which was sold by the gas company mainly as a fuel, together with a number of valuable by-products extracted during the gas purification processes. Gas works were usually sited in the lowest part of the district they supplied to avoid the cost of having to pump the gas downhill with increased risk of leakage from pipe joints due to the higher pressure. Gas leaving the retorts needed cooling and purifying before storage in large GASHOLDERS, from which it was distributed through underground pipes to customers.

Illuminating power was the earliest requirement of gas, so its candlepower was originally important; after the electric bulb displaced gas for lighting, the calorific value of gas for heating purposes became its primary quality. Retort design and gas purification methods were gradually improved, and by the 1870s a typical gas manufacturing works comprised the following items of plant through which the gas passed in sequence:

1. a retort house containing rows of retorts, heated by external furnaces in which the gas was made;
2. a HYDRAULIC MAIN to provide a water seal to prevent explosive gas blowbacks when a retort was opened for recharging;
3. a CONDENSER to cool the gas and allow liquid tar to drain out;
4. an EXHAUSTER which drew the gas from the retorts, through the hydraulic main and condenser, and pushed it on through the purification plant to the gasholder;
5. a SCRUBBER in which water removed ammonia from the gas;
6. purifiers to remove the last traces of unwanted contaminants by chemical reaction with lime or iron oxide;
7. a meter for measuring the volume of gas made in the works;
8. one or more gasholders;
9. a GOVERNOR to control the pressure at which the gas was distributed to customers at a constant level.

In addition, there would be a covered storage for incoming coal and outgoing coke; a boiler and steam engine to drive the exhauster; and a water pump for the scrubber.

Early retorts were heated by coke, about one-third of the coke produced in the retorts themselves being used for this purpose, the rest sold. Tar was also used as a fuel, giving higher temperatures. In the late 1880s, PRODUCER GAS made from low grade coal began to be used to fire the retorts, using regenerative furnaces. As cannel coal became scarce, lower grades of coal were coked, and the resulting poorer gas was enriched by mixing it with mineral gas-oil made in separate plants. The Peebles gas enrichment process, patented in 1893 by William Young (no. 12355), was a popular item of equipment.

By the mid-19th century there were over 900 individual gas companies operating in Britain. In the last quarter of the 19th century, electricity began seriously to challenge gas for lighting purposes, and eventually replaced it. Gas manufacture was then concentrated on domestic and industrial heating applications, and for some years as fuel for gas engine PRIME MOVERS until they too were replaced by electric motors.

After the discovery of North Sea natural gas in 1964, the manufacture of coal gas rapidly declined, and virtually all coal-gas-making plants are now shut down. Since gas works lack the aesthetic appeal of wind and water mills, they are rapidly disappearing and it is unlikely that more than a very few will be preserved as industrial monuments.

Gas was also made by carbonizing mineral and shale oils, and whale oil.

Chandler, D. and Lacy, A.D. *The Rise of the Gas Industry in Britain*, British Gas Council, 1949
Cotterill, M.S. 'The development of Scottish gas technology, 1817–1914', *Industrial Archaeology Review* V (1980/81)

Griffiths, J. *The Third Man: The Life and Times of William Murdock, Inventor of Gaslight*, André Deutsch, 1992
History of the Gas, Light, and Coke Co. 1812–1949, 1949
Stewart, E.G. *Town Gas, Its Manufacture and Distribution*, HMSO, 1958
Williams, T. *History of the British Gas Industry*, Oxford University Press, 1981

Developments in the coal-gas industry

1792	William Murdock lit his house by gas in Redruth, Cornwall.
1802	Birmingham Soho factory of Boulton and Watt lit by gas after further experiment and development by Murdock.
1804	Boulton and Watt commence selling gas making plant.
1805	Purification of gas by lime introduced by Samuel Clegg.
1806	Phillips and Lee's mill lit by gas in Salford, Lancs.
1807	Pall Mall, London, has gas street lighting installed.
1811	Stonyhurst College, Lancs., lit by gas.
1811	Hydraulic main invented by Samuel Clegg.
1812	Gas Light and Coke Company formed in London to supply gas from a central station. Eventually became the largest gas company in the world.
1816–17	Gas works output volume meter invented.
1816	Air cooled condenser and simple gas washer introduced.
1820	Refractory clay retorts introduced by John Grafton.
1820s	Gasholders of 15,000 cubic ft capacity in use.
1824	Outside guided, telescopic lift gasholders in use.
1825	Pioneer gas exhauster invented by S. Broadmeadow.
1844	Dry type, consumer gas meters introduced.
1848	Rotary gas exhauster perfected by Beale.
1859	Over 900 independent gas companies operating in Britain.
1860s	Gas being used for water heating and cooking in addition to lighting.
1861	Producer gas plants invented, using low grade coal.
1863	Institution of Gas Engineers formed.
1870s	Annular condensers introduced.
1874	Hydraulic stoking machine developed by William Foulis.
1876	Gas engine prime movers.
1886	Upright incandescent gas mantle by Carl Welsbach begins replacing open flame lights.
1890	Self guiding spiral lift gasholders.
1892–3	Peebles gas-oil enrichment plant.
1897	Inverted gas mantle introduced.
1900s	Mechanically fed, continuous output, vertical retorts.

gasometer, *see* GASHOLDER

gas turbine a heat engine PRIME MOVER in which hot gases or hot air expand as they pass through and rotate vanes attached to a central shaft, enclosed in a chamber. The kinetic energy created by the expansion is absorbed in driving the rotating shaft. Gas turbines were not successful until well into the 20th century, but several attempts at inventing one were made in the late 18th century and during the 19th century, and many patents were taken out. In 1791, John Barber of Nuneaton patented a gas turbine design (no. 1833) but never actually made one; John Ericsson, the Swedish born inventor, built one in 1826 using superheated air to drive it, but it was unsuccessful. It was not until materials became available which could withstand the high temperatures involved that gas turbines became a proposition, an outstanding example being the use of a gas turbine in jet propulsion by Frank Whittle in the 1940s.

gate 1. (or gait) in the 18th century, a trip or journey made with a coal waggon in Tyneside. **2.** a passageway between machines, such as the mule gate, the space where the spinner stands when working the machine. **3.** suffix which occurs in many placenames, where it is derived from the old Norse *gata*, meaning road or way: Saltersgate, for instance, is an old inn in Yorkshire on the old Saltway from Cheshire. Several placenames linked by a common word stem may indicate the route of an old packhorse track or route across country.

gatherer, *see* FOOTMAKER

gauge on a railway track, the horizontal measurement between the inner edges of the parallel rails. Although the gauge of railway tracks in Britain is standard today, it was not always so in the early days, and varied considerably between 1 ft 11½ in and 7 ft 0¼ in. When railways were being built, each line was laid down according to the design of the engineer concerned, without reference to other lines, and there was no inter-connection between them at first. Benjamin Outram proposed a common gauge across the country in 1799 of 4 ft 2 in between 'flanches', but this never materialized. George Stephenson, when building the Killingworth Colliery Waggonway, Northumberland, copied the gauge of an earlier 1762 wooden rail track, and this in due course became the standard national gauge of 4 ft $8\frac{1}{2}$ in, starting with the public mainline railway between Liverpool and Manchester of 1830.

However, this gauge was not adopted at first by other railway companies. In fact, at Crewe in Cheshire there were three gauges in the early 1840s – the Grand Junction Railway, the Crewe and Chester Railway, and the Manchester and Birmingham Railway, all differing from each other by small amounts. A notable deviation from the 4 ft $8\frac{1}{2}$ in gauge was the broad gauge of Isambard Kingdom Brunel (1806–59) at 7 ft, first used on the Great Western Railway between London and Bristol in 1838. This gauge was soon afterwards increased by $\frac{1}{4}$ in to give better clearance. By the end of 1844, there were approximately 2,236 miles of public railways in Britain, 2,013 of standard 4 ft $8\frac{1}{2}$ in gauge, and 223 of broad gauge. These different gauges first met at Gloucester, and through traffic, both passengers and goods, had to change trains – a source of great inconvenience, especially for goods. Such places were known as break-of-gauge points. A dispute soon arose as to which was the best gauge, and in 1845 a Royal Commission was set up to investigate both systems. In 1846 Parliament ruled that the 4 ft $8\frac{1}{2}$ in or narrow gauge should be the standard for the country. The Great Western Railway was a long time in complying: it was not until 1872 that they added a third rail to their existing lines to allow common running over their system by 4 ft $8\frac{1}{2}$ in traffic, the three rail track being known as mixed gauge. By 1892 the broad gauge had disappeared, and all passenger carrying railways in Britain operated on the standard gauge. There were, and still are today, some non-standard gauge mineral lines in existence.

The first railway in Ireland was the Dublin and Kingstown which opened in 1834 with a 4 ft $8\frac{1}{2}$ in gauge, but this was altered to the Irish standard of 5 ft 3 in in 1857. Since most of the early railways in other European countries were engineered by British engineers, the 4 ft $8\frac{1}{2}$ in gauge was adopted, except on the Iberian peninsular. The USA and Canada also adopted the British standard gauge.

Day, L. *Broad Gauge*, HMSO, 1985

gauging dock a place where a canal boat's draught is recorded. When a canal boat is made it is placed in a gauging dock where its immersion depth or draught is determined both when empty, and also with a series of known loads placed in it. Marks corresponding to each draught are cut into the side of the hull or made on metal plates attached thereto, to indicate the water levels; these marks could then be used to check loads for calculating tolls. Toll collectors had a book containing gauging data for each boat. Gauging docks are short side branches off the canal and are found either in boat yards or at wharves. Some gauging docks were fitted with large cranes for bodily lifting the boat out of the water for weighing.

Another method for checking loads for toll purposes, introduced in *c*.1810, was a hand held gauge, which comprised a hollow metal tube with a freely floating rod inside it graduated in inches. The tube could be placed in the water by the toll keeper alongside the boat's side and lowered vertically until a projecting arm rested on the boat's gunwale. The floating rod rose up and the freeboard could be read off and compared with previously recorded data for the boat held by the tollkeeper.

gauntlet track a pair of standard gauge rails laid centrally between the pair of broad gauge rails on a mixed GAUGE railway. This was only necessary where the track led onto a turntable, so that the rolling stock was positioned centrally and the load on the turntable balanced.

gauze a lightweight fabric of open net construction made in silk, cotton, etc., used in the 19th century for fine garments and hangings. The name comes from the town Gaza, sometimes spelt Ghuzzeh, in Palestine, where it originates.

gear cutting machine a precision machine for cutting gearwheel teeth. Toothed gear wheels for transmitting motion and power from one shaft to another have a long history. Up until the late 17th century gear teeth were filed by hand, but when more precision was necessary, as in mechanical clocks, greater accuracy was obtained cutting the tooth profile and maintaining more exact pitch by using a cutting machine. Robert Hooke developed a hand operated gear cutter in 1670 which was adopted by clockmakers; later, other inventors produced gear cutting machines, notably Christopher Polhem in Sweden in 1729, and Samuel Réhé in 1783, and by *c*.1820 John George Bodmer had invented a power driven gear cutter.

To maintain continuous contact between the surfaces of meshing teeth with a minimum of friction, cycloidal tooth profiles were considered best for a long time. (A cycloid is the curve traced by a point on the circumference of a circle as it rolls along a straight line.)

Clockmakers used this profile for decades, but such accurately cut gear teeth were not in general engineering use until the end of the 18th century. Joseph Whitworth (1803–87) invented a gear cutting machine in the 1830s, and more accurate gears gradually became available in general machine use. Around this time the involute tooth profile was introduced, which was shown to be better than the cycloidal profile, and became the standard tooth shape. (An involute curve is the path traced by the end of a taut cord as it is unwrapped from a base circle.)

Gear cutting machines were developed for cutting all kinds of toothed wheels: SPURS, BEVELS, HELICALS, etc. The early pioneers of textile machinery had to rely on clockmakers for their gear wheels, larger gears in windmills etc. being made by blacksmiths, but the introduction of gear cutting machines meant that large engineering concerns and machinery makers installed their own gear cutters, whilst firms specializing in gear cutting developed to provide a service to industry.

Woodbury, R.S. *History of the Gear Cutting Machine*, Massachusetts Institute of Technology Press, 1958

gearing transmitting rotation and power by intermeshing toothed wheels. The teeth on a driving wheel press against the sides of teeth on a driven wheel with a combined rolling and sliding action as successive teeth engage and disengage, causing the driven wheel to rotate in the opposite direction. The power that can be transmitted depends on the strength of the teeth. It is not known when toothed gearing came into use. Early industrial gears were made of wood (*see* LANTERN GEAR): stronger metal gear wheels were probably first made in number by clockmakers. These were hand made, and 18th-century pioneer inventors of textile machines got their gear wheels from clockmakers, usually in brass. Rough gear wheels in cast iron were being made for John Smeaton at Carron Ironworks in Scotland, in 1754, and John Rennie used wrought-iron and cast-iron gears in the ill-fated Albion Mills, London, in 1788. Up until about the mid-19th century, LINESHAFTING in textile mills was driven by a geared system from the PRIME MOVER. A vertical shaft passed up through the mill floors, and rotation and power was transmitted by BEVEL GEARS. Early metal gear wheels were inaccurately made, noisy, and jerky in action. Studies by mathematicians into the best geometric tooth profile to give a smooth action with minimum friction resulted in the cycloid profile at first, but by the late 17th century the involute form was found to be better, and became the standard profile. Superior machine-cut gears were introduced by the 1830s.

Gearing may be used to change the velocity of a pair of mating wheels and their shafts by having different diameter wheels and numbers of teeth. For parallel shafts, the larger of a mating pair of wheels is called a SPUR WHEEL, and the smaller one a PINION; the teeth are cut parallel to the shafts. Shafts intersecting at an angle can be connected together by bevel gears or by a WORM AND WORMWHEEL, with teeth cut according to the geometry of the connection. If the direction of rotation for driver and driven is to be the same, a third gear is put between them, called an idler, which does not affect the gear ratio between driver and driven.

Wooden teeth, called cogs, were used in corn mills. These teeth were hand shaped in a hardwood, and morticed into the rim of a cast-iron pinion, to mate with cast-iron teeth on the large spur wheel. This combination eliminated the risk of sparking, an important consideration in such a dusty environment.

genappe a smooth woollen yarn used for worsted manufacture, named after the town of Genappe in Belgium which specialized in this type of cloth.

General Enclosure Act 1801 an Act which simplified the enclosure of land for agricultural purposes by replacing the numerous private enclosure Acts which had been passed before. In the twenty years 1761–80, no fewer than 1039 private Acts were passed; but after the General Enclosure Act it was no longer necessary for individual Acts to be passed for each parcel of land.

'Geordie' lamp the nickname given to the miners' SAFETY LAMP invented by George Stephenson in 1815, which was the subject of controversy with the DAVY LAMP regarding priority of invention. The name 'Geordie' originated on Tyneside in about 1760 and is a local diminutive of George, a common name in that area at that period; on Tyneside a Geordie may also mean a coal miner, or a coal boat. Stephenson was moved to try and discover a safe means of illuminating coal mines particularly after the FIREDAMP explosion at Felling pit (also known as Brandling Main) in 1812, which killed 90 men and boys underground. Although the Davy lamp became the standard safety lamp, a sum of £1,000 was collected by Stephenson's supporters and presented to him in 1818 in recognition of his work.

German process, *see* CONTACT PROCESS

German steel, *see* SHEAR STEEL

gighole (or gigpit, killoddy) an old Shropshire dialect name for a hole dug in the ground in which a charcoal fire was lit so that wet RETTED HEMP and FLAX could be dried over it. Gigholes were used by domestic workers in rural areas preparing hemp or flax mainly for their own use.

gig mill a large diameter roller whose periphery is covered with short spikes against which woollen cloth is passed to raise a nap in one direction only. It was necessary to raise a nap on woollen cloth before it was sheared, to ensure a smooth finished surface with no random long fibres which might escape shearing if they had not been previously raised. Early gig mills had short wire spikes similar to CARD CLOTH and, because they could damage cloth if roughly used, or were deliberately used to stretch the cloth by unscrupulous clothiers, their use was banned by penal statute in 1633 to protect the consumer. Rowing, or the raising of a nap, was then carried out by hand-held TEAZELS. Later gig mills substituted king teazels for wires, and their introduction was greatly resented by hand rowers, particularly in Yorkshire where the destruction of such machines was carried out by the LUDDITES in 1812. *See also* CROPPING FRAME.

gill box, *see* SCREW-GILL DRAW FRAME

gilling the process of drawing out or DRAFTING textile fibres by the combing action of rows of pins, called gill pins, which are dragged through the fibres. This straightens and attenuates the fibres in preparation for subsequent spinning into yarn. This process is carried out in a SCREW-GILL or gill box which works in conjunction with rollers. Gilling is a preliminary process in the worsted industry for handling long wools (generally fibres over 8 in long).

gin 1. A horse gin was a primitive device for winding ore, water, or men up mine shafts, and for taking men down to the workings. The name probably is a shortening of the word 'engine'. Gins were also called whims. Fig. 28 shows two early types of gin or whim, and a detailed description is given under HORSE WHIM. A gin circle is the path trodden by horses working a gin, also more rarely called an engine race. **2.** a machine for removing seeds from the COTTON BOLL (*see* COTTON GIN).

gingham a lightweight cotton or linen fabric woven from dyed yarn to produce stripes or checks, and used for summer dresses and aprons. The name most likely comes from the Malayan *ging-gang* meaning striped, although an alternative possible source is the Anglicized version of Guingamp, a town in Flanders where such material was made. Gingham was being made in Manchester from the 18th century onwards.

ginging (or gingonin) the walled lining (often of stone) at the top of a mine shaft to strengthen it and prevent the sides from caving in; once solid rock was reached farther down the shaft, ginging ceased. Alternatively, it can mean the arching over discarded shafts to stop cattle etc. falling in. The word is particularly used in the lead mining area of Derbyshire, and is obscure in origin.

ginny ring, *see* HORSE MILL

gladden, *see* FLANNEL

glance a metallic ore of lustrous appearance (*see* COPPER, GALENA).

gland an assembly of parts designed to prevent leakage of a fluid, gas, steam, etc. from a vessel at the point where a rotating or reciprocating shaft emerges, such as from a steam engine cylinder, pump body, etc. It comprises a space called a stuffing box filled with a suitable PACKING material and some means of compressing it to make a steam- or water-tight joint, but allows movement of the shaft with minimum friction. The design of successful glands has occupied the inventiveness of many machine designers, particularly as fluid pressures have increased over the years. A sleeve encircles the shaft or piston rod which can be moved longitudinally and locked in position to compress the packing inside the stuffing box and tighten it to stop leakages. Sir Samuel Morland patented a plunger type pump fitted with glands in 1674.

glass a hard, brittle, homogeneous mixture of silicate, calcium, and soda ash, which being transparent is used for glazing windows, and for making drinking vessels and storage containers such as bottles; decorated objects such as vases, and ornaments are also made from glass, and sometimes coloured, as is stained glass for pictorial windows in churches, etc. Glass is made by heating the ingredients until they fuse together, and after an article is formed into the required shape, it is slowly cooled or annealed to remove any inherent stresses that may exist. Common window glass is made from fine sand (silicon dioxide), soda ash (sodium carbonate), and either lime (calcium oxide) or limestone (calcium carbonate), with a percentage of broken glass (cullet) added to act as a FLUX.

Glass was discovered some 5,000 years ago: objects were made by casting molten glass into moulds, or dipping a former made from straw and clay into molten glass and picking out the core when the surrounding glass shell was cool. Around 50 BC it was discovered that a blob of molten glass on the end of a long pipe could be blown out into a hollow shape, and the skilled craft of glass-blowing was developed over the

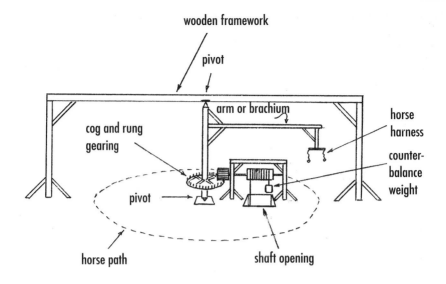

wooden framework

pivot

arm or brachium

cog and rung
gearing

horse
harness

counter-
balance
weight

pivot

horse path

shaft opening

Tyneside cog and rung gin (early 18th century)

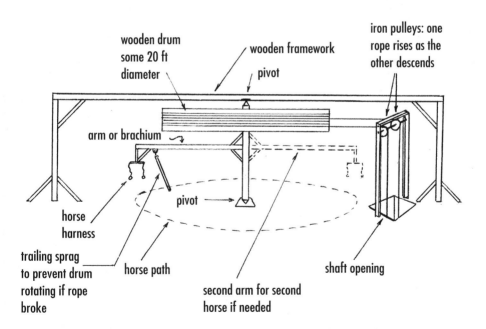

wooden drum
some 20 ft
diameter

wooden framework

pivot

iron pulleys: one
rope rises as the
other descends

arm or brachium

pivot

horse
harness

trailing sprag
to prevent drum
rotating if rope
broke

horse path

second arm for second
horse if needed

shaft opening

Scotch gin or horse whim (mid-18th century)

Fig. 28. Early winding gear for coal mines

following centuries, particularly in Venice. It was learned early that coloured glass could be made by adding small amounts of metallic oxides to the mix, and also that the unwanted green or brown tints in early glass, caused by the presence of iron traces in the sand, could be removed by adding manganese oxide. Glass blowers work together as a team called a CHAIR, producing domestic objects such as drinking glasses, etc.

By the Middle Ages glass making in Britain was mainly concentrated in woodland areas around London, where readily available fuel for the furnaces and potash (a crude form of potassium carbonate) could be obtained from the ashes of burnt bracken, beech, or oak (which was used as an alternative to calcium). The raw materials were heated in covered clay pots placed inside primitive furnaces which were heated from below, whilst completed articles were ANNEALED in an upper, cooler part of the furnace. When all the trees were used up around a glassworks, it moved to another forest site. The excessive deforestation of natural resources caused concern, and a law was passed in 1615 forbidding the use of wood as fuel for glass making. Glass makers then turned to coal and moved north to areas such as Newcastle upon Tyne, Stourbridge, and south-east Scotland where coal was being mined. By the end of the 17th century circular GLASS CONES appeared and continued in use until c.1830 when rectangular buildings housing furnaces began to replace them. Annealing was now carried out in separate long tunnel ovens called LEHRS in which the temperature gradually fell from just under glass melting temperature at the inlet to ambient temperature at the outlet, the glass article passing through to cool slowly.

Drinking glasses, vases, dishes, wineglasses, etc. were sometimes decorated: various methods were developed such as diamond point or copper wheel engraving, acid etching, enamelling, and straight cuts – made by rotating iron wheels fed with wet sand and subsequently polished by wood or felt covered wheels fed with pumice stone powder. Some articles were carved to give a decorative shape and finish. Cathedral and church windows have been glazed with stained glass since the 12th century; the production of such glass was very expensive and made in only small quantities for many centuries. When the glazing of domestic windows began in the 16th century, flat, clear glass production commenced. There were then three ways of making window glass: casting, which involved pouring molten glass onto a

metal plate, rolling it flat, and by grinding and polishing after annealing; the CYLINDER or broad glass technique; and the CROWN method. PLATE GLASS succeeded cylinder glass in the mid-19th century. A Window Tax had been introduced in 1691 and its abolition in 1851 resulted in a rapid increase in glass production and use.

In addition to common glass, lead crystal or flint glass made its appearance in 1675 as the result of work done in London by George Ravenscroft (1618–81). He used crushed flints for silica with the addition of lead oxide in place of lime to prevent internal crazing. He patented his process in 1674 (no. 176). Later, sand replaced flint, although this type of glass, used for domestic ware, is still called flint glass today.

Glass cutting wheels were treadle-operated at first, although some were water-powered. Eventually steam power was applied, and c.1830 press moulding of domestic glass articles was adopted in Britain, originating in the USA. Molten glass was pressed into a metal mould by a hand-operated plunger, the plunger forming the internal shape of the article, and the mould adding the outer surface decoration. This technique speeded production and cheapened the finished article. Examples of the glass maker's craft may be seen in many public museums, and some glass making firms have private museums which may be visited on application.

Barker, T.C. *Pilkington Brothers and the Glass Industry*, Allen and Unwin, 1960
Dodsworth, Roger. *Glass and Glassmaking*, Shire Publication No. 83, 1982
Douglas, R.W. and Frank, S. *A History of Glassmaking*, Foulis and Co., 1972
Louw, Hertie. 'Window glass making in Britain c.1660–c.1860 and its architectural impact', *Construction History* 7 (1991)

glass cone a conical brick structure in which glass articles were made. Such cones were in use in the mid-18th and early 19th centuries, and comprised a central furnace in which the glass was melted, the glass makers working in the annular space surrounding the furnace. The cone provided both chimney draught for the high temperature required in the furnace, and a covered, draught-proof working area for the men who worked around the furnace in teams known as CHAIRS. A typical cone would be about 80 ft high with a base diameter of 40–50 ft. Taller cones existed, the highest one known being 150 ft tall. The central furnace was fired from below and had side arches connected to the central hearth by flues or lunettes. Preliminary heating of the glass in clay pots took place in the side arches, and final melting in the centre. A number of openings in the circumference of the furnace enabled the glass makers to insert their irons to gather molten glass, which they brought to the working space to fashion into various shapes by blowing, etc. The glass articles were ANNEALED in the side arches to remove any residual stresses. Cone glasshouses were replaced by rectangular buildings c.1830, and today there are only about four still standing, none of which are in use.

glasswort a seashore plant, with the botanical name *Salicornia herbacea*, from which SODA was formerly made by burning, and used in the 17th century for making glass and soap. Another name for the plant is saltwort, and the burnt ashes were known as BARILLA.

glazing the creation of a smooth, shiny surface. The word comes from old English *glasen*, meaning glass or glass-like. Glazing is produced in different ways according to the material being treated. In paper making, waterpowered glazing hammers were once used to impart a smooth finish on high grade paper, replacing the old hand method of polishing the paper surface with a smooth stone or agate. In due course, glazing hammers were themselves replaced by calendering rolls; calendering is another name for imparting a smooth glazed finish.

Woollen cloth was given a smooth surface in a glazing press which comprised heated steel plates between which the cloth was placed, and the combination of heat and pressure produced the desired effect on the fabric. In pottery, the glazing of earthenware drain pipes and similar clay items is done by covering the articles with salt in the kiln. The salt volatilizes, producing the smooth, impervious, glass-like surface which is essential for such items. Salt glazing of pottery was introduced into the pottery district of Staffordshire c.1690 by the Dutch brothers David and John Elers, and was further developed by John Astbury around 1720. Other materials used for glazing pottery are lead and other metallic oxides, and feldspar (introduced in 1820). These glazes are applied to the articles by dipping them in a slip containing the glaze between the first and second final firing.

Metal tool blades were glazed or polished on a revolving leather-covered wheel impregnated with emery powder or silver sand, to delay surface corrosion of the steel. Finally, the glazing (or glossing) of gunpowder was done by tumbling it in barrels to round off the grains, and by adding black lead, to coat the grains and make them more resistant to moisture.

Gleynforth a type of cloth with a high linen content peculiar to Glemsford in Suffolk, and woven there in the Middle Ages.

gloom stove a special kind of oven for drying gunpowder without using any flames. The heat was obtained by radiation from red-hot iron plates placed inside the oven. The strange name is a derivation from the word gloaming, the glow from the setting sun.

glory hole an ancillary furnace in which glass articles may be reheated during their manufacture to keep them soft and workable.

glost oven a kiln or furnace in which BISCUIT is fired after it has been glazed.

Goad insurance plans scale plans of buildings such as mills, factories and warehouses, showing details of construction, number of floors, use, power sources, names of occupants, etc. They were produced by Messrs Charles E. Goad Ltd, of Old Hatfield, Herts., for insurance companies, so that fire risks could be assessed, during the period 1886–1970; regularly updated, they covered sixty towns, and are a useful source of information for industrial archaeologists.

Rowley, G. *British Fire Insurance Plans*, Goad Ltd, 1985

goaf (or gob) either the empty space left behind after coal has been removed in a mine, or the waste material or collapsed roof which has filled this space. A gob fire is a fire produced by spontaneous combustion of decomposing rubbish such as old discarded timbers, coal dust, etc., left in a goaf. The plural of goaf is goaves.

gob, *see* GOAF

goff an old Yorkshire dialect word for a water-powered trip hammer.

goffan a dialect word for an old mining surface excavation.

goit (or goat, gote, goyt) a northern dialect word meaning any watercourse or channel. It may be used to describe the channel cut in the ground to convey water from a point upstream to a WATERWHEEL, or for the similar channel which conveys the water away from the wheel back into the river downstream. Alternative words are leat or sluice.

Gooch link motion a mechanism used on stationary steam engines and locomotives for reversing the rotation of the engine and varying the CUT-OFF and expansion ratio (*see* Fig. 68c). Developed by Daniel Gooch in 1843, it is similar to the STEPHENSON LINK MOTION, the main difference being that the EXPANSION LINK is convex viewed from the engine crankshaft, and it is not raised or lowered, but merely oscillates about its mid-point. For this reason the linkage is also known as the Gooch stationary link motion, or fixed link motion.

The two eccentrics (*see* Fig. 68) are keyed on the engine crankshaft, one set for forward rotation, the other for reverse. Eccentric rods *ac* and *bd* are pivoted to the ends of the curved expansion link at *c* and *d*, the link being suspended from its mid point *e* from a fixed fulcrum *f*. The expansion link is slotted and a block *m* can slide in it. Block *m* is at the end of a link *mgh*, *h* being pivoted to the valve rod. A lifting link *gi* can raise or lower *mgh* by the driver tilting the bell-crank *ijk* via the reversing rod *kl*, thus altering the position of *m* in the expansion link. When *mgh* is raised so that *m* is coincident with *d*, the valve receives its motion from eccentric *bd* and the engine will run in one direction. The other eccentric *ac* merely oscillates end *c* of the expansion link without affecting the motion of the valve. Similarly when *m* coincides with *c* the valve is shifted within the valve chest to admit steam to the opposite side of the piston, causing the engine to run in the opposite direction, the valve now receiving its motion from eccentric *ac*. If *m* is in the mid position *e*, the valve is almost stationary and no steam is admitted, the engine remaining stationary. Intermediate positions between *e–c* and *e–d* reduce the valve travel and vary the cut-off point and hence the expansion ratio.

The Gooch linkage has the advantage over the Stephenson that the LEAD is constant for all cut-off points, but has the disadvantage that the line of thrust and pull on the valve rod is oblique. The open rod configuration is shown in the diagram; the eccentric rods can also be arranged to cross over each other, which alters the steam distribution, although the gear functions in a similar manner.

Good double-chain drafter a machine for preparing long fibres for spinning, such as hemp, jute, etc., when paralleling by CARDING (as for cotton, which has short fibres), and DRAFTING by rollers alone, is not practical. In 1871, John Good, an Irish-American, patented with A.V. Newton a double-chain machine which combed, drafted and spread long fibred materials (patent no. 2211).

Fig. 29 shows how the machine operated. The fibres are fed into the machine by a pair of feed rollers, and are picked up by raised gill pins fastened to an endless chain and carried forward at a relatively slow speed. When the fibres reach the end of the first chain, they pass onto a faster-moving, similar chain (usually five to ten times faster). The gill pins on the second chain first comb out the fibres until the friction on the slow chain can no longer hold the fibres; they are then drawn out or drafted corresponding to the difference in linear speed between the two conveying chains. The fast chain conveys the fibres into a pair of drafting rollers which rotate at a linear surface speed about 50 per cent faster than the fast chain to provide further drafting. Around half to two-

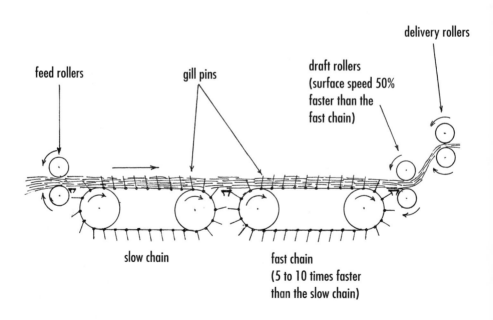

Fig. 29. John Good's patent double-chain drafter for long fibres

thirds of the total draft takes place at the transfer between the two chains, the remaining at the final rollers. The SLIVER delivered by the machine is then ready for further processing.

gooseneck a quick-release pipe connecting a TUYÈRE to the BUSTLE PIPE or main air blast pipe on a BLAST FURNACE.

Gossage tower a tower for trapping hydrochloric acid gas. Introduced by William Gossage at his alkali works in Stoke Prior, Worcs., in 1836–37, it comprises an absorption tower used in the LEBLANC PROCESS for the manufacture of sodium carbonate. The Leblanc process liberates acidic waste gases, which are passed up a Gossage tower through a deep bed of coke over which a descending stream of water passes. The coke presents a large wet surface area to the ascending gases and produces hydrochloric acid, which was formerly lost. The tower made the commercial production of hydrochloric acid possible, besides reducing a severe pollution hazard.

gossan soft, sulphide mineral matter, found in the upper parts of veins, and varying from light brown to dark red in colour. It often indicates that ore is present.

gounce, *see* TYE

governor a mechanical device for automatically controlling some function on a machine or engine. Most governors are used for regulating the speed of an engine by altering the energy intake to compensate for speed changes as the load on the engine varies. The two principal types of governor are the CENTRIFUGAL GOVERNOR and the inertia governor, the former of which is the more common. Other types of governor include the CATARACT CONTROLLER and BUOY CONTROLLER which control the frequency of strokes on BEAM STEAM ENGINES.

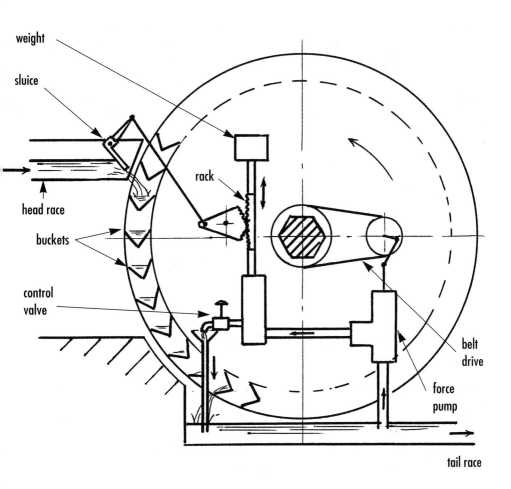

Fig. 30. Waterwheel governor attributed to Brindley, *c.* 1737

An ingenious way of controlling the speed of a WATERWHEEL, attributed to James Brindley (1716–72), is shown in Fig. 30. A force pump is driven by a belt from the waterwheel axle and draws water from the tail race. The water is forced into a vertical cylinder containing a ram, and an outlet pipe. The outlet is controlled by a valve which is manually set to allow a certain amount of water escape from the cylinder. The pressure generated inside the cylinder holds up the weighted ram, and a rack cut on its spindle engages with a pivoted quadrant which is connected to the sluice via linkages. If the wheel speeds up, the pump runs faster and sends more water into the cylinder. This raises the ram slightly, turning the quadrant, so reducing the sluice opening which slows the wheel back to its original speed. A different wheel speed is obtained by altering the amount of water escaping from the cylinder by adjusting the control valve by hand.

grandrelle yarn DOUBLED from two single cotton yarns of different colours, twisted together to make a yarn resembling a barber's pole. Grandrelle (or grandrill) cloth is material made from grandrelle yarn, used frequently for shirtings.

granite railway tramway built in 1820 between quarries on Haytor, Dartmoor, and the terminus of the Newton Abbot Canal at Ventiford Brook, Dartmoor, Devon. It replaced transport by packhorses, and was used for conveying large granite blocks, and the track itself is made from granite blocks with L-shaped rails carved in them. Small cast-iron points were used at intersections. The tramway was in use until the 1860s, and parts of it are still visible.

graphite a soft, black form of carbon, from which pencils are made. In Britain, graphite was discovered by shepherds in Borrowdale, Cumberland, in the 16th century, and used by them for marking sheep. The original finds were probably outcrops; later, graphite was mined from veins known locally as pipes. The material had several names at first, such as plumbago, wadd, blacklead, black-cawke, and kellow, but was renamed graphite c.1779 from the Greek *grapho*, meaning to write. It is a naturally occurring crystalline form of carbon containing about 96 per cent carbon, and 4 per cent iron, and found as a black, soft mass in igneous rocks.

Cumberland graphite was used in Italy as early as c.1580 as a writing and drawing medium, having been carried there by Flemish traders who bought it from British merchants. In the 18th century it had a medicinal use, and

was also used by dyers for making a fast, blue cloth dye. In 1795, a Frenchman called Conté mixed graphite powder with clay and moulded the mixture into thin sticks which were fired like pottery, and enclosed in a sandwich of thin wood slats to make the first true pencils, named from the Latin *pencillum*, meaning a paint brush.

The manufacture of pencils by hand became a domestic industry around Keswick, Cumberland, at first, until local factories gradually took over as demand rose. In the late 17th and early 18th centuries graphite was a very valuable commodity, and was used also for making cannonball moulds since it could withstand high temperatures without cracking or fusing. An Act was passed in 1751 making transportation the punishment for stealing or receiving graphite. Graphite paste was used in Victorian times as a grate polish; it is also a useful lubricant. The Cumberland deposits are now worked out, and supplies come from foreign sources today.

grasshopper engine alternatively known as the half-beam engine, a grasshopper engine gets its name from the peculiar nodding action of the overhead beam which is supposed to resemble the action of the rear legs of the grasshopper. This motion results from the configuration of the moving linkages by which the movement of the reciprocating piston is converted to circular motion at the crankshaft. Originally patented by William Freemantle in 1803, the design was developed by Oliver Evans (1755–1819) in Philadelphia, USA, soon afterwards, and used on small, single-cylinder rotative steam engines of up to 20 horsepower.

Fig. 31 shows a typical grasshopper engine. The piston rod from the vertical cylinder is pivoted to one end of the overhead beam at c, and the other end a is pivoted to a pair of rocking links (one either side of it) which are pivoted to the baseplate at o'. A pair of regulating radius arms (again one either side of the beam) extend from the pivot o on the engine frame, to the mid-point pivot b on the beam. The end a of the beam is equivalent to the central fulcrum of a normal full length beam, and it is from this that the alternative name of half-beam is derived. The drive down to the crank is via a connecting rod pivoted onto the half-beam also at the mid-point b. As the piston rises and falls inside the cylinder, it pushes and pulls end c of the half-beam up and down, and the regulating radius ensures that the piston rod follows a straight, vertical line, the rocking link moving through a small arc at a to accommodate this. The grasshopper design is

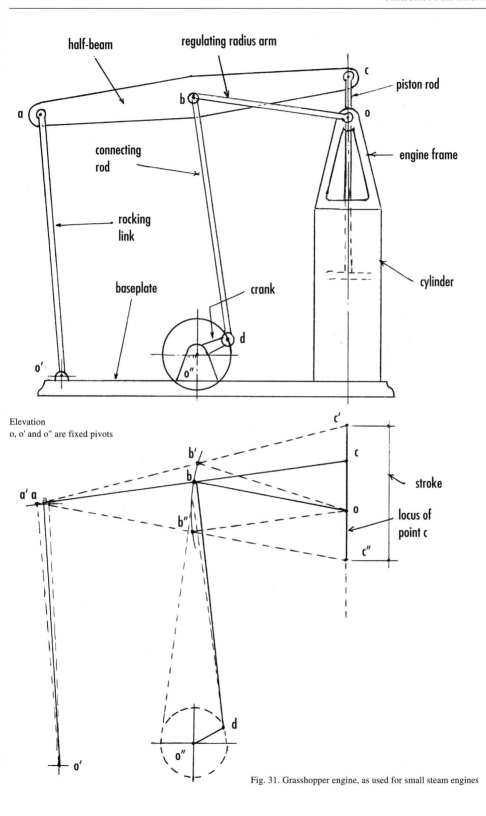

half-beam

regulating radius arm

piston rod

connecting rod

rocking link

engine frame

baseplate

crank

cylinder

Elevation
o, o' and o" are fixed pivots

stroke

locus of point c

Fig. 31. Grasshopper engine, as used for small steam engines

167

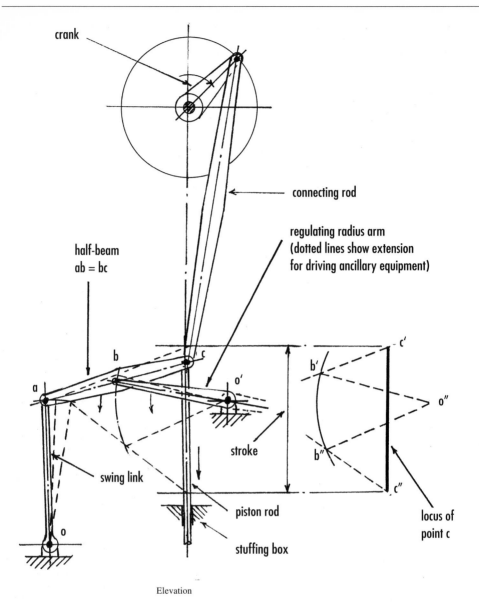

crank

connecting rod

regulating radius arm
(dotted lines show extension
for driving ancilliary equipment)

half-beam
ab = bc

b
c
a
o'
b'
o''
stroke
b''
swing link
c'
o
piston rod
c''
stuffing box
locus of
point c

Elevation

Fig. 32. Grasshopper, or half-beam motion; Fairbairn colliery winder, 1850s

therefore another STRAIGHT LINE MOTION necessary to prevent any side thrusts on the stuffing box since there is no crosshead and guide.

Sometimes the radius arm was extended beyond the centre line of the cylinder to drive ancilliary equipment such as an air pump on condensing engines. There are variations to the configuration shown on Fig. 31; for instance,

Fig. 32 shows a design for a colliery winding engine by William Fairbairn (1789–1874).

Clark, R.H. 'Some grasshopper engines', *The Engineer* CLXXIII (1942)

grassing the old method of bleaching cloth white by spreading it out in fields to bleach by the prolonged action of sunlight, also known as atmospheric bleaching. *See also* BLEACH CROFT.

graving dock a DRY DOCK where a ship or boat's bottom can be cleaned, or graved, of accretions, and repainted or tarred; repairs to the hull can also be carried out. Graving docks are sited at most docks of any size, or at boat repair yards. Small ones are provided at maintenance depots on canals for work on canal barges.

Great Exhibition of 1851 The Great Exhibition of the Works of Industry of All Nations, to give its full title, was the first truly international EXHIBITION of its kind to be held in the world. It was housed in the specially built CRYSTAL PALACE in Hyde Park, London. The idea of holding an exhibition of this magnitude originated with the ROYAL SOCIETY OF ARTS and a Royal Commission was formed, headed by Prince Albert (1819–61), which included eminent engineers of the day such as Isambard Kingdom Brunel and Robert Stephenson. The exhibition was opened on 1 May 1851 by Queen Victoria (1819–1901) and over 100,000 objects were displayed by over 13,000 exhibitors. There were four main divisions: raw materials, machinery and inventions, manufactured products, and sculpture and artistic works. Some 6 million visitors attended during the 141 days it was open to the public.

Besides those from Great Britain and the Empire, exhibits were shown by industrialists from all the developed countries of the time. The exhibition occurred at the time when Britain was regarded as the 'Workshop of the World', and was used as a stage to show off Britain's excellence in industrial and technical matters. There was a surge of orders from abroad for British goods following the exhibition, and out of the profit of £180,000 from it, land was purchased in south Kensington, London, for the later erection of several museums of national importance. Many exhibits from foreign nations were also greatly acclaimed, and the success of the venture spurred other nations to hold similar international exhibitions in later years.

A permanent Royal Commission for the Exhibition of 1851 still exists today for promoting scientific and artistic education from income from the Kensington estate.

ffrench, Y. *The Great Exhibition 1851*, Harvill, 1950
The Great Exhibition Official Catalogue, 4 vols, 1851

great lever, *see* BEAM (1)

great wheel the name for the simple spinning wheel in use in Britain in the 16th century, possibly earlier. It comprised a large wooden wheel, about 36 in in diameter with a wide flat rim, supported in a vertical plane by a wooden framework. At the other end of the baseboard a horizontal metal spindle was mounted at right angles to the wheel, and the spindle was rotated rapidly by means of a driving band which went round the large wheel and a small wooden pulley, called the whorl, attached to the spindle. To operate the wheel, the spinner stood with the wheel at her right-hand side, and attached the end of a SLIVER of wool or cotton, etc. to the free end of the spindle, the material having previously been CARDED. The sliver was held at an angle to the spindle which was then rapidly rotated by turning the great wheel by hand. At the same time the sliver was slowly drawn away from the spindle, attenuating the material whilst the rotating spindle applied twist, forming a yarn. The yarn, as it was spun, flicked off the end of the spindle at each revolution. When an arms length of yarn had been spun, the wheel was stopped, and the yarn brought round to lie at right angles to the spindle. Rotating the wheel again wound the length of spun yarn onto the spindle. The sliver was then brought round again at an angle to the spindle, and the process was repeated until all the sliver held had been spun into yarn. Thus, with the great wheel, spinning and winding-on were separate functions. The hand operations are shown in Fig. 33.

The great wheel was also known as the walking wheel on account of the step or two the spinner had to take towards the spindle and back again when drawing out the yarn, and the Jersey, or Guernsey wheel, where it was used for making fine yarn when stocking-making was an important industry in the Channel Islands. In Scotland, it was known as the muckle wheel. The great wheel was superseded by the so-called SAXONY WHEEL but the date when this happened is obscure. The main difference was the introduction of the FLYER which enabled spinning and winding-on to be carried on simultaneously, thereby speeding up the process and output. However, until the mid-18th century and the commencement of the Industrial Revolution, all yarn from which cloth, knitwear, and lace, etc. was made was hand spun, either by the ancient SPINDLE AND DISTAFF, or on simple spinning wheels.

Greek wheel an alternative name for a primitive WATERWHEEL also known as a NORSE WHEEL.

green vitriol, *see* COPPERAS

grège silk (or greige silk) raw filament silk; the word is of French origin.

grey cloth cotton cloth direct from a loom, woven in its natural colour from undyed yarn, and usually more cream or beige in colour than grey. Greys were usually intended for subsequent printing after BLEACHING.

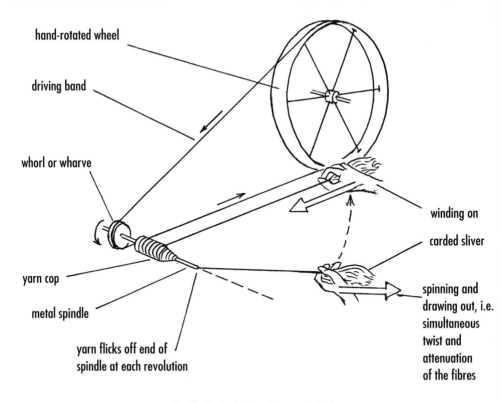

hand-rotated wheel

driving band

whorl or wharve

yarn cop

metal spindle

yarn flicks off end of
spindle at each revolution

winding on

carded sliver

spinning and
drawing out, i.e.
simultaneous
twist and
attenuation
of the fibres

Fig. 33. Hand spinning using a great wheel

grey room the department or warehouse attached to a cloth finishing works in which fabric as received from the weaver in its 'loom state' is stored awaiting processing. The area is so called because untreated cotton cloth is off-white in colour.

greys, *see* PEAK STONE

grid reference letters and numbers which locate a point on an Ordnance Survey map, normally used to give the location of an industrial archaeological site. The system used is the National Grid Reference (abbreviated NGR or GR). The reference comprises a pair of letters usually followed by a six-digit number when used with the 1:50,000 scale OS maps (1¼ in to the mile), or an eight-digit number for use with the 1:25,000 scale OS maps (2½ in to the mile), which locates a site to within 25 m (82 ft) on the ground.

National Grid references were first introduced around 1927, and amended in 1938. Britain and nearby surrounding seas are divided up into a grid of imaginary major squares with 100 kilometres (62.14 miles) sides, with their vertical sides running north to south. Each major square has a pair of unique reference letters allocated to it, called grid letters, and each square is subdivided into small squares of 1 km sides, numbered from 0 to 99; the horizontal numbers are called eastings, and the vertical are called northings. These lines and numbers are overprinted on OS maps, with the numbers round the edges. The grid reference is composed of, first, the grid letters of the major square; secondly, a three-digit easting number read off the horizontal line, with the third figure either estimated by eye or measured with a Romer card; and finally a three-digit northing number, determined in the same way. It is essential to state the grid letters since the numbers are repeated in every major square. It is also usual to prefix the map number to the reference. A typical reference would thus read: Map 118:SJ844763 (the map reference for the watermill at Nether Alderley, Ches.).

grieve a Scottish and northern dialect variation of 'reeve', meaning a colliery overseer.

griffe (or griff) that part of a JACQUARD mechanism which lifts the hooks selected by the PUNCHED CARD so that the warp threads attached to the hooks are raised. It comprises a rectangular iron frame with a number of thin metal blades passing across it, the blades arranged with their thin edges uppermost. The griff lies just below the rows of vertical hooks whose stems pass between the blades. Hooks which have been selected by the punched card are pushed into the path of the blades as the griffe lifts, whilst those hooks not selected are missed by the blades as they rise. The griffe is raised by the weaver depressing a foot treadle, and is actuated at each PICK of the loom (*see* Fig. 40). The griffe is equivalent to the tappets on a TAPPET LOOM. Griffe blades are sometimes called knives; the word comes from the French *griffe*, meaning claw.

grinding hull the building housing grinding wheels for sharpening edge tools such as scythes, shears, cutlery, etc. It often also included a GLAZING wheel for polishing the blades. The grinder sat astride, facing the revolving wheel, usually driven by water power, on a wooden framework known as a horse or horsing. A grinding hull is often known simply as a wheel in the Sheffield area.

grinding machine a machine tool which cuts or removes metal from a work piece by the abrasive action of carborundum or emery powder bonded into a wheel, which is revolved at high speed. Grinding machines were principally developed in the USA in the mid-19th century, although James Nasmyth invented a disk grinder in Britain in 1845.

Woodbury, R.S. *History of the Grinding Machine*, Cambridge, Mass., 1959

grindstones sedimentary sandstones, particularly the type known as millstone grit, used for grinding materials. Cut into flat circular disks of varying sizes, and also known as flat whetstones or hones, they were extensively used in the Sheffield cutlery industry, particularly grindstones from nearby Derbyshire. Other metal trades used grindstones for shaping and smoothing operations, and the paper making industry for grinding wood into pulp. By the end of the 19th century natural grindstones were gradually being replaced by better, synthetically produced abrasives.

gripper truck or car a mine truck used for underground transport in various kinds of mine, equipped with a device for gripping an endless moving cable which runs on rollers lying between the rails. The gripper car then moves at the same speed as the cable and tows other trucks behind it until the gripper mechanism is disengaged.

grist a meal or 'porridge' of crushed malt grains – husks and cracked kernels – which is the end product of a malt mill, and the feedstock for the MASH TUN. The material is collected in a grist case, a conical storage container.

grog clay which has been fired, or broken crockery, which is ground to a powder and added to some pottery clay mixes to make a hard product and reduce shrinkage during firing.

grogram (or grograin(e), grosgrain) a coarse woven fabric of silk, mohair or wool, or a mixture of these materials, often stiffened by gum and used for garments. The name comes from the French *gros-grain*, meaning coarse grain. The construction of the cloth is a variation of PLAIN WEAVE in which two consecutive picks pass over and under the same pair of adjacent warps.

groove (or grove) an old Derbyshire dialect name dating from the early 18th century, for the entrance to a mine, shaft, or pit. Miners were once called groovers. Like so many mining terms, it is probably of German origin, and may have come from an old German word *Grube* or *Grabe* meaning a ditch, hole in the ground, or mine.

groove ore a Derbyshire miner's term for the best grade of ore sorted out from a load of lead ore.

ground weave, *see* PLAIN WEAVE

grubbing, *see* OPENCAST WORKING

gudgeon (or goggyn) a pivot on which things can turn, usually only through a small arc. The word probably comes from the projecting bosses on either side of early cast-iron cannons which enabled them to be swung a little up or down for sighting. To some extent the word has been replaced by 'journal' where the main purpose is to form a bearing, but it is still used for some machine parts, etc. such as gudgeon pin, the pin which joins the end of a piston rod to the connecting rod in an engine.

gugg an old West Country term for an underground inclined plane in a mine with a double track; a single-tracked version was called a STIPE.

Guibal fan, *see* FANS AND BLOWERS

guidepost, *see* STOOP (1)

guilds (or gilds) medieval organizations of craftspeople for fixing the wages of their members and the prices of their products, and for maintaining standards of craftsmanship in the particular trade or industry they controlled. They were also once known as mysteries or misteries.

Guilds were town based, and had masters, JOURNEYMEN and APPRENTICES as members. Membership of the appropriate guild was compulsory for all who wished to practise the craft, and entrance fees and annual subscriptions were paid. Master craftsmen sold their products themselves, at guild controlled prices, and various crafts tended to congregate in the same part of the town, a practice reflected in surviving names and area names such as Corn Market, Tanners' Row and Shambles (for butchers). The length of apprenticeship varied from craft to craft, and journeymen had to show the guild their ability by making a 'masterpiece' before they were allowed to practise as masters themselves and take on their own journeymen and apprentices.

The guilds strictly controlled the activities of their members, and also acted as friendly societies, giving assistance during unemployment and illness, and benefits to widows and orphans. There were about seventy guilds in total, covering different trades and industries. The Weavers' Guild, founded in 1184, claims to be the oldest; others connected with the textile industry are the Dyers (1471) and the Clothworkers (1528), which was an incorporation of Shearmen and Fullers. The Goldsmiths (1327) was a very wealthy guild and acted as a financial institution before the existence of BANKS. Many guilds had their own meeting halls, and their members wore their own distinctive livery on special occasions; for this reason guilds are also known as livery companies.

Most guilds were based in the old established towns south of Birmingham. Cloth guilds in particular began to lose control when cloth making by men who were not members of the guild spread to villages. Since there were no guilds in the emerging new industrial towns in the north, textile manufacture developed there unhindered by guild restrictions. Whereas the guilds originally assisted in the growth of industry, eventually their restrictions hampered widespread expansion. Control over industry passed from the guilds to the government when the STATUTE OF ARTIFICERS was passed in 1563, and by the end of the 16th century the guild system was virtually dead. In its place grew the government trade and industrial policies known as the MERCANTILE SYSTEM. During the Industrial Revolution the growth of the FACTORY SYSTEM led to a gradual polarization of workers and employers into separate organizations. *See also* COMBINATION LAWS and TRADE UNIONS.

guillotine gate a vertically rising canal lock gate, rare on the canal system, but common on Fenland navigable rivers particularly the river Nene. A guillotine gate needs no PADDLES since it acts as its own paddle.

gunpowder manufacture the making of explosives from CHARCOAL, SALTPETRE, and sulphur. Gunpowder, the first explosive, came to Europe in the early 1200s from China where it originated a few centuries before. It is made from 75 parts saltpetre, 10 parts of sulphur, and 15 parts charcoal, and was imported into Britain from Europe until home manufacture commenced in Elizabethan days, encouraged by William Cecil (Lord Burghley, 1521–98). Saltpetre still had to be imported from Italy and India, and sulphur from Sicily, but charcoal was made from indigenous trees. Most gunpowder works were situated in wooded areas, Faversham in Kent probably being the earliest place in Britain where it was made, there being plenty of nearby timber for converting into charcoal, and rivers for water power; Faversham's proximity to the coast also kept down the transport costs of imported materials. By the 18th century gunpowder manufacture began to spread northwards to other rural wooded areas, such as the Lake District. Prior to 1760, the armed forces were supplied with gunpowder by private firms, but in that year the government bought works (in Faversham) and commenced state manufacture.

The principal manufacturing operations were first, the production of good quality charcoal – that made from juniper was considered to be the best – which by the 18th century was by distillation in sealed chambers. Secondly, each separate ingredient had to be ground to a powder, and then they were mixed in the correct quantities in an INCORPORATING MILL with water added to prevent explosions. The resulting damp paste was then granulated – a process called CORNING – and the grains dried. GRAPHITE was added to coat each grain with black lead to make it more resistant to moisture, and finally the powder was packed into oak kegs and barrels for storage and distribution. The graphite coating led to gunpowder's alternative name of black powder. Manufacturing gunpowder was a dangerous trade and many explosions with loss of life occurred. The buildings in which the various operations were carried out were widely spaced apart, in remote sites, with protective earth embankments between them, and plenty of trees around to act as shock absorbers. The buildings themselves were flimsy to lessen surrounding damage in the event of an explosion, and all spark creating materials were eliminated from the works.

Gunpowder was made in various grades of fineness according to its intended use: powder for cannons was coarser than that for muskets.

The first recorded use of gunpowder for mining and quarrying in Britain was in 1665 at Ecton copper mines in Staffordshire; it was not used in coal mines until several decades later. Another use was in fireworks. The safety fuse for exploding gunpowder, which comprised gunpowder in a waterproofed rope, was invented by William Bickford (1773–1834) in Cornwall in 1831. Guncotton, a more powerful explosive, was introduced in 1846, and dynamite in the 1860s. Very little gunpowder is made today: when manufacture ceased in a works, it had to be carefully cleaned, all traces of the powder removed in the interests of public safety, and the site abandoned. However, some of the old sites have been conserved.

Crocker, Glenys. *The Gunpowder Industry*, Shire Publications, Album no. 160, 1986
Hodgetts, E.A.B. (ed.) *The Rise and Progress of the British Explosives Industry*, Whittaker, 1909
Percival, A. 'The Faversham gunpowder industry and its development', *Industrial Archaeology* 5 (1968), 1–42

guss harness, *see* DOG BELT

H

hackling   (or heckling) the preliminary COMBING operation carried out on long fibred materials such as FLAX and HEMP. The fibres are divided up to a fineness to suit the quality and size of yarn to be spun, laid parallel, and short fibres (called tow) and any extraneous materials removed. Originally, hackling was done by hand by drawing a handful of fibres through a row of pins set in a wooden block. Later, the operation was mechanized: Joshua Wordsworth's patents (no. 6287, 1832 and no. 7657, 1838) laid the foundation of modern flax hackling machinery. Hackling is a combing operation which does not impose any draft, i.e. there is no relative movement between adjacent fibres.

A hackle or heckle is the name of a hand-held flax comb, also known as a hatchel or hetchell.

Hackworth radial valve gear   a mechanism used to reverse the direction of rotation of a steam engine and for altering the point of CUT-OFF and the EXPANSION RATIO. Invented by John Westley Hackworth (patent no. 2448) in 1859, it is one of the earliest radial valve gears. Radial valve gears differ from link motions in

that the valve derives its motion from a point on the eccentric rod (the radius), the point describing an elliptical path as the ECCENTRIC rotates. The inclination of the major axis of the ellipse is altered by the reversing control and this varies the valve travel. Fig. 68d shows the main features of this gear. Only one eccentric is needed as opposed to LINK MOTIONS which require two. The eccentric is keyed onto the engine crankshaft diametrically opposite the crank, and the eccentric rod *ab* terminates at a sliding block on which it is pivoted. Block *b* can slide in a straight slotted guide *cd* which is pivoted to a fixed fulcrum at its mid point *e*. A point *f* partway along *ab* is connected to the valve rod at *g*. Since end *a*, the centre of the eccentric, describes a circular path as the crankshaft rotates, and end *b* of the eccentric rod is constrained to move in a straight line, the intermediate point *f* describes an elliptical path. The direction of the major axis of this ellipse depends on the angular position in which the guide *cd* is held by the reversing rod. The valve receives a movement equal to the horizontal projection of the ellipse, and since *cd* can be tilted either side of vertical by the reversing rod, the valve travel can be altered. Maximum tilt of guide *cd* in one direction gives full forward rotation of the engine, whilst opposite maximum tilt gives full reverse rotation. When the guide is vertical, valve travel is minimal, and no steam is admitted to the cylinder; the engine is thus stationary. Other positions of *f* either side of centre give different valve travels and hence different cut-off points and expansion ratios.

The Hackworth gear is simple, and gives a constant LEAD (2). It was modified by Marshall in 1879.

hade   (or haid) the inclination of a mineral vein or lode from the vertical (*see* Fig. 73). The inclination rarely exceeds about 27° and was expressed in the early days of mining as so many feet per FATHOM. The hade is the complement of the DIP of a vein or seam. The word has been in use since the 1700s and is of uncertain origin, but may possibly be a dialect variation of head. If a vein is said to hade to the north, it means it inclines towards the north.

haematite ore   a particularly rich oxide of iron (containing about 70 per cent iron) found in its natural state. A red coloured variety is found around Ulverston and Whitehaven on the edge of the Lake District, and it is from this colour that the ore gets its name, i.e. blood colour. A brown variety is scattered elsewhere over Britain. Haematite iron is particularly pure, being virtually free from the injurious element phosphorus, and has been used for cast iron, wrought iron and later, steel manufacture. It was particularly important in the mid-19th century when its low phosphorus content (less than 0.03 per cent) made it the only iron to enable Henry BESSEMER (1813–98) to introduce his cheap steel process using pig iron from haematite ores.

hag master a dialect word for an overseer who hands out hags, another name for tasks. It usually concerns the cutting of canals.

haler, *see* BOW HAULER

half-beam engine, *see* GRASSHOPPER

half hand, *see* HALF-TIMER

half lock, *see* FLASH LOCK

half-timer (or half hand) a child or young person employed in a textile mill on a part-time basis, the other part of the day being spent at school. Half-timing was introduced in 1833 on the recommendation of the then Factory Inspector, L. Horner, under the FACTORY ACT of that year. It specified that children of nine to thirteen years of age were to attend a school not less than two hours per day and not to work more than nine hours per day in a mill. The Act marked the beginning of compulsory education for children, although it only applied to children working in textile mills, excluding silk mills; before this, no schooling was given to children of the working classes. The 1833 Act was amended by later Acts, the school hours increased, and the alternative of attending school a full day followed by a full day at work was allowed. Mill owners then employed their children in relays so as to keep the mills working continuously since many adult workers could not continue without child assistance. The half-time system was not finally officially abolished until the Education Act of 1918.

halite, *see* BRINE

Hall i'th'Wood wheel the first name given to Samuel Crompton's (1753–1827) spinning machine in 1779; it later became known as the MULE. The name comes from the building in Bolton, Lancs., in which he lived at the time of his experiments which led to the perfection of the mule.

Hall's process, *see* WET PUDDLING

halvans 1. an 18th- to 19th-century Cornish dialect word for discarded small pieces of ore (tin or copper), which may be the residue left over from an ore dressing process, and were thrown onto a heap with other unwanted material. The heap itself may also be called a halvan. A halvaner is a miner who dresses, i.e. cleans, ore. **2.** an old Cornish method of payment for a miner's labour. The wage was made up in two parts of equal value, one in

money, the other in the produce mined, i.e. half in money, half in kind. In this case the word halvans is derived from the verb to halve.

hammer blow the cyclical force or blow on a rail caused by unbalanced weights on a locomotive. To balance the reciprocating masses on a steam locomotive (i.e. the pistons, connecting rods, etc.) and reduce the swaying motion they produce, weights are added to a certain arc of the rims of the driving wheels. As the wheels rotate, the centrifugal force created by the weights causes alternating impact forces on the rails, or hammer blows. The rails must therefore be sufficiently strong and well supported to resist these forces which are additional to the static weight of the locomotive. Hammer blows must also be taken into consideration in bridge design. The hammer blows cause a variation in the pressure between the wheels and the rails and thus affect the TRACTIVE EFFORT. They vary with the square of the speed.

hammer mill, *see* FORGE

hammer pond a small reservoir for holding water to drive WATERWHEELS powering TILT HAMMERS and furnace bellows in early iron forges. These were usually constructed with earth dams, and the remains of such ponds, often still filled with water, are indications of the sites of old ironworks, although nothing may remain of the forge itself. Such hammer ponds today form attractive features in the Surrey and Sussex Weald, particularly in the St Leonard's Forest area, the site of the early iron industry in the south-east. *See also* WEALDEN IRON.

handle a framework set with rows of teazles, which was once drawn by hand across damp woollen cloth to raise a NAP. A handle house is a building with perforated walls (usually made by leaving out every other brick in every other course) to provide a through draught, in which teazles were dried. Such buildings are found in the old woollen districts of the West Country.

handloom weavers workers who manufacture cloth, first woollen, linen and silk, and later cotton, by hand on simple, mainly wooden looms. Before the Industrial Revolution, wool was the staple industry in Britain and employed the most workers. Weavers were traditionally men, working on their own looms in their own cottages or farms before the introduction of the FACTORY SYSTEM. Looms were mostly installed in top storeys above the living quarters with large, long windows to admit plenty of daylight, although some were placed in half cellars, again with large windows. Weavers could be divided more or less into two categories: the country-based weaver, often a subsistence farmer who combined both occupations; and the town-based weaver who generally relied on weaving alone for his living. Some weavers were self-employed, weaving the type of cloth they expected would sell well, taking them to the nearest weekly market to sell, and buying more yarn to bring back for the next week's work. Other weavers would work for a middle-man or putter-out (see DOMESTIC SYSTEM), who distributed yarn or raw wool to a number of domestic weavers; they would spin the yarn, or weave the cloth to his specification and be paid for their work. He would also supply REEDs and HEALDs if required. The putter-out would pass the finished cloth to his principal who would arrange for its sale.

In the early days of domestic weaving, the whole family would help in the manufacture of the cloth. Wives and daughters would spin raw wool on spinning wheels into yarn for the husband and sons to weave. As the demand for more cloth increased, the limited output of domestically spun yarn hindered cloth production, as yarn was in short supply. This promoted a number of spinning machine inventions, which in some twenty years in the second half of the 18th century resulted in a reversal of the situation, creating a shortage of weavers. As a result, handloom weavers around the 1790s were the best paid workers in Britain. It is said that in 1793, muslin weavers in Bolton, Lancs., could swagger about the town with £5 banknotes spread out under their hat bands. But their prosperity was to be short lived, as Edmund Cartwright (1743–1823) was inspired by the weaving bottleneck to invent his POWER LOOM in 1786. At first power looms could not weave cloth much faster than by hand (around 40–48 PICKS per minute), but improvements gradually increased their speed of working until by c.1815 power looms could produce cloth around five times faster than handlooms. By this time many weavers were working on employer-owned handlooms in small factories, although there was still a large number of domestic handlooms in use. The comparatively new material, cotton, was gaining ground on wool, and in 1800 had surpassed wool in output. It has been estimated that in 1815 there were some 334,000 employed in the cotton industry alone, including some 220,000 handloom workers; at this date there were fewer than 2,000 power looms.

By 1833 there were 85,000 power looms and the number of handloom weavers had already begun to decline rapidly; their wages had fallen disastrously and they could not compete against the high output from the machines. Industrial unrest arose among the destitute weavers and some rioting and destruction of power looms took place, particularly in Lancashire in 1812. Although wages were low, handloom weaving persisted mainly among immigrant Irish town weavers who were content with a low standard of living. During the 1820s and 1830s government grants assisted distressed handloom weavers to emigrate to Canada. By the 1840s the number of power loom weavers for the first time exceeded the number of handloom weavers, and by 1860 handloom weaving was almost extinct. The factory-based power loom had taken over and also brought about a reversal in the roles of men and women: power looms only needed supervision and one woman could attend to up to four looms, while men took over operating the spinning machinery. Handloom weaving probably lingered so long because of the independence enjoyed by the weavers and a natural resistance to change, plus the fact that it provided ideal employment for the whole family, which could be passed on between generations.

Bentley, Phyllis. *The Pennine Weaver*, Firecresta, 1971
Bythell, D. *The Handloom Weavers*, Cambridge University Press, 1969

hands a collective name for a workforce. The metonymical use of hands for workmen or employees dates from about the mid-17th century. As industry developed, the general term hands was gradually dropped as the division of labour brought about specialization of jobs, and employers began asking for people by their trade. Half hands was a term used in the cotton industry for HALF-TIMERS.

hank a standard length of yarn used in establishing its COUNT. The length of a hank varies according to the material under consideration: for measuring wool, the hank is 560 yd, and for cotton, the hank measures 840 yd or 7 LEAS.

Hanseatic League a trading partnership of north-western Germanic coastal towns, formed in 1241. Hamburg, Lübeck and Bremen were the three most important, and the League controlled the Baltic and North Sea trade routes until challenged by English, Dutch, and Scandinavian shipping in the 15th century. The League had depots in various countries, the main English one being in London at the Steelyard (an Anglicized version of the old German *Staalhof*, meaning a sample hall or courtyard). German merchants lived in the area to attend to their trade. The Hanse controlled trade with Britain for a long time, buying English wool to send to Germany, importing

Swedish iron into Britain, flax from Russia, etc. By the late 17th century its importance diminished, and the MERCHANT ADVENTURERS began to dominate British overseas trade. The buildings of the Steelyard were not demolished until 1863, although they had been closed by order of Elizabeth I in 1591; Cannon Street railway station was built on the site. Another Hanse depot in Britain was in Kings Lynn, Norfolk, once an important port, where there are 17th-century merchants' houses and the Hanseatic warehouse dating from 1428 still standing. The Hanseatic League is also known as the Hansards and the Easterlings.

harden (or harn, herden, hurden) dialect word for the cloth made from the hards of flax or hemp. Hards are the coarse parts of flax or hemp, separated in the HACKLING process.

harness the assembly of strong varnished linen cords hanging down from the hooks in a JACQUARD loom mechanism. Each cord includes an eye or mail through which a warp thread passes, and is weighted at its lowest extremity by a LINGOE. The assembly of cords is similar to the set of reins held by a coachman driving a four-in-hand, which may explain its name. The linkage controlling the raising and lowering of HEALDS in a DOBBY is also known as the harness.

Harris process a method of purifying lead, which depends on the interaction of lead with nitre, sodium hydroxide, and the impurities. A reagent cylinder containing molten caustic is submerged in a bath of molten lead and metallic salts are formed which are skimmed off the surface. The holding bath or kettle has a bottom discharge for the purified lead. When the salts turn from dark grey to white, most of the impurities are oxidized. The process may be repeated until the desired purity is reached, although silver may still remain, and is removed by another process if required. This method is known as the dry process. The so-called wet process is very similar.

hatchelling, *see* HACKLING

hat leather a circular packing of soft leather made with the cross-section of the ring in the shape of an 'L', leaving a central hole. It is used in hydraulic machines to prevent leakage of water or oil under pressure, and looks something like a top hat, hence the name. A hat leather would be used in a cylinder to seal a ram or plunger sliding inside the cylinder, or around the rod of a piston. The vertical leg of the 'L' is on the inside of the ring, pressed against the smooth surface of the ram or piston rod by the pressure inside the cylinder, but allows them to slide in or out of the cylinder. The leather is held in position by a metal ring.

hat making hats are made from several materials: straw, cloth, fur, silk and, most commonly, FELT. Felted woollen hats were being made by hand in London in the 16th century, the craft being controlled by the Feltmakers Company, founded in 1604. Another hatting centre in the early days was Bristol. Around the beginning of the 18th century the industry gradually moved north because of the high wages demanded by London workers. It settled particularly in the towns just south of Manchester such as Denton and Stockport in Cheshire. For a while at first, hat bodies in felted wool were made in the north and sent to London for finishing, but eventually the whole operation was completed in the north and the London hatting industry declined, apart from one or two long established and important firms.

In the early days, hats were made by outworkers as a domestic or backyard industry in a similar manner to hand weaving. Woollen sheets were felted and shrunk in an operation known as PLANKING and pressed onto shaped wooden blocks to make the bodies. They were then plated or ruffed (i.e. coated or covered) with a fine fur nap, such as beaver, or for cheaper hats, rabbit. The fur fibres, removed from their skin, were vibrated by plucking a hatter's bow which was suspended at its middle from the ceiling. The string was held against the fur fibres and this caused them to separate into a layer of equal thickness which facilitated the plating operation. This was followed by stiffening, dyeing, and final finishing and trimming.

Gradually hat factories were built and the former hand operations mechanized as demand for headgear increased. By the late 1820s, the making of woollen bodies was being done on machines, with woollen sheets wound onto revolving cones. Fur preparation and plating machines were invented in the USA, and were introduced into the British industry in the 1860s. This equipment blew loose fur fibres onto a fine mesh cone with internal suction, and hot sprays completed the plating.

The hat industry has always been subject to the vagaries of fashion, particularly in ladies' hats, which gave constant work to the milliners finishing and decorating them. The old beaver hat worn by men was a heavy, short type of top hat, which was ousted around the 1840s by the lighter silk top hat worn by the wealthier male. Bowlers, made from hard felt, were originally designed by a well-known hatter of 1850, a Mr Beaulier, from whose name bowler is derived. The soft trilby comes from the character in

George du Maurier's 1894 novel of that name. Fewer hats are worn today than formerly and there are not many hat factories still working. Remains of the old 18th- and 19th-century industry are scarce. There are traces of old backyard planking shops, and some former cotton mills were turned over to hat making for a while. Collections of hatters' tools are on display in some museums in hat-making towns.

The expression 'mad as a hatter' comes from the belief that the mercuric nitrate used in preparing fur for felting caused mental illnesses among some hat makers. The idea was popularized by Lewis Carroll (Charles L. Dodgson) in *Alice in Wonderland* (1865), but there are earlier references to the supposed malady among hatters. Dodgson was born in Cheshire, so would have some knowledge of the nearby hat industry.

Giles, Phyllis. 'The felt hatting industry, c.1560–1850, with particular reference to Lancashire and Cheshire', *Transactions of the Lancashire and Cheshire Antiquarian Society* 69 (1959)

Sadler, A. *175 Years of the House of Christy*, 1948

haystack boiler (or balloon boiler, beehive boiler) an early design of steam boiler shaped like a haystack (*see* Fig. 61a). Boilers dating about the time of the NEWCOMEN ATMOSPHERIC ENGINES, say 1712 onwards, were very primitive affairs capable of only low internal pressures. Originally they were made from copper sheets, and then from small wrought iron plates as these became available, riveted together. Usually they were circular in plan, with a lid, and set above a firegrate and ash pit. The hot gases from the fire were led round the outside of the boiler in a brick flue to extract more heat before being conducted to a chimney; this type of flue was known as 'wheel draught'. Steam pressures were not much higher than atmospheric, up to say 5 psi. These pressures were, however, all that was required by Newcomen engines, but in large volume. Large haystack boilers were built, some up to 20 ft in diameter, and although very inefficient they had surprisingly long lives, supplying Newcomen engines for as long as 100 years in some cases. Very frequently such boilers were positioned immediately below the cylinder of the engine with a direct steam connection to it.

head a word synonymous with pressure, used in particular in a hydraulic sense, usually for lower pressures. Water is normally taken as the standard for measuring head: the static pressure at the base of a column of water one foot high is 0.434 psi, so that the pressure generated by the head, or height of water, acting on an object, equals the height in feet multiplied by 0.434 to give psi. For example, the pressure on a PELTON

WHEEL from a reservoir sited high above might be stated as a head of so many feet. Quite large heads have been artificially created, a well-known example being that from a tank on the top of a specially built tower at Grimsby dock, erected in 1851 to provide a head of 200 ft for the hydraulic system for the dockyard. This generated a pressure of 86.8 psi.

In some cases the pressure generated by a column of mercury is used instead of water. Mercury is 13.6 times heavier than water, and then the head is expressed in inches of mercury. Barometric pressure was measured in inches of mercury before metrication, the average atmospheric pressure of 14.7 psi being equal to 29.95 in of mercury.

Static and dynamic pressures created by the flow of gases are usually measured in terms of inches of water as measured by water gauges connected to pitot tubes. The pressure against which water pumps have to operate is frequently given in terms of so many feet head. A head of steam is another loose way of expressing a pressure.

headgear the structure placed immediately over and above a mine shaft to support the wheel or wheels over which the winding rope passes. At early mines the headgear was constructed from timbers; later, these were made from iron or steel lattice girders. Some headgear carried sheaves for underground haulage cables in addition to the large winding wheels. In such cases a steam haulage engine would be sited close to the headgear to operate the haulage cable.

heading removing metallic ore or slate, etc. in the normal upwards direction from a BUNNING constructed in the roof of a level or gallery. The miner works on the bunning removing material above, making use of gravity to bring it down into the level from which it is carried away to the surface. Work proceeds upwards until the level above is reached, leaving a large cavern. The word is also used to describe a pilot tunnel driven into rock, etc. which is later opened out to the desired final dimensions.

headrace that part of a WATERWHEEL or WATER TURBINE installation which guides the incoming water onto the machine. Usually this is in the form of an open channel incorporating a flow controlling sluice.

headstock 1. the main mechanism of a spinning MULE from which all motions are obtained and which was driven by a belt from overhead LINESHAFTING before individual electric drives were introduced. It was called the rim in the late 18th century. Wright of Manchester, formerly an apprentice of

177

Arkwright, doubled the length of a mule by placing the headstock in the middle of the frame with carriages extending either side; previously the headstock was placed at one end of the frame. **2.** on a LATHE, that part of the machine, at one end of the bed, which houses the driving gears.

heald (or heddle, headle, yeald, or [rarely] gear) that part of a loom mechanism which raises and lowers the warp threads in accordance with the pattern of weaving which is being woven. The heald comprises a framework holding a large number of vertical wires, each wire having in the centre of its length a fine loop or 'eye', called a mail, through which a warp thread passes. When the heald is raised the warp threads are raised also to form the SHED through which the shuttle passes.

heapstead (or pit-heap) the buildings and surface works around a colliery shaft. A heap-keeper is a miner who overlooks the cleaning of coal on the surface.

hearth the lower part of a BLAST FURNACE in which the molten metal is collected, or an open fireplace fitted with some means of forcing air into the fuel lying in it to increase the rate of burning and temperature. The term is usually restricted to a metallurgical furnace of some kind.

heat 1. name sometimes given to the process of welding together a FAGGOT of small bars of wrought iron into a larger piece by hammering them together with a large flail hammer manually, or under a SHINGLING HAMMER. The pieces were heated to a high temperature (around 2600°F) to aid the welding action, hence the descriptive name. Metal heat-welded together was known as 'laid to' in the 18th century. **2.** in the steel making industry, complete process from feeding raw materials into the furnace to tapping the molten steel.

heat engine, *see* PRIME MOVER

heave, *see* THROW (3)

heck one of the small hooks fastened along the arms of a FLYER on a spinning wheel. The yarn being spun is hooked over one heck until a given amount is wound onto the bobbin. The spinning is then stopped and the yarn hooked over the next heck in line so that when spinning commences again, further yarn is wound onto the bobbin alongside the first amount. By moving the yarn from heck to heck, the thread is wound onto the bobbin more or less evenly along its length. On spinning MULES, etc., hecks are dispensed with on the flyers, the yarn being evenly wound onto the bobbin by a traversing mechanism which moves the yarn to and fro along the length of the bobbin.

heddle, *see* HEALD

Heilmann comber a machine for COMBING the fibres of cotton, worsted, flax, etc. to remove short fibres, clean out extraneous matter, and lay the fibres more or less parallel to each other. It was named after its inventor, Josué Heilmann (1796–1848) of Mulhouse, Alsace, in France, who took out a British patent for his machine in 1846 (patent no. 11103). It could handle short-fibred cottons which had previously been thought unsuitable for spinning into yarn, and in the cotton industry was used for HIGH COUNT cottons (80s to 250s and above) as well as being an important combing machine in the worsted industry.

Heilmann's machine was exhibited in Britain at the 1851 Great Exhibition and shortly afterwards his patent was purchased by an English syndicate for exploitation in Britain. It was a fully automatic, compact machine, intermittent in action, and the basic operating principle of one of its combing heads is shown in Fig. 34. The machine had six combing heads arranged side by side and delivered one combed sliver by combining the output from each head. Raw cotton was first CARDED and rolled up into a LAP before being placed on the machine, one lap per head, where it was slowly unrolled on a pair of wooden rollers and fed into a pair of feed rollers down a guide plate. The feed rollers rotated through small arcs intermittently, passing the lap a short length (*a–b*) at a time between a pair of metal nippers which gripped the material and pressed it down to be combed by a rotating combing cylinder. The combing cylinder had a series of combing pins over one segment of its circumference, which, together with a top retractable comb, performed the combing action whilst the material was held by the nippers. Diametrically opposite the pins, another segment of the cylinder circumference was covered by fine flutes. After the material had been combed, the nippers automatically moved forward, presenting the leading edge of the combed cotton to a detaching roller at the precise moment the fluted segment reached the roller to assist the forward motion of the cotton by compressing it between them. Since the nippers still held the trailing edge, the combed length broke away from the uncombed material and passed on, to where the leading fibres pieced up with the previously combed material on a guide plate to reform a continuous length again. The nippers then opened ready to receive the next piece of uncombed lap to be pushed forward by the feed rollers. The cycle then repeated itself. The output from each head was combined into one SLIVER by passing through a trumpet tube and coiled in a can. The combed-

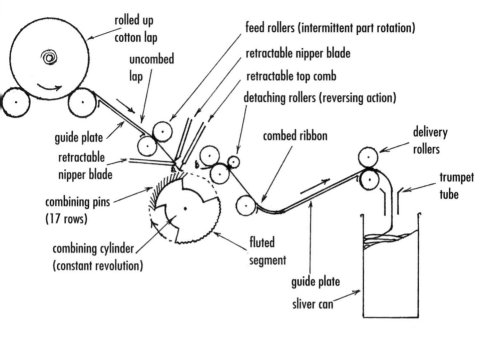

Fig. 34. Heilmann combing machine for cotton

out material was removed by other parts not shown in the diagram.

The Heilmann comber was improved and simplified, in particular by the Bolton firm of Dobson and Barlow and by other inventors such as Schlumberger, and is still in use. The flax and worsted industries used similar machines which worked essentially on the same principle. The Heilmann comber is also known as the rectilinear comb (because the combing action is in a straight line), the French comb, or the Continental comb. It is also known as a nip machine, after the gripping action on tufts of fibres during combing.

Burnley, J. *The History of Wool and Wool Combing*, 1889; reprinted by Kelley, New York, 1969

helical gears gearwheels with teeth forming a helix, believed to have been invented by Robert Hooke (1635–1703). Helical gears have teeth which are not parallel to the shaft axis as in most SPUR WHEELS, but are inclined at a small angle producing a helix. The advantage is that the load on each tooth as it comes into mesh with its opposite gearwheel is gradually taken up, avoiding the sudden impact loading inherent in spur gears. This also results in a particularly smooth transfer of power and a very regular transmission of rotation from the driver to the driven wheel.

There are two main types of helical gears, single helical and double helical. On single helical gears all the teeth are inclined at the same angle right across the face of the wheel, resulting in a side thrust along the axis of the wheel which needs to be resisted by some method. On double helical gears the teeth form a shallow 'V' across the wheel face: such a configuration eliminates any axial thrust because of the balancing effect of each 'leg' of the 'V'.

helve hammer, *see* TILT HAMMER

hemp the fibres from the stalk of the plant *Cannabis sativa* which grows in temperate zones. The stalks vary from 4 to 15 ft tall, the fibres lying just below the outer bark, and the plant has very little foliage except near the top. It is grown in Russia, Italy, India, and the Balkans; some has been grown in Britain particularly in Suffolk, Shropshire and Lincolnshire. In more recent times, the cultivation of hemp has been controlled by responsible countries, since the drug marijuana can be obtained from its stalks, flowers, and leaves.

Hemp produces long soft fibres which vary in colour from a greyish-brown to a light brown, and are about 77 per cent cellulose. The fibrous stems are prepared in a similar manner to FLAX

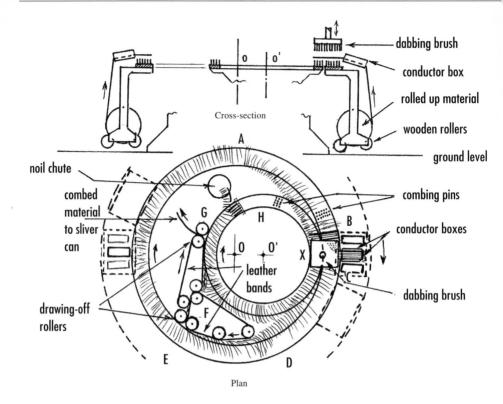

dabbing brush

conductor box

rolled up material

wooden rollers

ground level

Cross-section

A

noil chute

combed material to sliver can

combing pins

conductor boxes

G H B

O O' X

leather bands

dabbing brush

drawing-off rollers

F

E D

Plan

Fig. 35. Noble combing machine for worsted

before spinning to make a hempen yarn. The fibres are coarser and stronger than flax, and hempen yarn is used in the manufacture of ropes, and woven into a coarse fabric for sailcloth, of which large quantities were once required, and sacking. Most hemp was imported from India and Russia, and the industry in Britain became centred on factories in Dundee, Angus, Scotland by the early 19th century. The parallel JUTE industry of Dundee received a stimulus when imports of Russian hemp were stopped during the Crimean War of 1854–5.

After harvesting, hemp is either dew-rotted in two to three weeks, or water RETTED in seven to ten days, and HACKLED to extract the fibres. Long fibres are called line, whilst short and broken ones are called tow. Hemp is processed before spinning by being broken open from the bale and the fibres cut into suitable lengths, then spread into a continuous SLIVER ready for CARDING. It is then drafted and given a slight twist before being wound onto a bobbin.

The name hemp is loosely applied to other fibres which actually come from different plants. There is, for instance, sisal hemp, which is a leaf fibre obtained from the plant *Agave sisalana*, and Manila hemp, which comes from another plant leaf *Musa textilis* whose true name is Abaca. Most of these and true hemp form the raw material for ropes and twine.

In Shropshire hemp was grown in the 17th and 18th centuries in fields known as hemp butts; it was worked up into a canvas type of cloth called noggen, and also made into ropes. This rural, domestic industry persisted into the 19th century. The cloth and rope was mainly used by the cottagers themselves, very little being sold outside the area.

henna a privet-like shrub *Lawsonia inermis*, which grows in north Africa and eastern Asia, and was once used to produce yellow and brown dyes for cloth. Henna is the Arabic name for the plant.

Heslop steam engine a rotative beam steam engine patented by Adam Heslop in 1790 (patent no. 1760). It had a closed Watt-type cylinder which took steam from the boiler and exhausted into an open Newcomen-type atmospheric cylinder. This design was held to infringe Watt's separate condenser patent, but nevertheless many Heslop engines were built and used in northern and Shropshire coalfields, some until the 1890s.

hessian a coarse cloth made from HEMP and JUTE, and used as a wrapping material, e.g. packing bales.

higgler an itinerant dealer who went from house to house in country districts dealing usually in provisions, especially poultry and dairy produce. He would sell or exchange for small commodities from town shops, providing a service to isolated farms, villages, etc. before public means of transport became available, and before canals existed for bringing country produce into towns. The word is probably a variation of 'haggle', since a certain amount of bargaining took place in the exchange of goods. A higgler carried his goods on a horse, or even on his own back in baskets, etc.

hillocking searching old lead mine waste tips for pieces of minerals which have been thrown away in the discarded rubbish. The pile of discarded material is known in Derbyshire as a hillock.

Historic Scotland a government body responsible for the protection, preservation and conservation of historic monuments in Scotland. An agency of the Secretary of State for Scotland, it manages more than 300 properties of historical interest in Scotland, ranging from prehistoric sites to abbeys and castles, etc. and including some industrial buildings and structures. An annual multi-million pound Historic Buildings Grant Scheme for buildings repair is run by the Historic Scotland Heritage Policy Group which recommends grant awards by the Secretary of State for Scotland. Examples of repair grants for industrial buildings are those for the 18th-century No. 1 cotton mill at New Lanark, and the Stobcross crane at Finnieston, Glasgow. The headquarters of Historic Scotland are in Edinburgh. *See also* ENGLISH HERITAGE, CADW.

hit-and-miss governing a method for controlling the speed of a gas engine. Fig. 36 shows diagrammatically the essential parts of a hit-and-miss control. If the load on the engine decreases, it will speed up momentarily, causing the governor which is driven by the engine to speed up also. This causes the governor sleeve to rise as the rotating weights fly out to a bigger radius because of the increase in centrifugal force. The lever which is pivoted in the sleeve raises the distance piece so that the cam-driven pecker piece misses it. The gas inlet valve is

therefore not opened, so no gas enters the cylinder. This state of affairs continues until the engine speed falls as a result of the reduction in gas supply and the governor speed falls until the distance piece is again in position, so that gas is again admitted to the engine cylinder. Power strokes are missed intermittently in this manner, but every charge is at normal strength when entering the cylinder. Gas economy is achieved by this type of governing. Hit-and-miss governing is the normal method used on small gas engines.

hobbler (or hoveller) a man who helped haul ships or tow them into position in river estuaries and some coastal areas. Both hobbler and hoveller are 19th-century words in origin. In some cases it also meant a kind of pilot.

Hoffman kiln a kiln principally used in BRICK making which gives a continuous operation. Patented in England in 1859 in the name of Alfred Vincent Newton (patent no. 2918) in collaboration with the German engineers Friedrich Hoffman and Albert Licht, it comprises an oval annular kiln (originally circular in plan), with a central chimney. Some twelve to eighteen chambers can be constructed by movable partitions, and inside them bricks are placed, fired, and unloaded in a continuous sequence. Coal is fed through holes in the kiln roof, and ignited by circulating hot gases passing through the chambers in turn on their way to the chimney. The hottest zone gradually circulates round the stationary kiln at about 6 in per hour; air for combustion and the resulting hot gases are so controlled that the hot gases pass first through that chamber containing unfired, fresh bricks, to dry them. At the same time, cool incoming combustion air is arranged to pass over previously fired hot bricks to cool them prior to them being unloaded. The incoming air therefore picks up heat from cooling the bricks so that it is pre-heated when it enters the chamber where bricks are to be fired.

The Hoffman kiln was more economical in fuel consumption than the old batch process kilns, and reduced the time cycle, thanks to the continual heat exchange. Hoffmans were also used for the bulk production of powdered lime.

Hammond, M.D.P. 'Brick kilns: an illustrated survey', *Industrial Archaeology Review I* (1976), 171–92. Describes other types of kilns besides Hoffmans.

hog back a beam which has its lower edge straight, but its upper edge curving upwards to give an increased depth at mid-span. The design provides a greater resistance to the bending stresses which occur at the centre of the span due to the supported load, and the shape gets its

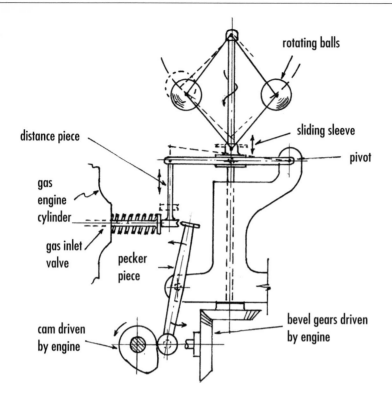

Hit-and-miss governor for a gas engine

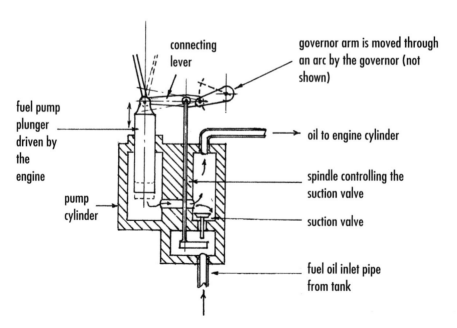

Spill control governor for an oil engine

Fig. 36. Governors for gas and oil engines

name from the resemblance to the back of a hog or pig. Usually the load is supported on the bottom flange of the beam which, if made from cast iron, is of substantial dimensions to provide enough material to resist the tensile stresses created there, cast iron being weak in tension. The opposite shaped beam, when the upper edge is straight and the lower curved downwards, is called FISH BELLIED.

hogshead a liquid measure of 52.5 imperial gallons. Pump outputs were reckoned in hogsheads per hour in Newcomen's day.

Holden comber a wool COMBING machine invented by Isaac Holden (1807–97), a Scottish inventor who lived for a time in Paris, but settled in Bradford, Yorks., in 1859. He patented his machine in 1856 (patent no. 1058). It is also known as the square or rectilinear motion machine, and was particularly suitable for very fine wools.

The machine comprises a slowly revolving circular comb with upstanding pins, with two wool feeding-on positions, a set of gills (see GILLING) and drawing-off rollers. SLIVERS of wool are fed by rollers working on an eccentric which throw or lash the leading edges of the wool onto the pins of the circular comb. The comb carries the fringe of wool round to the set of gills positioned close to the outer periphery of the comb. As each gill bar rises, its pins penetrate the overhanging fringe, and as the bar moves directly away from the circular comb, it combs that part of the wool. This is the so-called square motion. The comb continues in its rotation, passing the wool fringe to tangentially placed drawing-off rollers. As they draw the fringe off the comb pins, the combing of the fringe is completed. The wool then recombines with previously combed tufts to form a continuous combed sliver.

Holden's comber was largely superseded by the NOBLE COMBER which is more universal in the types of wool it can handle.

Burnley, J. *The History of Wool and Wool Combing*, 1889; reprinted by Kelley, New York, 1969

holland a kind of linen cloth originating in the 16th century in Holland, which strictly speaking is a province in the north of the Netherlands. In its unbleached state the material is known as brown holland, and when white is used for sheets, handkerchiefs, shirts etc.

Hollander (or beating engine) the roller beater used in paper making, invented by Dutch paper makers c.1650. It comprised an oval-shaped vessel, open topped, with a central divider which does not run the full length, stopping short of each end to give a flattened circular path around it. At one side of the divider a

heavy roller fitted with knives is rotated, and the paper-making rags are churned round and round in water, being cut into small pieces as they pass under the rotating knives cutting against a metal or stone bedplate. Hollanders were driven by water power and reduced rags to a pulp faster than the old stamps which they replaced.

hook in a JACQUARD loom mechanism, a vertical wire, hooked at the top, from which hangs a long weighted cord to below the level of the warp threads. The cord has an eyelet or mail, through which a warp thread passes. The hook is normally supported from below by resting on a bar, but when it is lifted by the GRIFFE BLADE it raises the warp thread to form the required SHED. Several hundred such hooks, closely spaced together in rows, constitute the full complement of the Jacquard (see Fig. 40).

Hooke's joint (or universal joint) a device for joining two non-parallel but intersecting shafts so that motion may be transmitted from one to the other, named after Robert Hooke (1635–1703). It comprises a fork attached to the end of each shaft, with the end of each arm of the fork making a bearing. The two forks are joined to a central, cross-shaped piece which has arms at right angles to each other, and the end of each arm is inserted in the fork bearings.

hooking term used in a bleach or dyeworks for folding pieces of finished cloth ready for despatch. In the 19th century this work was usually done by women.

hop a climbing herb *humulus lupulus* which is cultivated for its yellow female flowers (called cones) used to flavour beer and extend its life. Hops were introduced into Britain from the Low Countries in the 16th century, and are grown particularly in south-east England and the West Country where they are trained to climb up wires attached to tall posts. The cones are picked in late September and immediately dried in an OAST HOUSE. Hops are added to the beer during its manufacture when the WORT is boiled in a large copper vessel. They are delivered to a brewery in a sack traditionally holding 176 lb, and called a hop pocket.

hop kiln, see OAST HOUSE

hoppit 1. a wooden dish which holds the same amount of lead ore as the standard dish held by the BARMASTER, but is used at the mine for measuring ore. **2.** another name for a KIBBLE or large bucket used in mining for raising materials; usually cone shaped.

horizontal steam engine a steam engine in which the cylinder, crosshead, and crankshaft all lie in a horizontal line, as opposed to vertical designs. The earliest engines, BEAM ENGINES, had vertical cylinders. Richard Trevithick (1771–1833) built what was probably the first horizontal engine in 1802, but this configuration was not generally adopted until the mid-19th century, it being erroneously believed that excessive wear of the cylinder would result from it being on its side. Following successful railway practice in the 1840s, single-cylinder horizontal stationary steam engines of modest power were introduced into textile mills by the 1860s. As more power was needed when mills got bigger, larger horizontal engines were built of multi-cylinder design (*see* COMPOUNDING (1)), eventually reaching some 6,000 hp. The greatest disadvantage of large horizontal engines was the floor space required, and the more compact vertical designs were introduced to overcome this.

horse **1.** the wooden frame which supports the grain hopper above millstones. **2.** a mass of rock sometimes found in a mineral vein splitting it into two, with vein material or ore either side of it. The horse probably fell from the hanging wall of the vein during some early movement of the rock mass after the vein was partly filled with mineral and before the fissure was completely filled later on. *See also* RIDER (2). **3.** the wooden ladder used to reach the high parts of a pottery bottle kiln. **4.** the wooden framework on which a hand grinder sat astride when sharpening edge-cutting tools such as scythes on a revolving grindstone. The term was used particularly in Sheffield.

horse dolly, *see* DANDY CART OR WAGGON

horse gin, *see* HORSE WHIM

horsehair fabric fabric with a LINEN warp and horsehair weft, woven from horsehair imported from Australia, China, Siberia and south America. The manufacture of horsehair fabric for furniture upholstery was a cottage industry in certain parts of East Anglia, particularly in and around Lavenham, Suffolk. The hair was not spun, being sufficiently strong to be used on its own. Horsehair coverings on chair seats etc. were popular in Victorian times, the material being strong and long lasting. The width available was limited by the hand looms that were used in its manufacture, which did not use a shuttle; instead, a wooden lath with a hook cut in one end was passed across the shed, and a single horse hair attached and drawn through to make the weft.

horse mill a simple machine, worked by horses, to provide a power take-off for driving agricultural machinery. Horse mills were made in two sizes: there were large fixed mills and small portable ones. Most mills were used to drive farm machinery such as threshing machines, butter churns, etc. The oldest type, usually housed in a circular or hexagonal building, contained a vertical post on top of which a large wooden wheel could rotate in a horizontal plane. Around the rim of the wheel were wooden teeth, or cast-iron teeth bolted on in segments, which engaged with a pinion mounted on a horizontal shaft. The shaft passed through the wall of the wheel house, sometimes directly into a barn alongside, and terminated in a pulley to provide a power take-off. Suspended from the overhead wheel were harnesses to which horses could be hitched, so that by walking round in a circle, they drove the outside pulley. The pulley rotated at a fast speed as a result of the high gear ratio between wheel and pinion. A later improved variation had a compact gearbox lying on the floor with a take-off shaft also running along the floor. On top of the gearbox, a pair of radial wooden arms permitted horses to be hitched on to drive the mill as before, stepping over the take-off shaft at each revolution. Mills of this design were made in a range of sizes by agricultural machinery makers: smaller versions of the compact design were sufficiently portable to be taken out to the fields as required. This type was also known as tenant wheels, since tenant farmers could take them with them if they moved farms. In some farming districts, horse mills were known as ginny rings.

A horse mill was used on river craft in the 19th century in the USA, on what was called a teamboat. A pair of horses walked on a turntable fitted on the deck which drove side paddles.

Harrison, A. and J. 'The horse wheel in North Yorkshire', *Journal of Industrial Archaeology* 10 (1973)

horsepower the unit of mechanical power. Since the muscles of a horse had provided the main source of power in pre-machine days, it was natural that when attempts were made to measure the power developed by engines, comparisons were made to how many horses would produce the same power. Thomas Savery (1650?–1715), writing of his 'MINERS' FRIEND' in 1699, compared its output to the number of horses needed to maintain continuous working. Later scientists and engineers made estimates of the pulling power of draught horses, but it was James Watt (1736–1819) who eventually established the unit of power which is standard today. He needed to calculate the size of a steam engine to replace horses which were driving a logwood mill in Manchester in 1783. He estimated that 33,000 ft–lb was equal to the work done in a minute by an average horse, and from this designed his steam engine. Some two decades or so later, this figure was accepted in Britain, France and Germany, as the standard unit for measuring mechanical power.

Horsepower is used as a measure of the output from an engine, or of the power needed to drive a machine. It was once used to express the thermal output from a steam boiler, it being assumed that every 10 square ft of heating surface generated one horsepower. Thus, a Lancashire boiler of 900 square ft heating surface was called a 90 hp boiler. This was, however, an inaccurate assessment of a boiler capacity, and was replaced in due course by rating boilers by the number of pounds of steam generated per hour at a specified pressure.

Dickinson, W.H. and Jenkins, R. *James Watt and the Steam Engine*, 1927; reprinted by Moorland, 1981

horse pull-out a cut-out in the bank of a canal towpath to accommodate a sloping surface leading down to the canal bottom. Its purpose was to enable a horse which had fallen into the canal to be pulled out onto the towpath, the surface of the slope being ridged across to form rough steps to help the horse climb out. Horse pull-outs were usually sited at busy termini or canal basins where the likelihood of a horse accidentally falling into the canal was higher.

horse wheel, *see* HORSE MILL

horse whim substantial device constructed of timber, placed to one side of the shaft of an 18th- or early 19th-century coal or metal mine for hoisting up material (*see* Fig. 28). Whims were operated by horses, usually in pairs, or in the case of large constructions by four horses in two pairs. Smaller whims were operated by single horses. The horses would be worked in stints of about two hours or so, with spare horses resting and grazing nearby, waiting to take over. A whim comprised a large overhead rotating drum, typically 9 ft in diameter, arranged horizontally and supported on a timber framing. A vertical shaft to which the drum was attached rotated in a footstep bearing set in the ground, and another bearing held it in the overhead frame. Below the drum one or two arms projected horizontally in a radial direction to which the horse(s) could be harnessed. A rope would be wrapped round the overhead drum and carried to two pulleys, typically 3 ft in diameter, mounted over the shaft centre. Each pulley would guide the rope down the shaft, and when the horse(s) walked round a circular path, usually about 25–40 ft in diameter, the drum would be rotated, drawing up full tubs or baskets from the mine bottom by one pulley, and at the same time lowering empty containers down from the other pulley.

After the full containers had been emptied, the direction of the horse was reversed by his attendant and the process repeated to bring more material to the surface. Whims were also used to operate pumps or to raise water from mines in buckets. In former mining areas, their remains may be detected from the circular path trodden by the horses, often with an indication of where the central floor bearing was.

Another name for a horse whim was a horse gin: in the north, horse whims were sometimes called Scotch gins, and in some parts of the country they were called whimseys. The word whim, sometimes spelt whym, or whin, has an obscure origin, but it has been suggested that it is a corruption of the word engine in the same way that GIN also derives from engine. The horse arm has been called a *brachium* from the Latin *bracchium*, meaning arm.

hosiery industry the manufacture of knitted fabrics and garments; a hosier is a manufacturer or dealer in knitted goods. Originally, the word hosiery was reserved for stockings and socks, which were hand knitted until in the late 16th century a hand-operated machine was invented, known as a STOCKING FRAME. By the mid 1800s hosiery had come to mean all kinds of knitted fabrics as the old stocking frames were developed to make other garments. Hosiery may be made from many different materials – silk, wool, cotton, etc. – and the hosiery industry became the next in size and importance to the woven cloth industry. Knitted garments have an advantage over woven garments since knitwear shapes itself to the human form much better, being more elastic.

Hand knitting predates machine knitting by centuries. Knitting machines date from 1589 when the Revd William Lee (d. *c*.1610 in France), vicar of Calverton about seven miles north of Nottingham, invented the stocking frame for domestic use; using BEARDED NEEDLES, this produced a flat woollen (later in silk) fabric in plain stitch of constant width. Stockings were made from this material by cutting to shape and seaming. Lee tried to obtain a patent for his invention but was refused one by the government of the day who feared the threat it represented to hand knitters, of whom there were a large number. Lee took his machines to France where they were copied, and laid the foundation of the French silk knitting industry. After his death in France, his brother James brought the machines back to London and improved them so that finer fabric could be made.

Despite minor improvements, the stocking frame remained basically the same machine until 1758, when Jedediah Strutt (1726–97) adapted it to produce ribbed hosiery by adding extra needles, which had the effect of reversing the loop to make a purl stitch and produced a ribbed surface (purl or pearl comes from a Scots word 'pirl' meaning to twist). This machine was known as the DERBY RIB FRAME after Strutt's home town.

Matthew Townsend of Leicester invented the faster circular rib frame in 1847 (patent no. 11899), and the self-acting LATCH NEEDLE with David Moulden in 1849 (patent no. 12474). By the 1850s circular machines were being power driven. William Cotton (1786–1866) invented a wide machine capable of knitting twelve or more hose simultaneously, and solved the problem of mechanically widening and narrowing the fabric on the machine to produce fully fashioned (i.e. shaped) garments of all sorts. Garments had previously been made from constant width flat fabric, or tubular fabric cut and opened out, cut to shape and sewn together to make the finished article.

Hand-operated, home-based knitting frames persisted in use longer than hand machines in other branches of the textile industry, such as weaving. For this reason, water power was never applied to drive knitting frames. By the time power machines were being introduced into the industry, steam power had arrived and was directly applied to drive them. Working the hand frames was strenuous work performed by men; making up and seaming garments were done by women and girls, and when power knitters became available they were mainly looked after by women. The old hand frames were installed in the top storey (topshop) of dwelling houses, in separate frameshops built as extensions to the house, or in the back yard. Like weavers' cottages they had large windows to admit maximum daylight. Most frame knitters, or stockingers as they were known, were too poor to buy the frames on which they worked and had to hire them and pay a RACK RENT or frame rent to the owner. In the 18th and 19th centuries this was usually a master hosier, who employed spinners to make the yarn before passing it to the home-based knitter to produce the goods on a piecework basis, paid the knitter for his work and sold the goods on. The domestic knitting industry was concentrated in the east Midlands and was almost always overcrowded, resulting in low wages and unemployment when trade was bad. By the mid-19th century the use of hand frames declined, although a small number continued to be used for making special items such as shawls.

The machine-made lace industry is closely allied to the hosiery industry, since Jedediah Strutt's 1758 rib knitter was adapted to make lace in 1763 (see LACE MAKING).

Wells, F.A. *The British Hosiery and Knitwear Industry, Its History and Organisation*, 1972

hostmen a company of coal traders, colliery owners, etc. formed in Newcastle upon Tyne and incorporated in 1600 by Elizabeth I. The name comes from the medieval practice of hosting, i.e. introducing incoming merchants to others in the area for the purpose of trading. Hostmen were connected to the MERCHANT ADVENTURERS.

hot air engine (or caloric engine) an engine which uses air or the products of combustion as its working medium. Such engines came into use at the commencement of the 19th century. There were two versions: the open-cycle which used a fresh charge of air for each cycle, and the closed-cycle which used the same air over and over again. George Cayley (1773–1857) pioneered hot air engines, producing his first in 1807. He continued working on it until 1837 when he patented an improved design (patent no. 7351). He used the products of combustion from a coke-fired furnace directly in the engine cylinder. Meanwhile, a Scot, the Revd Robert Stirling (1790–1878), assisted by his brother James, had patented a closed-cycle design in 1816 (patent no. 4081) which included a REGENERATOR or heat exchanger for alternately absorbing heat from the air at the cooling phase of the four stroke cycle, and returning it during the heating phase. The hot end of the cylinder was heated externally by the gases from a solid fuel furnace. Improved versions were made for a number of years after 1816.

Shortly after Stirling's engine appeared, John Ericsson (1803–89), a Swedish engineer working in Britain at that time, patented his small open-cycle engine (patent no. 6409, 1833) which was successful for many years, being made in several fractional hp sizes. In 1877, small hot air engines of up to 1 hp were being made in Britain under licence from their American inventor, and at about the same time, even smaller engines by Robinson were available for domestic use, and sold in two sizes described as 1 manpower and 2 manpower!

The Stirling engine had two pistons working in the same vertical cylinder. The lower one, known as the cold piston, drove the engine, whilst above it another long piston containing the regenerator coils, and known as the DISPLACER, moved the air from the top hot end of the cylinder down an annular space surrounding it, through the regenerator, to the lower piston. The top of the cylinder was kept hot by gases from a furnace sited alongside playing on the cylinder end, whilst the bottom end was kept cold. The air was used over and over again, passing in sequence through the heating, expansion, cooling and compression stages without renewal.

Hot air engines were only practical for small power outputs. They were bulky and heavy, and needed an hour or so to heat up before full power could be reached. The hot end of the cylinder had to be kept very hot and metal failure was frequent because there were no metals available at that time which could withstand the high temperatures for long. They were, however, fairly economical on fuel and needed no steam boiler. By about the 1870s they had virtually disappeared, ousted by the GAS ENGINE.

hot blast pre-heated air used in a BLAST FURNACE for smelting iron, introduced by James Beaumont Neilson (1792–1865) of Glasgow (patent no. 5701, 1828). Neilson heated the incoming blast in a separate coal-fired chamber prior to the air entering the TUYÈRES. This raised the thermal efficiency of the blast furnace by some 30 per cent, and was soon adopted by ironmasters. Later, a regenerative pre-heater was developed by Edward Alfred Cowper (1819–93) in 1857 which used the waste gases from the blast furnace itself to raise the temperature of the blast. The adoption of hot blast by iron masters quickly resulted in the cheapening of iron and the consequent increase in its use.

Mackenzie, T.B. *Life of James Beaumont Neilson FRS: Inventor of the Hot Blast*, West of Scotland Iron and Steel Institute, 1929

hotching tub (or jig, jigger) a primitive device for separating unwanted rock from metallic ore by flotation. Introduced around the early 19th century it comprised a sieve hung on a lever over a water container. The BOUSE was placed on the sieve which was jerked up and down in the water so that the heavier ore sank onto the bottom of the sieve and the lighter rock could be removed and discarded. Hotching tubs were hand-operated at first, usually by boys, but later models were powered by water wheels.

hot short iron which is brittle when hot, i.e. at red heat. Short means brittle, in the same way that shortcake is friable. Metals which are hot short are difficult if not impossible to work at red heat. Hot short is also known as red short, and is caused by an excess of sulphur in the iron.

hot top, *see* DOZZLE

hotwell a tank holding hot water which acts as the feed tank for a steam boiler. Hotwells were introduced very early to conserve heat. Hot condensate from the eduction pipe of NEWCOMEN ENGINES was led into the hotwell, improvements to which were made by Henry Beighton (1686?–1743) of Coventry on a Newcomen engine installed near there.

house built term applied to engines, such as the Newcomen and some early Watt steam engines, which relied on the structure of the building housing them to act as part of the engine frame. The overhead beam was pivoted on one wall which was more massively built than the other three walls, and called the lever wall. Such designs were replaced by free-standing engines carried on baseplates independent of the building, which facilitated the erection of the engine, and relieved the building of any strain.

hovel the outer brick shell of a pottery kiln enclosing the oven in which the pottery items are fired. The hovel is a tall bottle-shaped structure, open at the top with access door to the oven at its base.

hoveller, *see* HOBBLER

huckster (or cadger, kedger) an old dialect word for an itinerant pedlar or hawker. Hucksters roamed the countryside before villages had shops, visiting outlying farms etc., and selling small wares such as needles and threads. They used packhorse tracks in remote areas, either carrying their goods themselves, or on a horse.

Hudson's Bay Company joint stock company operating under royal charter, founded by Prince Rupert in 1670. It had the monopoly of trade, mainly furs, in that part of North America where the rivers flow into Hudson Bay. Its privileges were transferred to the Canadian government in 1870, and it still operates today as a limited liability company.

huel an old Cornish word for a mine, later written as 'wheal' and sometimes appearing in the name of a mine, e.g. Wheal Victoria.

Huguenots French and Flemish Protestants who, persecuted in their own country because of their religion, fled to other countries. Many came to Britain in two main waves, first in the latter half of the 16th century and later towards the end of the 17th century. They brought with them considerable knowledge and expertise of the textile trades, particularly silk, which benefited Britain. Additionally, they brought other industries into the country such as lace making, glass making, and paper making. Many eminent scientists and technologists became British citizens, their descendants becoming integrated into the population. Many played important parts in scientific thought and invention in Britain, including Dr J.T. Desaguliers (1683–1744), the improver of Savery's steam engine; Dr Denis Papin (1647–1714) who resided in England 1681–7 and did early investigations into steam engines; Abraham deMoivre (1667–1754), mathematician, friend of Isaac Newton and fellow of the Royal Society; and Lewis (or Louis) Paul (d.1759), inventor of roller spinning, and son of a refugee. The brothers Henry and Sealy Fourdrinier (c.1809) invented the continuous paper-making machine which bears their name, while the Courtauld family established a silk industry in Braintree, Essex, which developed into the large, well-known textile firm of today. Finally, Henry Bessemer (1813–98), born in England of a Huguenot family, discovered a method of making cheap steel in the mid-1800s.

Hungry Forties the decade 1840–9, which was a period of widespread social and economic distress among the working population of Britain. The problems were brought about by bad harvests, dear bread and unemployment; the Irish Famine, created by the failure of the potato crop in 1846–7, made matters worse. The situation was relieved somewhat by the railway boom. This was the period when the CHARTISTS were active, and the PLUG RIOTS also took place during the period.

hunting the oscillation of rotative speed of a machine or engine about a given setting. When the speed increases above the mean value it causes the GOVERNOR slightly to reduce the steam flow to an engine so as to slow it down again. When the speed drops below the mean, the governor increases the steam flow to speed up the engine again. The aim of a governor is to minimize hunting to only a small amount so that a steady speed is maintained, a condition essential for some types of machinery being driven.

hunting tooth an extra tooth added to a gear wheel so that its number of teeth is not an exact multiple of the number of teeth on its mating pinion. This is arranged so that wear on the teeth is evened out, since the same pairs of teeth do not mesh as frequently as they would if the gear ratio were a whole number. This idea was particularly useful in the early days of gear cutting or casting, when the accuracies of tooth profile and pitch were not precise. Gearing in corn mills often had a hunting tooth introduced. The name comes from the searching action of the extra tooth as it meshes with different teeth in successive revolutions.

hurry 1. an Irish name for an inclined plane. **2.** name given in Midlands mines to a child assisting a coal miner by pushing or pulling loaded coal trucks from coalface to shaft bottom.

hurst 1. (or gantry) the massive wooden frame supporting the grinding wheels in a corn mill. **2.** a cast-iron collar into which the wooden shaft or helve of a TILT HAMMER fitted. The collar or hurst had trunnions cast on either side which formed the pivots for the helve.

hushing (or hydraulic mining, scouring) an old method of prospecting for, or extracting ores, coal, etc. lying near the surface. Hushing was used in hilly districts where mineral outcrops lay on the slopes, and it was possible to make a temporary earth or turf dam, higher up the hill above the area to be worked. Water was allowed to collect behind the dam, often aided by long drainage channels being cut leading to the pond. When sufficient water had accumulated, the dam was broken open, and the rush of water escaping down the hillside washed away the earth covering the deposits. The material sought was then dug out, saving the labour of removing the overburden. A fresh hush would be made alongside for extracting more material. Hushing scarred the hillside, caused the land below to become marshy, or possibly to block lower streams leading to flooding, and the method was not popular with landowners and farmers. The practice died out by the beginning of the 19th century.

Osborne, B.S. 'Patching, scouring, and commoners: the development of an early industrial landscape', *Industrial Archaeology Review* 1 (1976), 37–42

hutch 1. an old Scottish coal measure equivalent to two Winchester BUSHELS. **2.** a box for washing ore.

hybrid railway an early railway with a mixed form of haulage or traction. Before steam locomotives were powerful enough to haul loads up inclines, some early railways used stationary steam engines to pull the train of trucks and/or carriages with locomotive attached up the incline. On the other hand, some inclines were self acting (*see* INCLINED PLANE), whilst level stretches of the line might be horse drawn, or worked by steam locomotive.

Gale, W.K.V. and Hoskison, T.M. *A History of the Pensnett Railway', 1969*

hydraulic engine an engine worked by high pressure water. Originating in German mines in 1748, the first hydraulic engine made in Britain was by Westgarth Forster in 1765 for draining lead mines in Allendale, Northumb. A hydraulic engine uses high pressure water as its working fluid, and most engines for mine work were placed underground, fed from a water source on the surface. A pipe led down to the engine and the pressure generated by the head of water operated a piston through suitable valve gear which controlled the action of the engine automatically. The engine drove pumps which raised water from a lower level in the mine to a drainage sough higher up, but still below ground. The pumped water, plus the discharge from the hydraulic engine, drained away via the sough to a suitable stream, etc.

Such engines were also used to operate winding equipment, crushers, and haulage gear; they are sometimes known as water-pressure engines. The first such engines were single-acting only, the working stroke being effected by the hydraulic pressure, the return stroke by a counterbalance weight. Double-acting machines were introduced by Richard Trevithick (1771–1823) in Cornwall in 1799. They were further developed in the mid-19th century, particularly by William George Armstrong (1810–1900).

hydraulic lock water trapped inside a steam engine cylinder. When a steam engine stops, the steam inside the cylinder condenses into water and is trapped in the cylinder. Since water is incompressible, if the engine is started up again without releasing the water, either the full stroke of the engine is not reached, or at worst, the cylinder or end cap may be burst. Trapped water is released through manually operated drain cocks before restarting the engine.

hydraulic main in a gasworks, a large horizontal pipe positioned immediately after the retorts which provides a water lute or liquid seal between the retorts and other subsequent plant, to prevent gas blowing back as an explosive mixture when the retorts are opened for recharging with coal. Gas from the retorts enters the hydraulic main through dip pipes under water. The device was invented by Samuel Clegg (1781–1861) in 1811.

hydraulic mining, *see* HUSHING

hydraulic power power created by releasing the energy of a fluid under pressure. Before the transmission of electric power commenced in the early 20th century, water under pressure was used quite extensively as a means of power distribution, mostly operating heavy equipment. The method is still used today for certain purposes, although oil is almost invariably used as the pressure medium.

Hydraulic power was developed in the early 19th century using water as the pressure medium, hence the name hydraulic, which comes from the Greek *hydraulikos* (*hydor* meaning water, and *aulos* pipe). Water is virtually incompressible and, when pressurized, exerts an equal pressure in all directions. Pressure can therefore be transmitted over long distances by pipes full of water from a pressure source (e.g. a hydraulic pump) to the point of usage. About fifteen miles was the maximum economic distance. Pressures in the range of 700 psi to around 0.5 tpsi were popular, requiring strongly made pumping equipment and thick walled pipes to withstand the bursting pressure. Specially designed equipment to convert the pressure energy into some form of movement, linear or rotary, had to be developed to drive the users' machinery.

Hydraulic pumps are of the reciprocating kind and were mostly driven by vertical steam engines in the Victorian days. Hydraulic power is most easily used to operate equipment where intermittent linear movement is required, such as RAMS and JIGGERS. Rotary motion was achieved in hydraulic motors or in PELTON WHEELS. Hydraulic motors converted linear movement of plungers into rotary motion, and were made in a range of standard sizes. In the very early days of electrical generation, electricity for lighting purposes only (before electricity was used for power purposes) was produced by hydraulically powered Pelton wheels driving the primitive dynamos of the day.

Joseph Bramah (1749–1814) envisaged the use of hydraulic pressure to operate machinery as early as 1802, but it was not until a few decades had passed that hydraulic power began to be used more widely. The first users were railway companies who installed hydraulic systems to operate turntables, shunting capstans, etc. Isambard Kingdom Brunel pioneered the use of hydraulic equipment at Paddington station in 1851, whilst at the same time docks and harbours were using hydraulics to operate lock gates, cranes, warehouse lifts, etc. The first hydraulic crane was devised by William George Armstrong (1810–1900) in 1846 at Newcastle. Swing bridges were also being hydraulically operated. It was not long before the advantages of hydraulic power were extended from the private systems of railways and docks to public systems. Acts of Parliament were obtained for permission to build central pumping stations and to lay cast-iron hydraulic mains under streets to serve certain inner city areas. Hull was the first city to have a public hydraulic power supply in 1876, followed by London in 1883, Liverpool in 1888, Manchester in 1894, and Glasgow in 1895. The pumping stations comprised water storage tanks, steam boilers for driving vertical steam engines which powered hydraulic pumps, and ACCUMULATORS which, besides ironing out fluctuations in water pressure, provided a small reserve of water to meet peaks in water flow. From the pumping station a network of underground pipelines extended to serve consumers' premises. Lifts in offices and public buildings, cranes in warehouses, jet pumps for firefighting and cellar emptying, presses, organ motors in some churches, and some machine tools in workshops were all hydraulically operated; the consumer paid for water used, which was measured by meters installed on the exhaust side of the hydraulic equipment. In most cases the exhaust water, after passing through the high pressure equipment and meter, ran to waste. In some compact private systems, exhaust systems conveyed water back to the storage tanks for re-use, thus conserving water, but in extensive public systems it was not worth the cost of installing return pipelines. Some railway yards and docks also took water from the public system. If higher pressures were required than available in the public system, INTENSIFIERS were installed to boost the pressure. London, which had the largest public supply company, had at its peak period (c.1927) some 184 miles of hydraulic mains supplying about 8,000 users, including the machinery for lifting the BASCULES of Tower Bridge. There were six strategically placed pumping stations and accumulators around the city, and the company existed for ninety-three years until it went into liquidation in 1976.

Hydraulic power as described above enjoyed a period of some 50 years as a major source of power during the Victorian age, but by the beginning of the 20th century the electric motor and electrical transmission were sounding its death knell. Hydraulically operated machinery is still used today but driven electrically with individual closed circuit compact rotary oil pumps. Disused accumulator towers may still be found scattered around the country, silent reminders of the time when hydraulics reigned supreme.

Jarvis, A. *Hydraulic Machines*, Shire Publications, Album no. 144, 1985
McNeil, Ian. *Hydraulic Power*, Longman, 1972
Pugh, B. *The Hydraulic Age*, Mechanical Engineering Publications, 1980
Rouse, H. and Ince, S. *History of Hydraulics*, Constable, 1963

Main developments in the use of hydraulic power

year	
c.1647	Pascal enunciates principles of hydrostatics.
1749	Primitive water pressure engine in Hungarian mine.
1765	Water pressure engine at Allendale, Northumb.
1795	Hydraulic press patented by Joseph Bramah.
1812	Bramah patents idea of hydraulic power distribution by pipelines.
1836	Rotary motion first obtained by hydraulic pressure.
1846	Hydraulic crane patented by W.G. Armstrong.
1849	Grimsby hydraulic tower built.
1851	Hydraulic accumulator developed by W.G. Armstrong.
c.1853	Hydraulic jack by James Tangye and brother.
1875	Anderton Canal lift built, hydraulically operated.
1876	First public hydraulic power system starts up in Hull.
1880	Hydraulic rock drill used in Arlberg tunnel, Austria.
1883	London public hydraulic power system starts.
1888	Liverpool public hydraulic power system starts.
1891	Birmingham public hydraulic power system starts.
1894	London's Tower Bridge fitted with hydraulic machinery.
1894	Manchester public hydraulic power system starts.
1895	Glasgow public hydraulic power system starts.
1947–76	Public hydraulic systems abandoned, Hull first, London last.

hydraulic press a machine that uses liquid pressure to exert a large force on two platens so that items placed between them are pressed to a shape, compressed, or forced together. The invention of the first successful hydraulic press is credited to Joseph Bramah (1749–1814) in 1795 (patent no. 2045), although the 17th-century French philosopher Blaise Pascal had suggested one earlier. Early presses comprised a simple ram or piston working inside a cylinder; water was forced into the space behind the ram by a hand pump causing it to move slowly along the cylinder, generating a large force. An early use for such presses was the baling of cotton to reduce its volume before shipping. Loose cotton was placed between the two platens when wide apart and then brought together by pumping water into the cylinder to compress the cotton into a bale. Often two hand pumps were provided, one with a large diameter plunger to give a rapid initial closure of the platens by a low pressure, and a small diameter plunger pump for a final squeeze by high pressure.

Power driven pumps were introduced as presses got larger and more powerful, and small auxiliary return rams were fitted to speed up the return of the main ram after completion of its working stroke. Some presses were operated from hydraulic mains in those cities that had them, and often an INTENSIFIER was needed at the press to raise the mains pressure for operating the press. Special leather packings were needed between ram and cylinder wall to prevent leakage of the high pressure water, such as HAT LEATHERS and U-LEATHERS.

Other uses of hydraulic presses include baling cloth, seed crushing, and hot and cold metal forging and pressing. William George Armstrong (1810–1900) greatly developed the hydraulic press as an engineering tool. The hydraulic riveter and plate punch are specialized forms of hydraulic press. Oil instead of water as the operating fluid was introduced on self-contained presses to prevent rusting of rams, control valves, etc. A further use for hydraulic presses arose with the onset of the plastics and rubber industries.

McNeil, I. *Joseph Bramah: A Century of Invention 1749–1851*, David and Charles, 1968

hydraulic ram a self-acting device in which a large quantity of low pressure water is made to pump a small proportion of itself to a greater height than its source, or to a higher pressure. This is achieved by using the pressure rise resulting from suddenly interrupting the flow of water. The idea is credited to John Whitehurst in 1773, although his device was manually operated. A self-acting hydraulic ram was developed by Joseph Michael de Montgolfier (1740–1810), of hot-air balloon fame, in France in 1797. He said the regular hammering noise the pump made reminded him of the clashing of skulls between battling male sheep, and he called his device *coup de bélier* (*bélier* is the French word for ram). This explains how the device got its English name, since there is no RAM in the technical sense in the device.

Hydraulic rams were soon introduced into Britain: John Blake of Accrington, Lancs., was an early maker of them. The pump comprises a cast-iron vessel containing two disk valves horizontally placed: the impulse or spill valve, and a small delivery valve placed at a slightly higher level in the vessel. Water flowing through the vessel passes out to waste through the impulse valve until the dynamic pressure building up on the underside of the valve overcomes its weight, and snaps it shut. The momentum of the water flow suddenly interrupted causes a momentary rise in pressure inside the vessel which forces open the delivery valve, and a small quantity of water passes through it into the delivery pipe and is prevented from flowing back by a non-return valve. The delivery valve then closes as soon as the momentum is destroyed, causing a drop in pressure inside the vessel, which allows the impulse valve to open again so that the cycle can be repeated.

Hydraulic rams work intermittently, pumping a small quantity of the supply water either a considerable distance away, or to a height above the level of the activating supply, without any external power source. Uses include supplying water to farms, villages, and large country houses in remote districts from distant rivers and streams, provided a small head of water can be arranged to operate it. They are extremely reliable, and have been known to operate unattended constantly day and night for periods of well over half a century.

hydraulic winch, *see* JIGGER (1)

hydrochloric acid (or muriatic acid) a colourless, aqueous solution of hydrogen chloride gas, also known as spirit of salts. Hydrochloric acid was used with lime to make bleaching powder in the 18th century, the acid coming from the LEBLANC PROCESS. Its use declined with the introduction of the alkali SOLVAY PROCESS.

hypocycloid steam engine a design of vertical steam engine patented by Matthew Murray (1765–1826) in 1802 (patent no. 2632), which had no connecting rod. The piston movement was converted into rotary motion by a complex hypocycloidal gearing system. A hypocycloid gear is a gear in which a smaller rotating spur wheel meshes with the internal teeth of a larger wheel. This design of engine gave a low overall height, but not many were made as they were expensive to produce.

I

ice house a building for storing ice to keep food fresh. Ice houses were used prior to the introduction of mechanical REFRIGERATION for keeping food fresh for long periods. Pits filled with ice or snow and covered with straw were used by the ancient Greeks and Romans for this purpose, but the brick or stone built ice house was not brought to Britain from the Continent until the 1660s. A typical design was a chamber built partly into the ground or a hillside, cellar like, with a short entrance tunnel whose door was often shielded by an earth mound. Double air-lock doors gained admittance to the chamber, and a drain was included in the floor to run off any water which accumulated. Trees were usually planted around an ice house to give shade in summer time. Large country houses often had ice houses sited near a lake in their grounds, from which ice would be taken during winter and stored inside the ice house. Commercially run ice houses frequently imported ice from Norway; the USA was exporting ice in 1882, and hotels, fishmongers, restaurants, etc. were supplied with ice all through the year from this source. Ice blocks in properly constructed ice houses could last up to five years, and food could be kept for long periods as the ice slowly melted.

Mechanical refrigeration by compression/evaporation of ammonia was introduced in the 1890s, and ice houses fell into disuse. A few still survive.

Buxbaum, T. *Icehouses*, Shire Publications, 1992
Ellis, Monica. *Ice and Icehouses through the Ages*, Southampton University Industrial Archaeology Group, 1982

identification of metals Various methods of identifying the metal from which an artefact is made are available to the industrial archaeologist when a visual inspection is inconclusive. A simple rough guide is the spark test using a high speed grinding wheel, which may be portable. Each metal gives off its own particular pattern of sparks when touched by the revolving abrasive wheel. The trajectory and form the sparks take or 'spark picture' enable an experienced observer to identify the metal being tested, from the colour, brightness, presence or absence of side 'bursts' or 'forks'. The presence of carbon gives particularly bright sparks with bursts. The sketches in fig. 37 show the general appearance of the spark pictures created by some of the more commonly met irons and steels. Though quicker and cheaper than chemical analysis, the method is only indicative; other, more sophisticated methods of examination require the professional use of laboratory equipment, such as microscopes and spectographic analysers.

idler an extra gearwheel interposed between a driver and a follower to make a three gear train. Its purpose is to reverse the direction of the follower so that it rotates in the same direction as the driver. It does not alter the gear ratio between driver and follower.

Imperial preference system whereby British colonies were allowed to trade internationally provided they granted preferential duties on British-made goods entering their territory, and the duties on colonial goods entering Britain were lower than those on foreign goods. Introduced by William Huskisson, President of the Board of Trade, in the 1820s, the system was operated for about 100 years although it was relaxed during the period of free trade in the 1840s and 1850s. It is sometimes known as Colonial preference.

impulse turbine a rotor or wheel turned by the impulse or push from a jet. If a high velocity jet of fluid (e.g. water or steam) impinges on a surface at right angles to the jet, a force in the direction of the fluid flow acts on the surface. If the surface is attached to the periphery of a wheel free to turn on its axle, the wheel will revolve under the push or impulse received by the surface. A number of surfaces spaced round the wheel will ensure that rotation is maintained as the jet strikes each surface in turn. This is the operating principle of an impulse turbine, whether water or steam driven.

The PELTON WHEEL (Fig. 38a) is a well known impulse water prime mover. It comprises a fixed nozzle in which the pressure energy of the water is converted into a high velocity jet. The jet is directed at cups or buckets spaced round the circumference of a wheel, causing it to rotate at high speed, in air, inside an enclosing chamber. The buckets are specially shaped to allow the water to leave them with the minimum of energy loss, the spent water leaving at atmospheric pressure in a tail race.

The De Laval turbine (Fig. 38b) is a forerunner of several impulse steam turbines. It comprises a chamber containing a wheel which has a large number of curved blades on its circumference. Four (usually) fixed nozzles are equally spaced around the wheel, positioned to one side and pointing at an incline towards the ring of blades. High pressure steam is allowed to expand down to atmospheric pressure as it passes through the nozzles which gradually taper to a larger bore towards their exits. The steam leaves the nozzles at extremely high velocity and impinges on the blades turning the wheel at high speed. The steam passes across the blades and leaves the chamber at atmospheric pressure. The expansion of the steam therefore takes place in one pass across the wheel, i.e. in one stage, giving a compact machine of short axial length. Some De Laval machines were made in which there were two stages, i.e. two sets of fixed nozzles and rotating wheels in series mounted on the same shaft, the

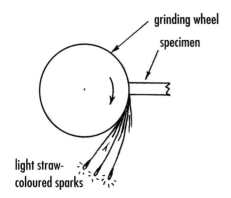

light straw-
coloured sparks

wrought iron bright sparks with a luminous
extremity. Any carbon present will give a small
burst at the extremity

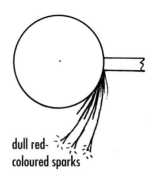

dull red-
coloured sparks

cast iron non-explosive sparks
thickening towards their ends

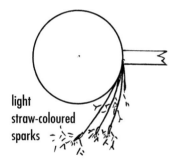

light
straw-coloured
sparks

mild steel thick luminous sparks
broken up by bursts which leave
the spark line at approx. 45°

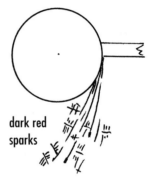

dark red
sparks

Mushet self-hardening steel
explosive side bursts leave the
spark line at right angles

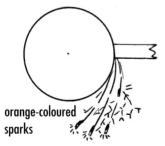

orange-coloured
sparks

high speed steel sparks vary in brightness as they
travel with interrupted lines. Luminous tips

Fig. 37. Spark pictures for some irons and steels

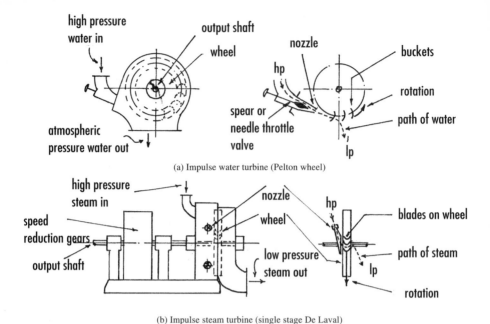

(a) Impulse water turbine (Pelton wheel)

(b) Impulse steam turbine (single stage De Laval)

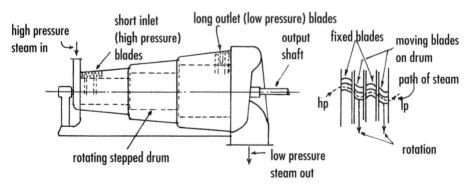

(c) Reaction water turbine (horizontal shaft Francis)

(d) Reaction steam turbine (Parsons)

Fig. 38. Impulse and reaction turbines

expansion being spread out over the two stages. Because of their high speed, De Laval turbines are only suitable for small units, and usually a speed reduction gear is necessary to bring the output shaft down to a practical speed.

See also REACTION TURBINE, STEAM TURBINE, WATER TURBINE.

inclined plane a prepared slope on which rails are laid to enable early tramroads and railways to negotiate a steep gradient. There are two types of inclined plane: gravity or self-acting, and power operated.

On gravity or self-acting inclined planes, loaded waggons may be arranged to pull up empty ones by an endless cable or chain running round ground level pulleys at top and bottom. One such system was patented in 1750 by Michael Menzies (patent no. 653). An incline may have twin tracks, one up, one down, or to economize only one track for most of the way with a twin section at the centre to give a passing place. If loaded waggons are to be pulled up, a water balance truck may be used. This would be filled with waste water at the top until its weight exceeded that of the loaded waggon, and emptied at the bottom. Some Victorian seaside cliff railways worked on this principle. A brake drum on the cable or chain under the control of a brakesman was necessary at the top of self-acting inclines. A well known self-actor, attributed to William Reynolds (1758–1803), was built in 1788 at Coalbrookdale, Salop., for handling coal and ironstone. Inclined planes were constructed on some canals where the gradient was too steep for locks. Boats were floated onto wooden frames, and loaded ones pulled up empty ones, the frames running on iron wheels on tracks. Self-acting inclines are called jig brows in the Lancashire coalfields.

On power operated inclined planes, a stationary steam winding engine was sited at the top of the incline to pull loaded waggons up the tracks by cable or chain. This system had to be used on the first railways because early locomotives were not powerful enough to climb steep gradients. The complete train, locomotive as well, was pulled up the incline, the locomotive taking over on level stretches of the line. The Liverpool to Manchester Railway had a steam worked incline in a tunnel at the Liverpool terminus which remained in operation for several years after the line was opened in 1830. Rope worked inclines were known as brakes in some parts of the country.

Lees, P.T.L. 'Excavations at Chatsworth Street Cutting, part of the original terminus of the Liverpool and Manchester Railway', *Industrial Archaeology Review* IV (1980), 160–70
Tomlinson, W.W. *North Eastern Railway*, 1915; reprinted by David and Charles, 1967
Williams, W.H. 'The canal inclined planes of East Shropshire', *Journal of Industrial Archaeology* 2 (1965)

incorporating mill a stone edge-runner grinding machine or mill for mechanically grinding and mixing the ingredients of GUNPOWDER. The amount of materials that could be incorporated at any one time was limited to 60 lb by the Explosives Act of 1860 for safety reasons. Early incorporating mills were horse driven; later, water power was used, and finally power was supplied by steam engines. Operating incorporating machinery was extremely dangerous, and most explosions which took place in gunpowder factories happened here.

Indian safflower, *see* TURMERIC

indicator diagram a diagram to scale, traced on paper, showing the cyclic conditions inside an engine cylinder. The first indicator was devised *c*.1794 by James Watt (1736–1819) to investigate what was happening inside the cylinder of a steam engine. It comprised a small diameter tube inside which a small piston worked against a calibrated spring. One end of the tube was connected to the engine cylinder, and the free end of the small piston moved a pencil up and down a sheet of paper on a vertical metal plate. The plate was arranged to slide horizontally and reproduce exactly the movement of the engine piston. Thus, a diagram was drawn out, reproducing to known scales the variation in steam pressure with piston stroke. The area of the diagram was an indication of the power being developed, and could also be used for setting the valves for steam CUT-OFF to give expansive working. Watt's indicator was improved by later engineers, and became a standard instrument for checking engine performance. The power measured by this method is known as the indicated horsepower of a cylinder. Indicators are also used on INTERNAL COMBUSTION ENGINES.

indigo (or anil, anile) a dye made from the plant *Indigofera*, imported from India and the West Indies; the name comes from the Greek *indikos* meaning Indian, since it was thought that the art of dyeing using this plant originated in India. It makes a blue vegetable dye, which largely replaced WOAD, and was often used with WELD to make a green dye. The plant was ground to a powder in an indigo mill and allowed to ferment; an insoluble dyestuff, it coloured textile fibres after oxidation by exposure to air. In the 18th century, Britain re-exported large quantities of West Indian indigo to Europe in addition to using it for home dyeing. After the development of synthetic dyes in the second half of the 19th century, demand for indigo decreased and cultivation of the plant rapidly declined.

indirect process of iron making the method of making wrought iron by first making pig iron (cast iron), and then decarburizing it to make wrought iron. The indirect process is based on the use of a BLAST FURNACE for making the pigs, which were then reheated either in a FINERY and CHAFERY forge – the earliest method which fell into disuse by the end of the 18th century – to decarburize the cast iron, or converting the pigs in a PUDDLING FURNACE. The puddling furnace was invented in 1783 and became the principal method of making wrought iron until the mid-19th century when cheap steel by the BESSEMER PROCESS began replacing wrought iron. Blast furnaces were introduced into Britain early in the 16th century from the Continent, and the indirect process of making iron began to supersede the direct process in which iron ore was smelted directly into wrought iron in the old BLOOMERY forges. *See also* IRON MANUFACTURE.

indoor stroke, *see* 'COME INTO THE HOUSE'

industrial archaeology the study of the tangible evidence of social, economic, and technological development from the onset of industrialization to the recent past. The study of past industries of necessity includes transport history, including turnpikes, canals and railways, also the living and working conditions of ordinary wage-earning people, set against the economic history of the country. The primary period of study is that known as the INDUSTRIAL REVOLUTION, usually accepted to be between the years 1750 and 1850, but time before this is not excluded for some industries, nor subsequent developments. Therefore, in general terms, the period 1700–1900 may be regarded as the 'classical' study period of the subject. Industrial archaeology is, nevertheless, an open-ended on-going subject, since the technology of today is the industrial archaeology of the future.

The subject may be divided into two main activities: FIELDWORK, covering the examination and recording of physical remains, and documentary research (*see* INFORMATION SOURCES) which gives information not deducible from a site. Recording of industrial sites and monuments is a valuable aid to their possible preservation by SCHEDULING or LISTING by appropriate authorities. Many of Britain's industrial sites and monuments of the 18th century have significant international importance.

Industrial archaeology grew rapidly in the 1960s and 1970s with the formation of local societies by interested and enthusiastic individuals. Most work in the subject is carried out by knowledgeable amateurs, there being little professional involvement at present. The ASSOCIATION FOR INDUSTRIAL ARCHAEOLOGY was formed in 1973 to support individuals and societies in their activities, and to represent the subject at national level. It co-operates with county SITES AND MONUMENTS RECORDS and the NATIONAL MONUMENTS RECORD in extending the recording of Britain's industrial heritage.

Palmer, Marilyn. 'Industrial archaeology: working for the future', *Industrial Archaeology Review* XIV (1991), 17–32

industrial buildings buildings which housed industrial enterprises, varying in shape and design according to the type of activity it houses, which determined fenestration and ventilation needs, the spacing of machinery, the requirements for movement of materials within the building, and so on. Provision for the in-house generation of power governs the size and position of buildings such as engine houses, steam boiler plant and chimneys. Certain industrial buildings therefore have distinctive, recognizable shapes, including maltings with their pyramidal roofs and small windows, multi-storey blocks of spinning mills, single-storey weaving sheds with their north light roofs, and warehouses with their emphasis on security and vertical loading slots. Other industrial buildings are less clearly related to the activity contained within their walls, and of course some have housed different industries during their history, and may have been altered or extended to suit at different dates.

The history of purpose-built factories can be said to start with the three-storey water-powered silk mill built in 1702 in Derby, no longer in existence. Mills for manufacturing other textiles followed some years afterwards, many based on the cotton mills of Richard Arkwright (1732–92). These were narrow span buildings, mostly made with load-bearing stone walls, and wooden floors and roof trusses. There was a rapid increase in the number of cotton mills during the period 1750–90. These early mills were simple, functional structures, designed by engineers or builders, with machinery driven by water power, and thus frequently built on the outskirts of towns or in rural areas. Canal-side warehouses followed mill construction, sometimes with shipping holes to facilitate the transfer of goods from boat to store.

Around the late 1790s, steam engines began to replace waterwheels in newly built factories, thus allowing mills to be erected away from rivers, and they were sited near coal supplies and in towns for their labour requirements. Boilers, chimneys, and engine houses became part of industrial buildings; tall engine houses were built for beam engines, and later, lower buildings with greater floor space for horizontal engines. Before electric lighting became available, many textile mills had their own gas-making plants. Mills became larger, packing in more and more machinery. New construction materials, such as cast-iron pillars and floor beams, permitted larger spans, and the FRAMED BUILDING was introduced, relieving walls of load carrying. By the 19th century FIRE-RESISTANT designs became common for textile mills. The buildings were now designed by architects, introducing some external decoration. Engine houses were often given special architectural enhancement, acknowledging the importance of steam as the source of power for the factory. Bricks replaced stone, and eventually steel frames and concrete floors were used for the building fabric. The ability to make glass in larger panes enabled large iron and glass structures to be erected. Vernacular buildings are also studied by industrial archaeologists, such as market halls and shopping arcades, which are often examples of ironfounders' skill, together with smaller railway stations, turnpike and canal toll houses, Cornish engine houses, coppice drying sheds and lighthouses.

Brockman, H. *The British Architect in Industry, 1841–1940*, Allen and Unwin, 1974
Davey, N. *A History of Building Materials*, 1961
Giles, C. and Goodall, J.H. *Yorkshire Textile Mills, 1770–1930*, HMSO, 1992
Jones, E. *Industrial Architecture in Britain, 1750–1937*, Batsford, 1985
Williams, M. and Farnie, D. *Cotton Mills in Greater Manchester*, Carnegie Publishing, 1993

industrial espionage spying on competitors and inventors to discover their trade secrets or machinery designs. The practice is not of recent origin: from the earliest days of the INDUSTRIAL REVOLUTION such practices were resorted to by the unscrupulous more frequently than is generally supposed. For instance, Abraham Darby I (1677–1717) visited Holland in 1706 to find out how cast iron hollow-ware such as cooking pots were cast. John Lombe (1693?–1722) paid a secret visit to Leghorn in Italy in 1716 to spy on the Italian silk manufacturing methods and returned to England with designs of the Italian machinery. He and his half-brother Thomas Lombe (1685–1739) built a silk factory in Derby soon afterwards. As news of Newcomen's steam engine spread to the Continent, Joseph Fischer von Erlach came to England disguised as a labourer to spy on an engine, c.1718, and later built one at Hesse-Cassel in Austria in 1722. Boulton and Watt had an effective system of spies to detect illegal poaching of Watt's engine patents, which were being flouted by a number of engine builders at the time. Stephen Wilson sent a spy to Paris in 1820 to discover details of Jacquard's device, which enabled him to patent card cutting equipment in Britain. Finally, two potters, Astbury and Twyford, gained employment at the brothers Elers' factory in the late 17th century, pretending to be simple minded to learn the secret of their superior pottery manufacturing methods, which Astbury afterwards improved. Many other examples could be cited.

Flinn, M.W. (ed.) *Svedenstierna's Tour of Great Britain 1802–3: the Travel Diary of an Industrial Spy*, David and Charles, 1973
Harris, J.R. 'Industrial espionage in the 18th century', *Industrial Archaeology Review* VII (1985), 127–38
Schinkel, Karl F. *The English Journey*, translated by F.G. Walls, Yale, 1993 (an account of a journey in 1826)
Woolrich, A.P. *Mechanical Arts and Merchandise: Industrial Espionage and Travellers' Accounts as a Source for Technical Historians*, De Archaeologische Pers, 1986

industrial housing, *see* BACK-TO-BACK HOUSING, INDUSTRIAL SETTLEMENTS

Industrial Revolution the term agreed by most historians to describe the transformation which occurred in the years 1750 to 1850, when the pace of industrialization in Britain increased considerably. Opinions differ as to who should be credited with coining the expression 'industrial revolution': Frederick Engels used it in his book *The Condition of the Working Class in England* in 1844, and Arnold Toynbee popularized it in his 1880–1 series of Oxford lectures. The word 'revolution' may appear inappropriate to some, since there was no short, sharp, sudden increase in industrial activity – it might be more appropriate to describe the hundred years as an 'accelerated evolution'.

There was, of course, a slow build up in some industries prior to 1750, but after that date the pace of industrialization did gain momentum over a comparatively short time. This increase in activity is shown graphically by a selection of pointers in Fig. 39. The rise in manufacturing productivity was textile led, as is confirmed by the steep rise in raw cotton imports in the first quarter of the 19th century.

A number of factors contributed to the rise of the Industrial Revolution, chiefly the application of capital to manufacturing by entrepreneurs, and the replacement of domestic hand methods

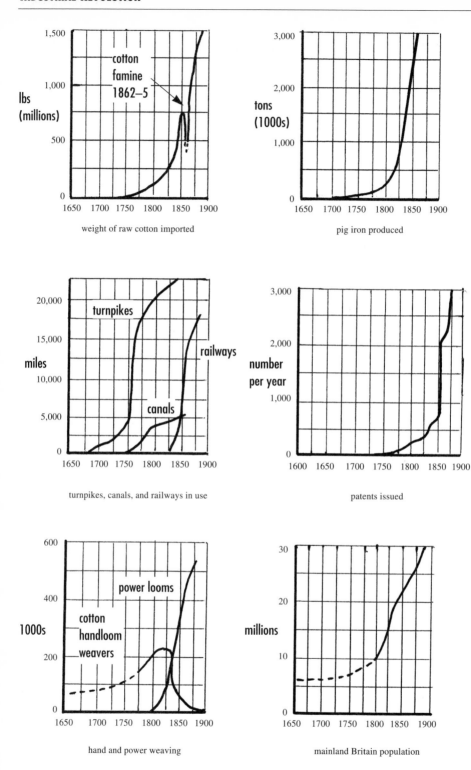

Fig. 39. Rise in industrial activity and population during the 18th and 19th centuries

by factory-based machines, first powered by water and later more effectively by steam, which resulted in greatly increased production (*see* FACTORY SYSTEM). Increased production created a worldwide demand for British industrial goods, textiles, machinery, etc; it also led to the development and invention of improved modes of transport for raw materials and finished goods. During the second half of the 18th century many pioneering inventions in textile machines were made; in the first half of the following century railways were invented, steam power extended in factories, and to drive ships. The number of inventions made in all industries is illustrated by the rise in the number of patents registered (*see* Fig. 39). Traditional hand crafts were largely destroyed by mass-produced, machine-made goods. The Industrial Revolution effectively changed Britain from basically a wood and water using economy to a coal, iron and steam using one. Britain led the world during this period, her lead more or less peaking with the GREAT EXHIBITION OF 1851, at which the fruits of British industry and inventiveness were displayed to all. Other countries, particularly Germany and the USA, were to have their own industrial revolutions later than Britain, and in due course caught up industrially.

The Industrial Revolution also brought about great social changes as the country entered the machine age. The period coincided with an increase in population, and with industrialization many people drifted away from rural life into often squalid, insanitary housing in industrial towns. Working and living conditions in manufacturing towns were bad: women and children were in general exploited, working long hours in dangerous and harsh conditions in mills, factories, and mines, until legislation brought about improvements (*see* FACTORY ACTS). A new middle class of wealthy mill owners and iron masters arose, as did professional engineers engaged in machinery making, canal, and railway building.

The period of the Industrial Revolution is the main area of study for industrial archaeologists, interpreting, and recording the physical remains of past industries and modes of transport, together with their social implications.

Ashton, T.S. *The Industrial Revolution, 1760–1830*, Oxford University Press, 1948
Flinn, M.W. *Origins of the Industrial Revolution*, 1966
Georgius Agricola (Georg Bauer), *de Re Metallica*, 1556, tr.
H.C. and L.H. Hoover, Dover, New York, 1920
Gimpel, J. *The Medieval Machine: The Industrial Revolution of the Middle Ages*, Pimlico, 1992
Hamilton, H. *The Industrial Revolution in Scotland*, Cass, 1966
Lane, P. *The Industrial Revolution*, 1978
Lines, C. *Companion to the Industrial Revolution*. Facts on File, 1990
Mantoux, P. *The Industrial Revolution of the 18th Century*, tr. M. Veron, Methuen, 1961

industrial settlements communities of workers' houses. Small groups of houses still exist in various parts of the country which are remains of settlements or communities built by employers for their workers. Frequently they are in what were, at the time of their building, remote areas; some still are today far from centres of population. Such communities were built to attract workers and ensure a captive labour force. Early textile mills were sited where water power was available, usually in the country away from towns, and since public transport was non-existent, putting up nearby housing was the only way of manning the mills. Similarly, many mines and quarries were of necessity sited away from towns, and local accommodation was essential.

Apart from economic necessity, some industrial communities were built by philanthropic employers to provide improved housing and better social conditions for their workers. Such settlements built by enlightened employers usually included a church, a reading room, school, but only rarely a public house – most settlements were built to encourage temperate living. Sometimes a co-operative store, a TOMMY SHOP or a Penny Bank (which took small deposits in pence) would be built. The standard of housing varied – some were better built than others by employers for reasons of prestige. Not all industrial communities were built by employers: in some cases workers built their own cottages on common land near their place of employment, but such settlements tended to be of poor quality and haphazard in layout. Dormitory-type accommodation was used to house mill apprentices, and similar barrack-type blocks were built in remote metal mining areas, the men living there during the working week, only returning home at weekends.

Often a settlement was named after the founder. For example, Saltaire, near Bradford, Yorks., on the river Aire, was built between 1851 and 1871 by the textile magnate Titus Salt for his workers. Another community near Bradford is Ripleyville, built in the 1860s by Henry Ripley to house workers for his dyeworks. Near Halifax, Edward Akroyd built Akroydon between 1849 and 1853 for textile workers. Many coal companies built houses for their colliers, and railway companies built small towns adjacent to their manufacturing and repair workshops: Crewe locomotive works is a good example. It started in 1843 by the Grand Junction Railway, and the number of employees rapidly rose to some 1,150, many housed with their families in the 250 company cottages. Three schools and a church were also built by the company. Similarly, some small towns owe their origin to the building of a canal.

Placing an industrial community in the remote countryside sometimes resulted in the creation of new farms and smallholdings in the neighbourhood to provide food for the workers and their families. There are examples of mill owners themselves building farms for this purpose, in addition to erecting housing.

Boyson, Rhodes. *The Ashworth Cotton Enterprise: The Rise and Fall of a Family Firm 1818–1880*, Clarendon Press, 1970
Challoner, W.H. *The Social and Economic Development of Crewe*, 1950
Darley, Gillian. *Villages of Vision*, 1978
Porteous, J.D. *Canal Ports: The Urban Achievement of the Canal Age*, Academic Press, 1978

'in fork' an old West Country expression used in the mining industry relating to the pumping of water from a mine. Forking water meant drawing it out of a mine; when the mine was pumped dry or the water inflow held in check, the engine was said to be 'in fork'. Thomas Savery, inventor of the 'MINERS' FRIEND', used the expression in 1702 and it was still in use in the 1860s. To fork can mean lift up.

information sources there are many documentary and other sources, both primary and secondary, of use to the industrial archaeologist and complementing FIELDWORK. Primary sources are those from which first-hand information is obtained and are therefore the most reliable, whilst secondary sources are those which have been compiled or repeated from the former. Primary sources may be consulted in a public record office, or a county or town archive, but some may be in private hands, with access depending on the attitude of the owner. The following lists the more important information sources:

Primary documentary sources include: parliamentary papers, e.g. Acts and Amendments, Returns of Mills and Factories, 1833–1905, and Reports of Commissions of Enquiry into industrial matters; company records and catalogues: personal papers, e.g. diaries, letters, wills and probate inventories, manuscripts, autobiographies (the National Register of Archives, established in London in 1945, maintains lists, indexes, and locations of manuscripts of businesses and industrial concerns from 1760, and of British scientists and engineers from 1600); maps and plans; parish registers; insurance company records;

population censuses (every ten years from 1801); PATENTS; solicitors records; special collections, e.g. Boulton and Watt papers (Birmingham library); town books (minutes and resolutions of town councils); rent and rates books, for occupancy of premises; engineering and architectural drawings; government statistics; port books; factory sale notices; exhibition catalogues; and the Business Archives Council records (since 1934).

Non-documentary primary sources include: museums, which as well as preserving machinery, vehicles, industrial artefacts, models and geological specimens may also demonstrate redundant crafts and industrial skills; oral history; sound, film and video recordings, e.g. of old machinery; preserved machinery or structures *in situ*; industrial sites, e.g. bloomeries, lime kilns; old photographs (from about 1850); paintings of industrial scenes (beware artist's licence!); and old picture postcards.

Secondary documentary sources include: newspapers (national, provincial and local), often held on microfilm or microfiche; technical journals and periodicals; proceedings and transactions of learned societies; proceedings of professional institutes; trade and commercial directories, e.g. Kelly's (from 1836); glossaries of industries and trades; gazetteers of industrial archaeological sites, surveys, etc.; biographies of inventors, engineers, industrialists, etc.; illustrated periodicals; encyclopaedias, e.g. early editions of *Encyclopaedia Britannica*, first published in 1766–71; bibliographies; industrial archaeology periodicals and other periodicals of related interest; publications of industrial archaeology and local history societies; books and booklets; university theses; and unpublished manuscripts, sometimes available in library archives.

Documentary searches might in some cases precede fieldwork, in which case the latter may confirm or find what physical evidence still exists; in other cases, documentary searches are made to fill out the results of fieldwork and add information which cannot be deduced from a site itself, e.g. ownership, production statistics, etc.

ingot a rectangular or square mass of steel which has been cast, when molten, into a metal mould and allowed to cool and solidify. It is then ready to be rolled into a desired shape in a rolling mill. In the middle of the 18th century ingot was frequently spelt lingot.

injector a device with no moving parts in which high pressure steam is allowed to expand to increase its kinetic energy and so entrain water and force both into a pressure equal to, or a little greater than, the steam itself. It was invented by Henri J. Giffard (1825–82) of France in 1858, and enables a locomotive to force water into its boiler without the need of a feed pump. It is also used on small steam boilers to eliminate the cost of a pump. Locomotives may therefore feed water into their boilers while stationary. The device was first used in England by Sharp, Stewart and Co. of Manchester in 1859. The exhaust steam injector was introduced in 1876 by Davies and Metcalfe.

inkle a kind of narrow, woven linen tape made on inkle looms, which wove several tapes at once. The tape was used as ties, etc. on clothing and for similar applications. Inkle possibly comes from a Dutch word *enkel* meaning single or narrow; inkle looms were introduced into Britain in the 18th century by the Dutch, and were also known as DUTCH LOOMS.

intake another name for a piece of land that has been enclosed by Act of Parliament, sometimes marked as such on Ordnance Survey maps. *See also* ENCLOSURE OF LAND.

intensifier hydraulic equipment, invented in 1869, which enables pressure to be increased or intensified above the supply or mains pressure. It comprises a cylindrical body inside which a RAM with two different diameters can move. The ratio of the areas of the two parts of the ram is in the same ratio as the desired increase in pressure. Mains water acts on that part of the ram with the larger area, forcing the smaller ram to move and thus raising the pressure of the water that it delivers. The action is intermittent only and is limited to the stroke of the ram. If a further supply of high pressure water is required, suitable valves must be incorporated in the device to allow the ram to return to its original position and be recharged with a fresh supply of mains water whilst pressure is maintained on the delivery side. Should a continuous supply of high pressure water be needed, two intensifiers are required side-by-side, arranged for each intensifier to operate the valves of the other, so that as one intensifier is delivering high pressure water, the other is recharging from the mains, and vice versa.

Intensifiers are used to raise the pressure from mains supply instead of using a high pressure pump. They are often incorporated in HYDRAULIC PRESSES where large forces are required intermittently, allowing the press to be worked off a public water supply.

internal combustion engine an engine, or PRIME MOVER, in which a mixture of air and fuel is ignited inside a closed cylinder, and the resulting explosion drives a piston to the opposite end of the cylinder, its movement turning a crankshaft via suitable mechanical parts. An internal combustion engine has a higher thermal efficiency than a boiler and steam engine combination.

The main fuels used are coal gas, oil, and petrol, although early attempts at inventing an internal combustion engine used different fuels. The first patent in Britain was that of Robert Street, who patented a primitive, intermittent-action, gravity-assisted engine in 1794 (patent no. 1983). His engine used turpentine as fuel, and drove a water pump. A later pioneer was Samuel Brown (1776–1852) who took out two patents (no. 4879, 1823 and no. 5350, 1826). The first was for an engine using coal gas as fuel, while the second used alcohol. His engine was in effect an ATMOSPHERIC ENGINE, similar in principle to NEWCOMEN's, since the power stroke was by atmospheric pressure acting on the piston. Brown made a pioneer run near London with a road vehicle powered by one of his designs in 1826.

The first successful GAS ENGINE was Lenoir's, developed in France in 1860. Ignition of the air–gas mixture was by an electric spark. OIL ENGINES were developed in the 1880s. Atomized oil in air was ignited either by an electric spark in some designs, or by a hot tube in others. Another type of oil-using engine is the Diesel engine, available by 1897; this is a COMPRESSION IGNITION ENGINE in which the high temperature necessary to explode the air–oil mixture comes from compressing air to a high pressure before oil is sprayed into the cylinder at the correct moment.

The PETROL ENGINE was developed in the 1880s, largely through the efforts of the two German engineers Daimler and Benz working independently of each other. Daimler's engine was working successfully by 1884, and was fitted to a motor cycle in 1886; ignition was by an externally heated tube attached to the cylinder. In 1885, Benz fitted his engine to a three-wheeler carriage, and in his case ignition was by an electric spark. Many engineers and inventors, mostly on the Continent and in America, subsequently developed and perfected the petrol engine. A possible reason why Britain contributed so little in the early days is that the steam engine and locomotive dominated prime movers in this country in the 1880s and 1890s, and there seemed little to be gained from the first internal combustion engines. However, internal combustion engines made rapid strides, the petrol and Diesel engines for road transport, and large Diesel units for ship propulsion.

Caunter, C.F. *The History and Development of Light Cars*, HMSO, 1957
Maxcy, G. and Gilbertson, A. *The Motor Industry*, 1959
Nevins, A. and Hall, F.E. *Ford, the Times, the Man, the Company* 1953
Rae, J.B. *American Automobile Manufacture*, 1959
Rolt, L.T.C. *Horseless Carriage: The Motor Car in England*, 1956

invention   a new and original idea for a machine, process, article, etc., upon which technological progress depends. In general, an inventor seeks to protect his or her invention by securing a PATENT which gives him or her a legal monopoly for a limited period in which to exploit the idea, in exchange for disclosing it.

Some inventions are the result of pure inspiration, others from steady work and experiments, often over many years, to solve a problem. A few inventions have come from accidental discoveries, and not all inventors have been directly connected with the industry to which their invention applied. For instance, the Revd Edmund Cartwright invented the first AUTOMATIC POWER LOOM in 1784 as the result of overhearing a discussion between cotton industrialists during a coach journey. He also made the first attempt at mechanizing wool COMBING in 1792, and there are several instances of others not connected with a particular trade or industry who have turned their mind to solving a problem outside their own sphere of interest. Industrial disputes have stimulated inventions, such as Richard Roberts' self-acting mule, invented to counter a crippling strike by hand spinners in 1824 (*see* 'IRON MAN').

Naturally, the invention and introduction of machines was greatly resented by hand workers in many crafts and industries who could see their livelihood threatened. This led to several periods of violent unrest in different industries at different times, such as machine-breaking by the LUDDITES. However, it is striking to note how very many inventions made during the Industrial Revolution were by workmen and artisans themselves, inventions which often caused considerable unrest among their own class. Most such inventions resulted from empirical approaches by practical people, and few were by scientific study or thought, with the possible exception of James Watt (1736–1819) of steam engine fame.

In some cases inventiveness ran from generation to generation in the same family, examples being John Kay (father) and Robert Kay (son) in the 18th century, and the Brunels, father and son, spreading over the latter part of the 18th and early part of the 19th century. Not all inventions were outstanding: many were small improvements on an existing machine or process, and many only had a short life of usefulness. Others took a surprisingly long time to spread within an industry, either because of conservatism and opposition to change, or because of lack of capital for implementing new discoveries. Many inventors were unable to benefit much from their invention, whilst others made fortunes, such as Richard Arkwright (1732–92), Henry BESSEMER (1813–98) and Samuel Lister (1815–1906) from his many worsted patents and manufacturing enterprises.

Baker, R. *New and Improved . . . Inventors and Inventions that have Changed the Modern World*, British Museum Publications, 1976
Rowland, K.T. *Eighteenth Century Inventions*, David and Charles, 1974

inverted syphon   a U-shaped pipeline or conduit which passes under an obstruction such as a river or cleft in the ground, to convey water from one side to the other. The free surface at the exit from the syphon must be at a lower level than the free surface at the inlet to the syphon, so that there is the necessary hydraulic head to maintain a flow. A well-known example of an inverted syphon is that constructed by James Brindley (1716–72) in 1753–6 which passed under the river Irwell to bring water to drive a waterwheel at a colliery at Clifton near Manchester. The inlet to his syphon was at a point in the river upstream of the exit on the opposite bank, the hydraulic head resulting from the inlet being several feet above the exit from the syphon.

Banks, A.G. and Scofield, R.B. *Brindley at Wet Earth Colliery: An Engineering Study*, David and Charles, 1968

inverted vertical steam engine   a type of steam engine in which the steam cylinders are placed above the crankshaft supported on a robust frame. This design was introduced about 1850 by James Nasmyth (1808–90), and is called inverted because until then, vertical engines had their cylinders on a baseplate with an overhead crankshaft. Nasmyth called his engine a 'Steam Hammer form of Steam Engine' because of its resemblance to his STEAM HAMMER, invented in 1839. Inverted vertical engines were greatly used in steamships.

IRIS   acronym for Index Record for Industrial Sites, a project run by the ASSOCIATION FOR INDUSTRIAL ARCHAEOLOGY for recording particulars about industrial sites, monuments, and landscapes, to enhance existing data held in county SITES AND MONUMENTS RECORDS and the NATIONAL MONUMENTS RECORD, where industrial archaeology is at present significantly under-represented. Recording is by volunteer industrial archaeologists throughout the country, filling in a standard AIA-IRIS Record form for each site, which is computerized to provide central indexes held by the SMRs, the NMR and the AIA. In addition to the recording of sites, the IRIS input when eventually completed will be an aid to possible statutory protection of important endangered sites and monuments.

Association for Industrial Archaeology, *Recording the Industrial Heritage: A Handbook*, 1993

iron next to aluminium, the most common metallic ore, estimated at around 5 per cent of the earth's crust. Not all of it is economically accessible, and iron rarely occurs naturally in a pure state: it is almost always chemically combined with some other element such as oxygen, carbon, or sulphur. Iron is the base metal from which all ferrous metals are made: cast iron, wrought iron, and steels, the latter being the most universal material used in engineering and construction. Iron has been known since ancient times, but it was not until the commencement of the INDUSTRIAL REVOLUTION that it began to be used in large quantities.

In Britain, rocks containing iron-rich compounds are fairly widespread and occur either in lodes or veins, or in beds. The iron content varies and can be as high as 70 per cent in some varieties of ore. The main impurities which may be present are manganese, silicon, sulphur and phosphorus. The principal varieties of British ores are: magnetite, an ore combined with oxygen; haematite (bloodstone), another iron oxide found principally in the Furness district of Lancashire and Cumberland, and also in South Wales; ironstone, a carbonate iron, found associated with clay in the coal measures; and pyrites, an iron-sulphide ore. Most British ores are carbonates.

Iron ore is quarried or mined according to where it is found. Outcropping ore was obtained by surface quarrying in medieval times. Later, BELL PITS were dug to reach deeper deposits, and eventually as deposits near the surface were exhausted and mining techniques improved, deep mines became necessary to extract the ores. Some ores are still obtained by surface working today, particularly in the East Midlands. To release the iron from its combining element, the ore has to be smelted in contact with some form of carbon. The unwanted element then combines with the carbon under the action of heat and may be removed as a slag, leaving more or less pure iron, which still contains a small percentage of carbon (usually 2–4 per cent) plus traces of the impurities mentioned above, depending on the source of the ore. Iron made from ores containing an appreciable amount of phosphorus is brittle when cold, a condition known as COLD SHORT, and is therefore unsuitable for making steel. When Henry BESSEMER first developed his process for making cheap steel in 1856, only pig iron from low phosphorus ores could be used: this prevented most British ores from being used, except for haematite which has a low phosphorus content (less than 0.03 per cent). Suitable ores had to be imported from Sweden and Spain to supplement haematite until in 1878 Sidney Thomas (1850–85) and his cousin Percy Gilchrist (1851–1935) changed the refractory lining of the Bessemer converter to one which allowed phosphoric ores to be used without the lining being destroyed by phosphorus attack (*see* BASIC LINING). *See also* IRON MANUFACTURE, PIG IRON.

Iron Act, 1750 an Act prohibiting the manufacture of most ironware in the American colonies, to protect the home industry and provide an export market for it.

iron bridges bridges whose principal members are iron castings. Bridges made from cast iron date from the late 18th century. The world's first substantial iron bridge is the famous road bridge spanning the river Severn at Ironbridge, Salop. Completed in October 1779, it comprises five semi-circular cast-iron ribs of 100 ft span supporting the roadway. The ribs are held together by wedges, no bolts or rivets being used. It was scheduled a national monument in the 1930s. The success of this bridge encouraged others to use what was then a new material for large bridges, and one of 236 ft span was erected over the river Wear at Sunderland, Co. Durham, in 1796, which was of different design to the Ironbridge one, Rowland Burdon's (patent no. 2066, 1795). Cast iron lends itself particularly to arch construction because of its high resistance to compressive stress. Cast-iron bridges became popular in the 19th century, with railways building many arches of moderate span. An outstanding design is Robert Stephenson's High Level double bridge at Newcastle upon Tyne; opened in August 1849, it has six 125 ft span cast-iron arches of four ribs each carrying the railway tracks, and the roadway is suspended from the arches by vertical wrought-iron rods. It is thus a bridge using two different materials, cast iron for compressive stresses, and wrought iron for tensile stresses. When rolled steel sections became available in quantity, bridges were constructed in this material, which permitted different design solutions.

Trinder, B. and Cossons, N. *The Iron Bridge*, 1979

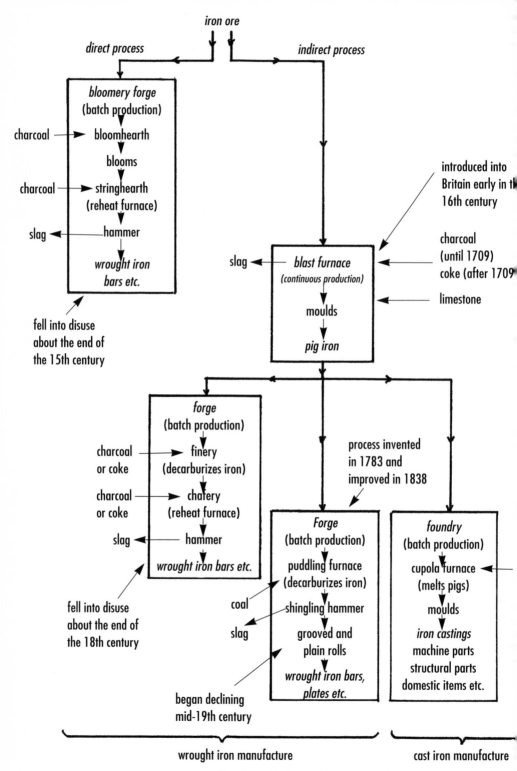

iron ore

direct process

indirect process

bloomery forge
(batch production)

charcoal → bloomhearth

blooms

charcoal → stringhearth
(reheat furnace)

slag ← hammer

*wrought iron
bars etc.*

fell into disuse
about the end of
the 15th century

slag ← *blast furnace*
(continuous production)

moulds

pig iron

introduced into
Britain early in the
16th century

charcoal
(until 1709)
coke (after 1709)

limestone

forge
(batch production)

charcoal
or coke → finery
(decarburizes iron)

charcoal
or coke → chafery
(reheat furnace)

slag ← hammer

wrought iron bars etc.

fell into disuse
about the end of
the 18th century

process invented
in 1783 and
improved in 1838

Forge
(batch production)

puddling furnace
(decarburizes iron)

coal

shingling hammer

slag

grooved and
plain rolls

*wrought iron bars,
plates etc.*

began declining
mid-19th century

foundry
(batch production)

cupola furnace
(melts pigs)

moulds

iron castings
machine parts
structural parts
domestic items etc.

wrought iron manufacture

cast iron manufacture

Flow diagram for iron manufacture

iron horse, *see* LOCOMOTIVE

'Iron Man' name given to the self-acting spinning MULE, patented by Richard Roberts (1789–1864) in 1830 (patent no. 5949). Roberts was asked by industrialists in the Manchester area to invent a self-acting mule to counter strikes by spinners using the hand-operated machines of the time.

iron manufacture the production of WROUGHT IRON and CAST IRON by various methods. Different methods of manufacturing irons have been used over the centuries, and these can be divided into two main classes: the direct process and the indirect process. In the DIRECT PROCESS, wrought iron is made directly from iron ore; in the INDIRECT PROCESS, cast iron is made first in PIG form, and wrought iron derived from the pigs in subsequent processes. Pig iron is also used to make iron castings by melting the pigs in a furnace and pouring the fluid metal into moulds. Whereas cast iron is extensively used today, wrought iron was replaced by cheap steel in the mid-19th century.

The most common routes used to manufacture both sorts of iron are shown in the simplified flow diagram. Old processes were often carried on after new ones were introduced for many years until they could no longer compete against the latest methods; there was no sudden switch from the old to the new. The earliest fuel used for providing the necessary heat was CHARCOAL and both processes used it until in 1709 successful experiments using COKE were made by Abraham Darby I (1667–1717) in his BLAST FURNACE at Coalbrookdale, Salop. Many blast furnaces gradually changed over to coke in due course, but a decreasing number continued using charcoal in remote areas, the last one not closing down until the mid-19th century in the Furness area of the Lake District. Today, blast furnaces use coke, and the pig iron they produce is used either for making castings in foundries, or for making steel. The direct process for making wrought iron fell into disuse around the end of the 15th century and the metal was then made by indirect processes until the arrival of cheap steel.

Ashton, T.S. *Iron and Steel in the Industrial Revolution*, Manchester University Press, 1924

Gale, W.K.V. *The British Iron and Steel Industry*, David and Charles, 1967

Gale, W.K.V. (ed.) *Griffith's Guide to the Iron Trade of Great Britain*, David and Charles, 1968 (reprint of 1873 edition)

Raistrick, A. *The Dynasty of Iron Founders*, Sessions of York, 1990

Schubert, H.R. *History of the British Iron and Steel Industry from 450 BC to 1775 AD*, Routledge and Kegan Paul, 1957

iron pyrites, *see* PYRITES

iron road, *see* PERMANENT WAY

Italian machine, *see* THROWING MACHINE

italians a kind of linen JEAN with a satin face, mostly used for linings. As its name suggests, this type of cloth originated in Italy.

J

jack 1. the fixed frame used in rope making which carries the hooks on which the rope strands are fastened. The hooks are revolved as the rope is formed to impart the necessary twisting action. 2. the pivoted horizontal bar which lowers and raises a SINKER in a knitting machine or stocking frame (*see* Fig. 69).

jacketing (or lagging) a means of keeping a steam engine cylinder hot by reducing the heat loss from its surface, thereby raising the thermal efficiency. A 'jacket' of wooden boards was fastened round the cylinders of BEAM ENGINES as insulation to conserve the heat. William Symington (1763–1831) formed a spiral flue round the cylinder of his engines and passed hot gases from the boiler through it. Later, annular spaces were made round the cylinder walls, and steam was passed through to keep the cylinder hot. This greatly reduces condensation of the live steam inside, enabling maximum power to be obtained. A steam jacket reduces heat loss by radiation from the cylinder, and is itself insulated on its outside surface.

jack frame a machine for the final reduction in cross-sectional area of a cotton SLIVER into a fine ROVING preparatory to spinning high COUNTS of yarn. A jack frame is in effect a second roving frame, and is only used for the preparation of rovings suitable for final reduction in fine spinning. It is the last of the series of machines fitted with flyers and bobbins. Jacking means to stretch a thread.

Jack-in-the-box, *see* CATARACT CONTROLLER

jack ring a device for taking a STONE NUT out of gear with a spur wheel in a corn mill when the mill is not working. It comprises an iron ring which, by turning a screwed rod, lifts the stone nut up its spindle out of gear. Turning the rod in the opposite direction lowers the stone nut back into gear, and a few more turns lowers the ring out of contact with the underside of the stone nut, which is then free to revolve when the mill commences working.

jack roller (or jackrowl) a simple windlass comprising a small diameter roller with handle which could be fastened across early shallow, small diameter coal or ore shafts in the 17th and 18th centuries. A rope could be wound round the roller to raise coal or ore from the bottom of the shaft. The term 'jack' is frequently used to describe something which is small.

jaconet a plain, medium weight, cotton fabric originally imported from India, but by the 19th century being made in Britain. The English name is derived from the Hindi *Jagannathi*, an early name of a town on the coast of the Bay of Bengal, now called Puri, where this type of cloth was first made.

Jacquard a mechanism for raising warp threads on a loom in the correct sequence required for weaving a complicated, or figured pattern. The correct sequence is controlled by a series of PUNCHED CARDS linked together, which are passed through the mechanism, each card being perforated by a predetermined pattern of holes which allows the correct warps to be raised in turn. The mechanism is named

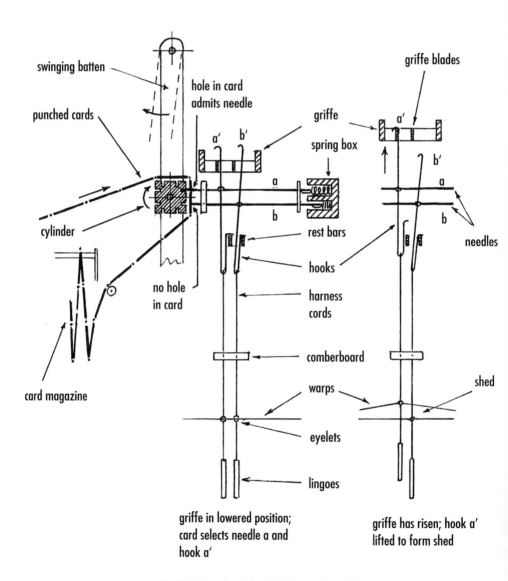

Fig. 40. Action of a single cylinder Jacquard mechanism

after its inventor, Joseph Marie Jacquard (1752–1834) of Lyon, France, who perfected his prototype machine in 1798, based on earlier work in about 1745 by another Frenchman, Jacques de Vaucanson (1709–82). It was a natural sequence to the older DRAW LOOM and was in fact first known as 'the new draw-loom engine'. In Britain, Francis Lambert patented a Jacquard type loom (patent no. 4442, 1820) and Stephen Wilson also patented a similar machine in 1821 (patent no. 4543).

The Jacquard comprises a framework containing the working parts which is mounted on top of the loom itself. Fig. 40 shows the main features of the mechanism. The punched cards are laced together to form a continuous sequence and held in a magazine awaiting use. They are led one at a time over a square section horizontal bar, called a CYLINDER (2), which revolves a quarter turn at each pick of the loom, drawing a fresh card into use each time. Facing the cylinder are several hundred horizontally positioned slim rods or NEEDLES which are spring loaded at their ends remote from the cylinder. Each needle has a small loop formed in its length through which a vertical wire hook passes. (In the diagram, only two needles and hooks are shown for clarity.) The hooks are arranged in rows closely spaced, and are normally supported from below by resting on support bars. Attached to their lower end are long cords hanging down past the warp threads and weighted at their extremity by long thin weights called lingoes. Each cord has an eyelet or mail formed in it at the warp level, and a warp thread passes through the eye. Surrounding the hooks, and just below them, is an open frame called a GRIFFE which has thin crossbars called blades or knives. A blade lies between each row of hooks, and lifts when the griffe is lifted. The cylinder has holes drilled in each of its four faces, one hole for every needle exactly in line with the needle. It is attached to a pivoted batten which swings it away from the needle ends to allow the cylinder to turn when a fresh card is brought into action. The card lies between the needle ends and the cylinder face, and is accurately positioned on the cylinder by registering on protruding pegs. When the cylinder is swung back into position it is pressed up against the needle ends. Where there is a hole in the card facing a needle, the spring pushes the needle into the hole in the cylinder behind the card. This swings the hook associated with the needle into the path of the griffe blade when it lifts. Where there is no hole in the card, the needle does not move and its associated hook is missed by the griffe blade

when it lifts. Those hooks which are lifted raise their attached cords and associated warps to form the required shed. When the griffe is lowered, the lingoes pull the warps and hooks down to their normal positions. The next rotation of the cylinder brings a fresh card into action and the sequence is repeated as many times as necessary to complete the design being woven. By then all the cards needed for the design have passed through the mechanism and the first card comes into action again to repeat the pattern, since the cards are linked into an endless chain.

The original Jacquard was used on hand-operated silk looms, and was not immediately taken up in Britain. It was later adapted for looms weaving other materials. Jacquards are made in various sizes designated by the number of needles, e.g. 400s, 800s, 1200s, etc. In fact each machine has eight extra needles, there being four per side for the SELVEDGE. Double cylinder machines were developed for faster working, and double lift machines with two hooks per needle and two griffes. Since the Jacquard lifts individual warp threads, it is capable of producing more complicated patterns or figures than the other warp sequence device, the DOBBY.

jagger lane, see PACKWAY

jagging carrying loads by packhorse. Another name for a packhorse is a jagger, and in the 16th century a jag was a load. The man in charge of a string of packhorses was called a jagger, although the word could also mean a pedlar or hawker. A further old meaning of jagger is a train of trucks in a coal mine.

jamdani (or jamdannie, jamdarma) a fine cotton, muslin-like, cloth usually with spots or flowers woven in it, and popularly made in Lancashire in the late 1700s. Although the word is of Persian origin, such cloths were woven in India, and imitated in Lancashire. Jamdani is also known as Dacca muslin.

japanning covering surfaces with a hard varnish called japan. Various materials, such as wood, papier mâché, metals, etc. can be lacquered in imitation of Japanese lacquer work, either for decoration or to give an anti-tarnish protection. A thin layer of a varnish called japan is applied and the article stoved at 200°F to give a hard, black, glossy finish. Japan is also used in making patent leather.

jarecock, see ARCHIL

jean a TWILLED cotton cloth used for garments since the 16th century. It is a kind of FUSTIAN, and was originally known as jene fustian, which became shortened to jean or jeanes. The name possibly comes from the French spelling of

Gênes for the city of Genoa in Italy. Jeanet or jeanette was a material resembling jean, dating from the late 18th century.

jene fustian, *see* JEAN

jenny an 18th-century hand-operated machine capable of spinning several yarns at once. The jenny (jeany in Scotland) was invented *c*.1767 by James Hargreaves (*c*.1725–78) of Oswaldtwistle, near Blackburn, Lancs. It was the first successful attempt at multiple spinning on one machine, designed to meet the shortage of cotton yarn existing at that time. Hargreaves' first machine had eight spindles, and was essentially a domestic machine, chiefly worked by women. It was developed by later inventors such as Haley, and eventually jennies of 120 spindles were in use, these large machines being operated by men in mills. By 1787 it was estimated that there were some 20,000 jennies at work in the textile industry.

Hargreaves had to move to Nottingham to avoid the violent local opposition to his machine from those fearing that unemployment would result from its greater output. Hargreaves did not take out a patent until 1770 (patent no. 962), but by then he could not enforce it as many jennies had already been made by others.

The jenny copied the hand movements of a spinster working a traditional wheel. It was intermittent in operation, spinning yarn in about 6 ft lengths between winding on. Fig. 41 shows the action of an early jenny. From the carriage position at *A* with the CLOVE open and spindles stationary, the carriage is drawn back to *B*, and the roving of length *A–B* passes through the clove, with the spindles stationary. With the clove shut, the spindles are then rotated by the handwheel and the carriage drawn back to *C*, applying draft and twist simultaneously. The spindles are stopped when *C* is reached. Extra twist is sometimes put in here. The spindles are then slowly reversed for backing off, the faller wire brought down, and the spindles slowly rotated to wind on spun yarn (which is now *B–C* long) as the carriage is returned to *A*. The cycle is repeated until the roving creel needs replenishing.

The jenny remained in operation in some mills for a surprising number of years. Although the MULE with its greater productivity was invented only some twelve years later, less progressive mills were still using jennies as late as the 1820s. Eventually the mule completely superseded the jenny.

Aspin, C. and Chapman, S.D. *James Hargreaves and the Spinning Jenny*, Helmshore Local History Society, 1964

jennygate (or wheelgate) that part of the floor which is traversed by a MULE carriage as it moves out, applying draw and twist to the yarn, and inwards as winding takes place.

Jersey wheel, *see* GREAT WHEEL

jersey wool a wool similar to the fine, choice wool once spun on the island of Jersey. It can mean a very fine woollen yarn, or wool which is combed and ready for spinning.

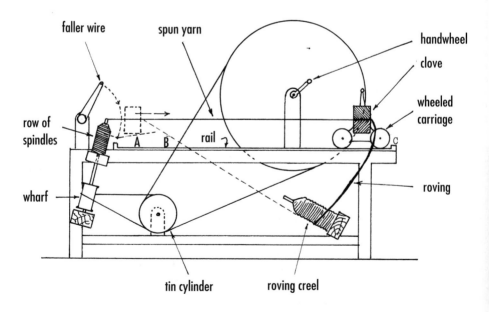

Fig. 41. Hargreaves' spinning jenny with Haley's improvements

jet condenser a vessel inside which steam is condensed back into hot water by mixing it with a fine spray of cold water. The first jet condenser was discovered by accident by Thomas Newcomen (1663–1729) when a faultily repaired leak in the wall of his steam cylinder allowed a fine spray of water to enter and rapidly condense the steam inside. Jet condensers can only be used where the combined cooling water and condensed steam may be re-used as boiler feedwater. *See also* CONDENSER (1)

Jew's house a medieval tin smelting furnace comprising a small, bowl-shaped, clay-built furnace measuring about 3 ft diameter by 3 ft deep. Peat was frequently used for fuel in Cornwall where coal is scarce, and the tin ore was melted using hand- or foot-operated bellows, and run into square moulds cut in granite blocks. The origin of the peculiar name is obscure.

jig 1. an old name used in Shropshire for a brake controlling the speed of trucks on a waggonway incline. **2.** *see* HOTCHING TUB.

jig brow, *see* SELF-ACTING INCLINE

jigger 1. a hydraulically operated stroke-multiplying crane. It comprises a vertically mounted hydraulic cylinder or jigger body with a top set of SHEAVES attached to its base, and another bottom set attached to the protruding end of the RAM. The pulleys in each set of sheaves are free to rotate on their axles. One end of a rope (or chain) is fastened to the jigger body, and loops round each pair of top and bottom pulleys in turn, to hang down with a hook at its free end. Admitting water under pressure to the jigger when the sheaves are nearest together causes the ram to makes its stroke, pushing the bottom sheaves further away from the top set. The hook rises a greater distance than the ram stroke, its travel being multiplied by twice the number of loops the rope makes between top and bottom pulleys.

Hydraulic jiggers on a warehouse at Albert Dock, Liverpool

Jiggers are in effect hydraulic CRANES or winches, and were used in warehouses where there was a hydraulic supply available. They were also used to operate lifts. The jigger was patented (no. 11343) by William George Armstrong (1810–1900) in 1846.
2. (or jig) *see* HOTCHING TUB. **3.** (or jolley) a machine for moulding circular hollow-ware pottery items such as plates, dishes, cups and saucers, etc. It comprises a revolving mould which forms the outer shape of the article, and a profiled former or jigger which shapes the inside. A lump of clay is placed in the revolving mould and the jigger pressed into it to complete the moulding. **4.** a hand comb for wool.

jim crow nickname for the swivelling tool holder on a PLANING MACHINE. It seems to have first come into use around 1842, and its origin can be traced to a Negro minstrel song that was very popular in the 1830s and 40s. This included the lines:

> Wheel about and turn about
> And do just so,
> Every time I wheel about
> I jump Jim Crow.

The song is of north American origin.

The name jim crow is also used for iron and steel rail bending and straightening equipment, originally operated by a hand screwed device, and later by HYDRAULIC POWER.

jockey pulley a pulley running on the outside of a belt to improve the effectiveness of a drive. The jockey pulley is so placed to increase the arc of contact of the belt round the driving pulley, or it may be used to take up belt slack. A jockey is usually held in a slot so that it may be moved closer to the belt, or in some cases it is weighted. The name obviously comes from the pulley 'riding' on the belt.

John Company, *see* EAST INDIA COMPANY

jolley, *see* JIGGER (3)

Jonval water turbine a parallel or axial-flow REACTION WATER TURBINE invented in France by N.J. Jonval in 1843, in which water descends through fixed curved guide vanes which direct the flow sideways onto curved vanes on the runner. These deflect the flow downwards, the reactionary forces imparted causing the runner to rotate. A diagrammatic cross-section through a Jonval turbine is shown in Fig. 83.

journal that part of a shaft which is in contact with and supported by a bearing which allows it to rotate. The word is also used to describe the bearing itself. Sometimes the journal part of a shaft or axle is called a neck. The origin of this meaning of journal is obscure.

journey **1.** the time taken to make glass from the beginning of melting of its raw materials. The word comes from the French *journée*, meaning a day's work. **2.** a train of trucks running on an incline at a coal mine, also known as a dukey.

journeyman a tradesman or craftsman who has served his APPRENTICESHIP and is skilled and qualified to work for a day's wages as an employee of a master. The word comes from the French *journée*, which originally meant a day's travel or a day's work. It was the ambition of most journeymen eventually to become masters in their own right. An apprentice became a journeyman usually at the age of twenty-one, and as a journeyman he often continued to live in the same house as the master who had trained him until in time he married and set up his own home. Frequently a ratio of apprentices to journeymen was maintained by the masters in each particular trade or industry. The introduction of the FACTORY SYSTEM saw the end of the days of journeymen as such. There was no social difference between journeymen and masters, as the position of journeymen was merely a stage in a man's career.

Joy valve gear a mechanism for reversing the rotation of a steam engine and varying the expansion ratio by altering the CUT-OFF point. Invented by David Joy (1825–1903) in 1857 (patent no. 929) and originally for marine engines, it was also applied to land-based stationary steam engines and locomotives. It differs from almost all other VALVE GEARS as it does not use an ECCENTRIC to obtain its drive. Instead, motion is obtained entirely from the connecting rod of the engine through a linkage system, as shown in Fig. 68g. In a simple application to a reversing stationary steam engine, a link *de* is pivoted from a point *d* near the middle of the connecting rod *bc*, and its lower end *e* is connected to a radius link *ef* which swivels about a fixed fulcrum *f*. From a point *g* on *de* another link *gi* is joined to *ij* which operates the valve rod. Near the end of *gi*, a block which slides in a curved slot is pivoted to *gi* at *h*. The slot is part of a WORMWHEEL whose centre coincides with *h* when the engine piston is on either DEAD CENTRE, and at these positions the slot is vertical. The slot on the wormwheel may be turned through an arc by rotating the handwheel attached to the worm which engages with the wormwheel. This inclines the slot to either side of vertical. As the point *d* on the connecting rod oscillates with the strokes of the piston, the sliding block moves up and down the curved slot. The direction of rotation of the engine and

the point of cut-off are controlled by altering the inclination of the slot from vertical. When it is vertical the gear is in mid-position and the engine will not drive in either direction. Later cut-offs occur as the slot inclination increases.

The Joy valve gear is simple and cheaper than most other valve gears and gives accurate valve action. It has the disadvantage that the connecting rod is weakened by the connection at *d*. However, the London and North Western Railway in particular standardized on this type of valve gear, although it was not used extensively elsewhere. It is classed as a RADIAL VALVE GEAR since the valve derives its motion from a point on a link (*gi* in the example given) which acts as the radius.

junk ring a metal ring for holding a packing material in place on a steam engine piston. A PACKING material is used to provide a steam-tight seal around the circumference of a steam engine piston: in the 18th and 19th centuries, junk (old rope saturated in tallow) was commonly used, and held in place by a removable metal ring called a junk ring. Later, metallic packings replaced junk, but the retaining rings were still called junk rings. The word junk probably comes from the Latin *juncus*, a kind of rush once used for making rope. *See also* OAKUM.

jute fibres taken from just beneath the bark of the stems of the plant *Corchorus capsularis* or *Corchorus olitorius*, mostly grown in India around Bengal, and in Pakistan; the name comes from the Bengali *jhota*, meaning a braid of hair. The plant needs ample rainfall and a warm climate; the stalks attain a height of 6–12 ft and do not have branches or leaves except at the tip. The fibres are spun into a yarn and are used for sacking, cordage, and backing material of carpets, linoleum, etc. A coarse cloth, HESSIAN, and some canvases are also made. The fibres, known as bast, are 5–10 ft long, soft and fine, coloured creamy-white to brownish-grey, and are about 66 per cent cellulose. They are strong but inelastic. After harvesting, the stalks are RETTED in a similar manner to FLAX for ten to twenty days in water. The stalks are then bent and beaten with wooden mallets to release the fibres which are then washed in water to remove any adhering unwanted matter. After being air-dried, the fibres are baled for delivery to the processor.

In Britain, the jute industry is mainly centred on Dundee, Angus, Scotland. This originated as a by-product of the Dundee Whaling and Fishing Company, founded in 1756, for early in the 19th century it was found that imported Indian jute mixed with whale oil could be woven into a coarse fabric and used for carpet backings, sacking, etc. By the mid-19th century so many jute mills were working in Dundee that it earned itself the name of *Juteopolis*. At the same period the manufacture of LINOLEUM was beginning, and rapidly expanded as the demand for cheap floor coverings for workers' houses grew. Linoleum uses a jute canvas base onto which a layer of linseed oil, resins and cork is applied. The industry was centred on Kirkcaldy in Fife, Scotland.

Jute is prepared for spinning in a similar manner to cotton. First, the compressed bales are opened and oil and water added. The fibres are then spread into a continuous SLIVER in, for example, a chain spreader, CARDED to make the fibres parallel, drafted in a DRAW FRAME and then a ROVING FRAME for further drafting with slight twist, and finally wound onto a bobbin. The natural brownish colour suits most purposes, but it can be dyed if required. Originally jute was hand processed; mechanical spinning was first introduced in 1832.

Juteopolis the name applied to Dundee, Angus, Scotland, in the 19th century because of the rapid rise of the JUTE industry which was centred on the town and surrounding area. As a result, Dundee expanded more rapidly than any other British town at that time, and a large number of jute mills were built.

K

kebbing a Lancashire dialect word for dredging a canal for coal, carried out by poor people searching for coal spilled at canal wharves during loading and unloading. Old perforated buckets on a rope were used to bring up pieces of coal.

keel 1. a small boat used on the Tyne from the early 17th century for transporting coal along the river from riverside STAITHES to collier ships waiting in the estuary. Keels were sometimes propelled by oar, sometimes by sail, and the men working them were called keelmen. They are remembered in the traditional folksong 'Well may the keel row'. The introduction of steam-powered paddleboats in 1822 heralded the demise of the keelmen, and by 1876 sea-going colliers could reach the staithes due to deepening of the Tyne by dredging and the removal of a low-level bridge, thus eliminating double handling of the coal. **2.** a load of coal equal to 8 CHALDRONS, and taxed accordingly. However, it was common practice for keels to weigh as much as 10 chaldrons to evade Customs tax on the 2 chaldrons excess.

Kehrrad German word for a reversing waterwheel. Such wheels comprise an OVERSHOT wheel with two sets of buckets side-by-side, each set facing in the opposite direction to its neighbour. A switchable LAUNDER enabled the entering stream of water to be directed into one or the other set of buckets, thus causing the wheel to rotate in one direction or the other. Kehrrads were used for driving machinery in either direction, and date from the late 15th and early 16th century.

kellow, *see* GRAPHITE

kelp seaweed, or the ashes which result from slow burning certain kinds of large seaweed. Kelp was once used as a form of alkali in glass and hard soap making; early glassworks usually had a kelp store. The gathering, drying, and burning of seaweed was once an important seasonal occupation around the coasts of Scotland and Ireland. Joseph Black (1728–99) was instrumental in developing the kelp industry, which for a while replaced the use of imported BARILLA as a source of alkali. Kelp production reached a peak of about 12,000 tons p.a. during the years 1807–9, involving the collection of some 150,000 tons p.a. of dry seaweed. However, its use in Britain rapidly collapsed after the end of the Peninsular War when importation of barilla resumed.

Rotted seaweed or kelp was also used once as an agricultural manure. Iodine is also made from kelp.

Kendal cloth a coarse woollen cloth, once woven in particular around Kendal, Westmorland. It was traditionally dyed green, using either Dyers' Greenwood, a plant of the bean family, or a dye made from the broom shrub, and was therefore also known as Kendal Green. Because of its strength and hard-wearing properties it was particularly worn by the poorer population. It was known all over England, and was mentioned by Falstaff in Shakespeare's *Henry IV*, Part One (1597–8): 'But, as the devil would have it, three misbegotten knaves in Kendal green came at my back and let drive at me; – for it was so dark, Hal, that thou couldst not see thy hand' (Act II, Scene IV).

kennet a kind of woollen grey cloth, plain woven in the 16th and 17th centuries mainly in Lancashire; it was frequently cottoned, i.e. processed to raise a NAP, and sold as Manchester cottons.

kep one of a pair of hinged devices for supporting a mine cage when it is at the top of a shaft. The keps swing out of the way when the cage descends.

kermes a fast red dye made from dried bodies of the insect *coccus ilicis*. Only the bodies of dead pregnant females are used, and the dye was sometimes known as kermes-grains. It was much used before the introduction of COCHINEAL. It was also known as scarlet grain, as the tiny insect bodies were formerly thought to be berries or grains.

kersey a coarse narrow cloth woven from long STAPLE wool and usually ribbed. Kerseys are narrower than BROADCLOTHS: an Act of 1465 fixed the size of a kersey piece at 18 yd long by 38¼ in wide (broadcloth was 2 yd wide). The name may come from the town of Kersey in Suffolk where an early weaving industry was set up by Flemish handloom weavers. In the West Riding of Yorkshire, four kerseys equalled one cloth piece.

kerseymere a fine twilled woollen cloth, similar in appearance to CASSIMERE but developed in Yorkshire. Kerseymere was first made in Yorkshire some twenty-five or so years after cassimere began production in the West Country, to compete against the latter. The name kerseymere may be a corruption of cassimere, and is wrongly associated with the cloth kersey which is a different, coarser material. Kerseymere generally was more heavily milled or fulled than cassimere. Unfortunately, both names were used rather indiscriminately in the 19th century which has caused some confusion as to which cloth was meant.

key a separate piece of metal, square or rectangular in cross-section, which is driven into grooves called keyways cut, or cast in a shaft and boss of a wheel to secure the wheel on the shaft. When sunk in this manner, half in the shaft and half in the wheel boss, torque is transmitted by the shear resistance of the key. There are other types of keys, such as the saddle key which is sunk into the wheel boss only and has a concave under surface which bears on the surface of the shaft. In this case torque is transmitted by friction only, and is only used on lightly loaded components.

kibble an iron bucket in which ore is raised from a mine.

kibbling mill a machine for coarse grinding corn, beans, etc. (to kibble means to grind coarsely). Small kibbling mills were hand-operated, while larger ones were power driven, and they date from the early 19th century. They are mostly used for grinding or crushing animal foods, and are also known as provender mills or kibblers.

kidder a two-ply or ingrain patterned carpet made by the intersection of two cloths of different colours in worsted or wool. Kidders date from about 1670, and the name is a shortening of Kidderminster, Worcs., where they were first made.

kier a metal vessel or boiler used in the bleaching or dyeing of yarn or cloth. Some kiers are open-topped, others have a lid which can be bolted on to make the vessel steam-tight. The word comes from *ker*, the Icelandic for vat.

kieve (or keeve) a large, circular wooden or iron open-topped vessel containing water into which tin or lead concentrate was slowly stirred. The mixture was allowed to settle, the fine particles falling to the bottom because of their higher density, and any other lighter material present lying on top of them. The kieve was then vibrated by hammering, known as tossing and packing, to cause the water to come to the top where it was skimmed off together with any unwanted foreign material. The recovered valuable material was then dug out, allowed to dry, and sent to the smelter. Kieves were also known as dolly tubs. In olden days they were operated by BAL-MAIDENS in Cornish tin streaming works.

killed steel fully de-oxidized steel, which gives sound ingots as it solidifies since almost no gas is evolved. In the days when CRUCIBLE STEEL was being made, steel was 'killed by fire', i.e. it was held in a molten state until the melter considered from experience that it was ready for TEEMING. Later, chemical de-oxidizing was introduced, usually by adding SPIEGELEISEN.

killoddy, *see* GIGHOLE

kiln 1. a general name for a structure in which heat is applied during the manufacture of some

Bottle oven pottery kiln at Coalport, Shropshire

commodity. Kilns may be made of brick or stone, and may in some cases have refractory linings. Typical examples are the kilns in which clay bricks and tiles are baked or pottery is fired. Hops are dried and barley malted in kilns, and powdered lime is produced from limestone in lime kilns. **2.** an ore storage hopper in Derbyshire.

king post truss a timber roof truss with a central vertical tie (the king post) connecting the ridge to the bottom horizontal tie beam. The king post also has a pair of inclined struts fastened to its base which are joined to the rafters at their mid points (*see* Fig. 57). This design, sometimes called a crown post truss, is used for moderate roof spans, and multi-span roofs.

King posts and bridles were added to the top of the beams of BEAM STEAM ENGINES to strengthen them.

kinney the corner of a glass-making furnace. The word probably comes from the French *coin*, meaning corner, or *cheminée*, meaning fireplace or chimney.

kip a hump at the top of a SELF-ACTING INCLINE to prevent ascending waggons running back down the incline under gravity when stopped. As the waggons came to a halt once over the kip, the tension on the haulage rope was reduced, enabling it to be more easily unhitched. Kip is a dialect form of cap, i.e. the top.

kirning an old Scottish mining term relating to a kind of opencast method of removing coal from seams lying just below the surface. Kirning means churning or turning over.

kissing the shuttle the action once performed by weavers when a fresh PIRN was fitted into a shuttle. The end of the thread from the pirn was sucked through a small hole in the shuttle by mouth, this method being quicker than trying to thread the end through by hand. The practice was believed to be harmful and to spread disease among weavers, so the need to suck the yarn through was removed in the 1920s by the simple idea of providing a fine slot in the shuttle leading to the hole, so that the yarn could be rapidly drawn into position by hand.

knitted wear, *see* HOSIERY INDUSTRY

knitting a method of producing a two-dimensional fabric by looping together adjacent rows of yarn or thread, either by WEFT KNITTING or WARP KNITTING (*see* Fig. 71). The origin of knitting is not known. The earliest method is weft knitting in which one continuous length of yarn is used to construct the fabric, using a pair of hand-held needles to make stitches which loop into similar stitches, made in a previous row, working from left to right, then reversing the fabric to continue with another row.

A knitted fabric is more elastic than a woven fabric, and is therefore particularly suitable for garments. It was not until 1589 that knitting on a simple hand-operated framework was devised by the Revd William Lee (d. *c.*1610), who copied the action of human hands in his machine: such machines were called STOCKING FRAMES since the first garments made on them were hosiery. Various improvements on Lee's machine were made in succeeding centuries, but the production of knitwear or hosiery continued to be mostly a domestic, cottage industry on hand-operated frames until the late 19th century. Eventually power-operated machines were developed, installed in factories.

Warp knitting was invented in 1775 by J. Crane and J. Tarrett. In this method, multi-lengths of yarn, each running the length of the fabric, are used side-by-side to fill up the width, similar to the warps in a woven fabric. Each warp is made to loop sideways into the adjacent warp, first to the right, then to the left, so that each stitch across the width of the fabric is made by a different warp. *See also* HOSIERY INDUSTRY.

knitting frame or loom, *see* STOCKING FRAME

knobstick 1. obsolete name for a man who worked during a strike or lock-out, who would today be called a blackleg. The term was sometimes applied to a non-unionist, or to a man working in a trade for which he had not served a proper apprenticeship. The term dates from the early 1800s, and was used by Frederick Engels in *The Condition of the Working Class in England* (1844); it was also the title of Allen Clarke's novel about an 1887 strike. Its origin is obscure. **2.** nickname for the boats of a carrier company operating in the Anderton (Ches.) area of the Trent and Mersey Canal. It is believed this unusual name may have come from the baton of authority carried by the company's boat marshall, which resembled a silver-tipped churchwarden's staff.
Wilson, R.J. *Knobsticks*, 1974

knock stone, *see* BUCKING (1)

kyanize a treatment for delaying decay in timber comprising a solution of corrosive sublimate, invented by the Irishman John Howard Kyan (1774–1850) and patented in 1832 (no. 6253). It was used to preserve timber railway sleepers and Brunel's continuous baulks, and also on wooden ships. It was superseded by CREOSOTE.

L

lace an openwork fine fabric made from linen, cotton, or silk threads, twisted, looped, or plaited together. The word lace comes from the Latin *laqueus* meaning a noose or net. The simplest form of lace is a fine net, a plain mesh without any ornamentation; net is often used as a synonym for lace, even if it is patterned. Patterns and designs can be made in the way the threads are connected together, and separate motifs may be added by an appliqué technique. Lace was extensively worn by the rich of both sexes in the 17th and 18th centuries – for ruffs, frills, cuffs, etc. – and other uses include curtains and table linen. The popularity of lace began to decline by the mid-19th century after a boom in the years 1821–31 known as twist net fever.

There are several types of lace made in different ways, such as BOBBIN LACE and NEEDLEPOINT. Originally a domestic handcraft, LACE MAKING became a factory industry in the second half of the 18th century.

Lowe, D. and Richards, J. *The City of Lace*, Nottingham Lace Centre, 1983

lace making originally a domestic hand craft, almost exclusively carried out by women and girls. The art of lace making was first brought to Britain by Flemish refugees in the 16th century. They introduced BOBBIN LACE MAKING into Devon and some other parts of England. An alternative hand method was NEEDLEPOINT LACE, which was introduced from Flanders or Italy, but since it was difficult to do and expensive, it eventually died out in favour of bobbin lace. A type of bobbin lace which imitated needlepoint lace was also made.

The domestic lace-making industry was conducted in a similar manner to hand spinning and handloom weaving in the early woollen and cotton industries. An agent supplied thread to the cottagers, and sold the finished lace, paying the women folk who worked in their own homes. The work involved long hours and was poorly paid, and was usually done to supplement the family income from other pursuits such as agriculture, mining, or fishing. Lace schools were set up where women and girls, some as young as five, were taught the craft.

Soon after the mid-18th century attempts were made to mechanize lace making by adapting the FRAME KNITTING machines of the hosiery industry. The two industries therefore were closely connected. The 1758 knitting machine of Jedediah Strutt for making ribbed knitted fabric was adapted in 1763 to make looped lace or network by John and Thomas Morris and John and William Betts (joint patent no. 807, 1764). John Morris later patented his Brussels point lace-making machine in 1781 (no. 1282). Robert and Thomas Frost of Nottingham jointly patented a machine for making figured lace and open network in 1784 (patent no. 1439). A bobbinet machine producing a plain hexagonal net was invented by John Heathcoat (1783–1861) in 1808 (patent no. 3151); his machine was nicknamed 'OLD LOUGHBOROUGH'. Meanwhile, John Leavers (sometimes spelt Levers, 1786–1848), Nottinghamshire framesmith, was secretly perfecting his machine which put intricate patterns into a lace mesh, which he eventually patented in 1828 (patent no. 5622). This machine was later improved by Hooton Deverill (patent no. 8955, 1841) who used a JACQUARD system to enable fancy lace to be produced. Another important lace-making machine was the Nottingham lace curtain machine of John Livesey, who took out a series of ten patents over a number of years (beginning with no. 13750, 1851).

The East Midlands rapidly became the lace making centre of England, and by 1850 Nottingham alone had over 100 lace factories with steam driven machinery. There were an estimated 3,600 bobbinet machines in the East Midlands, and the domestic lace-making trade was virtually finished. As in the textile industry elsewhere, working conditions in those early days were bad, with long hours worked by lace makers or twisthands, mainly women and children. Some factories had spare space which was rented to small firms who installed their own machines. Specialist lace-making machinery firms developed to support the industry. A worldwide export market was enjoyed, and overseas buyers came to the famous Lace Market in Nottingham. However serious competition gradually arose from France, Germany, and the USA in the 1870s. Furthermore, lace was very susceptible to the dictates of fashion, and demand declined towards the end of the Victorian period. A peak in output was reached at the commencement of the 20th century, since then lace has suffered a drop in popularity, and the industry has declined in importance.

Felkin, W. *History of Machine-Wrought Hosiery and Lace Manufactures*, 1867; reprinted by David and Charles, 1967

alls, Zillah. *Machine-made Lace in Nottingham in the 8th and 19th Centuries*, Nottingham Museum, 1964
alliser, Mrs Bury. *History of Lace*, 1902

ace runner a female worker who added mbroidery figures to lace net. Lace runners vere often employed as outworkers.

adder pit an early coal mine of shallow depth usually some 30–40 yd maximum) where ccess to the workings was by climbing down a eries of ladders with intermediate stagings. Tin nd copper mines were also reached in this nanner until mechanical winding was ntroduced. Coal mined in ladder pits was sually worked by the PILLAR AND STALL nethod, and the coal was carried up the ladders o the surface in baskets, or wound up by imple winches.

ade, *see* LEAT

ag a hardwood slat perforated with holes into vhich pegs are inserted to control the raising of hafts in a DOBBY. A number of lags are joined ogether to form an endless chain to produce the attern being woven.

agging thermal insulating material placed on ot surfaces such as steam engine cylinders, team pipes and boilers, to reduce loss of heat y radiation to the surrounding air. Lagging nay also be used to keep things cool. In the arly days of steam engineering, materials such s FELT were wrapped round hot bodies to keep he heat in as much as possible. Polished vooden strips laid longitudinally along engine ylinders, and held in position by brass bands vere popular. The word lagging is in fact elated to a Swedish word *lagg* which means a tave of a barrel, which a wooden lagged ylinder resembles. Steam piping was often nclosed in wooden troughs filled with sawdust n the mid-19th century. Later, an asbestos layer rotected by a hard plaster-like surface became ne common lagging material. Lagging is also nown as cleading or cladding, a variation of he word clothing.

airage a shed or enclosure in which cattle etc. re held whilst on their way to market or laughter. Docks often had such sheds, used uring the trans-shipment of live cattle.

iissez faire (French for 'leaving things alone') he political and commercial policy followed in 3ritain after the repeal of the Corn Laws in 846, characterized by non-interference and eregulation by government of foreign trade. 'ree competition of foreign goods with home roduced goods was allowed; import duties and ny encouragement to home-produced goods vere abolished. The industrialists who upported free trade believed that the industrial nterests of the country were best served by permitting capital to flow into those channels they were most naturally disposed to go. This economic liberalism was in direct contrast to the earlier MERCANTILE SYSTEM. Even so, duties were imposed on such items as tea, tobacco, and wine during the period of free trade to raise revenue. The period of *laissez faire* eventually ended soon after the end of the 19th century with the introduction of duties to protect home-based industries and preferential trade with colonial countries.

The INDUSTRIAL REVOLUTION paved the way for the introduction of *laissez faire* policies by placing in the hands of industrialists machinery and power sources for cheap manufacture of all manners of goods in bulk. The new railway system cheapened and facilitated the transport of raw materials and finished goods. The reduction and elimination of import duties on incoming raw materials and basic foodstuffs such as corn kept the prices of manufactured goods and the cost of living, and hence wages, down. There was little fear of foreign competition in the home market from other countries for many years since Britain virtually held a monopoly in the means of manufacture by machinery. Her low prices of goods abroad ensured a lucrative foreign market. Eventually, however, competition began to be felt from other countries, Germany and the USA in particular, as their industries developed, often with encouragement from their governments. This ultimately led to the abandonment of free trade in Britain as protective measures became necessary and tariffs were introduced.

Taylor, A.J.P. *Laissez-faire and State Intervention in Nineteenth Century Britain*, Macmillan, 1972

laithe house a dialect word used in Lancashire and Yorkshire to describe a house with a barn attached; a laithe or leath is a barn. Laithe houses are situated in rural areas and if WEAVERS' WINDOWS are also present, the 18th-century house occupants probably operated a dual economy of both weaving and subsistence farming. Some good examples of laithe houses still exist in the old wool areas such as Saddleworth near Oldham, Lancs.

lambreth a long settling flue or series of connected chambers for collecting ARSENIC particles or fume carried in the waste gases from a CALCINING kiln or furnace in which arsenopyrite is being treated, usually associated with tin mining in Cornwall. The word is obviously derived from labyrinth, which the long flues leading to the chimney resemble. The arsenical fume is slowly collected by gravity, and the lambreth is cleaned out periodically.

lampas (or lawmpas) a flowered silk fabric originally imported from China, but made in Britain from about the 1840s.

Lancashire boiler a horizontal cylindrical steam boiler with two internal firetubes and grates. In Manchester, William Fairbairn (1789–1874) and John Hetherington patented a shell-type steam boiler (patent no. 10166, 1844), which was an improvement on the older CORNISH BOILER, having an increased heating surface created by two firetubes and grates instead of one. First known as a double-flue tank, it soon gained the name of Lancashire boiler, and became the most common steam-raising boiler for factories, particularly in the textile industry. Thousands were made in a range of sizes, and in some installations banks of boilers supplied the steam requirements of large users.

Fig. 61c shows a typical hand-fired Lancashire boiler in its brickwork setting which forms three flues outside the boiler shell in which hot gases from the fires give up some of their heat to the water inside the boiler. The hot gases leave the firegrates and enter a common flue at the rear, passing under the boiler to the front where they split into two streams to return to the back again via side flues. There are thus three passes made, one inside the firetubes, and two outside the shell, before the cooled gases leave on their way to the chimney. The chimney draught at the grates is controlled by vertically sliding dampers in the side flues. The boiler is roughly two-thirds full of water, and the water level must be maintained above the top of the firetubes to stop them overheating with disastrous results. A precaution against low water level is the provision of FUSIBLE PLUGS in the crowns of the firetubes.

The original idea of having two firetubes and grates instead of one was that fresh fuel could be added alternately on each grate, so that there was always a brightly burning fire on one grate whose high temperature gases would ignite unburnt gases from freshly added fuel on the other. This would raise the efficiency of combustion and reduce smoke emission. Firing at a steady rate by mechanical STOKERS, which were soon added, eliminated the need for alternate firing.

Lancashire hearth a cast-iron water box for keeping the bottom of a hearth cool in a FINERY. It was introduced in the early 18th century in the north of England, from which it gets its name.

Lancashire loom a semi-automatic loom developed in Lancashire. Although it is self-acting, a Lancashire loom has to be stopped t recharge empty shuttles; full PIRNS are no automatically fed into the shuttle when the yar runs out. Replenishing empty shuttles is part o the duties of the weaver, and a diligent weave can keep a Lancashire loom running for 80 pe cent of its time. Early Lancashire looms wer made almost entirely from rough iron casting filed by hand to make them fit. Gear wheel were cast, and could produce sligl irregularities in the take-up mechanism whic wound on the finished cloth as it was bein woven. This resulted in weft-way streak detracting from the appearance of the cloth. A precision engineering became availabl machine-cut gears were substituted and oth components improved, enabling better qualit cloth to be woven at higher speeds.

Another characteristic is the position of th PICKING arm on the machine. A Lancashi loom is termed an overpick loom or horizonta side pick loom, meaning that the picking arn move across the top of the machine in horizontal plane to project the shuttle from sid to side.

The Lancashire loom is also known as th Blackburn loom since it was invented b William Dickinson of Blackburn c.1828, but n patented. It was later perfected by Jame Bullough, also of Blackburn, in 1841, by th addition of an automatic stopping motion an other devices. The Lancashire loom tends to b used for a variety of cloths on short productio runs, being a fairly flexible machine.

landsale the selling of coal directly at the p head.

landway a steep tunnel leading down to a co seam from the surface similar to a drift mine c adit, used as access to and exit from early min before vertical shafts were introduced.

lant (or land, leint) an old name for stale urin used in the Middle Ages and more rarely t later dates, in the FULLING of woollen cloth Lant was collected, and paid for, from houses i the neighbourhood of fulling mills, as a chea and convenient way of obtaining ammonia, th chief scouring agent used in the fulling proces It was mixed with water and wood ashes t make a liquor in which the cloth was pounde in FULLING STOCKS. Lant was also used in th bleaching of cotton. It was also known chamber-lye or, in the West Country, as sig (c zigg).

lantern frame the machine invented b Richard Arkwright (1732–92) in 1769 (pate no. 931) for preparing ROVINGS prior t spinning them on his WATER FRAME. Th lantern frame imparted some draft and twist to previously carded SLIVER, turning it into roving which was collected in coiled form in metal cans. It was because the cans resembled lanterns that the machine, which was in effect a roving frame, got its name.

Fig. 42 shows the main details of a lantern frame. Early machines had two cans and associated sets of rollers: the diagram shows the arrangement for one can only. Carded sliver was passed between two pairs of drafting rollers, the bottom, driven rollers being fluted, and pressure on the top front (i.e. second) roller was obtained by a weight suspended from it. The slightly drafted cotton strip was then passed between another pair of driven rollers mounted on top of the collecting can. These rollers added a little extra draft to the strip, and at the same time imparted some twist since they revolved with the can about a vertical axis. The revolving can and its rollers were driven via pulleys and cords from the same shaft which drove the drafting rollers. The roving as it entered the collecting can was thrown outwards against the can side by centrifugal force, and coiled itself in ascending coils. Only sufficient twist was given to the roving to provide enough strength for subsequent handling. The cans had doors in the side, and when they were full of roving the frame was stopped whilst they were emptied, usually by children in Arkwright's Cromford factory. The roving then had to be wound by hand onto bobbins to fit onto the water frame for spinning into yarn.

lantern gear an early form of gearwheel made from a circle of rods or staves mounted equidistant between two disks, and frequently

Windmill on Kos, Greece, showing wooden lantern and trundle gear

made from wood. The protruding teeth of the mating pegwheel or trundle meshed into the spaces between the rods. Lantern gear was used in particular in windmill and similar machinery. The gearwheel gets its name from its likeness to an old-fashioned circular lantern.

lap 1. the wide sheet of cotton delivered by a SCUTCHING MACHINE. A lap comprises cleaned cotton fibres lying in all directions forming a continuous sheet, usually lightly wound up into a roll and weighing about 40 lb. Preparation of a lap is a preliminary process before the material is passed to a CARDING engine. **2.** the distance a SLIDE VALVE in a steam engine has to move from its mid-position to open a port to the passage of steam. The face of the seat of a sliding D VALVE or a PISTON VALVE is made longer than the width of the steam PORTS it slides across. There are two extensions or overlaps, one known as the outer or steam lap, the other as the inner or exhaust lap (*see* Fig. 79). These overlaps are necessary because the ECCENTRIC which moves the valve is set at an angle in advance of the main engine crank to ensure smooth running. Laps were first introduced by Matthew Murray (1765–1826) around 1801. *See also* LEAD (2), ANGLE OF ADVANCE.

lapper, *see* ALNAGER

lappet a figured cloth with the figures raised on the surface. The figures are made by extra WARPS which do not interweave with other warps in the normal way, but are held in position by weft PICKS. The extra warps pass through a set of eyes placed in a sliding frame on a specially adapted loom called a lappet loom. The figures could be on a plain weave or gauze background cloth, and the end result imitated embroidery. Lappet was used in Victorian times for ladies' decorative wear, such as hats, dresses and petticoats.

lapping arranging linen cloth in folds a yard wide after weaving, and also after bleaching. A person employed to do this by hand was called a lapper, and there once was a lappers' union; lapping was later done by machine.

lastings a strong, twilled, woollen cloth which was very durable, and sometimes known as everlastings. It was popular for hard-wearing outer garments. Similar woollen cloth had the fanciful name *perpetuana* and was popular in East Anglia. Made in the 18th and 19th centuries, lastings was also used for the upper parts of ladies' footwear towards the end of the 19th century.

latch needle (or tumbler needle) a hooked knitting machine needle with a hinged latch over the hook which is opened and closed by the thread as a stitch is being formed, the

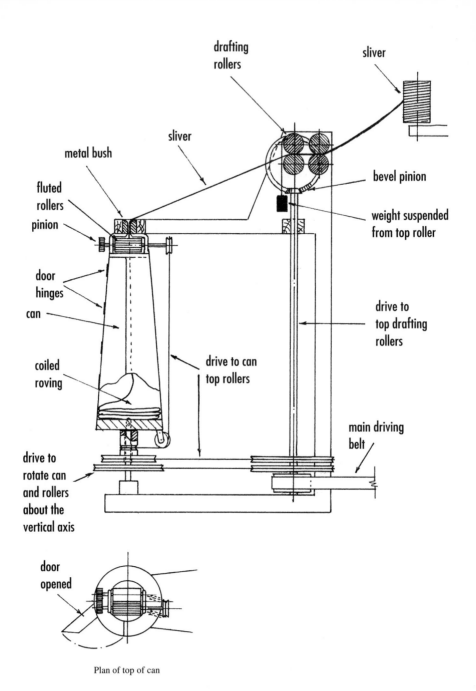

drafting rollers

sliver

sliver

metal bush

bevel pinion

fluted rollers

pinion

weight suspended from top roller

door hinges

can

drive to top drafting rollers

coiled roving

drive to can top rollers

main driving belt

drive to rotate can and rollers about the vertical axis

door opened

Plan of top of can

Fig. 42. Arkwright's lantern frame

completed stitch opening the latch ready to receive the next thread (*see* Fig. 72b). It is therefore self-acting. It was invented by Matthew Townsend and David Moulden (patent no. 12474, 1849).

lathe 1. a machine tool for making cylindrical items by an operation called turning. The origin of the lathe is obscure. Hand- and foot-operated pole lathes for turning simple wooden articles were in use in medieval times. By 1750, lathes were still made with wooden frames, small lathes being worked by hand, and large ones driven by waterwheels. Stronger machines with metal frames gave greater accuracy of turned work by the mid-18th century. Henry Maudslay (1771–1831) is credited with major improvements in lathe design. He introduced, around 1810, the screw-cutting lathe with change wheels for varying the speed, and the slide rest for holding the cutting tools. Further important improvements were made by Richard Roberts (1789–1864) *c.*1817, with the four-speed CONE PULLEY DRIVE and the self-acting saddle which automatically traversed the slide rest. Joseph Whitworth (1803–87) invented the split nut on the leadscrew in 1834 (patent no. 6566) which enabled the leadscrew to be engaged or disengaged at will.

Besides straightforward turning, lathes are used for facing circular items, screw cutting, and boring. Copying lathes were developed *c.*1818, the cutting tool following a master profile mounted alongside the copy being machined. Capstan or turret lathes were introduced from the USA in the 1860s, on which a number of different cutting tools are held in a rotatable holder so that a succession of machining operations can be made, saving tool-changing time for repetitive work.

Woodbury, R.S. *History of the Lathe*, Cleveland, 1961

2. (or lay), *see* SLEY

lattice girder the general name given to BRIDGE GIRDERS AND TRUSSES which are formed from a number of (generally straight) horizontal, vertical, and inclined members joined at their extremities to make a load-bearing open framework (*see* Fig. 12). Various designs have been patented by bridge designers and most are known by the inventor's name. The word comes from an old German word *Latta* meaning lath, referring to the crossing diagonals etc. joining the upper STRINGER to the lower stringer.

launder a trough for conveying water or molten metal. An example of a water-carrying launder is the wooden or metal channel conveying water from a headrace or mill dam to an OVERSHOT or PITCHBACK WHEEL in a water-powered installation. Often such a launder includes some means of controlling the water flow. A metal-conveying launder is used in a foundry to direct hot metal to a mould. An alternative name for a water launder is pentrough. The word has been in use since the mid-17th century, when it was sometimes spelt lander.

lawn (or lawnde) a fine plain woven cloth originally made from LINEN. Good quality lightweight cotton fabrics are also called lawns. The name possibly comes from the town of Laon, 87 miles north-east of Paris, France, where linen was, and still is, extensively woven.

lawnmower a machine for trimming grass using rotary cutters. The idea for the rotary lawnmower was copied from machines for shearing woollen cloth in the textile finishing industry by Edwin Beard Budding (1796–1846) of Stroud, Glos. (patent no. 5990, 1830). His employer, John Ferrabee, patented a similar machine for trimming the pile on cloth (patent no. 6058) the same year. The firm of J. and H. Ferrabee also made waterwheels, and corn milling and textile machinery.

lay 1. the swinging BATTEN of a loom, also known in some areas as a lathe or leath, all variations being dialect words. **2.** in some parts of Scotland, name also given to a turning LATHE.

layman the workman assisting the COUCHER in the hand method of PAPER MAKING. His principal job was to separate the sheets of paper from the woollen felts after they had been pressed in the screw press and put the felts ready for the coucher to use again. He also helped the coucher to handle large sheets made by the VATMAN.

layshaft, *see* COUNTERSHAFT

lea a measure of length for yarn which varies according to the material: for cotton, one lea equals 120 yd; for worsted, 80 yd; and for linen, 300 yd.

lead 1. a heavy, soft, non-ferrous metal with a low melting point at 327°C. Lead deposits were fairly widespread in Britain, and were extensively mined in Derbyshire, the West Riding of Yorkshire, Northumberland, Durham, north Wales, the Mendips of Somerset, and Shropshire. The deposits were usually found in hilly or mountainous country. In the 17th century there were thousands of small lead mines, but by the beginning of the 18th century many mines had been worked out. Today, there are many remains of former lead mining activities. Little lead was produced after 1950, but in its heyday lead was one of Britain's chief exports: in the 1820s Britain was the world's greatest producer of lead. The industry declined when lead extraction became uneconomic against the import of cheap lead from Australia and Spain.

There are two main sources of lead: first, GALENA, a lead sulphide, which varying in colour from a steely grey to a bright blue, and was the most mined variety; and secondly CERUSSITE, a lead carbonate. The ores are mixed with other rocks, and are frequently found in limestone areas. Deposits are found in veins, or rakes as they are usually called, or pipes or flats. Rakes occupy faults in the surrounding rocks: they may run almost vertically downwards for hundreds of feet, and can have considerable width. Pipes are approximately circular in cross-section, hence their name, whilst flats are more or less horizontal beds, varying from a few inches up to 20 ft in thickness. Veins are often interrupted by basalt which has no lead content, and was known as TOADSTONE by early miners. Veins are followed downwards by the miners, and the extracted material or BOUSE is sorted out on the surface. Galena normally comprises about 5 per cent of the total rock extracted, and has a lead content of roughly 85 per cent with 15 per cent sulphur. Cerussite contains about 83 per cent oxide of lead, and 17 per cent carbonic acid.

Early lead mining was by surface extraction from outcrops, and later BELL PITS were dug to reach lower deposits. When these were worked out and techniques and machinery were improved, deep shafts were sunk. In the early days, the metallics were separated from the bouse by breaking up the rock with hand-held hammers and picking the pieces of galena out. Later, horse-driven edge runners were used, and then power-driven rollers were developed to crush the material and various methods used to separate the lead-rich material from the waste, which was discarded. Water power was used to drive the machinery and operate winding gear at shaft heads.

Lead metal was obtained by SMELTING. A primitive method was by BOLE FURNACES until about the 17th century, then REVERBERATORY FURNACES were developed. Smelters were usually sited at, or close to, the mines. Fumes from smelting are poisonous, so long flues were built to carry the fumes away from the working areas to remote chimneys.

Lead was used in the manufacture of pewter, shot for firearms, flashing for roofs, pipes, paint etc., and was also used as a low friction bearing material in early machinery. The peak production from 347 mines was in 1856, when 99,514 tons of lead were extracted. The total output from 1700 till recent times has been estimated at 5 million tons, and during the period of greatest activity, 1854–71, some 90,000 tons per annum was averaged.

Burt, R. *The British Lead Mining Industry*, 1984
Crossley, D. and Kiernan, D. 'The lead-smelting mills of Derbyshire', *Derbyshire Archaeological Journal* CXII (1992), 6–48
Raistrick, A. and Jennings, B. *Lead Mining in the Pennines*, Longman, 1965
Willies, Lynn. *Lead and Leadmining*, Shire Publications, Album No. 85, 1982

2. the amount by which the inlet port of a steam engine is uncovered when the piston begins its stroke. In a steam engine cylinder and slide valve assembly the valve theoretically should be in its mid-position when the piston is at the end of its stroke. At this instant, the main crank is on DEAD CENTRE, and the radius arm of the ECCENTRIC which controls the valve movement is at a right angle in advance of the crank. In this position the valve would exactly cover and seal off the steam admission PORTS. In practice, in order to admit steam so that the piston can commence its stroke, the steam admission port must be open a small amount when the crank is on dead centre, and this small opening is called the lead. It is achieved by setting the eccentric so that its radius arm is slightly in angular advance of the right angle mentioned. Hence, fresh steam actually begins to enter the cylinder as the piston is almost at the end of its stroke.

The lead ensures smooth running of the engine with a minimum of throttling and wire-drawing of the steam during admission. *See also* LAP (2), ANGLE OF ADVANCE.

lead chamber process (or acid chamber process, English process) the method for making SULPHURIC ACID, also known as vitriol, developed by John Roebuck (1718–94) and Samuel Garbett (1717–1805) in 1746. They originally made the acid in small quantities for use in their precious metal refinery in Birmingham, but in 1749 opened a larger works near Edinburgh. They operated their process in secret for many years, not attempting to patent it until 1771, but by then they were too late in securing protection since many others were using the process. Shortly afterwards their business collapsed. By this time there was a great need for sulphuric acid in many industries – bleaching textiles, soda manufacture, etc. – making it an important basic chemical. The lead chamber process replaced the old slow method of distilling vitriol in glass jars. It involved burning a mixture of sulphur and SALTPETRE (nitre) in a furnace and passing the gaseous products of combustion into adjoining lead-lined chambers, where the sulphur dioxide was absorbed in a shallow bath of water to form dilute sulphuric acid. This was then concentrated further by distillation. The sulphur was originally imported from Sicily as natural brimstone, but when an excessively high duty was imposed by the Sicilian authorities in 1840, Spanish cupreous pyrites was substituted. An advantage of cupreous pyrites was that metallic copper could be extracted from the waste burnt residue and sold to metal refiners. Saltpetre was imported from Peru and Chile.

The lead chamber process continued in use until the early 20th century, peaking around the 1870s, when it was overtaken by the CONTACT PROCESS. Various improvements on the original process were made, notably by Charles Tennant (1768–1838) in 1803, but today it is obsolete. Little remains of the chambers since the high recovery value of the lead lining made their demolition worthwhile, but traces of their foundations and remains of their furnaces may still be found on some sites.

Gregory, S. 'John Roebuck: 18th-century entrepreneur', *The Chemical Engineer* No. 443 (1987), 28–31

leaf, *see* SHAFT (4)

lean yarn a woollen yarn which is tightly spun and taut. The opposite, more softly spun, is called lofty yarn. Lean yarn is stronger than lofty yarn, and is spun by the RING SPINNING process.

lease (or leash, or more rarely lays) the crossing of warp threads over a pair of rods (called lease-rods) prior to entering the HEALDS, the purpose being to keep the threads parallel and to act as a guide towards the healds. Lease-rods are also known as cross-sticks.

leat (or leet) a man-made water course for conveying water to or from a WATERWHEEL. The word is of south-west dialect in origin, and comes from an old word meaning 'to let'; in Scotland and the north of England, the word lade is frequently used. Other alternative names are goyt, flume, sluice and feeder. Not all leats are open channels: some are in the form of pipes or covered channels, while others may be open channels for part of their length, and become buried pipes where they pass under a spur on a hillside to avoid a long circuitous route round it, becoming open channel again when the obstacle is passed.

Leblanc process a chemical process for making sodium carbonate (soda ash) from common salt, developed by Nicholas Leblanc (1742–1806) in France in 1791. SODA is an important chemical, required in quantity for such purposes as soap and glass manufacture.

The Leblanc process involved decomposing salt with sulphuric acid in a REVERBERATORY-type furnace called a saltcake furnace, and then reheating the saltcake with coal and limestone to form black ash, which was allowed to cool. The soda it contained was leached out in tanks as a solution in water, and finally the water driven off by evaporation. It was a wasteful process, polluting the surroundings with hydrochloric fumes and creating large tips of solid waste material called GALLIGU. The reactions were only controlled by empirical methods.

John and William Losh introduced the process into England between 1802 and 1806 near Newcastle upon Tyne using brine from a nearby coal mine which had unexpectedly broken into a source of underground salt. In 1823 James Muspratt (1793–1886) built a factory for producing soda by the Leblanc process in Liverpool, and later one in Widnes, Lancs., in 1850. Although many improvements were made to the process, it still remained objectionable to nearby neighbourhoods and was responsible for the 1863 Alkali Works Act being introduced to enforce reduction of noxious emissions. The Leblanc process was replaced some ten years later by the SOLVAY PROCESS which was cheaper and did not create a pollution problem. The bulk production of soda by the Leblanc method really laid the foundation for the heavy chemical industry in Britain.

Gillispie, C.C. 'The discovery of the Leblanc process', *Isis* XLVIII (1957), 152–70
Gittings, L. 'The manufacture of alkali in Britain, 1779–1789', *Annals of Science* XXII (1966), 175

ledging room the office or counting house in a mill, etc. in which the financial accounts of the concern are kept in a ledger or account book.

left twist, *see* S-TWIST

legging the method adopted to propel canal boats through tunnels where no towpath existed. The bargees would lie on their backs head-to-head across the decks of the boats, with their shoulders against some fixed object on board, and 'walk' the boat along by their feet on the sides, or sometimes the roof of the tunnel. Early canal tunnels, such as the Harecastle tunnel on the Grand Trunk Canal, cut in 1766–77 by James Brindley near Tunstall, Staffs., were only 9 ft wide by 12 ft high. Legging had to be used to take the boats through its 2,880 yd length, the horses being led over the hill to rejoin the canal towpath on the other side. A similar method had also been used earlier on the underground canals serving the Duke of Bridgewater's coal mines at Worsley, Lancs. Here, the boatman used a broad canvas belt which had a 6 ft or so length of rope attached to it, and an iron hook at its end. He placed the belt round his body, and stood at the front of the boat, hooking the rope onto iron rings or staples fastened in the roof of the tunnel, which were spaced about every 10 ft. He then 'walked' the boat under him, pressing against the belt, until he was at the other end of the boat, when he unhooked the rope, walked to the front of the boat again, and repeated the procedure on the next roof ring. Many tunnels had gangs of professional leggers, and at the entrance to some the stone or brick hut in which they took their meals or waited to be hired may still be seen.

lehr (or lear, leer) a long, tunnel-like oven into which hot GLASS articles are placed by a TAKER-IN, so that they may be ANNEALED and allowed to cool slowly to remove any strain which may be present.

leish (or leash) the eyelet, or mail, in the vertical cord through which a warp thread passes in a HEDDLE assembly of a loom; alternatively it can be the name for the cord itself.

leitnagel Hund a hand-pushed waggon or truck originally used in German mines from about 1600, and which continued in use in some areas until as late as 1870. It comprised a wooden bodied, wheeled truck which ran on two flat wooden rails and was kept on them by a guide pin which hung beneath the front wheels and ran in a slot between the rails. The curious name comes from the German *leiten* meaning to guide or lead, and *Nagel*, a peg. The origin of Hund is obscure, but it has been suggested it is because the truck accompanied the miner everywhere, in doglike fashion. After the late 18th century such trucks became more generally known as spurnagel, from the German *Spur* meaning a track or trace. A variation in design to the guide pin was the use of two horizontal wheels beneath the truck body which ran between the rails. These types of trucks were known as Riesen, a word believed to be taken from *Riese*, a lumberjack's wooden slide down which logs were slid by gravity to lower valleys.

Leitnagel Hunds were used in mid-Wales and the Lake District mines, many of which were worked by German miners in the early 17th century. The use of guide pins or guide wheels to keep the trucks on the rails became unnecessary when flanged wheels were introduced c.1775.

Lewis, M.J.T. *Early Wooden Railways*, Routledge and Kegan Paul, 1970

lengthman an employee who maintains a section of a canal. Canal companies employed men to keep a watch on the condition of specified lengths of canal, and to carry out simple maintenance. Lengthmen were provided with canalside cottages, some of which may still be found. Railway companies still employ men for similar duties on the track.

leno (or lino) a lightweight muslin cloth used for ladies' veils, lightweight curtains, etc., made by crossing certain warps laterally over one another, with a normal weft. Crossing the warps prevents them from packing closely together and holds them firm, producing an open construction. Gauze is made in this manner. In France leno is called *linon*.

Levant red, *see* TURKEY RED

levee, *see* TRAINING WALL

level 1. a working tunnel or gallery in a mine. The term is also applied to tunnels used for draining mine workings when strictly speaking the floor is not level but has a slight fall in the direction of the flow of water. A boat level, or standing level, is a man-made underground watercourse leading into a mine which provides access to the working faces, and is used also for mine drainage and transport of material out of the mine. An alternative name sometimes used is stage. **2.** an above ground, man-made water course for bringing water from a distant source, e.g. across a moor etc., to work machinery in a mine by a waterwheel.

lever hammer a large hammer machine used in a forge which pivots through a small arc, the head being raised by CAMS rotated by a waterwheel or engine. There are various types of lever hammer such as the HELVE and the TILT. All are used to shape a BLOOM of hot iron by hammering it against a fixed anvil.

lever wall the substantial end wall of the building housing a BEAM STEAM ENGINE, which supports the pivots on which the beam rocks and also the weight of the PITWORK suspended from the outdoors end of the beam. The wall is so called because the engine beam was known as the great lever. Lever walls were replaced around 1850 by iron supports carried up from a bedplate when beam engines became self-standing and independent of the engine house.

liberty one of several districts in Derbyshire in which a miner could search for lead ore and enjoy certain rights. A liberty was often the same as a parish boundary.

licker-in a roller with a saw-toothed periphery which feeds the LAP of cotton onto the main cylinder of a CARDING engine (*see* Fig. 15). A similar feeding device is part of a wool SCRIBBLER.

lift conveyance for safely raising people or goods up to elevated floors in tall buildings, first developed in the USA by Elisha Graves Otis (1811–61) of Vermont, in the 1850s. Doubts had existed of the reliability and safety of lifts until he invented his safety device which prevented a lift falling in the event of rope failure: this was a leaf spring which was held in tension by the hoist ropes. A broken rope caused the spring to force a ratchet device to lock the lift 'cage' onto the vertical shaft on which it slid up and down. Otis spectacularly demonstrated the invention at the New York World Fair of 1853. The safety lift made the construction of tall buildings feasible. Its first use in a public building was on a store in New York's Broadway in 1857, the lift being powered by a steam engine.

lifting bridge bridge which either tips up (the drawbridge), or where the roadway rises vertically and remains horizontal. Drawbridges are hinged at one end and counter-balanced, some by balance weights at the end of the long overhead arms pivoted at their centre, others by low balance arms which descend into pits when the bridge is tilted up. Tilting bridges are more common than the other type which is generally restricted to small spans, an exception being the Newport lift bridge over the river Tees at Middlesbrough.

lig an old Yorkshire term for setting up a loom ready for weaving.

ligger 1. the nether or stationary bedstone of a pair of grindstones of a corn mill, etc. It is a dialect word used in some northern counties such as Derbyshire and Yorkshire. **2.** in the worsted industry, the person who feeds material into a CARDING machine.

lighthouse a building housing a light to warn coastal shipping of hazards, or to guide ships into a port or river estuary. Lighthouses date from ancient times. As both shipping and losses increased in Tudor times, a body was set up in 1514 to pray for sailors at sea and to lease authority to private persons to erect coastal lights on which they were empowered to charge a toll on passing ships. This arrangement lasted a number of years until eventually the body, which later became the Corporation of Trinity House, took over the erection and maintenance of lighthouses on the coasts of England, Wales, and the Channel Isles. A similar body, the Commissioners of Northern Lighthouses, became responsible for lighthouses in Scotland and the Isle of Man, from 1786.

The most famous lighthouse in Britain is probably the Eddystone, situated on a low reef of rocks which become submerged at high tide,

14 miles south-west of Plymouth. Four lighthouses have been built in succession on the Eddystone rocks. The first was by Henry Winstanley in 1698 and destroyed by storm in 1703. The second, built by John Rudyerd in 1708, was destroyed by fire in 1755. These two lighthouses were mostly built of timber and lit by candles. John Smeaton (1724–92) completed the third in 1759 in stone, with hydraulic mortar; this was removed undamaged in 1882 when it was deemed unsafe due to undermining by the sea of the rock it stood on. It was re-erected as a memorial to Smeaton on Plymouth Hoe. The present larger lighthouse was built by James Nicholas Douglass on an adjoining rock. Smeaton's lighthouse was also lit by candles – twenty-four, each weighing 6 lb – and it was not until 1858 that electric arc lamps were introduced for lighthouses, South Foreland being the first to be so lit in that year. The electricity for its lamps was supplied by a dynamo designed by Frederick Hale Holmes which was fitted with permanent magnets and driven by a non-condensing steam engine via a belt drive. Duboscq arc lamps were chosen. Progress with electric lighting for lighthouses was slow: and in 1880 there were still only five electrically lit lighthouses in Britain, and no more than ten in the whole world.

Many lighthouses were built from brick, whilst at Whitford Point in West Glamorgan, Wales, an unusual lighthouse was built in 1865 from large segmental cast-iron rings bolted together at their flanges. The Stevenson family, Robert (1772–1850) and sons Alan (1807–65), David (1815–86) and Thomas (1818–87) were all important builders of lighthouses and equipment. Robert introduced flashing lights, replacing the previously used fixed lights.

Hague, D.B. and Christie, Rosemary. *Lighthouses: Their Architecture, History and Archaeology*, Gomer Press, 1975
Mair, C. *A Star for Seamen: The Stevenson Family of Engineers*, Murray, 1978

lighting the provision or quality of illumination. Artificial lighting dates from ancient times. The earliest textile mills were lit by candles or oil lamps, which, besides only giving poor illumination, were a big fire hazard. When equipment for making gas from coal became available at the commencement of the 19th century, textile mills and other industrial concerns began installing their own private gas-making plant to light their premises resulting from William Murdock's experiments with gas lighting in 1792. One of the earliest mills to be lit by gas was that of Phillips and Lee of Salford, who installed some 900 gas lights in 1804 which allowed them to introduce night shift working, and make a saving on the cost of candles formerly used plus a reduction in fire insurance premiums.

At first, gas lights were naked flames from simple jet burners. It was discovered that if two jets impinged on each other, there was an increase in the emitted light. This resulted in the batswing and fishtail flat-flame burners of 1816–20, the latter invented by J.B. Neilson (1792–1865). A safer alternative to naked flames was the adaptation of the Argand oil lamp to gas. Originally invented by Aimé Argand, a Swiss chemist, this lamp burns with a circular flame inside a glass chimney with air introduced both inside and outside the ring of gas jets, giving improved combustion and a better light. From about 1820, the Argand became the main type of gas burner lamp in use. To eliminate corrosion of the jet holes in the simple burner, William Sugg used steatite (a heat treated kind of talc) at the jet orifices.

A great impetus to gas lighting occurred in 1885 when the Austrian chemist Karl Auer, Baron von Welsbach invented the incandescent gas mantle. This was a small hollow dome or pouch, called the mantle, made of cotton or a similar material, impregnated with a mixture of rare earths, mostly thorium with a small amount of cerium. Before use, the cotton supporting dome was burned away leaving the fused earths which glowed white hot in the gas flame. Hundreds of different highly decorative, gas lighting fixtures were made for domestic lighting, and the streets and factories of Victorian Britain were lit by gas for many years, until in 1870 electric lighting began to compete. Domestic and street gas lighting in existing installations continued in use, however, until after the First World War, when conversions took place and new installations put in electric lighting.

The possibility of using electricity for lighting purposes dates back to the beginning of the 19th century when Humphrey Davy noted in 1802 the exceedingly bright light emitted by an electric spark when a current was struck between the tips of two carbon electrodes. During the 1820s and 1830s, some experimental arc lights were exhibited in the USA, the current coming from batteries as in Davy's case. When direct current from generators became available, arc lamps began to be used in certain situations. Their first important application in England was for use in LIGHTHOUSES, South Foreland, near Dover, going into operation in December 1858. By 1867 arc lamps were on trial in selected London streets, and gas began to be seriously challenged for large lighting installations. Arc lights were never able to compete for domestic lighting because they were too large and cumbersome. Paul Jablochkoff (1847–1914), a Russian working in Paris, had some success with his arc lights, known as 'electric candles', and some were tried out in London in 1877.

The big breakthrough for electric lighting came with the invention of the incandescent filament contained in an evacuated glass bulb. Just as the Welsbach gas mantle relied on incandescence for its illuminating power, so did electric lighting, by raising a suitable high-resistance filament to white heat by the passage of an electric current. The discovery was made more or less simultaneously in the USA and England. Thomas Alva Edison (1847–1931) took out a British patent in 1879 (no. 4576), and Joseph Wilson Swann (1828–1914) of Newcastle was granted his patent two months later (patent no. 250, 1880) although he had demonstrated his invention in public during 1878. Both inventors started rival companies to manufacture electric lamps, and there was argument about priority of invention, but eventually they joined forces and the Edison and Swann United Electric Light Company was formed in 1881. The following year the first Electric Lighting Act was passed, and electric lighting rapidly spread. *See also* PUBLIC UTILITIES.

Chandler, D. *Outline History of Lighting by Gas*, 1936
Griffiths, J. *The Third Man: The Life and Times of William Murdock, Inventor of Gaslight*, André Deutsch, 1942
O'Dea, W.T. *The Social History of Lighting*, Routledge, 1958

light railway, *see* MINERAL LINE

lime a substance derived from limestone, a sedimentary rock mainly composed of insoluble calcium carbonate, and thus chemically similar to chalk. Limestone is fairly widespread across Britain, and since it has many important uses, has been quarried from early times. It is used as quarried as a FLUX for combining with impurities in the manufacture of iron and steel, producing a fluid SLAG which can easily be removed from the molten metal.

When strongly heated, limestone decomposes, giving off carbon dioxide, to leave a white powder known as quicklime (calcium oxide). This is done in a LIME KILN. Quicklime reacts with water (i.e. combines chemically with it) producing a large amount of heat, and results in a grey paste-like material (calcium hydroxide) known as slaked, or hydrated lime. Slaked lime is soluble in water allowing it to be used for many purposes. When mixed with sand and water it makes mortar, and this is probably its earliest use, certainly from Roman times. In Elizabethan times it began to be used agriculturally as an alkali to neutralize acidic soils. The lime was spread out on newly ploughed land to increase crop production. Other uses are in the tanning industry, candlemaking, glass manufacture, the manufacture of plaster, and for the bleaching of cloth. It was also used in the SOLVAY PROCESS for making soda ash. Other less important uses were to make a whitewash for painting onto cottage and barn walls where it had a disinfectant value, and as a method of illumination. The latter application involved playing a hot flame onto a ball of lime to produce a brilliant white light. This was discovered by Thomas Drummond (1797–1840) in 1825 and used for signalling and in theatres for stage work (the limelight). In the 16th and 17th centuries the residue from lime kilns was used to limeash the wooden floors of timber framed buildings where there were open fireplaces, as a fire resistant.

The use of lime in agriculture declined in the late 19th century because of a reduction in home production of corn as the quantity of imported corn increased following the repeal of the CORN LAWS.

lime blasting a primitive method used in mines and quarries to aid the extraction of rocks and minerals. A hole was bored in the rock and a quantity of quicklime packed tightly into it and plugged by a wooden plug which had a small central hole in it. When water was poured in through the hole in the plug, a rapid chemical reaction took place, with expansion and heat sufficient to fracture the surrounding rock which was then levered out with tools.

lime kiln a stone or brick structure for calcining broken limestone to make powdered LIME (quicklime). Powdered lime has important agricultural, construction and industrial uses, and has been made by burning broken pieces of limestone in kilns for centuries. Primitive kilns of the early 1700s, known as pie-, sod- or pot kilns, were little more than stone-lined shallow holes in the ground with a short, roughly built stone chimney to create some draught. They were sited in limestone areas, and when stone from the immediate area was used up, the kiln was abandoned and a fresh one built in a new spot. Limestone was broken up into small pieces, and fed into the kiln from the top, onto a charcoal fire. After burning for some time, the fire was allowed to go out, and powdered lime raked out through an opening left at the front of the kiln. Larger, more substantial and permanent kilns, several feet high, were later

developments. Built in stone, or sometimes in brick, they are usually circular in plan, although some are square, with an arched opening – the kiln 'eye' – at the front at ground level for feeding the fire and withdrawing the lime. Often a kiln would be built into a low hillside or slope to facilitate top loading of the limestone. Such kilns are known as draw kilns, and low quality coal or CULM was more commonly used as fuel instead of charcoal. Lime burning occupied several days, and some kilns were built in pairs so that one could be kept going while the other was being emptied to give continuity of production.

As stated, lime kilns are particularly numerous in, or very close to, limestone areas but some are sited a distance away, alongside canals, where stone and fuel could be cheaply brought to them and the lime taken away. Coastal sites are common in Devon and south Wales, where kilns were built on a beach or at the mouth of small river estuaries. Limestone and culm was brought to them in small coastal vessels, and the powdered lime taken back on the return journey. Some farmers built small kilns for their own, or local occasional use, while large kilns were built in rows for commercial production. By the early 20th century the use of lime kilns was declining, and bulk production using machinery for crushing the stone and burning it in HOFFMAN KILNS supplied modern needs.

Davies, P.B.S. *Dewisland Limekilns*, Merrivale, 1989
Searle, A.B. *Limestone and its Products*, 1935
Williams, R. *Lime Kilns and Limeburning*, Shire Publications, Album No. 236, 1990

lime pit, *see* PYE KILN

line **1.** the long fibres of flax, used to manufacture fine LINEN which takes its name from line. The short fibres of flax, called tow, can be used in a coarser variety of linen. **2.** in transport, a route, track or connected meaning. For example, it can mean the company operating a regular service between places, and is applied to railways, steamships, trams, etc. In railway parlance, a single track is referred to as a line, and there is an up line and a down line in a twin-track system. An up line usually refers to the track leading towards a London terminus or some other important city terminus, with the down line running in the opposite direction. There are also branch lines, loop lines, and so on. Line was used as a synonym for railway from the earliest days, as shown in George Stephenson's letter to his son Robert written on 23 February 1827 during the building of the Liverpool to Manchester Railway: 'The Bolton line which was clandistanly got from me when we were in parlament with the Liverpool bill has been given to me – a welsh line 9 miles long has been put in my hands, a line at Canterbury is in my hands likewise.' The very rails themselves are called train lines in everyday speech, and passenger ships sailing to a timetable are called liners.

linen a cloth or yarn made from FLAX, using the long vegetable fibres known as LINE. Linen yarn is stronger than wool and cotton, is less extensible, and virtually free from protruding 'hairs'. It is more expensive, and cloth made solely from linen is mainly used for table napery, shirtings, bedsheets, etc. LINT is usually made from linen cloth, whilst twines, cords, fishing nets and lines were made from linen threads.

Linen is probably the oldest textile made by man. It was used in ancient Egypt, and flax was the main vegetable fibre grown and used in Europe until the 18th century when imported cotton began to overtake it in quantity. The yarn was originally hand spun in Europe on the SAXONY WHEEL, also known as the flax wheel, but from the 1780s onwards Arkwright-type WATER FRAMES were adapted for the dry spinning of flax. John Kendrew and Thomas Forthouse of Darlington, Co. Durham, patented flax spinning machinery in 1787 (patent no. 1613), and Matthew Murray (1765–1826) invented similar machinery (patent no. 1971, 1793). Dry spinning machinery of those days was only suitable for producing coarse yarns, and in 1825 James Kay of Penny Bridge, near Ulverston, Lancs., patented a wet spinning process (no. 5226) which enabled finer yarns to be spun. Wet spinning originally meant soaking loosely twisted flax ROVINGS in cold water for five to six hours before spinning, which loosened the inherent gum binding the fibres together, allowing them to be drawn out further in the spinning process before the gum hardened again. The wet process originated in France c.1810. Later, the process was speeded up by drawing the roving through a bath of hot water attached to the spinning machine itself. The yarn could be DOUBLED if required to make a stronger, multi-yarn thread for twine, fishing line etc.

Linen yarn was used in the manufacture of FUSTIAN cloth from the 17th century onwards, where its superior strength was an advantage as warps over the weaker cotton which was used as weft. Later, stronger cotton yarn became available, enabling all-cotton cloth to be woven. Linen cloth straight from the loom has a natural brown colour, making bleaching necessary before dyeing. After bleaching and dyeing linen cloth was often BEETLED to close up the weave and put on a sheen. Beetling was later replaced by CALENDERING. In Ireland finished cloth was an important export, growing from 0.5 million yd in 1700 to 50 million yd in 1795.

Baines, Patricia. *Flax and Linen*, Shire Publications, Album No. 133, 1985
Rimmer, W.G. *Marshall's of Leeds: Flax Spinners 1788–1886*, Cambridge University Press, 1960

lineshafting overhead metal shafting transmitting rotational power to machinery. Before the gradual introduction of electricity to provide individual drives, power was distributed to machines by mechanical means. Overhead metal shafting ran above machines which were arranged in rows or lines, and power was transmitted by torsion along the shafting to turn pulleys spaced out above the machines. The final drive was by the tension in a flat, leather, endless belt connecting the lineshaft pulley to a similar pulley on each machine. Lineshafts were made from wrought iron at first, later from steel, and were built up from lengths of 20 to 30 ft each, joined by couplings. Support was by bearings hung from the roof or ceiling, or by bolting onto pads near the top of cast-iron building pillars. Normal speed of rotation for lineshafting was around 220 rpm. The driving pulleys were made in halves bolted together to facilitate addition to, and removal from, the lineshaft. The moving belts driving down onto the machines were often unguarded, and were a common cause of accident to workers. In a workshop or mill with many belt drives, a considerable amount of noise was created, a clear view around the area obscured, and also some light lost. Lineshafting ran continuously whilst the factory was working, and another big disadvantage was that all the lineshafting had to be run even though only one machine out of a number was needed. The lineshafting itself was driven from the PRIME MOVER, which in textile mills was either by a GEARED SYSTEM in early days, or later by rope or belt drives to a principal lineshaft on each floor. Other lineshafts on each floor would be driven off the principal by belts. In weaving sheds, lineshafts were often called countershafts. *See also* FAST AND LOOSE PULLEYS.

lingo(e) the long thin weight attached to the lowest end of each harness cord on a JACQUARD mechanism. Its function is to bring the warp thread which passes through the MAIL in the cord attached to the lingoe, down to its normal position by gravity pull, after it has been lifted by the hook to which the cord is attached. The word is said to be a variation of lingot, a mid-18th-century word for an ingot of metal.

linhay (or linney, linny) a lean-to extension to a building, usually open fronted. The origin of the word is obscure, but is possibly Cornish, and dates from the 18th century. China clay is stored in linhays in Cornwall.

linking up, *see* NOTCHING UP

link motion, *see* VALVE GEAR

linoleum a stiff material made from a paste of linseed oil, resins and cork, spread and pressed onto a backing cloth of jute or canvas. Introduced in the mid-19th century, linoleum rapidly became an important, cheap, domestic floor covering for which it is made in many colours and patterns. The word comes from the Latin *linum* (flax) and *oleum* (oil). It is popularly called lino.

linon, see LENO

linsey-woolsey (or linzie-wolzie) originally a textile fabric, woven from a woollen weft on a linen warp; later the name was applied to a coarse dress material woven from inferior wool on a cotton warp. The name may be a rhyming derivation from lin(t) (flax or linen) and wool, the original material from which it was made. Alternatively, the first part of the name of the cloth may derive from the village of Lindsey in the old woollen area of Suffolk.

lint 1. the loose fibres of GINNED raw cotton, which is compressed into bales for transport to a user. **2.** a soft linen fabric used for medical and surgical purposes after sterilization. It is made by scraping one side to raise a fine nap.

lint wheel a stone edge-runner wheel, often out in the open, which was used to SCUTCH flax stems, i.e. bruise and break open the previously RETTED stems so that the fibres (the LINE) could be extracted. The word is derived from line.

Linville truss a lattice-type bridge truss invented by Jacob H. Linville (1825–1906) in the USA. It comprises upper and lower horizontal STRINGERS joined together by vertical members at regular intervals. On the left-hand side of the centre of the truss, inclined members slope from bottom left up to top right between two adjacent verticals, and this arrangement is reversed on the right-hand side of centre, with a pair of crossed inclines at the centre itself (*see* Fig. 12). It is also known as an N-truss because the verticals and inclines form the letter N or N reversed.

list, *see* SELVEDGE

listed building a building, structure or monument of architectural, industrial, and historical importance which is legally protected against demolition or major alteration. Such buildings are covered by the Town and Country Planning (Listed Buildings and Buildings in Conservation Areas) Regulations 1990, and lists of these buildings are held by local authorities.

In England and Wales, there are three grades of building according to their individual importance or rarity. The lowest category is Grade II; Grade II* (Grade II star) covers the better examples of Grade II; and Grade I is reserved for the most important or rare examples. About 2.5 per cent of all listed buildings are Grade I, and about 5.5 per cent are Grade II star. A building has to be at least thirty years old (ten years in exceptional cases) before it can be listed. Corresponding categories in Scotland are Grades C (lowest), B, A (highest). Before a listed building or a fixture belonging to it can be altered, demolished, or removed, Listed Building Consent has to be obtained. If this is received, the Royal Commission on Historic Monuments has to be given thirty days' notice before work commences, to allow the Commission to visit the site to record it if it so wishes.

ENGLISH HERITAGE has been the statutory adviser to the Department of National Heritage and its predecessors on the listing of buildings and structures since 1984. English Heritage liaises with the MONUMENTS PROTECTION PROGRAMME, the Royal Commission on Historic Monuments and local authorities, and awards grants for conservation purposes. HISTORIC SCOTLAND has a similar duty for Scottish monuments and CADW for Wales.

Listed buildings include many industrial sites of historic importance which are or have been in receipt of grants. A listed building cannot be demolished until all possible adaptive re-use has been investigated, or a genuine and necessary redevelopment plan approved. Many former industrial buildings have been saved by skilful and sympathetic changes to other uses. An unlisted building which is considered to be of some interest, and is under threat or vulnerable, may none the less be given a temporary protection by being spot listed pending an investigation into its status. Groups of buildings may be protected by inclusion in a conservation area or a site of special scientific interest (SSSI).

Similar protection exists for scheduled monuments. The scheduling of ancient monuments, under Acts of various dates, first commenced in 1882. Scheduling mainly protects ancient monuments of national importance, ranging from prehistoric earthworks to historic buildings: in some cases a listed building can also be a scheduled monument. In 1994 there were some 14,400 scheduled monuments in England and Wales.

Lister comber a machine for combing out wool, mohair and alpaca, removing short fibres (noils) and any extraneous matter, and laying the long fibres more or less parallel to each other. It was used in preparing material for the worsted industry, and although only suitable for long fibred wools it could also be used for camel hair and cashmere. The machine is named after Samuel Cunliffe Lister (1815–1906) of Bradford, Yorks. – later Lord Masham – who invented it in collaboration with George Edmund Donisthorpe (1810–75). The Lister comber has a revolving circular comb like the NOBLE COMBER, and a swinging nip frame like the HEILMANN MACHINE, some interchange of ideas must have occurred during this period (1840s and 1850s) of intense activity by several Yorkshire inventors, and the influence of Donisthorpe, who was assisting both Noble and Lister around the same time is important.

Fig. 43 shows the main features of the Lister machine. Previously prepared wool is fed by rollers and pressed into the bed of upstanding pins of the gill box fallers A which are curved to fit the outer edge of the circular comb. As the fallers drop in turn to return to the front of the gill box, the jaws of a swinging nip frame B grasp the projecting fibres detaching a short length from the feed bulk, and pass it onto a carrying comb C. This in turn transfers the leading edges of the fibres onto the moving circular comb D, and they are pressed into the pins by the rapid up and down motion of a dabbing brush E. Thus, the fringe of trailing fibres hanging beyond the outer edge of the circular comb have been combed as they were drawn through the pins of the faller by the nip frame, whilst that part of the fibres held in the circular comb remain to be combed. The nip

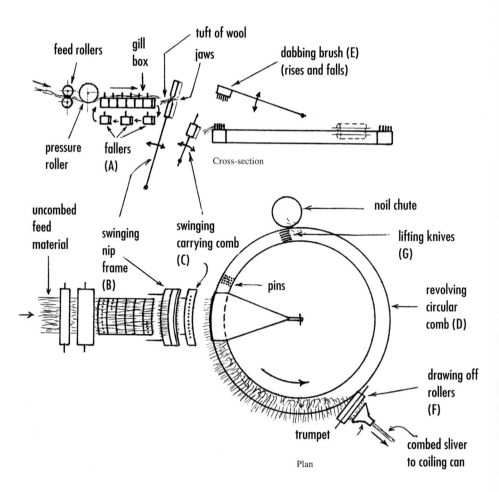

Fig. 43. The Lister comber

frame and carrying comb automatically return empty to their first positions so that the action can be repeated on the next length of fibres fed in by the gill box. The circular comb is thus continually fed with fresh partly combed material which is carried round until the drawing off rollers *F* are reached. These rollers grip the protruding fringe of material and draw the whole length off the pins, passing it in a continuous sliver into a can. Fibres too short to be drawn off remain in the comb until they are lifted out by knives *G* before the feeding in point is reached, and leave the machine as noils or waste.

The Lister comber was superseded by the more versatile Noble comber, which could handle all wools except those with extremely long or extremely short fibres. Lister took out many patents for fibre preparation, making a fortune from his inventions, and also built the large Manningham mill in Bradford in 1873. His silk combing machine of 1877 was popular in Britain for about a decade until that too was superseded. The Lister comber is also known as a nip machine from the gripping action on tufts of wool during combing.

Burnley, J. *The History of Wool and Wool Combing*, 1889; reprinted by Kelley, New York, 1969

'Little Germany' an area of old warehouses in Bradford, Yorks., near the railway station, which developed in the 1860s as a centre of woollen exports, particularly to Germany. Many German merchants and their agents settled in Bradford in this area, hence the nickname.

Roberts, J.S. *Little Germany*, 1977

'Little Giant' nickname given to Isambard Kingdom Brunel (1806–59) the eminent Victorian engineer, on account of his small stature, and the enormous contributions he made in the fields of transport and mechanical engineering.

Rolt, L.T.C. *Isambard Kingdom Brunel*, Penguin, 1970

'Little Ireland' notorious working-class slum area which arose on the banks of the river Medlock in Manchester in the first half of the 19th century. Occupied mostly by immigrant Irish mill workers, it comprised some 200 cottages housing about 4,000 inhabitants. Built of poor quality BACK-TO-BACK HOUSES in narrow twisting streets and courts, it was entirely surrounded by tall textile mills and its squalor was graphically described by Dr James Kay in his 1832 Report, *The Moral and Physical Conditions of the Working Class employed in the Cotton Manufacture of Manchester*. Friedrich Engels also referred to Little Ireland in 1844 in *The Condition of the Working Class in England*; but six years later the area was demolished by Manchester Corporation.

Clark, Sylvia and George, A.D. 'A note on "Little Ireland", Manchester', *Industrial Archaeology* XIV (1979)

'Little mester' a Yorkshire dialect description of a 19th-century self-employed cutler in the Sheffield area making cutlery by hand methods. 'Mester' was a dialect version of master.

llama a cloth made from the wool of the South American animal of the same name. Llama fabric is similar to ALPACA and was first woven in Yorkshire in the mid-19th century.

load 1. an old measure of weight used for various commodities, which varied considerably in different places. For example, in the 18th century a load of coal in Scotland was 3 cwt (336 lb), this being the maximum weight of coals in bags that a horse could comfortably carry over long distances; but in Lancashire a load of coal was 25 cwt (2,800 lb), whereas in Newcastle it was 20 cwt (2,240 lb). In Derbyshire a load of lead ore weighed about 585 lb, being equivalent to nine DISHES of ore; and a load of corn was 40 bushels (8 gallons), although this was a volumetric measure. These old weights were gradually replaced by units based on the imperial system. **2.** a measure of power used for atmospheric engines on mine pumping work. The engine load was defined as the weight of water on the pump piston (in pounds) divided by the area of the engine piston in square inches. This virtually equalled the steam pressure in the cylinder when steam was later introduced, ignoring losses due to friction, weight of pump rods, etc.

loading slot a line of openings or doorways in the outer walls of a warehouse arranged in a vertical line, one above the other, and opening onto each floor. Loading of goods into and out of the warehouse from the ground, canal, or railway siding was facilitated by this configuration. A projecting CRANE was sited above the highest opening. The openings are also known as loop holes, from the name of the defensive arrow slits in old fortifications.

location of industrial archaeology sites, *see* GRID REFERENCE

lock a construction to permit boats to change water levels on a CANAL. There are two types of lock: FLASH LOCKS, formerly used on rivers and comprising a single removable barrier, and canal pound locks which have two openable barriers. The latter are described below. The origin of pound locks is obscure: they may have been used in China in the first century AD, and were certainly in use on the Continent in medieval times. The first pound lock in Britain dates to 1564 or 1567 when one was made on the pioneering Exeter Canal. The word may come from the Anglo-Saxon *loc*, meaning an enclosure.

A typical canal pound lock comprises a stone-built, watertight boat chamber, sited at a point where a canal needs to change levels. The chamber is capable of holding a canal boat (some locks hold two boats side-by-side) and has a pair of vertically hinged heavy wooden gates at each end. The gates, when closed, form a V at the centre pointing towards the higher water level, so that water pressure forces them shut. Alternatively, some narrow locks have only one gate at each end which closes up against a ledge built in the stone lock wall to resist the pressure. Water can flow into or out of the boat chamber from a higher level, either through small openings near the bottom of the gates, or through passageways low down in the walls of the boat chamber. These openings are controlled by sliding paddles worked from above. When the water level is equal either side of the gates, they can be opened by pushing against a long arm set at waist height, called a balance arm. A variation to hinged gates is vertically rising guillotine gates. Paddles are not necessary in these gates, since they can be lifted only a short distance while water levels equalize, before being completely raised to allow a boat to pass.

A lock is operated as follows. A boat passing from high level to low, i.e. down the lock, has to ensure first that the boat chamber is full of water before entering, using the paddles if necessary. The top, or head gates and paddles, are closed when the boat is in the chamber, and the paddles in the lower or tail gates (or the side passages) are opened. The water in the boat chamber flows out to the lower level, the boat floating down with it. When the water levels either side of the tail gate are equal, the gates are opened, and the boat passes through, the head gates holding up the water at the higher level. The reverse procedure is followed for a boat passing up the lock.

The vertical distance between water levels either side of a lock is limited to around 16 ft, otherwise the lock gates become very tall and too heavy to move manually. If a height difference greater than this is to be overcome, several locks in sequence are necessary, with short POUNDS in between. This arrangement is called a FLIGHT OF LOCKS. If the ground gradient is steep, intermediate pounds are dispensed with, and each lock leads directly into the next, the tail gates of one lock form the head gates of the next lower lock. This configuration is called a STAIRCASE.

Many thousands of gallons of water pass down a lock each time it is used. Some canals which have water supply difficulties conserve some of the water by having side pounds; while the technique of allowing one boat up immediately followed by one boat down also conserves water. On some canals where water is constantly being added the locks have bypass channels to prevent pounds from overflowing.

locomobile steam engine a name sometimes used in Victorian days to describe a semi-portable, self-contained small steam engine and boiler unit. The steam engine was mounted on top of a horizontal boiler and drove the water feed pump and a power take-off pulley. Such units were intended for use on farms, in small factories and for export to overseas colonies where they were used on tea plantations, etc. Of robust, simple design, with an easily cleaned boiler capable of dealing with poor quality water and an enclosed, tamper-proof GOVERNOR, they were ideal for use where there was no or little technical knowledge or assistance available, and reliability was essential. Some units were mounted on wheels so that they could be hauled from place to place. The name locomobile was also given to early steam-driven passenger cars.

locomotive a steam engine on wheels which moves along a railway track under its own power. The word locomotive comes from the Latin *locus* meaning place and *motivus* meaning motion. Today the word locomotive refers to an engine which hauls freight and passenger coaches along a railway track, but in the 18th century it meant anything capable of self motion, and was applied to road using vehicles (*see* STEAM CARRIAGE). The world's first locomotive to run on rails was that by Richard Trevithick (1771–1833) which ran along a cast-iron tramway in 1804 at Pen-y-Darren, Wales. In 1812 a locomotive by John Blenkinsop (1783–1831) and Matthew Murray (1765–1826) hauled coal along a rack railway at Middleton colliery, Leeds, and shortly afterwards George Stephenson (1781–1848) built his first locomotive, the *Blucher*, for use at Killingworth colliery, Northumberland. His improved *Locomotion* ran on the Stockton and Darlington Railway in 1824. The most famous pioneering steam locomotive is Robert Stephenson's (1803–59) *Rocket*, virtually a BEAM ENGINE on wheels, which won the RAINHILL TRIAL in 1829 and later ran on the world's first true passenger railway, the Liverpool to Manchester.

Early locomotives met much opposition from landed gentry, across whose land railways were laid under Acts of Parliament, and from canal and turnpike operators, who resented competition from the 'iron horse' or 'vapour engine'. The advantages of steam traction over horse and barge were soon recognized, however, and the railway system rapidly spread.

The essential components of a locomotive are a steam boiler and firegrate; a non-condensing steam engine; mechanical arrangements to convert the reciprocating motion of pistons into rotary motion at the driving wheels; means of controlling speed and direction of travel; and a framework to carry everything. Additionally, sufficient fuel and water has to be pulled in a tender to give a realistic range of operation, and all this has to fit the GAUGE of the rails. Most pioneering locomotives ran on four wheels only, but by c.1834 extra wheels became necessary as locomotives got heavier to distribute the weight better on the rails. Wheel arrangement is used today to classify locomotives: in Britain, the notation invented by the American Frederick M. Whyte (1865–1941) is used. It consists of three digits indicating the number of wheels: first on the leading axle(s), if any; then the number of driving wheels; and finally the trailing wheels, if any. Thus, a 2-4-0 locomotive has one leading axle (two wheels), four driving wheels (two axles), and no trailing wheels.

At first, steam cylinders were attached to, or immersed vertically in, the boiler. Later, they were inclined at an angle, and finally arranged horizontally. A much better arrangement was the bar frame introduced by Edward Bury (1794–1858) in 1830, with the cylinders attached to it, relieving the boiler of strain. There are two alternative locations for cylinders: inside, between the frames, driving onto cranked axles, and outside the frames, driving directly onto cranks outside the wheels. Several mechanisms were invented for reversing direction and altering the CUT-OFF of steam to give expansive working (see VALVE GEAR).

By about 1850, the basic design of steam locomotives had been firmly established, and an estimated 2,500 locomotives were in use in Britain. During the years 1853–60 much attention was paid to changing the fuel from coke to coal, which resulted in the coal-burning firebox invented by Joseph Hamilton Beatie (1804–71). Most improvements after this were aimed at increasing the power and speed of locomotives, as better materials and improved mechanical engineering tools became available. The main developments of the locomotive are shown below.

Main developments in railway steam locomotives

1804	Trevithick's locomotive at Pen-y-Daren, Wales; world's first true railway locomotive.
1811–12	Blenkinsop's rack rail locomotive, Middleton, Leeds.
1813	Locomotive BOGIE patented by Chapman.
1814	Stephenson's *Blucher*, Killingworth, Northumb., with inside cylinders driving cranked axles.
1824	Stephenson's *Locomotion*, Stockton and Darlington Railway; four coupled wheels, weight 6.5 tons, 50 psi steam pressure.
1827	Hackworth's *Royal George*; six coupled wheels.
1828	Leaf springs introduced.
1829	Stephenson's *Rocket*, Rainhill Trial, Lancs.; weight 4.5 tons, 50 psi steam pressure. Ran on first true passenger railway, Liverpool to Manchester.
1830	Bar frames introduced by Bury.
1831	Outside cylinders attached to frame and not to boiler.
c.1834	Bogies common on locomotives.
1839	Locomotives now weighing 17 tons.
1843	STEPHENSON'S and GOOCH'S LINK MOTIONS.
1845	Locomotives now weighing 22 tons, 100 psi steam pressure.
c.1850	Compounding and steam brakes introduced.
1852	Locomotives now weighing 25 tons.
c.1853	Fuel being changed from coke to coal; improved combustion of coal.
1856	Ramsbottom's 'Duplex' safety valve; steam pressures now 130 psi.
1862	Steel boilers replacing wrought iron.
1863	Locomotives now weighing 35 tons, steam pressures 160 psi.
1886	Steel plate frames instead of wrought iron; locomotives now weighing 42 tons.

Ahrons, E.L. *The British Steam Locomotive, 1825–1925*, Locomotive Publishing Co., 1927
Casserley, H.C. *British Steam Locomotives*, Penguin/Bloomsbury, 1988

Nock, O.S. *British Steam Locomotives*, Handford, 1964
Stretton, C. *The Development of the Locomotive, 1803–1896*, 1896; reprinted by Bracken Books, 1989
Westcott, G.F. *The British Railway Locomotive, 1803–1853*, HMSO, 1958

Locomotive and Highways Act 1865 popularly known as the 'Red Flag' Act, the Act restricted the speed of self-propelled road vehicles to 4 mph, and required a crew of two to drive a vehicle with a man walking 20 yd ahead carrying a red flag to warn other road users of its approach. The Act was introduced as a result of pressure on Parliament by carriage and coach interests, the horse trade, and turnpike trusts (who feared damage to their road surfaces). The Act severely hindered the development of self-propelled road vehicles, which at that time were steam-powered (*see* STEAM CARRIAGE). The 1865 Act was replaced by the Highways and Locomotive Amendment Act of 1878, which was repealed on 14 November 1896; its removal is celebrated each anniversary by the London-to-Brighton Veteran Car Run. By 1896 the petrol INTERNAL COMBUSTION ENGINE had been invented and applied to cars, although it is estimated that there were only about seventy-five cars registered in Britain in that year.

Lord Montagu of Beaulieu, *The Brighton Run*, Shire Publications, 1990

lode 1. a mineral deposit, usually inclined to the vertical plane, in the form of a vein containing metal ores such as lead, copper, etc. The lode lies in a fault or fissure in the surrounding rock. The word is a variation of 'load', meaning the loading of the vein with valuable material. If the lode contains gold it is usually called a reef. Lodestuff comprises the metallic ore and GANGUE. A lode is generally a vertically inclined sheet-like intrusion which makes a line on the surface, or just below it, running across country sometimes for several miles. It is the result of faulting in the rock millions of years ago which allowed hot, mineral-bearing solutions to rise from great depths and solidify, filling the 'crack'.

A lode can contain more than one mineral in its composition. Sometimes several kinds of ores may be found in the same vein, but usually one ore predominates sufficiently to give its name to the lode. Lodes vary considerably in width and can measure from tens of feet down to only a few inches depending partly on the hardness of the surrounding rock: hard rocks usually have narrow lodes, and soft rocks wide lodes. A lode may not contain metallic ores everywhere along its length, and may be richer in some parts than others.

The angle of inclination of a lode from the vertical, the HADE, is usually uniform except where a change in the surrounding rock occurs when it can alter or even slope in the opposite direction. The side faces are known as cheeks or walls, with the upper face known as the hanging cheek and the lower the lying cheek. Sometimes the rock strata either side of a lode are displaced in relation to each other: a vertical displacement is called a throw, and a horizontal displacement a heave. Such discontinuities can vary from a few inches to several hundreds of feet, a downthrow being usually found below the lying cheek.

2. a dyke or embankment.

lodge a northern name for the water reservoir at a textile mill which is part of the steam raising plant and is used for recirculating condenser cooling water. Cooling water from the engine condenser is pumped into the lodge to cool off before it is used again. Ideally, a lodge is made large enough to hold enough water to supply the condenser for a day, and it therefore occupies quite a large part of the factory site. In some cases the cooling water entering the lodge is arranged to cascade down a number of steps like a waterfall, so that a larger surface area of water is presented to the air to increase the loss of heat and speed the cooling.

lofty yarn in the woollen trade, a yarn which is soft, bulky and springy; a LEAN YARN is stronger and more taut. Mules spun a more lofty yarn than ring spinners.

log mill a 17th- to 18th-century mill for grinding up LOGWOOD to make a dyestuff. A log mill housed machinery for chopping up, or rasping, imported logwood into small chips, and then grinding the chips into a powder under an EDGE MILL. Usually log mills were water powered, and are marked on old OS maps as logwood mill, or occasionally as Brazil mill.

logwood a natural dyeing material made from trees of the *leguminosae* variety, such as *Haematoxylon campechianum* found in the West Indies and Central America. First discovered in Honduras in 1662 by English colonists, it was imported into Britain as de-barked logs about 3 ft long, hence its name. The logs were ground into a powder in a LOG MILL, and used to make an inexpensive black dye for the textile industry, using GALL NUTS or ALUM as fixatives. Logwood was also known as blackwood, bluewood and compeachy. It superseded oak galls, sumac and iron salts which were formerly used for making black. Logwood is the only natural dyestuff used in any quantity today.

London Lead Company an early mining concern, sometimes known as the Quaker Company, incorporated in 1692, which worked lead mines in various parts of Britain: the company began mining in Derbyshire in 1721. It was responsible for introducing many advances in mining and smelting, such as REVERBERATORY FURNACES in Derbyshire in 1735, and built mining villages such as Nent Head in Cumberland. The company was wound up in 1905.

Raistrick, A. 'The London Lead Company, 1692–1905', *Newcomen Society Transactions* XIV (1933–4), 119–62

London time, *see* RAILWAY TIME

long ells a type of wool worsted serge woven in the West Country in the 18th century, exported in large quantities to China by the East India Company.

longlight window, *see* WEAVERS' WINDOWS

longwall a mining technique for extracting coal, also known as Shropshire working since it is said that the method originated there in the 17th century. The technique involves the removal of a long 'wall' of coal, a 100 yd or so long, and building up roof supporting walls from stone etc. at right angles to the coal face with access passageways between them or erecting a line of wooden props. After the extracted coal has been removed, a fresh 'wall' is cut out, and the supporting walls or props advanced correspondingly. This method allows all the coal to be extracted and replaced with supporting stone or props, as opposed to the PILLAR AND STALL method which leaves some coal behind. Longwall working is particularly suitable for mechanical coal cutting. Its disadvantage is that it can produce subsidence at the surface.

loom a machine for weaving cloth. A traditional loom comprises a framework with a horizontal back roller, the warp beam or warp roller, around which closely spaced WARP threads have been wound parallel to each other, stretched horizontally onto a front take-up roller, and fastened to it. From the warp roller, the threads pass over and under a pair of LEASE RODS, through the 'eyes' of the HEALDS, between the spaces in the REED, and onto the take-up roller. Usually there are several healds, which can be raised and lowered according to the type of cloth being woven. The reed is pivoted from below, and swings up against the last woven WEFT thread to consolidate it with the rest of the cloth, an action called BEATING UP. To weave cloth, a heald is raised which lifts those warp threads associated with it, the rest lying flat, to form a 'tunnel' or shed across the width of the loom. A shuttle, holding a small package of weft thread called a PIRN, passes across the loom through the shed, trailing a thread behind it. The reed then beats up this thread, the heald is lowered, and another is raised with different warp threads to form another shed. The shuttle returns to its original side, laying another weft thread across the loom. Cloth is woven by repeating these actions over and over again, the warp gradually unwinding from the warp beam onto the take-up roller. The shuttle has to be replenished with full pirns from time to time.

Primitive hand looms were of a vertical design, the warp threads hanging down in a simple wooden frame, and the weft threaded through from side to side. By about the 13th century primitive horizontal looms were in use. Weaving was a domestic industry at the beginning of the Industrial Revolution, with the shuttle passed across the loom by hand, and the healds operated by foot treadles. The maximum width that could be woven was determined by the reach of a man's arms; broader cloth needed two men passing the shuttle across the wide loom to each other. After the invention of the FLYING SHUTTLE in 1733, one man alone could weave BROADCLOTH, and at a faster rate. Patterned cloth needed a more complicated loom capable of making different shedding combinations, and at first this was done on a DRAW LOOM which required a man and a boy to operate it by hand; but by the 18th century, patterned cloth was being woven automatically on JACQUARD looms. Another automatic device for controlled shedding was the DOBBY. *See also* AUTOMATIC LOOM.

The Revd Edmund Cartwright (1743–1823) patented a power loom in 1785 (patent no. 1470), but it needed several redesigns before it was really workable; Richard Roberts (1789–1864) patented his power loom in 1822 (patent no. 4726). By the 1840s the LANCASHIRE LOOM appeared on the scene, and reigned supreme as the principal weaving machine for many years, with thousands being made. It was a semi-automatic loom with automatic BROKEN WEFT devices and other refinements, but had to be stopped to replace empty pirns in the shuttle every few minutes. This restriction was overcome in 1895 by the invention by James H. Northrup of the transfer system which enabled pirns to be changed without stopping the machine (*see* NORTHRUP LOOM).

Looms are almost invariably placed on ground floors in weaving sheds because of their weight and vibration. Good light is essential so that defects in the cloth may be easily detected as it is being woven; natural overhead light from a NORTH LIGHT ROOF is best.

An old spelling of loom is lumb.

Benson, Anna and Warburton, N. *Looms and Weaving*, Shire Publications, Album No. 154, 1986

Broudy, E. *The Book of Looms*, Studio Vista, 1979

Marsden, R. *Cotton Weaving*, Bell, 1895

loomer the person who fastened the ends of a warp assembly when it had almost run out on a loom to the ends of the new warp assembly which was to follow on, weaving the same pattern of cloth. This operation was originally done by hand on the loom, but in later times was done away from the loom by DRAWERS AND REACHERS. Sometimes a loomer was called a twister, because the ends of the warp threads were twisted together rather than tied.

loomshop the room housing the looms in a domestic handloom weaver's cottage. In general, wool loomshops were above the living quarters, whereas cotton loomshops were often below in a cellar, since the floor was usually kept damp to aid the weaving of cotton. In some houses, the loomshop was an area divided from the living quarters, holding a loom or two. Access to top storey loomshops was sometimes via a high-level door, often sited in the gable end of the building and sometimes with an external stairway, so that materials and WEAVERS' BEAMS could be taken into and out of the loomshop without passing through the living quarters. In terraced rows of weavers' cottages, a top loomshop often ran the full length of the terrace over the individual habitations; access was via the external stairs for the weavers, who might not all necessarily live in the terrace. *See also* TAKING-IN DOOR.

Morgan, N. *Vanished Dwellings*, Mullion Books, 1991 (a study of industrial housing in Preston, Lancs., with particular reference to cellar loomshops)

loop a rope sling used in 17th- and 18th-century coal and metal mines for raising loaded basket-type corves (*see* CORF) up the shaft.

loop hole the opening in the wall of a warehouse through which goods could be loaded into and out of the building, via an overhead crane; named after the defensive archer slots in old fortresses.

loose eccentric valve gear the method by which many early locomotives were reversed. First devised by George Stephenson (1781–1848) and Nicholas Wood (1795–1865) in 1816, the mechanism comprised an ECCENTRIC operating each of the two SLIDE VALVES, not fixed to the axle of the driving wheels, but free to slide a short distance along it either side of a central position. On each side of each eccentric a collar was keyed onto the driving axle, and a stud projected from the collar towards the eccentric: when the loose eccentric was slid up to a collar, the stud engaged it, and when the axle turned, it could drive the eccentric round also. The studs were so positioned that moving the eccentric up to one collar resulted in forward motion of the locomotive via the valve gear, whilst moving the eccentric in the opposite direction up to the other collar produced reverse motion. When the eccentric was halfway between the two collars, neither stud was engaged and the valve gear was inoperative. To reverse the direction of the locomotive, it was first brought to a standstill, and the eccentrics were disengaged from the driving studs by the driver depressing a foot treadle on the footplate, which moved them into the neutral position. A handle enabled him to lift up the ends of the eccentric rods, disconnecting them from the valve rods, and he could then manually move the valves backwards and forwards by levers to start the locomotive moving in the opposite direction. When it was moving slowly he lowered the eccentric rods into position and re-engaged the eccentrics by sliding them across to engage with the studs on the opposite collars by using the foot treadle again. The driving axle, now turning, continued to turn the eccentrics which automatically carried on operating the valves. The handles of the eccentric rods moved on the footplate all the time the locomotive was in motion.

Loose eccentric valve gear was not entirely satisfactory, and by about 1835 other designs of reversing gear were introduced using fixed eccentrics.

loriner (or lorimer, lorimar) a maker of horse mouth bits, spurs, and metal parts of harnesses. This was a specialized metal hand craft in the days when the horse was the only means of transport or source of power. Large numbers of loriners worked in small workshops near iron producing areas, particularly in and around Walsall, Staffs. Lorinery was also closely connected with the making of leather harness and saddles, of which Walsall became the centre, and both industries flourished until the horse was ousted in the early years of the 20th century with the coming of motor vehicles. There is a Loriner Livery Company still in existence today.

lot the duty paid by Derbyshire lead miners to a mine owner or owner of the mineral rights, usually one-thirteenth of the dressed ore, although this amount varied from time to time.

lough, *see* VUG

loupe, *see* BLOOM

lowder frame the massive framework supporting horizontal millstones at a level above the stone floor in an underdriven corn mill. The great spur wheel and stone nuts lie under the stones within the lowder frame.

lower orders, *see* WORKING CLASS

lubricants substances for reducing friction. Many materials and fluids have been used to make rubbing surfaces slippery and reduce friction in machinery. Vegetable oils and animal fats were used first, and by the 19th century mineral oils became dominant. James Watt (1736–1819) recommended olive oil as a lubricant in his steam engines. Castor, rape and sperm oils were also used, and greases were made from mineral oil, soda or lime soap. Animal fats were applied to bearings in devices known as 'suet' lubricators, and soaps and fats were used initially on early railways. Liquid oils were introduced later as bearing sealing designs improved. Individual lubricators to each bearing or sliding surface were normal, but towards the end of the 19th century forced lubrication, or oil pumped from a central point or reservoir through small diameter pipes to the points requiring lubrication, was introduced. Many patented devices were used for dispensing lubricants, and it was not until Beauchamp Tower investigated the theory of lubrication in 1883–5 that scientific principles were applied. Osborne Reynolds (1842–1912) developed further understanding of lubrication in 1886.

Adams, W.B. 'On railway axle lubrication', *Proceedings of the Institution of Mechanical Engineers* 7 (1853), 57–65
McDowell, D.M. and Jackson, J.D. *Osborne Reynolds and Engineering Science Today*, Manchester University Press, 1970
Reynolds, O. 'On the theory of lubrication and its application to Mr Beauchamp Tower's experimental determination of the viscosity of olive oil', *Phil. Trans. R. Soc.* No. 177 (1886), 157–234

lucam (or lewcome, luccam, lucomb) a projecting roofed gable built out over an external sack hoist on a water- or windmill. Its purpose was to enable the hoist to lift or lower sacks clear of the wall of the mill from the ground level, and also to protect the hoist from the weather. The word comes from the old French *lucarne*, meaning a dormer window. *See also* CAT HEAD.

Luddites textile workers opposed to the introduction of machinery who organized machine-breaking in the period 1811–16. There was very little violence directed towards people. The rioting started at Arnold on the outskirts of Nottingham, where sixty-three stocking frames were smashed on 11 March 1811. The agitation spread to Yorkshire, Lancashire, Derbyshire, and Leicestershire, the various gangs of machine breakers calling themselves Luddites after an imaginary or legendary leader called Ned Ludd of Leicestershire.

In 1812, Enoch and James Taylor of Marsden, Yorks., made cropping frames for the mechanical trimming of the nap on cloth, which had formerly been done by hand. Resentful hand workers formed a secret society on the lines of the first Luddites and destroyed many such machines around Colne, Lancs. Severe repressive measures by the government resulted in a mass trial of offenders in York in 1813; many of them were hanged and others transported. Trouble flared up again in 1816, brought about by the depressed conditions in the country following the conclusion of the Napoleonic wars, but by the following year repressive measures, and the restoration of more prosperous times, saw an end to the discontent. By 1817, it is estimated that 1,000 stocking frames and eighty lace machines had been destroyed in the Nottingham and Leicester area, and large numbers of other textile machines in Lancashire and Yorkshire. Only those machines belonging to employers who were paying starvation wages were broken in general.

Thomas, M.I. *The Luddites: Machine-Breaking in Regency England*, David and Charles, 1970

Lunar Society a society formed in 1766 by a group of engineers, industrialists, and scientists living in and around Birmingham, for pursuing their mutual interests in an informal manner. They met every month in members' houses on nights of the full moon, so that they could find their way home easily and safely. Among the members were James Watt (1736–1819), Matthew Boulton (1728–1809), Josiah Wedgwood (1730–95), Joseph Priestley (1733–1804) and Erasmus Darwin (1731–1802). The Society continued in existence until about 1802, with its period of greatest activity between 1775 and 1791.

Schofield, R.E. *The Lunar Society of Birmingham*, 1963

lunette a flue connecting the side arches in a glass melting furnace to the central hearth in a GLASS CONE. The word comes from the Latin *luna* meaning moon, and refers to the arched shape of the crescent moon.

lustring (or lutestring) a glossy, plain weave silk fabric, used for dress materials or ribbons. In the 17th century, this material was imported from Italy or France before manufacture began in Britain, probably in the 18th century. It was still used for ladies' gowns in the late Victorian era, and for lining curtains.

lye (or bowk, buck, ley) water made alkaline by the addition of plant ashes, and used in the old cloth bleaching process. Wood ash from ferns and kelp was a natural source of alkali. Cloth was boiled in lye in kiers to remove waxes etc. and then 'soured' in buttermilk. In the 19th century lye was replaced by chemical bleaching agents.

M

machine tools machines designed to remove surplus material from a work piece by accurately guided cutting tools. The principal functions machine tools perform are: planing, milling, or grinding to produce flat surfaces; turning or facing of circular or cylindrical items; drilling, boring, or slotting to make holes; making screw profiles and spirals; sawing; cutting of gear teeth, cam profiles, etc. by specialist machines; and automatic manufacture of small items such as nuts and bolts, with specialist machines. Since there is no universal machine capable of performing every function, machines have been designed over the years to perform a particular operation or group of operations.

The first machine tools relied heavily on the skill of the operator, since they lacked precision. Continual improvements resulted in greater machine accuracy and faster machining times, needing less and less contribution from the operator. At the same time, improved tool steels were developed as metallurgical discoveries were made, and drills, etc. were designed more scientifically. In the 18th century chilled cast iron and carburized iron were the only hard materials available for cutting tools, but by the end of the 19th century high speed steel and alloys gave faster cutting rates. *See also* BORING MACHINE; DRILLING MACHINE; ENGINEERING INDUSTRY; GEAR CUTTING MACHINE; GRINDING MACHINE; LATHE; MILLING MACHINE; PLANING MACHINE; SHAPING MACHINE; SLOTTING MACHINE; WOODWORKING MACHINERY.

Gilbert, K.R. *The Machine Tool Collection*, Science Museum, 1966
Kilburn, T. *Joseph Whitworth, Toolmaker*, Scarthin Books, 1987
Rolt, L.T.C. *Tools for the Job*, HMSO, 1987
Steeds, W. *A History of Machine Tools, 1700–1910*, Clarendon, 1962

madder a vegetable dye obtained from the root of the plant *Rubia tinctorium*, which was used in the early textile finishing industry for producing red and violet dyes. Alizarin is the colouring matter in madder. Madder was imported from Holland, France, Spain, and Italy, and also from India and the near East: in 1868, Britain imported some 23,000 tons of European madder. Some was also cultivated in England. The dye was prepared by crushing the roots and boiling them with ALUM in water in a madder mill. By the 1880s madder growing declined as synthetic dyes became available.

mail, *see* LEISH

mail coach horse-drawn coach used to carry mail, first introduced on 2 August 1784 by John Palmer (1742–1818), a theatre manager at Bath, between Bristol and London. This more than halved the time taken by the old method used by the Post Office of carrying the mail by post-boy on horseback. Other routes soon followed, and in 1786 a specially designed mail coach was patented by John Besant, a London coachmaker (patent no. 1574); with his partner John Vidler, Besant supplied them under contract to the Post Office until 1836. Mail coach services all over the country were developed by Thomas Hasker, and were well established by the commencement of the 19th century. Mail coaches used the best horses, had precedence over other road users and paid no tolls on turnpikes. Initially, they only carried letters – parcels had to be sent by stage coach or a carrier company – but after 1883 parcels were also carried. Passengers were also carried on mail coaches, and an armed guard was in charge. The routes followed by mail coaches became known as post roads.

With the coming of railways, the carrying of mail was gradually transferred onto trains as the rail system extended over the country. The Grand Junction Railway was the first to carry mail in 1837, using special mail coaches which also carried four inside passengers.

Clear, C.R. *John Palmer*, 1935
Copeland, John. *Roads and their Traffic, 1750–1850*, David and Charles, 1968
Vale, E. *The Mail Coach Men of the Late Eighteenth Century*, 1900

malleable iron an alternative name for wrought iron which reflects wrought iron's ability to be shaped and bent, unlike cast iron which is brittle and cannot be so worked.

malt house a large building in which barley is turned into malt for the BREWING and distilling industries. Barley is soaked in water, spread out on the floors of open rooms and allowed to commence germination under controlled temperature and humidity. The grains are regularly turned and raked to ensure uniform germination, and when tiny roots and shoots appear, they are dried in a kiln which prevents further growth. The substance is now called malt, or malted barley, and is used in the brewing of beer or the distillation of malt WHISKY. Malting may be carried out by a brewery or distillery, or by a specialist firm providing a service to these industries; before bout 1800, malting was often carried out by armers. It used coke and anthracite as fuel, 'hich did not contaminate the malt with an npleasant taste; peat is used for firing malt vhisky to add flavour to it.

Malt houses are recognized by their rows of mall windows on one or more low floors, and leir kilns with pyramid roofs and capped ents. Their internal construction is similar to lat of a textile mill, the floors supported on ows of cast-iron columns.

1alt mill a machine used in a brewery for onverting malt into GRIST. It comprises a pair f rollers between which the malt grains are roken into husks and cracked kernels before le grist is passed to the MASH TUN

Manchester Act 1736 Act which prohibited le manufacture of all-cotton cloth in Britain, esigned to protect the woollen industry against ompetition from the new, cheap, all-cotton naterials that were beginning to be imported rom India at that time. FUSTIAN (linen warp nd cotton weft) was permitted to be made, ubject to a tax of 3*d* per yard. The Act was epealed in 1774, largely through the efforts of ichard Arkwright (1732–92).

1anchester cottons, *see* KENNET

1anchester massacre, *see* PETERLOO

1anchester School name bestowed upon the NTI-CORN LAW LEAGUE by Benjamin Disraeli round 1840, because the leading personalities /ere from the Manchester Chamber of 'ommerce.

1an engine a device introduced in 1841 in 'ornish tin mines for bringing miners to the urface from the bottom of the shaft, liminating the exhausting climb of several undreds of feet up ladders at the end of a shift nderground. It comprised two vertical rods ide by side which extended down the mine haft, with small platforms attached to each rod t regular intervals. The rods were made to love up and down alternately, and a man tanding on a platform on one rod could step nto a platform on the adjacent rod, and was aised 12 ft at each stroke. In this manner, liners were soon brought to the surface one by ne.

The idea was the winning entry for a prize ffered by the Royal Cornwall Polytechnic ociety for the best machine for bringing liners to the surface, and was won by Michael ,oam. Originally powered by a waterwheel, the lan engine, as it came to be called, was onverted to steam power in 1843. The engine rove two large rack and pinion mechanisms /hich moved the rods up and down, and was irst installed in 1842 at the Tresavean mine. By 1862 only eight had been installed throughout Cornwall, mainly because many mineshafts were not vertical or did not reach the bottom in one drop. By the end of the 1800s several mines had installed cages on ropes both to bring men up to the surface and to take them down. However, a man engine continued in use at the Levant mine until 29 October 1919, when it collapsed, killing thirty-one men who were travelling on it at the time. The device was soon abandoned after this accident.

Manhattan engine a twin cylinder compound steam engine introduced in the 1870s which combined a horizontal and vertical configuration in the same machine (*see* Fig. 44). A horizontal engine and vertical engine on the same framework both drove onto the same crankpin: some makers placed the high pressure cylinder vertically with the low pressure cylinder horizontally, while others reversed this layout. A small number of such engines were built, and they were mainly used in power stations for electricity generation; the name comes from a power station in New York which used such engines.

manifold yarn a yarn made from more than one thread twisted together to produce a stronger yarn. This is done on a DOUBLING FRAME.

manure originally, the name given to any substance used to fertilize or sweeten agricultural land. References are found to the carrying of manure by canal boat, and this would have included materials such as lime, peat, peat-ashes, sea sand, and seaweed, which helped to improve agriculture. Such materials had earlier been carried by packhorse, but the coming of canals greatly cheapened the cost to farmers and enabled larger quantities to be delivered. It was only in more modern times that the word came to refer to dung.

maps diagrammatic representations of particular areas, showing positions of natural and artificial features. The larger scale maps of Britain are of interest to industrial archaeologists, particularly those dating just before, during, and after the INDUSTRIAL REVOLUTION, because they show the development of transport systems – turnpikes, canals, and railways – and the siting of mills, mines, factories, quarries, etc.

Early maps, such as Saxton's and Camden's did not show roads. Possibly the earliest maps of interest to the industrial archaeologist are the strip road maps of John Ogilby, who in 1675 published a series at 1 in to the mile which showed features of interest lying a short distance either side of roads, which were mainly

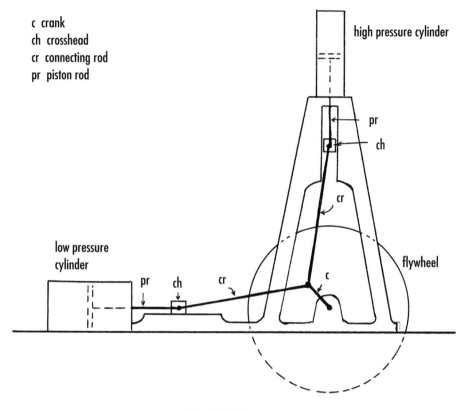

c crank
ch crosshead
cr connecting rod
pr piston rod

high pressure cylinder

pr

ch

cr

low pressure
cylinder

flywheel

pr   ch   cr

c

Fig. 44. A Manhattan engine

important post roads. These are among the earliest maps which were fairly accurately surveyed. Other useful early maps are the county maps such as Burdett's map of Cheshire (1777) and Yates' Lancashire (1786), which showed items such as windmills, forges, slitting mills, and so on, at a scale of 1 in to the mile. These maps and others of similar date were made as the result of prizes offered by the Society of Arts for accurate surveys. Estate plans, enclosure maps, are other sources of information.

The most reliable maps are those of the Ordnance Survey (OS), a government body established in 1791 with its headquarters in the Tower of London. Its origin was a survey made to determine exactly the difference in longitude between the meridians of Greenwich and Paris observatories, by mutual co-operation between the British Royal artillery and the French Academy. Mapping of Britain was carried on by the British Board of Ordnance, based on the principle of triangulation. An accurate base line 5.2 miles long was set up on Hounslow Heath,

London, and from this the whole country wa surveyed and maps made in different scales The 1 in to the mile series (known as the Firs Edition or Old Series) commenced with a ma of Kent published on 1 January 1801, and b 1853 the whole country had been mapped, wit different areas issued at various dates. Th larger scale 6 in to the mile maps or Count Plans were begun in 1846, and finished in 1896 The larger still 25 in to the mile series or Parish Plans also began in 1846, and finished in 1893 A 60 in to the mile series was produced fo certain towns.

Revisions are made to OS maps from time t time to keep them up to date: revisions to th early ones, for example, included the additio of railways. These early editions were printe in black only: coloured maps were no introduced on the 1 in series until the 1890s When studying OS maps, the date of surve printed on the margin is important since it ca pre-date the publication date by many years i some instances. Also it is important t remember that omissions occurred: if a mill mine, etc. is not shown on a map, it does not follow that it was not there when the map was surveyed.

Geological maps are also of interest to the industrial archaeologist. The first geological map was drawn up by William Smith in 1815 covering England and Wales on a scale of 1 in to 5 miles. Later geological maps are based on OS maps. Two types of maps are available: drift maps which show the geology of the surface, and solid maps which show the underground geology, known and suspected. *See also* GRID REFERENCE.

Close, Col. Sir Charles. *The Early Years of the Ordnance Survey*, 1926; reprinted by David and Charles, 1969
Lynan, E. *British Maps and Map-makers*, 1944
Smith, D. 'The representation of industry on large scale county maps of England and Wales, 1700–c.1840', *Industrial Archaeology Review* XII (1990), 153–77
Facsimiles of the OS First Edition 1 in maps have been republished by David and Charles in recent years.

marionette the mechanism at the end of the batten in a ribbon loom which activates the rows of shuttles, whose movements resemble those of marionettes (string puppets).

marl hole a quarry where pottery clay is obtained. Marl is a mixture of clay and carbonate of lime.

marmre (or marver) the slab, formerly of marble, later of iron, on which a ball of hot glass is rolled whilst attached to the end of the blowpipe prior to commencing blowing. Marvering the glass rolls it into a smooth regular shape, central on the end of the blowpipe. The word was brought over to England by HUGUENOT glass workers in the 16th century, and comes from the French *marbre* for marble.

Marseilles quilts (or Marsailles quilts) a compound fabric composed of two plain cotton cloths stitched together with a wadding in between, the stitching making a pattern and the outer cloths slightly bulging out because of the wadding inside. Used as coverlets, it was a speciality of Bolton, Lancs., in the 19th century. *See also* QUILTING.

mash tun a large vessel in which GRIST and hot water are mixed in a brewery or distillery to make WORT (unfermented beer). It has a perforated base through which the wort is drained off, and the remaining spent grist grains are sent to make cattle feedstuff. The mixing of grist and water is called mashing, which converts the starch in the grist into sugar. The wort passes to the boiling copper and hot water is sprayed into the mash tun to wash out any remaining sugar, an operation known as sparging.

mason's marks marks cut into a stone item by the stonemason who made it. Usually the marks were symbols made up from straight lines, since these are the easiest to make. They were cut so that the stonemason could claim payment for his work, and may still be found on some stonework. Another use of such marks was for assembly purposes, where Roman numerals were normally used: the edges of adjoining stones sometimes carried the same numeral, or stones were numbered in sequence. Similar assembly marks may be found on timber framed buildings.

masticator a powerful machine comprising a pair of heated cylinders revolving inside a chamber, and used for converting raw rubber into a soft plastic mass by being 'chewed' between knives or teeth projecting from the cylinders. The first masticator was built by Thomas Hancock (1786–1865) of Marlborough, Wilts., in a London workshop in 1820. It consisted of a large drum with externally protruding spikes, which could be rotated inside a slightly larger drum which had internally protruding spikes. The rotating and stationary spikes meshed with each other, and pieces of raw rubber introduced between them were torn to shreds or 'chewed' until they became a soft, warm mass. Hancock did not patent his machine, which he called a 'pickle' to hide its construction, and managed to keep it a secret for twelve years. Later machines had two spiked cylinders, and heat was added to the cylinders by steam. The plasticized rubber is compounded with sulphur and other additives whilst in a masticator prior to being moulded or extruded to shape and VULCANIZED.

maund an Indian measure of weight used for cotton. In Bengal a maund weighed about 82.25 lb.

McKinley tariff a protectionist tariff introduced in the USA in 1890 by President McKinley (1843–1901). It considerably reduced Yorkshire's textile exports to the USA, and that of tinplate from south Wales.

McNaughting a method of increasing the power output from an existing steam beam engine, patented by a Scottish engineer, William McNaught (1818–81) in 1845 (patent no. 11001). He fitted an additional short-stroke, high-pressure cylinder halfway between the central fulcrum of the beam and the flywheel end, and converted the existing cylinder to a low pressure cylinder. A new, higher pressure boiler was needed, but the conversion was cheaper than buying a complete new system. Many single-cylinder beam engines were so modified in the mid-19th century, and the alteration became known as McNaughting. *See also* COMPOUNDING (1).

'**Mechanical Age**' name coined by Thomas Carlyle (1795–1881), the historian, for the age he lived in; he bemoaned Man's 'becoming mechanical in head and heart', and noticed a growing materialism and decline in spiritual values.

mechanical stoker machines for automatically feeding fuel onto the fire of steam boilers and other furnace plant, introduced at the beginning of the 19th century as boilers increased in size. The main aims of mechanical stokers were smokeless combustion and economy in fuel consumption. Early designs of mechanical stokers were hand fed: the fireman kept a hopper full of coal by shovelling from a large bunker. The stoker mechanism fed coal from the hopper onto the furnace grate at a regular rate, which could be varied by the fireman according to the steam requirements of the boiler.

There are two main kinds of mechanical stoker: the coking and the sprinkler designs. There was great activity during the period 1819–41 by inventors of stokers, when several patents were taken out. The more important ones were: coking stokers by William Brunton (1777–1851), patent no. 4387 (1819) for a flat revolving grate, and patent no. 4685 (1822) for a straight line moving grate; a sprinkler type by John Stanley (patent no. 4692, 1822); an underfeed type by Richard Holme (patent no. 6503, 1833), comprising a tapered screw revolving in a trough below the grate feeding the coal up from below; and a travelling chain grate stoker by Johann Georg Bodmer (1786–1864) (patent nos. 6617, 1834 and 9899, 1843), which was later developed by John Juckes (patent no. 9067, 1841). Yet another type of stoker patented by Vicars and Smith (no. 378, 1879) comprised a grate with firebars which slowly reciprocated back and forward to carry small coal from a feed box to the rear of the firegrate, where the clinker fell over into an ashpit.

mechanician (or mechanicien, mechanitien) old word dating from the 17th century for a mechanic or machine builder. It was still used occasionally in Victorian times, but is now obsolete.

Mechanics' Institutes buildings where artisans could learn more about their craft, and the scientific and theoretical principles behind it, by attendance at evening lectures and the use of reading room facilities. The ideas of politician and reformer Jeremy Bentham (1723–90) led to the eventual formation of the Institutes, London's being founded in 1824 by George Birkbeck (1776–1841). Within twenty years there were some 200 Institutes in Britain with 50,000 members. However, they lost their original character and purpose, being swamped by clerks and shopkeepers, and the original artisan membership declined. By the 1850s interest waned and the movement began to wither away. There are still buildings with the words 'Mechanics Institute' over the door, mostly in industrial areas, and to some extent they can be regarded as the humble beginnings of today's professional engineering bodies.

Tylecote, Mabel. *The Mechanics' Institutes of Lancashire and Cheshire*, Manchester University Press, 1957

mechlin lace a type of lace originating in the city of Mechlin, now known as Malines, in Belgium. Dating from the beginning of the 18th century, it has the appearance of embroidery, and was popular in Victorian days.

medium piston name given by William Symington (1763–1831) of Wanlockhead, Dumfriess., to a second short-stroke piston lying in the base of his design of vertical atmospheric steam engine. This second piston acted as a pump to force air and condensate out of the condenser below. The condenser was integral with the cylinder, not separate as in Watt's engines, but separated from the main steam space by the medium piston. A separate air pump was not needed. The medium piston was counterbalanced so as to rise when the steam above it was being exhausted into the condenser. A diagram of the cylinder showing the medium piston appears in Fig. 45. When fresh steam entered the cylinder, forcing up the main piston, the medium piston was depressed, forcing out air and condensate from the previous stroke. When the steam exhaust cock opened, steam from the main cylinder passed into the condenser to be sprayed by a water jet, creating a partial vacuum. Atmospheric pressure forced down the main piston via the open top of the cylinder. The medium piston then rose under the action of the counterbalance, for the cycle to repeat. The main piston was connected to an overhead beam as for a normal beam engine. Symington patented his invention in 1787 (patent no. 1610).

Harvey, W.S. and Downs-Rose, G. *William Symington: Inventor and Engine Builder*, Northgate, 1980

meer (or mear, mere) a length of vein or other deposit of lead, usually a yard or two either side of 30 yd, although the actual length varied in different parts of the country. It is believed that the term arose from the practice in medieval Germany of a miner, on discovering a new vein, throwing his hammer in both directions along the length of the vein, to claim his working length. The earliest miners in Britain were

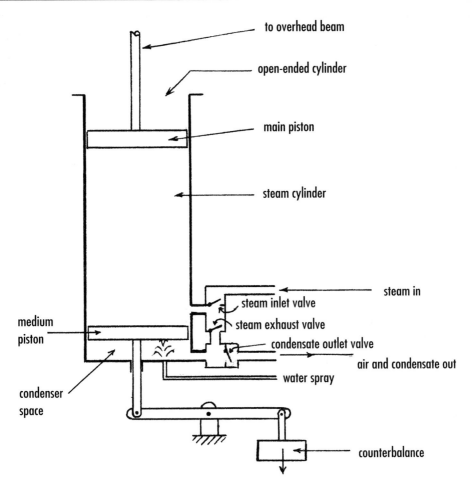

to overhead beam

open-ended cylinder

main piston

steam cylinder

steam in

steam inlet valve

steam exhaust valve

medium piston

condensate outlet valve

air and condensate out

water spray

condenser space

counterbalance

Fig. 45. Symington's steam cylinder with medium piston

frequently German, the concept of such a length measurement of a vein having been brought with them. Stakes were driven into the ground to mark out meers, or headstones set up with the miner's initials, or that of the mining company, inscribed on it. Such stones may still be found in lead mining districts. Sometimes a meerstone has a number only on it. The letter F usually follows the initials, this standing for 'founder', i.e. the finder of the vein. In addition to the meer length along the vein, a miner was allowed ground either side of the vein on which he could tip unwanted rock and construct his COE. This strip of land was known as a quarter cord, and was a quarter of the meer wide, i.e. about 7–8 yd.

A somewhat similar custom called bounding dates from medieval times in the tin mining areas of Cornwall. A tin miner on discovering a lode would claim a plot of land containing it by placing at each corner either a pile of three turfs, or a pole with a furze bush tied on top of it. The plot then had to be registered at the nearest STANNARY Court. Yet another old custom relates to the GALE system in the Royal Forest of Dean, west Glos.

meiler a word used in the early 19th century for a charcoal kiln. It comes from a German word meaning a pile of wood for making charcoal.

melton a strong, well fulled or milled woollen cloth, much used for overcoats. The name may come from Melton Mowbray, Leics., a hunting centre, where jackets and coats of this material were popular.

Men of Maudslay's a society formed by men

who had been trained in the London works of Henry Maudslay (1771–1831) and Joshua Field (1786–1863). They included: Richard Roberts (1789–1864), lathe designer and inventor of the SELF-ACTING MULE; James Nasmyth (1808–90), inventor of the shaper and STEAM HAMMER; Joseph Whitworth (1803–87), improver of many machine tools, who introduced the standard screw thread which bears his name; and Joseph Clement (1779–1844), builder of large planing machines. Maudslay is regarded as the pioneer of precision engineering: from a small workshop opened in 1797, he built up a prestigious mechanical engineering concern in London, manufacturing machine tools – many of his own invention – steam engines, both land and marine, and other machinery. He took on Joseph Field as partner in 1810, their firm being known as Maudslay, Sons and Field, and did work for Marc Isambard Brunel (1769–1849), as well as supplying engines for many of the large steamships of the day.

Nasmyth, James. *James Nasmyth, Engineer*, Murray, 1897 (see Chapters 7, 8 and 10).

mercantile system the economic and industrial policies followed by the government in Britain from the 16th to the mid-19th centuries. These arose out of a sense of nationalism, the desire to make the country self-sufficient and more powerful by developing trade with other nations, and the theory that gold and silver bullion were the only true wealth. Mercantilism followed the decline in the power of the GUILDS, when the regulation of industries passed to the government who issued decrees encouraging the import of raw materials not available in Britain, but not the buying in of manufactured goods from abroad. Overseas trade was regulated by duties, prohibitions, bounties and drawbacks; exports were encouraged to bring payments by bullion into the country.

To improve home industries, foreign workers were encouraged to settle in England during the 16th and 17th centuries, bringing in Dutch and Flemish craftspeople who introduced the NEW DRAPERIES, an influx of German miners, and HUGUENOT refugees with their silk weaving and cloth dyeing expertise. To improve overseas trade and secure foreign sources of raw materials, royal chartered companies such as the EAST INDIA COMPANY were given monopolies to trade in specified areas. The indigenous woollen industry was, at first, protected by several Acts against importation of cotton and silk fabrics. The emigration to the Continent of skilled mechanics and textile workers, and the export of machines or

drawings of them were forbidden by an Act of 1718, although it was often evaded. The manufacture of all-cotton goods in Britain was not permitted by law until 1774, when it was subject to a tax of 3*d* per yard (*see* MANCHESTER ACT).

The newly founded colonies were expected to contribute to the mother country's welfare by supplying her with raw materials and not competing against her industries. In return, Britain undertook to defend and develop the colonies, and give preference to colonial imports. However, as the colonies progressed, the restrictions imposed became increasingly irksome, leading eventually to the American War of Independence (1775–83). By the time the Industrial Revolution in Britain was well under way, mercantile policies began to be questioned and their efficiency doubted, which led to their eventual decline and replacement by a policy of *laissez-faire*.

mercerization a yarn or cloth finishing process invented by John Mercer (1791–1866) in 1850. The impregnation of cloth in a solution of caustic alkali makes cotton fibres stronger and more receptive to dyes: the caustic swells the fibres, makes them relatively smooth and round, and gives the cloth a lustre. Yarns can also be mercerized and used for sewing and embroidery; the yarn must be under tension during the process.

Merchant Adventurers a trading association which obtained a royal charter in 1407 and which principally exported English woollen cloth onto the Continent. At first, trading was mainly with the Low Countries and an important headquarters was established in Bruges; later, after this was lost, much trade was carried on with Germany and a centre in Hamburg was made. The organization reached its peak in the mid-16th century when it successfully rivalled the HANSEATIC LEAGUE. Soon after this, it was criticized by the British parliament as a monopoly, and lost many of its privileges in the 17th century. Its royal charter was lost in 1689 but the organization survived as a trading association in Hamburg until the outbreak of the Napoleonic wars. It was finally dissolved in 1808.

merchant bars wrought-iron bars in a finished state ready for the market, after the puddled bars have been piled, reheated, and rolled again into bar form. *See also* NUMBERED IRON.

mere, *see* FLASH

Merino wool a fine wool with a short staple length derived from the Spanish Merino breed of sheep. This breed was introduced into the colony of New South Wales, Australia, in *c.*1794, and wool from here was sometimes known as Botany wool, after Botany Bay. Before this, Australia had no indigenous sheep. From a flock of about 500 sheep in 1794, 100 years later there were around 50 million in New South Wales alone, and double that number in the whole of Australia. Export of wool to Britain from Australia commenced in 1810.

metallic packings metal sealing rings on engine pistons. To make a steam- or gas-tight sliding joint between the piston of a steam engine or internal combustion engine and the cylinder walls, low-friction, renewable rings are fitted in recesses in the piston sides. The first metallic piston rings were those patented by the Revd Edmund Cartwright (1743–1823) in 1797 (patent no. 2202). Other engineers and inventors patented other ideas, including John Ramsbottom (1814–97), whose invention (patent no. 767, 1852) was first applied to locomotives but soon adopted on all stationary steam engines. It consisted of steel rings of rectangular cross-section bent to a circle larger than the cylinder bore, with a short piece cut from it. The ring had a tendency to spring outwards against the cylinder walls when forced into position, thus making a steam-tight joint. Three rings were fitted per piston with staggered gaps. Many other patent metallic piston rings were invented: another design was of cast iron turned on the outside exactly to the cylinder bore, with spring strips fastened behind to press the ring against the cylinder walls, a cut having been made across the ring for flexibility. *See also* PACKING.

metewand (or metewood, meteyard) an old dialect word for a rod used for measuring cloth in the days of hand weavers; mete means to hand out or measure out. It was also known as a reel staff.

Meyer variable expansion valve a steam distribution valve with a means for varying the CUT-OFF in a stationary steam engine or locomotive while it is running. This is done by two valves working in the same steam chest. Fig. 63b shows a cross-section through a Meyer valve. The main slide valve, called the distribution valve, has another slide valve, called the expansion valve, sliding on its back. Each valve is driven by its own ECCENTRIC. The distribution valve is similar to an ordinary slide valve, but is extended at each end to incorporate two admission ports. It is driven by the main eccentric, and controls the exhaust from the cylinder. The expansion valve comprises two plates or blocks screwed onto a spindle, one by a right-hand thread, the other by a left-hand thread. The function of the expansion valve is to cut off steam at any desired point in the piston stroke by closing ports in the distribution valve. Steam can only enter the cylinder when the inlet port is uncovered by a plate or block. The distance between the two plates can be varied whilst the engine is running, by rotating the spindle connecting them. The screw threads either draw them closer together or farther apart, depending on which way the spindle is turned. As the gap between the plates is increased, the cut off occurs earlier in the stroke. The expansion valve spindle can be turned manually by a handwheel, or automatically by a GOVERNOR. Hand control is usual on locomotives, governor control on stationary engines. The valve was invented by the railway engineer Jean Jacques Meyer (1804–77) of Mulhouse, France.

Milan Decree, *see* CONTINENTAL SYSTEM (2)

mild steel ordinary, bulk produced steel, with a low carbon content of about 0.1 per cent, or 0.25 per cent at most. It is the common steel used for general purposes in structural and manufacturing industries: its low carbon content means that it cannot be hardened, and is free cutting. Mild steel was first produced cheaply in bulk by the BESSEMER PROCESS in 1855.

mill any factory fitted with machinery for the purpose of manufacture, or a machine for processing materials. The earliest known use of the word as a noun is a reference to a corn mill in AD 961. The word comes from the Latin *molinum* and the Old English *mylen*, meaning to grind. There are thus water mills and windmills, for grinding corn etc., and mills for grinding or crushing many materials, such as a flint mill. Over the years the word came to mean any factory fitted with machinery for manufacturing, such as cotton mill, bobbin mill, paper mill, etc.; it thus has a very loose and wide meaning. A milling machine is a machine tool capable of removing metal from a work piece to produce a flat surface, or to cut grooves or profiles; a millhand is a factory worker. An old spelling for mill is mylne or milne.

milling, *see* FULLING, MILLING OF CLOTH

milling machine a versatile machine tool capable of producing flat surfaces over limited areas, cutting profiles and, by adding extra equipment or using special cutting tools, creating a variety of formed shapes and spirals. There are three types of milling machines – the horizontal, the vertical, and the universal. Each type comprises a robust vertical column or pillar with a movable 'knee' which can slide up and down the front of the column carrying a saddle and table. The top of the column encloses the spindle on which the cutters are mounted. The saddle and table combination on the knee provides horizontal traverse and crossfeed movements, whilst the knee itself gives vertical movement. On the horizontal machine, the cutters are mounted on a horizontal spindle, driven by gearing from the column, the projecting end of the spindle being supported by a removable arbor which is suspended from an overarm carried off the top of the column. The arbor can be removed to enable cutters to be placed on the spindle. The vertical machine has a vertical spindle driven from the column which projects downwards over the centre of the work table. The universal machine is similar to the horizontal model but has a swivelling table enabling spirals and gear teeth to be cut, thus increasing the flexibility of the machine. Horizontal machines can be converted into vertical machines by removing the horizontal spindle and overarm and substituting a vertical milling attachment.

The work piece is clamped onto the table using T-slots provided, and metal is removed by the table passing backwards and forwards under the rotating cutting tool and moving sideways a small amount (the crossfeed) after each cut so that a fresh path is presented to the cutter. The rotating cutters have several cutting edges, whereas fixed tools on, for example, PLANING MACHINES, have only one.

Milling machines originated in the USA. A pioneering horizontal machine was made there by Eli Whitney about 1818, but was not exploited commercially until some 30 years later by F.W. Howe, also in the USA. In 1860, the vertical version made its appearance in the USA, introduced by W.B. Bement. Joseph Rogers Brown of the well-known American machine tool makers, Brown and Sharp, developed the universal miller in 1862 specifically for cutting the spiral flutes on twist drills, which had only been invented a year or two previously. By this date, milling machines began to be used in increasing numbers in Britain, and soon became essential tools in engineering and production workshops. The introduction and adoption of milling machines was coupled with the use of specially shaped cutting tools, also invented by Brown.

Woodbury, R.S. *History of the Milling Machine*, Massachusetts Institute of Technology Press, 1960

milling of cloth shrinking woollen fabrics by pressure between rollers. Milling of woollen cloth replaced the old FULLING stocks in the mid-19th century. John Dyer of Trowbridge patented a rotary cloth milling machine in 1833, which gave better control over the shrinkage process than the old method. Cloth was stitched at its ends to form an endless band, and passed between weighted rollers mounted over a water trough containing soap and an alkali or acid (depending on the type of fabric). The shrinkage and closing up of the weave were obtained by pressure and friction.

millstone circular, flat stone, mainly used for grinding corn and other meal into flour. Millstones are mostly made from a sedimentary sandstone, particularly millstone grit, and have been used for grinding flour in water- and windmills for centuries. There are two varieties, solid stones and segmental stones. Solid stones are represented by indigenous British stones such as PEAK STONES, and by CULLIN STONES imported from Germany. Segmented stones or FRENCH BURRS came from France and were made up from several pieces bound together by iron hoops. Millstones can vary in size from around 3 ft up to 8 ft in diameter, and from 8 to 12 in in thickness. Millstones were usually cut to size on site from suitable large stones found on a moor, or quarried in the usual manner: abandoned 'wasters' may still be found in millstone grit areas.

Corn is ground between the surfaces of two millstones – the finely balanced top runner, usually rotating at about 130 rpm, and the stationary bottom bedstone. A pattern of grooves, called furrows, is cut in the opposing surfaces of the stones to guide the flour to the periphery. The grinding takes place on the flat surfaces between the furrows, and fine sharp ridges are cut on them for this purpose. These surfaces have to be re-cut about every two to three weeks of constant use by a skilled stone dresser. The stones are housed inside a wooden 'box' called a tun or vat, which has a chute directing the flour into a waiting sack. A fine clearance must be maintained between the grinding surfaces, and this is controlled by TENTERING. Millstones may be driven from above or below. Water millstones are driven from below, called an underdrift drive, whereas windmills may be driven in either way, though the overdrift drive is more common. Millstones were also used for grinding dye woods and similar materials in the textile industry, and for crushing ores under their weight; in this case they were used in a vertical plane, as EDGE MILLS.

In 1862, ROLLER MILLING of corn was introduced, and the demand for millstones declined as flour production by water- and windmills fell into disuse.

Major, J.K. 'The manufacture of millstones in the Eifel region of Germany', *Industrial Archaeology Review* VI (1982), 194–204

Tucker, D.G. 'Millstone making in the Peak District of Derbyshire', *Industrial Archaeology Review* VIII (1985), 42–58

Tucker, D.G. 'Millstone making in England', *Industrial Archaeology Review* IX (1987), 167–88

mill time an ingenious device dating from the early 19th century which was used in some textile mills to show how the rate of production of the whole mill varied. This was done by comparing the speed of the machinery against the passage of time. A twin-dial clock was placed in the manager's office: the lower dial was driven by a pendulum as in a grandfather clock and showed the correct time, labelled 'clock time'; an upper dial had a clock mechanism driven through suitable gearing from the factory LINESHAFTING and was labelled 'mill time'. When the lineshafting was running at its correct speed, the 'mill time' clock kept correct time; if the mill ran slow, a discrepancy between the two clock dials appeared, the 'mill time' lagging behind the 'clock time'. The manager would then instruct the water supply to the waterwheel to be increased, or the steam engine speeded up, so as to maintain the desired production rate. In this manner the output from the mill could be checked and regulated. The device was also known as an engine clock.

minder an alternative name for an operative spinner in charge of a pair of MULES; a minder would have two young assistants helping him called PIECERS.

mine an underground excavation made for extracting coal, metallic ores, salt, gems, etc. Coal is generally mined in fairly flat country, the coal lying in near-horizontal seams of varying thickness, accessed from the surface via vertical shafts or sloping tunnels. A coal mine is also known as a pit or a colliery, a word obviously derived from the word coal. In some 18th-century literature, a coal mine is described as a coal work, and occasionally the word field has been used as a synonym for mine. Metal mines usually occur in hilly or mountainous districts because the veins, which tend to be near-vertical or steeply sloping, are more easily detected where they outcrop on a hillside. There are probably mineral deposits below flat country, but they are usually covered by thick alluvial deposits and not easily found. Metal mines in general follow the ore vein downwards, whereas a coal mine extracts coal sideways along the seams from the access shaft. In addition to the access point(s), there are surface working areas associated with mines, such as winding and water pumping machinery, mineral dressing floors or coal sorting areas, waste tips, and some means of transporting the mined material away. In remote districts, miners' cottages were often built by the mine company close by.

The word mine is also used in some areas instead of seam in the naming of particular coal seams. For example, Arley mine is a coal seam which stretches over a wide area in the Lancashire coalfield, and is mined in several places, each colliery having its own name. *See also* MINING INDUSTRY.

mine cage an enclosed, box-like platform, or tiered platforms, used for raising and lowering materials and men vertically in a mine shaft, by a cable from a winding engine. Cages replaced the baskets which were used in early mines. At first, cages had no sides nor guide rails in the shaft, and accidents occurred. Normally two cages are used, one ascending with full tubs, the other descending with empties. Wheeled tubs ride on rails placed on the cage floor. The first metal cage is believed to have been used by Hall in a Durham coal mine in 1835.

mine haulage steam engine a steam engine working an underground cable haulage system in a late 19th-century coal mine. Underground transport of coal was improved by the introduction of an endless moving cable, onto which coal trucks could be attached. Steam engines drove the cable system, and various arrangements were in use at different collieries. At some, the engine and boilers were sited near the shaft at ground level, with the haulage cable going down the shaft on guide pulleys and along the main roadways. At other collieries, the engine was placed underground near the shaft bottom, with steam piped down from boilers on the surface, whilst at some collieries the boilers were also underground.

Mineral and Battery Works, Company of an organization founded by Elizabeth I in 1568 for the production of BRASS (an alloy of copper and zinc), and to encourage new methods of metal working. Brass in sheet form, called brass battery, was hammered into hollow-ware such as domestic pots and pans. Brass was also drawn into wire, and the company also became involved in producing drawn iron wire. The company had certain privileges granted under the royal charter with leases of mines particularly in Keswick, Cumberland, and Tintern, Monmouthshire. German miners were largely employed in the early days, particularly in Keswick. At Tintern, the company developed a type of iron, called osmond iron, used for wire drawing. In 1668, the company was combined with the Company of MINES ROYAL into the United Society of Mines Royal and Mineral and Battery Works.

Donald, M.B. *Elizabethan Monopolies*, 1955
Hammersley, G. *Daniel Hechstetter the Younger*, 1988
Rees, W. *Industry before the Industrial Revolution, Incorporating a Study of the Chartered Companies of the*

Society of Mines Royal and of Mineral and Battery Works, 1968

mineral line private railway, often only a few miles long, used for transporting metallic ores, coal, slate, etc. from a mine or quarry to a nearby sea port or canal basin. Most early railways were initially mineral lines. George Stephenson's first locomotive *Blucher* (1814) hauled coal at the Wylam colliery, near Newcastle upon Tyne, Northumb., as did John Blenkinsop's locomotives on the rack railway at Middleton colliery, near Leeds, Yorks. (1811–35). The Ffestiniog Railway in north Wales, opened in 1836, was horse drawn initially, conveying slate from the slate mines down to the sea at Portmadoc. Normally passengers were not carried, although some mineral lines did commence carrying passengers; the Ffestiniog Railway started carrying them in 1865, two years after steam locomotives had been introduced on the line. Mineral lines are also known as light railways, the operation of which was covered by an Act of 1868.

Many but not all mineral lines were NARROW GAUGE RAILWAYS (e.g. 1 ft 11.6 in): the Stockton and Darlington Railway, a mineral line initially opened for coal traffic in 1825, was laid at what was to become the standard gauge (4 ft 8½ in) by Stephenson. Some narrow gauge mineral lines terminated at later-built standard gauge railways, the material carried being transferred into standard sized waggons. To avoid this double handling, pick-a-back flat waggons were provided on some standard gauge lines, the narrow gauge trucks being transported on them to their destination.

Boyd, J.I.C. *The Ffestiniog Railway*, Oakwood, 1959
Dean, I. *Industrial Narrow Gauge Railways*, Shire Publications, Album No. 145, 1985

'Miners' Friend' name used by Captain Thomas Savery (*c.*1650?–1715) to describe his 1 hp 'steam engine' or PULSOMETER in a pamphlet he published in 1702. His invention, patented in 1698 (patent no. 356), was claimed to 'raise water by the impellent force of fire'. In actual fact, the lift obtained from the device was inadequate for raising water from mines, but several were used where low lifts were needed, such as for supplying buildings with water, and recirculating water to existing waterwheels. Since only primitive boilers were available in those days, only low pressures could be used, although attempts were made to use high pressures with disastrous results. The 'Miners' Friend' was superseded by Thomas Newcomen's ATMOSPHERIC ENGINE around 1712, although because Savery's patent did not expire until 1733 its existence prevented

Newcomen from patenting his more successful engine. However, a Savery type engine was still being used in Marshall's flax factory, Leeds, in 1791 for light pumping work, and one was in use as late as 1820 in Kentish Town, London, for raising water for a waterwheel which drove machinery in an engineering works. It was because of the allusion to the use of fire in the patent that early steam engines were often called fire engines. *See also* SAVERY ENGINE.

Jenkins, R. 'Savery, Newcomen and the early history of the steam engine', *Newcomen Society Transactions* III (1922–3) and IV (1923–4)
Savery, T. *The Miners Friend; or an Engine to Raise Water by Fire*, 1702; reprinted in Edinburgh, 1969

mine safety hook a hook or link of special design to protect MINE CAGES against overwinding at the headgear. Accidents can occur if overwinding by the engine takes place, and patent devices have been invented to safeguard the cage against damage which could happen if it crashes against the headgear. An early design was by John Knowles (patent no. 2401, 1856), but the most used one is that invented by Edward Ormerod of Atherton, Lancs. (patent no. 2350, 1867). It is a self-detaching hook, comprising three specially shaped plates connected by a central pivot, which form a link between the shackle attached to the winding rope and the shackle attached to the mine cage. A soft metal pin holds the plates in position. The rope passes through a conically shaped collar in the headgear: should overwinding take place, the plate link enters the collar and the outer edges of the outside two plates strike against the inner surface of the collar. This causes them to turn slightly on the central pivot, shearing the soft metal pin which releases the centre plate to which the winding rope shackle is attached. The rope continues upwards, but projections near the top of the two side plates lock over the top of the collar, thus supporting the cage which remains suspended over the mine shaft. The Ormerod safety hook is also known as the butterfly hook, because the two outer plates resemble the shape of the wings of a butterfly.

mine shaft a vertical or inclined excavation giving access to an underground mine. Unless cut through solid rock, most mine shafts are lined to prevent the walls collapsing. A shaft may be used for access to and from underground by miners, for winding up material, for ventilation, and for pumping water out of the mine. Cornish lead and copper mine shafts were usually rectangular (around 8 ft by 6 ft) in the 1860s, frequently timber-lined, and one shaft was used for all purposes. Later, the shafts became larger with multi-compartments to separate the various activities, and later still, circular shafts became popular. Stone and brick linings have also been used, and in Derbyshire lead mines, stone lining or walling at the top of a mine shaft is known as GINGING. Oval shafts in coal mines in the 18th century were often fitted with a BRATTICE divider, so that winding of materials could take place on one side of the brattice and water pumping on the other. Metal lining by segments bolted together, known as TUBBING, replaced brick and stone in more recent times.

Most coal mines at one time had only one shaft, but after a disastrous accident at Hartley colliery in Northumberland, in 1862, when its single shaft became blocked by a broken part of the engine beam, resulting in the loss of 202 men and boys, two shafts were made compulsory by law. Besides giving an alternative route for escape or rescue, the second shaft brought great improvements in ventilation. One shaft became the downcast shaft, down which fresh air was drawn or blown; and, after circulation through the underground workings the air was drawn out via the second or upcast shaft.

Mines Royal metal mines once claimed by the Crown if the value of any gold or silver found exceeded the value of the base metal mined. The custom dates from 1568 when Elizabeth I founded the Company of Mines Royal by granting a charter for the mining of copper, mainly in Keswick, Cumberland. This arose out of the policies of William Cecil (Lord Burghley, 1521–98) who encouraged the mining of copper and iron in Britain to make the nation independent of foreign sources for the manufacture of cannon and other munitions. The royal claim overrode the local ownership of mineral rights.

In 1668, the Company of Mines Royal was combined with the Company of MINERAL AND BATTERY WORKS to form the United Society of Mines Royal and Mineral and Battery Works. The Mines Royal Acts of 1689 and 1692 freed all lead, copper and tin mines from claims by the Crown, which increased the prospecting for, and mining of, these ores. Any gold or silver then found in the base metal could be extracted by refining processes without fear of confiscation by the Crown.

Donald, M.B. *Elizabethan Monopolies*, 1955
Rees, W. *Industry before the Industrial Revolution, Incorporating a Study of the Chartered Companies of the Society of Mines Royal and of Mineral and Battery Works*, 1968

minikins (or myniken) a kind of BAYES: minikin was a 17th-century coarse, plain weave worsted cloth, woven in Norwich in the days of

hand weavers. It was usually made from warp which had been handspun on a ROCK, and weft which had been spun on a wheel. FRIZADOES was a similar cloth.

mining industry the removal of useful materials from underground. The main activities of mining are prospecting, extraction, and removal of unwanted materials by dressing or washing at the surface. Prospecting requires a knowledge of geology and mineralogy, and involves techniques such as searching for outcrops, boring trial holes and examining the rock cores, or sinking speculative shafts. The method used depends on what material is sought. Coal and some forms of iron lie in horizontal or near-horizontal layers or seams, whilst non-ferrous ores lie in vertical or near-vertical veins or lodes.

Mining has a long history. The earliest method of extraction was by following an outcrop along. As deeper deposits were sought, BELL PITS were dug, then later, shallow ladder pits, and eventually deep shafts as mining techniques improved. Coal is removed either by PILLAR AND STALL or by LONGWALL methods. Metals are removed by stopeing (*see* STOPE), or following the vein down. Slate may be mined or quarried.

The main problems the mining industry has to overcome are removal of underground water, the provision of adequate ventilation, and the hazards of dangerous gases. The first application of steam power was to pump water out of mines. Drainage by gravity through small tunnels or soughs to lower outlets was another method, where the contours of the land permitted. Ventilation problems increased as the length of galleries increased. One early method was to maintain a fire at the bottom of one shaft so as to induce fresh air to circulate through the workings from another shaft; later, mechanically driven fans superseded dangerous underground ventilation fires. The invention of the SAFETY LAMP in 1816 reduced the risk of fires and explosions in coal mines. Mined materials were removed at first by winch or ladder from shallow mines; the HORSE WHIM was then introduced, and finally steam driven winding engines.

Metal mining in any quantity dates from the 16th century when German miners were invited to mine COPPER near Keswick; there is thus a German influence in mining, and many mining terms have a German origin. COAL was being mined in all the principal coalfields of Britain by the beginning of the 18th century. In the mid-19th century Britain was the world's biggest supplier of TIN, but little is mined today. The historic centre for IRON mining was in the Weald of Kent and Sussex in the 16th and 17th centuries.

Burt, R. *A Short History of British Metal Mining Technology in the Eighteenth and Nineteenth Centuries,* De Archaeologische Pers, 1982
Galloway, R.L. *A History of Coal Mining in Great Britain,* 1882; reprinted by David and Charles, 1970
Nef, J.U. *The Rise of the British Coal Mining Industry,* 1932; reprinted by Frank Cass, 1966 (2 vols)
Richardson, J.B. *Metal Mining,* Allen Lane

mispickel the principal ore from which ARSENIC was obtained, also known as arsenopyrite. It is a sulphide of iron and arsenic found associated with lead and copper veins, and was extensively mined in the 19th century in Devon and Cornwall to produce arsenic.

mitre wheel one of a pair of mating bevel gear wheels which transmit power through two shafts meeting at 90° to each other. Each mitre wheel has the same number of teeth so that the speed of rotation of each shaft is the same.

mixed gauge, *see* GAUGE

mixer a large, usually gas-fired, container at a steel works in which molten iron is kept hot until a BESSEMER CONVERTER needs it. Several BLAST FURNACES feed metal into the mixer so that a uniform iron results as feed for converting into steel in the converter.

mockado an inferior woollen cloth. First made in Flanders, it began to be made in England around Norwich by Flemish refugees in the 16th century, and was used for clothing until the late 17th century when it fell out of fashion.

mocket a Staffordshire word of obscure origin, dating from the late 17th century, for the large square knob-end of a BLOOM of iron.

mock lead, *see* BLENDE

mohair an animal fibre used in the textile industry, which comes from the Angora goat, native in Turkey, and later introduced into South Africa. It has a fibre length of 4–10 in and is strong, lustrous and springy. A mohair fabric may be pure or mixed with wool or cotton. Titus Salt (1803–76) built the well-known mohair mill at Saltaire, near Shipley, West Yorks., in 1851.

moiré a silk fabric with a clouded or watered appearance. This effect is given in the CALENDERING of the material. Moiré was, and still is, used for garments and their linings.

moleskin a heavily wefted, uncut FUSTIAN, in which the face of the cloth is slightly raised to imitate the skin of a mole. It is a hard wearing fabric, often used for outdoor working garments, such as navvies' trousers.

monorail a railway system on which trains are suspended from an overhead single rail, first patented in 1821 by Henry Robinson Palmer (patent no. 4618). Two short lines to his design were built: one, built in 1825 at Cheshunt, Herts., in a brickworks, and known as the Patent Suspension Railway, was horse drawn; and the other, built in 1826 at Deptford naval docks in London, was hand-powered. The difficulty with these was that the loading of the 'trucks', which were slung pannier-like either side of the rail, had to be carefully balanced. Not many monorail systems were developed until much more modern times.

Monteith process, *see* DISCHARGE BLEACHING

Monuments Protection Programme (MPP) an ongoing review of the country's monuments and sites by ENGLISH HERITAGE, with the view of selecting those deserving statutory protection by LISTING and SCHEDULING.

mood an old Sheffield term describing the construction or manufacturing process of the blade for a scythe or similar edge cutting tool, which in the 18th century comprised a CRUCIBLE STEEL strip sandwiched between two wrought-iron strips. The whole was heat forged into one piece with the centre steel being drawn slightly out to form the cutting edge when the blade was sharpened. The word mood is a variant of mould; the craftsman moods (moulds) the blade to shape under the hammer.

mordant a substance used with DYES which combines with them and fixes the colour onto the fibres of the cloth. In the early days of dyeing, many substances were used as mordants, such as ALUM, GALL NUTS, FUSTIC, stale URINE, SORREL root, and metallic salts such as salts of iron, tin, and chrome. A dye could sometimes be made brighter if the cloth was treated again by the same mordant, or in some cases by a different mordant. It was also possible in some cases to produce different colours by using different mordants with the same dye. The use of mordants was empirical at first, and it was not until *c.*1782 that their true action was discovered by P.J. Macquer (1718–84). Mordants were called bases in the late 18th century; the word mordant comes from the Latin *mordere,* meaning to bite.

mortice wheel a gear wheel which has wooden teeth fitted into mortice slots. Such gear wheels were used extensively in wind- and water mills.

mosing mill (or mozing mill) mill which used young TEAZLES gently to raise a nap on woollen cloth as part of the finishing process. The teazels were fixed to a roller against which the cloth passed. Early machines were worked by hand by one man and a boy. The device was first introduced in the West Country in the early 17th century to replace the GIG MILL.

moss **1.** a measure used for reeled silk. Three skeins of silk are called a moss, and twelve mosses make a book, i.e. thirty-six skeins, which weighs about 10 lb. **2.** a northern name for PEAT.

mosser a pillow-shaped lump of slag often found on sites of old bloom smithies and early iron refineries. These were discarded during the processing and usually thrown into a pile nearby. Sometimes mossers may be found built into old stone walls nearby, which were constructed at a later date using what material lay to hand.

mote **1.** in mining terminology, a straw filled with GUNPOWDER to act as a fuse for igniting a shot. **2.** an ancient arrangement for raising water from a well. The wall of the well is built up above the surrounding ground level, and a ramp built leading up to the top of the wall. A pulley is mounted over the well and a rope passes over it and hangs down the well, terminating with a bucket. To raise the bucket, the man or animal pulling the rope walks down the ramp, so that gravity helps to overcome the weight of the heavy bucket. **3.** a small tuft or imperfection on the surface of a cloth. A mote knife is a sharp blade fitted in a CARDING machine to remove motes.

'mother of all' the assembly mounted at the front of a spinning wheel which carries the SPINDLE, FLYER and WHARVES.

motion block, *see* CROSSHEAD

moulding box (or flask) a wooden or metal container, usually in two parts, the COPE (top) and DRAG (bottom), used for casting or moulding small iron items. The shape of the item is formed by a pattern pressed in dry moulding sand held in the box, the joint between the cope and drag occurring at the parting plane. When the molten metal has cooled, the box is opened by removing the cope from the drag and the casting is ejected, the box being used over and over again for fresh castings. Abraham Darby I (1677–1717) obtained a patent (no. 380, 1707) for casting iron smallware in such moulding boxes. Some moulding boxes have more than two parts, depending on the complexity of the item being cast.

mousseline the French word for MUSLIN. Muslin is only made from cotton, but confusingly there are two muslin-like fabrics made in other materials, which have the word mousseline in their name. *Mousseline-de-laine* is a muslin-like lightweight woollen fabric (in Britain this name was often shortened to delaine); and *mousseline-de-soie* is a muslin-like thin silk fabric. Both fabrics were popular for ladies' dresses.

muckle wheel, *see* GREAT WHEEL

muck rolling mill a rolling mill under which wrought-iron BLOOMS which have been hammered under the SHINGLING HAMMER are rolled into bars ready for further processing. The origin of the word muck is obscure, but there is possibly some connection with the Celtic *muc* meaning pig (pig iron?). The mill is also known as a forge rolling mill.

mughouse term used in the mid-18th century for a cottage with a pottery kiln attached.

mulciber a fanciful name sometimes used in the 19th century to describe a metalworker. Mulciber is the surname of Vulcan (Latin *Vulcanus*), the god of fire, or the hammer god of classical literature, and Vulcan is the patron of metalworkers.

mule a machine for SPINNING cotton yarn, originally invented in secret by Samuel Crompton (1753–1827) in Bolton, Lancs. It got its name because it was a hybrid spinning machine combining the principles of Hargreaves' JENNY and Arkwright's WATER FRAME. Crompton did not patent his invention, but was persuaded to disclose its design in 1779 on the promise of money from local cotton manufacturers, many of whom later reneged once they had the details.

Crompton's first mule spun 48 yarns simultaneously by hand, producing yarns finer and stronger than other contemporary machines, and enabled the weaving of British muslins equal to Indian imports. He used three pairs of weighted drafting rollers on a stationary frame, and placed the revolving spindles on a moving carriage to draw out the yarn as it was being twisted. Operation was intermittent, as the actions of drafting, twisting, stretching, and winding onto the spindles were not continuous. Several improvements were made by later inventors and the size of the machine gradually increased, to 150 spindles by 1790, and within a few more years to 400 spindles.

At first, only the carriage movement and spinning were power driven, with BACKING OFF and winding on performed manually. Fig. 46 shows the basic principles of a mule of around 1800: this machine was power driven from the lineshaft for moving out the carriage and twisting, stretching and drawing out the yarn. Cop formation was done by manually using the FALLER and COUNTER-FALLER wires. Automatic winding on was patented by William Eaton in 1818 (*see* COPPING MOTION). Each cycle of operation of a mule spun about 5 ft of yarn per spindle in approximately 15 seconds, giving about 1,200 ft per hour per spindle. The complete mechanization of the mule was unsuccessfully attempted by Edmund Cartwright (1743–1823), and it was not until 1830 that the first successful self-acting mule was patented (no. 5949) by Richard Roberts (1789–1864). He introduced some ingenious improvements such as the QUADRANT.

A mule required skilled spinners, since the speed of the rollers, the carriage movement, and spindle speed could all be varied independently of each other to produce different types of yarn. Different types of mule were made. Woollen mules used only one pair of feed rollers, and applied little twist to give soft yarns. Mule spinning was the mainstay of yarn manufacture in Britain for many decades, producing yarn for cloth for both the home market, and export. Fully automatic machines with up to 1,500 spindles were made, with complicated mechanisms controlling delicate operations. High productivity was reached. Mules were

placed in pairs facing each other so that one spinner with his assistants could supervise both machines from the wheelgate in between.

Mules were eventually superseded by RING SPINNING, developed in the USA and adopted by progressive firms in Britain from about the 1850s, although mule spinning continued for many years. No new mules were made after the early 1920s, and mule spinning is obsolete today. *See also* Fig. 64.

Catlin, H. *The Spinning Mule*, 1970; reprinted by Lancashire Library, 1986

French, G. *Life and Times of Samuel Crompton*, Adams and Dart, 1970

Thornley, T. *Self-acting Mules*, Heywood, 1893

mule gate the passage between the front of a pair of spinning MULES in which the spinner works, controlling and supervising the operation of the machines. The mules are

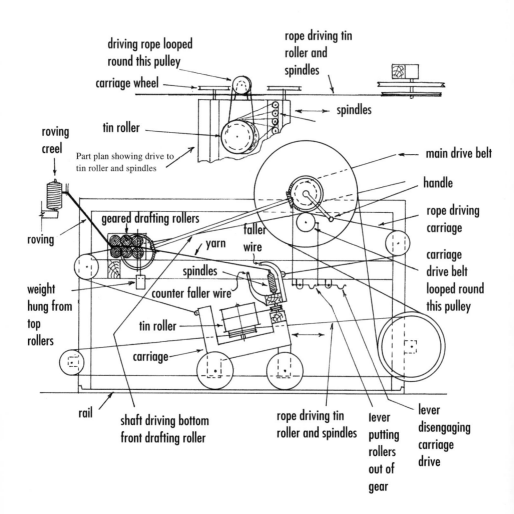

Fig. 46. Spinning mule, *c.* 1800 (NB much of the gearing, etc. is omitted for clarity)

arranged facing each other so that the spinner merely has to turn round from mule to mule.

mull a thin plain-woven MUSLIN. The word is a shortening of mulmull, which itself comes from *malmal*, the Hindi name for this material. Mull was used in bookbinding, for keeping and packing butter in Victorian times, and for dresses.

multi-tubular boiler a steam-raising boiler fitted with a number of tubes in the water space. The hot gases pass through the tubes which collectively provide a large heating surface. Multi-tubular boilers are used where rapid steaming is required, the locomotive boiler being a good example. Marc Seguin invented and patented a tubular boiler for locomotives in 1827 in France. A year or two later, Robert Stephenson (1803–59) included a multi-tubular boiler in the design of the *Rocket*, prompted by the idea put to him, independently of Seguin, by the treasurer of his locomotive building firm, Henry Booth (1788–1869). All locomotives have multi-tubular boilers, as have marine boilers; the latter have large diameter shells of short length and are often built as two boilers placed back-to-back. Some vertical boilers are also fitted with a nest of firetubes to increase the heating surface area. Another boiler which was popular for a while which incorporated some firetubes was the FAIRBAIRN–BEELEY BOILER of *c*.1895, shown in Fig. 9.

mundic a Cornish word of Celtic origin for iron PYRITES, once used for making sulphuric acid, and also known as fool's gold because it can be mistaken for the precious metal.

mungo recovered wool made from shredded old woollen or mixed fibre materials, such as tightly woven or heavily fulled cloth, known as hard rags. It was first made *c*.1834 by George Parr of Batley, Yorks., and an apocryphal story of how it got its name is that when the process was first being tried, the foreman had difficulty with it; on reporting to his superior that 'it would not go', he was told 'it mun go', meaning that it must go!

Old rags are sorted into qualities, then ground or pulled to shreds in a DEVIL, until they are in a condition similar to new raw wool. Cotton and any other threads present are then removed by CARBONIZING, and the all-wool result, called extract, is then ready for scribbling and carding and spun in the usual way. The woven cloth product, also known as mungo, was mostly used for blankets, overcoating, and military uniforms. Mungo production became a Yorkshire speciality in what is known as the heavy woollen area around Dewsbury. An older, similar material using soft rags is called SHODDY.

municipal engineering, *see* PUBLIC UTILITIES

Muntz metal a type of zinc-copper alloy invented in 1832 in Swansea, south Wales, by the English metallurgist George Frederick Muntz (1794–1857), and covered by two patents (no. 6325, 1832 and no. 11410, 1846). Otherwise known as 'yellow metal', it was particularly used for sheathing the hulls of wooden ships, replacing copper which was previously used.

murex a Mediterranean sea snail, *Murex brandaris* or *Murex purpura*, which yields a yellow fluid that becomes a purple dye when exposed to sunlight. It was known as the Tyrian or royal purple dye, after Tyre the Phoenician city where it was first used, and was known in Britain in Shakespeare's time. The colour is more a crimson than purple. Before synthetic dyes superseded it, murex was imported from Mediterranean sources.

muriatic acid (or oxymuriatic acid) a 19th-century bleaching term for HYDROCHLORIC ACID, derived from the Latin word *muria* meaning brine.

Mushet steel a self-hardening alloy steel containing chromium, manganese, and tungsten, discovered by Robert Forester Mushet (1811–91) around 1861. It was known as RMS steel (or Mushet's Special Self Hardening Steel), and was the first specialized tool steel. It did not soften when heating up while cutting other steels and iron, but actually hardened. It was originally made in secret in the Forest of Dean area, Glos., and not patented until 1867 (patent no. 88). Later, its manufacture was transferred to Sheffield.
Osborn, F.M. *The Story of the Mushets*, 1952

muslin (or muslina, mussolin) a fine, delicate, woven cotton fabric with an open weave. Its name comes from Mussolo, a town in Iraq, where it is believed the cloth originated. It was also extensively woven in India from hand spun yarn, and was imported into Britain in the 18th century by the EAST INDIA COMPANY. It was highly regarded here, being a much finer cloth than calico, and was popular for ladies' garments.

Many attempts were made in Britain to copy muslin, notably in Paisley, Scotland, but it was the invention of Samuel Crompton's MULE in 1779 which eventually permitted large scale production of the fine fabric. Bolton, Manchester, and Stockport became the muslin weaving centres for British muslins, which equalled in fineness those made in India. Muslins were usually woven in lengths of 20 to 30 yd, and sold in half lengths (demis). Many were given Indian names, such as BALASORE muslin, which was used for making handkerchiefs, and named after the port on the east coast of India from where it had been formerly imported. Muslins were made plain, spotted, striped, and patterned, and were exported in large quantities to tropical eastern countries. This trade, plus that of other British cottons, caused a great decline in the domestic hand spinning and weaving industries of India where the weavers could not compete with the cheaper, mass-produced cloth from Britain.

muslin wheel an early name for Samuel Crompton's spinning machine, which eventually became known simply as the MULE.

Mystery or Mistery, *see* GUILDS

N

nail a cloth measure equal to one-sixteenth of a yard, i.e. one nail is 2.25 in. The origin of the word is not clear.

nail making formerly a domestic based craft industry dating from the 16th century. The nail maker worked at home, where his small smithy was housed in an outhouse and contained a hand-blown hearth and anvil for heating iron strips to form the point and head of each nail by hand. Often his wife and children worked with him. The nailer would obtain strips or rods of iron from a forge equipped with a SLITTING MILL, make the nails, and sell them to middlemen or dealers called FOGGERS. Nailers tended to congregate in areas close to where iron was available. Some tens of thousands were engaged in making nails by hand around Walsall and other Midland towns in the 1740s, and nails were made in other parts of the country, such as around Warrington in Lancashire. The work was poorly paid, involving long hours to make a barely subsistence wage, due in the main to the high competition among the nailers themselves. By the 19th century master nailers emerged who had accumulated sufficient capital to build a row of nailers' terraced houses with smithies attached. They put work out to the nailers, and sold the combined output to wholesalers or exporters.

The nails made in these early days are known as cut nails. They were rectangular or square in cross-section, having been cut from iron sheets received from the slitting mill, the sheet being the thickness of the nail. Nails made by machine were introduced in the late 18th century by Thomas Clifford who patented machinery in 1790 (patent nos 1762 and 1785). These were similar to cut nails but were stamped from the iron sheets. Other machines were invented later which made nails from round wire, and these superseded cut nails, with high rates of continuous production possible, making nails from coils of wire on automatic machinery.

Bodey, H. *Nailmaking*, Shire Publications, Album No. 87, 1983

Court, W.H.B. *The Rise of Midland Industries, 1600–1838*, Oxford University Press, 1938

Neff, W. *Victorian Working Women*, Cass, 1966

nankeen a kind of cotton cloth originally made in Nankeen, China, from a naturally yellow variety of cotton. It was imitated in Britain by being made from ordinary cotton and dyed yellow, and was used in the 18th and 19th centuries for underclothing, trousers and ladies' dresses.

nap a soft feel to the surface of a cloth or carpet, obtained by raising the fibres of the material, and shearing them to a uniform short length or height. Velvet is an example of a cloth with a nap. An alternative word is pile (from the Latin *pilus* meaning hair), a term usually reserved for carpets.

narrow cloth (or kersey) hand woven cloth up to about 36 in wide. The width of the cloth was restricted to a man's reach as he passed the shuttle across the loom. The growth in production of narrow woollen cloth in Yorkshire is given below:

year	no. of pieces × 1000	yards × 1000
1740	58.6	–
1750	78.1	–
1760	69.6	–
1770	85.4	2,255.6
1779	93.1	2,659.7
1790	140.4	4,582.1
1800	169.3	6,014.4

Source: Heaton, H. *The Yorkshire Woollen and Worsted Industries*, 1965

After the invention of the FLYING SHUTTLE in 1733, wider cloths or BROADCLOTH could be woven by one man, and by *c*.1760 the production of broadcloths had exceeded that of narrow cloths. Broadcloth is a more useful dimension for making up into items than narrow cloth, and gradually the production of narrow cloth declined.

narrow gauge railway railways with a GAUGE less than the standard of 4 ft 8½ in. Many different gauges have been used ranging from 3 ft down to as little as 15 in, with gauges around 2 ft being the most popular. Narrow gauge railways were mainly developed as private MINERAL LINES but some also carried passengers and goods, whilst others were built for passenger traffic from the start, and usually known as light railways. Many narrow gauge railways were built in remote and mountainous areas where their construction cost was less than that for a standard gauge line. Many, fairly short narrow gauge lines were built in Caernarvonshire, Wales. They were often horse-operated at first, but specially built steam locomotives were adopted in later days. Their popularity declined with the building of better roads and the rise of road transport for the conveyance of minerals, etc. A small number of narrow gauge railways have been taken over by preservation and restoration societies and run as tourist attractions. The Ffestiniog Railway in north Wales, for instance, closed in 1946, but the Ffestiniog Railway Society was formed in 1954 and passenger traffic resumed the following year. Some of the original locomotives are still in operation.

Boyd, James I.C. *The British Narrow Gauge Railway* (several regional volumes), Oakwood Press
Dean, I. *Industrial Narrow Gauge Railways*, Shire Publications, Album No. 145, 1985
Lewis, M.J.T. *How Ffestiniog got its Railway*, Routledge and Kegan Paul, 1968

National Archaeological Record (NAR) a division of the NATIONAL MONUMENTS RECORD which is held by the ROYAL COMMISSION ON HISTORICAL MONUMENTS, ENGLAND (RCHME), comprising a register of archaeological sites and monuments up to 1945.

National Buildings Record (NBR) a collection of photographs of buildings, founded in 1941 to try to photograph important buildings before they were destroyed by aerial bombing, although many were lost before they could be recorded. Work continued after the war, and in 1963 the NBR was transferred to the ROYAL COMMISSION ON HISTORICAL MONUMENTS, ENGLAND (RCHME). Today, the collection contains over 1.5 million photographs as well as some measured drawings. It includes buildings of interest to industrial archaeologists, such as factory buildings and industrial housing, railway stations, steam engines and windmills. The NBR is at the RCHME headquarters in London, and is accessible to the public.

RCHME *Fifty Years of the National Buildings Record, 1941-1991*, Trigon Press, 1991

National Monuments Record (NMR) the national register and record of historical structures, monuments and landscapes, directed in England, by the ROYAL COMMISSION ON HISTORICAL MONUMENTS (RCHME). The register was created in 1964, and includes the NATIONAL BUILDINGS RECORD and the NATIONAL ARCHAEOLOGICAL RECORD (NAR). Some industrial sites are included. Similar registers are maintained in Wales and Scotland.

National Record of Industrial Monuments (NRIM) an expanding collection of record cards issued by the Council for British Archaeology on which details of industrial sites, etc. are recorded in a standard form from information provided by industrial archaeologists working in the field. Description of the item, its National Grid reference, its condition and any known information about possible future demolition, and notes about any documentary or photographic sources are included on the record card. The NRIM has been administered by Bath University since 1965, which maintains a set of cards; copies are also held by the Council for British Archaeology and the NATIONAL BUILDINGS RECORD. The NRIM is not to be confused with the National Survey of Industrial Monuments which had been set up earlier jointly by the Council for British Archaeology and the Ministry of Public Buildings and Works (the forerunner of the Department of the Environment). *See also* IRIS.

navigation an early name for a canal, also called a cut. There are many canalside pubs with the name Navigation Inn which perpetuate the old name for a canal. The skilled and unskilled workmen or labourers who built the canals were called navigators from about the 1790s and this was shortened to 'navvy' around the 1830s; previously, navvies were known as 'cutters'. After the canals, navvies built the railways. Some 250,000–300,000 were employed in the 1840s on railway construction. They were in general a hard-living, rough lot of men, who lived in temporary camps close to the route of the canal or railway on which they were working, often terrorizing the nearby villages with their activities and drunken behaviour. Many navvies came from Ireland, and a number from the Fens district of Lincolnshire. Railway navvies were known as bankers in some districts.

Coleman, T. *The Railway Navvies*, Penguin, 1968
Hanson, H. *Canal People*, David and Charles, 1979

Navigation Acts attempts to protect British shipping against foreign competition, dating from the 14th century. The Navigation Act of 1651 prohibited imports from certain countries except in British ships manned by British crews. It was introduced in an attempt to compete against the dominant hold on world shipping by the Dutch in Cromwell's time (1599–1658). A later Act of 1660 contained several new provisions and laid down the principles by which British shipping was regulated for nearly two centuries, with occasional modifications. The British colonies in USA were regarded as outposts of the mother country, and the same restrictions on use of foreign shipping was applied. However, by the late 18th century American ships were allowed to carry goods to Britain following the loss of the US colonies after the War of Independence (1775–83). In 1849, the Navigation laws were repealed, and in 1854 foreign ships were allowed to engage in UK coastal trade.

needle the horizontal, spring loaded, fine rod on a JACQUARD mechanism, which has a loop or eyelet formed in its length through which a vertical hooked rod passes (*see* Fig. 40). The horizontal movement of a needle is controlled by the punched cards. Where there is a hole in the card opposite the end of the needle, it enters the CYLINDER and pushes the vertical hook into the path of the GRIFFE blade so that the attached warp thread is raised when the griffe is lifted. Where there is no hole in the card, no needle movement occurs, and the appropriate warp thread is not raised.

needle making, *see* PIN AND NEEDLE MANUFACTURE

needlepoint lace (or Brussels point lace) a hand-made lace, introduced from Italy or Flanders, which involved making button stitches on a foundation fabric, and was difficult and expensive to produce. A point net lace machine was patented in 1781 by John Morris (patent no. 1282).

needle stick (or doffing stick) a wooden rod with a row of projecting pins or needles, used to take SLIVER off a hand-rotated CARDING engine, such as that patented by Daniel Bourn in 1748 (patent no. 628).

Neilson pre-heater an arrangement for pre-heating combustion air for a BLAST FURNACE, invented by James Beaumont Neilson (1792–1865) of Glasgow (patent no. 5701, 1828). It comprised a nest of curved cast-iron tubes in a brick chamber over a firegrate, sited before the TUYÈRES. Air was passed through the tubes, picking up heat from the fire.

net strictly, a plain, open lace which may have square or hexagonal openings (*see* LACE MAKING). However, the word net is often used as an alternative to lace, even though the fabric has figures and designs worked on it, e.g. net curtains.

nether stone, *see* BEDSTONE

Newcastle road, *see* WAGGONWAY

Newcomen atmospheric engine a single-acting, non-rotative BEAM ENGINE worked by atmospheric pressure. Invented and developed over several years by Thomas Newcomen (1663–1729) and his assistant John Calley (d. 1717), it was the first successful self-acting engine in the world. It was invented to operate underground pumps to dewater mines in Cornwall. A vertical, open-topped cylinder contained a piston, the latter connected by a chain to an overhead, centrally pivoted, timber beam. The other end of the beam was attached by another chain to the heavy wooden PUMP RODS which passed down a mine shaft to operate underground water pumps. A primitive steam-raising boiler was positioned immediately beneath the cylinder and was in communication with it via a stop valve. The engine was of massive construction with boiler and cylinder placed inside a tall engine house adjacent to the mine shaft. The end of the beam connected to the pump rods projected from the house through a slot in the wall. The beam pivots were supported by the wall, an arrangement known as HOUSE BUILT.

The action of the engine is as follows. The unbalanced weight of the pump rods slowly pulled their end of the beam down, which raised up the piston inside the cylinder at the other end of the beam. The piston drew in steam from the boiler at a very low pressure, only 1 lb per square inch or so above atmospheric pressure, which was the maximum the boiler could then produce. The stop valve was closed by a linkage from the overhead beam called a PLUG ROD as the beam moved, and another plug rod opened a water valve to spray cold water into the cylinder below the piston. This rapidly condensed the steam, creating a partial vacuum, and atmospheric pressure acting through the open top of the cylinder forced the piston down. This raised the pump rods which operated the pumps, lifting water out of the mine. Thus, the power stroke of the engine was effected by atmospheric pressure, the steam merely being used as a means of creating a vacuum below the piston.

Newcomen engines worked slowly, used a lot of coal, and were restricted in speed to the time the boiler took to make more steam after completion of a power stroke. Newcomen used two controlling devices to regulate the engine speed – the BUOY CONTROLLER and the CATARACT. The first recorded Newcomen engine was at Dudley, Staffs., in 1712, installed to dewater a coal mine. It had a brass cylinder of 21 in diameter, 7 ft 10 in high, and pumped 10 gallons of water from a depth of 153 ft at each stroke. By 1762, cast-iron cylinders of 74 in diameter were in use. Although slow and inefficient, the atmospheric engine was the only engine available for dewatering mines for some sixty years. It was also used for pumping water supplies. As a result of a loosely worded patent of Thomas Savery, Newcomen was unable to patent his invention, and died before Savery's patent expired (*see* MINERS' FRIEND). Many improvements were made to the atmospheric engine, particularly by John Smeaton (1724–92) in the 1760s, who raised its thermal efficiency. Atmospheric engines were superseded by true steam engines which used steam for their power stroke, and since pressures higher than atmospheric were, by then, available, greater power was obtained. In the 18th century Newcomen type engines were often called common engines or vacuum engines.

Jenkins, R. 'Savery, Newcomen and the early history of the steam engine', *Transactions of the Newcomen Society* III (1922–3) and IV (1923–4)
Rolt, L.T.C. and Allen, J.S. *The Steam Engine of Thomas Newcomen*, Moorland, 1979

Newcomen Society short name for the Newcomen Society for the Study of the History of Engineering and Technology, founded in 1920 and incorporated in 1961. It is based at the Science Museum, London and has a branch at Sheffield, Yorks. Its published *Transactions* are an authoritative source of information for industrial archaeologists.

new draperies new types of woollen and worsted cloth first introduced into Britain by immigrant Flemish weavers who settled mainly in Norwich, Colchester, and other East Anglian towns in the 16th century. New draperies were finer, lighter fabrics than those previously woven by English weavers (*see* DRAPERIES). They were not controlled by the restrictive rules and regulations of the woollen guilds, nor subject to ALNAGE, and consequently their manufacture flourished.

Kerridge, E. *Textile Manufacturers in Early Modern England*, Manchester University Press, 1985 (covers the period 1500–1760)

New York World Fair, 1853 the USA's first international exhibition modelled on the GREAT EXHIBITION OF 1851 held in London. It even had a 'palace' similar to London's Crystal Palace, but as a result of poor planning and the fact that the crystal palace leaked rain, spoiling many exhibits and drenching visitors, the exhibition was a failure and suffered a financial loss.

nicking laying claim to an abandoned lead mine. In the early days of lead mining in Derbyshire, if a mine was left abandoned, providing it was not due to waterlogging, another miner could claim it by asking the BARMASTER to nick (i.e. cut a notch) in the wooden frame of the stow (windlass). If three successive undisputed nicks were made at weekly intervals, the ownership of the mine passed to the new claimant under the mining laws.

niddy-noddy a frame to skein and measure the length of woollen yarn, so called from its nodding action.

nip frame (or nip comb) that component in the mechanism of a combing machine which grips uncombed feed material between its jaws, and transfers the tuft which it breaks away from the feed bulk, onto the next operating stage. The jaws open and close as required. Nip frames are used in HEILMANN and LISTER COMBERS.

Noble comber a machine for combing out wool, cleaning out extraneous matter and short fibres (or NOILS) and laying the combed long fibres more or less parallel to each other as required for WORSTED spinning. It is named after James Noble of Leeds, Yorks., who took out several combing patents (chiefly no. 894, 1853) to cover the invention he made in association with George Edmund Donisthorpe of Bradford, Yorks. The latter was precluded from appearing as a joint patentee by the terms of his agreement with Samuel Cunliffe Lister, whom he had also assisted in improving wool combing (*see* LISTER COMBER). Noble had worked for over forty years gradually perfecting his machine. His comber handles almost all wools except those with extremely long or extremely short fibres, and is the most popular wool comber in the worsted industry. It is fully automatic, combing out the long fibres which become worsted TOPS, and separating out the noils which are sent to the woollen or felting industries.

Fig. 35 illustrates the basic operations of the machine. It comprised a large circular ring of upstanding combing pins, surrounded by a number of feeding devices called conductor boxes which fed previously prepared rolls of woollen SLIVERS inwards over the combing pins. In the diagram the rolls of slivers sit on wooden rollers lying below the combing ring; in Noble's original 1853 machine the slivers were mounted above the ring. The whole assembly slowly rotated at about 4 rpm. In the central space, a smaller ring of upstanding combing pins was placed eccentrically so that its outer edge nearly touched the inner edge of the large ring at one point *X*, all the pins being at the same horizontal level. The smaller ring rotated in the same direction as the larger outer ring at the same peripheral speed at point *X*, so that the pins on each ring came together and parted at the same speed. As the conductor boxes passed through segment *A–B*, a length of sliver was gradually fed inwards over the pins until it covered all the pins on the outer and inner ring at *B*. While passing through segment *B–C*, the fibres were pushed down into the pins by a rapid up and down motion of a dabbing brush. As segment *C–D* was passed through, the fibres were separated into two paths as the rings diverged, some fibres remaining on the outer ring, others on the inner ring, this giving the combing action. In segment *D–E* moving leather straps brushed the fibres sideways and directed their leading tips between drawing-off rollers, at *F* for the outer ring and at *G* on the inner ring. At *G* the fibres from both rings rejoined and were taken off the machine as a continuous combed sliver and coiled in a can. During the remainder of the complete rotation of the outer ring segment *E–A*, any excess length of fibres which had escaped being drawn off at *F* was removed. Any short fibres left in the inner ring were lifted out of the pins by knives *H* and directed down a noil chute. The cycle then repeated itself when the feeding-in point was reached again.

Various improvements were later made to the machine by others. The rolls of sliver awaiting combing were placed below the comb rings, and modern Noble combers have two inner rings of smaller diameter than the original single ring, with two feeding-in points, making in effect a double machine. The combed slivers from each half of the machine are combined into one.

Burnley, J. *The History of Wool and Wool Combing*, 1889; reprinted by Kelley, New York, 1969

noil the short unwanted fibres combed out of wool which is being prepared for WORSTED. Noils are sent to woollen manufacturers, where they are blended in with other wools. Noil is known as pinion (from the French *peignon*, meaning combing) in the West Country; an old spelling is noyl.

non-condensing steam engine a STEAM ENGINE from which the spent, exhaust steam either passes out to the atmosphere and is lost, or in some cases is used as process steam in a factory. A locomotive is an example of a non-condensing steam engine.

non-dead-centre steam engine a patented design of twin-cylinder, inverted vertical steam engine, which can be started irrespective of the position of the crank. Invented in Glasgow and patented by W.Y. Fleming, P. Ferguson, and G. Dixon (patent no. 4079, 1891), it was originally intended for marine use. For this application the principal advantage was to enable frequent stopping and starting of a ship's engine during manoeuvring of the vessel. The design was also used in a small number of engines for driving textile mills.

DEAD CENTRE situations were avoided by connecting each piston rod to a corner of a triangular shaped member which replaces a pair of conventional connecting rods. The 'triangle' was connected at its third corner to a single crank, and the geometry arranged so that the crank would turn irrespective of its stopped position. Another feature of the design was that the crankshaft lay in plan, at right angles to the line of cylinders instead of in line with them, as in conventional twin-cylinder engines which have two cranks.

noria a simple, ancient device for raising water, comprising an endless chain of pots or pitchers secured between a pair of ropes which pass over a top wheel. The lower end of the chain dips into the water, and as the chain revolves water is scooped out and discharged at a higher level as the pots go over the top wheel. The noria was the forerunner of the CHAIN PUMP, or bucket elevator. The word is Spanish, and comes from an earlier Arabic word; norias were used in Spain and the East.

Norse wheel (or Danish wheel, Greek wheel) a primitive design of WATERWHEEL dating from the 8th century. It comprised a horizontal wooden wheel with usually six to eight protruding vanes, mounted on the lower end of a vertical shaft or tirl. The tirl passed through the stationary BEDSTONE of a pair of grinding stones to support the upper RUNNER STONE which was fastened to it. The wheel was usually sited on a suitable slope such that water from a stream could be directed onto one side of the wheel, turning it by impact against the vanes, and falling clear to continue on its way. The rotating wheel directly drove the runner stone mounted above it, grain being introduced into a central hole, to be ground between the rotating and stationary surfaces. The wheel was enclosed in a simple building or hut to make a primitive corn mill of low power (about 0.5 hp at most). The Norse wheel is a forerunner of other vertical shaft waterwheels such as the FRANCIS TURBINE of 1840. A surviving example is Click Mill at Dounby, in Orkney.

north light roof a roof design common on weaving sheds, comprising a sawtooth profile with unequal slopes forming each ridge (*see* Fig. 57). The steeper slope is glazed and the other solid, and wherever possible the glazed slopes face north, or near north. This configuration gives the best overhead daylight illumination essential for weaving, without glare from the sun. It is frequently called a shed roof, and sometimes a dog-tooth or ridge-and-furrow roof.

Northrop loom an automatic power loom invented in 1894 by James H. Northrop, a Yorkshireman from Keighley who had emigrated to Massachusetts, USA, and still in use. Its main feature is the automatic transfer of weft PIRNS to the shuttle without stopping the loom. This is achieved by a cylindrical magazine holding twenty-four full pirns positioned at one end of the loom (usually the right-hand end), and a feeler device at the opposite end. The feeler touches the pirn in use each time it arrives in the box at that end, and when it senses that the pirn is almost empty, it operates a mechanism at the magazine end which ejects that pirn when it arrives at the magazine end. A fresh full pirn is immediately fed into the shuttle without stopping the loom, and the magazine indexed round to present the next full pirn ready for insertion. One weaver could oversee the working of several Northrops due to the automatic changing of pirns. However, the loom was slow in being adopted in Britain.

notching up a term used on steam railways for moving the gear lever of a locomotive towards the centre of the notched quadrant in the driver's cab, from either the forward running position or the reversing position. Notching (or linking) up shortens the travel of the steam valve and reduces the CUT-OFF, saving steam which works more expansively. The term was still used even if a screw reverser was fitted instead of a notched quadrant.

noyal a type of canvas sailcloth, named after the cloth made in the town of Noyal near Rennes, France. Its manufacture in England was introduced by the HUGUENOTS in the 18th century.

nozzle a Cornish term for the housing or chest containing the double-beat valves (*see* BEAT) on BEAM STEAM ENGINES.

N-truss, *see* LINVILLE TRUSS

numbered iron wrought iron graded according to its quality. Common grade, usually called merchant or crown bar, was also known as No. 2 iron. This, when broken up into short lengths, repiled or faggoted, heated and re-rolled into one piece again, was sometimes known as No. 3 iron, and was of better quality than No. 2 iron. Alternatively, No. 2 iron was also known as Best iron or B iron, whilst No. 3 iron was also known as Best Best iron or BB iron.

nut 1. the small gearwheel or pinion fastened on the millstone shaft which takes its drive from the spur wheel. Its teeth are usually made from a hard wood such as hornbeam or appletree. **2.** the internally screwed part which screws onto a bolt to clamp or fasten machine components etc. together. Nuts have flats formed on their outer sides so that they can be tightened up or unscrewed with the aid of a spanner. Early nuts were usually square, i.e. they only had four flats; later, hexagonal nuts became standard.

oakum old, unravelled tarry rope, called junk, used for caulking (stopping up) the joints between the planks of wooden sailing ships. Picking by hand (i.e. unravelling) old ropes was frequently the task set for inmates of the workhouse, or the recipients of parish relief, particularly women, or prisoners in jail. The use of oakum for caulking economized on the import of HEMP from India. Oakum was also used in stuffing boxes, as piston packing in early steam engines such as NEWCOMEN ATMOSPHERIC ENGINES, and for stuffing mattresses.

oast house (or hopkiln) a kiln for drying HOPS. It comprises a tall, usually circular but sometimes square, building, topped by a conical cowl or cap, known as a granny, which has an outlet or ventilation slot through which the hot air can escape. The cowl can rotate under the action of the wind on a projecting vane so that the vent is always on the leeward side and the escape of hot air is not hindered. The hops are spread out on an upper floor in the kiln, covered by a fine netting, and dried by the heat rising from a fire maintained at ground floor. To avoid contaminating the hops by smoke, charcoal or anthracite is used since these are virtually smokeless fuels. Attached to the kiln is a rectangular building, in which the hops awaiting drying and fuel are stored, and the warm, dried hops allowed to cool before being compressed by a simple press into long sacks called pockets.

Oast houses are outstanding features in hop growing districts. The word oast possibly comes from the Latin *aestus* meaning heat. Very few oast houses are in use today: most have been converted into residences, and hops today are dried under factory conditions.

Walton, Robin A.E. *Oasts in Kent – 16th to 20th Century: Their Construction and Equipment*, Christine Swift, 1985

oil engine an INTERNAL COMBUSTION ENGINE developed in the late 19th century, and usually made as a stationary, horizontal unit, competing against gas engines. Oil engines were mainly used in locations where TOWN GAS had not yet reached, and were cheaper and more compact than steam engine plant. Oil can easily be transported and stored, and has a higher calorific value per lb than coal. Most oil engines were single cylinder, running on the

OTTO CYCLE. The biggest problem to overcome was to atomize the oil sufficiently to form an explosive mixture with the correct amount of air within the engine cylinder. Two solutions were developed: the vaporizing method, and spray injection. The vaporizing method, devised by Dent and Priestman in 1886, used paraffin oil, and had a vaporizer heated by the exhaust gases to gasify the fuel before it was drawn into the cylinder; ignition was by spark or hot spot. In spray ignition, invented in 1890 by Herbert Ackroyd-Stuart (1864–1927), the oil was sprayed into the cylinder as a fine mist by a pump, and ignited by a hot spot or tube.

Oil engines working on these principles were soon superseded by Diesel engines, introduced soon after 1893, in which ignition is achieved spontaneously by the high temperature reached by compression alone, without the application of any external heat or spark (*see* COMPRESSION IGNITION ENGINE).

Clerk, D. *The Gas, Petrol, and Oil Engine*, 2 vols, Longmans Green, 1916
Evans, A.F. *The History of the Oil Engine, 1680–1930*, Sampson Low, 1932

oil of vitriol the old name for SULPHURIC ACID, made by heating COPPERAS.

Oldham coupling a means of joining two shafts which are parallel to each other but not in line, providing they are not too far displaced. It comprises a disk keyed to the end of each shaft with a slot cut diametrically across its face, and another disk of similar diameter with a protruding tongue on either face, these tongues being at right angles to each other. The tongues are a sliding fit in the slots on the other disks, and this disk is placed between the other two so that each tongue fits into its corresponding slot on the shaft disk. As the shafts rotate, the central disk describes a circular path equal to the distance apart of the shafts, the tongues sliding to and fro across the slots at each revolution. Thus, the motion of one shaft is transmitted to the other with uniform velocity.

'Old Loughborough' nickname by which John Heathcoat's (1783–1861) bobbinet lace-making machine was known, which he invented in 1808 (patent no. 3151) in the town of that name. The machine was later known as the plain net machine. It made a plain hexagonal net, and imitated hand-made pillow or BOBBIN LACE. In 1816, the LUDDITES smashed Heathcoat's machines during riots, causing him to move to Tiverton in Devon, and set up business there. In 1813, Heathcoat patented improvements to the original machine (patent no. 3673).

old man workings the name given to early worked-out areas of veins by lead miners. Sometimes when a vein was being worked, evidence was discovered of part of it having been worked (and unrecorded) by earlier mining activity. This, of course, would only be near the surface, since early mining techniques did not reach down very far.

oliver a small lift- or TILT HAMMER worked by foot and used in smithies for shaping nails, bolts, and similar small, forged articles. It comprises a framework supporting the hammer arm, anvil, and the former's pivoting arrangements. The hammer arm is connected by a rod to an overhead spring which returns the hammer after a blow has been struck, and a chain runs to a foot treadle. Since the hammer is operated by the foot, the user has both hands free to attend to the work being performed. The somewhat strange name has an obscure origin. Seventeenth-century hammers were known as hollipers, and used a wood spring-pole, often made from a holly branch (hence the name) to return the hammer. Oliver may be a derivation of holliper. In the nail-making trade, olivers were known as tommy hammers. Olivers were also used in early BLOOMERIES before water-powered hammers were introduced, where they were used by smiths working up a bloom at a STRINGHEARTH. It has also been suggested that an oliver was used by smiths not wishing to employ a striker or mate to use a hammer.

open belt a power transmitting belt which connects two pulleys in such a way that there is open space between the two pulleys, and the direction of rotation of the second pulley is therefore the same as that of the first. For flat driving belts, this means that the inner surface of the belt passes round each pulley in turn. The converse, for reversing the direction of rotation, is the CROSSED BELT.

opencast working removing coal, ore, etc. from open pits or ditches. Mining by opencast working, or shallow mining, has been used for centuries. In the 17th century opencast coal mining was known as footrid in Staffordshire, a word derived from 'ridding', i.e. getting rid of the top soil to expose the underlying coal. Other old words for opencast working include grubbing (from the old German *Grabhan*, meaning a grave or ditch in the ground), and goffan, a dialect word for an excavation. Working tin and copper by opencast methods was called stockwork in Cornwall.

Coal is still removed by opencast mining today, from seams too shallow for underground mining; the old supporting pillars of coal left by past shallow mining are recovered. Opencast extraction of ironstone is also used.

open hearth furnace a gas-fired, steel-making

furnace comprising a shallow, refractory-lined hearth, and incorporating a REGENERATOR. This type of furnace was originally developed in Britain by Charles William Siemens (1823–83) in 1856, from an idea of his brother Frederick (1826–1904). The fuel used was PRODUCER GAS made in equipment the brothers had patented in 1861 (patent no. 167), preheated in the regenerator. The Siemens furnace was actually first used by the glass making industry in Britain, but in 1863–4 Pierre-Emile Martin (1824–1915) used one in France for making steel from pig iron and steel scrap. Combining the processes from both inventors, the Siemens–Martin steel-making process (an alternative name for the open hearth furnace) was evolved. Steel was made using pig iron decarburized by some iron ore plus steel scrap, and since the reactions in the furnace were slower than in the then-used BESSEMER CONVERTER, better control over the process was possible. The open hearth furnace began to supersede the Bessemer process as the principal method for mass producing steel, and by about 1900 was almost universally in use in Britain.

Two types of steel are made depending on whether the furnace is lined with acid or basic refractories. The former lining could only be used with iron ores with few or no phosphorus impurities. Since the majority of ores are phosphoric, most open hearth steel is basic steel. Fuel oil, gas from coke ovens, and blast furnace gases have been used as fuel, and some furnaces tilt for ease of emptying.

Fig. 52 shows a Siemens–Martin open hearth regenerative furnace. Air and gas flow, shown from left to right, is reversed after about 20 minutes when the products of combustion have heated up the right-hand generator bricks, which are then ready to preheat the cold incoming air and producer gas which are directed through them.

Ordnance Survey National Grid, *see* GRID REFERENCE, MAPS

ore the metalliferous matter found naturally in the earth in veins or beds. The metallic content is usually the result of volcanic activity in prehistoric times. Ores are either quarried or mined; the earliest ores were discovered by accident where they outcropped onto the surface. As knowledge of their appearance and composition increased with the study of geology, ores were prospected for and methods of winning them and their subsequent treatment developed. Metals are combined chemically with other elements, pure metals being only very rarely found. The elements most commonly found in combination are oxides, sulphides, phosphates, silicates and carbonates. After extraction, ores require DRESSING before the metal content can be obtained by SMELTING, and usually a refining operation is necessary afterwards. The depth to which ores are mined depends on their economic value which has fluctuated over the centuries, plus the difficulty of reaching workable deposits. An alternative name for ore used in some old documents is 'mine'; an old spelling of ore was ewer.

The commonly mined ores in Britain (see individual entries) are listed below.

Oregrund iron, *see* DANNEMORA IRON

ore hearth an early type of simple heating furnace for smelting ores. William Humphray was given letters patent in 1565 for smelting

Metal	Ore	Composition	Alternative name(s)
arsenic	mispickel	sulphide of iron and arsenic	
copper	chalcocite	sulphide of copper	copper glance
copper	malachite	cupric carbonate	
copper	chalcopyrite	sulphide of copper and iron	copper pyrite
copper	cuprite	oxide of copper	
iron	haematite	oxide of iron	bloodstone
iron	siderite	iron carbonate	shale ironstone; chalybite
iron	iron pyrites	sulphide of iron	fool's gold; mundic
iron	magnetite	oxide of iron	
iron	clay ironstone	carbonate of iron	
lead	galena	lead sulphide	lead glance
lead	cerussite	lead carbonate	white lead
tin	cassiterite	oxide of tin	tin stone
tungsten	wolfram	tungstate of iron and manganese	wolframite; wolframium
zinc	calamine	zinc carbonate	
zinc	blende	zinc sulphate	black jack; sphalerite; mock lead
zinc	smithsonite	silicate of zinc	

lead in an ore hearth sited near Beauchief in Derbyshire.

ore slide, *see* BUDDLE

organzine (or organza) a strong thread of silk intended for use as warp thread, made from several strands twisted together to form a 'rope'. The strands are twisted in the opposite direction to that of the component threads. *Organzino* means extra twist in Italian.

orleans cloth a cloth made from a cotton warp and a worsted weft, so named since it is reputed to have first been made in the French city of Orleans. Its manufacture became a speciality of Bradford in the early 19th century.

ornamentation in iron decorative work in iron, both wrought and cast, which has a long history of artistic use both architecturally and on machinery. Ornamental wrought ironwork has its origin in the provision of security devices – window grilles, gates, and railings, etc., the blacksmiths of the day adding some form of decoration for their more wealthier customers. Jean Tijou (*fl.*1680s), a HUGUENOT refugee living in England, was a master of decorative ironwork in the late 17th century, and inspired the development of the skill and art through many pupils. Besides exterior wrought ironwork, interior examples still exist as banisters for staircases in large country houses and as screens etc. in churches. Decorative wrought ironwork is made by hand, hammering, twisting, and heat forging the bars

into the various designs and patterns. A fine example of wrought-iron is the 1719 gates to Chirk Castle, Clwyd, North Wales.

In the 16th century some elementary decoration was sometimes added to cast-iron firebacks. One way of doing this was to press rope stiffened by glue or pitch into the sand mould to form borders and designs on the front surface of the fireback. The wider introduction of cast iron in the 18th century enabled ornamentation to be easily added by carving the patterns in wood, and figures not possible on hand worked wrought iron were produced. Wrought-iron articles such as gates were copied in cast iron down to the rivet heads which often held the separate pieces of wrought iron bars together.

Decorative ironwork was the hallmark of Regency period architecture (1811–20) with widespread use of verandahs, bandstands, seaside piers, roof trusses in market halls, shopping arcades, etc. Its use continued into the Georgian and Victorian periods, and by the late Victorian age a bewildering selection of ornamental railings, gates, balconies, circular stairways, etc. was available from the catalogues of iron merchants; the skill of the iron founder was displayed at the GREAT EXHIBITION OF 1851 and in the well-known gates near Alexandra Gate, Hyde Park. All manner of themes were used to add decoration to cast-iron structures and machines: foliage representation was a popular theme, with vine

These iron gates at Warrington in Cheshire were cast at Ironbridge for the 1851 Great Exhibition

and acanthus leaves and bunches of grapes; while classical lines in the form of Greek fluted columns, complete with appropriate capitals, were used to decorate the ENTABLATURE of large beam pumping engines, particularly those operating public water supplies. Two good, preserved examples are at Papplewick, Notts., and Abbey Lane, Leicester. Some cast-iron roof trusses in textile mills and other industrial buildings were given decorative treatment. Machines too occasionally had ornamental frames as was the fashion at the time.

Fearn, Jacqueline. *Cast Iron*, Shire Publications, Album No. 250, 1990
Lister, Raymond. *Decorative Wrought Ironwork in Great Britain*, Bell, 1957
Lister, Raymond. *Decorative Cast Ironwork in Great Britain*, Bell, 1960

oscillating steam engine a compact design of steam engine which eliminates a connecting rod by having the piston rod directly attached to the crank. The cylinder is supported on trunnions projecting from its sides, at or near the centre of its length, to allow it to oscillate or rock through an arc to follow the rotation of the crank. The trunnions are hollow and form the steam inlet and exhaust outlet to and from the valve chest mounted on the cylinder (*see* Fig. 47).

The first oscillating engine was invented *c.*1785 by William Murdock (1754–1839), the motion of the slide valve being given by the rocking of the cylinder. One such engine was fitted to the first iron-hulled paddle steamer, the *Aaron Manby*, in 1822. John Penn (1805–78) developed the idea further around 1842–3 for marine use, where the compactness of this design was an advantage for driving paddle steamers, and they became very popular. A 500 hp twin-cylinder oscillating engine of Penn's manufacture replaced Brunel's original engines in the *Great Britain* in 1852. The design is now largely obsolete, but the same principle is used on small oil pumps etc.

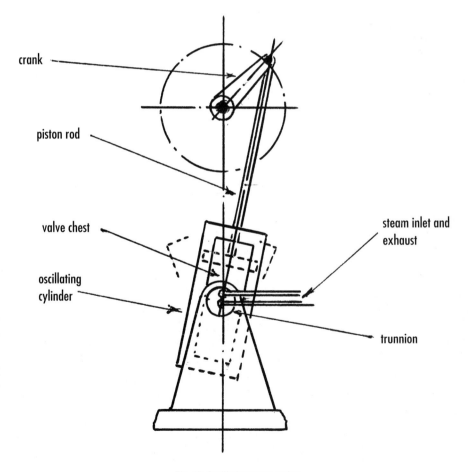

crank

piston rod

valve chest

oscillating cylinder

steam inlet and exhaust

trunnion

Fig. 47. Oscillating steam engine

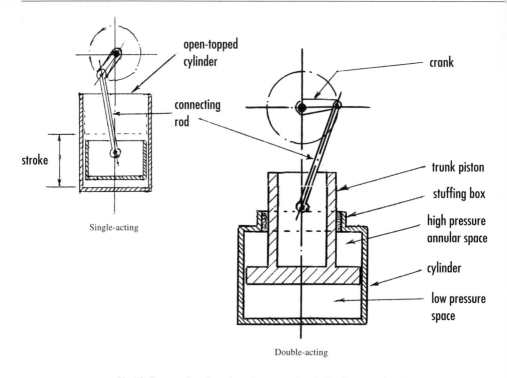

Fig. 48. Cross-sections through trunk steam engines (valve chests not shown)

Osmond iron a particularly pure and ductile Swedish iron, held in high regard in Britain and imported until Britain achieved more-or-less self sufficiency in iron production. It came from bog or lake ores, and was imported into Britain via Danzig, the trade being mostly in the hands of the HANSEATIC LEAGUE. It was also known as Danzic iron.

In the 16th century somewhat similar ores were discovered in south Wales and English Osmond iron production commenced in Tintern, Monmouth. The iron was particularly suitable for WIREDRAWING, and was developed by the COMPANY OF MINERAL AND BATTERY WORKS for that purpose.

osset loom (or ossett) a narrow hand loom. The origin of the word is obscure, but it has been suggested that it is a dialect derivation of worsted. Ossett, or ousett was a kind of woollen cloth.

Otto cycle the thermodynamic pressure-volume cycle for gas and petrol engines, which is also known as the constant volume cycle since the heat is received and rejected at an almost constant volume within the engine cylinder. The cycle is named after Nicholaus August Otto (1832–91) who developed the sequence in his 1876 gas engines. The Otto cycle may be four stroke or two stroke. Otto's four stroke cycle comprises a sequence of two revolutions of the engine which then repeats itself. The strokes are suction, compression, working or explosion, and exhaust, the admission and exhaust of the working fuel being controlled by the opening and closing of valves at the correct times. In the two stroke version, introduced by Dugald Clerk (1854–1932) in 1880, an externally pressurized fresh gaseous charge forces out the burned gases near the end of the working stroke, thus eliminating the suction and exhaust strokes. There is thus a working stroke for every revolution of the engine.

outcrop a stratum of a mineral such as coal etc. which comes naturally to the surface, perhaps because of the contour of the ground, or the inclination of the stratum itself. Horizontal strata can outcrop on a hillside, or underground inclined strata can outcrop on level ground, or there may be a combination of both configurations. The earliest coal mines were the working of outcrops by driving DRIFTS into the hillside. Coal seams running out to the surface are sometimes called crop seams.

P

outdoor stroke the vertical distance swept through by the outside portion of the beam of a CORNISH BEAM ENGINE, to operate underground pumps in the mine shaft. On some engines the outdoor stroke was less than the indoor or piston stroke, giving the engine a slight mechanical advantage. This was achieved by the beam not being pivoted at its centre.

overdrift the drive to the grinding stones of a corn mill which comes from above. Almost all windmills are overdrift, although there are a few exceptions when the drive comes from below, in which case it is said to be underdrift.

overlooker head spinner in a cotton spinning mill, responsible for the operation of the machinery and quality of the product. He was also known as a mule gaffer in those mills which spun by MULES.

overshot wheel a design of WATERWHEEL in which the water is fed onto the wheel at a point just above the top centre (*see* Fig. 84c). The weight of water filling the buckets on one side only of the wheel causes it to be unbalanced and rotate. The direction of rotation of the wheel at its top is the same as that of the flow of water. This configuration can only be used where there is sufficient difference in level between the LEAT bringing the water to the wheel and the TAILRACE taking the water away, the diameter of the wheel being suited to this distance.

owling nocturnal smuggling of wool from England to the Continent. The export of wool was prohibited by law in the 17th century to protect the home British industry. An obvious reference to the night owl.

Oxland and Hocking calciner (or Oxland tube calciner) an ore roasting furnace or CALCINER invented by Robert Oxland and John Hocking II (patent no. 2950, 1868). It comprised a firebrick-lined iron cylinder, 4–6 ft in diameter and 25–30 ft long, held at a slight incline and slowly rotated about its long axis. A firebox at the low end provided heat, and ore fed in at the high end was calcined as it slowly tumbled down the cylinder in the hot gases.

Oxland process the method for separating WOLFRAM from tin developed by Robert Oxland of Plymouth, in 1844. Wolfram has a similar specific gravity to tin and is difficult to separate from it; Oxland converted wolfram to tungstate of soda, from which tungsten can be extracted. The process was first carried out at Drakewalls mine in east Cornwall.

oxymuriatic acid a late 18th–early 19th-century bleaching term, first used by Lavoisier (1743–94), for chlorine; it is sometimes known as oxygenated muriatic acid.

packet a boat providing a passenger service to a regular timetable on a canal or short sea crossing; also known as a passage boat. Canal packets were often fitted up with first and second class cabins with facilities for serving food and drink. They were crewed by a captain or master, a steersman, a stopman (to assist at locks), and a boy to attend to the towing horse. Frequently, the master's wife and a young woman assistant served passengers' refreshments. Some canal packets carried goods as well as passengers. Packet boats were usually towed by one horse with speeds up to about 4 mph including passage through locks; horses were changed at staging points on long journeys by horse contractors. Faster services were provided on some canals by FLYBOATS.

In Scotland, canal packets were known as track boats. A Scottish poet, James Maxwell, described a Forth and Clyde Company's track boat operating in the late 1780s as follows:

> For here a cabin in each end is found,
> That doth with all conveniences abound.
> One in the head, for ladies nine or ten,
> Another in the stern, for gentlemen,
> With fires and tables, seats to sit at ease;
> They may regale themselves with what
>   they please.
> For all utensils here are at command,
> To eat and drink whate'er they have at hand.

Canalside pubs called 'The Packet' indicate that a packet boat once operated along the canal.

packhorse a horse or pony for carrying goods in packs slung across its back. Before roads were suitable for wheeled traffic, goods were transported on wooden frames called crooks or crubs, slung across the saddles of horses or ponies. Galloway ponies were especially used in the Pennines. Packs or pannier baskets containing the goods were strapped to the frame and hung down either side of the horse. A packhorse could carry about 250 lb, and walk up to about 25 miles in a day depending on the terrain. Packhorse routes or packways were followed across country, crossing rivers and streams by PACKHORSE BRIDGES, and along paved causeways over soft ground. Late in the 17th century, guide posts where packways crossed were made obligatory under a 1697 statute, and some may still be found on open moorland (*see* STOOP).

A single packhorse would carry a handloom weaver's pieces to market, or a chapman's wares from village to village. Strings of packhorses, known as jags, under the control of a carrier or packman, would carry finished goods for manufacturers. Up to thirty or forty horses walking in single file, the lead horse carrying a warning bell, were not uncommon. Letters were sometimes entrusted to a carrier, and considerable distances were covered to regular timetables by some. 150 packhorses took cloth from Manchester to Bridgnorth, Salop., each week in 1766, several days' journey; at Bridgnorth, the cloth was transferred onto boats for forward travel on the river Severn. Every town and village on a packhorse route had an inn for stabling the horses, and a lockable store for the packs overnight. Journeys were preferably made in daylight due to the unreliable state of tracks and the risk of robbery. Travellers with only one, or a few packhorses would form a convoy for mutual protection and help.

By the end of the 18th century road improvements permitted more wheeled traffic, and much greater loads could be carried on canals. The use of packhorses therefore declined, except in remote areas where roads were scarce or still in poor condition. The importance of packhorse transport can be judged by the number of Packhorse Inns scattered around the country on former packhorse routes.

Drake, M. and D. *Early Trackways in the South Pennines*, Pennine Heritage Network, 1981
Raistrick, A. *Green Roads in the Mid-Pennines*, Moorland, 1978

packhorse bridge a bridge over a stream or river on a packhorse track. Early bridges were probably wooden affairs, but these were replaced in the 16th century by more durable stone structures. Single arched bridges are narrow and hump-backed (to allow the passage of extra water when the river is in spate), with low parapets, to allow packhorses to cross without their side panniers being obstructed. The horses would cross one after the other in a line, and often a length of stone paving either side of the bridge led them onto it. Wider rivers were crossed by bridges with more than one arch. Many packhorse bridges still stand, often in picturesque situations, with old packhorse tracks converging onto them. The parapet walls have now usually been raised for safety reasons.

The packhorse bridge at Swanside Beck, Lancs.

packing material, also known as stuffing, used to form a seal between moving parts in an engine, machine, etc. and prevent the escape of fluids such as steam and water. Packing is used in the STUFFING BOX of a steam engine cylinder where the piston rod enters it, and a different form of packing is used on hydraulic machinery to contain the high pressure water or oil inside the cylinder at the circumference of the moving ram. Packing is also needed round the circumference of pistons.

Many materials have been used as packing, some of animal origin, others of metallic construction. The packing used round the edge of NEWCOMEN STEAM ENGINE pistons comprised a leather flap with a layer of water on top to provide a seal. OAKUM was also used as a packing material. James Watt's piston packing was hemp rope and tallow, squeezed and held in position by a JUNK RING. Many patents were taken out for types of packing: for instance, in 1797, the Revd Edmund Cartwright patented the first expanding metallic piston packing (patent no. 2202); in 1823, William Jessop II invented a spiral-spring packing ring for pistons (patent no. 4770); and in 1852, John Ramsbottom invented a split piston ring for locomotives (patent no. 767). For water-using machines, Sir Samuel Morland (1625–95) invented hat-leather rings for his metal plunger water pump, while Henry Maudslay invented cup-leathers for Bramah hydraulic presses in 1798. Asbestos fibre packings for resisting high temperatures were introduced c.1870. See also METALLIC PACKINGS.

packing floor the intermediate access floor built round large, early BEAM STEAM ENGINES at a level just below the top of the steam cylinder so that the STUFFING BOX could be easily reached for adjustment and repacking. Other floors were the DRIVING FLOOR and the BEAM LOFT.

packway route followed by PACKHORSES over remote country, moorland, etc. Packways may often be traced by remains of CAUSEY STONES, STOOPS, wayside stone horse drinking troughs, and PACKHORSE BRIDGES over streams and rivers. Most packways were just wide enough to take packhorses walking in single file, but some were widened to take wheeled vehicles when the traffic of goods increased beyond the carrying capacity of packhorse trains.

In some parts of the country, mostly in the north, a packway is called a jaggerway or jagger lane, derived from the word jag, another name for a packhorse. In the south, packways may be called galley lanes, and this is derived from the Galloway breed of pony commonly used as packhorses.

Hey, D. *Packmen, Carriers, and Packhorse Roads: Trade and Communications in North Derbyshire and South Yorkshire*, Leicester University Press, 1980

paddle 1. the means for controlling the flow of water into and out of a canal lock compartment. The flow of water is regulated by a cover or 'door', called a paddle, which slides across the opening, its movement controlled by operation of a mechanism at ground level. A rack and pinion gear is a common mechanism, but there are other methods in use. When the water levels either side of the gates are more or less equal, the heavy gates can be opened by turning the balance arm through 90°. Paddles on the gates themselves are called gate paddles, and those controlling water flow through the side walls are called ground paddles. Paddles are often called sluices in southern counties, and cloughs in the north. **2.** the removable vertical boards on a flashlock; also known as cloughs, slackers, or slats in various parts of the country. **3.** see FLOAT BOARD (2). **4.** see FLOAT BOARD (1).

paduasoy a strong corded silk fabric used in the 18th century for clothing. The name is possibly a corruption of the French *pou-de-soie*, a kind of say or serge silk known in England since the early 17th century. The French name is associated with the city of Padua, Italy, which was famous for its silk fabrics.

palm oil an oil extracted from the fruit of the palm tree. Supplies first began to reach Britain from Nigeria, west Africa, in 1772, when the oil was used in the manufacture of candles and soap. Later it was used in certain foodstuffs. Imports into Liverpool rose dramatically in the first half of the 19th century, from 55 tons in 1785 to 30,000 tons in 1851.

paper and card substance made from vegetable fibres which is formed into flat sheets in various qualities according to its intended use, e.g. as stationery, to receive printing (books, newspapers, etc.), for wrapping purposes or for wallcoverings. The word paper comes from the Greek *papuros*, meaning the papyrus or water reed, the pith from which was used in ancient Egyptian times to make a writing surface. Paper consists of a thin web of cleaned vegetable fibres which have been pulverized and macerated before being strained through a fine wire sieve from a water solution (*see* PAPER MAKING). It is therefore a thin cellulose felted sheet which, when sized, will take ink or coloured areas without them running. Unsized papers are also used, such as tissues, crêpe paper, blotting paper, and the coarser types of brown wrapping paper. There are two basic types of paper – laid paper, which is formed on a sieve of fine wires laid parallel to each other, and woven paper which is made on wires arranged criss-cross, as in plain woven cloth. Laid paper is the oldest; woven was introduced in 1757. Designs or lettering made in fine wire superimposed on the base sieve, or impressed into the paper by a DANDY ROLL, cause a slight thinning of the paper which becomes visible when a sheet is held up to the light. This is the WATERMARK, and is added as a trade mark or for security reasons (e.g. on banknotes).

Card, or cardboard, may be either thick, stiff paper (pulpboard) or several sheets of paper pasted together (pasteboard) to make a stronger sheet. Cardboards are made in several qualities depending on their use. The cheaper, coarse grades are mainly used for packaging (cartons, boxes, etc.), whilst the finer grades are for resisting hard wear such as playing cards, Jacquard cards, etc. The word card comes from the Greek *khartes*, meaning papyrus leaf. Thick paper mixed with glue, known as papier mâché (from the French meaning chewed paper) may be moulded into objects and was popular in the Victorian era; in fact, in 1833 even cottages were prefabricated in papier mâché and sent to Australia!

paper making an art which originated in the Far East; manufacture commenced in Britain in the late 15th century. At first, paper was made by hand methods from torn up linen or cotton rags (wool is not suitable for good quality paper). The rags were beaten up in water to a pulp by large water-powered stamps, similar to fulling stocks in appearance. The pulp was sometimes boiled in caustic soda or lime to remove impurities, and sometimes bleached if a fine quality white paper was to be made. The pulp was then made into paper, a sheet at a time, in a mould made up of a sieve of closely spaced, parallel, fine copper wires, by a pair of skilled workmen – a VATMAN and a COUCHER – working in unison. The wet paper sheets were piled on individual woollen felt pads, and squeezed under a screw press to express excess water. The sheets and felts were then separated, and the former hung on ropes in a drying loft to dry slowly in an air stream. If intended for stationery or printing, the sheets were dipped in a warm gelatine size, and dried a second time.

Various improvements were made to speed up the process and mechanize it. In about 1650 the HOLLANDER roller beater was invented, and in the 1820s resin and alum were added at the beating stage, removing the need for separate sizing and a second drying. Early in the 19th century, wood fibres began to replace old rags, and eventually wood pulp and waste paper became the major raw materials. Esparto grass from Spain and north Africa was introduced *c*.1860. Making paper in a continuous length began with the FOURDRINIER MACHINE in 1807; this was improved in 1820 by a steam drying section patented (no. 4509) by Thomas Bonsor Crompton (1792–1858). By about 1830, half the paper made in Britain was by machine, and by about 1860 that proportion had risen to 95 per cent. *See also* PAPER MILL.

Shorter, A.H. *Paper Making in the British Isles*, 1971

paper mill a factory where paper is made. In the early days of making paper by hand, small workshops, usually family-run affairs, were more or less integrated with domestic quarters. Often these were three storeys high, with one or two vats on the ground floor where the paper was made, the living quarters above, and a drying loft on the top storey. The building was sited in a river valley so that water power could be used for working the stamps (*see* PAPER MAKING), and it was placed with its long side facing the prevailing wind which blew through vertical movable shutters in the drying loft. A hand turned screw press was used on the ground floor for squeezing water out of the paper sheets.

By the 1860s paper was being made by machine, and a typical paper mill would comprise reservoirs and filter beds for controlling the quality of the water; a rag store; sorting room; rope chopper; dusting house; HOLLANDER beating house; boiling kiers; bleach house; paper making machines; paper cutting machines; glazing house; warehouse; and a boiler house for providing the necessary steam for process and power purposes. A copious supply of water has always been essential for paper making, once to work the stamps, and later for steam generation. Most old paper mills are therefore sited in river valleys, close to towns which were both a source of rags and a nearby market. Due to the similarity of location and facilities, old bleach works were often converted to paper making. Modern paper mills contain complex, automatically controlled machines, producing paper at a fantastic rate from wood pulp. They tend to be sited near ports where imported wood fibre is unloaded.

parallel motion system of linkages developed by James Watt (1736–1819) for guiding the unsupported end of the piston rod in a straight line. It is more compact than his THREE BAR MOTION which it superseded. He included it in his patent no. 1432, 1784, and it is an elegant solution to the problem. The parallel motion comprises three short bars, arranged to form a parallelogram with the main beam making the ourth side, and pivoted at each corner. The unsupported end of the piston rod is attached to one corner of the parallelogram and also pivoted, whilst another corner is attached to a swinging arm called the regulating radius, which is pivoted either from the framework of the engine or the wall of the engine house. The configuration is shown in Fig. 77. As the main beam rocks in an arc, the end of the piston rod attached to the system is constrained to move in a straight vertical line over the length of the engine stroke. In actual fact if the beam could rock to the full extent allowed by the linkages, the path or locus of the point at which the piston rod joins the parallelogram describes arcs at each extremity of its traverse. However, since the beam can only rock an arc equivalent to the stroke of the piston, the piston rod end moves only in the central part of the locus which is a straight line. Overstroking of the piston is prevented by stops set to limit the rise and fall of the beam.

The necessity for ensuring that the piston rod rose vertically in a straight line became evident when Watt introduced DOUBLE ACTION working, since with double action the piston had to be directly connected to the beam by rigid links so that the upward thrust could be transmitted to the beam. In earlier single-acting engines the power stroke was only downwards, and the free end of the piston rod could be attached to the BEAM ARCH by a chain. A chain cannot transmit a push, but it can pull the beam downwards which it did when the power stroke occurred.

Parallel motion was also used on early locomotives, such as *Puffing Billy* of 1815; it is also known as a straight line motion.

parchmentry the collective name for braids, cords, tassels, fringes, and other trimmings which were hand woven in the 17th century by passementiers. The word comes from the French *passementerie* which has the same meaning.

Paris Exhibition, 1855 international exhibition sponsored by Napoleon III, spurred on by the success of the GREAT EXHIBITION OF 1851 in London and held in the Palais de l'Industrie on the Champs Elysées. It was less successful than the London exhibition – there were fewer visitors, and it lost money. It was too soon after 1851 to show any new technical or industrial advances, apart from the first European showing of the Singer Sewing machine.

parish road a ROAD maintained by the parish through which it runs. Parish roads were forerunners of turnpikes, and were maintained by STATUTE LABOUR.

parison a glass-making term for a partly finished article, whether partly blown or in an intermediate stage in a moulding sequence.

Parkes process a method for recovering silver from lead, patented by Alexander Parkes (1813–90) in 1850 (patent no. 13118). His invention comprises a CALCINING furnace of several floors with a central vertical shaft with arms attached, which, when the shaft rotates, stir the molten lead ore. Silver is separated from the lead by adding zinc in the ratio of about one cwt of zinc per ton of lead. When the mass cools, the zinc crystallizes and abstracts the silver as an insoluble compound floating on the top, and is skimmed off. The silver is then separated from the zinc by dissolving in muriatic or sulphuric acid. Usually a second de-silvering treatment is needed before the silver is finally obtained. A low-silver dross from the previous charge is added to the new charge to aid the process.

parliamentary fare fare of 1*d* per mile, charged on a third-class train. Under the Regulation of Railways Act of 1844, all public railway companies were obliged to provide at least one third-class train per day travelling at not less than 12 mph, with covered carriages fitted with seats, stopping at every station, at the fare of 1*d* per mile; this became known as the parliamentary class, and the trains as parliamentary trains. The first railway in Britain to carry third-class passengers on all trains was the Midland Railway in 1872. Third class was renamed second class on all railways in 1956, second class having disappeared many years before this. The 1844 Act was also known as the Cheap Trains Act.

parliamentary fence the fence which railways have to maintain by statute to isolate the permanent way from the surrounding land for safety. Such a precaution was enforced from the early days of railways.

parrot coal, *see* CANNEL

passage boat, *see* PACKET

passementerie, *see* PARCHMENTRY

patchings a term used particularly in south Wales, for old shallow mine workings on a coal outcrop. A patch was usually named after the individual miner working it.
Osborne, B.S. 'Patching, scouring and commoners: the development of an early industrial landscape', *Industrial Archaeology Review* I (1976)

patent a monopoly granted to an inventor by the state which gives him or her the right, for a specified time, to use the invention exclusively, and to stop others from using it. In exchange for this monopoly he has to pay regular annual fees to the state whilst the monopoly is in force, and at its commencement disclose the invention by publishing a detailed specification of it. Patents are granted providing the invention is novel and involves some ingenuity. Under an Act of 1833, a claim for the features thought to be novel had to be included in the specification.

The word patent is a shortening of the Latin *litterae patentes* meaning open letters. Letters Patent, as the documents were originally called, were issued by the sovereign conferring a right or privilege, and were written on unsealed open sheets so that they could be read by anyone. Originally, Letters Patent were issued for any sort of monopoly, whether for trading (as for the Company of MERCHANT ADVENTURERS), for the right to search for ores, to manufacture some commodity, or to exploit an invention. The purpose was to benefit the economy of the country by fostering industry, and in early days to provide extra income for the sovereign from the fees. Gradually, the word patent alone came to mean the protection given to an inventor for a limited time, to enable him to gain a financial benefit from his idea(s) in exchange for disclosure, so that all could benefit in due course when his monopoly had expired.

The history of patents for inventions began in Britain with the granting of privileges in the 1400s and 1500s for periods up to twenty years. Several of these early patents were for the manufacture of glass. Under the Statute of Monopolies of 1623/4, the law governing patents was firmly established (although case law existed prior to this) and the period of protection was set at fourteen years. This figure was chosen because it represented two successive generations of apprenticeship (seven years apiece), considered sufficient time for an inventor to train apprentices and journeymen in his invention and reap the profits from their work. The period of fourteen years remained in force for nearly 300 years.

The application procedure for patents was very cumbersome throughout the Industrial Revolution. Patents could be registered in several different places with different bodies, until the system was tidied up by the Patent Law Amendment Act of 1852 which established one governing body, the Patent Office, and streamlined the procedure. Before this inventors would often include more than one invention in a single patent to save time and expense. Under the 1852 Act separate patents had to be taken out for each distinctly different invention, and specifications had to be more detailed. At first, patents only covered England and Wales, and if protection was required in Scotland and Ireland, separate patents had to be taken out in those countries. However, the 1852 Act consolidated these into one patent which covered all areas of

the British Isles.

Until 1835, a private Act of Parliament was needed to extend the duration of a patent beyond fourteen years, which was usually on the grounds that the inventor had not been able to earn an adequate reward from his invention. For example, in 1775 James Watt applied for a twenty-five year extension to his patent (no. 913, 1769) for the separate condenser, realizing that the initial outlay could not be recouped by 1783, and the original patent did not therefore expire until 1800. It was also extended to cover Scotland. Patents can also be cancelled if evidence can be provided after issue that the invention is not novel; this happened to Richard Arkwright's second patent (no. 1111, 1775) which included a roving machine previously invented, but not patented, by Thomas Highs in 1767. Arkwright's patent was revoked in 1785.

The study of patent specifications is a rich source of information for industrial archaeologists, and the rate of issue of patents indicates the quickening rise in technology, although the numbers alone do not measure the rate at which new machines and processes were introduced into industry. Inventions also vary in quality: some may be breakthroughs, whereas many are only slight improvements to existing machines. A large number of patents were not renewed for their full period of fourteen years, since they proved to be commercially unsuccessful. Nevertheless, the following table roughly indicates the rapid rise in inventiveness over the period of the Industrial Revolution:

Decade	Number of patents	Decade	Number of patents
1740–9	82	1800–9	924
1760–9	205	1820–9	1453
1780–9	477	1840–9	4581

Source: *Abstract of British Historical Statistics*, 1963

By 1854 almost 14,500 patents had been issued. The cost of taking out a patent and paying the annual fees was a big obstacle for poor inventors: many inventors of early textile machines were ordinary working men, and it was difficult for them to finance a patent when the wage of, for example, a handloom weaver averaged only £1.00 per week in 1806. Samuel Crompton (1753–1827) did not patent his spinning MULE for lack of funds, and disclosed it on the promise of financial reward from local Bolton businessmen, which in the event totalled only £70. Although he was later awarded £5,000 by the government, this was still an inadequate figure.

Numbering of patents

The first patent was issued to Aaron Rapburne and Roger Burges in 1617 for map making. Subsequent patents were numbered sequentially in chronological date of issue up until no. 14359 of 26 July 1853, and these are known as the Old Series. On 1 October 1852 a new series was commenced, starting at no. 1 again, for patent applications received and granted after that date. There was thus an overlap of almost ten months whilst patents from the Old Series were being processed by the Patent Office. On 1 January 1853 patent numbering commenced again with no. 1, and each succeeding year started again at no. 1 on 1 January until 1916, when sequential numbering irrespective of the year recommenced with no. 100,001 on 1 January to avoid any possible confusion with earlier patents. Thus between 1852 and 1916 the year must be quoted as well as the number to identify a particular patent. Today, a different set of numbers is in use.

Patent collections

Collections of patents are held in twenty-five public libraries in Britain and at the National Library of Wales, Aberystwyth, whilst the biggest collection, which includes selected foreign patents, is held at the Science Reference Library, London. Together, these holdings form the Patents Information Network for the country.

Davenport, Neil. *The United Kingdom Patent System – A Brief History*, Kenneth Mason, 1979
Dutton, H.I. *The Patent System and Inventive Activity during the Industrial Revolution, 1750–1852*, Manchester University Press, 1984
Macleod, Christine. *Inventing the Industrial Revolution: The English Patent System 1600–1800*, Cambridge, 1988
Woodcraft, B. *Alphabetical Index of Patentees of Inventions, 1617–1852*, 1854; reprinted by Evelyn, Adams and Mackay, 1969

patent sail a type of WINDMILL sail invented by William Cubitt (1785–1861) in 1807 (patent no. 3041) which combined the principles of Meikle's SPRING SAIL and Hooper's REEFING SAIL. The sail comprised a number of hinged

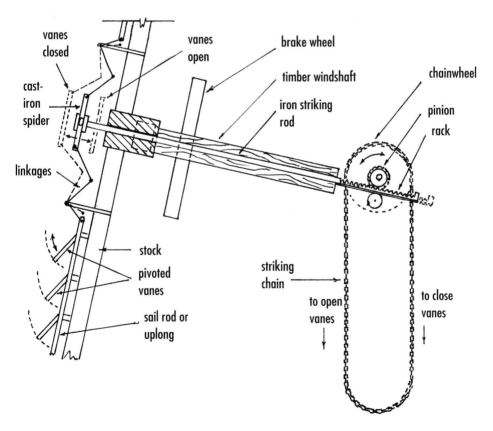

Fig. 49. Cubitt's patent sail mechanism, 1807

vanes or shutters which could be opened or closed according to the wind strength, without stopping the mill to make the adjustment. Fig. 49 shows the principle, the main feature being the striking rod which made the adjustments. Each vane was pivoted on the main members of the sail and connected to a rod or upalong bar, which ran the length of the sail. This in turn was joined through a system of linkages to a cast-iron component called a spider, located at the centre of the sails. The spider had a leg for each sail, usually four, and rotated with the sails on a stationary iron striking rod which passed through a clearance hole in the centre of the windshaft. A collar either side of the spider kept it in position on the striking rod. The other end of the striking rod protruded beyond the windshaft and terminated in a rack which engaged in a pinion. Mounted on the pinion spindle was a chainwheel which could be turned by the miller pulling on an endless chain. When the pinion was rotated, it moved the striking rod via the rack along the centre of the windshaft. This caused the spider to be either pushed farther out, or drawn closer in, since it was held between the two collars on the striking rod. Movement of the spider activated the linkages simultaneously on each sail, altering the angle of the vanes as the upalong bar tilted them on their pivots. With all the vanes fully open, the miller was said to have 'put the power off', and with them closed, to have 'put the power on'. A weight could be hung onto the chain according to the power required, and when the force of the wind acting on the sails overcame the effect of the weight, the vanes were opened, letting the wind blow through them, known as 'spilling the wind', thus controlling the speed of the mill machinery.

patron saints and gods saint or deity who is supposed to watch over the interests of a particular country, craft, or profession. Patron saints date back to medieval times and the GUILDS, when various crafts adopted a saint as a symbolic representation of their craft or profession. Saints and gods and their symbols which are of interest to industrial archaeologists are listed below.

saints

blacksmiths and metalworkers	St Dunstan (*c.* 925–988)	Chosen for his skill as a farrier. He was archbishop of Canterbury in 961, and is usually depicted with pincers or tongs in his right hand. Saint's day: 19 May.
brewers	St Augustine of Hippo (345–430)	Bishop of Hippo in north Africa in 395. Saint's day: 28 August.
builders	St Vincent Ferrer (1350–1419)	Saint's day: 5 April.
carpenters	St Joseph	Carpenter and husband of the Virgin Mary, and lawful father of Jesus. Usually depicted holding a building staff. Saint's day: 19 March.
charcoal burners	St Anthony the Great (*c.* 260–356)	Saint's day: 17 January. Symbol: a firebrand.
clothworkers	St Homobonus (d. 1197)	Saint's day: 13 November.
dyers	St Maurice (d. *c.* 287)	Saint's day: 22 September.
engineers	St Ferdinand III (1199–1252)	Saint's day: 30 May. Symbol: a greyhound.
forgemen and tanners	St Clement (d. *c.* 1000)	Saint's day: 23 November. Symbol: an anchor, since he was martyred by being thrown into the sea tied to an iron anchor.
merchants	St Nicholas of Myra	Bishop of Myra in the early 4th century and the original Santa Claus (Santa Nikolaus) with connections with the Lombards (13th-century Italian merchants). Saint's day: 6 December.
miners	St Barbara (d. *c.* 303)	Saint's day: 4 December. Symbol: a tower.
spinners and wheelwrights	St Catherine of Alexandria	Christian martyr said to have been tied to a revolving wheel on the order of the Roman Emperor Maximinus in AD 307. Saint's day: 25 November, also known as Candle Day or Cattern.
tanners	St Clement (*see under* forgemen)	Saint's day: 23 November

weavers	St Severus of Ravenna	Symbol: a loom. Also St Maurice, shared with dyers. Saint's day: 25 November
wheelwrights	St Catherine of Alexandria (*see under* spinners)	
woolcombers	St Blaise (Blase, Blasius) (*c.* 289–316)	Bishop of Jersey, said to have met his death by having his flesh torn with iron combs similar to those used to comb wool by hand. Saint's day: 3 February. Symbol: a woolcomb.
wool weavers and merchants	St John the Baptist	Saint's day: 24 June. Symbol: a lamb carrying a flag.
gods		
engineers	Mercury (Roman) or Hermes (Greek)	Represented everything that needed dexterity and skill. He is depicted carrying a caduceus, a rod entwined by two serpents, also known as the peace wand. Day: 25 May.
metalworkers	Vulcan (Roman) or Hephaestus (Greek)	The god of fire and working of metals, also known as Mulciber the Hammer god. Day: 23 August.
weavers	Arachne	The Greek goddess of spinning and weaving, daughter of a dyer. In Greek mythology she was changed into a spider and her cloth into a cobweb.

pattern a full-size wooden or metal copy of an article to be cast. A simple pattern is made in one piece, but a pattern for a complex shaped article would probably be made in several pieces or sections. Patterns have to be made slightly larger than the dimensions of the finished casting to allow for the contraction which takes place as the molten metal cools to room temperature. Hollow cavities and holes in a finished casting are made by sand cores placed in the mould, and broken out after the casting is cold. Large metal articles are cast in the shape left by the pattern in the foundry casting floor. Small articles are cast in sand-filled MOULDING BOXES or flasks. Moulds for simple circular items such as bowls are made by strickle boards – wooden boards profiled on one edge to the required shape, and rotated about a central peg in the sandy loam mould, to sweep or strike out the outer shape of the item to be cast.

Pattern making dates from the earliest days of iron casting. The skill of iron founders peaked in Victorian days when highly decorative cast ironwork was made, particularly for architectural work. *See also* ORNAMENTATION IN IRON.

Pattinson process a process patented in 1833 (patent no. 6497) by Hugh Lee Pattinson (1796–1858), a Tyneside metallurgical chemist, for extracting silver from lead by a crystallization process. Lead is heated and crystallizes at a certain temperature, whilst any silver present is still molten and is skimmed off. The process is repeated several times, increasing the concentration of silver each time. The more efficient PARKES PROCESS superseded this method.

pawl a pivoted catch which engages in the gap between the sloping teeth of a RATCHET to prevent reverse movement. The pawl can be permanently maintained in contact with the ratchet by means of a spring, or it can be thrown into or out of contact manually as required. When movement between the pawl and ratchet takes place, the pawl slides across the backs of the ratchet teeth.

Peak stone (or Derby grit stones, greys) a millstone made from stone quarried in the Peak District, Derbys. Peak stones are normally made from one piece of rock and are used mainly for heavy grinding work, such as for barley, oats, peas, and the softer grains of wheat.
Tucker, D. Gordon. 'Millstone making in the Peak District of Derbyshire: the quarries and the technology', *Industrial Archaeology Review* VIII (1985), 42–58

pearl ash (or pot, potash, ashes) another name for potassium carbonate, used in the early days of chemical BLEACHING by chlorine. Use of pearl ash was replaced in the 18th century with cheaper lime by bleachers making their own 'chemick' at the bleachworks.

peasy a word used in Derbyshire to describe a low grade lead ore of small size, i.e. like peas.

peat a turfy substance comprising dead vegetation resulting from the accumulation over centuries of the remains of mosses and marsh plants compressed into layers near the surface. It is largely used as a fuel, being dug out in blocks and air dried before use. Peat can be regarded as the youngest geological member of the coal series, brown coal being the next oldest. The right to dig out peat, known as turbary, existed from medieval times. Peat was used to make CHARCOAL on occasions, especially when timber from forests became scarce. It is known as turf in Ireland, and moss in northern England.

peg mill another name for a windmill of the POST MILL type. The word was used mostly in Lancashire and dates from the 14th century.

peg warping, *see* WARPING MILL

Pelton wheel an IMPULSE WATER TURBINE named after Lester Allen Pelton (1829–1908), a British mining engineer working in California, USA, who developed it *c.*1870 (*see* Figs 38a and 83). It is particularly suitable for high heads of water and comprises a wheel with hemispherical cups arranged round the circumference. A jet of water from a nozzle at the base of a long pipeline impinges on the cups and revolves the wheel at a high speed. Pelton wheels are therefore used where a high water pressure is available, such as in mountainous country. It is usually necessary to gear down the speed of the wheel to drive most machinery. Pelton wheels have also been used as a means of obtaining rotation from hydraulic mains. A minimum head of about 500 ft is needed otherwise the runner or wheel becomes too large for a useful power output. Multi-jet, multi-wheel machines with a common chamber, the wheels running on the same shaft, have been made.

penistone (or pennystone) a coarse, woollen, narrow cloth, particularly woven in the 17th and 18th centuries around the town of that name in west Yorkshire, but now obsolete. Although now involved in steel making, Penistone was once a busy wool hand weaving area and had a CLOTH HALL dating from 1768.

penitent, *see* FIREMAN

penstock **1.** a sluice gate for controlling the flow of water. **2.** a pipeline leading water into a water turbine, usually down from an elevated reservoir or pond.

People's Exhibition, *see* GREAT EXHIBITION OF 1851

perching and burling the examination and rectification of finished cloth as part of the cloth dressing operation. Perching meant pulling the cloth across two overhead bars or rollers spaced parallel to each other and a yard or so apart, and examining that part hanging down in a good light. The word comes from the Latin *pertica*, meaning pole, referring to the two horizontal bars or perches over which the cloth was slowly pulled. The same device was used earlier when blankets etc. were dressed by hand CARDS to raise a NAP. A burl is a tuft, knot, or lump in a woollen cloth, and BURLING means to remove any such irregularities found in finished cloth as part of the final dressing it receives. Any small rents or holes found are also repaired, and any specks or parts of threads which have not taken the dye are removed.

permanent way (or iron road) a synonym for a final, completed railway track or line, as opposed to a temporary track or way laid by a contractor. The expression first came into use around the late 1830s when railway construction was beginning. The rails of early railways were supported either on STONE BLOCKS or transverse timber sleepers which were completely covered by ballast, leaving only the rails themselves visible; this is why in contemporary drawings or prints, only the rails of the permanent way appear.

pernambuco, *see* BRAZIL WOOD

perpetuana (or perpet) a 16th-century woollen fabric favoured by Puritans, receiving its name from its longlasting perpetual quality.

Persian berries an old yellow dyestuff used on cotton and wool, once imported via Aleppo in Syria. The dye matter comes from the unripe berries of the shrub variety *Rhamnus infectorius*, which is related to buckthorn.

Persian wheel, *see* SAKIA

Peterloo massacre (or Manchester massacre) the occasion on 16 August 1819 when magistrates in Manchester, expecting a riot, gave orders for the yeomanry to disperse a large, orderly crowd of 50–60,000 working men and women gathered in St Peter's Field, Manchester, to hear Henry Hunt (1773–1835), a Radical politician, address them on parliamentary reform. In the stampede which followed, eleven people were killed and some 400 injured, including many women and children. The name was coined in imitation of Waterloo, the famous battle at which Napoleon was defeated four years earlier. Manchester's Free Trade Hall was built on the site of St Peter's Field.

There was great public indignation at the disastrous way the meeting had been handled, and Peterloo became a potent symbol of the repression of working people. Percy Bysshe Shelley (1792–1822) wrote a long poem, *The Mask of Anarchy*, immediately afterwards which was highly critical of the authorities concerned. Agitation for parliamentary reform continued long after Peterloo, and in 1832 the first Reform Act was passed, which began to address the need for representation in parliament of the new industrial towns with their large populations. *See also* SIX ACTS, 1819.

Marlow, J. *The Peterloo Massacre*, Rapp and Whiting, 1969

petrol engine an INTERNAL COMBUSTION ENGINE which uses a mixture of air and petrol as fuel, the combustion of which is by an electric spark. Possibly the first engine to use petrol was that patented by George Brayton in the USA in 1872, but it was not very successful, and the real advances were not made until the following decade, mainly in Germany. The petrol engine operates on the OTTO CYCLE and may be of two-stroke (one engine revolution per cycle) or four-stroke (two engine revolutions per cycle) design. Gottlieb Daimler of Germany developed his high speed petrol engine in 1884, whilst Karl Benz, also of Germany, developed his in 1885. Daimler's engine was ignited by a hot tube, and that of Benz by an electric spark; the latter method soon became the preferred ignition source. The petrol engine was rapidly applied to road transport vehicles and has today become the main means of propulsion for the lighter type of private transport – cars and motor cycles – with a huge industry worldwide manufacturing the vehicles and relevant components, and refining petrol from oil.

Clerk, D. *The Gas, Petrol, and Oil Engine*, 2 vols, Longmans Green, 1916

pewter a grey alloy of 80–90 per cent tin, and 10–20 per cent lead. Pewter has been known since Roman times, and was used extensively from the Middle Ages until about the end of the 18th century for drinking vessels, plates and other tableware. The alloy sometimes had small amounts of copper, antimony or bismuth added to it. In the early 17th century it was discovered that dissolving pewter in nitric acid produced a salt which aided making a scarlet dye from COCHINEAL. Pewter articles were cast in sand or clay moulds, and finished by hammering the surface smooth; printer's type was once made in pewter. Little pewter is made or used today.

Philadelphia Centennial Exhibition, 1876 international exhibition held to celebrate America's independence and to promote national unity after the Civil War, which had ended eleven years earlier. It was a great success: some 8 million visitors saw that the US had become a powerful, inventive, industrial nation. Among the exhibits, the first generation of electricity by steam was shown by a big Corliss beam engine which was the focal point of the event. This engine had 40 in diameter cylinders with a 10 ft stroke, and ran at 36 rpm, developing 1,400 hp. Two shafts 108 ft long drove machinery in the building. Also on show was British-born Alexander Graham Bell's (1847–1922) telephone, invented the previous year.

philosophy word used until about the mid/late 18th century to describe what today would be called science. Natural philosophy was the study of natural things and phenomena, and included subjects such as mechanics, hydrostatics, physics, chemistry, etc., whilst experimental philosophy covered experiments and investigations to prove theories and apply scientific principles. Scientists of the day were called philosophers, and a number of literary and philosophical societies were formed in towns and cities, such as Manchester's, founded in 1781; in their heyday these were a source of advancement in technology and scientific thought. Many eminent engineers, mill owners, etc., of the day were members of such societies. Philosophy comes from the Greek word *philosophos*, meaning lover of wisdom or knowledge.

phlogiston theory an erroneous theory of combustion current for many years in the 18th century. Phlogiston (from the Greek *phlogizo*, meaning to set on fire) was thought to be a weightless, inflammable substance present in all combustible materials, which when they were burned was taken up by the air and absorbed in it. This theory was put forward by the German chemist Georg Ernst Stahl (1660–1734) in 1702, and was accepted by many, but not all, scientists of the day.

The mid–late 18th century was a period of great activity and new discoveries in chemistry, and there was a growing interest in finding out the nature of heat, and its role in thermal processes in metallurgy and in steam generation. Joseph Priestley (1733–1804) isolated oxygen in 1774, and called it dephlogisticated air, believing in the phlogiston theory at that time. (Phlogisticated air was the old name for nitrogen.) But three years later, the French chemist Antoine Laurent Lavoisier (1743–94) published the true theory of combustion showing the importance of oxygen in the chemical reaction of burning, this put an end to the phlogiston theory.

photography the process of recording pictures by chemical action of light on light-sensitive film. Joseph Nicéphore Niépce (1765–1833) of France took the world's first photograph at Châlon-sur-Marne in 1826; many improvements followed and by 1850–60 photography was becoming fairly general in Britain. This is of relevance to industrial archaeologists since reliable pictures of machinery, buildings, etc. were for the first time becoming available; earlier drawings and paintings were the only pictorial records, and these were sometimes inaccurate. An early photograph taken in 1851 shows a Nasmyth steam hammer in Manchester, with the inventor himself standing by it. In spite of the introduction of photography, line drawings continued to be used as illustrations in books and catalogues for another fifty years. The arrival of the picture postcard, based on photography, is a useful source of Victorian industrial scenes, modes of transport being frequently shown on such cards.

Today, photographic recording of industrial buildings, machinery, sites and artefacts is an important part of industrial archaeology, as the past industrial scene gradually disappears, especially where buildings are under threat of demolition. Aerial photography is increasingly being used over industrial areas – low-level oblique angle shots being particularly useful – whilst evidence of past industrial activity in remote sites can often be best detected and photographed from the air.

phthisis the old name for pneumoconiosis, lung disease associated with mining caused by breathing in dust, and known as collier's lung in the coal mining industry. The word comes from the Greek *phthino* meaning decay. Because of inadequate ventilation underground, most 19th-century Cornish tin miners died by the age of thirty-five from this disease. Another source of phthisis was the dust inhaled by needle pointers from dry sandstone *c*.1790, the condition being known as pointer's rot. The introduction of exhaust fans and hoods in the 1840s reduced this occupational disease in needle making.

pick a single thread of WEFT in a cloth. In machine weaving, the shuttle carrying the weft is projected across the width of the cloth by the oscillating picking stick or arm of the loom. One such pass is called the pick, and the speed of a loom is measured in the number of picks per minute. The pick is sometimes called a shoot. Cloth construction is partly designated by the number of picks per quarter inch in the longitudinal direction.

On the early hand looms, the shuttle was projected across the cloth by jerking strings which slid striking blocks along rails propelling the loose shuttle. The strings were brought together at a central point and attached to a wooden handle called a picking stick, or in some parts of the country, a pegging stick. This arrangement is called the FLYING SHUTTLE.

The picking stick simulates the action of the human arm in throwing the shuttle across the width of the loom alternately from side to side. A loom with its picking stick or arm placed level with the plane in which the shuttle moves and oscillating horizontally, is called an overpick loom, and is characteristic of a non-automatic LANCASHIRE LOOM. Other designs of looms have their picking arm pivoted at the base of the machine and oscillate in a vertical plane to strike the shuttle: these machines are called UNDERPICK LOOMS.

picking, *see* BATTING

pickle-pot a crude type of condenser used on later NEWCOMEN steam engines. It comprised a small vessel sited below the main cylinder and directly attached to it by a large pipe. An outlet from the pickle-pot contained a non-return valve which allowed flow outwards only. Cold water was injected into the pickle-pot instead of into the cylinder when the vacuum was to be created; fresh incoming steam entering the cylinder blew out condensate and air from the pickle-pot through the non-return valve. The device was an attempt to evade Watt's separate CONDENSER patent, but was really an infringement, and was not a very satisfactory arrangement.

picric acid a synthetic dyestuff producing a yellow colour, first made in 1771 by Peter Woulfe (*c*.1727–1803) from indigo and nitric acid and used for dyeing wool without the need for a mordant. It was also used during the First World War for making explosives.

piece a length of cloth, in particular that woven by the handloom weavers. The actual length varied according to the material and with time: for instance, a piece of muslin was at one time 10 yd; calico 28 yd; and Irish linen 25 yd. The length of a piece was gradually increased in the late 1700s by employers as they drove manufacturing costs down. Dodd's *Textile Manufacture* (1844) states that a piece of cotton cloth varied from 24 to 47 yd in length, and from 28 to 40 in in width. The term piece is therefore a very indeterminate description of a length of woven fabric. In the West Riding of Yorkshire, four KERSEYS equalled one piece.

Handloom weavers in the 19th century wove woollen pieces of 42 yd length which would take about eighteen days of fourteen hours per day to weave. When completed each piece would be taken to the clothier and fresh yarn obtained for the next piece. The journey to the clothier would be made once every three weeks. Handloom woollen weavers in Yorkshire took their pieces to CLOTH HALLS for sale.

The term piecework originates from the practice of paying a workman by the number of pieces or items he makes, as opposed to payment by time. A piece is also known as a CUT.

piece hall, *see* CLOTH HALL

piecening joining together by hand the separate strips of carded material as they were fed into a SLUBBING FRAME so that it had a continuous feed. This work was usually done by children or young persons called pieceners in the late 18th and early 19th centuries. By 1827 a machine had been invented to do this automatically (*see* PIECER (2)).

piecer 1. a young person employed to assist a spinner on a spinning MULE, whose job was to piece together or join broken threads. There were different classes of piecers, progressing with age and experience from little piecer, to cross piecer, and finally to side (or big) piecer. Eventually piecers would themselves become spinners when the opportunity arose. Traditionally, piecers were paid by the spinner and frequently were his own children. Piecers also replenished ROVINGS as they ran out, removed (doffing) full COPS of spun yarn, and kept the mule clean. In some textile districts to piece up broken threads is called to get up.

2. a machine for joining separate carded strips from early CARDING engines into continuous SLUBBING lengths. Early carding machines delivered separate strips of material some 10–12 in wide, rolled loosely into 'sausages' with their length equal to the width of the machine. These had to be joined to form continuous 'ropes' by hand, either by women or children called PIECENERS, before proceeding to the next process. The first machine to perform this task automatically was invented by James Whitaker in 1827 (patent no. 5486). The piecer stood at the end of the carding machine and received each separate carded strip onto a moving conveyor of V-shaped trays. A certain number of trays were inverted intermittently, depositing a set of strips onto a wide belt moving at right angles. The tipping motion was timed so that the leading end of one set of strips slightly overlapped the trailing end of the previous set. The strips then passed between oscillating rubbing bands which rolled the overlapping ends together to join them into continuous slubbings, which were finally automatically wound onto bobbins by the same machine. Piecers were replaced by CONDENSERS fitted to the end of the carding machine by the mid-19th century, which enabled the carder to produce continuous slubbings.

pig the bar or block of lead which is cast in a mould at a lead smelter. It usually has the name or symbol of the lead company moulded on it, and can weigh anything from 112 to over 300 lb, there being no standard weight. The origin of the word is the same as for PIG IRON. The name pig may also be applied to copper blocks.

pig boiling process, *see* WET PUDDLING

pig iron the end product of an iron BLAST FURNACE, sometimes known as rough iron in the early days of iron making. The molten iron is cast into moulds hollowed out in a sand bed: the channel along which the molten metal flows feeding the rows of moulds is called a sow, and each individual piece of solidified iron, a pig. These names are attributed to an early metallurgist, John Rovenzon (*fl.*1613) who likened the configuration to a sow with a row of piglets suckling at her side. Each pig weighs in the order of one cwt, capable of being handled by a man. Similar shaped pieces of other cast metal, such as lead, are also called pigs.

Pig iron is the raw material from which other items are made by subsequent remelting in foundries and forges, and is an important basic commodity in the engineering and structural industries. Some idea of its importance may be gauged from the fact that the output of pig iron in Britain rose from 25,000 tons in 1720 to 250,000 tons in 1806, and to a massive 6,300,000 tons in 1875.

pile a raised surface on a textile fabric, cloth and carpet, formed by warps or wefts rising above the surface of the ground or backing cloth. The pile may be left as loops after weaving, or the loops may be cut. Most pile fabrics have a pile on one side only: the heaviest one-sided pile is carpet, the lightest a fine velvet. Cut pile may have been formed either by the warps (e.g. velvets and moquettes) or by the wefts, e.g. corduroy. Terry towelling has uncut looped pile on both sides. The word pile comes from the Latin *pilus*, meaning hair.

piling, *see* FAGGOTTING

pillar and stall (or bord and pillar working) an early method of working a coalfield originating in the north-east. Coal was extracted from roads or galleries which made a grid of empty spaces, usually at right angles to each other, called the stalls. Uncut coal was left in between as rectangular blocks or pillars to support the roof. It was an inefficient way of getting coal since often more than half the potential coal was left behind as pillars, but the method was used well into the 19th century until LONGWALL working was introduced. In Scotland the method was known as room and stoop, stoop corresponding to pillar.

Similar methods of underground working are adopted in slate and stone mines when chambers are left where the material has been extracted, with pillars to support the overhead rock; but the name pillar and stall seems to be reserved for coal mining.

pillow lace, *see* BOBBIN LACE

pilot-cloth a windproof cloth with a raised nap, usually dyed blue, and used for overcoats and uniforms, particularly for mariners. Top quality pilots are all wool, whilst lesser qualities use cotton and wool mixtures.

pin and needle manufacture Today, pins are made from steel wire, but in the early days of pin making brass pin wire was drawn down from a brass rod, cut into lengths, then pointed, the head formed, and whitened i.e. given a coating of tin. Most of the work was performed by women and children in what was one of the worst sweated industries. The finished pins were stuck into paper in rows ready for sale to haberdashers, etc. by children called stickers. Larger quantities were sold loose by the pound. There are several centres of pin manufacture such as Birmingham, Dublin, Gloucester, and Warrington, besides London. Eventually manufacture was mechanized: Lemuel Wellman Wright patented a pin-making machine in 1824 (patent no. 4955).

Needles were first made from thin iron sheet, slit into fine strips and rolled in sand and water until round. The eyes were made by splitting open one end and heat welding the extremity to leave a small hole. Points were made by grinding, and hardening was done by packing the iron needles in charcoal and heating them for long periods until the carbon from the charcoal was absorbed into the iron turning it into steel. Polishing was done by wrapping a large number in a tight hessian bundle with oil and an abrasive powder, and the bundle rolled back and forth for several hours (*see* WHEE-WAH). Redditch was once an important needle-making centre in Britain. In 1786, Ezekeil Reed took out a patent in America for making needles by machine.

Ashton, T.S. *The Records of a Pin Manufactory, 1812–1814*, 1925
Davies, J. *Pinmaking*, Gloucester Folk Museum, 1978
Davies, J. *Needlemaking*, Shire Publications, Album No. 71, 1981
Rollins, J.G. 'The Forge Mill, Redditch', *Journal of Industrial Archaeology* 3 (1966), 84
Rollins, J.G. *The Needle Mills*, Society for the Protection of Ancient Buildings, 1970

pinch the narrowing of a canal where it passes under an ACCOMMODATION BRIDGE. The canal was reduced in width to allow one boat at a time to pass under the arch so as to reduce the cost of the bridge.

pinion 1. the smaller of a pair of toothed gear wheels working together; the larger wheel is called a SPUR WHEEL. The term is usually only used when the small wheel is considerably smaller than the spur; where there is little difference between the wheel sizes they are usually described as a pair of gearwheels. The minimum number of teeth a pinion can have is normally ten to twelve, otherwise the individual teeth become too weak to transmit much power. The name comes from the Latin *pinea*, meaning a pine cone. **2.** *see* NOIL.

pinion wire, *see* WIRE

pipe a long and narrow vein of lead ore lying more or less horizontally, and usually a side branch off a main vein. Graphite veins were also known as pipes in the Lake District.

pirn the small package of WEFT yarn wound on a bobbin which fits into a SHUTTLE of a loom for weaving cloth. About twenty to thirty pirns of weft to the lb are normal, depending on the size of the shuttle. Pirns are wound from larger packages of yarn in the weaving shed.

piston the cylindrical metal disk which slides to and fro inside the cylinder of an engine, or in a compressor or pump, etc. The Frenchman Dionysius (Denis) Papin (1647–1714) is credited with the invention of the piston *c.*1690. A piston may move under pressure from steam or exploding gas, etc. in an engine, and transmit its motion via PISTON ROD and CONNECTING ROD to rotate a crank. Alternatively, it may be driven by some means to displace a fluid such as air in a compressor, or water in a pump. Pistons have to be a close fit inside cylinders to prevent leakage past them, and this is achieved by circumferential seals which do not create undue friction on the cylinder walls. In NEWCOMEN ATMOSPHERIC ENGINES, sealing of the vertical moving piston was very primitive: a leather ring, upturned at its edges, was secured on top of the piston, and a layer of water a few inches deep provided the seal. Later, grooves were cut or cast in the sides of pistons, and tallow-soaked rope was held in them by removable metal rings, called JUNK RINGS. John Ramsbottom (1814–97) introduced METALLIC PACKINGS in the mid-19th century, for use on locomotives and stationary steam engines.

An engine piston may receive pressure on one side only as in single-acting engines, or on both sides alternately, if double-acting. Pistons on single-acting force pumps are normally called plungers; the pistons of lift pumps are often called buckets.

piston rod the rod attached to the PISTON in an engine mechanism, which passes out of the cylinder through the STUFFING BOX. The rod slides to and fro with the motion of the piston, transmitting the thrust and pull of the power strokes to the CONNECTING ROD. To maintain the line of action of the outer end of the piston rod in a straight line and prevent it bending or straining the stuffing box, it is guided by a CROSSHEAD which runs on slides. On early beam engines the free end of the piston rod was guided in a straight line in the absence of a crosshead by a lever system known as a PARALLEL MOTION.

piston valve a form of steam engine SLIDE VALVE for controlling the flow of steam into and out of a cylinder. (*see* Fig. 79).

pit brow lasses name given in Lancashire to female surface workers at a coal mine. Women and girls were prohibited from working underground in coal mines by the Mines Act of 1842. However, they continued to be employed near the top (brow) of the mine shaft, removing stones and rubbish by hand, and breaking up large lumps of coal. In 1885, some 1,400 pit brow lasses were still employed for this purpose in the West Lancashire coalfield alone.

pitchback wheel a type of waterwheel where the incoming supply of water leaves a LAUNDER near the top of the wheel, and drops onto the paddles or buckets of the wheel which rotates in the reverse direction to that of the incoming flow (*see* Fig. 84d). It is also known as a back-shot wheel and more rarely as a high breastshot wheel. The famous 'Lady Isabella' wheel at Laxey on the Isle of Man is a pitchback wheel with a wheel 72 ft 6 in diameter, built in 1854.

pitcher a baked earthenware mould made from a master mould, and used in pottery for making the thin raised ornamentation which is added to the surface of items such as vases, for example, on Wedgwood jasperware. A thin layer of clay is pressed into the pitcher, eased out by a spatula, and placed onto the vase or item to be so decorated.

pit load an old weight measure for coal equal to thirty baskets each weighing 120 lb; one pit load therefore equalled 3,600 lb.

pitman, *see* CONNECTING ROD

pitstead (or pit ring) a forest site where CHARCOAL burning has taken place. A pitstead comprises a cleared, level circular area, about 30 ft across, in which a pile of COPPICE or cordwood was made for controlled burning. The charcoal burner's hut would often be placed to one side, or nearby if several pitsteads were close together. Pitsteads may still be discerned in some wooded areas; since the soil area has been fertilized by a prolonged dropping of wood ashes, it may grow different plants from its surroundings.

pit wheel the primary gearwheel in a water mill mounted directly on the main shaft inside the mill building, the waterwheel itself being attached to the other end of the shaft revolving in the wheel pit. The pit wheel is usually a large bevel wheel and mates with the WALLOWER.

Pitchback waterwheel and launder at New Abbey, Dumfries & Galloway

pitwork collective name for the reciprocating PUMP RODS, BALANCE BOB, etc. of a beam engine operating on a mine shaft.

place names can often give an indication of an industrial activity which once took place in a neighbourhood, as can the name of a pub, field, street, or part of a name. A few examples include black (bleach in Anglo-Saxon), e.g. Blackburn, Lancs.; bole hill, indicating an early metal smelting site; croft, an old bleaching field (e.g. Whitecroft, Lancs.); ginn, a place where a horse gin once stood; linacre or linneyshaw, a flax growing field, from line (flax); pandy, the Welsh for fulling mill (e.g. Tonypandy,

Glamorgan); saltcote, a place where salt was made (e.g. Saltcoats, Cumbria); sinder or cinder, an early metal working site (e.g. Cinderford, Forest of Dean); and whitefield, a bleaching field. Pub names associated with particular activities, such as Founders Arms, Finishers Arms, or the Corner Pin (which refers to hand block printing) are frequently found in industrial areas. *See also* GATE (3)

plain weave the simplest form of textile weaving where each WEFT thread passes alternately over and under adjacent WARPS at right angles to produce an unpatterned, even-surfaced cloth (*see* Fig. 50). Plain weave is also

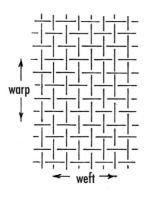

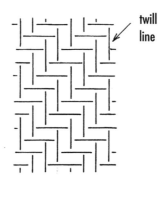

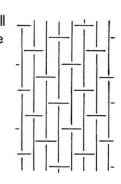

Plain weave

Twill

Satin

If warp and weft have the same count and setting (pitch), the cloth is said to be 'square'. If the warps are more closely set than the weft (say twice as many to the inch) the warp tends to wrap round the weft which lies almost straight, and the cloth becomes almost warp faced with a weft-way rib. The above shows a square weave.

The above shows a '2-and-2' twill, i.e. each weft passes successively over 2 warps, under 2 and repeats with the warp doing the same. In a '2-and-1' twill, the weft will pass successively over 1 warp, under 2, over 1, and so on, while the warp will pass under 1 weft, over 2, and repeat. This is known as a 'jean'. The twill line may zigzag up and down at narrow intervals to give a herringbone twill.

In the above satin, each warp thread passes over 4 wefts to give a repeat of the pattern every 5 threads. This is known as a '5-end satin'; an end is a single warp thread. The length of warp passing over the several wefts is known as the 'float'. The floats are distributed so as to break up any tendency to form a twill line. The longer the float the more vulnerable is the cloth to damage.

Fig. 50. The construction of three textile weaves

called calico weave, tabby, or ground weave. Variations are possible: for instance, if two consecutive picks of weft are repeated, crossing over and under the same adjacent warps, the weave is called GROGRAM. In plain, TWILL and SATIN weaves, the pattern of interlacing is regular and repeats itself over only a few threads. More complicated weaves are possible using DOBBY mechanisms.

plaiting a bleaching term, meaning folding cloth on itself. Boys used to do this by treading the cloth down in a KIER before it was boiled during the night, until machinery was invented to do this.

planing machine a machine tool for producing large flat surfaces on metal objects. It comprises a large work table which slides backwards and forwards along a substantial guide bed, passing under a stationary bridge which spans it. The horizontal member of the bridge may be raised or lowered on its two side uprights to accommodate the height of the item being planed, which is clamped onto the reciprocating work table. The horizontal bridge member carries a saddle which is traversed across the width of the machine, and a pivoted tool holder called a CLAPPER BOX is attached to the saddle. The tool on early planers cut surplus metal away only on the forward stroke of the work table, and swung clear on the return stroke. Later machines cut on both strokes, thus reducing machining times.

Planing machines date from the latter part of the 18th century. Richard Roberts (1789–1864) of Manchester made a hand-operated machine in 1817 which was soon improved by Joseph Clement (1779–1842) in 1825, but still manually operated. The first successful power driven planer was invented by Joseph Whitworth (1803–87) in Manchester in 1842: this was a self-acting machine with an automatically swivelling tool, christened a JIM CROW, which made a cut in each direction of the work table movement. Many other inventors improved the basic machines, which became bigger and more accurate as the need arose for planing larger items. By 1862 William Fairbairn (1789–1874) had made a self-acting planer which could take work pieces up to 20 ft long by 6 ft wide.

planking shaping of the body or crown of a felt hat. In the early days of felt HAT MAKING, planking was a domestic or backyard industry, the hatter working for a master and often combining hat making with farming or some other occupation. Small planking shops developed, and when hat-making factories came into being, planking was carried out by groups of men working round a pot or kettle of boiling water. The water was acidulated by weak sulphuric acid, and sheets of wool were shrunk and felted by hand on planks sloping down towards the kettle. Usually there were eight planks spaced around a central kettle making eight working places, and as the wool was felted it was pressed or blocked onto blocks of wood shaped in the required form for the finished hat. By the mid-19th century the operation had been mechanized.

plansifter a large box inside which long thin trays with mesh floors are constantly shaken in a horizontal orbit to grade stock received from BREAK ROLLS in a grain roller mill. The tray meshes vary in fineness from wire to silk and are brushed to assist the passage of the stock through the sieves. The various grades of stock are directed separately to reduction rolls for further reduction in particle size. The boxes containing the sieves are suspended from flexible canes.

plantations an early name for the first British colonies overseas, such as those on the east coast of North America and the West Indies, where cotton, sugar, indigo, and tobacco estates were cultivated by settlers or planters. In the early days, trade from the plantations was controlled by the British government, the plantations being regarded as extensions of Britain and economically subordinate to the mother country. In return, Britain defended the plantations, but their export trade was allowed only with Britain, and could only be carried in British or colonial ships. This is sometimes called the 'Old Colonial System'. As the plantations or colonies became more self-reliant, resentment arose in the American ones regarding the restrictions on trade and carriers, culminating in the Declaration of Independence on 4 July 1776. By the 1850s all restrictions on trade had been completely eliminated.

plat a dialect word for a flat surface, i.e. a base, platform, etc.

plate girder a solid fabricated BRIDGE GIRDER, which comprises a wrought iron or steel plate web riveted to top and bottom plate flanges with angle irons at the corners (*see* Fig. 11).

plate glass glass formed into a thin sheet by rolling, first invented by Bernard Perrot in 1687 in France, and not manufactured in Britain until 1773 at Ravenhead, St Helens, Lancs. Plate glass is made by casting molten glass into flat iron moulds and rolling it to the required thickness. Afterwards it is slowly ANNEALED and allowed to cool for up to fourteen days, then ground and polished. It had superseded CROWN GLASS by the mid-19th century.

plateway metal track for the movement of wheeled vehicles, the forerunners of EDGE RAILS used by railways. The first plateways were made by fastening flat iron strips or plates on top of wooden timbers to provide a hard wearing surface for truck wheels to run along. Such plateways were used in mines, both underground and on the surface, and gave no guidance to the wheels.

In about the 1780s, John Curr began using angled plates of an L cross-section to guide waggon wheels along the track. The upright 'legs' of the plates were placed facing each other on the inside of the track, and these kept waggons running along the horizontal 'legs'. Any debris which accumulated on the running surface could be swept away to the outside of the track. Labourers employed to do this were called creasers on north-east plateways. Such plateways were mainly used on mineral lines, and their use still persisted in a few places until the early 20th century. An advantage of a plateway was that ordinary road-using waggons and trucks of the right gauge could also run on them, as the wheels did not need flanges. Plateways were superseded by edge rails at the end of the 18th century; flanged wheels provided the guidance, but restricted their use to the rails only.

The men who maintain and lay new rails today on the permanent way are still called platelayers. Sometimes called TRAMROADS.

plating hammer a powered hammer, part of a forge, which is used for flattening iron bars etc. into plates, for instance to make shovels, plating hammers are usually water powered in the 18th and early 19th centuries.

plug 1. a simple valve or cock comprising a cylindrical piece which can be rotated about its long axis in a surrounding body, the latter having inlet and outlet holes in line with each other. A hole of equal bore passes transversely through the cylinder, and when in line with the inlet and outlet holes in the body, allows a fluid to pass straight through. By rotating the cylinder through $90°$ the through passage is cut off, thus stopping the flow. A plug is thus a simple control valve, usually used for on–off duties. The origin of the word is obscure, but Thomas Savery (1650?–1715) used plugs to control the cycle of his elementary steam engine. Plugs were also used to control the various actions on the Newcomen steam engine: a long rod, called a PLUG ROD, hung from the overhead beam and as it rose and fell with the rocking of the beam, opened and closed plugs in correct sequence so that the engine ran automatically. **2.** a solid metal cylinder with an external thread which

may be screwed into a threaded hole to seal or 'plug' it. Infrequently used outlet holes, such as drainage holes in boilers etc., are fitted with solid plugs merely as a simple way of stopping up a hole, which can be opened when required by unscrewing the plug.

plug and feathers (or stope and feathers) tools used in the early days of mining and quarrying for extracting rocks and minerals, etc. After boring a hole, or finding a suitable natural crevice or crack in the rock, two half-round iron bars (the feathers) were placed in the cavity, flat sides facing each other. An iron wedge (the plug) was then driven between them, the wedging action bursting apart the immediately surrounding rock which was then removed by other tools. The plug and feathers method replaced the older WEDGE AND GROOVE method in the early 19th century.

Plug riots name given to an outburst of industrial discontent in 1842–3 arising out of depressed economic conditions, which resulted in low wages and unemployment. It was mostly confined to the northern textile areas, particularly Lancashire, beginning in Blackburn in August 1842 and spreading through Rossendale. Mills and mines were stopped by gangs removing the drainage plugs from steam boilers, thus bringing operations to a halt. The stationary incline winding engine on the Bolton and Leigh Railway was also attacked. Some CHARTISTS were among the rioters. Order was enforced by the military, and four men were killed by the soldiers at a riot in Preston.

Rose, A.G. 'The Plug riots of 1842 in Lancashire and Cheshire', *Trans. Lancs. and Ches. Antiquarian Soc.* XVII (1957)

plug rod (or plug trees, plug frames) the wooden rod (usually of square cross-section) which hung down from the overhead beam of a Newcomen type steam engine to operate the valves controlling the working of the engine. The plug rod had a slit cut in an appropriate place through which levers operating the various valves or PLUGS protruded. Pegs were placed across the slit through holes, and as the overhead beam moved up and down, the plug rod followed the movement, the pegs depressing or raising the levers accordingly. Some variation in the speed of operation of the engine was possible by varying the position of the pegs, a series of holes being provided in the plug rod for this purpose. So that the valves would act quickly, they were provided with pivoted balance weights which tipped over once they passed their centre, to open or close the valve rapidly, an action the slow moving plug rod could not do.

plumbago, *see* GRAPHITE

plummer block   a journal bearing for supporting a rotating shaft. The word comes from the Latin *plumbum* (lead), since early plummer blocks had renewable split sleeves made of lead in which the shaft rotated. Lead was used because of its low frictional resistance. The sleeves were carried in a cast-iron box. Later, 'brasses' were used in place of lead, and shallow grooves were cut in the bearing surfaces to hold lubricating oil or greases.

plush   a silk or cotton cloth with a soft nap longer than velvet, used in the 17th and 18th centuries for expensive garments, coverings and footmen's liveries. The name comes from the Latin *pilus*, meaning hair.

pointer's rot, *see* PHTHISIS

point of suppression, *see* CUT-OFF (1)

poling   a method for refining and toughening copper during smelting by removing its oxygen content. The molten metal is covered with wood-charcoal or anthracite to prevent oxidation, and greenwood logs, usually birch (the poles) are plunged into the molten metal. The reducing gases from the burning poles remove dissolved oxygen, and when the correct oxygen content is reached, the copper is said to be tough pitch, and is cast into ingots. If there is too much oxygen in the metal, making it brittle and unusable, the copper is said to be underpoled; if there is too little, it is said to be overpoled.

Poncelet water turbine   an inwards, radial-flow, REACTION WATER TURBINE developed in 1826 by Jean Victor Poncelet (1788–1867) in France. The first machine to his design was built in New York in 1838. Later, it was improved by James Bicheno Francis, leading to the mixed-flow FRANCIS WATER TURBINE.

Poncelet waterwheel   a type of improved UNDERSHOT waterwheel developed by Jean Victor Poncelet (1788–1867) in France, which greatly raised the efficiency of previous undershot wheels. He substituted curved metal paddles or vanes for the flat wooden boards formerly used, the advantage being that the energy lost by impact on the flat surface was reduced. The incoming water flowed smoothly up the curve of the paddle, and receded in a similar manner as the paddle left the TAILRACE. This streamlining also permitted air to escape into the wheel centre, and raised wheel efficiency from about 20 per cent to around 60 per cent. Fig. 84f shows a cross-section through a Poncelet type paddle.

pontil   (or punty, puntee) an iron rod which is attached to a blown globe of hot glass so that it

may be spun in the furnace mouth to form the flat disk in CROWN GLASS manufacture. The word comes from the French *pointée*, meaning a rod or spike. Pontils are also used to carry finished glass articles to the ANNEALING oven.

poplin   in the 17th century, a fabric made from silk warps and jersey (worsted) wool weft, particularly in East Anglia. It had a PLAIN WEAVE with a slightly ribbed surface, caused by having more ends per inch (warp threads) than picks per inch (weft threads). It was a popular material for light garments. Later, poplin came to be made from cotton with the same surface texture, and was extensively used, as it is today, for shirts and dresses. The name comes from the French *popeline* which had a papal connection, the cloth being first made in Avignon which was the papal seat in the 14th century and continued in papal ownership until 1797. Avignon was an early silk growing area.

poppet valve   (or puppet valve) a mushroom shaped valve with a conical seating face on its underside which registers with a similar face on the aperture or port in which it works. The angle of the seat is usually 45°. Such valves are used in pumps, and Watt used them as steam valves. They operate in a vertical direction, as opposed to SLIDE and PISTON VALVES which move sideways. In some pumps the seats were once made from LIGNUM VITAE or holly – both hard, durable woods. The lift of poppet valves is limited by a stop acting on the valve stem. In some designs, rapid closure is assisted by springs. They are also known as mitre, conical, or mushroom valves.

pop valve, *see* SAFETY VALVE

porcelain   a non-porous, translucent form of fine POTTERY. There are two types of porcelain, soft and hard. Originating in China in the 6th century, hard porcelain was greatly admired in Europe and many attempts were made to copy it. The first attempts produced soft porcelain which was being made in Lambeth, London, in 1671 and called Delftware after the town of Delft in Holland which was famous for its pottery. Other potteries in London's Bow and Chelsea districts were making soft porcelain in the 1750s from a white clay.

The first successful hard porcelain to be made in Europe was in 1709 at Meissen, Germany, and was known as Dresdenware in Britain. William Cookworthy (1705–80), a Plymouth chemist, patented a hard porcelain in England (patent no. 898, 1768) using KAOLIN and burnt ground flint. By the 1780s hard porcelain was being made in the Potteries, as well as in Derby and Worcester.

Porcelain articles can be made thinner and more delicately than other types of pottery. A type of porcelain lying between hard and soft porcelain known as BONE CHINA was developed around 1800.

Hughes, B. and T. *English Porcelain and Bone China, 1743–1850*, Lutterworth, 1955

porcupine drawing a method of producing worsted ROVINGS without twist. The material is passed over a revolving brass cylinder, called a porcupine, whose circumference is covered by inclined rows of gill pins (*see* GILLING). The porcupine is set as close as possible in advance of a pair of drafting rollers, and combs the fibres just before DRAFTING. The resulting SLIVER then passes between top and bottom horizontal moving leather bands, which also reciprocate sideways in opposite directions to gently roll or rub the sliver into a round roving without imparting any twist. It is also known as the Continental or French system of drawing.

port an opening or passageway for a fluid of some sort entering or leaving a machine, or in a furnace. Examples include steam ports in a steam engine cylinder; water inlets and outlets to a hydraulic machine; and air and gas openings in an open hearth steel furnace. The opening and closing of a port is usually controlled by some form of valve gear or damper. In a steam engine, port opening and closing is automatically controlled by the VALVE GEAR which is driven off an ECCENTRIC, and port design is critical. Ports must be adequately sized so that steam flow is not throttled, and the length of the passageway kept short so that a minimum volume of steam is held in it.

porter bar an iron bar which is temporarily welded to a ball of puddled iron so that it may be removed from a PUDDLING FURNACE and carried to the next operation.

post a term used in the days of hand PAPER MAKING for a pile of alternating wet sheets of paper and woollen felts that could be accommodated in the screw press for squeezing out the excess water. Normally, a post contained six quires of paper (a quire is twenty-four sheets), i.e. 144 sheets in total. The word post was also used for the size of printing paper measuring 15$\frac{1}{2}$ in by 19 in.

posting a private form of road transport before the railway age. There were three forms of post travel for those who could afford not to travel in public stage coaches. First, post chaises and postilion could be hired from posting inns on a mileage basis. A post coach was usually pulled by two or four horses with the postilion riding on the leading near horse,

and no driver on the coach itself. Horses would be changed at other posting inns en route. Secondly, horses could be hired to pull one's own carriage; and finally, one could hire riding horses. In 1779 an annual licence had to be paid by the proprietor of a post inn for operating a post chaise service, or for hiring out horses, and a mileage tax had to be paid to the first toll-keeper passed.

post mill (or peg mill) a type of windmill construction where the whole wooden body containing the internal machinery and the sails is turned into the wind about a massive vertical timber post called a pintle. Post mills date from the 12th century and early ones usually only worked one pair of stones. The body was turned manually around the pintle by pushing a projecting tail pole at ground level until the sails faced into the wind. The post or pintle is supported on a trestle of massive timbers, the horizontal cross members of which rest on short brick piers. On some post mills the trestle is open to the atmosphere, whereas in others it is enclosed in a roundhouse which protects the timbers from the weather and provides some storage space.

post road a road used by the royal mail, ridden by post-boys on horseback at first, and later by mail coaches. Post roads were therefore the fastest and best roads between towns, and had post inns where post horses could be changed about every twenty miles. Travellers in a hurry would use post roads, hiring post horses at the inns (*see* POSTING), hence the expression 'post haste', meaning with great speed. Post comes from the Latin *posta* meaning place.

Robertson, A.W. *Great Britain's Post Roads, Post Towns, and Postal Rates, 1635–1839*, 1961

potash pits stone-lined pits up to 10 ft across, found in forests or areas which were once wooded, where potash was once made. Potash or caustic potash is the common name for potassium hydroxide, and got its name from this early way of producing the alkali: wood (usually birch twigs or green bracken) was burned to ash in iron pots, and the potassium hydroxide which was present in the wood remained in the ashes. This was sold to fullers or cloth merchants to make soft soap or LYE by the addition of lime and tallow, and used in the BLEACHING or FULLING of cloth. Making potash by this method died out by about 1850. Potash or wood ash was also used in the making of GLASS in the days of early forest-based glassworks, and in SOAP MAKING.

pot bank a factory where pottery is made, comprising the clay preparation sheds, moulding, kilns for firing, etc.

pot iron iron produced in small quantities by a process developed by the brothers Charles and William Wood in the early 1760s. The method is known as the stamping and potting process, or the Shropshire process. Cast-iron pigs were first heated in a FINERY in contact with coal which removed unwanted silicon, but the iron absorbed sulphur from the coal. To remove the sulphur and carbon, because the iron was too brittle to use, the iron was broken up into small pieces under heavy stamps, and packed into clay pots fitted with lids, together with a lime FLUX. Several pots were heated in a reverberatory type furnace, and the lime absorbed the sulphur whilst the carbon was virtually removed by the high temperature to make wrought iron.

The stamping and potting process was short-lived, being carried on for only a few decades, and was eventually superseded by Cort's DRY PUDDLING process of 1784.

potter's clay, *see* BALL CLAY

potter's rot a disease that can be caught from glazing porcelain with a lead glaze. Its incidence was reduced when feldspathic glazing was introduced in 1820. *See also* FELDSPAR.

pottery industry the manufacture of ceramic articles. Once a hand craft, pottery developed into a factory-based industry in the mid-18th century. Pottery is made from natural clays to which other materials are usually added to obtain certain qualities, and after being shaped, is hardened by heat. There are different classes of pottery – EARTHENWARE, STONEWARE, PORCELAIN, BONE CHINA, and TERRACOTTA – the main differences between them lying in their hardness and texture, brought about by the composition of the clay mix and the degree of heat used in firing. The first four types are frequently known as 'china' in common parlance, an indication of the origin of the finer types of these ceramic materials. Pottery may be useful or decorative, and porous or non-porous according to its intended use. Besides domestic pottery such as tableware and ornaments, other branches of the industry provide items such as sanitary ware, ceramic tiles, and industrial items.

The art of the potter is very old: pottery artefacts found at archaeological sites have been intensively studied, and are used today as dating aids. In medieval times pottery was crude and mostly made in monasteries, but later became a home-based hand craft, with the throwing wheel and firing kiln sited at the master potter's own cottage near to where suitable clay could be found. It was largely due to the organizational abilities of Josiah Wedgwood (1730–95) that a factory-based pottery industry came into being in the 1750s, centred on the five towns in Staffordshire known as the Potteries. He introduced mass production of cheap earthenware utensils by flow-line methods and the use of power machinery, together with the division of labour. China clay was brought from Cornwall, FELDSPAR from Derbyshire, and flint from Sussex and Kent to his factory, and local coal was used for firing the kilns.

There are three main ways of using clay for making pottery articles: throwing, pressing, and slip casting. Throwing, used in its old meaning of twisting or turning, is by the potter's wheel. Deep, circular articles such as pots and vases were made by hand, the potter moulding a lump of clay into shape as it revolves on the horizontal round table. Shallow hollow-ware such as plates and saucers are made by pressing flat slabs of clay into moulds, whilst non-circular, irregular shapes such as ornamental figures are cast by pouring liquid clay (slip) into porous moulds which are broken open after the clay has set. After shaping by any of the three methods the soft clay articles require hardening by heat. They are carefully stacked inside a bottle oven or kiln, some being placed inside protective ceramic SAGGARS and fired. Pottery when removed from the kiln, is known as BISCUIT, and if it is to be made impervious to liquids, it has to be glazed by baking on a 'glass hard' coat. Various materials have been used for glazing. Salt glazing is variously attributed to the Dutch brothers, David and John Elers, working in Bradwell, Stoke-on-Trent, *c*.1690, or to John Astbury (1688–1743) who developed the process around 1720 at Shelton, Staffs. Damp salt was thrown into the kiln at the height of a second firing, and the vapours arising settled on the surface of the pottery, which when cold resulted in a transparent glossy coating.

Other materials have been used for applying a glaze, such as powdered galena (lead), which was once dusted onto a coating of wet slip or a flour paste so that it would stick, before the second firing. Later, the healthier method of dipping the articles into a liquid lead oxide was adopted. Manganese, copper and cobalt oxides have also been used for glazing or to colour the pottery, as well as protect any decoration such as painting which may have been applied. The second firing is carried out at a lower temperature in what is known as a GLOST OVEN.

Baker, Diane. *Potworks*, Royal Commission on the Historical Monuments of England, 1991
Hughes, B. and T. *English Porcelain and Bone China, 1743–1850*, Lutterworth, 1955

Lockett, T.A. *Davenport Pottery and Porcelain*, David and Charles, 1972

Reilly, R. *Josiah Wedgwood, 1730–1795*, Macmillan, 1993

Thomas, J. *The Rise of the Staffordshire Potteries*, Adams and Dart, 1971

pound a stretch of water between successive locks on a canal. A side pound or pond is a basin alongside a lock into which almost all the upper half of water from an emptying lock may flow by gravity for storage, instead of passing down into the lower pound or level. When the lock is refilled, water from the side pound enters first, before the upper half is drawn from the upper pound or level. This economizes on the use of water and enables one lockful of water to pass two boats. Sometimes two separate locks are built side by side, one for up traffic, the other for down traffic, each lock then acting as a side pound for the other whenever possible. Steam engines were also used to pump all the lockage water into side pounds.

A turning pound is a widening of a canal to enable a canal boat to be turned round.

pouse FLAX dust, created during HACKLING. It can cause a disease of the throat or lungs known as Hacklers' disease, and a person suffering from this is said to be poucey (or poucy).

powder store a secure building for storing GUNPOWDER. When gunpowder was used in mining and quarrying, its storage in secure and safe magazines, or powder houses, was essential. These were small, brick or stone buildings with solid walls, sited some distance away from the working area. Remains of such buildings may sometimes be found in abandoned quarries. In sailing days, ships carrying gunpowder had to unload it at a powder house remote from the wharves, before entering the dock.

power loom (or steam loom) a power driven cloth weaving machine. The power loom stems from the invention of the Revd Edmund Cartwright (1743–1823) who took out his first patent in 1785, but the first power looms were very clumsy and needed stronger yarn because they worked faster and subjected the yarn to greater strain. Power looms did not therefore come into general use until about 1815 after several improvements had been made. More rapid progress in their adoption was made in the worsted industry than in the woollen trade since worsted is naturally stronger than wool; by about 1845 worsted hand looms were almost a thing of the past. By 1825 it has been estimated that there were 30,000 power looms in England, working on all types of yarn, and by 1833 the number had risen to some 85,000. Richard Roberts (1789–1864) contributed to the success of power looms in 1822 with his designs, and other inventors added refinements to the power loom, making it automatic in operation and faster. Whereas men had operated hand looms, the application of power and automatic working meant that loom supervision became a female job, one woman attending to several looms at once.

Power looms were called steam looms in the 19th century since by this date steam engines had largely taken over from waterwheels for driving mills and weaving sheds; very few power looms were driven by water power.

Pratt truss a bridge lattice truss invented in 1844 by Caleb and Thomas Willis Pratt, father and son, in the USA, and used for medium spans (*see* Fig. 12). It comprises upper and lower horizontal STRINGERS joined at regular intervals by vertical members. On the left-hand side of the centre of the truss inclined members slope from top left to bottom right between adjacent pairs of verticals, and on the right-hand side they slope from top right to bottom left; the centre pair of verticals have crossed sloping members. The truss is therefore made up of a series of triangular spaces.

premium royalty charged by Boulton and Watt for the use of their steam engines. In areas where the price of coal was high, such as Cornwall, they charged one-third of the cost of the fuel saved by their engine compared with a NEWCOMEN ENGINE with the same DUTY. This premium was to be paid annually for twenty-five years, or if preferred, a down payment equivalent to ten years could be made. Another alternative was a payment per 10,000 strokes made by the engine as registered on a mechanical counter. Elsewhere where coal was cheap, or where coal mines valued their waste or surplus coal at nothing, a premium based on a horsepower year was: a figure of £6 per hp year for the London area and £5 per hp year for country districts was common. After 1795, when Watt's condenser patent (no. 913, 1769) was within five years of running out, separate annual charges were dropped, and the price of the engines was adjusted to include an amount equivalent to the premium.

presser the component on a knitting machine which closes the open hook of a BEARDED NEEDLE at the appropriate moment during the knitting sequence.

presser wire, *see* FALLER WIRE

pressure a force exerted on a surface by a weight, or a gas, liquid, or vapour under compression. Pressure is a form of energy: the pressure of steam in a steam engine, for instance, is converted into kinetic energy by moving the piston along the cylinder to do work. Pressure is measured by its force or weight per unit area. In Britain, Imperial units of pounds per square inch (psi) were used before metric or SI units were introduced in the 20th century. In practical terms, positive pressures above atmospheric pressure (approx. 14.7 psi, or the pressure exerted by a column of mercury 29.9 in high) are called gauge pressures since they are measured by pressure gauges. Negative pressures, i.e. partial vacuums or suctions, are expressed in terms of inches of mercury. The very low suctions and pressures of chimney draught and ventilation fans are usually measured in inches water gauge by water-filled manometers (1 psi equals 27.7 in of water). Positive pressures occur in steam engine cylinders, and negative pressures in steam condensers or pump suction pipes.

Pressure has played an important part in steam engineering, as higher and higher pressures were used for developing more power, as shown in the table below. A few exceptions to the steady rise in pressures were made by designers in advance of their times: for instance, Trevithick's locomotive of 1804 used 50 psi, and Gurney's steam carriage of 1835 ran at up to 120 psi on occasions.

year	working steam pressure (psi)	engine
1712	1–2	Newcomen atmospheric engine
1788	4–6	Watt rotative beam engine
1829	40	Stephenson's *Rocket* locomotive
1843	15	Brunel *Great Britain* steamship
1845	120–150	McNaught compound beam engine
1870	150	triple expansion compound engine
1880	160	locomotive

In water and hydraulic engineering, the term HEAD is often used instead of pressure.

pressure compounding reducing steam pressure in steps in a PRIME MOVER. Examples of pressure compounding are a single tandem-compound steam engine, which reduces the boiler steam pressure in two steps, first in the high pressure cylinder and secondly in the low pressure cylinder; and a Parsons reaction steam turbine, which reduces the steam pressure in a number of small drops as the steam passes through each successive stage of the rotor.

prime mover a machine, such as an engine, which is supplied with energy from a natural source and converts it into mechanical power. Examples include WATERWHEELS, STEAM ENGINES, INTERNAL COMBUSTION ENGINES and WINDMILLS.

The common denominator for all prime movers is that they ultimately depend on heat as their energy source. Steam and internal combustion engines draw their heat from the fuel burnt, i.e. coal burnt in the furnace of a boiler in the case of a steam engine, and gas, oil or petrol exploded in the cylinders of an internal combustion engine. Waterwheels and windmills receive their energy from the heat of the sun: in the case of waterwheels, the sun's heat is responsible for the evaporation–precipitation cycle for the water which flows down the rivers which drive the wheels; while winds are caused by air temperature differences in different locations, warm air rising and cooler air blowing in to take its place. Because of their dependence on some form of heat energy prime movers are also known as heat engines, particularly steam and internal combustion engines.

Two other kinds of prime mover relying on natural sources are muscle power, human or animal, represented for example by a hand wound winch or a HORSE WHIM; and gravitational pull, utilized in a self-acting incline (*see* INCLINED PLANE), or the out-of-balance created by the full buckets on a WATERWHEEL.

priming 1. the state in which a steam boiler is said to be when minute particles of water are carried up into the steam and out of the boiler. This may be because there is insufficient steam space above the water level, or because the boiler is being forced, which causes excessive turbulence in the water. Priming should be avoided, because any water carried over into the steam mains may accumulate in the cylinder of a steam engine and cause loss of power. **2.** filling the body of a water pump with water before it can commence pumping. This must be done to expel any air, otherwise suction lift cannot be started.

producer gas a gas produced, in general, from low grade fuels such as sawdust, wood chips, brown coal, etc. or alternatively from graded coke or anthracite. Producer gas comprises mostly carbon monoxide, hydrogen, and nitrogen, with a calorific value of 120–180 BThUs per cubic ft dependent on the fuel used. It was cheaper than TOWN GAS, and was used for powering GAS ENGINES, and for firing furnaces such as pottery kilns, open-hearth steel furnaces, etc., but not for lighting purposes. Experiments for producing this type of gas began in the mid-19th century, and by the 1880s many plants were in existence, mostly small for specific duties. Frederick and Charles William Siemens invented a gas producer (patent no. 167, 1861) for their open-hearth steel-making furnace using cheap powdered coal. Another name associated with producer gas equipment is that of Joseph Emerson Dowson.

The gas is made in a vertical, firebrick-lined, steel cylinder, which is fed at the top with fuel through a double-door device called a charging bell, which allows the fuel to drop into the gas-making chamber without an escape of gas. A hearth is at the base of the cylinder with firebars which support the column of burning fuel. Gas is drawn off by a fan near the top of the chamber, and combustion air (1.25–1.5 times the gas volume) is sucked in at the base. As fresh fuel descends, it passes first through a distillation zone, where volatiles join the ascending gas stream, then through reduction zones where the carbon monoxide is largely formed, and finally through an oxidation zone where it is burned to ashes. These are extracted from below the firebars. To enrich the gas, small amounts of water are dribbled into the fire near the base. After leaving the chamber, the gas is passed through a purifying tower to remove tarry deposits created by combustion and any fine particles entrapped in the gas, and then cooled before being piped to the furnace or engine. By the 1880s small producer gas plants were being attached directly to gas engines, the movement of the piston creating the necessary draught to draw air into the system; for this reason producer gas was often known as suction gas.

projector name by which an inventor was sometimes known in the 17th and 18th centuries.

propellor, *see* SCREW (2)

prospecting searching ground surfaces with the prospect of finding valuable minerals, coal, metal ores, etc. hidden below. Before today's scientific methods and knowledge of geology were developed, primitive means were used, including simple observation. For instance, examination of hillsides after heavy rain could sometimes show coal outcrops previously hidden. Discoloured spring water seeping out onto the surface might indicate the presence underground of a metal ore – for example, brown or rusty coloured water can indicate iron; and sometimes the type of vegetation growing at a spot indicates a particular mineral is near the surface. Some plants have a liking for certain metalliferous soils, such as certain cresses and members of the alyssum plant.

Another method of prospecting was shoding, a dialect word meaning searching around for small pieces of ore lying on or near the surface which signal a vein nearby, which can be confirmed by digging. Copper, lead, and tin have been found in this way in the past. In the 16th and early 17th centuries coal seams were sometimes searched for, or their direction confirmed, by using divining rods in a similar manner to that used when dowsing for water. Divining rods – usually forked branches of hazel, rowan, or willow – have been found in old coal workings. Metallic lodes were divined in Elizabethan times in Cornwall, by persons sensitive to the presence of the ores. It is believed that this rather haphazard method was introduced into Britain by German miners. Tin and lead have been discovered by examining the gravel in the beds of rivers and streams for traces of minerals, and following them upstream until the approximate source is found.

Once the existence of an outcrop was proved or suspected, much of the labour involved uncovering it could be avoided by HUSHING. Alternatively, primitive hollow drills might be hammered vertically into the ground and periodically withdrawn to examine the earth core for minerals. Huntington Beaumont demonstrated such borehole techniques for prospecting for coal, known as percussion drilling, as early as 1606. In Cornwall, the practice of COSTEANING was used to trace the direction of a tin lode in rock.

prunella name dating from the 17th century for a strong, hard wearing cloth, originally made from silk, and later from worsted. It was woven with a two by one, or three ends, TWILL and was formerly much used for barristers' and clergymen's gowns etc. Later it became fashionable for the uppers of ladies' shoes.

public utilities water, gas, electricity supplies, etc., provided for public use. Today's hygienic living conditions in developed countries date only from the mid-19th century when the provision of clean water, sewage disposal, and gas and electricity supplies for domestic, commercial and industrial users was developed. Prior to this, there were no satisfactory water supplies nor adequate sewers in the rapidly expanding industrial towns of Britain during the late 18th and early 19th century, and living conditions for working people were extremely unhealthy.

Some attempt at supplying clean water to London had been made by Hugh Middleton (1555–1631), when he brought water from springs near Ware, Herts., in 1609–13 via a man-made water course some 38 miles long known as the New River, parts of which can still be traced. The population of Britain almost doubled over the period 1801–51, and the increase was mainly concentrated in towns and cities where industry was rapidly being established. Overcrowding of the working population in jerry-built, insanitary conditions nurtured epidemics of cholera and smallpox, and gradually it was recognized there was a correlation between the epidemics and a lack of pure water. Investigations by Edwin Chadwick (1801–90) led in 1842 to his *Report on the Sanitary Conditions of the Labouring Population of Great Britain.* This report initiated the setting up of the first Board of Health by the government in 1848. The Board was, however, short lived, mainly due to resentment by local authorities of state interference, and it was abolished in 1854. The need for some regulation of health affairs continued to be recognized, and in 1875 the first Public Health Act became law. This empowered local authorities to provide clean water supplies, water-borne sewage collection and treatment before disposal, and such amenities as public baths and washhouses, and isolation hospitals for infectious diseases.

Some local authorities were already supplying water to their towns for drinking and street cleansing purposes before the Act. Sheffield, for instance, had a reservoir in 1830 from which water was pumped into the city, whilst Nottingham was supplying pumped water for 1*d* per week per house in the 1830s. Joseph Bazalgette (1819–91) of the Metropolitan Water Board built London's main drainage sewers during the years 1858–75, and Thomas Hawksley (1807–93) built over 150 waterworks during his lifetime. A professional class of municipal engineers arose to design and construct water and sewerage schemes. The Sanitary Act of 1866 applied to workshops and industrial concerns, and was supervised by inspectors appointed by local authorities. As the result of improved living conditions, the death rate in the country steadily declined from 1848.

Public gas supplies date back to 1798, when William Murdock (1754–1839) is credited with the first application of coal gas to LIGHTING at the Soho ironworks in Birmingham. A cotton mill was lit by gas in Salford in 1804, and the Gas Light and Coke Company began lighting London streets in 1812–20. By 1823 over fifty towns had gas street lights, provided by private companies. Local authorities were empowered to supply towns with gas from 1848, and ten years later there were nearly 1,000 gas works in the country. The first public electricity supply was not created until 1881, when Holborn streets were lit in London; the first Electric Light Act was passed the following year. By the 1890s, electric power was beginning to spread across the industrial scene, and development and usage of electricity rapidly spread in the early 20th century.

Industrial archaeology interest in public utilities lies in the study of surviving buildings and machinery, etc. dating from the days when these services were first developed. There are reservoirs for water storage dating from the 1830s and 1840s in many parts of the country, particularly those serving the woollen and cotton towns of the Pennines. The first reservoirs had earth dams with puddled clay cores, stone faced on the water side. Masonry dams were introduced in the 1890s. Most towns installed steam driven pumps, either to raise water from wells and boreholes, or to force it up to high level reservoirs or water towers. Pumps were also needed to move sewage and street drainage water to sewage farms by the 1850s. Generally BEAM STEAM ENGINES were preferred for such pumping duties, and most dated from the 1850s and 1860s. Some fine examples of large Victorian beam engines have been preserved in their often cathedral-like, ornamental houses, although very many have been scrapped or replaced by electrically driven pumps. Outstanding installations are at Ryhope near Sunderland, Co. Durham, at Papplewick, Notts. and at Kew Bridge, London. Many gas holders still exist, now storing natural gas, with the original gas-making and purification plants scrapped.

'Beam engines in Greater London', *Greater London Industrial Archaeology Society Newsletter*, January 1970
Binnie, G.M. *Early Victorian Water Engineers*, Telford, 1981
Dunsheath, P. *A History of Electrical Engineering*, Faber, 1962
Engels, F. *The Condition of the Working Class in England*, 1845; English edition reprinted by Granada, 1969
Lewis, R.A. *Edwin Chadwick and the Public Health Movement, 1832–1854*, 1952
Linsley, S.M. *Ryhope Pumping Station*, 1973
Robins, F.W. *The Story of Water Supply*, Oxford University Press, 1946

puddled clay clay treated to make it watertight and used to line the bottom and sides of a canal. The clay was mixed with some sand and a little water, 'puddled' or chopped and kneaded about by spades, or trampled underfoot by the boots of the navvies, until it was reduced to a semi-fluid, plastic state. The puddling action made the mixture watertight as long as it was kept wet; unworked clay on its own is not watertight.

Used by James Brindley to line his Bridgewater Canal in the 1760s, it became the standard method for making watertight canals. Puddled clay is also used as impervious core for earth dams.

puddler's candles flames from burning carbon monoxide in an iron PUDDLING FURNACE. A critical stage in the melting of iron in the puddling process was when the molten mass began to 'boil': when this occurred, bubbles of carbon monoxide burst up through the surface of the molten metal and burned to carbon dioxide with a blue flame. These flames were known as puddler's candles, and could last for up to half an hour, during which time the iron had to be continuously stirred. When the flames disappeared it signified that all the carbon had been removed and the pure iron was ready for leaving the furnace.

puddling furnace a reverberatory furnace for producing wrought iron from cast-iron pigs by a stirring process. Wrought iron was produced by decarburizing pig iron in reverberatory type furnaces, and two historical methods were used – first 'dry' puddling, and later the 'wet' puddling process.

Dry puddling Although the brothers Thomas and George Cranage had partly anticipated the true puddling process (patent no. 851, 1766), the credit for dry puddling belongs to Henry Cort (1740–1800) with his patent no. 1420 in 1784. In his process, the lining of the furnace bath in which the pig iron was heated was made of a siliceous sand, and only 'white' CAST IRON was used. Cort's process was wasteful of iron, up to 30 per cent being lost, but it remained in use for half a century until the improved 'wet' process was invented.

Wet puddling This was patented by Joseph Hall, Richard Bradley and William Barrows in 1830 (patent no. 7778). A reactive bath lining called FETTLING was used, which greatly reduced metal loss. The wet process, also known as pig boiling, completely replaced Cort's earlier method, and became the standard way of making wrought iron for almost a century. Fig. 51 shows a cross-section through a wet puddling furnace. It comprised two chambers, a firebox and ashpit at one end, separated from the furnace bath by a low firebrick wall known as a bridge. A sloping refractory arch spanned the bath, and heat from the fire reflected or reverberated from it onto the cast-iron pigs held in the bath. The hot gases left the furnace via a flue, either to a chimney, or from several furnaces to a waste

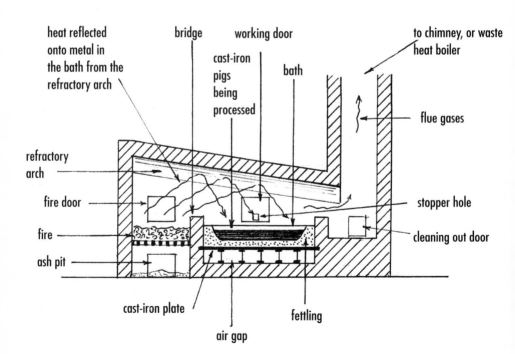

Fig. 51. Cross-section through a puddling furnace

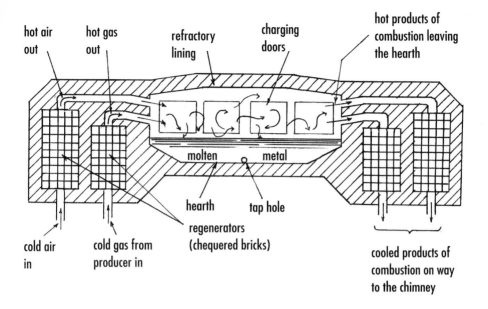

hot air out

hot gas out

refractory lining

charging doors

hot products of combustion leaving the hearth

molten metal

hearth

tap hole

regenerators (chequered bricks)

cold air in

cold gas from producer in

cooled products of combustion on way to the chimney

Fig. 52. Siemens-Martin open hearth regenerative furnace

heat boiler where steam was raised to drive the associated SHINGLING HAMMER. Conversion from cast-iron pigs into wrought iron occurred in three stages in the furnace. In the first stage, the temperature reached was above the melting point of cast iron, but below that of wrought iron; the metal did not become fluid but stayed in an extremely hot, pasty state. In the second, boiling stage, an oxidizing atmosphere was maintained above the bath, and the metal continuously stirred, i.e. puddled, by iron bars to induce decarburization and removal of impurities. When all the carbon had been burnt out, the metal was removed in the third stage, by being rabbled into white hot balls of wrought iron and taken in tongs to a shingling hammer to be shaped into blooms. A charge of 5 or 6 cwt of pig iron could be converted into four balls of wrought iron, each weighing about 120 lb, in a two-hour cycle. During the second stage, the metal surface became very agitated as bubbles of carbon monoxide burst through. It was this similarity to water boiling that gave the process its name. (*See also* PUDDLER'S CANDLES.)

Working a puddling furnace was extremely arduous and dangerous work, involving heavy labour and exposure to hot conditions. Mechanical puddling was introduced in the USA in the 1870s and was adopted by some firms in Britain soon afterwards. The demand

for wrought iron declined when cheap steel became more abundant and puddling furnaces became redundant, although one or two firms still continued to use them in Britain well into the present century.

Brough, J. *Wrought Iron: The End of an Era at Atlas Forge, Bolton*, Bolton Metropolitan Borough, 1981
Mott, R.A. *Henry Cort: The Great Finer: Creator of Puddled Iron*, The Metals Society, 1983

pug mill a mixing machine for loam or clay, used in the brick-making and pottery industries. It prepares the clay for subsequent operations, at the same time expelling air from the mixture.

pulley block, *see* BLOCK

pulping stone, *see* EDGE MILL

pulsometer a steam operated pump with few moving parts, based on the device invented by Thomas Savery (*c.*1650–1717) – *see* 'MINERS' FRIEND'. A pulsometer pump comprises a casing divided into two equal chambers with a common steam inlet at the top. A rubber ball is constrained to move sideways at the top of the chambers to cover and uncover the steam entrance to each chamber in turn. A common water inlet is at the bottom of the casing with a non-return valve controlling the way into each chamber. Near the bottom of each chamber is a water outlet which joins a common pump delivery pipe. Steam enters one chamber, the ball closing off the other, and steam pressure forces out water lying in the chamber into the delivery pipe. As the water level falls its lower temperature condenses the steam, causing a partial vacuum which pulls the rubber ball across to the other side, and sucks in a fresh volume of water into the chamber. The steam now enters the second chamber and forces out the water which had been sucked into it by the previous cycle. The sequence then repeats itself automatically. The pulsometer needs priming to start off, and although it is rather extravagant in steam, and can only pump a few feet, its big advantage is its simplicity; it can also handle a certain amount of suspended solids in the water. A pulsometer pump was developed by Hall in 1876.

pump a power-driven machine or device for raising a liquid or forcing it along a pipe, etc., or for compressing a gas. There are several types of pump, many known from ancient times, and mostly used then for moving water from one level to another. Pumping action is either by reciprocating or rotating a specially shaped component inside a closed chamber.

A suction pump is placed above the free surface of a liquid; a 'drowned' pump is placed below the liquid or immersed in it. In the latter case the fluid flows to pump by gravity. In a suction pump a sub-atmosphere is created inside the pump's inlet pipe by the action of the moving part, and the normal atmospheric pressure acting on the free surface surrounding the inlet pipe forces the liquid up the pipe. For cold water, the maximum theoretical height the water will rise is about 34 ft, but in practice this is reduced to about 25–30 ft for a well-made pump. On the delivery side of the pump, the limiting factors are the pressure the pump can stand, and the power available to drive it.

Water is the most common liquid pumped, for town and industrial use, raising unwanted water from mines, supplying water for steam raising, etc. Thames water was raised for London by pumps driven by tidal waterwheels sited in the arches of old London Bridge from 1582 to 1822. Shallow mines were dewatered by a kind of primitive pump comprising continuously running chains (*see* CHAIN PUMP) as described by Georg Bauer in 1556 (*see* Fig. 53a). The invention of the ATMOSPHERIC STEAM BEAM ENGINE by Thomas Newcomen in 1712 enabled water to be raised from deeper mines. BEAM ENGINES were particularly suitable for operating reciprocating pumps sited down the shaft, worked by the weight of long and heavy PUMP RODS.

Fig. 53b shows a type of pump, the bucket pump, which was used in early mines. It comprised a vertical chamber with an inlet CLACK VALVE at the bottom, an outlet pipe at the top, and the bucket or 'piston' which slid up and down. The bucket incorporated another clack valve. Each clack allowed water to flow upwards only, and snapped shut against any reverse flow. As the bucket rose, previously raised water inside the chamber was lifted and passed out at the top, through a non-return valve, not shown, whilst an equal amount of water was drawn into the chamber through the bottom clack. When the bucket descended, water was transferred through the bucket clack to above the bucket. The cycle was then repeated by the next stroke. In deep mines, bucket pumps were arranged one above the other, as shown in Fig. 53c, each pump delivering water to the one above; this was called shammelling in Cornish mines. At East Pool, Cornwall, Taylor's engine, still standing, worked seven pumps, raising water 1,700 ft. Bucket pumps are more or less obsolete today.

Beam engines were often used for water and sewage pumping by local authorities in Victorian days, some engines lasting over 100 years on this duty. Some engines worked two pumps, a bucket pump raising water from a well, and a force or ram pump to distribute water at pressure in the mains. A horizontal ram pump is shown in Fig. 53d. In the absence of heavy pump rods, the vertical rams were weighted by several tons. The steam cylinder of the engine raised the weighted ram, which descended under gravity forcing the water into the mains. Force pumps may have a ram or a piston, and may be single- or double-acting. Hydraulic pumps and boiler feed pumps are other examples of force pumps, forcing water against a high pressure.

In the 1850s the centrifugal pump was developed, pioneered by J.C. Appold (1800–65) and James Thomson (1822–92). Fig. 53e shows a centrifugal pump. A specially shaped impellor rotates at high speed inside a spiral casing, which creates an outward radial pressure and a partial vacuum at the centre. The inlet is therefore at the centre of the pump, and the delivery led off at the circumference. Centrifugal pumps will deliver water up to about 30 ft high; greater heights or pressures are obtained by placing several pumps in series in one block, each pump delivering into the eye of the next pump, building the pressure up at each stage.

Other types of pump have been invented, such as the rotary radial with sliding vanes in an eccentrically placed rotor, dating from Elizabethan times. The PULSOMETER, with no moving parts, is another. *See also* HYDRAULIC RAM.

Bale, M.P. *Pumps and Pumping*, Crosby Lockwood, 1901

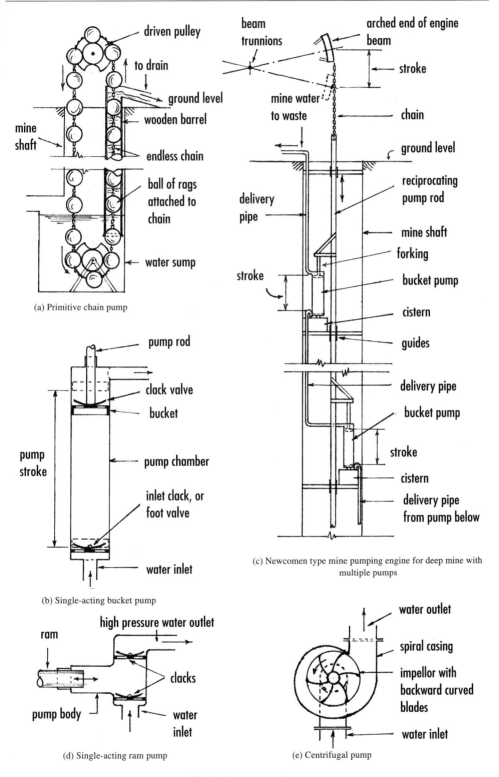

(a) Primitive chain pump

(b) Single-acting bucket pump

(c) Newcomen type mine pumping engine for deep mine with multiple pumps

(d) Single-acting ram pump

(e) Centrifugal pump

Fig. 53. Various types of pump

pumping plate, *see* SWASH PLATE

pump rods long, timber 'rods', joined together and hung from the BEAM ARCH of a beam engine, such as a NEWCOMEN ATMOSPHERIC ENGINE, which pass down a shaft of a mine to operate lift pumps for raising water from the workings. The rods were usually made from Baltic fir or pine, these being low density woods, to reduce the weight as much as possible, and were made in 40–60 ft lengths of rectangular cross-section and joined by bolts and FISH PLATES. The rods passed between roller guides at intervals down the shaft over the dry lengths. The wet lengths, which were immersed in the water being pumped out of the mine, weighed less because of their buoyancy. On very deep mines, the pump rods were balanced by BALANCE BOBS at ground level to relieve the weight on the engine beam and reduce load on the engine. The rods were also called pump spears, probably a variation of the word spar, a length of timber.

In operation, the power stroke of an atmospheric engine raised the rods, at the same time raising water in the lift pump. At the end of the stroke, the rods fell under their own weight, at the same time lifting the engine piston to the top of the cylinder ready for the next power stroke.

punched card the means for automatically controlling the design of cloth woven on a JACQUARD loom. A large number of cards are laced together to form an endless long loop, and each individual card has holes punched in it in certain places according to how the warp threads are to be raised to make the design. Each card passes through the loom mechanism in turn, and determines how the SHED is formed for that pass of the shuttle. A simple design may only need a hundred or so cards, whilst an elaborate design might require thousands. Special punching machines are used to perforate the cards; one such machine was patented by Stephen Wilson (patent no. 4795, 1823).

purifier a machine used in a roller mill when producing white flour. It comprised a vibrating tray which brought the lighter brown bran particles to the surface of the flour, where they were drawn off by an air current aided by brushing. The 'cleaned' flour then passed through a fine mesh before being conveyed away for further milling.

pusher lace lace made on the patterned twist-lace machine developed by Samuel Clark and James Mort of Nottingham in 1812. The carriage carrying the bobbins was traversed across the machine by a long device called the pusher, hence the name of the machine and its product. Pusher lace is an imitation of hand-made BOBBIN LACE.

putter a person who pushes waggons or trucks underground in a coal mine, taking empty ones to the coal face, filling them, and pushing them to the shaft bottom. Women and boys were used as putters in the early days of coal mining. The word is used on Tyneside; it is possible that it comes from the German word *Pütt*, meaning mine or pit.

putting-out system, *see* DOMESTIC SYSTEM

pye kiln (or lime pit) a primitive kiln for making lime. These 'kilns' date from the 16th century, when lime was known as a 'sweetener' for sour soil. A pye kiln comprised a long shallow pit dug into the ground, some 30 ft long by 10–15 ft wide, with wind holes cut in the sides leading down to fire spaces in the base of the excavation. Broken limestone and coal were piled into the pit in layers to form a heap rising above the surrounding ground, and then covered with soil. The 'pye' was set alight and left to burn slowly for several days to form lime powder, which was then dug out and used on the land. Such primitive pits were in use until the end of the 18th century, often sited at limestone quarries.

pyrites combinations of metals with sulphur or arsenic. Two common pyrites are iron pyrites and copper pyrites (chalcopyrites). Iron pyrites or MUNDIC is a hard, natural substance, brass coloured, properly an iron bisulphide comprising about 46 per cent iron and 54 per cent sulphur. It burns with a blue flame. In the late 18th and early 19th centuries iron pyrites was burnt and the fumes condensed to obtain sulphur for the manufacture of sulphuric acid. When iron pyrites occurs in coal, it is known as fool's gold, or coal brass: the name fool's gold dates back to Elizabethan times when the navigator Martin Frobisher (1535–94) brought to England samples of a supposed gold mineral which proved to be only iron pyrites. Copper pyrites is a sulphide of copper and iron, and is the most common ore for copper. Most copper pyrites was imported from the famous Rio Tinto district of southern Spain. The word pyrites comes from the Greek *purites*, meaning fire; an early use of the substance was to obtain sparks by percussion, a property known to the ancient Greeks.

Q

quadrant   a spinning mule mechanism controlling spindle rotation during winding. A problem when winding spun yarn onto the spindle of a MULE is that as the diameter of the COP increases, the speed of rotation of the spindle has to decrease. The quadrant mechanism is the solution adopted by Richard Roberts (1789–1864) in his self-acting mule and included in his patent no. 5949 of 1830. It was so designed that its action is governed by the movement of the carriage, and it controls winding-on and cop build-up during the inwards run of the carriage.

Fig. 54 shows the main features. The quadrant arm turns through an arc of 90° about a centre fixed in the mule framework at the opposite end to the drafting rollers, and is operated by a belt-driven pinion which meshes with the teeth cut in the curved part of the arm.

The pinion is driven from the main drive of the machine which also moves the carriage in and out. The arm has a radial screw along which a nut travels and which can be moved up and down by turning a handle attached to the free end of the screw. A winding chain stretches from the nut onto a winding drum positioned on the carriage, and is wound round it to an anchoring point. The winding drum is geared to the TIN ROLLER through a ratchet drive, and the tin roller drives the spindles. When the carriage runs in (winding-on), the ratchet drives the tin roller and spindles. On the outward run of the carriage, the ratchet 'free wheels', the spindles then being driven at speed (spinning) by another drive not shown.

The action of the mechanism is complex. When starting to form a new cop, the nut is at the bottom of the screw near the centre of rotation of the quadrant and the arm in a near vertical position, the carriage out. As the carriage runs in to wind on, the quadrant arm slowly turns towards the drafting rollers. The movement of the carriage causes the winding drum to be rotated as the chain unwinds from it, this in turn slowly rotating the spindles, the whole movement being synchronized with the

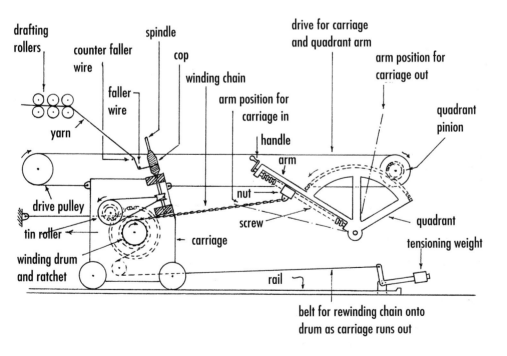

Fig. 54. Roberts' quadrant for regulating the speed of winding-on of yarn on a self-acting spinning mule

action of the faller and counter FALLER WIRES, and the cop is built up. When the carriage reverses and runs out to spin the next length of yarn, the chain is rewound onto the drum by the belt positioned near the floor, and the quadrant arm returns to the near vertical position again, ready for the cycle to be repeated. As more yarn is wound onto the spindles and the cop diameter increases, the spinner winds the nut farther up the screw a little at a time. This has the effect of slowing down the speed of rotation of the spindles since less chain is unwound from the drum as the quadrant arm comes down.

The action of Roberts' quadrant was not precise and depended greatly on the skill of the spinner in judging how much to wind up the nut to produce a well formed cop. However, the mechanism, with later improvements, became the standard device to control winding-on on automatic mules.

Quaker Company, *see* LONDON LEAD COMPANY

Quakers' Line a name by which the Stockton and Darlington Railway of the 1820s was known in its early days, because of the large amount of money invested in it by Quaker families such as the Pease and Backhouse families of the north-east, the Gurneys of Norwich, etc.

quality governing a method for controlling the speed of a GAS ENGINE. In this method the gas supply to the engine is not cut off as it is in HIT-AND-MISS GOVERNING, but is reduced by the governor throttling the gas supply in a similar manner to throttle governing a steam engine. Since the separate air inlet supply remains unaffected, weak mixtures result when the engine speeds up. The weaker mixtures reduce the power of each explosive stroke, causing the engine speed to fall until the mean speed is again reached and the governor restores the gas strength. The reverse happens when the engine speed falls. The disadvantage of this method is that with varying mixtures either side of mean speed, incorrect ignition timing results, and thermal efficiency suffers.

quant post the vertical shaft which drives the runner stone in an overdriven windmill. It comprises a metal shaft, often cast iron of square cross-section, on which the STONE NUT is mounted. The upper end of the quant runs in an overhead bearing, and its lower end terminates in a two-pronged fork. The fork fits into two slots provided in the runner stone, and by this means rotates it. In some designs it is possible to take the quant out of its top bearing easily to disengage the stone nut from the spur wheel when the mill is not working, a universal joint allowing this to be done. The word quant possibly comes from the Greek *kontos* meaning pole. Other names for a quant are crotch spindle and crutch pole.

quantity governing a method for controlling the speed of a GAS ENGINE. The governor controls both the gas inlet and the air inlet valves by throttle control. If the engine speeds up the increased speed of the governor throttles back the air and gas supplies to the engine cylinder keeping the air–gas ratio more or less constant, but a lesser quantity enters causing a reduction in power per charge. This slows down the engine until the governor resumes its normal speed and restores the normal charge; the reverse happens when the engine slows down. The advantage of this method over QUALITY GOVERNING is that the thermal efficiency is better maintained. Quantity governing was usually used for governing large gas engines.

quarrying the extraction of stone, slate, etc. from an area open to the sky, either by cutting into a hillside forming a cliff, or digging down to make a crater. Quarries occur where the wanted material outcrops onto the surface, or lies just beneath it. Some quarrying is, however, carried out by a mixture of open-air quarrying and shallow mining.

Quarrying is a very old industry. Stone has been used as a building material from early days, and thousands of defunct quarries exist all over Britain where all the material has been extracted, or an economical point has been reached where the cost of further work is not worth the value of the material won. Local geology once determined what ready-to-hand building material would be used for the construction of dwellings, bridges, churches, etc., and this was responsible for the distinctive appearance of towns and villages in some parts of the country. For example, the older buildings in Dorset villages are built from the warm-coloured local stone, whilst the local millstone grit has produced the more sombre towns of north-west England. The coming of canals, followed by railways, eased transport of building materials to places remote from where they were quarried, and more variety was introduced into buildings everywhere.

Certain types of stone having special qualities have always been used on important buildings, often brought at great expense from quarries considerable distances away. One well-known quality stone is Portland stone, an oolite limestone from the Isle of Portland, Dorset, which has been quarried since the 14th century. It is a freestone that can be carved to provide ornamentation, and was greatly used in rebuilding London after the Great Fire of 1666, when it was brought round the coast and up the Thames; it was used in the reconstruction of St Paul's Cathedral, begun in 1675. Other notable London buildings built from Portland stone include Somerset House (1771–81), and the National Gallery (1834–37). By the mid-1800s there were over fifty quarries working in Portland. Another important stone is Purbeck marble (actually a Jurassic limestone capable of being polished) which also comes from Dorset and was quarried at a large number of sites. It provided the columns of Salisbury Cathedral, and the Thames embankment in London was constructed in the 1850s from Purbeck stone. A liasic limestone called Ham stone was quarried in Somerset, and went into the building of Montacute House in the same county in 1588–1601.

Granite, a hard stone, not easily decorated, has been quarried in Devon and Cornwall, Scotland, the Shap area of the Lake District, for centuries. London's Tower Bridge (1886–94) and the Eddystone lighthouse (1882) are two prominent structures made from Devonshire granite. The famous granite quarry at Haytor on Dartmoor even had a horse-drawn tramway in 1820 composed of grooved granite blocks for carrying granite blocks down to a canal (*see* GRANITE RAILWAY). Granite quarrying on Shap Fell commenced in the mid-1860s. Aberdeen, in Scotland, is built on granite, of granite, earning the sobriquet 'Granite City'. In addition to use on buildings, the hard-wearing property of granite has been used for road surfaces, particularly in the mill towns of the north-west (*see* SETT (3)). Sandstone and millstone grit are two other stones that have been extensively quarried, particularly in east Lancashire and west Yorkshire, and used in many Pennine towns. Splitstone roofs as well as walls made from these materials are a feature in many older buildings in this area.

The old method of winning stone in a quarry was by a line of hand-hammered PLUG AND FEATHERS; the rough block of stone so split off the cliff face was horse-drawn on sledges or carts to a level part of the quarry to be dressed into shape. Later, blasting by GUNPOWDER superseded the old hand method.

The slate quarries of north Wales became important in the mid-18th century, and some very large quarries have been worked where the slate deposits have been found, the slate being removed in terraces often of great depth. The blocks of slate were then split by hand into various sizes and thicknesses and trimmed to various dimensions of roof tiles. To bring the slate down from the inland quarries to the coast for shipment, narrow gauge railways were built (*see* MINERAL LINES). At the Lake District quarries, blocks of slate were once brought down the steep fell slopes on wooden sledges guided by a man running in front, a highly dangerous operation (*see* TRAIL BARROW); later, self-acting tramways were built. Usable waste from the slate quarries was used as walling material in cottages, farm buildings, etc. In the second half of the 19th century railway transport boosted the use of Welsh slate for the roofs of the expanding industrial towns, but the industry declined when alternative roofing materials were introduced and demand fell.

Clay is another important quarried material: it is the basis of brick manufacture, and as stone became increasingly expensive, bricks took over as the principal walling material throughout Britain. Clay is also the basis for TERRACOTTA which was popular in the 18th and 19th centuries. Pottery clay was dug from MARL HOLES wherever a suitable quality was found. Other materials quarried include limestone, used in the iron and steel industry and for cement making; some metallic ores, e.g. copper on Anglesey; and simply stone that was crushed for road making, railway ballast, aggregate for concrete, etc.

Since many quarries were situated in remote areas, away from villages and towns, quarry owners often had to build quarrymen's cottages close to the place of work. Alternatively, at some sites, dormitories were built for the quarrymen, who lived there during the working week and returned home at week-ends. Remains of such dwellings can sometimes be found at abandoned quarries, together with traces of the machinery used on the dressing floors, or inclines with ruined brakehouses at their top down which the stone was lowered. Some abandoned quarries have become flooded, and all are dangerous places to explore. Some remote quarries have been left unfenced, and falling rock from the cliff face is another hazard.

In northern England a quarry is also known as a delph; and an 18th-century spelling sometimes found is querry.

Bezzant, N. *Out of the Rock*, Heinemann, 1980
Greenwell, A. and Elsden, J.V. *Practical Stone Quarrying*, Crosby Lockwood, 1913
Hudson, K. *The Fashionable Stone*, Adams and Dart, 1971
Lindsay, J. *A History of the North Wales Slate Industry*, David and Charles, 1974
Stanier, P.H. *Quarries and Quarrying*, Shire Publications, Album No. 134, 1985

quarter 1. in cloth measure, four NAILS or 9 in, i.e. one-quarter of a yard. **2.** a volumetric grain measure of eight BUSHELS, which varied in different parts of the country. **3.** a measure of coal meaning one-quarter of a CHALDRON, which varied considerably in different parts of the country. **4.** a fourth part of a hundredweight, i.e. 28 lb. This meaning of a quarter superseded all others with the introduction of the Weights and Measures Act of 1878, when standards of length and weight,

the yard and the pound respectively, superseded all previous measures then in use in Britain.

quarterbars strong diagonal struts which supported the vertical centre post of a POST MILL.

quarter cord a unit of length used in lead mining of 7.5 yd being a quarter of a MEER (normally 30 yd). It was used to measure along a lead vein, or at right angles to the vein.

queen post truss a timber ROOF TRUSS, similar to a KING POST TRUSS but with two

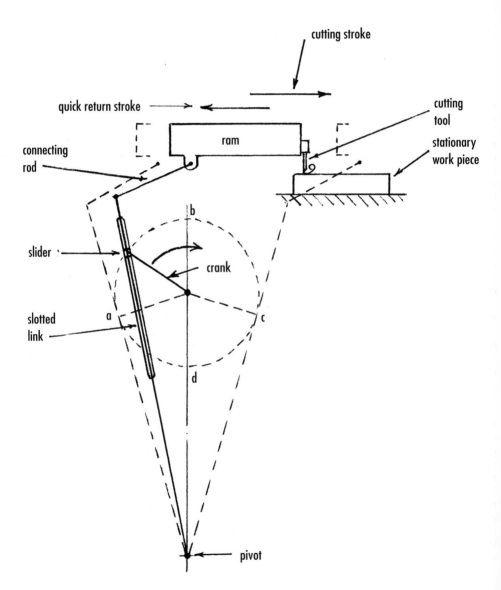

Fig. 55. Whitworth quick return mechanism. The cutting stroke occurs as crank turns through arc abc. The quick return occurs as crank turns through arc cda.

vertical ties (the queen posts) spaced a distance apart, joining the rafters to the horizontal bottom tie; and with inclined struts running from their base to the rafters. A queen post construction is used when the span is greater than about 30 ft, which is the maximum for a king post truss (*see* Fig. 57). An advantage of a queen post truss is that the space between the two vertical posts may be used for attic storage.

quercitron the black, or dyers' oak of north America, the inner bark of which was used as a yellow dye, and in tanning. The name is short for querci-citron, which comes from the Latin *quercus* for oak plus *citrus* for lemon. The name was coined *c.*1784 by Edward Bancroft, who discovered its use as a vegetable dye. To produce the yellow shade in cotton and wool, it was mordanted with ALUM. Quercitron was replaced by synthetic dyes in the 19th century.

quicklime, *see* LIME

quick return mechanism invented by Joseph Whitworth (1803–87), a mechanism used on SHAPING MACHINES and SLOTTING MACHINES to speed up the machining of the work piece. Fig. 55 shows its main features. The driving crank rotates at constant velocity and a slider at the crankpin end slides along a slotted link which is pivoted at a point vertically below the crank shaft centre. As the crank rotates, the slotted link oscillates about its pivot. Attached to the free end of the slotted link is a short connecting rod which transmits motion to the ram carrying the cutting tool. The ram moves backwards and forwards horizontally across the work piece in slides. The configuration of the mechanism is such that the ram moves quicker when the crank is turning in the lower arc *cda* of its rotation than in the upper arc. Thus, the cutting stroke is made whilst the crank is rotating in the upper arc *abc*, and the non-cutting idle return is made more quickly, hence speeding up the completion of the work.

Other means of producing a quick return motion have been invented, such as the use of oval gear wheels.

quilting a cloth with a diagonal pattern representing a padded or layered bed quilt. Bolton, Lancs., was well known during the 18th century for its quilting: Joseph Shaw was making quiltings there in 1763, and there was a Marsailles Quilt Weavers Society about that time (*see* MARSEILLES QUILTS). Quilts were also known as counterpanes.

quoin a large, dressed, rectangular stone laid at the corner of a building. The long side of a quoin makes a stretcher on one wall face, and its short side a header on the wall at right angles. They are laid in alternate courses to form stretchers and headers on each wall face. Hollow quoins have a concave curve at one corner, which forms the surface against which the rounded edge of a canal lock gate turns, making a kind of hinge.

R

rabbet a springy wooden board placed above a HELVE HAMMER in such a position that the hammer head strikes it as it is raised by the revolving cams; the elasticity of the rabbet assists the downwards fall of the hammer head, adding to the force of the blow. The word comes from the French *rabattre*, meaning to beat down. A rabbet is also known as a spring beam or recoil arm.

rabbling the working of molten iron in a puddling furnace. The operation comprises stirring the molten mass to assist in its decarburizing to produce a ball of wrought iron. The stirring was done manually, using a long iron bar called a rabble, or sometimes a puddling tool; the work was arduous and subject to heat from the open door of the furnace. The size and weight of the wrought iron ball was limited to that a man could physically handle.

race a passage, a channel, or path along which something can pass. The word has many applications, usually implying speed. For instance, a rope race in a textile mill is the narrow space through which the driving ropes from the engine flywheel pass on their way up to the LINESHAFTS on the various floors. A shuttle race is the board on which the shuttle slides as it passes through the SHED on a loom during weaving. A mill race is the channel along which water passes to and from a waterwheel driving a mill: this is often described as a headrace when the channel approaches the wheel, and a tailrace when leading the water away from the wheel.

raceboard, *see* SHUTTLE

rack 1. a straight, flat metal bar with teeth cut into one side, into which a toothed PINION meshes. Rack and pinion are used to convert rotative motion into longitudinal movement in various mechanisms. A typical application is when a rack is attached to the vertical arm of a

PADDLE in a LOCK gate: and when the meshing pinion is turned, the paddle is raised or lowered to control the water flow. Another use of a rack was by John Blenkinsop (1783–1831) on the Middleton Colliery Railway, Leeds, Yorks., in 1812 (patent no. 3431, 1811). The rails on which the locomotive ran had teeth forming a rack cast on one side; a large cog wheel on the locomotive engaged the rack to provide the drive. In the 18th century a rack and pinion was often called a rick-rack.

Around 1784, James Watt (1736–1819) was using a device known as a rack and sector for obtaining a straight-line motion for pumps, etc. from his beam engines. A rack was cut into the free end of the vertical PUMP RODS, and another rack, the sector, was cut in an arc at the end of the overhead beam. This was in effect part of a large diameter pinion at the end of the beam. The teeth in the arc engaged in the teeth on the straight rack on the pump rod, and as the beam rocked, the pump rods were raised and lowered accordingly.

A rack and freewheel was used on the Otto-Langen gas engine, c.1876, to give rotary motion, and was also used by William Symington (1764–1831) in his 1787 patent for a steam driven beam engine.

2. *see* TENTER FRAME.

rack dam a dam placed across a moorland stream to form a shallow pond upstream. Its purpose is to collect silt etc. carried down by the water by allowing it to settle in the pond because of the slow flow rate. Clear water flows over the dam cill, and the silt is dug out of the pond periodically and discarded. Rack dams would be used upstream of factories sited in moorland areas when clear process water was required, such as for bleaching of cloth.

racking term used in the brewing industry for filling casks with beer.

rack rent the maximum economic rent that can be charged for property; it can also mean an excessive rent. Owners of knitting frames charged domestic knitters of the east Midlands rack rent or frame rent. In some cases where the frame was installed in a workshop not owned by the knitter, space or standing rent was also charged in addition to frame rent. Frame rent was abolished by Act of Parliament in 1874.

radial valve gear a mechanism for reversing or altering the CUT-OFF point in a steam engine, in which the SLIDE VALVE receives its motion from a point on the linkage which describes an ellipse, i.e. it is 'radial'. Examples of radial valve gears are those of HACKWORTH and JOY.

railcar a self-contained passenger coach with its own tractive unit. Several steam railcars were built to operate on the early railways, the first in 1847. Its designer, James Samuel (1824–74) built other railcars in collaboration with William Bridges Adams (1797–1872) in succeeding years for operation on the Bristol and Exeter Railway and the Eastern Counties Railway. Railcars mostly ran on branch lines, and some were used solely for conveying railway staff about the system.

rail coach passenger carrying coaches, similar in appearance to a stage coach, first introduced on the Stockton and Darlington Railway in 1822. The coaches operated singly, each pulled by one horse, with the coach wheels running on rails. The service was operated daily except Sundays; soon after starting it, the Stockton and Darlington Company let the operation off to contractors.

rails strips on which wheeled vehicles can travel. A system using such rails is called a railway today, although earlier names were WAGGONWAY, PLATEWAY and TRAMROAD. Various materials have been used for making the rails, commencing with wood, then cast iron, wrought iron, and finally steel. Various shapes of rail were also developed, all intimately connected with the type of wheel to run along it. They are also known as lines or, less commonly, metals.

The use of rails started in the mining industry, where the need arose to be able to move heavy loads of coal, ore, etc. over rough ground, both inside the mine workings and on the surface. The most rudimentary rail could be considered as a single line of wooden planks on which wheelbarrows could be pushed, or barrow-ways, on which a man both pushed and guided the barrow. When four-wheeled trucks, capable of holding more than wheelbarrows, were developed, twin lines of rails became necessary, and the idea of providing a means of guiding the truck to prevent it coming off the rails was probably introduced at the same time. U-shaped rails, or rails with a raised flange at one side which provided some guidance for flat-rimmed wheels, were probably copied from ruts worn in common roads. Another way for guiding a flat-rimmed wheeled truck was to incorporate a guide pin hanging between the front pair of wheels, which ran in a central slot between the flat wooden rails (*see* LEITNAGEL HUND). Wooden rails were used from the Middle Ages until about the 1790s, when iron began to supersede wood; such rail systems were known as waggonways. Wooden flanged wheels running on flat rails were also in use during this period.

Cast iron strips or bars were first fastened on top of wooden rails to reduce wear at

Coalbrookdale, Salop., in 1767 by Richard Reynolds (1735–1818). Soon afterwards, L-shaped rails in cast iron for unflanged wheels were invented by John Curr at Sheffield in 1787. This type of rail or plateway became very popular for a number of years. However, it was weak, and collected dirt kicked up by towing horses on the surface where the wheels ran, increasing the frictional resistance.

The edge rail, made in wrought iron, was introduced in 1808 and patented by John Birkenshaw (patent no. 4503, 1820). This rail needed flanged wheels to provide guidance, and because it was stronger and did not accumulate dirt on the higher, narrow running surface, it soon superseded the cast-iron plate rail. Various designs of edge rail followed and eventually one, known as the bullhead rail, became the standard rail for railways. The first steel rails were tried experimentally in 1857, and today all modern rails are made from steel.

Bland, F. 'John Curr, originator of iron tram roads', *Newcomen Society Transactions* XI (1932)

railway a system of tracks of parallel metal rails upon which freight and passengers are transported in trucks and coaches. The forerunner of railways arose out of the need to move heavy loads in mines over rough ground (*see* RAILS). In due course, flanged wheels running on edge rails became standard, but there was no common GAUGE. The rails, or PERMANENT WAY as it soon was called, were supported at first on STONE BLOCKS without cross ties; when transverse wooden sleepers superseded stone blocks the gauge was more accurately maintained. Gradually, two main gauges emerged over the country: the broad gauge of 7 ft ¼ in favoured by the Great Western Railway, and the NARROW GAUGE of 4 ft 8½ in over the rest of the country. In 1846, the narrow gauge was made standard by parliament, and the broad gauge system had to conform. Railways of necessity have to be kept as level as possible by the construction of CUTTINGS and EMBANKMENTS, since the maximum gradient a locomotive can climb is about 1 in 14 (7 per cent).

From the earliest days of railways, an Act of Parliament had to be obtained so that land on the intended route could be compulsorily purchased. The first Act was in 1758 for the Middleton Colliery, near Leeds. Another early railway was the Surrey Iron Railway between Wandsworth and Merstham, opened in 1803, which was built by William Jessop (1745–1814). Some years later, George Stephenson (1781–1848) constructed the Stockton and Darlington Railway which opened in 1825 for goods traffic. Interest in this new form of transport grew rapidly, and the Liverpool to Manchester Railway was opened in 1830 (*see also* RAINHILL TRIALS). This railway was originally intended for carrying goods, but soon passenger carrying became of greater importance.

The success of the Liverpool to Manchester Railway heralded in a rush of financial investment in new railways all over the country (*see* RAILWAY MANIA). Competing canals were bought up and closed by the new railway companies; and railways competed against each other, resulting in unnecessary duplication of lines between certain cities and industrial areas. Whereas in 1830 only 100 miles of railway were open, by 1870 there were 15,000 miles of railway (excluding mineral lines). Competition between railways was eventually recognized as being contrary to the interests of shareholders and the public, and a series of amalgamations took place in the 1840s and 1850s leading to the formation of the Midland Railway, the London and North Western Railway, the Lancashire and Yorkshire Railway, etc.

Booker, F. *The Great Western Railway*, David and Charles, 1985
Ellis, H. *British Railway History: Vol. 1, 1830–76, Vol. 2, 1877–1947*, Allen and Unwin, 1954, 1959
Jackson, A.A. *The Railway Dictionary: an A–Z of Railway Terminology*, Alan Sutton, 1992
James, L. *A Chronology of the Construction of Britain's Railways, 1778–1855*, Ian Allan, 1983
Lewis, M.J.T. *Early Wooden Railways*, Routledge and Kegan Paul, 1970
Ransom, P.J.G. *The Victorian Railway and How It Evolved*, Heinemann, 1990
Robbins, M. *The Railway Age*, Penguin, 1965
Simmons, J. *The Railways of Britain: An Historical Introduction*, Routledge, 1961
Snell, J.B. *Early Railways*, Weidenfeld and Nicolson, 1964

railway clearing house a central office dealing with railway financial accounts. In the early days of railways, different companies had tracks connecting towns, and difficulties arose when through journeys were made involving trains passing over different companies' lines. Money had to be apportioned between the companies concerned, and this sometimes led to disputes, and frequently, financial chaos. The situation was resolved by K. Morison, who suggested a system to be set up modelled on the already existing cheque clearing house for London bankers. The London-based railway clearing house came into being in January 1842, with Morison as its first manager. Besides sorting out receipts, records were kept of the movement of rolling stock when it was not on the tracks of its owner. The smooth operation of the clearing house greatly facilitated through traffic across inter-connecting lines owned by different railways, both for passengers and freight.

'Railway King' nickname by which George Hudson (1800–71) of York became known on account of his involvement in railway promotions in the 1830s and 1840s.

Lambert, R.S. *The Railway King*, 1934
Peacock, A.J. and Joy, D. *George Hudson of York*, Dalesman Books, 1971

railway mania period of mad speculation in railways in the mid-19th century. Following the success of the Liverpool to Manchester Railway, the 1830s, 1840s and 1860s saw great activity in promoting railways all over the country, and these years became known collectively as railway mania. It closely mirrored the CANAL MANIA of 1790–7 in the way it developed. The mania can be divided into three phases: the years 1834–7, largely promoted by Quaker entrepreneurs, during which some £50 million was invested; the years 1844–7, mostly due to the activities of George Hudson (1800–71), the 'Railway King', in which some £200 million was invested and 2,000 miles of track opened; and 1864–6, which was mainly contractor led for extensions to existing lines. By 1850, there were some 6,000 miles of track opened employing 9,000 in running the many separate companies. In 1843, twenty-three Acts were passed for new railway companies; in 1844 there were forty-eight Acts; in 1845, 108; and in 1846, 272.

It became necessary for newly promoted companies to buy out competing canals because Railway Bills could not be obtained without coming to some arrangement with competing canal companies, or because the railway company wanted to use the route of the canal for building the railway. In 1845, five canals were bought by railway companies, totalling some 78 miles; in 1846 seventeen canals were bought, totalling 774 miles; and in 1845 a further six were bought, totalling another 96 miles. In these three years about one-fifth of the total canal mileage in Britain had been bought. Those canals which were lined with factories held out the longest. Many canal companies sold out to the railways because they could not compete for one reason or another. Many of the closed canals became derelict, while others were filled in.

During the railway mania, many ill-considered projects were promoted and a good deal of investors' money was lost, but by 1850 the sound schemes had provided the country with the basic network of tracks connecting manufacturing areas to the big towns and ports.

During the second phase of the mania, a certain amount of consolidation took place with some companies buying up others or amalgamating, thus reducing the total number of separate railways in the country. The 1844–7 mania was largely responsible for the widespread financial crisis in the country which came to a head in 1847, created by the enormous amount of money tied up in railway construction.

Lewin, H.G. *The Railway Mania and its Aftermath*, 1936; reprinted by David and Charles, 1968

'Railways, Father of English' person principally responsible for the birth of the railways. It can be argued there are two contenders for this title: Edward Pease (1767–1858), a Quaker businessman of Darlington, Co. Durham, and George Stephenson (1781–1848), the famous railway engineer of Newcastle upon Tyne. Edward Pease promoted the Stockton and Darlington Railway, opened in 1825, encouraged and financed George Stephenson and later George's son Robert, and supported the development of early railways. On the other hand, George Stephenson built the first successful steam locomotive *Blücher* in 1814, and went on to construct many early railways including the Liverpool and Manchester, the first true twin-track public railway, opened in 1830.

railway time the standardizing of time across Britain. Time, in relation to the passage of the sun across the sky, was a localized affair up until the 1840s. For instance, midday in Truro, Cornwall, when the sun was immediately overhead, was about twenty minutes behind midday in London, since Truro lies considerably to the west of London. In the days of the horse-drawn coach, guards on mail coaches carried timepieces which were regulated to gain or lose according to the direction of the journey, so that they agreed with local time at the various stopping places. As the railway system rapidly spread across the country, it became necessary for time to be standardized everywhere so that a national rail timetable could be established. The time as measured by the Royal Observatory in Greenwich, London (established in 1672) was taken as the standard for the country, and all railway clocks were set to agree with it. This synchronization became known as 'railway time' or 'London time'. London time was included in Bradshaw's famous *Monthly Guide*, which commenced publication in December 1841 with timetables for forty-three lines, and gave footnotes for converting local times to Greenwich time. In 1852 the telegraph was completed along all main lines, and this enabled time signals to be transmitted from London to all distant destinations to ensure that standardization was maintained throughout the country.

Rainhill trials trials to decide the mode of traction for the Liverpool to Manchester Railway. The trials were held by the promoters of the railway in October 1829 at Rainhill, Lancs., to decide whether locomotives or stationary haulage engines should be used to move trains along the line. A £500 prize was offered to the best entry, which had to comply with certain specifications. Four entries took part: the steam locomotive *Rocket* by George and Robert Stephenson; the steam locomotive *Sanspareil* by Timothy Hackworth; the steam locomotive *Novelty* by John Braithwaite and John Ericsson; and *Cyclops*, a truck on which a horse walked on an endless platform which turned the wheels, designed by Thomas Brandreth. The Stephenson's *Rocket* won, and they were awarded the prize on the last day. The Liverpool to Manchester Railway was officially opened on 15 September 1830, with locomotives hauling the trains. The ceremony was unfortunately marred by an accident which killed William Huskisson, a former President of the Board of Trade and MP for Liverpool, the first fatal railway accident.

Burton, A. *The Rainhill Story: The Great Locomotive Trial*, BBC, 1980

raising and shearing process of creating the nap on woollen cloth after fulling, by teasing the surface and cutting the raised fibres with shears to a uniform height to give a smooth pile or nap. Before machinery was invented to do this, raising was done by hand-held TEAZELS, and shearing was by large hand shears with curved blades which required skill and strength to use them. Shearing was also known as cropping. Boys combed out loose woollen hairs from teazels so that they could be re-used, a job known as preeming in Yorkshire.

Raising a nap was mechanized by the development of the GIG MILL in which revolving teazels performed the task. Power shearing, first invented in 1787 by the brothers Enoch and James Taylor of Marsden, near Huddersfield, Yorks., used a cumbersome machine which simulated the action of hand shears (*see* CROPPING FRAME). This machine caused a violent resistance to its introduction by the shearmen of Yorkshire, but by the mid-19th century hand shearing was extinct. In 1815, two other machines for shearing woollen cloth were patented in the West Country: one by Jonah Dyer of Wotton-under-Edge, Glos. (patent no. 3885) and the second, a rotary machine, by

Stephen Price of Stroud, Glos. (patent no. 3951).

rake 1. a Derbyshire name for a lead vein or mine. A rake is usually an oblique, near vertical, lead vein, sometimes called a pipe, although the more exact meaning of a pipe is a near horizontal branch from a rake. **2.** a North East dialect name for a train of CHALDRON coal waggons.

raker the leading animal of a PACKHORSE train, which carried a tinkling bell to warn others of the approach of the train, and to guide following horses in darkness, etc.

ram the plunger or piston in a hydraulic cylinder. A ram is usually longer than its diameter, and of constant cross-section, although telescopic rams are made with varying diameters along their length. A ram is the principal part of a hydraulic press, and exerts a large force on a work piece placed between the press platens. The reciprocating plungers on water pumps are also called rams, and such pumps are often called ram pumps. The ram described here is not the same as a hydraulic ram.

ramie (or rhea) a Malayan word for the fibres from the stem of the nettle-like plant *Beehmeria nivea*, which is woven into linen-like cloth. Ramie was first introduced into England in 1845 and comes from China (where cloth woven from it is known as grass-cloth), Jamaica, and the USA. Its fibres can vary from 4 in to as long as 72 in, and it can be spun with less twist than other fibres of similar length. Cloth made from ramie is strong, smooth, and very durable. It is used for tapestries, furnishings, and towellings, and is very resistant to moisture.

rash an old name for a smooth fabric of either silk (silk rash), or worsted (cloth rash), which is a kind of SAY. The name probably comes from the Latin *rasus*, meaning smooth or shaven.

ratch (or reach) the distance between the nip of one pair of DRAFTING rollers and the nip of the next pair in the sequence. This distance is set slightly greater than the longest fibre length of the material being processed (*see* Fig. 24).

ratchet a wheel or bar with inclined or sloping teeth which works with a pivoted PAWL or catch to permit motion in one direction only. There are two types of ratchet: circular wheels with ratchet teeth cast or cut around the circumference; and straight bars with ratchet teeth along one edge. The shape of the teeth permits the pawl to slip over their backs when relative motion is in one direction, but reverse movement is prevented by the pawl locking into the gap between two adjacent teeth.

Ratchets have many uses. Reverse rotation on capstans is prevented by circular ratchets and pawls; a bicycle freewheel is an everyday rotational example. Straight ratchets are used, for example, on the PADDLE mechanisms of canal lock gates to prevent the paddle falling down under its own weight as it is being raised. When it is lowered, the pawl is disengaged. A ratchet and pawl pair can be used to convert linear movement into rotary. William Symington (1764–1831) used a ratchet drive to obtain rotary motion from the reciprocation action of his beam engine (patent no. 1610, 1787).

An old spelling of ratchet was rochet, and in the 18th century ratchets were often known by the onomatopoeic name clicks.

rattler, *see* DAMSEL

raven-duck a kind of canvas cloth used for sails in the mid-18th century and later. The word probably comes from the German *Rabentuck*, a coarse cloth.

reach, *see* RATCH

reaction turbine a prime mover which is rotated by the reaction from forcing a moving fluid to change direction. If a high velocity jet of water or steam is compelled to change its direction, a side acting force is required to bring this about. If the jet is directed onto a curved surface which forces the jet to turn away from its original direction, the pressure the surface exerts on the jet supplies the side force the jet needs to make the change in direction. The curved surface experiences a reaction in the opposite direction and equal to this side force. Should the curved surface be attached to a wheel free to turn on its axle, the reactive force will cause it to rotate, and if a number of similar surfaces or vanes are spaced round the wheel, constant rotation will result, as each vane in turn experiences the reactive force. This is the operating principle of reaction turbines. Representative water and steam reaction turbines are described below.

There are many different designs of reaction water turbines. All operated drowned, i.e. they are completely full of water, being sited below the free surface where atmospheric air has no access to them. For this reason, reaction turbines are often called pressure turbines. The FRANCIS machine, for example, comprises a ring of fixed guide vanes which direct the flow of water inwards onto a runner which has curved vanes on its periphery. The curved vanes on the runner cause the direction of flow to be changed as the water passes between them, and the reactive force on these vanes causes the runner to rotate. Part of the pressure energy in

the water is converted into kinetic energy in the guide vanes, and a further drop in pressure occurs in the runner. The water leaves at atmospheric pressure, and the power is developed in the single stage, there being only one runner. Fig. 38c shows a small horizontal shaft Francis machine; a larger Francis turbine is shown in Fig. 83.

The Parsons machine is a well-known reaction steam turbine (*see* Fig. 38d). It comprises a horizontal rotating drum which increases its diameter in steps towards the low pressure end of the turbine. Attached to the circumference of the drum are rings of curved blades radiating outwards. These rotate between similar blades curved in the opposite direction, which are fixed and radiating inwards from the outer casing which encloses the drum. High pressure steam is admitted into the annular space occupied by the rings of blades at the smallest end of the drum, and flows axially towards the largest end, passing alternately between fixed and moving blades. The fixed blades direct the steam between the drum blades, which change the direction of the steam, and the reactive force experienced by the drum blades rotates the drum. As the steam passes through successive rings of blades, it expands with a loss in pressure. The increasing diameter of the drum and longer blades as the exit is approached accommodate the increase in volume of the steam as its pressure decreases, until the steam finally leaves the turbine, either at atmospheric pressure or below it if connected to a condenser. The total expansion of the steam is therefore controlled to take place in a series of small expansions at each stage, resulting in a machine which is long axially compared with its diameter.

Rebecca Riots civil disturbances which occurred in 1839 and 1842–3 in Carmarthenshire, Pembrokeshire and Breconshire, when Welsh tenant farmers, dressed as women, went about at night destroying tollgates. They objected to having to pay tolls on what they considered to be too many tollgates in the areas, and were also protesting against excessive rates, tithes, and an unfair system of landholding. The riots were suppressed by military force. The rioters took their name from a Biblical passage in Genesis 24:60 which reads: 'When Rebecca left her father's house she was told "Let thy seed possess the gate of those which hate them".' The bands of farmers responsible for the riots called themselves Rebeccaites.

re-circulating engine, *see* WATER-RETURNING ENGINE

recoil arm, *see* RABBET

rectilinear comb another name for the HEILMANN COMBER and HOLDEN COMBER. It describes the essential operation of these machines, which is to comb out the material in a straight line, whereas other combing machines work more on a circular action.

'Red Flag' Act, *see* LOCOMOTIVE AND HIGHWAYS ACT 1865

red short, *see* HOT SHORT

reduction of a metal the thermal process by which oxygen is removed from a metal in the presence of another material called a reducing agent. This is done by heating the materials until the chemical combination between the metal and oxygen is separated. For example, if oxide of lead is heated in a furnace in the presence of charcoal, carbonic acid is produced and the lead is reduced to its metallic state. Similarly, oxygen is removed from iron ore in a blast furnace leaving metallic iron, the reducing agent being coke.

reduction rolls the final rolls for producing fine flour in a roller mill. They are precision-set, smooth iron or steel rolls, between which the flour is finally passed before it is bagged. A train of rolls is used, the flour passing through each pair of rolls in sequence.

reed a comb-like arrangement of flattened wires or dents fixed in a frame and carried on the SLEY of a loom. Its purpose is to keep the warp threads (or ends as they are called) in position and evenly spaced, to form a back guide for the shuttle as it passes across the loom, and when moved towards the weaver by the rocking of the sley, to BEAT UP the weft against the edge of the already woven cloth. The pitch of the dents determines the fineness of the cloth, i.e. the number of ends per inch. A 90 reed, for instance, means there are 90 threads per in across the width of the cloth being woven. In the early days of loom design, reeds were made from thin slivers of cane or bamboo. An early improvement was the substitution of thin polished metal dents, introduced *c.*1730 by John Kay (1704–*c.*1780) who was a reed maker in Bury at that time. These were more durable and enabled finer fabrics to be woven.

Reed marks in a cloth are faults which appear as lines running down the length of the material due to the warp ends tending to group themselves together, especially when there are several ends in the space between dents.

reefing sail (or roller sail) a design of windmill sail invented by Stephen Hooper in 1789 (patent no. 1706), in which each sail comprised a number of small roller blinds which were coupled together in such a manner that they could be manually adjusted simultaneously to vary the opening between each roller, according to the strength of the wind. The sail could therefore be reefed, i.e. the amount of surface exposed to the wind reduced, by rolling up the 'blinds' to control the speed of the sails. The sails were reefed by moving the SPIDER at the centre.

reeling 1. drawing off silk filaments from silkworm cocoons. Several filaments, around eight to twelve, are reeled together to make a single silk thread, since a single filament on its own is too weak to use. The filaments are not twisted together, but adhere to each other by the naturally inherent gum which coats them. Reeling of silk takes place in factories called filatures, and is carried out in the country of origin of the silk. The raw silk is exported in skeins. **2.** winding the yarn from cops or bobbins into HANKS. This is done on a machine called a reel, which comprises a horizontal row of lightweight hexagonal frames or cages, known as swifts or flys, which are rotated a certain number of times to give a pre-determined length of yarn, with the yarn wound round the flys. The number of turns of each fly depends on the COUNT of the yarn. The bobbins or cops are held on a row of spindles in front of the reel, and the flys are collapsible to facilitate removal of the hanks. A large spinning mill has several reels arranged in a reeling room. Hanks are formed into bundles when exported, the bundles compressed into a uniform size for economical carriage. Cotton yarn in this form was once exported to Indian handloom weavers.

reeling staff, *see* METEWAND

refrigeration the production of low temperatures by mechanical means, used for making ice and for cooling storage chambers containing perishable food. The principle of preservation of food is that of preventing activity of bacteria by the reduction of temperature. The word refrigeration comes from the Latin *frigus*, meaning cold.

That freezing food can preserve it for long periods was known in ancient times. The earliest form of refrigeration was by ICE HOUSES. These led in time to the manufacture of small domestic ice boxes in Victorian times. These were made with slate walls, thermally insulated on the outside; ice was placed inside, onto which the food, fish, meat, etc. was directly placed to keep it cold. The ice had to be replaced from time to time; supplies could be bought from butchers.

The mechanical production of cold commenced in the 1830s when Jacob Perkins (*fl.*1827–34) invented a vapour-compression machine, which, however, was not in commercial use until some twenty years later. Further developments took place in the USA during the 1860s. An ammonia-absorption machine was patented by Rees Reece in 1867 (patent no. 1621), and in 1874, A. Bell and J.J. Colman produced their open-cycle air machine (patent no. 3577). This system was used in the first refrigerated ships bringing frozen meat to Europe, such as the *Strathleven* from Australia to London, and the *Dunedin* from New Zealand, in 1877 and 1882.

The Bell–Colman system comprised a driven compression cylinder and an expansion cylinder, with a cooler in between. Air drawn from the thermally insulated cold storage chamber was compressed in the compression cylinder, passed through the cooler in which cold water constantly circulated, and was then expanded to a lower temperature in the expansion cylinder, before being returned to the cold chamber. Heat was thus extracted from the cold chamber at the same rate as heat entered it through its walls, thus maintaining a constant low temperature inside. The Bell–Colman cycle is, in effect, a reversed HOT-AIR ENGINE. Other early cycles were closed ones, using brine as the refrigerant. Heat was pumped from a brine tank into the circulating cooling water, and the cold brine pumped through pipes lining the walls of the storage chamber. Brine was suitable since it freezes at a temperature lower than that required in the chamber. Other refrigerants are carbon dioxide, and ammonia for closed-cycle systems.

The vapour-compression refrigerator compresses a suitable vapour, then condenses it to a liquid by cooling and removing its latent heat. The liquid is then passed through a throttle valve to reduce its pressure, and it returns to a vapour by taking up its latent heat again from the cold store or domestic cabinet; the cycle is then repeated again.

Woolrich, W.R. 'History of refrigeration – 220 years of mechanical and chemical cold, 1748–1968', *Am. Soc. Heating and Refrigeration Eng's. Journal*, July 1969

regenerator a pair of large brick chambers adjacent to a Siemens steel-making furnace which act as air pre-heaters. Each chamber is filled with bricks with spaces between them to allow a through passage for either waste gases or combustion air. The bricks are called checkers and they provide a large surface area. The waste gases leaving the furnace are directed through one chamber, and the incoming combustion air through the other. The hot waste gases heat up the checkers as they pass through, and after a certain time, the flows are switched round so that the cold combustion air now passes through the hot checkers. The air picks up heat from the checkers cooling them down, whilst at the same time the gases start to heat up the other chamber. The flows are continually switched from one chamber to the other whilst the furnace is in operation, the checkers being alternately heated and cooled in sequence. Thus the cold combustion air is pre-heated at no expense, the regenerator acting as a heat exchanger, raising the thermal efficiency of the furnace and reducing fuel consumption.

The regenerative furnace was patented by Frederick Siemens (1826–1904) in 1856 (patent no. 2861). It was first used in GLASS-making furnaces and for pre-heating air for iron blast furnaces, but by 1866 was being used for steel manufacture, and for heating gas retorts in the late 1880s. Where PRODUCER GAS is the furnace fuel, such as in the SIEMENS–MARTIN open-hearth steel furnace shown in Fig. 52, there are four chambers, two each side of the furnace, and both the combustion air and the producer gas are pre-heated in separate chambers before combining on entering the hearth.

regulating radius the link or arm in James Watt's PARALLEL MOTION which connects the system of parallel bars to the frame of the engine, to produce a straight line motion for the free end of the piston rod. It is also used in his earlier THREE BAR MOTION, where it is pivoted from the engine house wall (*see* Figs. 76 and 77).

regulator valve the control valve in the steam pipe from the boiler to the cylinders on a locomotive, which regulates the supply of steam to them and hence the power and speed of the locomotive. It is placed in the cab and is hand-operated by the driver.

reheater in stationary steam engine practice, a reheater was a vessel through which superheated steam passed on its way to the inlet of the high pressure cylinder of a COMPOUND engine. Steam exhausting from the same cylinder, on its way to the low pressure cylinder, also passed through the reheater without making contact with the superheated steam, passing through different passageways. Heat was exchanged between the two steams, the superheated steam giving up some of its heat to the other, which had the effect of drying it to eliminate or reduce condensation losses in the low pressure cylinder, thus raising the thermal efficiency of the unit.

reheat furnace a furnace in which puddled wrought iron bars are reheated before they are converted into MERCHANT BARS. It is sometimes called a reheating mill or welding furnace.

reservoir a man-made 'lake' for storing water. Reservoirs may be fed naturally by streams, rivers or springs, or in the case of smaller mill LODGES which are part of a recirculating system, they are topped up from other sources. Most reservoirs are formed by damming river valleys using gravity or arched DAMS, while in some cases natural lakes are improved. Reservoirs are sited at places higher than the points of water usage, so that gravity flow through pipelines may be stored to bring supplies down. Water is stored for a number of reasons, of which four are the most important. First, reservoirs are sited at CANAL summits to replace water lost in the system due to seepage, evaporation, and the downward flow of water as locks are used. Secondly, it is stored to provide a power supply: water was stored to regulate the flow to mill and factory waterwheels, and to provide a reserve in times of drought. Damming Pennine valleys began in the 1820s. Thirdly, water was stored against drought for large water users such as cloth finishers, paper makers, etc., where it was crucial to the manufacturing process; and fourth, it is stored for public water supply. Increasing population forced cities to go farther afield for their water: for instance, Liverpool built the Anglezarke reservoirs near Bolton, Lancs., in 1847–55, and further storage at Vyrnwy, mid-Wales in 1882–91. Public water reservoirs were first constructed c.1830: Thomas Hawksley (1807–93) built over 150 public waterworks including many reservoirs. A few towns were supplied with filtered water from canals, e.g. Dublin in the mid-19th century, where the canal served as a reservoir.

Damming a river to form a reservoir often interfered with the RIPARIAN RIGHTS of downstream users, and COMPENSATION WATER had to be provided to them from the reservoir. (Sometimes a reservoir is erroneously called a dam.)

retort the chamber in which bituminous coal is heated externally to make TOWN GAS. It is not known who first discovered that gas could be made by distillation of a fuel such as wood or coal, but experiments were being made as early as the 17th century. George Dixon, a colliery owner at Cockfield, Co. Durham, used coal gas to light his house c.1780 by distilling coal in an old kettle on a fire. However, it was William Murdock (1754–1839) who, having lit his house and an outside lamp in 1792 by making gas from coal in an iron vessel situated in the yard, persuaded his employers, Boulton and Watt, to continue investigations into GAS MANUFACTURE at their Soho works, Birmingham. By 1802 their works was lit by gas, and shortly afterwards they commenced making gas plants for sale.

The early retorts were horizontal vessels made from wrought-iron plates: several were placed side-by-side in a row and heated externally. Coal was placed inside the retort, sealed, and heated to around 700/800°C. When all the gas had been drawn off via vertical ascension pipes, the retort was opened, residue coke removed, and after allowing the retort to cool off, it was recharged with fresh coal. Gas was thus made by a batch process. By 1820, retorts were being made from refractory brick with iron fronts, doors, etc. and temperatures raised to over 1000°C. Inclined retorts were tried next, and finally vertical retorts which allowed continuous operation, fresh coal being fed in at the top, and coke discharged and quenched at the bottom. Large numbers of retorts were placed in lines in the retort houses of gas works, and were known as retort benches. Various fuels have been used to heat up the retorts: as much as one-third of the coke made was consumed in early retorts, and tar was also used, as well as PRODUCER GAS, made at the gas works from low grade solid fuels. The surplus coke made was sold where it had several other uses. An EXHAUSTER drew the gas from the retorts and passed it to the purification plant.

retting the decomposition process used to free FLAX fibres from unwanted woody tissue, in effect a rotting process. After the stems have been pulled from the ground, the beets or bundles of stems are soaked in water. This water retting is carried out in ponds, field dams, or stone troughs for ten to fourteen days, and causes the fibres, which are just below the outer skin of the stems, to be loosened and the other stalk tissue chemically decomposed. After air drying, the stems are bruised and broken so that the unwanted material, called boon or shove, can be beaten off. This scutching operation was originally done by hand, or under stone edge-runner wheels called lint wheels. By the mid-18th century, machinery was used in SCUTCH MILLS.

The simplest form of retting is known as dew retting, where the pulled flax is merely spread out in the field and left to the mercy of the elements, being turned over from time to time. This method could take between twenty and thirty days, and if a dry spell occurred the flax would have to be watered. Long holes dug in boggy ground, called lint holes, were also used for retting; for this reason retting is sometimes known as bogging.

return connecting-rod engine, *see* STEEPLE ENGINE

return crank a short crank fixed at an angle outside the main crank, and pointing back towards the crankshaft. It acts as an ECCENTRIC on locomotives fitted with WALSCHAERT VALVE GEAR controlling outside cylinders.

reverberatory furnace a design of metal melting furnace in which the heat from the fire is reflected or reverberated onto the metal from an overhead firebrick arch or sloping roof. A reverberatory furnace consists in essence of a horizontal brick structure with a grate at one end on which the fuel burns on firebars. The hot gases are drawn over a low wall, called the bridge, into an adjoining chamber which has a sloping refractory roof above a bath, in which the metal being smelted is placed. The roof slopes towards the end farthest from the fire. The heat given up by the hot gases is reflected down by the roof onto the metal bath. The gases leave the furnace at the far end via a flue to a chimney stack which provides the draught for the fire. Charging doors are positioned at the firebox and metal bath for fuel and metal respectively. The molten metal is also extracted from the door above the bath.

A coal-fired reverberatory furnace was invented by the Cranage brothers, Thomas and George, who were foremen at the Coalbrookdale ironworks in the days when it was managed by Richard Reynolds (1735–1818). It was used for converting hard and brittle cast-iron pigs into malleable wrought iron. This design and process was patented in 1766 (patent no. 815), the method of stirring the iron during melting being known as puddling. The Cranage process was soon improved by Peter Onions (*fl.*1780) in 1783, and by Henry Cort (1740–1800) in 1785. Reverberatory furnaces are also used for smelting lead, and are sometimes known as air furnaces. The PUDDLING FURNACE is a typical example of a reverberatory furnace and is shown in Fig. 51. In Derbyshire lead smelting terminology, reverberatory furnaces are known as cupolas.

reversing gear mechanisms for machines and engines that need to be reversed: examples include winding engines at mines, marine engines, drives to rolling mills, and locomotives. Before the introduction of steam power, winding at mines was often done by HORSE WHIM: reversal was simply done by turning the horse round and walking it in the opposite direction. Where water power was used, OVERSHOT waterwheels with two parallel sets of buckets were constructed, one set for turning the wheel in each direction. To reverse the wheel, the launder feeding water onto the buckets was swivelled from one set to the other. Early steam winding engines were often reversed by stopping the engine on a DEAD CENTRE and manually setting the flywheel to go in the opposite direction.

On slow moving rotative BEAM ENGINES on reversing duty (e.g. mine winding), a simple reversing device known as the GAB VALVE GEAR was used (*see* Fig. 68a). This comprised a specially shaped component (the gab) fastened on the valve rod which moved the valve by pins driven by ECCENTRICS pushing against it. On some such engines, the valve had to be worked by hand until the engine was going in the right direction, and the eccentric rods then slipped into position on the gab. Similarly, early locomotives in 1825 had no reversing gear: the direction of travel had to be determined by manually operating uncoupled valve rods before they were reconnected to the eccentric rod for automatic working.

As engines and locomotives became larger and more powerful, more sophisticated steam valve gear came into use, and mechanical reversing gears were invented. These may be divided into two main classes: LINK MOTIONS, and RADIAL VALVE GEARS. Link motions derive their action from two eccentrics per steam cylinder mounted on the engine crankshaft and joined by a slotted link. A system of levers brings either one or other eccentric into operation, causing the engine to run one way or the other. Radial valve gears generally use only one eccentric per steam cylinder, and the valve receives its motion from a point on an oscillating radius arm with means incorporated for reversing the rotation. Both types of valve gears have been used on stationary engines, marine engines, and locomotives. In the pioneering days of steam locomotives, scores of different valve gears were invented and patented. Another important function of a reversing gear is that it also enables the CUT-OFF point to be varied at will, thus controlling the steam expansion ratio leading to efficient working and saving of steam. For this reason reversing gears are often called expansion gears. For details of the more popular and proven reversing gears, *see* ALLAN STRAIGHT LINK MOTION; GOOCH LINK MOTION; HACKWORTH RADIAL VALVE GEAR; JOY VALVE GEAR; STEPHENSON LINK MOTION; and WALSCHAERT VALVE GEAR; and corresponding diagrams in Fig. 68.

Lake, Charles S. and Reidinger, A. *Valves and Valve Gears for Steam Locomotives*, TEE Publishing Co., reprinted 1981

rewinding process through which cotton yarn is passed so that bulky piecings, slubs, and other faults can be removed to give a trouble-free yarn for weaving. Both weft and warp yarns are rewound, weft into pirns for the shuttles, and warp onto beams. Such rewinding was done on automatic machinery.

rhea, *see* RAMIE

ribbon loom, *see* DUTCH LOOM

rider 1. an 18th-century commercial traveller or representative of, say, a textile firm, so called on account of his mode of transport. He would travel the country on horseback carrying his samples in bags thrown across the saddle bow, and was also known as a bagman. Riders frequently travelled in company for mutual safety due to the twin dangers of poor roads and highwaymen. The coming of the railways put an end to this mode of transport. **2.** a Derbyshire lead mining term for a mass of COUNTRY ROCK which divided a lead vein into two. Alternative local names are HORSE, craunch and stalch.

ridge and furrow roof, *see* NORTH LIGHT ROOF

riffle a groove or raised ridge across a vibrating table, used as an ore classifier in DRESSING operations. The riffle collects the larger, heavier material, the finer running off the edge of the table.

right-angle-strut truss a simple roof truss (*see* Fig. 57) suitable for spans of 15–40 ft, comprising a pair of triangles made up of members whose long sides form the rafters, and joined at the top to form the ridge. One or two struts within the framework of the triangles meet the rafters at right angles and run down to the horizontal bottom tie.

right twist, *see* Z-TWIST

rim an old name for the HEADSTOCK of a spinning mule; the large driving wheel, in particular, was so called.

rimmer 1. (or rimer, rymer) a wooden horizontal beam in which vertical PADDLES may be slid up or down on a FLASH LOCK. The paddles fit together and when lowered block off the flow of water, the rimmer holding them in position against the water pressure. **2.** Scottish name for the iron hoop round a top millstone.

ring the circular metal ring used with a TRAVELLER on a RING SPINNING FRAME. The ring provides the stationary track around which the traveller is dragged by the yarn as it is wound onto the revolving spindle tube. The inner circumference of the ring is 'beaded', i.e. raised, so that the traveller, which is sprung over the ridge, cannot fly off, and is constrained therefore to move in a circular direction

imparting twist to the yarn at the same time. The ring is carried on a traversing or lifting bar which moves the ring up and down the central spindle to wind a well formed COP. Rings with slightly different sizes of central hole are used depending on the COUNT of yarn being spun: smaller diameters are used with high counts, and larger diameters for low counts.

ringer a long iron bar for stirring molten iron in a FINERY. The term comes from the French *ringard*, meaning poker.

ring gear a large diameter iron ring, usually built up in segments, carrying gear teeth and fixed to the side of a waterwheel. The drive to the mill machinery is taken off the ring gear by a pinion, which because of its smaller diameter rotates the power take-off shaft at a faster and more useful speed than that of the waterwheel itself.

ring spinning frame a textile spinning machine in which yarn is twisted by a small eyelet running round a stationary RING surrounding a rotating spindle. A stationary metal ring surrounds a vertical, rapidly rotating spindle, and a small C-shaped eyelet or traveller is free to slide round the inner raised beaded edge of the ring (*see* Fig. 56). Yarn from the usual drafting rollers is led through the traveller and is wrapped round a removable tube slipped over the spindle. As the spindle rotates it drags the traveller round the ring, but at a slightly slower speed because of friction between ring and traveller and air resistance. Twist is thus applied to the yarn, and the spindle winds yarn onto the tube because of the speed differential. The ring is arranged to move slowly up and down the tube as spinning proceeds, so that yarn is evenly wound onto the tube to give a well-formed cop. Spindles are spaced out in rows along the machine frame, up to 200 per side. The yarns balloon out at the spindles due to centrifugal force, and anti-ballooning devices, not shown on the diagram, control this within limits to prevent interference between spindles. The diameter of the ring and weight of the traveller depend on the count of the yarn being spun (*see also* Fig. 64).

Ring spinning is a direct descendant of Arkwright's WATER FRAME and the THROSTLE FRAME; the traveller and ring perform the same function as the HECKS on the FLYER. This method of SPINNING was invented by John Thorp (1784–1848) in the USA in 1828, with improvements by Addison and Stevens in 1829. It was not widely adopted in Britain for several years because of prejudice by master spinners who were accustomed to the throstle and MULE, but by the 1870s ring spinning was replacing

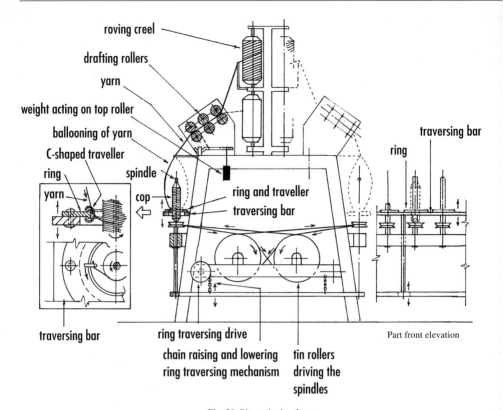

roving creel

drafting rollers

yarn

weight acting on top roller

ballooning of yarn

C-shaped traveller

ring

yarn

spindle

cop

ring and traveller

traversing bar

traversing bar

ring

ring traversing drive

chain raising and lowering
ring traversing mechanism

tin rollers
driving the
spindles

traversing bar

Part front elevation

Fig. 56. Ring spinning frame

mule spinning. Ring spinning is a continuous action, in contrast to mule spinning which is intermittent in operation, and ring spinning frames are more compact – three can fit in the same floor space as one mule. Being automatic, they also need less skilled supervision.

riparian right the ancient right of a water user, such as a water-powered mill, to extract water from a river. The word comes from the Latin *riparius*, meaning river bank. If the supply of water is disturbed, say by the building of a dam, COMPENSATION WATER has to be continually passed downstream to owners of riparian rights.

ripple a coarse metal comb, through which FLAX stalks were pulled to remove the seeds which were collected and sent for making linseed oil or cattle fodder. The old method was to pull the stalks through the ripple by hand, the ripple being fastened to teeth pointing upwards along the top of a portable wooden frame; the operation was carried out in the flax fields. Later, machines were invented to do this in flax processing factories.

river navigation transport of goods and people by river boats and coastal vessels. This has

always been important in Britain: British rivers are numerous and penetrate far inland, and gave a ready-made system for easy transportation to and from those towns built on them, or nearby. By the 17th century the population was steadily increasing, accompanied by a drift away from the country into the towns. Roads were in very poor condition, and land transport was expensive and unreliable. There was a need to improve rivers and extend the length they could be navigated, and letters patent were granted to individuals and corporations to do this in return for a monopoly as carriers, or toll takers, on the river they had improved. River navigation was of course, closely associated with coastal trade. For example, SEA COAL was brought for many years from Newcastle by coastal vessels sailing down the east coast and up the Thames to London.

Andrew Yarranton (1616–*c*.1684) carried out much work on rivers, and Parliament passed several Acts in the 1660s for river improvements. The work included deepening shallows, creating towpaths, removing weirs or building FLASH LOCKS, and in some cases straightening out bends. Compensation had to be paid to corn and fulling mills for weirs removed, and to landowners for towpaths made across their land. River boats varied in design and size according to the river they navigated. Large boats could carry up to 130 tons, and were usually square rigged with one sail. Severn sailing trows were usually 16–20 ft wide by 60 ft long, and could carry from 40 to 80 tons plus a small crew. When there was no wind, teams of men, called halers, towed the boat along the towpath. Later, they were towed by horses, as were canal boats at a later date. Some rivers were improved to carry a specific commodity, such as salt in Cheshire, and cotton to Manchester. By 1727, there were some 1,100 miles of navigable inland rivers in England, bringing a large part of the country within 15 miles (or one day's travel) of their banks; by then CANALS were being cut to join up rivers and extend the network available for water carriage.

Summers, D. *The Great Ouse: The History of a River Navigation*, 1973
Willan, T.S. *River Navigation in England, 1600–1750*, Cass, 1964

roaching cask (or roching cask) a large, wooden, conically shaped cask, in which hot ALUM liquor is held while it cools and crystallizes. After about seven to ten days, the cask is dismantled to remove the crystals, and any liquid left in the centre is drained off by boring a hole into the solid block for re-use.

road locomotive, *see* STEAM CARRIAGE

roads load-bearing routes for wheeled and non-wheeled traffic. Most roads in Britain are public rights of way: a very small number are privately owned, some of which may be used on payment of a toll. A rail*road* is a specialized means of transport reserved only for those conveyances with wheels made to run on guide rails (*see* RAILWAYS).

The Romans were great road builders, but after they left Britain, roads deteriorated until in the Middle Ages they became well-nigh impassable in winters, and very little better in summers, as a result of poor maintenance. Travel was mainly by horseback, for conveyance of both passengers and goods. Wheeled traffic cut enormous ruts, which turned into quagmires in winter. An attempt was made in Elizabethan times to improve matters by the passing of an Act in 1555 which made parishes responsible for maintaining roads within their boundaries. An unpaid waywarden was given powers to call on able-bodied men for four days' labour per year (later increased to six days per year) to repair those roads passing through the parish. This was known as Statute labour. A sum of money could be paid in lieu of providing active labour by those who could afford it. These requirements were unpopular and carried out irregularly: parishes objected to working on roads which they hardly used themselves, the benefit (if any) being gained by through travellers.

It was not until wheeled traffic increased when stagecoaches were introduced in the 17th century that serious attention was given to improving the condition of British roads. To encourage road maintenance, trusts were set up under parliamentary Acts, the trusts being mainly composed of local landowners who undertook the upkeep of stretches of road by charging a toll on all users except pedestrians. This threw the cost of road maintenance on users. Roads under the control of trusts were known as TURNPIKES and the right to charge tolls at gates was usually granted for a period of twenty-one years, renewable on application on expiry. Although the first one was in 1663, the real commencement of turnpiking did not take place until 1695–6. By 1830 there were nearly 4,000 turnpike trusts controlling about 22,000 miles of main roads, with nearly 8,000 toll gates and side bars. This represented about one-fifth of the estimated total road mileage at that time, with the remaining mileage still covered by the 1555 Act. Although improvement of main roads resulted from turnpiking, the trusts did not prosper financially, and they gradually declined in the late 19th century; more and more were not extended as they came up for renewal. The turnpikes did, however, lay down the outline of the modern road system, with bridges being built to shorten routes between places separated by rivers, etc.

In 1835 a rates levy on parishes for road maintenance (as opposed to turnpikes) was substituted for Statute labour. This too was not popular; in 1878 responsibility for half the cost of main roads was transferred onto county authorities, and in 1888, the whole upkeep of all roads except those within boroughs was passed to county councils, with government grants.

Although the development of the road system was principally driven by commercial pressures as the transport of raw materials and finished goods increased, some roads were built for military purposes, notably those constructed by General George Wade (1673–1748) in the Highlands of Scotland between 1726 and 1740, and by his successor, General William Caulfield (d.1767). These roads were built as a precaution against Jacobite uprisings to facilitate troop movements.

An early road builder was horse dealer-cum-soldier John Metcalf (1717–1810) of Yorkshire, known as 'Blind Jack of Knaresborough'. Reputed to be blind, but probably partially sighted, he built some 180 miles of good turnpike roads in the north of England on sound principles. It is thought he learned something of road building whilst serving under General Wade in Scotland: he preceded George Stephenson in using bundles of heather as foundations in soft marshland. Other important road builders were John Loudon McAdam or Macadam (1756–1836), a Scot from Ayr, who used broken stones on a bed of loam, topped by gravel to give a slightly elastic road; and Thomas Telford (1757–1834), another Scot from Dumfriesshire, whose roads were more solidly built and cost more than Macadam's, but lasted longer. Telford paid particular attention to the gradients, on his roads which he kept below 1 in 30 by forming EMBANKMENTS and CUTTINGS where necessary. He also built a large number of bridges.

Heavy goods had long been transported by RIVER NAVIGATION, and the cutting of CANALS in the late 18th century followed by the coming of the RAILWAYs meant that roads lost some of their importance for a while. Passenger traffic moved from stagecoach onto the railways, and many goods, particularly perishables, left the canals for the railways. It was not until the inventions of pneumatic tyres, the petrol INTERNAL COMBUSTION ENGINE, and tar spraying of roads to keep down dust towards the end of the 19th century that roads regained their importance. The speed restriction of four mph maximum, introduced by the LOCOMOTIVE AND HIGHWAYS ACT 1865 for self-propelled road vehicles was removed in 1895, and road traffic began to compete against the railways.

Copeland, John, *Roads and their Traffic, 1750–1850*, David and Charles, 1968
Reader, W.J. *Macadam: The McAdam Family and the Turnpike Roads, 1798–1861*, Heinemann, 1980
Rolt, L.T.C. *Thomas Telford*, Penguin Books, 1979
Webb, S. and B. *The Story of the King's Highway*, 1913 (reprinted 1963)

road steamer, *see* STEAM CARRIAGE

roasting of ores heating finely ground ores and concentrates to eliminate any sulphur present, by allowing free access of air to convert the sulphur into oxide. This is achieved in a roasting furnace which has a shallow hearth in which the ore is continually RABBLED (stirred) to give easy access to air. Heat input is assisted by the sulphur itself burning. In the 1860s, roasting furnaces with several hearths were introduced, the charge falling onto each hearth in turn via the action of mechanical rabbling. Roasting is often a preliminary process before actual smelting, particularly in copper production; it also reduces the bulk of the ore.

Rochdale pioneers the name given to the twenty-eight flannel weavers of Rochdale, Lancs., who in 1844 founded a small shop on co-operative lines with a capital of £1.00 per head. They were inspired by the ideals of Robert Owen (1771–1858) who advocated the principles of mutual help as early as 1821. By cutting out the middleman, and by bulk buying, they enabled local worker-members to obtain cheaper food and consumable items, and broke down the TRUCK SYSTEM. Many other similar stores soon developed following the success of the Rochdale experiment, and eventually the widespread Co-operative movement evolved, commencing with the Co-operative Wholesale Society in Manchester founded in 1862.
Bailey, J. *The Co-operative Movement*, 1952

rock an alternative name for a DISTAFF. Rock-spun yarn was yarn spun by hand using the distaff and spindle and whorl, as opposed to wheel-spun yarn which was spun on a spinning wheel. Rock-spun yarn was normally used for warps in the early days of hand spinning. The origin of the word is obscure. Rock Day was the name given to 7 January, also known as St Distaff's Day; being the day after the twelfth day of Christmas, this was said to be the day on which women returned to spinning after the festival of Christmas.

rod iron straight lengths of iron of small cross-section. In the early days of wrought-iron manufacture, the metal was forged into thin bars and hand cut into narrow strips for such industries as NAIL and WIRE making. By the early 17th century SLITTING MILLS were replacing hand methods and circular rods could be made from thin forged strips, the smaller sizes for nailers and wire drawers, the larger sizes for chain makers, etc. Such material was known as rod iron. As well as nails, the smallest sizes were used in making CARD CLOTH and combs for the textile industries.

rolag the soft, spongy, roll of wool or cotton fibres, made by hand carding the material before it is spun on a spinning wheel. The spinner holds the rolag in one hand and feeds it to the spinning wheel to turn it into yarn. The fibres lie transversely across the length of a rolag after carding, and are brought longitudinally parallel to each other as they are teased out by the spinner's fingers. Rolag comes from a Gaelic word meaning a roll.

roll boiling an old process for preventing woollen cloth from 'spotting' after rain, and to impart a permanent damp-resistant lustre. The process was invented by J.C. Daniel in Wiltshire (patent no. 4391, 1819), but this patent was cancelled in 1826 when it was discovered that a similar method had been tried earlier in Yorkshire, although later abandoned. After RAISING, the cloth was wound on a wooden or perforated metal cylinder, and immersed vertically into cold water heated by steam jets. Roll boiling is also known as hot water patenting.

roller chain small metal rollers linked together to make an accurately pitched chain. Endless roller chains transmit power over short distances by connecting together chainwheels which have specially shaped teeth on their circumference to receive the rollers. A textile machinery manufacturer, James Slater, developed chain drives in his Salford, Lancs., factory around 1864. His factory was later taken over by Hans Renold who improved the chains he found there, and patented the bush roller chain in 1880 (patent no. 1219). Roller chains are made in various sizes: the simple chain comprises pairs of inside flat side plates or links, connected to pairs of similar outside side plates by a pin. A short tube or roller is held between the inside plates, and the pin passes through it and is riveted to the outside plates. Duplex and triplex chains are made, comprising in effect two or three simple chains riveted side by side for added strength. A common example of a simple roller chain is that used on a bicycle connecting chainwheel to rear sprocket. Roller chain drives are particularly useful for transmitting power between shafts at slow speeds where the tension involved would be too great for a leather belt. The maximum operating speed for a roller chain drive is around 1,250 ft per minute, unless special lubricating arrangements are made.

roller mill a corn or other grain grinding establishment, in which the meal is ground to a flour between revolving chilled iron or steel precision rolls instead of between the flat surfaces of a pair of millstones. This method was invented in Hungary by the Swiss Jacob Suizberger in 1834. Introduced into Britain in the late 19th century, roller mills soon superseded the old traditional water and windmills, producing flour in bulk from imported foreign grain. Roller flour mills are mostly sited at or near the ports where the grain enters the country and were at first mostly steam driven, although some smaller units were driven by water turbines. Later, electric power took over the large units.

Roller mills are large affairs with high-capacity grain storage silos and grinding machinery arranged on several floors. After preliminary cleaning, the grain is passed through a number of spirally fluted rolls in sequence to break open the grains; the resulting stock is sifted and graded, and finally fed through plain rolls to produce the type of flour required. The stock is taken from machine to machine by totally enclosed conveyors, and finally bagged for collection by users.

roller sail, *see* REEFING SAIL

rolling mill a machine for shaping iron or steel bars into items of various cross-sections, such as structural girders, railway rails, and plates. This is achieved by passing the metal whilst white hot between pairs of hardened steel rolls, which in the case of non-flat items, are profiled to produce the required cross-section. The power-driven rolls are held in a massive strong frame, and cannot be forced farther apart once the gap between them has been set to the required dimension. The metal is sufficiently plastic whilst hot to be pressed or squeezed into shape, several passes through the rolls being necessary to reduce it to size. To produce girders, for example, a series of specially profiled grooves are cut into the surface of the rolls across their width. This leaves a number of gaps of differing shapes across the width between a pair of nearly touching rolls. The gaps are designed gradually to produce the final cross-section in stages as the metal bar is passed through each gap in turn in the correct sequence. As the final shape is approached, the bar increases in length as metal is displaced by the rolling action on it. To roll plates, the rolls are not grooved, being plain across their width, and they are gradually brought closer together after each pass of the hot metal until the final thickness of plate or sheet is reached. In some cases, metals (such as lead) are rolled cold.

Rolling mills date from before the commencement of the Industrial Revolution. John Hanbury of Pontypool, Wales, developed wide rolls so that thin iron sheets could be rolled in *c*.1696. Henry Cort (1740–1800) made iron bars by grooved rolls at Funtley near Fareham, Hants. (patent no. 1351, 1783). Early rolling mills were two high, i.e. there were two rolls mounted one above the other, water driven, with the rolls rotating in opposite directions. The metal being rolled had to be manhandled back to the feed side over the top of the rolls between passes, the rolls rotating always in the same directions. Later, reversing rolls were introduced, the direction of rotation of the rolls being reversed after each pass so that reduction of metal could be obtained in either direction. Three-high rolls were invented in Sweden by Kristofer Polhem in 1734, and were introduced into England soon afterwards. Three-high rolls always rotate in the same direction, which enabled the first pass to be made between the lower pair of rolls, and the second pass between the upper pair. This speeded up the rolling process since no time was lost whilst the rolls were reversed or the metal passed back to the feed side, as in the case of two-high rolls. Production was further speeded up by arranging a series of rolls in line so that the stock could be rolled by passing through each pair of rolls in rapid sequence. Such an arrangement is known as a FORGE TRAIN.

romal (or romall) a silk, or fine cotton square, used as a handkerchief or headscarf. Such fabrics were woven in cotton in south Lancashire and north Cheshire in the late 18th century. The word romal or romall is of Persian origin.

roof truss the wooden or metal structure supporting the roof of a building, and comprising a number of straight struts and ties joined together at their extremities. A roof truss is designed to carry the weight of the roof covering, additional loads such as snow, wind pressure, and any loads to be hung from it inside the building. Roof trusses are needed for curved, ridged and sloping roofs. The majority of flat roofs do not require trusses since they are carried on solid beams, except those flat roofs of exceptionally wide spans carried on LATTICE GIRDERS which may be regarded as a truss. Traditional roofing materials include split stones, slates, bitumen felt-covered wooden boarding, tiles, and corrugated iron sheets. Many industrial roofs include glazing to admit daylight to the working space or storage area below, and ventilators of various designs are often included, particularly where fumes etc. are emitted in the industrial process being housed.

The earliest material used for roof trusses was timber; later, iron and steel were used. The introduction of the FACTORY SYSTEM brought about the building of textile mills and weaving sheds, and timber trusses were used to support the roofs. Carpenters used a variety of joints where the different members met, and hardwood pegs were frequently used as fasteners. Various designs of truss were developed as the spans needed increased in dimensions; early mills were narrow, because the width between walls was restricted to the maximum that a timber truss could safely span. Greater widths were obtained by supporting the ends of abutting trusses on a transverse beam

running down the length of the building and carried on a row of cast-iron pillars. The maximum span for wooden trusses was c. 40 ft. Some trusses were strengthened by wrought-iron rods and cast-iron shoes, plates, etc.

Metal trusses enabled larger spans to be made giving clearer floor space free from intervening pillars. Wrought-iron angle, tee and channel sections were used for struts and compression members, whilst rods or eye bars and flats were used for ties and tension members, or alternatively angle irons. Metal trusses were made by structural engineers. Rivets were used at joints, the individual truss members being fastened to metal plate cleats. By the mid-19th century, steel sections began replacing wrought iron. During the Victorian period cast-iron roof trusses were used quite frequently, often of ornamental design. Whilst these tended to be mostly used in public buildings such as market halls and shopping arcades, a number were used also in industrial buildings. Cast in sections, they were bolted together on site, sometimes with wrought-iron ties.

Fig. 57 shows several of the designs most commonly used in industrial buildings. There are many other variations.

rook an old coal measure of weight used in the Midlands, and approximately equal to 30 cwt (3,360 lb).

room and power a phrase commonly displayed on signs outside early cotton mills which were partly empty and had space available for industrial renting. Aspiring men would rent space, install one or two machines, connect up to the overhead LINESHAFTING and go into business on their own in a small way. Those who prospered would eventually go on to build mills of their own, and many firms had beginnings in this manner in the early days of the textile industry. Some mills therefore housed several small independent businesses in the spare space not being worked by the owner. A similar fate has befallen many mills today, although the small businesses operating in them are frequently not connected with the textile trade as they were in the early Victorian times.

The phrase 'room and power' was mainly used in the weaving industry; the equivalent term used in spinning was often 'space and turning'. Some mills were built by speculators with the intention of renting off space to several small occupiers, and could be regarded as 'public' mills.

room and stoop, see PILLAR AND STALL

Roots' blower a positive displacement air blowing machine invented in the USA by the two Roots brothers in 1866. It comprises two

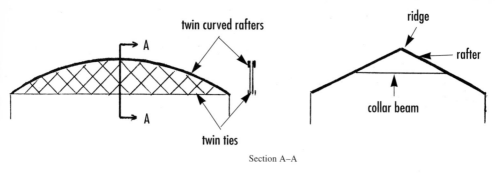

Section A–A

Belfast truss (timber) (moderate spans)

Collar beam truss (timber) (small spans)

Crescent truss (metal) (large spans)

French truss (metal) (40–60 ft spans)

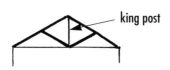

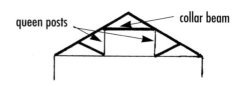

King post truss (timber) (spans up to about 30 ft)

Queen post truss (timber) (up to about 40 ft span)

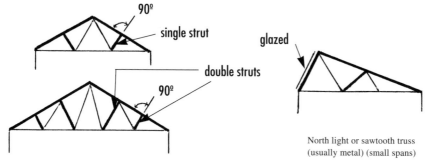

North light or sawtooth truss
(usually metal) (small spans)

Right-angle strut trusses (usually metal)

━━ strut (compression member)
── tie (tension member)

Fig. 57. Roof trusses used in industrial buildings

rotors shaped somewhat like the figure eight, arranged at 90° to each other and driven at a constant speed of rotation. They rotate inside a similar shaped casing, one rotor turning inside one 'loop' of the casing, the other inside the other. As they rotate, air is drawn into the casing on one side, compressed between the rotors, and blown out on the opposite side of the casing. Originally used to draw air through mines to ventilate the workings, the machine was soon used to provide blast air for blast furnaces since it is capable of delivering air at quite high pressures.

rope driving transmitting power via a round rope. The LINESHAFTS of late 19th-century textile mills were driven by ropes running in V-shaped grooves cut into the rim of the engine flywheel and in similar grooves in pulleys fastened to the lineshaft. Rope driving superseded the geared systems previously used, and was first developed in the USA, spreading to Britain in the 1870s; a flax mill in Dundee, Scotland, was using rope drives in 1875. Hemp ropes were used at first, but cotton was soon found to last longer. Thomas Hart of Blackburn, Lancs., invented the 'Lambeth' rope, and this rapidly became a popular driving rope. The circular cross-section rope wedges itself against the sides of the V groove, which increases the frictional grip and improves the efficiency of power transmission. The drive is usually arranged so that the taut (driving) strand is on the lower side, with the slack (return) side uppermost. This increases the arc of contact on both the flywheel and driven pulley, increasing the frictional grip further. The ropes passed up through a space known as the ROPE RACE from the engine flywheel to each floor in turn. Large powers could be transmitted by groups of ropes, the ropes often running at speeds of up to 7,000 ft per minute.

The advantages of rope drives were quietness, and cheaper installation costs over geared systems; if a rope should break it could soon be replaced or rejoined, whereas a gear failure on the old system meant a more serious interruption in mill production. With the onset of electrical power, rope driving became obsolete, as did the large stationary steam engine which drove all the machinery in the mill. Electric motors were at first fitted to drive each lineshaft, and later, lineshafting was dispensed with and each machine fitted with its own individual electric motor.

rope making Before the invention of synthetic fibres, ropes were made from natural fibres such as coir (from the coconut palm), cotton, flax, hemp, jute, manila (fibres from abaca

leaves, a wild type of banana), and sisal (spiky fibrous leaves of the plant *Henniquin*). The fibres were twisted together to make a yarn, and a number of yarns further twisted together to make up a rope.

Ropes may be divided into two main categories: those used for carrying loads such as rigging on sailing ships, crane and mine winding ropes, etc., and those used for transmitting power such as driving ropes. Other, less important uses for rope and twine are for fishing-net making, coiled basketware, packaging, etc. In all cases, the preliminary processes are HACKLING the fibres, and spinning them into yarn. To make round ropes a number of yarns are twisted together to make a strand, and three (sometimes four) strands are twisted together (or 'laid' in rope-making terms) to form the finished rope. To prevent the rope untwisting, the strands are wound in the opposite direction to the yarns which compose them. Flat ropes were made by stitching strands together, side by side. This construction was once used for winding ropes at collieries, its advantage over round ropes being that it could wind up upon itself on a narrow drum (*see* WINDING DRUM).

Ropes were once made by hand in ropewalks in standard lengths of 120 fathoms (720 ft). A ropewalk had to be straight and about 1,320 ft long to enable a standard length of rope to be made, since as the twisting proceeded first the yarns and then the strands shortened. The equipment used in rope making was simple and comprised two frames, one at each end of the ropewalk. A stationary frame called a jack had a number of hooks which could be made to revolve together by a man turning a handle, which turned the hooks via gearing or a belt drive. Yarn was attached to each hook, brought to the other frame called a traveller which had one hook free to rotate, and mounted on a weighted trolley. As an assistant turned the hooks on the jack, the rope maker held a circular hardwood block called a top between the strands near to the traveller. The top had three deep grooves cut in its circumference, equally spaced, and to make a three-stranded rope, a strand was slotted into each groove. The rope maker slowly walked towards the jack pushing the top along, and the rope formed itself behind the top as he walked along, pulling the traveller along as shortening occurred. At one time, every port and many inland towns had ropewalks: and although not in use today, old ropewalks can often be traced in town plans or street names. HEMP was extensively grown around Bridport in Dorset for naval rope making until the mid-19th century; hemp ropes were used in collieries until about 1840 when an iron stranded wire rope invented by Andrew Smith (patent no. 8009, 1839) began to be used.

Rope making began to be mechanized in the late 18th century. Edmund Cartwright (1743–1823) invented the 'Cordelier' rope-making machine in 1792, and Marc Isambard Brunel (1769–1849) also designed machinery for this purpose. Machines needed less space than ropewalks. Cotton driving ropes for textile mills were introduced in the 1860s.

rope race the narrow space between a pair of walls which extended from the ground floor up through successive floors to the top floor of a spinning mill in which ran ropes transmitting power from the engine to each floor LINESHAFT. The rope race was sited directly opposite the engine FLYWHEEL and a pulley fastened to each lineshaft projected into this space. The distance each pulley projected varied so that groups of ropes from the flywheel had an uninterrupted access to each pulley in turn. The flywheel rim was grooved with a number of grooves equal to the combined total of the grooves in all the lineshaft pulleys, and a group of ropes connected each lineshaft pulley according to the power that floor required, the lengths of each group of ropes depending on the distance between the centres of the engine flywheel and pulley concerned.

A somewhat similar arrangement was used in rope-driven weaving sheds, which are almost invariably single storey. Here, pulleys at the end of each adjacent lineshaft were connected together by ropes, and with the engine normally centrally placed, the drive was passed horizontally from engine to each lineshaft in turn. Sometimes the line of pulleys was arranged in a narrow passageway called a rope alley divided from the work space by a wall.

rotary cloth shears a machine for shearing woollen cloth by a rotary action. Several rotary cloth shears were patented, but the most successful one was invented by John and William Lewis and William Davis, all from Gloucestershire (patent no. 4196, 1818). It became known as a lewis.

rotative steam engine steam engine which produces rotary motion. The first rotative steam engine dates from 1779. Prior to this steam engines could only produce reciprocating motion indirectly via a rocking beam; when rotary motion was obtained, again indirectly via a beam, the potential use of the steam engine was greatly extended since it could then drive machinery. Later, the beam was dispensed with, and rotary motion was obtained via a connecting rod and crank. The STEAM TURBINE was the first successful *direct* rotative steam-using prime mover, in which steam rotates a shaft without any intermediary mechanism. *See also* BEAM STEAM ENGINE.

roucou, *see* ANNOTTA

rough iron, *see* PIG IRON

roundhouse **1.** the circular or polygonal building enclosing the base of a POST MILL. **2.** a locomotive roundhouse is an engine shed, circular in plan, with rails radiating from a central turntable, thus allowing easy movement of the locomotives.

roving a soft, pliable 'rope' of loosely twisted textile fibres made in a preparatory operation prior to the final drawing out and twisting in a spinning machine to the required yarn or thread size. Another name for a roving is a slubbing.

roving bridge a bridge crossing over a CANAL at a point where the towpath changes sides. It is arranged so that a horse towing a barge can walk from one towpath to the other without the need to unhitch the towrope, thus saving time. One towpath carried under the arch leads to an upwards sloping path which turns through 180° to join the road level; the opposite towpath stops short of the arch and leads to a straight slope up to the road level (*see plan*). The momentum of the barge keeps it going whilst the horse crosses the bridge, the tow rope passing over the bridge parapet, and towing recommences when the horse takes up the slack rope and continues on its way. Roving bridges are also known as turnover, crossover and changeline bridges, and in some parts of the country as snake bridges.

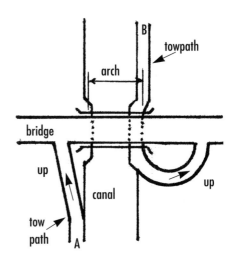

Plan of a roving bridge

Roving bridge on the Macclesfield Canal, Greater Manchester

roving frame a machine for the final attenuation of cotton SLIVERS into a continuous strand of small cross-section prior to the actual spinning into yarn on a MULE or RING SPINNER. The object is to reduce a sliver after it has passed through a SLUBBING FRAME into a roving, which is lightly twisted a little more so as to resist the tension of being drawn off its bobbin by the spinning machine. A roving frame is very similar to the preceding slubbing frame, but its component parts are smaller: the sizes of the spindles and bobbins are decreased but their number increased, perhaps up to 140 per machine. It is fitted with a CREEL on which bobbins from the slubber are mounted, and the slivers are drawn through three pairs of rollers to draw out the sliver to its reduced dimensions, which is wound onto small bobbins by a FLYER. The continuous strand is now called a roving, and is ready for the final process of spinning into yarn.

For the finer COUNTS of yarn, a second frame is used, called a JACK FRAME, which reduces a roving considerably further to make the final spinning easier.

row a Staffordshire name for a coal SEAM. *See also* COAL MEASURES.

rowing, *see* FRIZZING

Royal Commissions on Historical Monuments organizations for recording national monuments in England, Scotland and Wales. There are three government commissions: the Royal Commission on Historical Monuments (England) (RCHME), in London; the Royal Commission on Ancient and Historical Monuments of Scotland, in Edinburgh (RCAHMS); and the Royal Commission on Ancient and Historical Monuments in Wales, Aberystwyth (RCAHMW). All three Commissions were appointed in 1908 to make inventories of monuments such as earthworks, castles, buildings, etc. of outstanding or historical significance, which include a relatively small number of buildings and sites of interest to industrial archaeologists. The Commissions are purely recording bodies: they can make recommendations on what to preserve in case of sites threatened with demolition, but have no power to implement their recommendations. The Commissions publish reports and surveys of industrial archaeological interest from time to time, and have emergency recording teams who record sites and buildings under threat. Included in the Commission are the NATIONAL BUILDINGS RECORD and NATIONAL MONUMENTS RECORD.

Falconer, K.A. and Thornes, R. 'Industrial archaeology and the RCHME', *Industrial Archaeology Review* IX (1986), 24–36
Hay, G.D. and Stell, G.P. *Monuments of Industry – An Illustrated Historical Record*, HMSO/Royal Commission on the Ancient and Historical Monuments of Scotland, 1991

Royal Institution of Great Britain founded in March 1799 by Benjamin Thompson, Count Rumford (1753–1814), with the objective 'to diffuse the knowledge and facilitate the general introduction of Useful Mechanical Inventions and Improvements, and to teach by courses of Philosophical lectures and Experiments, the application of Science to the common purposes of life'. Its headquarters are in London, where important pioneer discoveries were made in its laboratories, particularly in electricity and chemistry. Humphry Davy (1778–1829) and Michael Faraday (1791–1867) were both employed by the institution in its early days.

Royal purple, *see* MUREX

Royal Society society which began with informal meetings of a group of scientific men about 1645, and was incorporated by Royal Charter in 1662 under the patronage of Charles II. Early members included Robert Boyle (1627–91), Christopher Wren (1632–1723) and Robert Hooke (1635–1703). The Society encouraged scientific investigation and inventions, and had great influence on the development of science and technology in the 18th and 19th centuries. Its headquarters were in Gresham College until 1710, Crane Court till 1780, Somerset House until 1857, and in Burlington House, London since 1857. It was largely responsible for instigating the GREAT EXHIBITION OF 1851 held in London. The Society began publishing its *Philosophical Transactions* in 1665 and *Proceedings* in 1800, both of which are an invaluable record of the progress in science.

Royal Society for the Prevention of Cruelty to Animals (RSPCA) a society, extremely well known today, which was founded in 1824 following an Act of 1823, primarily to protect coach and canal horses from abuse and overwork.

Royal Society of Arts, *see* SOCIETY FOR THE ENCOURAGEMENT OF ARTS, MANUFACTURES, AND COMMERCE

rubber an elastic material, which can be either natural or synthetic. Natural rubber was first introduced into Europe in the 15th century, when Christopher Columbus brought rubber resin back to Europe from Haiti; but it remained undeveloped until the 18th century, after investigations by French explorers in the Amazon forests. Synthetic rubber is a modern development of the 20th century.

Rubber is made from latex exuded from certain trees such as *Hevea brasiliensis* or *Ficus elastica*, which grow in well drained soil lying up to 10° north or south of the equator. The bulk of rubber comes from the *Hevea* tree which originated in the Brazilian jungles and the islands of the West Indies, but in the last quarter of the 19th century the tree was introduced into the Far East, where it was cultivated in extensive plantations. The French called the resinous gum *caoutchouc* in the 1730s from the Caribbean word *cahutschu* (from *caa* and *u-chu*, meaning the tree that weeps). In Britain the first use in the 1770s of small pieces of the imported material was to erase or rub out pencil marks, and from this, and because the pieces came from the West Indies, it got its English name India rubber, or simply rubber.

The milky latex is tapped from the trunk of a rubber tree by incisions made into the inner bark where the latex vessels lie, and collecting the slow latex flow in small cups. In the Brazilian jungles, native tappers collected the latex and coagulated it on a flat stick rotated in the smoke of a wood fire until a lump of smoked rubber, called a biscuit, had built up. The biscuits were floated down river to traders on rafts. Much later, in rubber plantations, the treatment was more sophisticated: the latex was first treated with ammonia to stabilize it, coagulated by adding acetic or formic acid, then concentrated in a centrifuge before being shipped to users in bales.

Before rubber can be turned into something useful, it has to be vulcanized. VULCANIZATION changes its physical properties, preventing it from softening when warmed or hardening when cold; vulcanized rubber can be moulded, extruded or calendered as required. Rubber has many useful properties, amongst which may be mentioned elasticity, imperviousness to many liquids, toughness, and electrical insulation. The earliest use of rubber was for the manufacture of waterproof footware. It has very many industrial uses, and with the development of road vehicles in the early 20th century, tyres soon became its largest single consumer. *See also* RUBBER INDUSTRY.

rubber industry an industry which developed in the early 19th century. For many years, imported RUBBER remained a difficult new material to work in Europe, and remained a curiosity from the New World. By 1770 rubber had found its way to England, and in 1791 Samuel Peal discovered that dissolving it in turpentine made a rubber solution which he applied to cloth to make it waterproof, although at that time it was not a commercial success. The main founder of the rubber industry was Thomas Hancock (1786–1865) of Marlborough, Wilts., who invented the MASTICATOR in 1820, which by a shredding action converted unmanageable chunks of intractable crude rubber into a workable plastic substance that could be moulded into useful articles. A few years later he discovered that masticated rubber would dissolve in naphtha and produce a rubber solution superior to that of Peal's. He invented a machine (patent no. 7344, 1837) for spreading the rubber solution onto cloth, and in 1834 combined with Charles Macintosh (1766–1843) to make the well-known waterproof clothing.

The next developments in the industry came from the USA, where in 1832 Edwin M. Chaffee of Roxbury, Mass., invented the two-roll RUBBER MILL which replaced the masticator, and the three-roll CALENDER in 1835. These inventions were shortly followed by the accidental discovery of the hot VULCANIZATION process by Charles Goodyear (1800–60) of Philadelphia in 1839, which enabled the rubber mixture to be moulded into articles which did not lose shape when heated or cooled. In 1846, Alexander Parkes (1813–90) of Birmingham, England, discovered the cold process of vulcanization, but this vulcanized only thin articles, such as rubber gloves. It was about this time that pneumatic tyres were first made: Robert William Thomson (1822–73) invented a tyre called the 'aerial wheel' using rubber tubes, but no interest was aroused in it since his invention was premature for the road users of the day. In 1888, John Boyd Dunlop (1840–1921) a veterinary surgeon of Belfast, Ireland, re-invented the tyre.

In the early days of the rubber industry, most of the raw rubber was tapped from trees growing wild in the jungles of Brazil. In 1825, Brazil exported only 30 tons of rubber: the tonnage increased to 1,467 in 1850, and to 21,260 by 1897. However, since the demand for rubber was outstripping the supply from Brazil, some 70,000 seeds from the *Hevea brasiliensis* tree were brought from Brazil in 1876 to the Royal Botanic Gardens at Kew, London, by Henry A. Wickham (1846–1928) for the India Office. From the seedlings grown at Kew, rubber plantations in Singapore and Malaya were established in 1877 and 1881 respectively, and from these beginnings the large rubber cultivation industry was built up in the Far East. By 1920, some 3 million acres were under cultivation, producing 300,000 tons of rubber a year and greatly exceeding the Brazilian output.

By the commencement of the 20th century,

attention to making rubber and rubber-like substances by artificial means had reached a practical stage, and the synthetic rubber industry was born, later to be accelerated by the exigencies of World War I.

Cook, J. Gordon. *Rubber*, Muller, 1963
Schidrowitz, R. and Dawson, T.R. *History of the Rubber Industry*, Heffer, 1952

rubber mill a pair of closely spaced, steam heated, hollow steel rollers, one rotating faster than the other and both lying in the horizontal plane. They masticate raw rubber in the nip between the rolls, turning it into a soft, warm, dough-like mass.

The first rubber mill was invented by Edwin M. Chaffee of Roxbury, Mass., USA, in 1832. The rolls masticate the raw rubber between their nip with a tearing action as the faster roller pulls the rubber into the nip, whilst the slower roller tends to hold it back. The rubber forms a thin sheet round the slower roll and is removed periodically. The work performed on the rubber heats it up, and the combined mastication and heating change the physical characteristics of the material from a tough, elastic rubber into a soft, almost non-elastic dough. At this stage, sulphur and other ingredients are thoroughly mixed into the rubber whilst it is still in the mill, a process called compounding.

rubbing rollers vertical rollers, usually wooden, placed on the corners of canal bridges on the towpath side, and held top and bottom in simple bearings so that they could rotate. They were fitted where the canal made a bend at the bridge, so that tow ropes could press against the rollers instead of rubbing against the stone or brick sides of the bridge, thus reducing wear on the rope. Rollers may still be found on some canal bridges, or evidence of where they once were. Where rubbing rollers were not fitted, grooves worn in the bridge sides by the ropes are often visible; the grooves were worn by grit embedded in the tow ropes, this being picked up from the towpath as the ropes dragged along. Rubbing rollers damaged in the same way were easily replaced.

rubble reel an enclosed rotary sieve used for removing foreign matter from wheat before grinding commences in a ROLLER MILL.

ruck, *see* SPOIL HEAP

ruling gradient the steepest gradient permitted by the specification laid down for the construction of a road or railway. CUTTINGS or EMBANKMENTS are necessary in hilly country so as not to exceed this gradient. Thomas Telford (1757–1834) stipulated a ruling gradient of 1 in 30 on his roads. In railway terms, a gradient or incline of 1 in 60 (1.67 per cent) is classed as severe, and the steepest gradient with smooth rails was 1 in 19 (5.26 per cent) in Britain.

runner 1. the rotating wheel in a WATER TURBINE, fitted with vanes onto which the flow of water acts. 2. the top rotating grindstone of a pair of millstones. To ensure a runner revolves in a truly horizontal plane, it is usually balanced by molten lead poured into a number of evenly spaced recesses around the circumference of the top surface.

russel a woollen cloth used for garments in the 16th century. The origin of the name is obscure, but possibly comes from Rijssel, the Flemish name for Lille, where a similar fabric was made. It is not to be confused with RUSSELL CORD.

Russell cord a ribbed or corded cloth with a cotton warp and a woollen or worsted weft, dating from the second half of the 19th century, and popular for lawyers' and scholastic gowns. The origin of the name is unknown.

russet a coarse, homespun woollen cloth usually of reddish-brown colour, although it could be grey or neutral. It dates from the 14th century and was used to make clothes for country people.

rynd (or rind) a metal cross-piece fastened to the end of a QUANT. The rynd is recessed into the top, runner stone of a pair of millstones to support it and transmit rotation.

S

sack a measure once used by corn millers for the volume of grain. One sack equalled 4 BUSHELS; in terms of weight, one sack weighed around 2 cwt, varying with the type of grain – a sack of flour was reckoned to weigh 280 lb. The grinding capacity of mills was stated as so many sacks per hour. The term is obsolete today.

safety fuse a textile 'rope' with a gunpowder core which burnt at a predetermined rate. A safe fuse for exploding gunpowder was invented by William Bickford and Thomas Davey at Tuckingmill, Cornwall, in 1831 (patent no. 6159) which reduced accidents in mines during blasting. This replaced the unreliable, dangerous fuses made from reeds and goose quills which were formerly used.

safety lamp a portable lamp for providing illumination in coal mines, so designed that it will not readily ignite FIREDAMP or other gases in the mine. Prior to its invention there were many mining disasters caused by the ignition of gases by the naked flames miners once used to light up their working area. Several attempts were made in the early 19th century to make a lamp which could be used with safety in gaseous mines. In 1813 Dr William Reid Clanny (1776–1850) of Sunderland invented his 'blast' lamp, which used bellows to supply air to the lamp, but it proved to be too unwieldy and did not come into general use. Two years later George Stephenson invented his 'GEORDIE' LAMP whilst at the same time Humphry Davy produced his design in 1816. Eventually the DAVY LAMP became the generally accepted standard, although Stephenson's lamp was used extensively by his supporters in the north-east coal mines for many years. Davy's lamp was improved in 1840 by L. Meuseler of Liège, Belgium, and J.B. Marsant of France in the 1870s.

The principle on which the success of the safety lamp rests is that the flame is encased in a fine wire gauze which, whilst it admits air and hence oxygen to maintain the flame, prevents heat from the flame being communicated to any combustible gas which may surround the lamp.

safety valve (or pressure relief valve, pop valve) a pressure-relieving valve fitted to pressure vessels such as steam boilers to allow the contained pressurized fluid to escape harmlessly to atmosphere when a pre-set internal pressure is reached, thus protecting the vessel from damage or rupture, and consequent possible explosion.

Safety valves are either of the deadweight, weighted-lever, or spring-loaded designs. The earliest boiler safety valves were usually of the deadweight type. This basically comprises a small circular outlet from the top of the vessel in the steam space, which is sealed by a vertically guided spindle loaded with weights. The total weight is so related to the area of the outlet that when the total upward internal pressure equals or slightly exceeds the downward closing force, the spindle lifts and allows the steam to escape until the internal pressure falls sufficiently to allow the valve to reseat. The alternative weighted-lever design is very old, and comprises a lever pressing the valve down on its seat; it was first used by Denis Papin (1647–1714) in the mid-17th century on his steam digestor (*c*.1682).

Weighted safety valves are not suitable for moving applications such as on locomotives and ships, and springs are substituted since they are not affected by movement or vibrations etc. Timothy Hackworth (1786–1850) used spring-loaded safety valves on his locomotives in the 1830s. The duplex spring-loaded safety valve was invented by John Ramsbottom (1814–92) in 1855 (patent no. 1299) for use on locomotives. This has two valve openings, closely spaced with a central tension spring holding them both closed by a crossbar. Should one valve lift before the other, the spring leans slightly towards the closed valve, easing the pull on it and permitting it to open also. The two valves allow steam to escape more rapidly than a single valve, thus reducing the excess pressure more quickly. Stationary steam boilers also use spring-loaded safety valves.

All pressure vessels must have a safety valve fitted by law.

safflower a thistle-like plant, *Carthamus tinctorius*, the dried petals from which were used to make yellow, pink and red dyes. It was imported from Egypt and India, where it was cultivated for centuries. It is also known as dyers' thistle.

saffron a cloth dye giving a yellow colour, and also a food flavouring and colouring agent, made from the dried stigmas of the flower *Crocus sativus*, otherwise known as the saffron crocus. The flower was grown around the old wool town of Saffron Walden in Essex until the end of the 18th century, and being the most important industry of the area, gave its name to the town. Saffron also had a medicinal use.

sagathy a kind of woollen SERGE, which was being made in England in the 18th century and was used for men's outer clothing until the late 19th century. Silk SAYS were also known as sagathies. The origin of the word is unknown.

saggar (or segger) a baked, fireproof clay container inside which fine pottery items are placed before being fired in a kiln. An earlier word was shrager, dating from the late 17th century, which may come from the German word *schragen*, meaning to prop up. The name saggar was introduced about the mid-18th century and is thought to be a corruption of the word safeguard; its purpose is to protect the ceramic ware from the naked flames and smoke in the kiln.

sails the revolving arms of a windmill, also known as sweeps. Most windmills had four sails, although more than this number have been in use. Usually the sails of a windmill revolved anti-clockwise when viewed from outside. Various designs of sails were developed over the years, with the aim of automatically reducing the surface offered to the wind as wind

strength increased, to prevent damaging overspeed. Sails are attached to a shaft known as the windshaft, which rotates in bearings. The windshaft is tilted off the horizontal a few degrees so that the lower path of the rotating sails will clear the wide base of the mill tower, this wide base giving greater stability to the structure. This slight tilt also throws some of the wind thrust, and weight of the sails themselves, onto a thrust bearing at the opposite end of the windshaft, relieving the front bearing of some of the load. The drive to the internal machinery of the mill is taken off the windshaft by a large gearwheel.

For details of patented designs, *see* REEFING SAIL, SPRING SAIL and PATENT SAIL.

sakia (or sakhia, saqiya) an ancient Eastern irrigation device comprising a vertical wheel with earthenware pots attached to its periphery, which was turned by a horizontal wheel worked by oxen or asses similar to a HORSE WHIM. The pots dipped into a river and raised water to a higher level into irrigation channels. This was the forerunner of the SCOOPWHEEL, and is sometimes called a Persian wheel, or more rarely a Chinese wheel.

salt a compound of basic or acid radicals, with whole or part of their hydrogen replaced by a metal. Such salts are known as sulphates, nitrates, phosphates, etc. depending on the acids from which they are derived. The salt discussed below is the common or household salt, sodium chloride, which has been an important commodity and necessity of life since ancient times. Its many uses include the seasoning of food during cooking and as a condiment; the preservation of meat and fish before REFRIGERATION; the curing of skins and hides; and the glazing of pottery. It is an important ingredient in soap manufacture, a constituent of bleaching powder, and was used in the manufacture of sodium carbonate (washing soda) by the LEBLANC PROCESS of 1791. There are two principal methods of obtaining natural salt: from seawater, or from rock salt, the former being the earliest source.

There were two methods of making salt from seawater, both dating from about the 13th century. One was to dig up salty sand from sea-washed flats between tides, and tip it into wooden troughs filled with straw or rushes to act as a filter. The troughs had perforated bottoms, and when seawater was poured in, salt was leached out and collected in buckets. The collected salt was then boiled in lead pans in a SALTCOTE, often using peat as fuel to drive off remaining water. The damp salt was removed, drained and dried in hanging wicker baskets.

Salt made this way was called sandsalt. It was sold in an old measure called a mett, equal to about 8 bushels. The other method was to collect seawater from an incoming tide in shallow ponds called SALT PANS dug in the shore. The pans were then blocked off, trapping the seawater which was allowed to evaporate naturally to concentrate the BRINE. Final evaporation was carried out in heated metal pans until the salt crystallized. Both methods were part-time summer occupations, usually combined with farming. There were four main marine salt producing areas in Britain: south Hampshire, Flintshire and Denbighshire, Tyneside, and Scotland along the Forth. Tyneside and Scottish salt producers mostly used coal fired shallow iron pans.

Rock salt exists in saliferous beds below ground. Rock from inclined beds never comes to the surface as an outcrop, since ground water forms a salt solution with it which can reach down to 200–400 ft below the surface. This natural salt solution is known as wild brine, and where discovered, was pumped up to the surface and processed in the same manner as seawater. Rock salt may also be mined from lower depths by conventional mining methods, via vertical shafts reaching down to the saliferous bed(s). Rock salt was discovered in Cheshire around 1690 near Northwich, and an important salt extraction and processing industry developed there and in surrounding areas, many million tons of salt having been extracted from underground. These sources of salt are called salterns or wiches: the names of those towns in Cheshire where salt is found end in the suffix '-wich', although this suffix is not an infallible guide to the presence of salt, since many placenames ending in '-wich' are derived from the Old English *wice*, meaning wych-elm.

A later method of extracting rock salt was to drill cavities in the salt bed, fill them with water, and pump the brine so formed up to the surface into large shallow metal pans. The unwanted water was driven off by heating the pans, and a final drying of the crystalline salt in stoves or ovens. This method of selecting where to make the underground cavities was preferable to taking wild brine from the naturally formed 'pools', the extent of which was not known, since the latter method resulted in subsidence at ground level, a feature evident in and around the Cheshire wiches. Rock salt is brownish in its natural state, and only becomes white after refining for household use.

Salt was once carried by packhorse from where it was made to be sold in towns and villages throughout the country. The routes taken by the packhorse trains are known as saltways and may often be traced by placenames containing the word 'salt' or 'salter', such as Saltfield, Saltersgate and Salterford. With the coming of canals, especially as salt using industries developed, salt in greater bulk was carried by water wherever possible. A tax (gabelle) on salt was introduced in 1702 and not finally abolished until 1823, and then mainly to make the manufacture of cheap bleaching powder possible. Bonded storehouses were built to assist tax gathering: in Scotland, such storehouses were called girnels or girners. Marine salt loses up to one-seventh of its bulk whilst in store, and merchants preferred to buy salt at least three months old on account of this.

Bridbury, A.R. *England and the Salt Trade in the Later Middle Ages*, Oxford University Press, 1955
Crump, B. 'Saltways from the Cheshire Wiches', *Transactions of the Lancashire and Cheshire Antiquarian Society* LIV (1940), 84–142

saltcote (or saltcoat, saltern) a house or cottage where salt was either stored or made by boiling salty water. Saltcotes were often sited on a coast where sea salt was extracted, but some were in inland salt bearing areas.

saltern, *see* SALTCOTE

salt pans large, shallow pits or ponds, dug close to the sea, which could be filled with seawater by an incoming tide and blocked off to allow the seawater to evaporate naturally in the sun, leaving a SALT deposit which was later dug out. Salt pans date from medieval times, and were still in operation up till about 1800 in Britain. Metal salt pans were also used, heated by peat, wood, or coal to speed up evaporation. Remains of old salt pans may still be found around the coast in a few remote or undisturbed places, and former sites are sometimes indicated by placenames which include the word pan, e.g. Harley Pans on the north-east coast, and Prestonpans near Edinburgh. The salt obtained from natural inland brine springs was evaporated in a similar manner; such salt was known as wich salt.

saltpetre a white crystalline salt substance, with the chemical name potassium nitrate. It is the main constituent of GUNPOWDER, supplying the oxygen necessary for the explosion. It occurs naturally in warm climates and was imported into Britain from India in the second half of the 17th century; it can also be produced artificially, and in Elizabethan times a recipe was purchased from Germany for making it from long piles of dung, lime, black earth, and urine, called nitre beds, from which the salts were scraped. In the 19th century a cheaper source was found in the Chile saltpetre or

CALICHE (soda nitre), from which potassium nitrate was made using potassium chloride. Saltpetre also occurs naturally in small quantities as a white effervescence on the surface of damp, and sometimes new, walls. It is possibly from this that it derived its name, since in Latin *sal petrae* means the salt of stone. Prior to its regular importation from India, saltpetre scraped off stable walls was used in gunpowder manufacture. Another early source was pigeon dung from dovecotes.

samson 1. a small type of wooden winch used to increase the pressure on a screw press in the days of making paper by hand. The pile of alternating wet paper sheets and felts was placed in the screw press, which was tightened down to expel water from the paper, and the samson, which was placed alongside the press, used to exert the final pull on the screw press lever for maximum pressure. The name comes from the ancient Hebrew hero (Judges 13–16) who possessed phenomenal strength. **2.** a screwed metal clamp used by wheelwrights for drawing together rim segments (felloes) when fitting on the iron tyre.

sand bed a sand floor in which feeding channels and moulds are made, along which molten iron from a BLAST FURNACE is run when the furnace is tapped. The main feeding channel from the furnace outlet is called the sow, and arranged in rows on either side of it are the sand moulds of particular size which made the pigs. PIG IRON is thus the end product of the blast furnace, the pigs being cast in the sand bed. The sand is a special type known as moulding sand. Flat iron items may also be cast in a sand bed.

sanderswood (or saunderswood) a dye made from the powdered wood from the evergreen tree *pterocarpus santalinus* which grows in the East Indies and Ceylon, used to dye wool brown. The related sandalwood tree is used in perfumery.

sapan wood a dyewood imported from the East Indies, which comes from a tree known as *sapang* in Malayan. It produces a red dye.

sarn the Welsh name for a CAUSEWAY.

sasse a 17th-century word for a sluice or lock on a waterway. The word is no longer in use, although the French word *sas*, meaning an airlock, is obviously related to it.

sateen a cloth woven so that the WEFT mainly appears on the surface, giving a glossy appearance. It may be in silk or cotton, and was used mainly as linings for garments, or sometimes as dress material. The pattern of weaving is complementary to that of SATIN.

satin a form of weaving in which the WARP

mostly appears on one surface of the cloth. This is achieved by arranging for the warp threads to pass over several WEFTS in succession before passing under one (*see* Fig. 50). The long lengths of warp on the surface are called floats, and because they are not held in place as frequently as they would be in PLAIN WEAVE, satins are more vulnerable to damage and wear. When silk is woven as a satin fabric it results in a smooth, lustrous finish on the side where the floats are. The fabric is popular as a fine dress material.

This form of weaving is complementary to SATEEN, where the weft predominates on one side.

Savery engine an elementary steam 'engine' working on the atmospheric principle, and named after Thomas Savery (*c*.1650–1715). Such simple 'engines' were sometimes used downstream of an OVERSHOT waterwheel, where they raised water up into a cistern placed just higher than the wheel. The cistern fed water onto the wheel, thus using the water over and over again. Savery engines were also used to dewater mines.

A Savery engine comprised a long, vertical cylinder or tube fed with steam from a boiler. The lower open end of the cylinder terminated below the surface of the water in the TAILRACE. Steam was admitted into the cylinder, then cut off, and condensed by an injection of cold water. This caused a vacuum inside the cylinder, which sucked water up from the tailrace, the atmospheric pressure acting on the free surface of the tailrace water forcing some up into the cylinder. A valve closed, trapping water in the cylinder, which then ran out by gravity into the cistern when an outlet valve opened, and the cycle then repeated. The Savery engine was cheap, with hardly any moving parts to wear out. Joshua Wrigley (d.1810) of Manchester was a well known maker of these engines: he arranged for them to be self-acting by using the rotating waterwheel to operate the various valves. Some such engines were still working as late as 1800, but were eventually replaced by Watt engines. Savery engines were also known as blow engines in the 18th century. *See also* 'MINERS FRIEND'.

Hills, R.L.'A steam chimera: a review of the history of the Savery engine', *Newcomen Society Transactions* 58 (1986–7), 27–44

sawney 1. a disastrous event on a spinning mule when all the yarns break simultaneously. The origin of the word is uncertain, but a sawney in Scots means a simpleton. **2.** an old dialect word for a windlass at the top of a coal pit. A sawney-tenter was a man who worked such a windlass.

sawpit the place where tree trunks were sawn into planks by hand. A sawpit comprised a rectangular pit about 6–8 ft deep, over which the trunk could be laid horizontally. Sawing was by a long sawblade with a cross handle at each end, with the pitman, often an apprentice sawyer, standing in the pit below the log, and the sawyer standing above. The saw was moved up and down, the top man guiding it and the pitman cutting by pulling on the downstroke. Sawpits were replaced by saw mills, water-powered at first, later by other prime movers. Mechanized sawing was at first by frame saws which imitated the action of the old sawpit using straight rip saws; later, circular saws came into use.

In the old sawpits, the pitman's job was not an enviable one, since he became covered in sawdust, unlike the sawyer. This gave rise to the old saying that a person in a better position is a 'top sawyer', i.e. is superior.

saw-tooth truss a roof truss used for small spans with a saw-tooth overall shape braced by vertical and diagonal members (*see* Fig. 57). The construction is used particularly for weaving sheds and is known as a NORTH LIGHT ROOF since it allows plenty of daylight to enter the working space below when facing that direction.

Saxony wheel a treadle-operated spinning wheel fitted with a FLYER to give continuous spinning and winding on. Generally believed to have been invented by Meister Jurgen of Brunswick, Saxony, around 1530, this type of wheel was used by German mining families to supplement their income by spinning FLAX. There are two types of wheel, the horizontal and the vertical. Both operate in the same way, the latter being more compact since the spinning head is mounted above the wheel. The Saxony wheel differs from the great wheel in two important ways: first, the treadle freed both hands of a spinner for feeding in the ROLAG, and secondly, the flyer made spinning and winding of yarn onto the bobbin simultaneous and continuous, apart from the occasional stop to move the yarn onto a fresh HECK on the flyer. By comparison, spinning and winding on were separate, intermittent actions on a great wheel. The Saxony wheel was thus a faster machine, and the spinner could sit at its side. It was a domestic machine, usually worked by the women and girls of a family: when the demand for yarn in the mid-18th century outstripped the capacity of domestic, single-spindle wheels, the JENNY with its multiple spindles took over. The Saxony wheel is known by several alternative names, such as flax wheel, Dutch wheel, and Scots wheel.

say a fine fabric with a texture resembling that of SERGE. In the 16th century says were partly silk, but subsequently they became all wool.

scabbling, *see* CABBLING

scantlings an old word for dimensions; it may come from the French *escantillon*, meaning a measuring tool or gauge. Originally, scantling had a ship-building usage in Britain, referring to the cross-sectional dimensions of timbers, and later crept into engineering usage also. It is rarely used today.

scarfed beam, *see* FLITCHED BEAM

scarlet grain, *see* KERMES

scheduled monument, *see* LISTED BUILDING

'Schemer, The' nickname by which James Brindley (1716–72), the pioneering English canal builder, was known in Leek, Staffs., in the 1740s. He acquired this reputation in his early days when working as a millwright for his skill in improving existing machinery and inventive genius.
Boucher, C.T.G. *James Brindley, Engineer, 1716–1772*, Goose, 1968

Science Museum Fund an annual amount of public money allocated by the government and administered by the Science Museum, London, to assist local authorities and other sources in the purchase or preservation of items of scientific and technological interest. Usually, the Fund matches each pound raised by the body wishing to make the purchase. Mostly artefacts, such as machinery, vehicles, buildings, etc. qualify if considered worthy, but documents may also be included. The Fund was set up in 1973, and a similar Fund is operated in Scotland by the Royal Scottish Museum, Edinburgh. It is by this financial assistance that many items of interest to industrial archaeologists are conserved in museums, etc.

scoggan the device for automatically operating the valves on a NEWCOMEN ATMOSPHERIC ENGINE by the movement of the beam. The word is of Cornish origin, dating from the earliest days of the atmospheric engine.

scoopwheel a large diameter wheel with buckets fastened to its circumference. Such wheels, steam driven by beam engines, enabled the Fens to be rapidly drained in the 1830s by lifting water out of field drains into nearby rivers and sluices. Wheels mainly around 30 ft diameter were used. Scoopwheels were also used in the tin mining industry in Cornwall.

scoria (pl. scoriae) an 18th-century word used for slag or dross, the layer of impurities which floats on molten metals during smelting or refining. When cold, scoria is a hard, brittle, lava-like material usually discarded or used as road-making material. The word comes from the Latin *scoria*, meaning dross; an Anglicized spelling sometimes found is scory. Scorification is the formation of slag.

Scotch boiler a marine type, compact steam boiler, introduced about 1862. It comprised a short, squat shell with a diameter almost the same as its length, with flat ends strengthened by end-to-end ties or stays. Three, or sometimes four, furnace tubes led from the front to an internal vertical combustion chamber surrounded by water, near the far end. Multiple return, small diameter firetubes conveyed the hot gases from the combustion chamber to an external gas uptake fastened to the front of the boiler; this led in turn to the ship's funnel(s). The firegrates were nearly as long as the furnace tubes. Banks of such boilers were often sited back-to-back in steamships; they were capable of rapid response to steam demands.

Scotch crank engine (or Scotch yoke) a compact design of engine in which a connecting rod is dispensed with, giving a short baseplate (*see* Fig. 58). The crosshead incorporates a T-shaped extension, the top of the T being at right angles to the line of stroke of the piston, and has a slot formed in it. The crankpin slides up and down the slot as the crankshaft revolves. This design is used for engines of moderate power only, and is also used on small pumps.

Scotch gin, *see* HORSE WHIM

scotchman an 18th-century name for a travelling draper, packman or pedlar. These itinerant salesmen travelled remote country areas selling small goods to outlying farms and village communities. Often they operated on a credit system, payment for their goods being accepted in weekly instalments. Many originated from Scotland and it is possible that this explains the origin of the name, although it

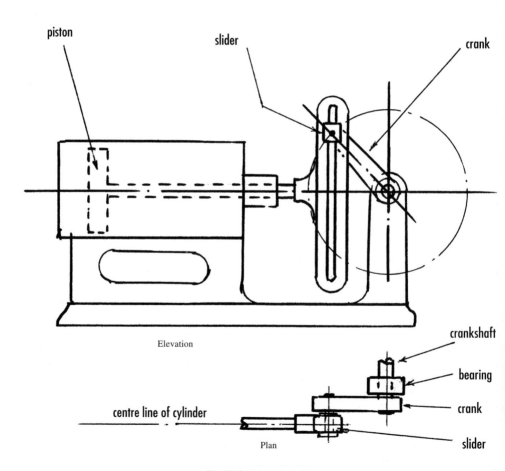

Fig. 58. Scotch crank engine

was equally applied to English pedlars. When travelling from place to place they generally used packhorse routes and there was obviously some risk involved since they carried goods and money: this is instanced by the murder in 1838 on Rivington Moor, near Bolton, Lancs., of one such pedlar, himself a Scot. The spot is marked by a cast-iron inscribed post known locally as Scotchman's Stump.

Scotch mill, *see* BARKER'S MILL

Scotch yoke, *see* SCOTCH CRANK ENGINE

scouring a south Wales term for HUSHING.

scow a flat-bottomed boat used as a lighter for unloading a cargo ship. The term comes from the Dutch *schouw*, a ferry boat.

scowle an old, abandoned opencast iron ore site in the Forest of Dean. A quarry is said to scowle when its sides cave in.

screw **1.** a small metal item used for fastening things together. Screws have a helical ridge and groove, or male thread, cut round their outer surface. Woodscrews taper to a point and cut their way into wood; setscrews are cylindrical and flat ended, and screw into prepared holes which have similar, but internal female threads. Screws are made in many sizes and have a variety of heads. They are comparatively recent in origin, dating from the early 19th century; before accurate screw threads became available, other methods of fastening objects together were used, such as pins, wedges, and rivets. *See also* SCREW THREADS. **2.** a propeller for moving a ship. A marine screw usually has two to four blades, set in a helical manner at the end of a shaft protruding from the stern of a ship. When revolved at speed, it produces a thrust, driving the ship forward, as it 'screws' itself through the water. Screw propellers were demonstrated about 1825 or 1827 by Robert Wilson (1803–82), and two screw propeller patents were taken out in 1836, one (no. 7104) by Francis Petitt Smith (1808–74), and the other (no. 7149) by John Ericsson (1803–89). It was the advantage of screws over paddles that made Brunel change to screws during the building of the *Great Britain* in 1839. The superiority of screw propellers over paddle wheels was finally convincingly demonstrated by the famous tug-of-war between the screw driven naval ship *Rattler* and a similar sized vessel, the *Alecto*, which the *Rattler* won easily.

screw-gill draw frame a machine for paralleling long textile fibres. A well-known screw-gill drawing frame, or gill box as it is sometimes called, was patented in 1833 by Samuel Lawson and William King Westley (patent no. 6464). Its purpose is to draw out the longer type of textile fibres and is used

extensively in the worsted industry. The screw-gill is also known as a spiral frame.

Fig. 59 shows the device, which works in conjunction with drafting rollers. The main parts of the screw-gill are the feed and drafting rollers, two pairs of screws, and a set of faller bars fitted with gill pins. The feed rollers pass the fibres to be gilled onto the travelling faller bars, at the same time exerting a pull on the fibres as they are held in the nip of the rollers. The gill pins on the rising faller bars penetrate the mass of fibres and, because of their greater forward speed, gradually draw out and comb through the fibres until they are eventually released by the feed rollers. The straightened and attenuated fibres are carried forward by the faller bars until they are fed into the nip of a pair of drafting rollers which, travelling at a faster surface speed than the gill pins, pull the fibres through the pins, so attenuating them further. The faller bars are driven forward by a pair of screws – hence the name – and when they reach the end of their travel, are lowered by a cam mechanism onto a similar pair of screws which return them underneath to the feed end. Here they are raised up again by cams to repeat their drafting action on fresh fibres. The fibres are thus first combed by means of back draft in which the rollers hold and the pins comb, and then drawn out by means of front draft in which the pins hold and the rollers draft, i.e. the rollers either hold or draft, aided by the gill pins. In worsted preparation, the wool is gilled a number of times at each succeeding machine as it passes through the various processes.

screw threads helical ridges and grooves of accurate pitch. Engineering screw threads are termed male if on the outside of a bolt, etc. or female if inside a hole. There are different thread profiles for different purposes. When used to fasten things together, the profile is usually in the form of a 'V' or a modification of it, and the tightness between the male and female threads relies on the pressure and friction between the mating surfaces, i.e. the flanks of the 'V'. Until about 1860, there was no unified, standard screw thread in Britain, each workshop making its own, and therefore there was no interchangeability. Joseph Whitworth (1803–87) introduced the standard V-shaped screw thread which bears his name, and other specialized threads were developed from it.

If a screw thread is to be used for transmitting a force (e.g. as on a FLYPRESS), or for moving an object along (e.g. the lead screw on a lathe), a square profile is used; there is less friction, and no oblique bursting force on the

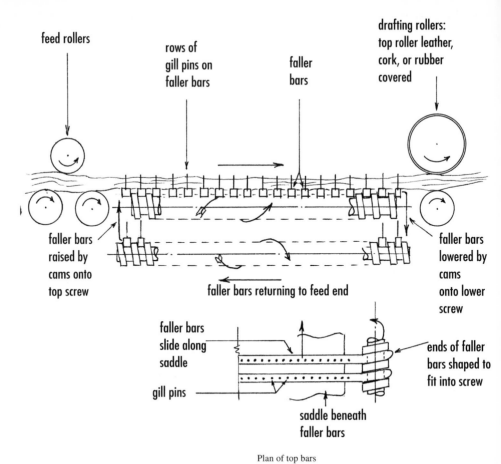

Fig. 59. Screw-gill draw frame or gill box for long fibres

female component. There is however, no universal profile for square threads in the same sense as for Whitworth threads.

scribbling the term used in the woollen industry for the fibre preparation process known in the cotton industry as CARDING. A scribbling machine comprises a series of rotating cylinders covered with CARD CLOTH which produces a continuous flossy sheet of wool. Earliest scribblers were hand or horse driven, but water power was soon applied. Such machines date from around 1780, and were adapted from the cotton industry. The word is possibly derived from scrub, i.e. to scour with a brush (which card cloth resembles), although no water is involved in the scribbling process. The card cloth in a woollen scribbling engine has stronger wires than are used for carding cotton.

scrin a Derbyshire dialect mining term for a narrow side-branching vein or rake of lead leading off a main vein. Usually scrins are short in length and only a foot or less in width. It is a possible variation of 'string', or may come from an old Dutch or German word for fissure or crack.

scrubber that part of gas purification equipment for removing ammonia and any residual tar by water-washing the gas. It comprises a metal tower, usually cylindrical, inside which are a number of shelves or ledges. Water is continuously sprayed over these and the gas is caused to flow across them in series in contact with the water, which 'scrubs' out the impurities mentioned. Scrubbers date from the mid-19th century.

scry (or scroy) a dialect word used in Kent and Sussex for a sieve, such as that used in a corn mill.

scutching machine a machine for cleansing already opened raw cotton, and forming the fibres into a continuous wide LAP or sheet in preparation for CARDING. The scutching machine (known as a picker in the USA) was invented in 1797 by Neil Snodgrass of Johnstone, near Glasgow, and not patented; it was later improved by William and Andrew Crighton of Manchester (patent no. 1128, 1854). Various forms of the machine were developed, of both vertical and horizontal design. The name comes from the early use of scutches or rods for beating dirt out of cotton masses and also for dressing flax. The machine breaks up cotton masses, and using an air stream draws the fibres onto a perforated drum to form the lap, which is then consolidated by a roller system. Once the cotton has been separated into loose fibres floating in the air stream, any unwanted impurities such as seeds, leaves, sand etc. which were present in the BALE drop out under gravity and are removed. Fine dust is sucked out.

Fig. 60 shows a cross-section through a typical scutcher of horizontal design. The raw cotton, having been opened up from its compressed condition in the bale, is spread out on a creeping lattice-feed mechanism which delivers it to some feed rollers. These slowly feed the cotton 'lumps' into a closed compartment in which a pair of high speed beaters revolve. The beaters break up the pieces of cotton without damaging the fibres, which are then drawn further into the machine by an exhaust fan, and passed across grids in the base into which the heavier impurities fall. The fibres, now floating in the air stream, are drawn onto the periphery of a large drum made of fine wire mesh. Any dust left in the fibres is drawn through the mesh by the air stream but the cotton fibres remain held on the drum surface. The drum slowly revolves and the cotton is

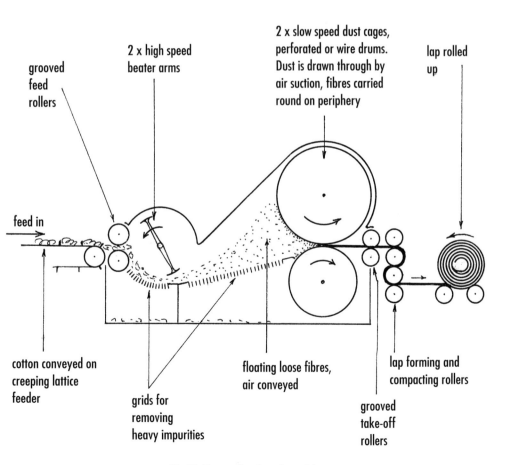

Fig. 60. Cross-section through a scutcher

removed from it by a pair of rollers as a wide loose sheet. This is consolidated via a lap-forming series of compacting rollers, and the finished lap is wound into a roll. The lap comprises fibres arranged randomly, i.e. in all directions, and is passed to the carding engine for the next part of the process.

Flax is also subjected to a scutching action to break off the unwanted woody core and bark (*see* SCUTCH MILL).

scutch mill machinery for preparing FLAX for later processes. For flax preparation, machinery was introduced by the mid-18th century to replace the former hand operation of breaking away the unwanted woody tissue from the fibres. A scutch mill often comprised a long horizontal shaft rotated by a waterwheel which drove a number of stands or berths (working stations) in a row. Each stand would have four to eight rotating arms or flails which beat a handful of previously bruised flax stems thrust into their path by a workman. This treatment removed the ligneous matter and left the fibres ready for further processing. By the 1830s, there were over 1,000 scutch mills in Ireland, mostly concentrated in Ulster, and by the 1860s the number had increased to some 1,500, but a steady decline took place after this peak had been reached.

scythe grinding sharpening scythes and similar tools to provide a cutting edge. In the 19th century hand scythes, sickles, shears and similar agricultural edge cutting tools were made in small forges. Each forge would have a grinding shop where the tool blades would be hand sharpened on a revolving sandstone, belt driven from a LINESHAFT. A typical arrangement had a large wheel about 6 ft diameter, astride which a grinder sat facing the wheel; the lower part of the wheel dipped into a water trough to keep the wheel wet during the grinding, and prevent overheating the metal blades and affecting their temper. After grinding, the blades were polished (glazed) against the rim of a leather-covered wheel which had an abrasive powder embedded in it, to prevent corrosion of the metal. Grinding was a hazardous job, and men suffered from silicosis as a result of inhaling stone dust. *See also* GRINDING HULL.

sea coal coal found on the seashore. From as early as the 14th century pieces of coal were gathered from the seashore in the north-east of England, particularly around Tyneside. This coal was washed up by the tide from seams which outcropped there, and as demand rose, the outcrops themselves were mined. Such coal became known as sea coal (spelt sea cole in

early documents). Most of it was shipped to London down the east coast, since this was the best route, the roads of the day being inadequate for carrying loads. In 1700, Newcastle upon Tyne shipped nearly 550,000 tons of sea coal to London, and some thirty years later this quantity had risen to close on 750,000 tons. The name sea coal was also used by Londoners since it reached them by sea, and there is still an Old Sea Coal Lane where a coal wharf was once sited. In 1667 a tax was levied on coal landed in London to help pay for rebuilding the city after the disastrous fire of 1666.

Smith, F.R.S. *Sea-Coal for London*, Longmans, 1961

Sea Island cotton the name of the cotton variety *Gossypium Barbadense*, grown along the coasts of South Carolina, Georgia, Florida, and the nearby offshore American islands. This variety of cotton was amongst the earliest obtained from North America, and was of excellent quality. It is a fine, silky cotton with fibres around 1.7 in mean length, around 0.0064 in mean diameter, and of consistent quality. Its excellence is due to a very favourable climate and soil, and it has always been used for fine spinning, i.e. cottons of high COUNTS. The cotton has smooth black seeds unlike most other cottons which have furry green seeds, and is therefore also known as black seed cotton.

It is believed that Sea Island cotton originally came from the Bahamas, and was sent to Georgia in 1786 by refugee colonials loyal to the British crown who had settled in the Bahamas after the American War of Independence (1775–81). Cotton grown on the islands of the West Indies was sometimes called Sea Island cotton because of its similarity.

seam 1. an old word for a packhorse load, the weight of which varied in different parts of the country and with different materials. 2. a stratum or layer of coal; one of the series that make up the coal measures. A coal seam lies on its seat earth and is separated from the seam above by a layer of sandstone or shale. Coal seams can vary in thickness from 1 in up to as much as 20 ft, but the thickness and coal quality can vary from place to place. They lie more or less horizontally below the surface, or may dip at an angle. The deepest seams are the oldest chronologically: each seam is associated with its own suite of fossils, which depends on the epoch in which the coal was laid down, and this feature enables the same seam to be identified when it reappears, vertically displaced, on the other side of a fault. Coal seams have local names, and the same seam may be known by another name where it reappears in another coalfield: for example, the Gowthorpe Seam in West Yorkshire is known as the Top Hard Coal in the Nottinghamshire and Derbyshire fields. In Lancashire seams are called mines, e.g. the Silkstone Seam of Yorkshire is called the Bullion Mine in Lancashire. In Staffordshire a coal seam is known as a row.

Bands of ironstone and fireclay are often found in close association with coal seams.

seat earth, *see* FIRECLAY

secondhand mistress an intriguing job title for a female worker employed in finishing off lace. It once was a domestic hand industry.

second motion shaft shaft connecting a prime mover to mill gearing. In early textile mills driven by geared systems, the drive from the prime mover (waterwheel or beam engine) was carried into the building by a horizontal shaft, sited either above or below ground. This was called the second motion shaft, and it terminated in a BEVEL GEAR which drove another bevel at 90°, i.e. it changed to a vertical shaft which carried the drive up to the various floors.

seersucker a thin, striped linen or cotton fabric with a puckered or crimped surface, originally made in India. The name is a corruption of the Persian *shir o shakkar* which literally means milk and sugar, but somehow came to mean a striped linen garment with the characteristics described. In the 17th century seersucker was used for upholstery, and later for garments. The puckered surface is made by feeding into the cloth different sets of warps at different tensions during weaving.

seger cone a small cone a few inches high made from a clay and salt mixture which will soften and bend over at a definite temperature; various mixtures are made to provide a range of temperatures. The cones are placed in a pottery kiln where they can be observed, and are used as an approximate determination of the kiln temperature during the firing. They are designated by numbers according to their softening temperatures, and are named after Hermann August Seger (1839–93), the German ceramics technologist who invented them.

self-acting incline, *see* INCLINED PLANE

self-acting mule, *see* 'IRON MAN'

self-open (or shack, shake-hole) a Derbyshire expression for a natural underground cavity found in limestone rock during lead mining. Sometimes self-opens were used for drainage from the mine workings, or for storing unwanted rock, called 'deads'. Peak Cavern, near Castleton, is a good example of a large self-open.

selvedge (or selvage) the strengthened edge on woven cloth, usually about 0.25 in wide,

obtained by a few doubled warp threads. Its purpose is to resist the drag of the weft as it returns for the next PICK, and to improve the appearance of the cloth; it also helps to prevent the edge of the cloth from fraying after weaving. It is also known as list or listing.

serge originally a silk fabric, and later used to describe woollen materials generally with a TWILL weave, popular in the 16th century as bedroom hangings and for durable clothing. The fabric was originally imported from France and called serge-de-Nîmes in England, but when French Huguenot refugees began to manufacture it in East Anglia in the 17th century the name was shortened to serge. Subsequently, the name was applied to twilled worsted, or a fabric of worsted warp and woollen weft, which being very durable and hard-wearing is extensively used for outer garments, suitings, etc.

sericulture the production of silk by rearing the mulberry silkworm and reeling silk from its cocoon. Practised in China as far back as 3000 BC, by the 15th century its secrets had been discovered and sericulture was being practised in Italy and France. An attempt was made in Britain in the late 17th century to cultivate the silkworm so that refugee HUGUENOT silk workers could be supplied with an indigenous raw material, but the experiment was unsuccessful.

servitor (or blower) the member of the team of glass blowers who does the preliminary shaping of blown articles; servitor means assistant. *See also* CHAIR (2).

set the number of ends, i.e. warp threads, per inch in a textile fabric.

sett 1. an old dialect word for a metal mine. It could also mean the amount of work done, or an area of a mine to be worked, i.e. a mine lease. Setting has the meaning of to lease or let. **2.** one of the natural stones forming a packhorse causeway. An early name sometimes found in literature for these paving stones is eases. **3.** a shaped stone block used to pave a road surface. Setts of granite or sandstone measuring about 6 in deep by 3–4 in wide by 6–9 in long were laid on roads subject to heavy wear from iron tyred wheels in textile districts in the 19th century. On some inclines a sandstone central strip with granite setts either side can be found. This combination was to provide a horse with a better grip on the sandstone setts, the wheels of the cart running on the granite. A configuration in which setts are laid in curves and arches across the paved area goes under the German name of Kleinpflaster, and in addition to the decorative effect, provides a smoother passage for poorly sprung vehicles since the wheels cross the joints at an angle, reducing the jolting which is more noticeable when the joints are in line.

Settlement, Law of a law of 1662 relating to entitlement to parish relief by the poor and destitute. At this time, families receiving parish relief, or those living close to the margin of subsistence and expecting to have to claim parish relief, were frightened to leave their parish to seek better employment elsewhere; if they did, they would lose their right to relief, since it was only paid to those residing in their parish of origin. Newcomers to a parish could be forcibly removed to their last parish of settlement, at the latter parish's expense, within forty days of arrival if they were likely to become a burden on the new parish.

The law was relaxed in 1795 by the Poor Law Removal Act, but nevertheless the general effect of the Settlement Act was to starve the burgeoning industrial towns of labour and to perpetuate unemployment in agricultural areas.

settling flue (or condensation flue, lambreth) a long brick flue, sometimes let into the ground and often tortuous, leading from a SMELTER to a distant chimney, along which fumes from the smelter pass. Its purpose is to encourage poisonous particles carried from the smelter to settle out or 'condense' along its length, to reduce emission from the chimney, and to recover metal which would otherwise be lost. Such settling flues are attached to lead smelters and arsenic CALCINING kilns. The collected contents of the flue are dug out periodically and returned to the smelter or kiln for reprocessing. Such flues date from the 1770s. *See also* CONDENSER (2).

'Seven Wonders of the Canals' These are said to be:

1. The Pontcysyllte aqueduct near Llangollen, Denbighs., north Wales. Built by Thomas Telford (1757–1834), and opened in 1805, it carries the Llangollen Canal in a cast-iron trough on eighteen masonry piers, 127 ft above the river Dee.
2. The Barton swing aqueduct near Manchester. Designed by E. Leader Williams (1828–1910) and opened in 1893, it carries the Bridgewater Canal across the Manchester Ship Canal, and may be swung to one side to allow ships to pass along the ship canal.
3. The Anderton lift, near Northwich, Ches. Designed by Edwin Clark (1814–94) from an idea by E. Leader Williams, it was completed in 1875, and enabled boats to be raised or lowered between the river Weaver and the Trent and Mersey Canal, a vertical distance of some 50 ft.
4. The five-rise staircase locks at Bingley, West Riding of Yorks. Built by John Longbotham (d.1801), and opened in 1774, they raise the Leeds and Liverpool Canal 60 ft up a steep incline.
5. Standedge tunnel, on the boundary between Lancs. and Yorks. Planned by Benjamin Outram (1764–1805), this is the longest British canal tunnel, 5,698 yd long, and takes the Huddersfield Narrow Canal under the Pennines from Diggle to Marsden. It was completed in 1811, having been begun in 1794.
6. Burnley embankment, which carries the Leeds and Liverpool Canal across the town for about 0.75 mile in a straight line. The engineer was Samuel Fletcher (d.1804).
7. The flight of twenty-nine locks at Devizes, Wilts., constructed as part of the Kennet and Avon Broad Canal by John Rennie (1761–1821) in 1810.

The eighth wonder is said to be the first Harecastle tunnel, near Kidsgrove, Staffs. It is 2,880 yd long, taking the Trent and Mersey Canal under a ridge of high ground. Commenced by James Brindley (1716–72), it was completed by Hugh Henshall (d.1817) in 1777.

shaduf, *see* SWAPE

shaft a term whose several meanings nearly all relate to something which has a length greater than its width. **1.** a metal rod or axle, circular in cross-section, which transmits power from one point to another by torque. Examples are a LINESHAFT and a crankshaft. Before iron and steel became common, some shafts were made from wood, and sometimes square in cross-section. **2.** a vertical or inclined excavation, such as a MINE SHAFT, giving access to an underground mine, etc. A downcast shaft is where fresh ventilating air is drawn into a mine, and an upcast shaft is where the vitiated air is withdrawn. **3.** the central vertical space in a BLAST FURNACE in which the ore, fuel, and flux are melted. Early blast furnaces had square shafts, but by the mid-17th century tapering circular cross-sectioned shafts became common. **4.** a shaft (or leaf) of HEALDS comprises two parallel flat wooden laths, between which the healds are stretched which control the movement of the warp in a loom.

shaft furnace a primitive, tall chimney-like furnace, square or circular in cross-section, used for smelting ore or for heating clay for bricks or pottery. Such furnaces date from the 16th century, and at first they were made high enough to create a sufficient natural draught, the fuel (mostly charcoal) being either mixed in with the ore, or sometimes burnt in a separate fireplace at the base of the shaft. Later, first hand- and then water-powered bellows were added to obtain higher temperatures, and later still BLOWING ENGINES, the height and diameter of the shaft being increased to give greater throughput. Eventually, the shaft furnace developed into the BLAST FURNACE for iron production, or the smaller CUPOLA FURNACE used in foundries to remelt metals for making castings.

shake-hole, *see* SELF-OPEN

shalloon a light, closely woven, worsted cloth, chiefly used for coat linings and women's dresses. The name comes from Châlons-sur-Marne, France, where this type of cloth was woven, which was imitated in Britain. Shalloon weaving was introduced in the Halifax, Yorks., area about the beginning of the 18th century and soon became the speciality of that town.

shammelling an old Cornish mining term for lifting water or ore in stages. Water was pumped up from deep mines by a series of pumps, each pump delivering water to the pump above, while ore was shovelled from one platform (a shammel) up onto a higher platform. A shammel engine was an engine which raised water part of the way up a mine shaft. The word comes from the Old English 'shamble', which meant a wooden bench or counter.

shantung a kind of silk cloth made in imitation of the silk originating from Shantung in north-east China. Chinese shantung was made from silk from the wild silkworm, and was left undyed; shantung made in Britain is dyed.

shaping machine a machine tool for producing flat surfaces, slots, etc. on small work pieces by cutting away surplus material. The basic parts of a shaper are a pedestal supporting a ram which moves horizontally in guideways with a reciprocating motion. The cutting tool is held in a CLAPPER BOX positioned at the front end of the ram, and the work piece is clamped onto a table supported by the pedestal and positioned below the ram. The table may be adjusted vertically to accommodate the size of the work piece, and either it, or the tool, may be capable of sideways traverse. Besides cutting flat surfaces or slots, keyways may also be made on a shaper.

Marc Isambard Brunel (1769–1849) designed a machine similar to a shaper c.1805 for use in Portsmouth naval dockyard for shaping wooden ships' BLOCKS. But James Nasmyth (1809–90) is usually credited with the invention of the metal cutting shaper in 1836 at his Patricroft works, near Manchester. Joseph Whitworth (1803–87) added his QUICK RETURN MOTION soon afterwards, which reduced machining time by speeding up the return (non-cutting) stroke of the ram.

shearing, *see* CROPPING FRAME

shear steel a type of steel made in the early days of steel making, used in particular for cloth shears, cutlery, and other edge cutting tools and implements. It was made by heat welding a pile of bars of BLISTER STEEL together, and work-hardening the piece under a hammer in a forge to make a steel capable of providing a sharp and durable cutting edge when ground. There was single shear steel, made as described, and double shear steel which was single shear steel bent back on itself and hammered down to its original unbent thickness. Ambrose Crowley's Winlaton forges near Newcastle upon Tyne was the main source of British shear steel in the 18th century, until Sheffield production outstripped it by the end of the century. At the same time, this type of steel was also imported from Westphalia, and is also known as German steel.

sheave 1. a grooved wheel or pulley in a lifting device over which a rope or chain passes. A sheave works as one of a pair of similar wheels, with the rope anchored to the frame holding the top wheel, and passing over both wheels. When the rope is pulled, the sheaves are drawn towards each other by a distance equal to half the distance the rope is moved. This gives a mechanical advantage of two, and by arranging several pairs of sheaves side-by-side on each axle, the mechanical advantage is increased by the number of pairs of sheaves involved. This is the basis of manual lifting blocks and is also used in reverse on hydraulic JIGGERS, where the short stroke of the hydraulic ram is multiplied by the sheaves to raise a load a useful distance. **2.** the circular central part of an ECCENTRIC, round which the strap fits and slides as the sheave rotates.

shed (or shedde, sheed) the horizontal open passage formed by the raising of selected warp threads across the width of a loom. The shuttle passes through the shed, leaving a length of weft thread behind it which is BEATEN UP by the REED against the previously woven part of the cloth to consolidate it. The shed is then reformed for the reverse pass of the shuttle, and in this way the up and over configuration of the weave is made, the warp threads passing over and under the weft threads according to the type of weave being constructed. The shedding motion is obtained on the loom either by the raising and lowering of HEALDS in the case of TAPPET or DOBBY looms, or by similar movements of JACQUARD HARNESSES. The word shed has the meaning of to separate or divide.

Sheffield plate a kind of silver plating, developed in 1743 in Sheffield by Thomas Bolsover (1705–88), made by fusing or soldering thin sheets of silver onto both sides of a thicker sheet of copper, and rolling the sandwich down to a thin sheet. It was used for buttons, candelabra, coffee and tea services, etc. as a cheaper substitute for solid silverware, and was made principally in Sheffield and Birmingham until the late 19th century. A fine silver wire was soldered onto any exposed edges to cover the copper. Joseph Hancock (1711–91) also developed the process.

shell boiler a steam-raising vessel comprising a large diameter drum – the shell – which contains water in its lower part and steam above. Most shell boilers have an internal firegrate with a flue or in some cases, tubes, through which the products of combustion pass on their way to a chimney. Various types of shell boiler are shown in Fig. 61.

Simple shell boilers were horizontal cylinders supported on brickwork with an external firegrate beneath to heat the water. A variation on this was the HAYSTACK BOILER. Shell boilers with internal firegrates gave better heating and fuel economy: the first such boiler was the CORNISH BOILER, followed soon after by the LANCASHIRE BOILER. These are of horizontal design, and similar, though smaller boilers of vertical design are also available. The locomotive boiler is a shell type boiler fitted with a large number of tubes through which the hot gases pass, the tubes collectively giving a large heating surface for rapid steaming.

Shell boilers are limited in the pressure that may be generated within them, the upper limit usually being around 200 psi. Pressures in excess of this are dangerous and can cause explosions if the stresses raised in the shell, often weakened by corrosion, become too great. Nevertheless, shell boilers, particularly the Lancashire boiler, were mainstays of industry in the days of the steam engine for powering mills etc., whilst the locomotive boiler reigned supreme for railways, traction engines, road rollers, etc. As higher steam pressures were called for, particularly when steam turbines were introduced for electric power station work, WATERTUBE BOILERS were introduced. *See also* VERTICAL BOILER.

Nasmyth-Wilson steam-operated shingling hammer at Bolton, Lancs.

shillibeer (or shellibere) the first name for an omnibus, so called after George Shillibeer (1797–1866) who introduced horse-drawn buses in London in July 1829. He also patented a mourning carriage and hearse combined in one vehicle, which was also known as a shillibeer (patent no. 9086, 1841).

shingling hammering of an iron bloom while still in a plastic state to force out slag, and to consolidate the metal into a block. The operation is carried out in a shingling hammer, which comprises an anvil placed beneath a massive frame carrying a vertical steam-operated hammer or a HELVE HAMMER, in the days before steam power was available. The word shingling comes from the French *cingleur*, which is a squeezing machine.

shipping hole an entrance in a warehouse into which a canal penetrates the building so that canal boats may be loaded and unloaded under cover, and in a secure area.

ships The main interest for the industrial archaeologist in ships lies in their engines and boilers, method of propulsion, and the materials of construction used for the hull.

Apart from ancient galleys, manned by banks of oarsmen, the movement of air captured by sails was the only means of propulsion for ships for centuries, and the universal material for hull construction was timber. Shipping was extremely important to the British economy, and by the 18th century shipping was the second biggest employer after agriculture. During the Industrial Revolution many of the country's raw materials were imported from abroad – cotton, silk, dyestuffs, iron, etc. –

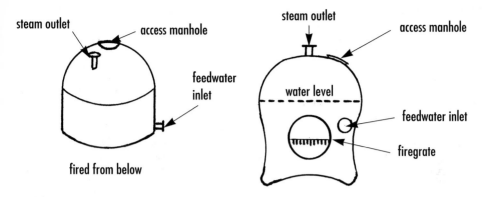

(a) Haystack or balloon boiler (flat sides and base, externally fired, brickwork setting not shown)

(b) Waggon boiler (curved sides and base for strength, internally fired, brickwork setting not shown)

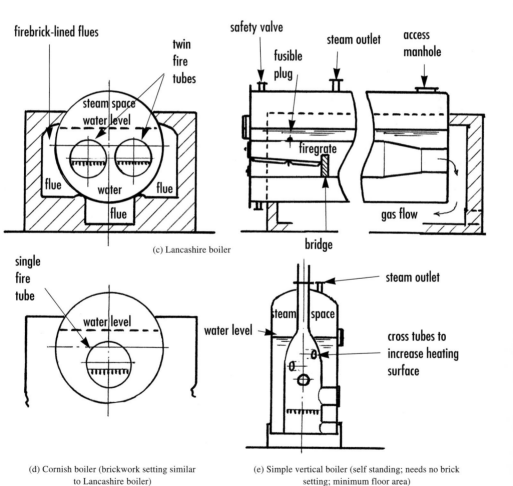

(c) Lancashire boiler

(d) Cornish boiler (brickwork setting similar to Lancashire boiler)

(e) Simple vertical boiler (self standing; needs no brick setting; minimum floor area)

Fig. 61. Shell type steam boilers

333

whilst certain foodstuffs such as tea and coffee had to be brought in to feed the rapidly growing population. Additionally, finished goods had to be exported to overseas markets.

When the steam engine was invented, it was soon applied to boats and ships as a means of propelling vessels which was independent of the vagaries of the winds. The first method was to drive revolving paddle wheels. Since early steam engines could be unreliable, ships in the pioneering days of steam were usually fitted with sails as well, on a belt-and-braces basis. The use of steam developed more quickly on ships than on steam road carriages and locomotives in the early 19th century: large, slow moving Watt-type BEAM ENGINES could be fitted or adapted on board where there was more space available than on a locomotive. There were fewer problems involved than those facing railway pioneers: there was no gradient to overcome, no special tracks were needed; the capital expenditure needed to provide a sea-based mode of transport was considerably less than that required for a reasonably sized railway; and no Act of Parliament was required to obtain a route. However, although there were no space restrictions for fitting a steam engine into a sea-going vessel, the space occupied by fuel for a long voyage was at the expense of cargo space. This was partly overcome by restricting the fuel space and creating coaling stations at strategically placed ports for refuelling. The need to reduce fuel space encouraged the development of more efficient engines and boilers, so that less fuel was consumed; in this respect, marine engine design led the way for greater efficiency and economic use of fuel. This was largely met by COMPOUNDING, Alfred Holt (1829–1911) being a leading exponent of this development.

The earliest steam ships had traditional wooden hulls, and were driven by paddle wheels either placed on each side or at the stern. The idea of using a paddle wheel obviously came from the waterwheel where, instead of moving water rotating a wheel on a fixed site, driving a wheel round in comparatively still water would cause the ship to move along. The earliest experiments on paddle wheels were conducted on inland waters with small boats. William Symington (1763–1831) patented a steam engine for driving a tug boat (patent no. 2544, 1801) which was fitted into the second *Charlotte Dundas* and launched on the Forth and Clyde Canal in 1803. She had a wooden hull with a stern paddle wheel, and was powered by a double-acting cylinder of 22 in diameter and 4 ft stroke, using coal as the fuel.

The first steam ship to run a regular service was the *Comet*, which operated on the Clyde in 1812 between Glasgow and Greenock. She was built by Henry Bell (1767–1830) and had a wooden hull driven by two pairs of side paddles arranged in tandem. Seven years later the *Rob Roy*, built by David Napier (1790–1869), commenced a regular passenger and mail service across the Irish Sea between Glasgow and Belfast, and two years later she began the first cross-Channel service between England and France.

By the end of the 18th century wrought iron in rolled plate form was becoming available through the work of Henry Cort (1740–1800). Since wrought iron is stronger than timber, it began to be used for ships' hulls, and the *Aaron Manby*, built 1821–2, was the first iron hulled paddle steam ship. She was built in sections in Tipton, Salop., taken to London, assembled and fitted with an engine with two oscillating cylinders designed by Aaron Manby (1776–1850). After trials on the Thames, she was exported to France for working on the river Seine.

Attention was now focused on the possibility of steam driven paddle ships being used for longer voyages, particularly for crossing the Atlantic. The *Savannah* had made the crossing from the USA to Britain in 1819, but only part of the way by steam, the rest under sail. There was considerable discussion at the time as to whether a steam ship could carry enough fuel to make the crossing. A Canadian paddle ship, the *Royal William*, made the crossing in 1833 entirely under steam, and five years later, Isambard Kingdom Brunel's first ship, the *Great Western*, commenced regular trans-Atlantic runs, a service which lasted for eight years. She was a wooden hulled ship with two enormous steam engines with 73.5 in diameter cylinders by 7 ft stroke, driving side paddles.

Alternative means of propulsion were now being investigated. In 1836 experiments were under way using screw propellers instead of paddle wheels. Two inventors applied for patents within two months of each other: Francis Pettit Smith (1808–74) in May (patent no. 7104) and John Ericsson (1803–89) in July (patent no. 7149). Ericsson fitted his propeller in the *Francis B. Ogden* in 1837, and Smith put his design in the *Archimedes* in 1838. The superiority of screw propellers over paddle wheels was demonstrated effectively in the famous tug-of-war of 1843: Brunel was building the *Great Britain* intending to use paddle wheels, but the performance of the *Archimedes* made him change his mind after conducting careful trials with her, and *Great Britain* was fitted with a screw. She was launched in 1844 with an iron hull, as well as sails. After a short spell on trans-Atlantic voyages, she operated between Liverpool and Melbourne, Australia for many years.

By the 1850s there was a gradual move away from wooden hulled vessels with paddle wheels to iron hulled vessels with screws, and after cheap steel became available in 1880, steel hulls were introduced. As ships grew larger and larger, docks had to be built or enlarged to accommodate them. Britain enjoyed a supreme place in shipbuilding in late Victorian days: in 1890 the tonnage of British ships accounted for nearly half that of the world, but later years saw a decline against fierce competition from other countries.

Corlett, E.C.B. *The Iron Ship*, Moonraker Press, 1980
Emmerson, G.S. *John Scott Russell: A Great Victorian Engineer and Naval Architect*, Murray, 1977
Paffett, J. 'Ships' hulls since Cheops: an engineer's view', *Industrial Archaeology Review* X (1987), 84–99
Spratt, H.P. *The Birth of the Steam Boat*, Griffin, 1958

shire, *see* BOON

shirs small pieces of vegetable matter caught up in raw wool, picked up by the sheep whilst grazing.

shoddy a cheap woollen cloth made from recycled soft woollen rags, such as old knitted goods, discarded worsted cloth, and any loosely woven woollen materials. Shoddy was first made in Yorkshire *c.*1809, after experiments by Benjamin Law, the 'Shoddy King', who devised a machine for tearing old rags to shreds so that they could be recovered and re-used. A later improvement to the preliminary process was the invention of the GARNETTING machine by Charles Garnett in 1859, which produced a finer material. The shredded material then underwent a series of processes similar to that of MUNGO to make the final cloth. Sometimes new wool was added in a preparatory stage to enhance the end result.

The origin of the word shoddy is obscure, but since the material is a cheap inferior cloth, the word has come to mean anything of poor workmanship or quality in everyday language. The fortune of the shoddy (and the more superior mungo) industry was very dependent on the price of new raw wool. When the price of the latter was high, shoddy and mungo manufacture prospered, but declined when the cost of raw wool fell.

Jubb, S. *The History of the Shoddy Trade*, 1860

shode (or shoad) small pieces of ore found lying on or near the surface indicating the presence of a vein in the immediate neighbourhood. Many minerals have been discovered by shoding (i.e. searching), as shown by the remains of shoding pits where excavations have been made. The word is probably of Cornish origin.

shoe (or slipper) the chute down which grain tumbles from the feed hopper to direct it into the eye of the RUNNER stone in a corn mill. The shoe is vibrated by the action of a DAMSEL or CLAPPER to ensure an even flow of grain into the stones.

shoot (or shute) the WEFT in a cloth.

shot tower a tall tower with means for melting an alloy of lead and arsenic at the top, from which lead shot or pellets are manufactured for use in firearms and by fishermen. The molten metal is poured through a perforated zinc tray, and allowed to fall some 100–150 ft through the air inside the tower into a water bath at the base; the globules solidify and form perfect small spheres as they fall. The water bath prevents deformation which would result by impact on a solid surface. It is said that this method of making lead shot was discovered by accident by William Watts, a plumber of Bristol, who took out a patent (no. 1347) in 1782. He built Britain's first shot tower about 1787 in Bristol, which is now demolished. The arsenic is added to the lead to harden it. Before Watt's invention, lead shot was cast in metal moulds.

shove, *see* BOON

shuttered sail, *see* SPRING SAIL

shutting (or shutying) a blacksmithing term for forge-welding two metal parts together when hot. The term is also used in CHAIN MAKING, to mean joining together the ends of a link.

shuttle 1. the boat-shaped holder which carries the weft thread wound on a COP or PIRN bobbin on a loom. It is usually made from a hard wood with a metal pointed tip at each end, and an eye at one end through which the WEFT thread is passed. The bobbin is replaced with a full one when all the weft has been used in weaving, the shuttle being rapidly thrown from side to side of the loom paying out the thread at each pass or PICK. The shuttle passes through the SHED made in the warps by the loom mechanism, gliding across the RACEBOARD. *See also* FLYING SHUTTLE. **2.** a junction where two water channels meet with suitable gating, so that the flow may be directed either way as desired. **3.** a sluice or gate controlling the flow of water onto a waterwheel.

Shuttle Club an association formed by Yorkshire clothiers in 1733 to cover legal costs if they were prosecuted by John Kay for using his FLYING SHUTTLE illegally.

Siamese engine name given in the mid-19th century to a design of steam engine in which the piston rods from two side-by-side cylinders were connected to a common T-shaped crosshead with a single connecting rod driving the crank. Such engines were used on ships in the 1840s. The name comes from the famous male twins Chang and Eng Bunker (1811–74), born in Siam (now Thailand), who were permanently joined at the breastbone and were exhibited as curiosities in various countries, including Britain.

side lever engine a design of BEAM STEAM ENGINE introduced *c*.1800 in which, instead of a single overhead rocking beam, there are two beams positioned alongside the cylinder, one either side, giving a lower overall height. Such engines were popular for marine work and had also short strokes compared with their cylinder bores, again to reduce height. Side lever engines were also used in textile mills by William Fairbairn (1799–1874). *See* Fig. 62.

side pound, *see* POUND

side weir a sideways exit from a canal controlled by a gate, sluice, or boards held in vertical slots, which enables excessive water to be discharged into a nearby river to control the level of water in the canal. It is sometimes called a waste weir or spillway.

Siemens–Martin process, *see* OPEN HEARTH FURNACE

sifter (or dresser, jog-scry) a device in a corn mill for sieving loose flour or meal to grade the size and separate oversize material, which is returned to the grindstones. It usually comprises a box into which the flour etc. is emptied: the box contains sieves of different mesh size and is automatically vibrated to give a shaking action, being suspended by leather straps to allow this.

silk the fine thread produced by the caterpillar *Bombyx mori* of the silk moth. It differs from all other textile raw materials as it is in the form of a continuous filament and not composed of individual short fibres. The caterpillars or silk worms, about 3 in long, feed on the leaves of the mulberry tree, either the *Morus alba* or the *Moras nigri*; the worm eats for from 35 to 42 days, after which it begins to spin a cocoon around itself. To do this, it extrudes a twin thread, one from each side of its head through

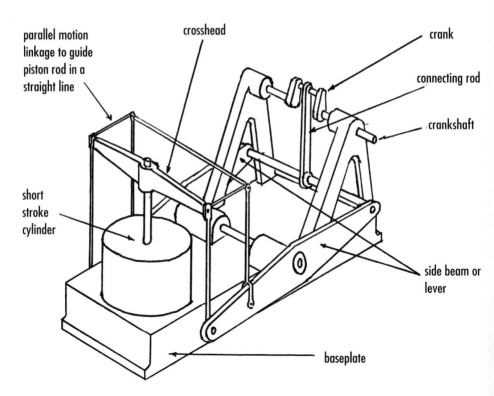

Fig. 62. Side lever steam engine

exit holes called spinerets, at the same time waving its head in a figure of eight motion to deposit layers of round, smooth threads inside the cocoon. After about three days the cocoon is made, and the worm is killed by stifling it by steam or heat to prevent it changing into a moth and forcing its way out of the cocoon, thus destroying the silk filament. A 1 lb weight of silk worms produce about 10–12 lb of silk in a year. An early name used in Britain for a cocoon was a cod.

Sericulture, the breeding of silk worms for the production of silk, dates back to ancient times in China. It was introduced into Europe in about the 6th century and was particularly cultivated in Italy, where the making of silk yarn was a secret process. Attempts at sericulture in Britain took place in the late 17th and mid-18th century to try to supply the French HUGUENOT refugee silk workers with an indigenous raw material, but the experiment did not develop, and raw silk was imported from India and Italy. Later, France developed a sericulture and silk industry centred mainly around Lyon.

To prepare the silk for use it is first unwound from the cocoon. This highly skilled operation is called reeling, and several cocoons have to be unwound together to make a thread strong enough for further processing, the individual filaments being too fine to use singly. Secondly, several reeled threads are twisted together to make a stronger silken yarn. This operation is called silk throwing (*see* THROWING MACHINE, THROWING MILL).

Silk was always an expensive luxury in Britain, its lustrous property being highly prized, and it is easily dyed. The silk industry in Britain was mainly concentrated in London, Derbyshire, north Cheshire around Macclesfield, some in Manchester, and also around Braintree in Essex. The growth of the industry was, however, slow in the 18th century, due to competition from cheap imports. The industry does, nevertheless, have the distinction of being the pioneer in the establishment of the first true factory – that of Thomas Cotchett, who opened a water-powered silk mill in Derby in 1702.

In addition to throwing reeled silk to make a thread, WASTE SILK is spun to make a thread in a similar manner to that of cotton.

silk weaving an industry which, like other textiles, existed both as a domestic and later, as a factory industry. Domestic weaving was carried out on hand looms in weavers' garrets, top storey rooms above the living quarters running the full width of the house from front to back with long, large windows front and back to give plenty of daylight. Many such houses still exist today in silk towns, e.g. Macclesfield, Ches. With the coming of the factory system, power looms were installed in mills by the early 19th century and silk throwing mills provided the silk yarn for weaving.

Weaving of silk began in Spitalfields, London, and Canterbury, Kent, in the 15th century as the result of an influx of Flemish refugees who brought their skills with them and settled in these areas. By the 18th century the industry had concentrated in the area between Manchester and Derby with some work being done in Paisley, Scotland, and the southern centres declined.

Silk fabrics were woven on simple wooden broad looms by hand, using plain weaving at first, but figured fabrics became available by the end of the 16th century. These were woven on DRAW LOOMS which required the assistance of a boy to activate the SHEDDING by hand to create the pattern being woven. By about 1820 the JACQUARD mechanism had been introduced into Britain from France, although difficulties were encountered in fitting the mechanism into the existing weavers' garrets because of the extra height needed to fit the mechanism on top of the loom. Soon after this, metal framed power looms began to be built, and Moses Poole (*fl.*1817–52) obtained a patent (no. 6981, 1836) for fitting the Jacquard mechanism to a power loom. By now weaving had become mainly a factory activity, although some domestic weaving persisted.

In addition to weaving broad silk, silk had been woven into ribbons and braids on narrow looms from the early days. The early looms wove plain-weave ribbons etc. singly, but by the late 17th century DUTCH LOOMS were weaving up to twelve ribbons simultaneously. In 1760 Joseph Stell invented a method which permitted the weaving of patterns and figures on ribbons (patent no. 753).

The British silk industry gradually declined in the face of cheaper imports, and today the amount of silk woven is only a shadow of that produced around the time of the GREAT EXHIBITION OF 1851.

In the silk industry, thread for warps is called organzine, and weft is called tram.

Calladine, A. and Fricker, Jean. *East Cheshire Textile Mills*, Royal Commission on the Historical Monuments of England, 1993
Warner, F. *The Silk Industry of the United Kingdom: Its Origins and Development*, 1921

silver a metallic element, brilliant white in colour, whose chemical symbol is Ag from the Latin *argentum*. It can occur in natural form, but is usually found as a compound with sulphur, chlorine, and in association with lead and copper ores. The average yield in lead is in the order of 16 oz per ton of lead. The chief silver ore is argentite or silver sulphide.

Silver has been known from ancient times. It was mined in mid-Europe and Germany in the late Middle Ages, and later in the 16th century extensive supplies were brought to Europe from South America by Spain. It has always been a valuable metal, and has been used for coinage, decorative articles, bullion, etc. It can be separated from its compounding element by several methods: CUPELLATION from the lead ore GALENA; the PATTINSON PROCESS of 1833; and the PARKES PROCESS. Silver in thin sheet form is the main constituent of SHEFFIELD PLATE.

Silver Cross the name given to the inland system of trunk CANALS which linked the four principal navigational rivers of England – the Mersey, Severn, Thames, and Trent – and through them connected with the surrounding seas. The system effectively connected Runcorn on the Mersey, Stourport on the Severn, Oxford on the Thames, and Derwentmouth on the Trent. The final link completing the Cross was made in 1790, with its centre at Birmingham. It was James Brindley (1716–72) who christened this important group of canals, also simply known as the Cross. The canals forming the group are the Trent and Mersey, the Staffordshire and Worcestershire, the Coventry and the Oxford.

simple lines or cords attached to the warp threads in a DRAW LOOM. They pass through holes in a board to keep them separate, and are tensioned by weights. They were pulled in strict rotation by a draw-boy standing at the side of the loom to produce patterned cloth by raising certain warp threads to form the SHED for the SHUTTLE to pass through.

Sims compound engine a form of tandem COMPOUNDING of early BEAM ENGINES introduced by James Sims in the 1840s in Cornwall (patent no. 8942, 1841). He mounted a high pressure steam cylinder directly on top of a low pressure one, the steam passing from the top cylinder to the bottom one, with both pistons on a common piston rod. After some popularity, his principle lost favour and the WOOLF method of compounding became the standard.

Harris, T.R. 'James Sims and the compound engine', *Engineering* CLV (1943)

singeing of cloth passing a woven fabric across a bank of burning jets of gas, or over a hot copper plate at speed, to burn off any raised small fibres or hairs, which produces a smooth cloth of even thickness and improves its appearance. It is a preliminary process in the bleaching of cotton cloth, and is also known as gassing. Thread intended for LACE MAKING was singed in the 19th century by passing it through a coal gas flame: this gave a more compact appearance by burning off loose fibres and slightly raised the COUNT by reducing the hank weight.

single-acting the power stroke from a piston working inside a cylinder, such as a steam engine, in one direction only. All early steam engines, such as Newcomen's, and Watt's earliest, were single-acting with the power stroke downwards; this pulled the overhead rocking beam down through an arc equivalent to the stroke by means of a chain. The return stroke, upwards, was caused by the weight of the PUMP RODS taking their end of the beam down, the chain attached to the piston rod end pulling the piston up in the cylinder so that the next power stroke could begin. James Watt (1736–1819) introduced DOUBLE-ACTING on steam engines in 1782.

singles yarn the end product from a spinning machine, i.e. a single thread. When a stronger yarn is required, more than one thread is twisted together to form what is called a manifold yarn, an operation carried out on a doubler (*see* DOUBLING).

sinker 1. a component in a knitting machine representing the moving needle of a hand-held pair of knitting needles. It is a specially shaped thin metal bar which pushes a length of yarn over the machine needles to form a new loop. Sinkers were first used by the Revd William Lee in his STOCKING FRAME of 1589, and were called jack sinkers since they hung from horizontal metal bars or jacks (*see* Fig. 69). Lead sinkers are extra components added later by Lee's brother James to produce finer knitted fabrics. They were so called because they were fixed to a transverse bar by being embedded in molten lead. **2.** a man employed to construct a mine shaft. The sinking of a shaft was usually contracted out by a mine company to a firm specializing in this type of work.

sintering the fusing of powders into cakes or solids by heat. It is a method of preparing powdered ores and concentrates for smelting by heating in a sintering furnace, and was introduced around the end of the 19th century. Sinter coal is another name for a caking coal; the word is derived from cinder.

Sites and Monuments Records (SMRs) registers and records held by counties of those historic sites and monuments which lie within their boundaries. The records are used to aid planning, and include some sites of interest to industrial archaeologists. Each county has a Site and Monuments Officer who maintains the register.

Six Acts of 1819 collective name given to the six parliamentary measures to control public disorder introduced immediately after PETERLOO and also known as the Gagging Acts. They covered the restriction of public meetings; quicker trials of political agitators; a ban on drilling of private persons; powers to seize seditious and blasphemous literature, and arms; and an extension of stamp duties on newspapers and periodicals. The measures were repealed at various dates towards the end of the 19th century.

sizing hardening and strengthening warp threads by dipping them in a cereal paste or size to increase the coherence of the fibres. This enables the yarn to resist better the treatment they are subjected to during weaving. *See also* WARP SIZING, DRESSING FRAME.

skaws, *see* SLAG

skein a length of yarn in HANK form based on its weight, not on any standard length.

skew arch an arch, such as part of a bridge, which has its axis at an oblique angle to its face, such as an arch which carries a railway across a road not at 90° to the road. If constructed from brickwork, the courses of bricks under the arch would lie in an oblique line across the axis of the roadway. The skew arch is said to have been originated by William Chapman (1749–1832) around 1788 on the Kildare Canal in Ireland. When the brick courses are skewed across an arch, planes of weakness are avoided which could develop when the bricks are laid at right angles to the walls of the arch. The advantage of a skew bridge is that it avoids a double bend where a road crosses a railway at an angle, which would occur if an arch of minimum span (i.e. at right angles to the railway) were used. The first skew arch across a railway is probably that at Rainhill Station on the Liverpool to Manchester Railway: this crosses the line at an angle of 34°, giving a safer road crossing with no impediment to or slowing down of traffic. A skew bridge was called a swin bridge in northern dialect, swin meaning to cross diagonally.

skin wool, *see* SLIPE WOOL

slabbing mill a rolling mill which produces slabs of steel wider than they are thick for subsequent rolling into plates, sheets and strips. *See also* COGGING MILL.

slack belt drive a method for intermittently taking power from a continuously rotating pulley to drive some other machinery, also known as a band CLUTCH.

slag the impurities which float as a layer on top of molten metal during smelting and refining processes. These are skimmed off and frequently dumped as unwanted material forming slag heaps, although some slags have a further use as road materials or fertilizers. Old slag heaps are often the only remains of former furnaces, etc. long abandoned and destroyed, and the metallurgical examination of the slag may reveal the type of activity which was once carried on at the site and the processes used. Slag is also known as dross, cinders, or skaws.

slag hearth a furnace for remelting lead slag to recover more lead. It is only economic when the price of lead is high enough to warrant the expense of running the furnace.

slasher a machine for applying protective size to yarn intended for warp. This type of machine was jointly invented by James Bullough, John Walmsley, and David Whittaker, and patented by them in 1853 (patent no. 2293). It got its name from its rapid working. *See* WARP SIZING.

slate a metamorphosed sedimentary rock of a clay or silt grade, found principally in north Wales, the Lake District, and north Cornwall. It can be easily split along planes of natural cleavage into thin smooth sheets of uniform thickness (the term comes from the old French *esclat*, meaning to splinter or burst). Its impervious nature makes it particularly suitable as a roofing material, which is its main use. Slates vary somewhat in colour, the most common being the grey-blue or purplish-blue Welsh slate. Green slate (containing chlorite) is found in the Lake District, and a reddish tinge (containing haematite) may be found in Cornwall and elsewhere.

Slate is quarried or mined in large pieces which are sawn to size and split by hand into thin sheets and trimmed to various standard sizes for roof slates. Larger slabs have been used for items such as kitchen sinks, paving flags, mantelpieces, gravestones, and thin sheets for school writing slates in Victorian days. Suitably sized blocks not good enough for splitting and left untrimmed were often used as local building materials for farms and cottages and for boundary walling.

Digging for slate commenced in a small way as a cottage industry in the early 18th century for local consumption. By the late 18th century entrepreneurs had taken over and slate production increased. The coming of the canals and later the railways enormously widened the market for slate roofing materials, and large numbers of houses and factories in the emerging industrial towns were roofed, in particular, by Welsh slate. Large quarries were cut into the hillsides of north Wales, and extraction from underground caverns was also developed. Quarries were worked in terraces, and inclines and light railways built to bring the slate from its source down to the dressing sheds. Because the quarries were often remote, NARROW GAUGE RAILWAYS such as the Ffestiniog Railway were constructed to transport the slate to the nearest harbour or rail head, where coastal vessels or standard gauge railways conveyed the slate to more distant markets. Slate output peaked around the end of the 19th century, when some 500,000 tons were quarried per annum, most of it Welsh. In a few decades demand had declined: cheaper clay roofing tiles replaced slates and its main market was lost. Very few quarries are working today, and large tips of discarded waste debris scar the countryside around the deserted quarries.

Slate was usually quarried by gangs of four men working as a team. There would be two rockmen extracting the blocks of slate from the quarry face, one man splitting the blocks into thin sheets, and the fourth, the dresser, trimming them to size. Power for the machinery, such as saws, was from WATERWHEELS or PELTON WHEELS. Houses were often built nearby for the miners and quarrymen and their families; alternatively, barrack-like accommodation was provided, the men living there during the week, and returning to their homes at weekends.

Isherwood, J.G. *Slate from Blaenau Ffestiniog*, AB Publishing, 1988
Johnson, P. (ed.) *Ffestiniog Railway Gravity Trains*, Ffestiniog Railway Heritage Group, 1986
Lewis, M.J.T. and Denton, J.H. *Rhosydd Slate Quarry*, Cottage Press, 1974
Lindsay, J. *A History of the North Wales Slate Industry*, David and Charles, 1974
Williams, M. *The Slate Industry*, Shire Publications, Album No. 268, 1991

slave trade   shipment of slaves from Africa to the New World during the 18th and part of the 19th century, to work on cotton and other plantations. Slave trading was based on the Triangular Trade. Ships sailed from England to the west coast of Africa with woollen goods, steel swords and ironmongery which were traded with local chiefs for slaves; the slaves were shipped to the West Indies and the east coast of North America, where they were sold to work on sugar, tobacco, and cotton plantations; and on the return journey to England, coffee, rum (made from sugar cane), tobacco and raw cotton were brought. Cotton became the most important commodity brought back, and North America became the main

source of supply for the British cotton industry in the 18th and 19th centuries.

Slave trading by Britain commenced in 1709, when one ship sailed from Liverpool with fifteen slaves brought back from Africa. This disreputable trade developed over the next hundred years to become a lucrative business. England was not alone in slave trading, with the French, Dutch, Portuguese, and Danes all taking part, although to a lesser degree. Many millions of slaves were shipped across to the New World, usually under the most inhuman conditions aboard ship. In 1807 Britain prohibited slave trading by Act of Parliament, and another Act in 1833 liberated nearly 800,000 slaves in the British West Indies. It was not until after the American Civil War (1861–5), which arose largely out of the slavery question, that slavery was finally abolished in the southern states of North America; the cotton industry in Britain suffered a decline during the American Civil War as supplies were cut off (*see* COTTON FAMINE).

sleeper   1. the transverse supporting beam for railway rails, usually of timber, to spread the wheel loading and maintain GAUGE. Sleepers were once known as dormant timbers. **2.** a cord of the harness which bears the WARP in weaving.

sley   (or slay, sly) the movable part of a loom which may be pivoted at its base (underslung), or from above (overslung), and which oscillates through a small arc in the vertical plane. The sley carries the REED, the raceboard or shuttle race (*see* RACE) and the shuttle boxes; the arms carrying the sley are called the sley swords. The warps pass through the reed, and when the sley moves towards the weaver, the reed presses (BEATS UP) the weft against the edge of the already woven cloth to consolidate it. The sley has many other different names used in different parts of the country, including lathe, lay, batten and beater.

Sleying a loom means threading the warps through the reed when preparing a loom for weaving. The reed on a stocking frame is known as a slay-bar.

slide valve   a valve controlling the flow of a working medium into and out of an engine cylinder, by a sliding action. There are two types of slide valve: the D-valve and the piston valve. The valves can control steam, water, gas, and air, according to the working medium of an engine.

In D-valves, the moving part of the valve is shaped like a letter D laid on its back. Fig. 63a shows a long D-valve as invented by William Murdock (patent no. 2340, 1799) for double-acting steam engines. The valve slides to and fro across the cylinder PORTS inside a valve chest which is bolted onto the engine cylinder. It receives its motion automatically from a rod driven by an eccentric on the engine crankshaft. High pressure steam from the valve chest enters the cylinder when one port is uncovered by the valve, and simultaneously the other port exhausts spent steam via the hollow space within the D. The ports become inlets and exhausts alternately as the valve slides across them. Improvements were made by Matthew Murray (patent no. 2632, 1802) by introducing LAPS on the valve face, and a LEAD (2) on the ECCENTRIC, to permit expansive working.

A development from the simple D-valve by Jean Jacques Meyer (1804–77) involved a second slide valve called an expansion plate, which worked on top of the main D-valve (*see* Fig. 63b). Steam could not enter the cylinder until the ports in the D-valve and expansion plate lined up. The latter was worked by a separate eccentric, and the distance between the two 'plates' could be altered by rotating the eccentric rod. This drew them either closer together, or farther apart by the left-hand and right-hand screw threads shown, so that the point of steam cut-off could be varied while the engine was running. A further variation of the D-valve is the Trick valve, designed to increase steam flow at small cut-off (*see* Fig. 63d).

Piston valves operated in the same way as D-valves: two small pistons rigidly connected together slid to and fro inside a cylindrical valve chest instead of D-valves (*see* Fig. 79). Piston valves were introduced in the 1820s and are preferred for high pressure steam. Simple slide valves were also used in Lenoir gas engines to control air and gas inlet and exhaust by on–off action (*see* Fig. 63c).

slime pit a large shallow pit dug into the ground, in which the final process for recovering the finest particles or dust of, for example, lead from crushed ore, takes place. Water from the ore washing process is directed into the pit so that the fine particles carried along will settle out in the bottom. Periodically, the water is run off, or the pit allowed to dry out by natural evaporation, and the lead slime dug out and fed into a smelting furnace to recover as much metallic lead as possible. A slime pit is also known as a catch pit.

slip clay reduced to the consistency of cream by adding water, and used to give a smooth coat to rougher ceramic surfaces or, when coloured, to decorate pottery. Slip is also used in the slip-casting process for making irregularly shaped articles such as figurines or pottery flowers,

when it is poured into plaster-of-Paris moulds; a master of the article is made first, from which working plaster-of-Paris moulds are made for the slip-casting process. After the slip has been poured into the mould it is allowed to stand and the moisture contained in the slip is gradually absorbed by the porous mould, until a thin, uniform layer of clay is left adhering to the inner surface of the mould. When the correct thickness is reached, any surplus slip is poured out and after allowing the clay to harden sufficiently for handling, the mould is broken open and the cast hollow article taken out for firing and subsequent processing. The working moulds are thus used only once.

slipe wool (or skin wool) wool from slaughtered sheep, removed by painting the skin with lime.

slitting mill a machine for dividing wide iron strip or sheet into narrow strips, rods, or bars, by passing the material through rollers designed to cut or shape it to the desired cross-section. The raw material is made red hot before slitting to soften it, and cut or shaped whilst hot.

Slitting mills originated in Europe and were introduced into England at Dartford, Kent, by a Belgian immigrant *c*.1590. Hot iron strip was passed through rotating disk cutters driven by water power. Richard Foley (1580–1657) slit iron in a mill near Stourbridge in 1628 for NAIL makers. Henry Cort (1740–1800) patented grooved rolls for iron bar production at Funtley, near Fareham, Hants., as part of his DRY PUDDLING patent (no. 1351, 1783). This method greatly increased the output of iron bars over the old TILT-HAMMER method of bar making. Early slitting mills were not very efficient until steam power was harnessed to drive them, when the greater power enabled faster production rates and thicker material to be cut.

sliver a thick 'rope' or strand of soft, untwisted, continuous cotton with approximately parallel fibres, as delivered from a CARDING MACHINE. It is therefore one of the first preparation processes towards the final spinning of cotton into yarn, and the sliver is usually coiled in a tall cylindrical metal can before passing to the next operation to further attenuate the 'rope' into a ROVING. Although the fibres in a sliver are approximately parallel, a certain amount of tangling is necessary to give coherence to the 'rope'.

slope reel an inclined hollow cylinder or reel, made with a silk fabric gauze or skin, which is slowly rotated above a tray, the whole enclosed in a chamber. Corned, i.e. granulated, GUNPOWDER is fed in at the higher end of the sloping cylinder and is tumbled inside it to

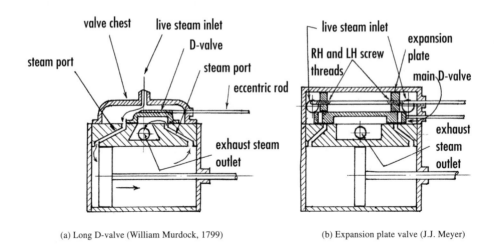

(a) Long D-valve (William Murdock, 1799)

(b) Expansion plate valve (J.J. Meyer)

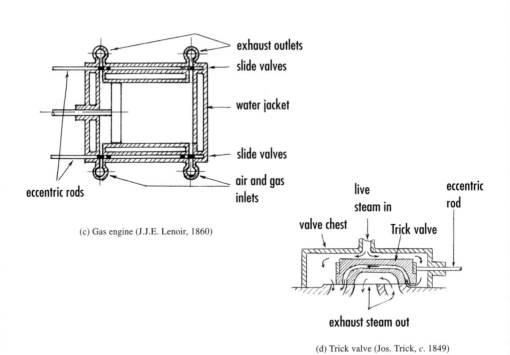

(c) Gas engine (J.J.E. Lenoir, 1860)

(d) Trick valve (Jos. Trick, c. 1849)

Fig. 63. Slide valves

remove any dust adhering to the 'grains', the dust passing through the silk fabric, which acts as a fine sieve, into the tray. When dusted, the gunpowder is removed and finally dried, the collected dust being sent for reprocessing.

slope shaft, *see* DRIFT MINE

slotting machine a machine tool similar in general appearance to a SHAPING MACHINE but in which the head or ram carrying the cutting tool moves in a vertical plane. It is used principally for cutting keyways etc. in the work piece. James Nasmyth (1808–90) developed this type of machine in 1862. Some slotters are hydraulically operated.

slub a fault in a yarn due to a point where some of the fibres are not, or hardly, twisted. Slubs can cause trouble during weaving, although sometimes slubs are deliberately formed at intervals in a yarn to give certain effects in the finished cloth. To slub means to give a light twist.

slubbing frame (or slubbing billy, speed frame) a machine for further attenuating a SLIVER of cotton after it has been through a DRAW FRAME. The object is to reduce the cross-sectional area as another step in preparation for spinning, and here the drawing out of the sliver is such that it is necessary to twist it only slightly in order to preserve its cohesion and rounded form.

Slubbing is achieved by passing one sliver through three pairs of DRAFTING rollers, each pair of rollers rotating faster than the previous pair; the increase in speed draws out the sliver to a smaller dimension. The sliver then passes to a FLYER carried on a revolving spindle, which imparts a slight twist and winds the sliver onto a bobbin. A slubbing frame will carry up to about sixty spindles and will therefore deliver that number of bobbins of lightly twisted cotton strands ready for the next attenuation operation before final spinning into yarn. Sometimes the cotton strands from a slubbing machine are given another pass through a second slubber (or intermediate slubber as it is sometimes known) for cotton intended for fine spinning, i.e. high COUNTS. Intermediate slubbers usually have more spindles and wind onto smaller bobbins, and sometimes two slivers from the first slubber are DOUBLED in this machine. A slubbing is another name for a ROVING.

sluice a mechanical means or valve for controlling the flow of water from a canal, harbour, reservoir, etc., often in the form of a sliding or hinged gate. It is also used as an alternative name for a lockgate PADDLE, and for a LEAT.

slurcock a cam-shaped piece of metal which is slid along a straight iron bar placed near the rear of a STOCKING FRAME, to strike against the spring bars which release the sinkers one by one to form the preliminary loops in the yarn (*see* Fig. 69). To slur means to slide.

slurgall a fault in knitted fabric in the horizontal direction caused by trapping or tightening of the thread during feeding it onto the needles.

smallware textile articles of narrow width such as tapes, ribbons, braids, handkerchiefs and scarves, in cotton, linen, silk, or woollen fabrics. Such articles would be sold by haberdashers, milliners and drapers, and were also carried by a CHAPMAN from farm to farm or village to village. Smallwares were woven on special looms (*see* DUTCH LOOM).

Smeatonian Society society of engineers founded in 1771, named after John Smeaton (1724–92), which was the first society of professional engineers.

smelting the process by which metal is obtained from its ore by the combined action of heat and fluxes. This results in two layers in the melting pot or bath. The layer floating at the top comprises a slag which consists of the GANGUE and fluxes, whilst below is molten impure metal. The slag is skimmed off, and the molten metal often refined in a separate process. Smelting of iron is carried out in a BLAST FURNACE, the iron ore being mixed with a lime flux, and a carbon fuel – CHARCOAL in the early days, COKE later. Other metals such as lead are smelted in furnaces without intimate contact with the heating fuel, as in a REVERBERATORY FURNACE where the fuel is burnt in a separate chamber; here the hot products of combustion are reflected down onto the metallic charge from an overhead refractory roof.

smithy (or forge) the workplace of a blacksmith or ironsmith, where iron was worked into useful artefacts from early times. Blacksmiths made weapons and armour in the Middle Ages, and items such as locks, hinges, spades, ploughshares, and tools for other trades. Iron horseshoes were introduced by the Celts, and the farrier (from the Latin *faber ferrarius*, meaning maker in iron) or shoesmith was a specialized blacksmith once in great demand before mechanization, making horseshoes by hand. There was a Company of Farriers with a royal charter in the 1670s. Machine-made horseshoes were introduced from the USA in the 1870s.

The blacksmith's main material was WROUGHT IRON, usually in bar form, from which he made all manners of agricultural implements and machinery, and architectural items such as grilles, gates and railings, often of a decorative nature. Scythe blades were made from CRUCIBLE STEEL when this material became available. The blacksmith made the metal parts for early looms, spinning machines, locomotives, coaches, waggons and carts, and the iron tyres for wheelwrights. When wrought iron was superseded by STEEL, the blacksmith turned to mild steel.

A smithy or forge comprises a hearth, bellows, anvil and bosh (quenching trough), and a large collection of tools for forging different shapes. A small forge would have hand-operated bellows, while a large industrial forge would have water-powered bellows, and power hammer and shears.

Old BLOOMERIES were known as smithies, and the word appears in some placenames, such as Rockley Smithies in Yorkshire.

smock mill (or frock mill) a windmill with a stationary timber body which contains the grinding machinery, and which supports a rotating cap in which the sails rotate. The cap can be turned into the wind to keep the sails rotating. The name is said to derive from the resemblance of the mill body to a rustic wearing a smock (a long outer garment, usually of linen).

smutter a cleansing or separating machine used in a corn mill for removing smut from grain before it is ground. Smut is a disease caused by the parasitic fungi *Ustilaginales* which attacks grain and looks like lumps of soot, from which it gets its descriptive name. A smutter is driven off an auxiliary shaft from the main drive of the mill.

snake bridge, *see* ROVING BRIDGE

snarl a 'knot' or kink in spun yarn caused by too much twist at one point. The yarn curls back to form the snarl when tension is released.

snifting valve (or blow valve) the small diameter outlet pipe from near the base of the cylinder of a NEWCOMEN ATMOSPHERIC ENGINE through which air (plus a small amount of steam) was expelled by steam coming into the cylinder. A non-return valve in the pipe prevented air from being sucked into the cylinder when the vacuum was later formed under the piston. The snifting valve was found necessary to enable accumulating air, brought in by each cylinderful of fresh steam, to be expelled; otherwise it became gradually impossible to create a satisfactory vacuum. The name arose from the sniffing sound made by the air leaving the end of the pipe.

soaking pit a furnace for holding hot steel ingots to equalize their temperature before they are hot rolled in a STEEL-making or ROLLING MILL complex.

soap making the process of making soap, which consists in essence of boiling either vegetable oils or fats in an alkaline solution until saponification occurs. There are two kinds of soap, soft soap (potassium stearate) and hard soap (sodium stearate).

In the late Middle Ages soap was made in the home, but by the late 16th and 17th centuries demand had increased mainly for the FULLING of woollen cloth, and manufacture commenced commercially. Soft soap was the first to be made in Britain, using caustic potash made from the ashes of burnt bracken or wood, tallow, and somewhat later whale oil. Hard soap was imported at that time from Mediterranean Europe, where it was made from the ashes of burnt BARILLA and olive oil. Often known as Castile soap, it was an expensive luxury. By the 18th century English hard soap was being produced from imported barilla, or Irish and Scottish KELP. Hard soap increased in quantity until by the late 18th century it had surpassed that of soft soap, and soon virtually superseded it, whilst by then domestic manufacture had almost ceased. In the 1830s palm oil from the west coast of Africa was imported in large amounts for soap manufacture. The use of alkali of vegetable origin began to be replaced in the 1820s when soda from the LEBLANC PROCESS became available. This was preferred because it was more concentrated and of consistent quality.

Soap manufacturers had to register with the Customs and Excise authorities and pay a duty, first imposed in 1711. Hard soap could only be made in the presence of an Excise officer, who checked the weight of the ingredients for tax calculation. In 1840 weighing was abolished, and a volumetric gauging substituted. Soap duty was in force with amendments until 1853 when it was finally abolished: in 1816 it was running at 3*d* per lb. Soap makers concentrated in or near ports, such as Bristol, Liverpool, and Warrington, where they had ready access to their imported materials, and inland soap manufacture declined.

Soap was boiled in vessels called coppers. Originally these were made of cast iron, then later, larger ones from riveted wrought-iron plates. The early coppers were heated by external coal fires, but later, steam coils inside the copper were introduced. When thoroughly boiled, salt was added to separate glycerine, water, and any excess alkali from the mixture, and the soap floated on the top as a kind of curd. Adding salt was called salting out. The hot soap was transferred into wooden bottomless boxes, called lifts, which were held in an iron frame of standard dimensions to cool. When solid, the soap was removed and cut into bars by being forced through an array of taut parallel wires (like a cheese cutter). In general, soap making was an unsavoury process in the 19th century, emitting objectionable smells and clouds of escaping steam; soaphouses were usually sited on the outskirts of towns away from habitation as far as was possible.

In late Victorian days, large industrial combines making soap and soap-related products came into being, a notable one being that started by William Hesketh Lever (1851–1925). He began his working life at the age of fifteen, cutting up soap in his father's grocery business, and by 1885 was making 'Sunlight' soap in his own factory at Port Sunlight, Cheshire, going on to found the multinational Unilever Company.

The word soap comes from the Old English 'sape'; it was sometimes spelt sope in the 18th century.

Gibbs, F.W. 'The history of the manufacture of soap', *Annals of Science* IV (1939)
Gittins, L. 'Soapmaking and the Excise laws, 1711–1853', *Industrial Archaeology Review* I (1977)

soapwort   the perennial plant *Saponaria officinalis*, a member of the pink family, which grows 2–3 ft high; its gummy sap was used as a mild detergent for removing grease from wool in 17th- and 18th-century FULLING mills.

Society for the Encouragement of Arts, Manufactures, and Commerce   a body founded in 1754 by William Shipley (1714–1803) to encourage useful arts and inventions in Britain by financial rewards and presentation of medals. For example, since spinning was a bottleneck restricting the manufacture of cloth at that time, the Society offered a prize of £50 in March 1761 'for the best invention of a machine which can spin six threads of wool, flax, cotton or hemp, at one time by one person'. A second prize of £25 was offered. In 1763 the Society awarded the first prize to George Buckley for his six-thread machine. In 1764 a prize of £100 was offered for the greatest improvement in the STOCKING FRAME, and this was won by Samuel Unwin (1712–99), a merchant hosier and cotton spinner of Sutton-in-Ashfield, Notts. (patent no. 1009, 1772). In 1788 the Society gave a gold medal to Abraham Darby III (1750–89) for his part in building the Iron Bridge at Coalbrookdale.

There were six committees in the Society: Agriculture, Chemistry, Colonies, Manufactures, Polite Arts and Trade. Its first industrial exhibition was held in 1761, and a repository of machines and models submitted to it by inventors was kept. The Society published *Transactions* from 1783 to 1851. Its title was shortened to the Society of Arts, and after acquiring royal patronage in 1908 it became known as the Royal Society of Arts (not to be confused with the ROYAL SOCIETY). The Society now has its headquarters in London.

Hudson, D. and Luckhurst, K.W. *The Royal Society of Arts, 1754–1954*, 1954

Society for the Protection of Ancient Buildings (SPAB)   an amenity society founded in 1877. A windmill section was formed in 1931, and water mills were added a few years later; this section deals with all molinological matters.

soda   a general name used for some of the compounds of sodium in common use, such as sodium carbonate. The word comes from the old Latin name *sodanum* for GLASSWORT, a seashore plant which was once a source of soda. Sodium, an alkaline metallic element, does not exist by itself in nature since it is extremely reactive, but it is common when combined with several other elements. It was, however, being separated in metallic form in France in 1854 by H.E. Sainte-Claire Deville by reducing caustic soda with carbon, and was used in an expensive and now obsolete way of making aluminium.

The main compounds of sodium have specific uses. Sodium carbonate, also known as soda ash or washing soda, is a white alkaline crystalline solid, used in the manufacture of glass, hard soap, and for softening water. A method for producing sodium carbonate was invented by Nicholas Leblanc in 1787 (*see* LEBLANC PROCESS). This was later superseded by the process developed by Ernest Solvay in 1863 (*see* SOLVAY PROCESS). Sodium chloride, or common SALT, has many uses, and exists naturally in liquid form as brine (in seawater) and in a solid, as rock salt. Sodium hydroxide, also known as caustic soda, is made by treating quicklime with a hot solution of sodium carbonate, and is strongly alkaline (hence its description 'caustic'). It is used in hard soap and dyes, and was used for making aluminium in the mid-19th century. Sodium nitrate, also known as SALTPETRE, is used in the manufacture of gunpowder, glass, and as a fertilizer; and sodium bicarbonate, or baking soda, is added to bread etc. during baking as a raising agent.

soke mill (or manorial mill) a corn mill (usually a water mill) owned by the medieval lord of the manor, at which all his tenants were obliged to have their corn ground. A toll, called a multure or mulcture, had to be paid to the lord when the corn was ground, and grinding was supposed to be done within 24 hours of receipt of the corn. The toll varied between one-twentieth and one-twelfth of the quantity ground. Such feudal rights continued well into the 19th century in some rural areas. When water-powered textile mills were built, the prior right to the water by the soke mill (its RIPARIAN RIGHT) had to be taken into account by a mill sited on the same watercourse.

sole the lowest level or gallery in a mine, or the floor of a level or SOUGH.

sollar 1. (or saller) a Cornish name for a platform supporting a ladder in a mine shaft. 2. a Cornish mining term for a raised floor or platform under which an airstream passes.

Solvay process (or ammonia-soda process) a chemical process for making sodium carbonate (soda ash) discovered by Ernest Solvay, a Belgian chemist, in 1863. By saturating a concentrated solution of sodium chloride with ammonia and passing carbon dioxide through it, sodium hydrogen carbonate is precipitated and ammonium chloride remains in solution. The Solvay process replaced the older LEBLANC PROCESS since it was cheaper and did not produce the pollution associated with the latter. Solvay uses limestone, ammonia and salt (brine) as its raw materials. The British use of the process commenced near Northwich, Ches., about 1873 by Ludwig Mond (1839–1900), a German chemist working in Widnes, and John Tomlinson Brunner (1842–1919) of Everton, Liverpool, who obtained a licence from Solvay to work his process in England. Mond made many improvements to the original Solvay process, particularly a method of producing cheap ammonia. The Solvay tower is the vertical reaction vessel in which carbonation of the ammoniacal brine takes place.

sorrel (or sorel) a group of several allied plants, of the sorrel variety, including the important variety *Rumex acetosa* which has acidic leaves, from which the roots were used to make a reddish-brown dye. It was also used as a MORDANT.

sough (or suff) a small underground tunnel for draining a mine into a suitable river or stream lying in a nearby valley below the level of the point in the mine being drained. Typical downwards gradients of soughs were about 10 ft per mile; some were a few miles long to reach a discharge point. Their exit was usually stone arched, and sometimes they were paved along their length, or where porous ground was met. Long soughs frequently had vertical ventilation shafts along their length. In some cases, short soughs were also used as access to the mine. The exit of a sough is often called its tail.

Soughs were sometimes tunnelled by the miners of the mine company, but large undertakings were frequently done by sough companies formed specially for the purpose. A sough company was usually paid by taking a percentage of the ore won after the water level in the mine had been lowered from its original position. In this manner, abandoned mines which had previously been waterlogged were re-opened.

Soughs are also known as day levels or adits. In north-east England, a drainage sough is called a watergate, and the same name is used for drainage tunnels from Derbyshire lead mines. A sough can also mean an open ditch or gutter in some districts.

souring the treatment of cloth or yarn by dilute acid as part of the old BLEACHING process. Buttermilk, and later dilute VITRIOL (sulphuric acid) or dilute hydrochloric acid were used. The acids were known as sours, and the purpose of souring was to neutralize the cloth after BOWKING and before GRASSING. The use of dilute sulphuric acid for bleaching was first suggested by Francis Home (1719–1813) of Edinburgh in his book on bleaching, published in 1756.

After the introduction of chemical bleaching, the final process before the cloth was washed and dried was known as white souring. This comprised soaking the cloth in a weak acid to neutralize and remove any chemick (solution of bleaching powder).

sow the main feeder from a BLAST FURNACE to rows of PIGS, along which molten iron is directed when the furnace is being tapped. The name is attributed to the early metallurgist, John Rovenzon (c.1613) who, it is said, likened the feeder to a sow lying with her piglets feeding from her in a row. After the pigs have solidified and been removed from the sow, it is broken up and returned to the furnace for remelting.

space and turning, *see* ROOM AND POWER

spalling (or spaling) the manual process of breaking up pieces of metallic ore on the dressing floor before it is sorted. The term comes from the German *spallern*, meaning split.

Spanish bugloss, *see* ALKANET

sparging the practice of spraying hot water into a MASH TUN during emptying, to remove any residual sugar.

spark pictures, *see* IDENTIFICATION OF METALS

spear the connecting rod joining the end of the overhead beam to the crank on a rotative BEAM STEAM ENGINE. The term is probably a variation of the word spar. The long timber bars hanging down the shaft of a mine to operate the underground pumps by the rocking motion of the beam were also called pump spears.

speed cone a means of driving a machine at different speeds by a belt from a shaft running at constant speed. Two types of speed cone have been used in the days when power transmission was by belting: stepped speed cones, and infinitely variable cones. Stepped cones were often used on machine tools to give different fixed speeds of operation, whilst the other type was commonly used on textile machinery, e.g. cone drums on spinning machines.

Stepped cones comprise sets of adjacent pulleys – three or four is usual – arranged opposite one another so as to form a series of pairs of pulleys, the smallest pulley on one shaft being opposite the largest pulley on the other. By shifting the connecting belt from one pair of pulleys to the other by means of the BELT STRIKING GEAR, the speed ratio is altered. The diameters of each pair of pulleys depends on the speeds of the shafts, and the diameters must also be such that the same belt will operate on both without alteration in length.

Cone drums comprise a pair of wide tapering pulleys arranged opposite each other, the smallest diameter of one being opposite the largest diameter of the other. As with the stepped cones, the connecting belt or rope can be moved along the cones to vary the speed ratio between driving shaft and driven shaft. The profiles of the cones must permit the belt to run at any point along their width without alteration in its length, and because of the gradual taper the speed ratio can be infinitely varied between the highest and lowest ratios.

speed frame a general name given to a series of machines which successively reduce the diameter of ROVINGS before the final spinning into yarn. Usually there is a set of three such frames: first a SLUBBER, followed by an intermediate frame, and then a roving frame. If fine yarns are to be spun, a fourth speed frame called a JACK FRAME is added.

Speenhamland system an early 19th-century outdoor relief scheme for agricultural labourers, devised by local magistrates, at the Pelican Inn, Speenhamland, near Newbury, Berks., in 1795 to alleviate endemic distress among agricultural workers. Its main feature was that low wages were to be supplemented out of the rates by an amount related to the price of bread and the size of a family. The system rapidly spread throughout rural districts in the south of England, and an Act soon followed extending it to the whole country, but it did not have much effect in the north or parts of the Midlands, nor did it reach Scotland and Ireland.

Although intended to be humane, the system in fact had the opposite effect: it tended to keep wages low because farmers knew they would be topped up out of the rates, which soon rose to meet the cost. It also encouraged early marriages with resulting larger families among the poor, since the 'dole' rose with the size of the family. The system reached its height during the Napoleonic wars, when labourers were discouraged from moving to seek work elsewhere for fear of losing their right to relief which could only be obtained in their parish of origin. Industry therefore tended to be starved of workers at a time when it was expanding. The system was eventually replaced by the Poor Law Amendment Act of 1834. *See also* SETTLEMENT, LAW OF.

sphalerite, *see* BLENDE

spider the cast iron component located at the centre of rotation of the sails of a windmill, which activates the linkages to open and close the vanes on each sail. The spider rotates with the sails and has as many 'legs' as there are sails, usually four, sometimes five or six. *See also* PATENT SAIL.

spiegeleisen (or spiegeliron) an alloy of iron, manganese, and carbon used in steel making. It has a white, crystalline, lustrous appearance, taking its name from the German *Spiegel*, meaning mirror, plus *Eisen*, meaning iron.

spill control a method for governing the speed of OIL ENGINES. Fig. 36 shows diagrammatically the arrangement for spill control of an oil engine. The fuel pump plunger is driven from the engine and its outer end is connected by a lever to a small arm which can be partially rotated by the governor (not shown in the diagram). Between the pump plunger and the governor arm a spindle enters the spill valve assembly, terminating in a flat lever which projects under the suction valve stem.

When the engine is running at normal speed, as the pump plunger rises up and down the spindle also rises up and down, lifting and dropping the suction valve, so allowing oil to be pumped to the engine cylinder in a measured quantity. If the engine speeds up, the governor, which is also driven by the engine, speeds up and the arm is moved through an arc. This has the effect of altering the stroke of the spindle causing the suction valve to seat later, and since it remains open longer a lesser quantity of oil passes into the engine cylinder and more is 'spilled' back into the tank. The reduced supply to the engine causes it to slow down until its normal speed is restored, by which time the governor will also have slowed down and resumed its normal position, altering the lever which controls the spindle movement back to its normal position. The reverse happens when the engine slows down, and more oil is pumped into the cylinder until normal speed is regained. The amount of oil reaching the engine is thus regulated according to the power demand on it.

spindle in the textile industry, an essential component in spinning machinery. It comprises a short, small diameter, metal rod which is rotated at speed, and yarn may be spun directly onto it in some machines, whilst in others it is the means for rotating removable bobbins which receive the already spun yarn.

The principle for spinning directly onto a spindle is the basis for several machines. The simple medieval hand spinning wheel had only one spindle: the twisting of a yarn using a spindle is achieved by holding the yarn at a certain angle to the rotating spindle and allowing it to slip off the spindle tip. This puts one twist into the yarn for each revolution of the spindle. When sufficient twist has been put it, the yarn is wound onto the spindle, and the process repeated. The wheel was developed c.1767 by James Hargreaves into the JENNY, which had eight spindles at first; later jennies were made with up to eighty spindles. Samuel Crompton invented the hand-worked MULE which had forty-eight spindles in 1779, and later power driven mules of 1800 had some 400 spindles. By the 1920s, mules with 1,200 spindles were being made. Thus, there has been a continual increase in the number of spindles a machine can operate.

Other spinning machines which use spindles as the means for rotating removable bobbins placed on them, are represented by Richard Arkwright's WATER FRAME of 1769, and RING SPINNING FRAMES, introduced around the mid-19th century. On the former machine, the actual twisting of a yarn is done by revolving FLYERS, and on the latter twist is put in by a traveller running round a metal ring at high speed. In both cases, the spun yarn is wound onto the bobbin held on the spindle.

The size of a spinning machine, or a spinning mill, is given in terms of the number of spindles. The number of spindles in a mill can run up to many thousands, this figure being the cumulative total of all the spindles on individual machines. In 1870, a large mill would have around 50,000 spindles, and eventually a mill of 221,520 spindles was in operation in Rochdale, Lancs., during the 1914–18 war. When mule use was at its peak, there were an estimated 50 million spindles in operation in Lancashire alone.

spindle and whorl the earliest form of hand implement used for spinning fibres into a yarn, and the primitive forerunner of the hand spinning wheel. The simple device comprises a short round stick (the spindle), about 12–15 in long and made of wood or bone, with a notch cut into it near one end and weighted at the other end by a disk-shaped piece of wood, clay, or stone (the whorl, sometimes called the wharve) fastened to it. To use, a short length of previously spun yarn is fastened into the notch, and the spindle suspended in the air from one hand, the whorl hanging at the lower end. The fibres to be spun are placed as a bundle in a DISTAFF, and the short length of previously spun yarn is attached to this bundle. The spindle is given a quick turn to set it spinning, the whorl acting as a FLYWHEEL to maintain the spin. Whilst the spindle is spinning, the spinner allows fibres to be drawn through the fingers of one hand from the distaff as they are spun into a yarn. The spindle slowly descends, the weight providing draft as more fibres are spun into yarn, and before the whorl hits the ground, or the spindle stops turning, the spinner stops the motion. To prevent the twist running up into the distaff, the fibres are clamped in the other hand near the distaff. After stopping the spindle, the yarn is removed from the notch and wound onto the spindle as far as the point where it was prevented from twisting, and fastened back into the notch again. The process is repeated, spinning other short lengths until all the fibres in the distaff have been converted into yarn.

This simple device could spin any sort of fibre, and being portable, could be used anywhere, even when walking about if necessary. It was mostly used by women. Yarn made this way was, of course, highly labour intensive, and the spindle and whorl was eventually replaced by the more productive hand spinning wheel.

Spindle City nickname for the industrial city of Lowell, Mass., USA. Lowell, named after its creator, Francis Cabot Lowell (1775–1817), was an important early textile town in the United States, founded in 1822. F.C. Lowell, a Boston merchant, visited Britain to study textile manufacture and machinery before he set up his mill. In its Victorian heyday, some 175 cotton and woollen mills were in operation in the area, running about 930,000 spindles.

spinning the combined drawing out and twisting together of short fibres to form a yarn or thread. The origin of spinning is lost in antiquity. Several naturally fibrous materials can be spun to make a yarn or thread: those of animal origin include sheep's wool, mohair and alpaca, whilst examples of vegetable origin include cotton, flax, and hemp. Silk is not fibrous, being a continuous filament, so although filaments are twisted together to form a single thread (a process called throwing) silk is not spun, as defined. Yarn is used in weaving cloth, knitting, carpet making, and so on, and thread for lace making, sewing threads etc. The bulk of yarn is used for cloth manufacture: it can be spun in different diameters, known as COUNTS, and the amount of twist varied according to the intended use. A well twisted hard yarn is used for warps, a less twisted softer yarn for wefts. The technique of spinning varies somewhat from material to material. In each case, preparatory work is needed before spinning can commence. In general, this involves bringing the individual fibres more or less parallel to each other: this is done by SCRIBBLING wool, COMBING worsted, and CARDING cotton.

In spinning, the short, 'hairy' fibres, previously made parallel, are drawn out (drafted) over each other until they lock firmly together, and twisted (spun) into a continuous long yarn or thread. The first known way of doing this was by the hand-held SPINDLE AND WHORL. Slow and laborious, this process was nevertheless used for centuries in ancient times. Speed of production was increased with the invention of the simple one spindle spinning wheel. In the mid-16th century the FLYER was invented, which enabled spinning (draft and twist) and winding of yarn onto the bobbin to be done simultaneously. By the mid-18th century, the FLYING SHUTTLE greatly increased cloth production, and a shortage of yarn occurred. This spurred on the invention of several multi-spindle machines in the remarkably short period of twelve years: the JENNY in 1767, the WATER FRAME in 1769, and the MULE in 1779. The SELF-ACTING POWER MULE came in 1830, and RING SPINNING in the 1850s. The chronological development of spinning machines may be summarized as follows:

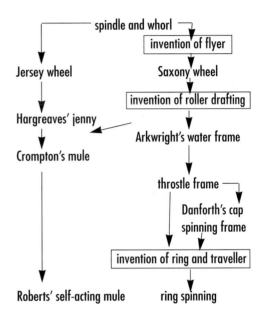

The actions involved in preparing and spinning the four main textile materials are shown in the following table. The basic principles of mule and ring spinning are shown in Fig. 64.

machine	twist applied by	draft applied by	winding on by
spindle and whorl	rotation of spindle	gravitational pull, and spinner's fingers	hand with spindle stopped
Jersey wheel	rotation of spindle	spinner's fingers	rotation of spindle
Saxony wheel	rotation of flyer	spinner's fingers	differential speed between flyer and spindle
jenny	rotation of flyer	pulling clove away from spindles	faller wire and spindle rotation
water frame	rotation of flyer	rollers	differential speed between flyer and spindle
throstle	rotation of flyer	rollers	differential speed between flyer and spindle
mule	rotation of spindle	rollers, and outward run of carriage	faller wire and spindle rotation
ring frame	traveller running round ring	rollers	differential speed between traveller and spindle

The main sequence for preparing and spinning four of the most common fibres is summarized below.

wool	*worsted* (long-fibred wool)	*cotton*	*flax*
1. sorting: fleeces sorted into various qualities and heavy impurities removed	1. sorting as for wool	1. bale breaking: compressed raw cotton opened out	1. hackling: preliminary combing to separate short fibres (tow) from line
2. wet scouring: remaining dirt removed followed by drying	2. wet scouring as for wool	2. mixing: cotton from different bales mixed to even out quality	2. sorting: line sorted into lots according to quality
3. blending and oiling: wool oiled to replace natural lubricants lost in scouring	3. blending etc., as for wool	3. willowing: impurities removed by air stream	3. scutching: to remove woody tissues
4. scribbling: produces a lap	4. gilling: fibres made straight and parallel	4. scutching: produces a lap	4. gilling: produces line slivers
5. carding: produces slivers	5. combing: removes short fibres (noils) and long fibres (tops) combed into slivers	5. carding: produces slivers	5. drawing and doubling: to produce uniform slivers of equal weight
6. slubbing: produces rovings	6. drawing: slivers attenuated into rovings	6. slubbing: preliminary twist put in to produce rovings	6. roving: slivers converted into rovings
7. spinning: final twist and draft put in to produce yarn	7. spinning: rovings spun into yarn	7. spinning: final twist and draft put in to produce yarn	7. wet spinning: rovings passed through hot water to soften inherent gum before spinning into linen yarn
	8. folding: (if required) two or more single yarns twisted together to make stronger	8. doubling (if required) two or more single yarns twisted together to make manifold yarn (stronger yarn)	

Marsden, R. *Cotton Spinning: Its Development, Principles, and Practice*, Bell, 1891
Morton, W.E. and Wray, G.R. *An Introduction to the Study of Spinning*, Longmans, 1962

spinning gallery a relic of the days when farming was often combined with spinning. Spinning galleries are open fronted verandahs giving plenty of daylight, and usually sited on an upper floor of an old farmhouse. The women of the household would sit at their wheels and spin wool into yarn on the gallery; washed wool or yarn was also hung on the gallery to dry. A few such galleries may still be seen on old farmhouses in the Lake District.

spinning mill usually implies a cotton spinning mill or factory in which raw cotton is spun into

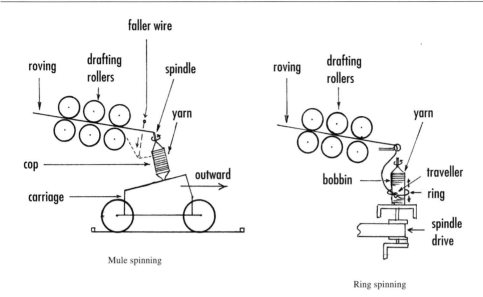

Fig. 64. Basic principles of mule and ring spinning of yarn

yarn or thread, undergoing many processes as it is changed from a mass of tightly packed, tangled fibres into a smooth continuous thread. The end product of the spinning mill may be used for manufacturing cloth in a weaving establishment, as a sewing thread, for lace-making, etc. Some spinning mills have a weaving shed attached.

Spinning mills were the natural development from domestic yarn production by hand as the factory system was introduced. Early spinning mills were small and water-powered (*see* ARKWRIGHT-TYPE MILLS). As mills increased in size and steam power replaced waterwheels, the multi-storey mill was developed. Spinning mills are rated according to the number of spindles they contained: they are designed to produce fine, medium or coarse yarns, and usually fitted out with specific machinery for spinning one class of yarn only.

A typical 19th-century spinning mill comprised fibre preparation machinery, yarn spinning machinery for producing WEFT and WARP, a warehouse for finished yarn, offices, and steam raising boilers and steam engine, together with power transmission equipment to drive the machinery. The main operations that are carried out on the cotton are:

1. opening of the bales of raw compressed cotton.

2. mixing of cotton from different bales to even out the quality.

3. cleaning the cotton massed fibres to remove rubbish. This is done in SCUTCHERS, machines which form the cotton fibres into a wide flat web known as a LAP, in which the fibres lie in random directions, carried out in a BLOWING ROOM.

4. CARDING, where the fibres in the lap are 'combed' into a parallel longitudinal direction and delivered in a soft, untwisted 'rope' called a SLIVER. This is performed in a carding engine.

5. drawing: in a DRAW FRAME, several slivers are drawn together and slightly attenuated into one 'rope' to even out the composition.

6. DRAFTING: further attenuation of the sliver with the addition of a slight twist also reduces the cross-sectional area of the 'rope', which is now known as a ROVING and is wound onto a bobbin.

7. spinning: the final reduction in cross-sectional area and increase in length, with more drafting and twisting to produce the yarn. This is done on a spinning machine proper, initially a MULE giving way later to a RING SPINNER. Yarn so produced will be fine, medium, or coarse, depending on the type of goods the mill is designed to make.

Warp yarn is more tightly spun than weft yarn.

8. doubling is sometimes undertaken in some mills, whereby two or more yarns are twisted together to form a single, stronger yarn or thread.

These activities are carried out on different floors of the mill, the preparatory machinery being usually on the ground floor, or in a basement. The machines are driven by flat leather belts running on pulleys spaced out along overhead LINESHAFTING on each floor. The lineshafting is turned by rope drives from the steam engine flywheel which is sited at ground level; the rope drives run in a vertical corridor called a rope race, which is either sited at one end of the building or, in a double mill, in the centre, with lineshafting stretching out on either side. Sketch plans of a typical four-storey mule spinning mill of about the 1870s are shown in Fig. 65. *See also* COTTON MILL.

Giles, C. and Goodall, I.H. *Yorkshire Textile Mills, 1770–1930*, HMSO, 1992 (deals mainly with wool, but cotton and other fibres are included)
Williams, M. with Farnie, D.A. *Cotton Mills in Greater Manchester*, Carnegie, 1992

spinning wheel (or cottage wheel) a spindle for spinning yarn, driven by an endless band running over a wheel. The origin of the spinning wheel is obscure. In medieval Europe it began replacing the ancient SPINDLE AND WHORL for making yarn from fibrous materials such as flax and wool. An early design was the GREAT WHEEL or walking wheel, which spun yarn in short lengths and was stopped every so often to wind the yarn onto a bobbin. The addition of the FLYER in the mid-16th century, making the SAXONY WHEEL, enabled spinning and winding on to proceed simultaneously, and the spinner could now sit down and operate the wheel with a treadle. A vertical arm projecting above the wheel, the DISTAFF, held a bundle of carded material waiting to be spun.

Spinning by wheel was a domestic occupation, usually carried out by women; the word spinster has come to mean an unmarried woman, and the distaff side of a family means the female branch. It took several spinners to keep a handloom weaver fully occupied, and in the late 18th century single-spindle spinning wheels were gradually replaced by hand JENNIES which could spin several yarns at once. Today spinning wheels are still used in small numbers in craft industries.

Baines, Patricia. *Spinning Wheels, Spinners, and Spinning*, Batsford, 1977

spiral gear, *see* WORM AND WORMWHEEL
spirit of salts, *see* HYDROCHLORIC ACID
spoil heaps heaps of discarded materials from mining, smelting, tunnelling and similar activities, which can be of industrial archaeological interest. The presence of old spoil heaps, often overgrown, indicates the site of a former mining or smelting activity, although all other evidence such as buildings may have long disappeared. Some spoil heaps are not self evident, but can be recognized by the fact that the type of vegetation covering them is different from the surrounding area. In some cases, a lack of vegetation can give a clue. These surface effects are usually created by the presence of discarded minerals lying just below the ground, which control the type of plant which will grow there. For example, the wild sandwort will tolerate lead, and is known as leadwort in some mining districts. Other examples are the calamine violet which will grow on soils polluted by zinc, and the alyssum and cress families which will grow on metalliferous soils.

Analysis of material from spoil heaps will usually determine what went on earlier at the site. Some spoil heaps have been reworked at a date after the original material was thrown away. This usually indicates either that a better process had been developed which enabled previously discarded material to be recovered, or that the improved economic value of the material made it worthwhile reworking the old waste.

There are many local names for spoil heaps. The large heaps associated with coal mining are known in Lancashire as dirt tips or rucks; in recent years some old tips have been landscaped and turned into leisure areas. Spoil heaps from Cornish tin and copper mines are known locally as burrows. Waste stone and gangue heaps at old lead mines are known as hillocks in Derbyshire, and waste from shale oil mining in Scotland are known as bings. Metallurgical waste is called a slag heap, and waste material associated with granite quarrying is called tirr in Scotland. The waste from the old Leblanc soda ash process was known as galligu.

In addition to mining waste and so on, spoil heaps often are still visible from tunnelling activities by railways and canals.

'spoilt child of the State' name sometimes used of the early British woollen industry because it was the first home industry to be protected by the government. As early as 1258, the export of wool was forbidden and the importation of foreign woollen cloth prevented

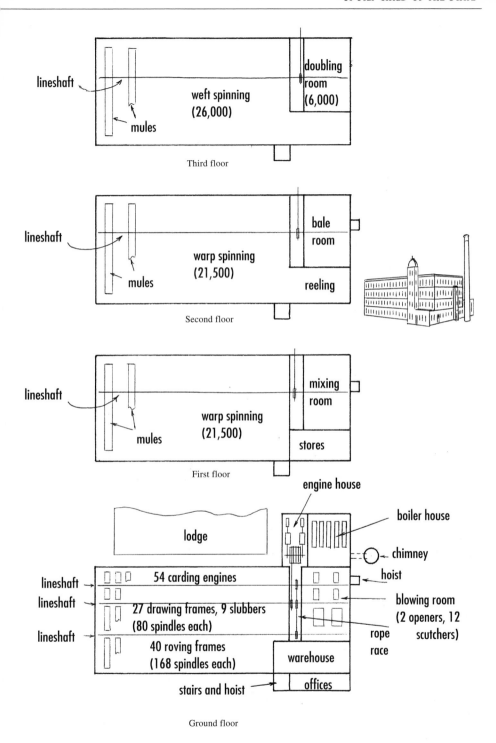

Fig. 65. Typical four-storey mule spinning mill of *c.* 1870s with 1,000 hp engine, with 75,000 spindles plus preparatory machinery (spindles per floor shown in brackets). Source: Marsden, R. *Cotton Spinning*, 1891

to protect the home industry. Later protection by various bans on the importation of competing cloths were made, and in 1660, the export of wool from the British Isles was prohibited by Act of Parliament to ensure adequate supplies for home weavers. This embargo was not removed from the Statute Book until 1825.

When the East India Company's imports of printed cotton goods from India began to threaten the home woollen industry, the influential wool trade lobbied parliament and obtained an Act in 1700 prohibiting such imports. To further protect the home industry against competition, an Act was passed in 1719 making it illegal for skilled textile workers to emigrate to European countries to help foreign manufacturers. In due course, all these protectionist Acts were repealed, and eventually cotton cloth manufacture in this country outstripped that of wool in quantity. *See also* BURIAL IN WOOL.

spool rack, *see* CREEL

spout, *see* COAL TIP

spring beam, *see* CATCHWING, RABBET

spring sail (or shuttered sail) an early adjustable windmill sail devised by Andrew Meikle (1719–1811) around 1772, in which pivoted, Venetian-type shutters could be set at different angles according to the strength of the wind. An iron control rod ran along the WHIP of each sail, from an adjusting box near the free end to a leaf spring fastened to the whip near the central boss. A handle projecting from the box enabled a pinion to be turned, which engaged with a rack cut in the end of the control rod. When turned, the pinion moved the box towards or away from the central boss, and since the box was connected to sail rods running the length of the sail, these also moved, and in doing so altered the angle of all the shutters on the sail. The miller stopped each sail in turn so that he could adjust the angle of the shutters by operating the adjusting box from ground level or from a raised platform surrounding the mill structure. The shutters remained at the angle he had set them in a normal wind, but in a strong gust, the greater pressure forced them open, allowing the wind to spill through the sail and protecting the mill from overspeed. As soon as the gust died away, the spring returned the shutters to their original angle.

Thirty-five years later, a mechanism which allowed the shutters to be adjusted without stopping the mill was invented by William Cubitt (*see* PATENT SAIL).

spring shuttle, *see* FLYING SHUTTLE

sprocket a toothed wheel with teeth designed to engage with the links of a chain to transmit motion or power. A sprocket is usually the smaller of a pair of wheels in a chain transmission, the larger wheel being known as the chain wheel. The word sprocket is of unknown origin.

spur wheel the larger of a pair of gearwheels connecting two parallel shafts. The teeth on a spur wheel may be cut straight across the wheel and parallel to the shaft, or be inclined at an angle to the shaft to form a helix (*see* HELICAL GEARS). The smaller gear of the pair is called a pinion. The great spur wheel is the large diameter gear which drives the STONE NUTS in a corn mill.

square a large open-topped vat, usually rectangular, in which beer is fermented, sometimes called a working tun; yeast is added to the beer whilst it is in the square. Squares were introduced in Yorkshire breweries by Timothy Bentley in the mid-1790s, and are still in use.

square motion comb another name for the HOLDEN COMBER. The first patent for an elementary square motion comber (patent no. 12289), was taken out in 1848 in Samuel Cunliffe Lister's name, although his partner at that time, Isaac Holden, was the inventor of the idea and developed the machine into the successful wool comber which bore his name.

stack 1. (or shaft) a chimney for discharging the products of combustion from a boiler, furnace, etc. high into the air. On a locomotive it is known as a funnel. **2.** an old Shropshire weight measure of coal which varied according to place and time, from 26 to 40 cwt.

staddling a foundation or platform. It is also an old dialect word for the pier of a bridge, also known as a starling or steerling. A staddle is a support.

stage, *see* LEVEL (1)

stagecoach a horse-drawn coach for conveying the fare-paying public along specified routes. Stagecoaches were introduced about the mid-17th century and were usually pulled by four horses, who were changed at the end of each stage of the journey at staging inns, where stabling was kept for this purpose. Some 10–15 miles was a typical stage. Passengers travelled either inside the coach or outside (seated on top); four to six could travel inside, paying a higher fare and up to fourteen outside on some coaches. Stagecoaches also carried parcels.

When stagecoaches were first introduced they travelled at about 4 mph due to the poor condition of the roads, and only ran in the summer months for the same reason. As roads were improved, speeds of 8–10 mph by the early 1800s became common. In 1700, York was a week distant from London, Tunbridge Wells or Oxford 2 days, Dover 3 days, and Exeter 5 days. Passengers would be accommodated in the stagecoach inns overnight. In the 1830s it is estimated that there were some 3,000 coaches in operation, employing 150,000 horses. 1,500 coaches left London daily on short and long journeys. By 1837, the heyday of coaching had been reached, and competition from the new, faster railways began their decline. For a while stagecoaches continued to operate in areas not yet reached by the railways, but as the system expanded, more and more coach companies disappeared. At first, some stagecoaches, complete with their passengers, were actually carried for part of their journey on the new railways, mounted on flat trucks.

Bird, A. *Roads and Vehicles*, Arrow, 1973
Copeland, J. *Roads and their Traffic 1750–1850*, David and Charles, 1968

stage waggon horse-drawn vehicles, equivalent to the passenger stagecoaches, for transporting goods and materials by road. Stage waggons operated regular services between certain towns using four-wheeled carts, usually drawn by at least two horses, and more when heavy loads were involved. Waggoners reckoned on one horse for every ton carried. Passengers were sometimes carried as well. Naturally stage waggons were slower than stagecoaches: around 3 mph was normal, with about 20 miles covered in a day. The well-known firm of carriers, Pickford, founded in the 18th century, was conveying goods in 1776 from Manchester to London by van in four and a half days twice weekly. Raw materials, finished goods, machine parts, etc. were transported in this manner until the spread of canals took some of the bulk freight. Stage waggons continued operating in areas not served by canals, although later the railways took most of the transport of goods off the roads. The widespread importance of waggon traffic may be judged by the large number of inns and pubs around the country bearing the name Waggon and Horses.

staircase locks a succession of closely spaced canal LOCKS with no POUNDS in between them. A staircase is used to overcome a steep rise in the ground, and is arranged so that the top gate of one lock is the bottom gate of the one above. A good example of a staircase is the Bingley Five-rise, on the Leeds and Liverpool Canal:

opened in 1774, it raises the canal 60 ft in a short distance.

staithe an erection or staging placed on the bank of a river, harbour or seashore, to facilitate loading coal into a ship moored against it. A staithe comprises essentially a chute or chutes down which loose coal can be tipped from a truck straight into the hold of a coal ship. The word is of Scandinavian or German origin. Staithes had begun to be built on Tyneside by 1700, and in addition to chutes positioned over the river for loading KEELS or ships if on the coast, other chutes were incorporated which allowed coal to be discharged to a storehouse when desired. Coal was therefore also stored at staithes rather than at the pit, so that quick delivery could be effected. A large staithes complex might store tens of thousands of CHALDRONS of coal. When coal was drawn from the stockpile, it was barrowed to lower chutes to load the keel.

staking on, *see* FASTENERS
stalch, *see* RIDER (2)
stalk, *see* CHIMNEY
stammet (or stammel) a coarse woollen fabric, usually dyed red and popular as undergarment material, which was being woven in East Anglia in the 17th century.
stammin 1. (or tamin) a coarse narrow cloth of worsted, which was made in Norfolk as early as the 15th century and continued to be made there for some 200 years. The cloth was used for clothing. **2.** the warp threads in an upright loom.
stamping and potting process, *see* POT IRON
stampmaster, *see* ALNAGER
stamps crushing machines used in ore dressing. They are usually arranged in banks, side by side, with four, six, eight or more crushing heads or stamps driven by a revolving horizontal shaft which has cams spaced along its length. The heavy heads are raised by the cams and fall by gravity in the simpler designs to crush the pieces of ore, which are placed in a bowl anvil beneath each head. Early stamps were made from massive timbers with the crushing head iron shod at its base; later machines were constructed from iron. The driving cam shaft was turned by water power at first, later by other prime movers such as beam steam engines. There are dry and wet stamps: dry stamps were the earliest types which operated without water, while wet stamps were more efficient. The water, which was arranged to flow over the ore whilst it was under the stamps, helped in the crushing process, and was also used to empty the anvil bowls. A secondary beam, operated from the top of the

sweep arm or connecting rod of the main beam engine, was arranged to work a pump for supplying the water to the stamp grates.

The simple design of stamps is known as a Cornish stamp; a later design of the 1850s called a Californian stamp, rotated the head at each stroke to even out wear on the hammer surface. An improved design, the Husband pneumatic stamp, was introduced in the 1870s. It had a patented oscillating cylinder, the head being connected to a piston inside a cylinder which was lifted by a crankshaft. As the cylinder was raised, the air below the piston was compressed, which lifted up the stamp head. As the crankshaft continued turning, the air above the piston became compressed which forced the head down at a speed greater than it would have reached falling by gravity, thus delivering a greater blow. The Husband stamps ran faster and were quieter than the old mechanical stamps, and crushed about eight times as much ore in the same time.

Stamping mills were also known as knocking mills or clash mills.

stand pipe a tall, open-ended vertical pipe connected to a pipeline, to ensure that the pipeline pressure at that point cannot exceed the head pressure from the stand pipe. Stand pipes were sited at municipal water pumping stations to reduce pressure fluctuations in the distribution main caused by pulsations from reciprocating pumps. They also protected the engines from possible damage should the main burst, resulting in a sudden loss of load.

stang a handle, particularly the lever that operates a strap fork mechanism. *See* FAST AND LOOSE PULLEYS.

stank 1. a dam across a waterway with removable horizontal boards so that water behind it may be emptied, or its level lowered, by removing all or some of the boards. 2. a watertight wall in a mine.

stannary a tin mine, or tin mining district. The word comes from the Latin *stannum* for tin, and has been in use since about 1201. Stannary Courts, or Courts of the Stannaries, were bodies regulating tin mining in Cornwall and Devon on similar lines to the lead BARMOTE of Derbyshire; they were only abolished in 1897. Cornwall was divided into four Stannaries, each with its own court. Until 1752, representative assemblies of tin miners called Stannary Parliaments were held. The heir to the British throne holds the title 'Lord Warden of the Stannaries', and tin miners were once called stannators. Stanniferous veins are veins or rocks containing tin.

Lewis, G.R. *The Stannaries: A Study of the English Tin Miner*, Harvard University Press, 1924

staple 1. the length and quality of a textile fibre. Staple lengths vary according to the material: short staple is generally only suitable for the coarser and lower quality yarns, and long staple is suitable for the better yarns. 2. some kind of hole or shaft in the ground. It can be a vertical shaft connecting different levels in a coal mine, often made to aid ventilation, or a deep hole at ground level, into which the counterbalance of a DURHAM WINDER fell to assist the starting of the engine.

starling (or steerling) a wedge-shaped projection either side of a bridge pier, to protect the foundation in the river bed from erosion by the water and damage by any floating object. The starling is built parallel to the river flow and is also known as a cutwater. Both starling and steerling are corruptions of the old word 'staddling'.

starvationer the nickname given to the narrow canal boats used on the Bridgewater Canal, and in the coal mines at Worsley, Lancs., because the 'ribs' of the boat showed on the inside of the hull, giving a starved appearance. The boats were particularly narrow so that they could enter the underground waterways which led to the coal seams. They were propelled when underground, by walking the boat along, hauling on a rope attached to hooks in the tunnel roof (*see also* LEGGING).

stationary steam engine a steam engine working at a fixed location. It may refer to an engine positioned at the top of an incline to haul up trucks, or complete trains at the beginning of the railway era, or any land-based steam engine such as a mill engine, as opposed to marine engines, steam carriages, etc.

Main developments of stationary steam engines
year

year	
1698	'Miner's Friend' pistonless steam engine by Thomas Savery
1712	Atmospheric beam engine by Thomas Newcomen
1767–74	Improvements to Newcomen type engine by John Smeaton
1769	Separate condenser by James Watt
1780	Rotating crank patented by James Pickard
1781	'Sun and Planet' motion patented by James Watt
1782	Double-acting beam engine by James Watt
1782	Expansive working by James Watt

1787	Conical pendulum governor applied to a steam engine
1799	D-slide valve invented by William Murdock
1800	High pressure beam engine by Richard Trevithick
1807	Self-standing 'table' engine patented by Henry Maudslay
c.1825	Horizontal steam engines introduced
1825	Cornish beam engines introduced
1840s	Inverted vertical engines by James Nasmyth
1845	Compounding of beam engines by William McNaughton
1849	Fast-acting steam valve invented by George Corliss in USA
1860s	Large horizontal mill engines
1884	Central valve engine by Peter Willans
c.1900	Drop valves introduced
1908	Uniflow engine by Johann Stumpf in Germany.

Hayes, G. *Stationary Steam Engines*, Shire Publications, 1979
Hills, R.L. *Power from Steam: A History of the Stationary Steam Engine*, Cambridge University Press, 1990

Statute labour, *see* ROADS

Statute of Apprentices, *see* ARTIFICERS, STATUTE OF

Statute of Artificers, *see* ARTIFICERS, STATUTE OF

staunch a FLASH LOCK on a river navigation. Many staunches are of the guillotine type, such as those on the river Narr in Norfolk. A similar device, comprising a horizontal beam connecting gateposts across a lock, is called a stride on the river Thames, and a galley beam in East Anglia.

steam the vapour into which water changes when boiled. Steam has two main uses – as a heating medium in industrial processes or for space heating, and as a power source when under high pressure for driving engines. Steam is formed when the latent heat of vaporization is supplied to water at its boiling point to cause the change in state. Steam itself is invisible, but when escaping into air, minute droplets of hot water are formed by condensation with the cooler air, creating a visible white plume. Fuel is burnt in a boiler to generate steam under pressure, and as it leaves the boiler, the steam usually contains a small amount of water moisture; in this state it is called 'wet', and the percentage of pure steam present is called its 'dryness fraction'. If there is no moisture

present, the steam is said to be 'dry and saturated' (i.e. saturated with heat). If further heat is added, the steam becomes 'superheated'; its pressure is not altered, but its volume increases. When driving a steam engine or locomotive, steam should be dry or superheated, since any moisture carried over from the boiler into the engine cylinder causes loss of power.

There has been a steady increase in steam pressures from Watt's days in the search for more and more power (*see* PRESSURE). Steam has a great expansive power. For example, one volume of water produces about 1,670 volumes of steam at boiling point (212°F), and this property is used to economize on the quantity of steam used by an engine and hence the amount of fuel used by the boiler. By cutting off the amount of steam let into a cylinder soon after the commencement of the piston stroke, the expansive power of the steam completes the stroke with falling pressure (*see* CUT-OFF). The amount of expansion allowed is restricted to about three times the inlet volume, otherwise the cylinder has to be so large that condensation problems arise. This is overcome by passing the steam into larger and larger cylinders in succession, to accommodate the increasing volume of the steam (*see* COMPOUNDING (1)). If steam is condensed back into water inside a closed chamber, a partial vacuum (sub-atmospheric pressure) is formed because of the great reduction in volume from steam to water. This property is used on condensing steam engines to increase the overall pressure drop from inlet to condenser, and give more power output. Newcomen used this idea on his engines to create a vacuum under the piston so that atmospheric pressure could provide the power stroke.

The French physicist Henri Victor Regnault (1810–78) published tables giving the pressure–temperature relationship of steam up to a pressure of 24 atmospheres (approximately 350 psi) in 1843–7, and his figures remained in use until c.1915 when they were revised.

steam carriage a road vehicle powered by a steam engine. Steam carriages date from the late 18th century and precede railway locomotives by some thirty or forty years. William Murdock (1754–1839) experimented with a small carriage driven by a GRASSHOPPER ENGINE in 1785; William Symington (1764–1831) tried unsuccessfully to get financial backing in 1786 to build a full-sized steam carriage which drove the road wheels by racks and ratchets; but it was Richard Trevithick (1771–1823) and his cousin Andrew

Vivian who built the first really successful steam carriage in Britain (patent no. 2599, 1802). In 1803 they demonstrated another steam carriage on London streets. Several other inventors followed, among them Goldsworthy Gurney (1793–1875) whose steam coach travelled from London to Bath in 1829; Charles Dance used a Gurney coach to run a regular passenger service between Cheltenham and Gloucester in 1831. Gurney's vehicles had FLASH BOILERS for rapid steaming, and burned coke to avoid making smoke. Steam driven omnibuses were running in London and some other cities by 1834.

Opposition to steam carriages came from STAGECOACH proprietors and TURNPIKE TRUSTS, who imposed high tolls on steam coaches; when the railways developed, they too joined in the opposition. Private steam cars were also made. The LOCOMOTIVE AND HIGHWAYS ACT 1865, with its speed restriction, was a hindrance to the development of steam cars, but they were still being made as late as 1903 when they were exhibited at the first motor show at Crystal Palace. Steam road carriages were also known as locomotive carriages and road steamers.

Davison, C. St C.B. *History of Steam Road Vehicles*, HMSO, 1953
Harris, T.R. *Sir Goldsworthy Gurney*, Trevithick Society, 1975
Kidner, M.W. *The First Hundred Road Locomotives*, Oakwood Press, 1959

steam coal   a low volatile class of coal particularly suitable for raising steam in boilers. A typical analysis is around 85 per cent carbon, 5 per cent ash, 4 per cent hydrogen, and 2 per cent nitrogen and sulphur.

steam engine   an external combustion heat engine which converts the pressure energy in steam into useful mechanical work. Steam engines as prime movers have been used for some 250 years, powering machinery, ships, and providing traction for road and rail transport. A steam engine depends on an external boiler for generating its working medium, which is converted into useful work by a steam-tight piston moving backwards and forwards inside a cylinder or, in large engines, more than one cylinder. The reciprocating motion of the piston is translated into either a vertical up and down motion in a beam engine, or into rotary motion by a connecting rod turning a crank, the latter motion being the more useful. Steam engines can be divided into SINGLE-ACTING or DOUBLE-ACTING, and may be CONDENSING or NON-CONDENSING. Engines have been made in many configurations, sizes, and operating speeds.

The first steam-using engine was Newcomen's single-acting ATMOSPHERIC BEAM ENGINE of 1712, which was not a true engine using the pressure energy of steam for its power strokes. Later, double-acting beam engines were developed from it, using steam pressure to give much greater powers. At first these engines only gave the same reciprocating motion, but by 1780 rotary motion was obtained, making the engines much more useful since they could now drive machinery. Two years later, EXPANSIVE WORKING was introduced, with a resultant economy in boiler fuel consumption. Beam engines are of the indirect design, in as much that work is obtained via the intermediate action of a beam. By dispensing with the beam and translating the motion of the piston straight into rotary motion by connecting rod and crank, a more compact, direct design results. Most steam engines are of direct design with their cylinders arranged either horizontally or vertically, but beam engines still have a special use for pumping water or sewage in PUBLIC UTILITIES, a duty for which they are particularly suited.

By the end of the 18th century steam engines were competing against WATERWHEELS for driving machinery. The use of the former meant that mills etc. were now independent of a water supply to drive a wheel, giving greater choice of location. There followed many years of improvement to engine design as better boilers, superior engineering, and metallurgical developments permitted higher steam operating pressures and larger and more powerful engines to be built. The large STATIONARY ENGINE reached its peak in the late Victorian period with multi-cylinder, horizontal, condensing engines of 2,000–3,000 hp, driving spinning mills or winding coal from deep mines.

Steam engines were applied to road transport when Gurney's STEAM CARRIAGE ran from London to Bath in 1829, but the use of steam on the road had only a comparatively short history. Steam locomotives date from 1804 with Trevithick's pioneering run in Wales, and by 1830, the first true public railway was opened in Lancashire. Steam was the mainstay for railways for some 130 years until the introduction of diesel–electric locomotives this century. Marine steam engines, driving vessels propelled by paddlewheels, were running a regular service on the Clyde in 1812. Sea-going vessels powered by steam were soon sailing the oceans, and in fact, marine engine design led the way in raising engine efficiency: fuel economy was important on long voyages, to give maximum space for cargo, and fuel-saving ideas developed for marine use were copied onto stationary land engines (*see* SHIPS).

Buchanan, R.A. and Watkins, G. *The Industrial Archaeology of the Stationary Steam Engine*, Allen Lane, 1976

Dickinson, H.W. *A Short History of the Steam Engine*, 1936; reprinted by Cass, 1963

Farey, J. *A Treatise on the Steam Engine, Historical, Practical, and Descriptive*, 1827; reprinted by David and Charles, 1971

Hayes, G. *Stationary Steam Engines*, Shire Publications, 1979

Watkins, G. *The Stationary Steam Engine*, David and Charles, 1968

Watkins, G. *Textile Mill Engines*, 2 vols, David and Charles, 1970–1

steamer a popular name for a steam driven road carriage in the early to mid-19th century. It can also mean a steamship.

steam hammer a large, powerful, forging hammer, operated by steam. It comprises a vertical double-acting steam cylinder mounted at the top of a massive framework, with a hammer block or head attached to the lower end of the piston rod. The hammer rises and falls in vertical guides directly above a bottom anvil on which the item to be forged is placed. Steam to the cylinder can be controlled from ground level, and it is possible to control the blow from the hammer very precisely.

The idea of a steam hammer was conceived by James Hall Nasmyth (1808–90) in 1839 for forging the crankshaft for the paddle steamship *Great Britain*, but I.K. Brunel, the ship's designer, changed his mind and screw propulsion was substituted instead. Nasmyth's steam hammer was therefore not built at that time. The first steam hammer was actually built at Le Creusot, in France, some time before 1842. This was the result of Nasmyth's business partner showing Eugène Schneider (1805–73), of the Le Creusot Ironworks, Nasmyth's sketch of the hammer during Schneider's visit to the Patricroft works whilst Nasmyth was away. Nasmyth discovered a hammer in use at Le Creusot when he visited Schneider later on, and immediately took out a patent (no. 9382, 1842) on his return to England. A further patent (no. 9850, 1843) based on the ideas of Robert Wilson (1803–82), Nasmyth's works manager, made the hammer self acting.

In addition to its principal use for forging, the steam hammer was adapted for SHINGLING wrought iron, for pile driving, and for hewing and dressing stone. Steam hammers soon replaced the old TILT HAMMERS, since a more powerful blow could be generated, and larger work could be accommodated on the anvil.

Nasmyth, J. *James Nasmyth, Engineer*, ed. by Samuel Smiles, Murray, 1897

steam horse, *see* LOCOMOTIVE

steam loom, *see* POWER LOOM

steam turbine a prime mover in which steam is expanded inside a closed chamber, and the kinetic energy created is partly absorbed in rotating vanes or blades attached to a central drum or disk. There are two principal types of steam turbine, reaction machines and impulse machines. In the REACTION TURBINE, the steam expands progressively from high pressure passing in stages through alternate rows of blades fixed to the outer casing, and blades attached to the central drum which is free to rotate. The kinetic energy is continuously developed at each stage in turn, as the steam is directed by the fixed blades onto the drum blades. The drum is rotated by the reaction between the steam flow and the blades attached to the drum as the kinetic energy is absorbed. This is known as pressure compounding, i.e. the total pressure drop through the turbine is divided into a series of small stages. In the IMPULSE TURBINE, the high pressure steam is first expanded in nozzles with diverging bores losing pressure and gaining velocity, and directed onto blades fixed to a rotating disk in one stage. There is no change in pressure across the ring of blades, which are rotated by the impulse they receive from the steam jets impinging on them. There may be further stages in some impulse turbines before the steam leaves the machine. When there is more than one stage in an impulse turbine, it is known as velocity compounding. A third type of turbine combines both principles in one machine, i.e. it comprises a high pressure impulse stage (or stages), followed by lower pressure reaction stages. Such a machine is known as a disk and drum turbine, an impulse-reaction turbine, or a combination turbine.

It may be considered that the first steam turbine was that by Hero of Alexandria (2nd century BC) who demonstrated a toy reaction turbine in his AEOLIPYLE. However, successful full-sized steam turbines were not to appear until late in the 19th century although many patents were taken out in the first half of that century, amongst which may be mentioned Richard Trevithick's in 1815; John Ericsson's in 1830; Timothy Burstall's in 1838; James Pilbrow's in 1842; and Robert Wilson's in 1848. None of these was successful. It remained for Charles Algernon Parsons (1854–1931) to develop the first really successful turbine when he patented a multi-stage non-condensing reaction turbine (patent no. 6735, 1884). (*See* Fig. 38d.) This ran at 18,000 rpm for steam entering at 80 psi. Soon after, he had a 50 hp machine driving an electric generator. Besides this use, turbines were soon applied to marine work. Parsons equipped a 100-ton vessel the *Turbinia* with three turbines driving three propellers, and spectacularly demonstrated the superiority of this form of prime mover over existing marine engines when he outsped naval vessels at the 1897 Jubilee Naval Review at Spithead.

Much development on turbines took place in the 1880s, resulting in the invention of continental designs such as the single-stage impulse turbine by Carl Gustav Patrik De Laval in Sweden in 1889, and the multi-stage impulse turbine by Auguste Rateau in France in the same year. In the USA, the velocity compounded impulse turbine was developed by C.G. Curtis (1860–1953) in 1896. This machine was often made with a vertical axis as an alternative to the more usual horizontal axis; the reaction turbine is always made with a horizontal axis.

The advantages of turbines over reciprocating steam engines are compactness, economy of steam, and less wearing of parts. Turbines are ideally suited to drive electric generation plant, for which they are still used, since they are capable of higher speeds of rotation than high-speed reciprocating engines which they soon replaced for this duty. They cannot be reversed, so for marine work it is necessary to have separate low-power turbines for reversing. The De Laval turbine (*see* Fig. 38b) runs at extremely high speed, and is only suitable for small power units; usually a speed reduction gear is necessary to bring the speed down to a practical figure for driving machinery, etc.

Appleyard, R. *Charles Parsons: His Life and Work*, Constable, 1933

Parsons, R.H. *The Development of the Parsons Steam Turbine*, Constable, 1936

steam wheel an abortive device invented by James Watt (1736–1819) in 1775 in an attempt to make a rotative machine. It was a possible forerunner of the STEAM TURBINE.

steel an alloy comprising a solid solution of iron and carbon, the latter ranging from about 0.1 per cent to about 1.7 per cent. Small amounts of other elements are normally present in steel, such as manganese, silicon, phosphorus, sulphur, and oxygen. Many of these come from impurities in the iron ore from which the steel is made, but in some cases certain elements are deliberately introduced in controlled amounts into the metal while it is molten to produce particular properties in the final steel, then known as an alloy steel. The mechanical properties may be modified by later heat treatment. Steel will take a sharp edge, and can be hardened if sufficient carbon is present by sudden chilling, whereas slow cooling will produce a soft steel. Intermediate degrees of hardening are by tempering processes.

Typical applications of the higher carbon steels are: 1.4 per cent carbon: lathe tools; 1.2 per cent: twist drills, watch springs: 1.0 per cent: woodworking tools; 0.8 per cent: chisels; 0.6 per cent: general cutting tools. Steel with a carbon content of up to about 0.25 per cent is known as MILD STEEL, and is the common steel used for general purposes. Steel is equally strong in tension and compression which makes it more useful than CAST IRON which is strong in compression but weak in tension, and is brittle.

Steel today is made from BLAST FURNACE pig iron, but other methods were used before this (*see* STEEL MANUFACTURE). The first bulk production of steel was by the BESSEMER PROCESS in 1856. Estimates of production before this are difficult to make, since no reliable records were kept, but the quantity was small compared with the production after 1856. British steel production rose from 703,000 tons in 1875 (about 40 per cent of the world's total) to 3,916,000 tons in 1896 and to 6,230,000 tons in 1900.

steel and flint mill an early primitive lighting method used by coal miners underground. It comprised a portable hand-operated device of geared wheels, one of which rubbed against a piece of flint causing a shower of sparks to give some illumination. It was invented by Carlisle Spedding (1696–1755) of Whitehaven, Cumberland, *c*.1740. Although originally thought to be safe because it was believed that the temperature of the sparks was too low to cause trouble, several explosions in coal mines were caused by it; but it was still safer than candles, the only other form of illumination current at that time. The steel and flint mill was mainly used in northern mines, but its use was discontinued by the end of the 18th century when the DAVY LAMP replaced it. It is sometimes known simply as a flint mill. Usually a boy was employed to turn the handle and provide some light for the miner.

steeling hammer in a forge, a hammer reserved for drawing out iron bars to smaller dimensions by repeated hammering whilst the iron is hot; this work-hardens the iron to give a steely composition. In the 18th and early 19th centuries steeling hammers were water-powered.

steel manufacture the process of making iron take carbon into a solid solution. STEEL was expensively made in the Middle Ages for swords, etc. in very small quantities. By the early 17th century greater amounts were being made from bar iron by the CEMENTATION

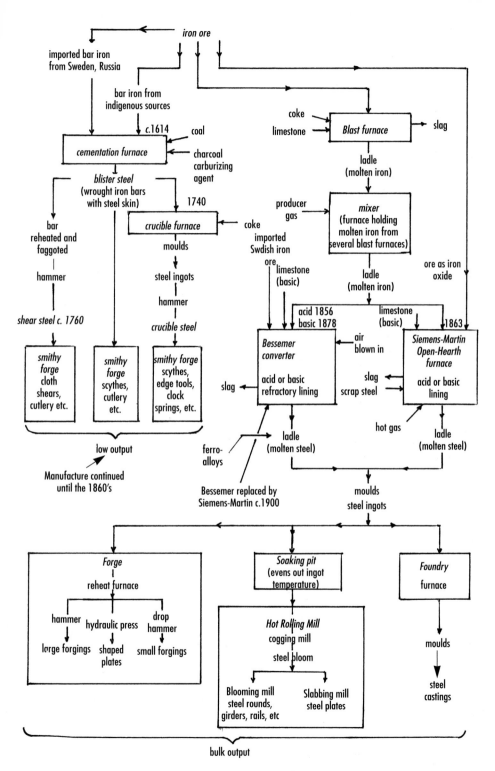

Flow diagram for steel manufacture

PROCESS, making what was known as BLISTER STEEL. This was in effect a wrought iron with a steel skin. It was, however, not very consistent in quality, and Benjamin Huntsman (1704–76) began making a superior steel known as CRUCIBLE STEEL in 1740. Another improved steel made from blister steel a few years later was known as SHEAR STEEL since its main use was for making cropping shears for the textile finishing trade.

The output of these types of steel was small, and as demand for more and more steel arose in the 19th century, efforts were made to produce cheap steel in bulk. This was first achieved in 1856 by Henry Bessemer (1813–98) who converted blast furnace PIG IRON into steel by blowing air into an acid refractory-lined vessel holding molten iron, called a converter (*see* BESSEMER STEEL). The oxygen in the air oxidized the carbon in the iron until the desired percentage was reached. At first, only pig iron with a nil or very low percentage of phosphorus could be converted into steel, but eventually the more abundant phosphoric ores could be used due to the discovery in 1878 of BASIC LININGS for the converter. Meanwhile, another approach to making cheap steel in bulk was being made in Britain and France. Charles William Siemens (1823–83), a German working in Britain, developed a shallow reverberatory type of furnace, fired by PRODUCER GAS pre-heated in a heat regenerator; Pierre-Emile Martin (1824–1915) also used one in France for making steel from pig iron, scrap steel, and some iron ore. Combining these in the 1860s, the Siemens–Martin OPEN HEARTH regenerative steel-making process came into being. In time it superseded the Bessemer process, as it gave better control, could use scrap steel, and was more economic in fuel consumption. It could make either acid or basic steel, depending on whether the hearth lining was a basic or acid refractory. More basic steel is made than acid.

If steel from the steelworks is intended for a ROLLING MILL, hot ingots are placed in a furnace called a SOAKING PIT to equalize their temperature before they are hot rolled into structural sections, plates, etc. If going to a forge or foundry, they are reheated or melted there for subsequent working. Cold rolling is done when the steel becomes thin with a large surface area which would cool rapidly; such as sheets or strip.

The flow diagram of steel manufacture on page 361 shows the main methods which have been used over the years.

Barraclough, K.C. *Steelmaking before Bessemer*, 2 vols, Metals Society, 1984
Barraclough, K.C. *Steelmaking 1850–1900*, Institute of Metals, 1990
Gale, W.K.V. *The British Iron and Steel Industry*, David and Charles, 1967
Schubert, H.R. *History of the British Iron and Steel Industry from 450 BC to 1775 AD*, Routledge and Kegan Paul, 1957

steeping soaking barley in warm water for about 50 hours to induce germination when it is later spread out on the floor in the MALT HOUSE. *See* BREWING INDUSTRY.

steeple engine a compact, free-standing steam engine, introduced *c.*1810, and built mainly in small sizes; David Napier (1790–1869) is credited with its invention. It was mostly used to power workshops and small factories. It had two piston rods side-by-side, which passed either side of a horizontal crankshaft mounted immediately above a single vertical cylinder (*see* Fig. 66). The piston rods extended to an overhead crosshead which ran in vertical guides, and a connecting rod descended back to the crank and crankshaft. The engine acquired its name from its resemblance to a church steeple, although horizontal versions were also made; it is also known as a return connecting-rod engine.

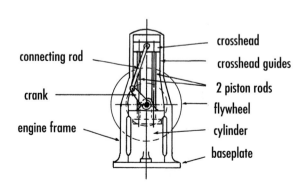

connecting rod

crank

engine frame

crosshead

crosshead guides

2 piston rods

flywheel

cylinder

baseplate

Fig. 66. Steeple steam engine, *c.* 1810 (vertical design)

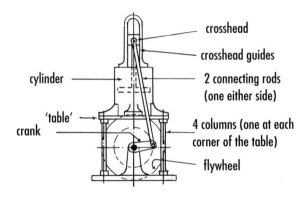

Fig. 67. Table steam engine, *c*. 1807 (inverted vertical design)

steining a method of sinking a shaft or well; the word is also used for the lining to the hole. A circular hole is first dug, and a circular curb laid in the base. Brickwork is then built onto the curb for a few vertical feet. Working inside the 'tube' or steining, more earth is excavated below the curb and the steining allowed to sink under its own weight, building the brickwork up to suit. The process is repeated until the required depth is reached.

stemples 1. wooden pieces fixed to the side of a mine shaft, a man's stride apart from each other, so as to form a kind of stairway or ladder by which the shaft could be descended or ascended. These were used in early mining practice in shallow shafts. **2.** (or stulls) various kinds of supports used underground in mines. For instance, timber or stone bars placed across narrow openings to support DEADS stacked above them are known in some areas as stemples, as are wooden platforms on which miners stand to reach overhead ore when working overhand stopeing in lead mines (*see* STOPE).

stentering the process of stretching moist fabrics widthways to their correct size after BLEACHING or DYEING. When wet, cloth has a tendency to shrink and cockle sideways, and stentering brings it back to its original dimension. This is achieved by passing the cloth through a stenter, which grips the SELVEDGES and pulls the fabric out to its correct width whilst it is dried by hot air.

Stephenson link motion a mechanism used on stationary steam engines and locomotives for reversing the rotation of the engine and varying the CUT-OFF and hence the EXPANSION RATIO. It was first invented by William Williams, a young draughtsman, and developed further by William Howe (1814–79) in 1842 whilst he was working for Robert Stephenson & Co. The mechanism was first fitted to a North Midland Railway locomotive by Robert Stephenson in the same year, and became known as Stephenson's link motion. It was the most commonly used REVERSING GEAR, as it was simple and gave a fairly good steam distribution in the cylinders, although the valve LEAD (2) varies as the linkage is altered.

Fig. 68b shows the gear in outline. It comprises a pair of ECCENTRICS keyed on the engine crankshaft, one with its ANGLE OF ADVANCE set for forward motion, the other with the same angle for reverse. In the diagram, *a* and *b* are the centres of the eccentrics, and *ac* and *bd* the eccentric rods which are connected to the ends of a curved, slotted link *cd* called the EXPANSION LINK. This link is suspended from point *e* on the bell-crank *efg* which is pivoted about a fixed fulcrum *f*. The expansion link is concave viewed from the engine crankshaft, and it can be raised or lowered by operation of the hand lever and catch working in a notched quadrant via the reversing rod *gh* and the bell-crank. Sliding in the slot in the expansion link is a block *i* which is joined to the valve rod, and the latter being constrained to move horizontally by guides. Block *i* can occupy any position between *c* and *d* depending on where the hand lever is. When it is at the top of *cd*, the valve receives its motion from eccentric *bd*, whilst the other eccentric *ac* merely oscillates end *c* without affecting movement of the valve. If the expansion link is raised so that *i* comes to the bottom of the slot, the position of the valve is altered and it comes

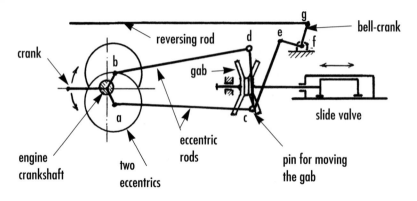

(a) Gab valve gear

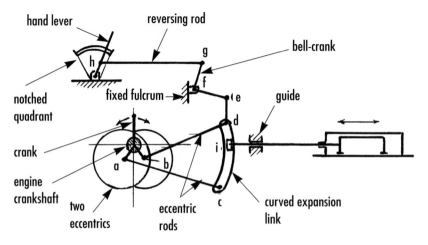

(b) Stephenson link motion – open rods

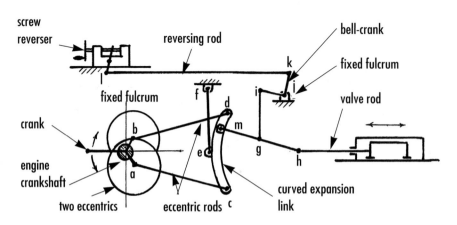

(c) Gooch link motion – open rods

Fig. 68. Steam engine reversing gears

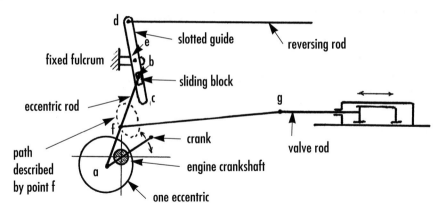

(d) Hackworth radial valve gear

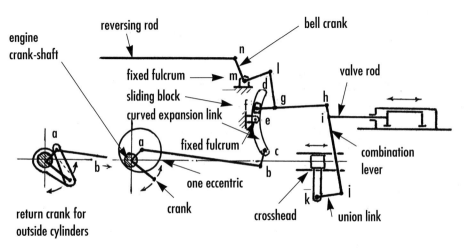

(e) Walschaert valve gear for inside cylinders

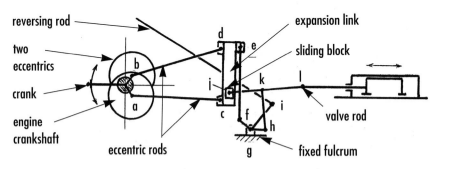

(f) Allan straight link motion

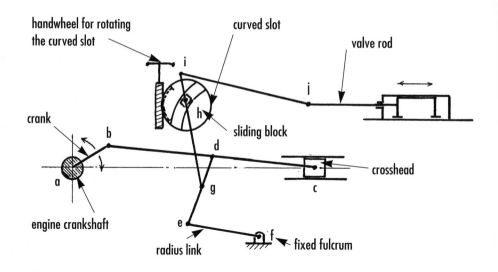

handwheel for rotating the curved slot

curved slot

valve rod

crank

i

i

h

sliding block

b

d

crosshead

a

g

c

engine crankshaft

e

f

fixed fulcrum

radius link

(g) Joy radial valve gear

under the sole influence of eccentric *ac*. Such shifting of the valve means that when steam is admitted the engine rotates in the opposite direction.

When *i* is in the mid position of the slot, it is under the influence of both eccentrics which tend to cancel each other out; the engine will then not run in either direction. Other intermediate positions either side of centre results in *i* being activated by both eccentrics, one more than the other, which reduces the travel of the valve altering the point of CUT-OFF. The closer *i* is to centre of *cd*, the earlier is the cut-off and the greater the expansion ratio of the steam. On locomotives, changing the position of the hand lever is called notching (or linking) up when it is moved towards the centre of the quadrant (from either direction) to reduce the cut-off and save steam. When the eccentric rods are as shown in Fig. 68b, the linkage is said to have open rods. They can cross over each other (called crossed rods) and if so the steam distribution is different, but the same result is achieved.

In 1856, John Ramsbottom (1814–92) invented the screw reverser, which gives infinite adjustment of cut-off, rather than stepped adjustment corresponding to the notches in the quadrant. The screw reverser is shown on the GOOCH LINK MOTION in Fig. 68c. Its disadvantage is that it is slower to operate than the hand lever reverser.

Since the Stephenson expansion link is raised or lowered to reverse the engine rotation, it is also known as the shifting link motion. Fig. 68 also shows other designs of reversing gear which are described under the relevant entries.

steps brass, gunmetal, or WHITE METAL renewable liners fitted into bearing housings to provide a low-friction surface on which a shaft can rotate. They are usually made in two halves with the joint positioned where the least pressure occurs, i.e. at the point of least wear. Some steps are made up from more than two pieces, whilst in cases where the pressure is always in the same direction, such as in locomotive axle boxes where the load is always downwards, only a top step is employed. The word has the meaning of a surface, curved in this case, on which a rotating shaft or journal is supported. Steps are also called brasses, even when they are not made from that material.

stipe a West Country term for an underground inclined plane with a single track. A double tracked incline is called a GUGG.

stoapway, *see* STOPE PIPE

stock cards larger versions of hand-held textile CARDS. As the demand for cloth increased in the 18th century, the preparation of wool and cotton for spinning became bottlenecks. Until the carding operation was mechanized and output greatly increased, attempts were made to increase the output of carded material by introducing devices known as stock cards. A

Canal lift, Anderton, Cheshire

typical stock card of the 18th century comprised a sloping wooden bench (the stock) covered with card cloth, with a similar sized board also covered on its underside with card cloth, suspended from overhead on a cord from a pulley and counterbalanced. Stock cards were operated by men sitting astride a seat facing the bench; a quantity of material to be carded was spread onto the lower surface, the upper card brought down onto it, and the material carded between the two. Such devices increased output considerably over hand cards.

stockinger man who produced knitted goods on a hand STOCKING FRAME, so called because the earliest machine-made knitted items were stockings. It is reputed that the first pair of frame-made cotton stockings made in England were by a stockinger called Draper in Nottingham in 1730, using Indian yarn.

stocking frame a machine for making knitted fabrics or hosiery by the WEFT knitting method. The first stocking frame was invented by the Revd William Lee (d. *c*.1610) in 1589 for making hosiery. His application for a patent was refused for fear of its effects on the livelihood of hand knitters. Much later, the machine was adapted to make knitted wear, but retained the word 'stocking' in its name. Lee's frame was worked by hands and feet, and comprised a knitting mechanism on an iron carriage which could be slid backwards and forwards and raised and lowered as required, the whole supported in a wooden framework. Depressing treadles caused certain parts of the machine to operate, the operator (stockinger) sitting at the frame. Its operating principle was that a number of closely spaced horizontal fixed needles held the knitted article as it was made, and specially shaped thin plates, called sinkers, hung down between the needles and formed new loops by certain movements, and added them a row at a time, gradually building up the finished article. Lee's original frame made eight stitches per inch, and was later improved to twenty stitches per inch. Since the frame required considerable strength to operate, most stockingers were men.

Fig. 69 shows the main parts of a knitting mechanism, and Fig. 70 the sequence of movements when a new stitch is made. Hooks on the fixed, spring-steel, bearded needles (*see* Fig. 72a) were closed by a presser bar, and sprang open again as the latter retracted. When a beard was depressed, a loop of yarn could pass over it. The sliding carriage holding the

367

pivoted jack could be slid backwards and forwards, or up and down by the stockinger. At the front of the jacks, sinkers hung down, and the jacks were held level by spring latches at their other end. A metal cam, called a slurcock, could be traversed across the latches to release the jacks, allowing the sinkers to fall a predetermined distance in between the needles. A loop of yarn was formed between each pair of needles, extra yarn being drawn in from a bobbin (not shown in Fig. 70). The carriage was pulled partway towards the stockinger so that the sinkers pushed the loops under the open beards; it was then raised to lift the sinkers clear of the needles, and the presser brought down to close the hooks, trapping the loops of yarn. Pulling the carriage further towards him, the stockinger pushed the previously made row of loops on top of the closed beards. The presser bar retracted, and a final pull on the carriage knocked the previous row of loops off the beards to hang over the new loops trapped inside the hooks. The sinkers were then brought back to their original position, at the same time lifting the completed knitting onto the straight part of the needles, with the jacks latched back level again. The cycle was then repeated to make the next row of knitting.

It was not until 1758 that a real development on the stocking frame was made. This was by Jedediah Strutt (1726–97), who fitted an extra row of vertical needles between the horizontal ones to make purl stitches, and form a raised rib on the surface of the fabric. This machine is known as the DERBY RIB. Eventually power driven frames capable of making shaped knitted garments were invented (*see* FULLY FASHIONED), and by then, the once extensive hand knitting industry had disappeared. The knitting industry is now mostly concentrated in the east Midlands and around Hawick in Scotland.

A stocking frame is also known as a knitting frame or, more rarely, as a knitting loom. *See also* HOSIERY, WARP KNITTING, WEFT KNITTING.

Felkin, W. *History of the Machine-wrought Hosiery and Lace Manufactures*, 1867; reprinted by David and Charles, 1967

Wells, F.A. *The British Hosiery and Knitwear Industry: Its History and Organisation*, David and Charles, 1972

stockwork working clusters of small veins of tin or copper occurring near the surface, by opencast methods.

Stokoe condenser, *see* CONDENSER (2)

stone block sleepers supports for early railway tracks. Early tram and PLATEWAY rails, and the first EDGE RAIL tracks of railways, were placed on individual stone blocks instead of transverse sleepers. The stone blocks, usually weighing between 150 and 200 lb each, were placed in

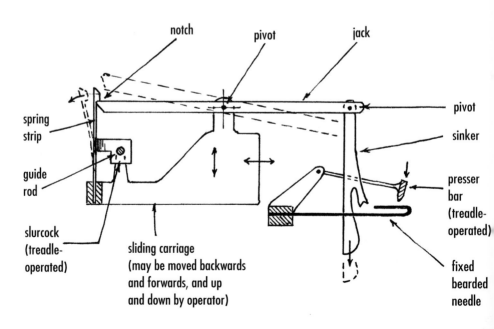

Fig. 69. Main parts of a stocking frame

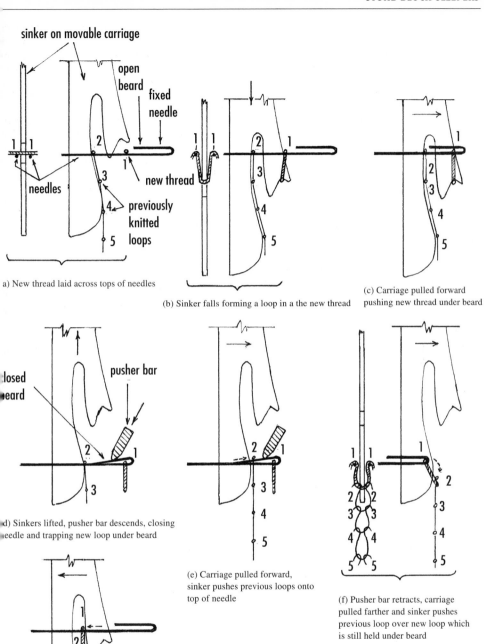

a) New thread laid across tops of needles

(b) Sinker falls forming a loop in a the new thread

(c) Carriage pulled forward pushing new thread under beard

d) Sinkers lifted, pusher bar descends, closing needle and trapping new loop under beard

(e) Carriage pulled forward, sinker pushes previous loops onto top of needle

(f) Pusher bar retracts, carriage pulled farther and sinker pushes previous loop over new loop which is still held under beard

g) Carriage moved back, sinker slides new loop off needle ready to repeat the cycle

Fig. 70. Sequence of stocking frame motions (only one sinker and pair of needles shown for clarity)

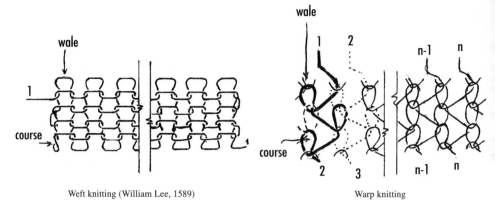

Weft knitting (William Lee, 1589)

Warp knitting

Fig. 71. Construction of knitted fabrics

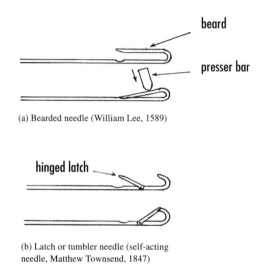

(a) Bearded needle (William Lee, 1589)

(b) Latch or tumbler needle (self-acting
needle, Matthew Townsend, 1847)

Fig. 72. Machine knitting needles

the ground under each rail, and not cross tied. The rails were held down onto the blocks by iron spikes driven into previously drilled holes, a central levelled area having been made on the top surface of the block to receive the rail. *See also* WAGGONWAY.

Baxter, Bertram. *Stone Blocks and Iron Rails*, David and Charles, 1966

stone nut the toothed pinion which takes the drive from the spur wheel in a corn mill to rotate the millstones. In an underdriven mill the stone nut is mounted on the stone spindle; in an overdriven mill it is mounted on the QUANT. Stone nuts are usually cast iron with wooden teeth mortised into them. Appletree wood was often used. Wooden teeth working with the cast-iron teeth on the SPUR WHEEL gave quiet running and eliminated risk of sparks, a very important advantage in such an environment. The nuts were usually arranged so that they could be taken out of gear with the spur when the mill was not working as a precaution

Stone block sleeper on the Bolton to Leigh railway, 1828

gainst accidental starting of the mill. This was sometimes achieved by a JACK RING which raised the nut off tapered splines on the stone spindle. Another way was to take the quant out of its top bearing to disengage the stone nut from the spur wheel when it was stationary; this was possible by incorporating a universal joint in the quant to allow this sideways movement, or by slotted bearings called glut boxes.

stoneware a hard, liquid-tight form of earthenware POTTERY which is partly vitrified, made from a clay and flint mix fired at a high temperature (1200–1300°C). A glaze is not necessary unless it is required to provide a smoother surface or a colour (iron oxide is frequently used for this purpose), or to protect a decoration. Josiah Wedgwood's (1730–95) Jasperware, invented in 1774, is an example of stoneware: it is named after jasper, a kind of quartz, which it resembled, and is decorated with raised ornamental figures and motifs. Josiah Spode II was associated with the development of stoneware at the beginning of the 19th century. Stoneware is acid proof, so has many uses in the chemical industry.

stoop 1. a dialect name for a stone post or pillar acting as a waymarker or guidepost on desolate, remote stretches of PACKHORSE tracks. They were often placed where they could be seen from a distance, e.g. on the skyline, or at crossing points and junctions. Large numbers were erected under legislation of 1697, and mileages to the nearest towns were added after 1738. Several stoops still stand on moorlands, and some have names, such as Illescholes Milestone in the Pennines, near Todmorden, Yorks. A Yorkshire spelling is steup. 2. in coal mining, the column of coal left undisturbed to support the roof of the galleries. Stoop and room is another name for the PILLAR AND STALL method of working.

stope the space left after a metallic ore, such as copper, has been excavated from the vein or LODE. Stopeing means working away the lode in steps by excavating the ore horizontally, layer by layer. Removing the ore from above is called overhand stopeing, and is the preferred method since gravity assists removal; digging ore out from below is called underhand stopeing, and here the ore has to be lifted out. Most veins or lodes are near vertical and fairly narrow. Where the vein slopes to one side, the upper wall of the stope is known as the hanging wall or hanging cheek, and the lower wall the foot wall or foot cheek, or lying cheek, since this is the wall on which a miner working in the stope can gain some foothold. Stope is probably a variation of the word step.

stope and feather an alternative name for primitive mining and quarrying tools (*see* PLUG AND FEATHER).

stope pipe (or stoapway, stope tree) a wooden pipe made from bored out lengths of trees and joined together to form a continuous pipe, through which water was pumped from coal mines by NEWCOMEN ATMOSPHERIC ENGINES in the early 18th century.

stop grooves and planks vertical grooves cut in the stone sides of a canal opposite each other at strategic places, into which planks could be dropped across the canal to act as a dam. These were used when the water had to be drained away for maintenance purposes, or to contain water in the event of emergency bursts. Sometimes a hand crane was permanently fixed on the towpath to help lift the planks.

stop lock a lock at the end of one company's canal where it joins another company's canal. Such a lock was often provided to prevent loss of water from one canal to the other, some canals having more difficulty in providing make-up water at the higher levels than others. They were also installed so that boats would have to stop when passing from one canal to another, and usually a toll house was situated at the lock.

stow (or stowe, stoce, stowce) a Derbyshire name for a small hand-operated winch or windlass erected over the shaft of a lead mine, by which lead ore was wound up in buckets or baskets. Small stows were also placed along the line of a lead vein, usually a MEER apart, as markers to show possession of the vein. An alternative name for a stow was a turntree.

straight line motion a system of linkages which guides the free end of the piston rod of a BEAM ENGINE in a straight line in the absence of a CROSSHEAD and guides. Three motions were used: THREE BAR MOTION, PARALLEL

MOTION, and GRASSHOPPER or half beam motion. James Watt (1736–1819) invented the first and second of the above when he introduced double-acting on his beam engines; this was because it was necessary for the piston to be able to push as well as pull the beam, and there were no machine tools capable at the time of making accurate guides for a crosshead.

straining hammer a water-powered hammer used for elongating iron rods and reducing their diameter before passing them on for drawing into wire. It was introduced into Britain from Germany in the 17th century.

strake a long, shallow wooden box used for washing away lighter waste material from heavier ore particles; it was also known as a tye.

strap 1. another name for a flat leather belt for driving machinery. **2.** the outer ring of an ECCENTRIC to which a connecting rod is fastened.

strap fork, *see* BELT STRIKING GEAR

streaming a method of extracting TIN from the gravels and sands of river beds. In Cornwall and Devon, prehistoric erosion of tin LODES brought CASSITERITE or tin stone down into the gravels and sands of river valleys, from which it could be extracted by a washing process. The tin bearing gravel was shovelled out by hand and spread out on a slightly sloping trough called a tye, which had water flowing down it. Material lighter than the tin was washed away, and the tin pieces collected for later smelting. The deposits were worked in sections, moving along as each section was worked out.

Tin streaming pre-dates extracting tin ore by mining, and was carried out from medieval times until the 18th century. Leats were dug to bring water to the tyes, and remains of old workings may still be traced today by abandoned leats, piles of debris, pools of water and old dams. Streaming was also used to extract more tin from the residue of mine waste.

strength of materials a property essential to know so that structures and machinery are safe in use and economic in the amount of materials used. Early engineers, builders and inventors relied upon experience, judgement or empirical knowledge, or arrived at their final designs by a process of trial and error, in the absence of accurate information. As the traditional materials, stone and timber, began to be replaced by metals in the 18th century, it became necessary to determine the strength of the latter and how they resisted the forces imposed upon them. Theoretical investigations into the elasticity, resistance to bending, tension and compression of materials had been done as

scientific curiosities, particularly in France, and practical applications of the theories were beginning to be made. Thomas Young (1773–1829) did work in Britain on the elasticity of materials before the end of the 18th century, and Leonard Euler (1707–83), a Swiss mathematician, developed his formula for the strength of columns in 1757 which has been in use ever since. An English book, popular with engineers of the day, was Peter Barlows' (1776–1862) *An Essay on the Strength and Stress of Timber*, published in 1817. Thomas Tredgold (1788–1829) published *A Practical Essay on the Strength of Cast Iron* in 1822, which was highly regarded. William Fairbairn (1789–1874) and Eaton Hodgkinson (1789–1861) conducted many important experiments on cast iron, wrought iron, and the strength of riveted joints, steam boilers, and tubular bridges, the latter in connection with designing the Conwy and Britannia bridges in north Wales; their results were published in *Useful Information for Engineers* in 1856. Two years later W.J. Macquorn Rankine (1820–72) published his *Manual of Applied Mechanics*.

A private testing laboratory was set up in Southwark, London, by David Kirkaldy (1820–97) in 1865, which remained in use until 1974. The advent of railways gave a great impetus to finding out the strength of materials for locomotive design, bridge building, retaining walls, etc.; and ship building in iron and steel also demanded more knowledge of the behaviour of materials. Advances in the quality control of manufactured materials permitted a greater reliance to be placed on them when under load.

Timoshenko, S.P. *The History of Strength of Materials*, 1953; reprinted by Dover Publications, 1983

stride, *see* STAUNCH

strike in mining terminology, the horizontal direction at right angles to the direction of the DIP of a rock or seam (*see* Fig. 73).

striking rod the iron rod which passes down the centre of the windshaft of a windmill and which opens or closes the vanes on PATENT SAILS.

string 1. an old woollen weaving measure of 2 yd 3 in, used in payment by the piece. **2.** a thin vein of ore or coal. **3.** a steel bar $\frac{3}{16}$ or $\frac{1}{4}$ in square, from which triangular and half-round files were made by hand methods.

stringer the long continuous member in a lattice girder or truss, also called a chord or a boom.

stringhearth a hearth in a BLOOMERY forge used in conjunction with a bloomhearth. It was a separate hearth in which a smith reheated a

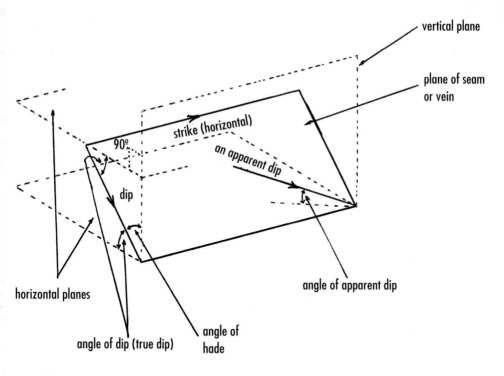

Fig. 73. Mining terms relative to seams and veins

(angle of dip) + (angle of hade) = 90°

bloom which had been formed direct from iron ore in the bloomhearth. The bloom was then hammered to force out entrained slag, several reheatings being necessary before a suitable state was reached. The name stringhearth comes from one meaning of the verb 'to string', i.e. to tighten, which comes from the Latin *stringere*, meaning to draw tight; thus, a bloom is squeezed or 'tightened' by hammering. An old spelling is stryngherth.

stripper and grinder the job description for the skilled mechanic who maintains the critical close settings and cleanliness of the working parts of a cotton CARDING machine. For good carding, the points of each wire must be kept very sharp and free from any turn-up which creates a hook. Sharpening card points and maintaining a level surface around the circumference requires skilful hand grinding, and regular stripping away of accumulated short cotton fibres and rubbish from between the wires is essential so that the cards may work effectively.

stroke the reciprocating motion, or the distance travelled, by a piston in an engine, or a plunger in a pump, etc. A stroke can be in either direction inside a cylinder or pump body. A two-stroke engine completes one cycle in two strokes of the piston, i.e. in one revolution of the crankshaft; a four-stroke engine completes its cycle in two revolutions. Cylinder capacities are defined by piston diameter and stroke.

Struve ventilator a positive displacement air pumping machine in use in the 1840s for ventilating mines. It comprised two large vessels somewhat like gasholders which were moved up and down in a water seal alternately, and drew in air from the mine workings via the UPCAST shaft, and expelled it to the surrounding atmosphere. Typical dimensions were hollow cylinders of 18 ft diameter with an 8 ft stroke, slowly driven by steam engines. The ventilator was patented by William Price Struve in 1846 (patent no. 11127).

Stückofen a primitive forerunner of a BLAST FURNACE for producing cast iron from iron ore using charcoal fuel. The furnace was developed mainly in Germany in the Middle Ages, and comprised two vertical truncated cones joined at their widest dimension, which was around 5 ft in diameter, with a 2 ft diameter bottom and top. The total vertical height usually varied from 10 to 16 ft. Normally two TUYÈRES side-by-side were sited near the base, with an opening or breast opposite them. After the furnace had been pre-heated with the breast temporarily closed with fireclay, iron ore and charcoal were fed in at the top. The iron was continuously reduced at tuyère level as it descended inside the furnace, and when about 1 ton was deposited in the base, the blast was stopped, the breast broken open, and the metal lifted out in a hot solid mass or bloom, called a *Stück* or *Wulf* in Germany (i.e. a piece or lump). Any sulphur or phosphorus present in the ore remained in the bloom, so the end product was cast iron.

The Stückofen was developed into a true blast furnace by the end of the 17th century by increasing both its height and blast pressure, and running off molten metal into pig moulds.

stuff (or stoffe) a textile material of any kind, but especially worsted, which is distinguished from wool by the absence of a nap or pile. The word comes from an old French word *estoffe*, meaning material. A stuff mark is a weaver's mark woven into the material.

stuffing box a circular metal sleeve projecting from the casing of a steam cylinder or a pump body at points where a sliding or rotating shaft passes through. Its purpose is to prevent leakage of steam, water, etc. from the cylinder or body by the compression of a PACKING material around the shaft by another metal sleeve called a gland. Soft packing may be used, or alternatively some form of metallic packing. The stuffing box is cast on the cylinder cover in the case of a steam engine, its bore being larger than the piston shaft diameter by twice the thickness of the packing to be employed. The gland is forced down onto the packing by a ring of bolts to keep it in place and seal the annular space round the piston rod, yet allow it to slide to and fro with each stroke of the engine. James Watt (1736–1819) was the first to use a stuffing box when he introduced a closed cylinder *c*.1776 on his steam engine, previous engines having had open-ended cylinders.

A similar design feature is used to seal hydraulic machinery where rams move in and out of cylinders. Here the sealing is usually done by flexible leather rings which are so shaped that the internal fluid pressure acts on them and makes a tight joint, yet allows movement of the ram or plunger.

stulls a Cornish mining term for timber supporting waste rock backfilled into excavated STOPES in a tin or copper mine.

S-twist a left-hand or anticlockwise twist given to a yarn. When yarn is twisted or DOUBLED, it can be twisted either to the right or to the left: these directions are taken relative to the direction of rotation of the spindle or FLYER, being either clockwise or anticlockwise. In a simple spinning wheel, when the spindle turns anticlockwise viewed from its free end, the yarn twists into a spiral form right to left towards the spindle. This is called S-twist, after the direction of the slope of the central portion of the letter S. FLAX is often spun with S-twist, because most of its cell walls have a left-hand spiral and the fibres tend to lie naturally in this direction. The reverse twist is known as Z-TWIST.

S-twist (or left twist)

styth (or stythe, stith) an old North-country dialect word for foul air in a mine, otherwise known as BLACK DAMP or choke-damp. It is of obscure origin, but possibly comes from an old word 'stive', meaning to suffocate. Styth was in use at the beginning of the 18th century and continued to be used for well over a century, as is evidenced from an 1863 Tyneside song:

> But did they face the deadly styth,
> Where scarce a single breath held life.

suction gas another name for PRODUCER GAS. A suction gas engine is a gas engine directly coupled to a gas producer, the outward stroke of the engine providing the necessary suction to draw air into the gas generator or producer vessel.

sugar industry Sugar as a sweetener was imported into Britain from the Near East in the Middle Ages, the word itself coming from the Arabic *sukkar*. By the 1620s, British colonists began sugar-cane growing in the West Indies and were producing a raw brown sugar using Negro slaves brought to the islands on one leg of the TRIANGULAR TRADE. The sugar cane *Saccharum officinarum* was cultivated on estates, harvested, and immediately processed in local sugar mills. Pieces of cane were crushed between parallel rollers, and the juice extracted was subjected to several successive boilings, with lime added to neutralize inherent acids. It was then concentrated by evaporation to a thick syrup. When the syrup cooled it was moulded into conical shapes ready for shipment to Britain. The thick residue (molasses) was sent to distilleries to be made into rum. In the early days the rolls were driven by wind or water power, but by the late 1780s Boulton and Watt were sending ROTATIVE STEAM ENGINES to the sugar mills of the Caribbean.

The raw brown sugar was refined in small refineries sited at or near sea ports such as Bristol, Liverpool and Lancaster into white granulated cones, the so-called sugar loaves. As demand grew, the refining became concentrated in large units and sugar was mass produced, the small units gradually disappearing. Refining involved washing off any molasses film left on the raw sugar, melting the sugar in hot water and clarifying to remove any impurities. Further lime was added and decolourizing done using carbon absorbents such as bone char. The liquid was then crystallized in vacuum, steam-heated pans, and dried in rotary driers by hot air. The vacuum pan was invented by Edward Charles Howard (1774–1816) and patented in 1813 (patent no. 3754). Sugar was subjected to a duty in Britain of $1\frac{1}{2}d$ per 1 lb in 1846.

An alternative source of sugar from the sugar beet (*Beta vulgaris*) was discovered in Germany in 1747, and by the mid-19th century large quantities of sugar were coming from Germany and France. The cane sugar industry in the West Indies began declining at this time as competition was felt from cheaper sugar from other sources in the world.

Although there are some remains of the early sugar industry in the West Indies, there is little left of the early refineries in Britain apart from some old warehouses. Most of the output of sugar is in the form of granulated white, but there are some other types made. The confectionery and biscuit industries were built up on cheap sugar imports in the 1870s. In addition to being a sweetener of beverages, sugar is used in brewing and soft drinks, and since the 1730s has been used as a preservative by boiling fruit in it to make jams.

Deerr, N. *The History of Sugar*, 1949–50
Stiles, R. 'The Old Market Sugar Refinery, 1684–1908', *Bristol Industrial Archaeological Society Journal* 2 (1969), 10–17
Wright, Neil and Ann. 'Hamilton's Sugar Mill, Nevis, Leeward Islands, Eastern Caribbean', *Industrial Archaeology Review* XIII (1991)

sulphur house a large room or building constructed in brick or stone, used for BLEACHING cloth. The pieces of wet cloth were hung in rows and sulphur burnt in pots to produce sulphur dioxide fumes, which rose among the cloth to bleach it, the fumes escaping through vents in the roof. The advantage of this early method of bleaching was that it was independent of the weather, which played an important part in the alternative method of bleaching outside by sunlight. Sulphur houses went out of use in the early 19th century when chemical bleaching commenced.

sulphuric acid a highly corrosive acid (when diluted) made from either sulphur or PYRITES, and an important industrial chemical. It is a colourless, oily liquid in its concentrated form, and its old name was vitriol, oil of vitriol or green vitriol. It has many uses, among which may be mentioned the manufacture of bleaching powder, dyestuffs, mordant manufacture, explosives, alkali manufacture, metal refining, and in the 18th century as an aid to croft bleaching in a dilute concentration. It was originally made from COPPERAS by an oxidation and hydrolysis process; later, two other processes for making sulphuric acid were introduced, the earlier one being the LEAD CHAMBER PROCESS (sometimes called the English process), and the more recent one the CONTACT PROCESS (also known as the German method). Joshua Ward (1685–1761) may be regarded as the founder of the sulphuric acid industry in England when, in 1736, he made small quantities of acid in glass vessels in Twickenham, London. He was succeeded in 1746 by John Roebuck (1718–94) who, with Samuel Garbett (1717–1805), developed the lead chamber process. Various improvements were made, and the lead chamber process reached its peak in the 1870s, but soon after began to be overtaken by the contact process.

Dickinson, H.W. 'History of vitriol manufacture in England', *Newcomen Society Transactions* 1 (1937–8)
Fleck, A. *The British Sulphuric Acid Industry*, Chemistry and Industry, 1952

sumac (or sumach) dried and ground up leaves from various shrubs, used to make a dye in the early days of cloth DYEING: it produced an iron-grey, black, or yellow colour depending on which MORDANT was used with it. A common sumach was obtained from the leaves and shoots of the shrub *rhus coriaria*, found in southern Europe. It was also used in the tanning of leather. *See also* FUSTIC.

summit level the highest level stretch of a CANAL, or POUND, from which water flowed to lower levels as locks were operated, etc. Summit levels had to be supplied with fresh water to maintain the correct depth of water in the system, this make-up coming from reservoirs placed higher up, or in some cases from water pumped up from lower levels.

sumpter pot a cast-iron bowl about 18–24 in diameter, into which molten lead from the ORE HEARTH was run.

sun and planet motion a mechanism patented by James Watt (1736–1819) in 1781 (patent no. 1306) to overcome the CRANK patent of James Pickard registered the previous year. The idea was suggested by William Murdock, Watt's assistant, and it enabled Watt to proceed with a ROTATIVE STEAM ENGINE. The mechanism comprised a large gearwheel fastened to the output shaft of the engine (the sun), around which a smaller gearwheel (the planet) rotated, held in mesh with the sun by an arm. The planet wheel was fixed to the end of the engine connecting rod, and as the piston rod moved in and out of the cylinder, the planet wheel described a circular path round the sun wheel, causing it to rotate. The configuration caused the sun wheel to make two rotations for every cycle of the engine, thus giving the output shaft a speed of twice that of the engine.

A number of sun and planet engines were made, but the device was dropped when Pickard's patent expired, and Watt's later engines used the conventional crank to obtain rotation. The sun and planet motion was the last of five alternative methods for converting the reciprocating motion of a beam engine into rotary motion covered in Watt's 1781 patent, but it is believed to be the only one of the five which he actually used.

superheat the extra heat stored in steam, above that which it can store at saturation point corresponding to its pressure. When steam is first formed in a boiler at a given pressure, a corresponding temperature is reached, and the steam will consist of a mixture of actual steam, and a small quantity of water at the same temperature. This is known as wet steam, and when sufficient heat has been supplied to convert the proportion of water into actual steam as well, the steam is then said to be dry or saturated. To achieve this condition all the latent heat of evaporation necessary to cause the change of state of all the water into steam has been supplied. It is then possible to force extra heat into the steam, raising its temperature higher without any increase in pressure. This is done in a superheater, which comprises a nest of small bore pipes situated at the rear of the boiler in the path of the leaving hot gases. Since this extra heating is done away from contact with the water from which the steam is formed,

a rise in temperature of the steam inside the pipes is achieved without the pick up of any further water.

The advantage of superheated steam over wet or dry steam is that the thermal efficiency of the steam engine system is increased, fuel consumption is reduced, and the formation of water in the cylinders is eliminated or greatly reduced. This latter advantage results from the fact that the steam can lose several degrees of temperature before it arrives at its saturation temperature at which water begins to form. The use of superheated steam was held up until suitable PACKING materials were invented that could withstand the higher temperatures, but after c.1855 superheat began to be used, initially in marine practice, to save fuel. By c.1880 superheat began to be used in mill engines, and soon became common practice. Superheating was once known as surcharging.

Surat cotton cotton grown in the areas north of Bombay, India, of the *Gossypium Indicum* and *Gossypium herbaceum* varieties. A less favourable climate means that Surat cotton is inferior to American cottons, having short, coarse fibres of non-uniform length, averaging around 0.65 in long with a diameter around 0.00084 in. It is used for coarse cotton spinning of low COUNTS.

During the American Civil War (1861–5), when supplies of raw cotton were prevented from reaching Britain, Surat cotton was substituted, but without much success, especially where fine spinning was concerned. These attempts to keep the industry going gave rise to two well-known poems by Lancashire dialect poets which bemoan the poor quality of the cotton from this source and the difficulty of spinning it: *Th' Surat weyver* by William Billington and *The Shurat weaver's song* by Samuel Laycock. *See also* COTTON FAMINE, SEA ISLAND COTTON.

surcharge, *see* SUPERHEAT

surface condenser a vessel inside which steam is condensed back into hot water by passing over the cold surfaces of a nest of pipes through which cold water is circulated. Surface condensers are always used in marine plants, where seawater is used as the cooling medium, and on land installations where the cooling water is unsuitable for re-use as boiler feedwater. *See also* CONDENSER (1).

surnames family names, which date from the 14th century in Britain, and which by the 16th century were fairly well established. Their origins may broadly be divided into four main categories: those derived from place-names; those derived from relationships, e.g. son of;

nicknames; and those derived from an occupation or office. The latter can be of interest to industrial archaeologists, since frequent occurrence of a surname in a particular area, especially in parish registers, is often a guide to a past industry of that area. Some of the less obvious occupational surnames include Arkwright, maker of wooden chests (arks); Ashburner, maker of potash from wood ashes, for making soft soap; Barker, a tanner (oak bark was used for curing leather); Blumer or Bloomer, an ironworker (from the old Saxon *bloma* for lump of metal); Bowker, a bleacher of cloth; Cartwright or Kortwright, a maker of wooden carts; Challoner, a shalloon or coverlet weaver; Chapman, a middleman between spinners and weavers; Cropper, a wool shearer; Draper, a textile merchant or retailer; Fuller, a woollen cloth fuller; Jagger, a man in charge of a packhorse train; Jenner, an engineer, usually military; Lister, a dyer (from the Middle English *litte*, meaning to dye); Milner, a corn miller (from the Old Norse *mylnari*, a watermill); Naylor, a nail maker; Sawyer or Sayer, a worker in a timber sawpit; Shearer or Sherman, a finisher of woollen cloth; Sly, a sley maker, part of a loom; Smyth(e), or Smithers, a blacksmith, farrier, hammerman, or metalworker; Tucker, a fuller of woollen cloth; Walker, a fuller, either from the Flemish *walche*, a fulling mill, or the Old English *wealcere*, a fuller; Wainwright, a maker of wooden waggons (a wain is a farm waggon); Webb or Webster, a weaver; and Wright, a carpenter or joiner. The above is only a small selection of occupational surnames. Fransson (see below) identified 165 surnames connected to the textile industry alone, and 108 to the metal industries.

Addison, Sir W. *Understanding English Surnames*, Batsford, 1978

Fransson, G. *Middle English Surnames of Occupation*, Lund, 1935

surveying the accurate measurement of that part of the earth's surface where it is intended to make a road, canal, or railway, which is an essential preliminary before work can commence. Estimates of the probable cost are based on surveys, from which the need for earth moving, construction of bridges, etc. is deduced. The Romans had instruments to aid the laying out of their long distance roads, and the manufacture of accurate surveying instruments began in the 16th century in Britain. The building of the canal system gave impetus to surveying, since the need to maintain levels over long stretches was important: knowledge of the terrain was necessary in deciding where embankments or cuttings were to be made, where a level contour was to be followed, and where locks had to be made. James Brindley (1716–72), the pioneer canal builder, often reported on what he called 'ochilor serveys' (ocular surveys), but he obviously used some instrumentation to aid his surveys in 1762 for the Duke of Bridgewater. Railways also required surveying before an application to build could be laid before Parliament, and here the gradients that the locomotives of the day could climb had to be carefully worked out. All the pioneer locomotive engineers were also surveyors. Among the early surveying instruments are the hodometer or measuring wheel, introduced in the 17th century, and the theodolite for measuring horizontal and vertical angles, introduced by Jesse Ramsden (1735–1800) in 1787.

Surveying larger areas of the earth's surface led to the production of land MAPS and sea charts. The first accurate survey of the whole of Britain was carried out by the Ordnance Survey department, set up in 1791; maps to different scales were published in subsequent years, and revised from time to time as new roads or railways were built, or towns enlarged, etc. Surveying is also required for underground mining, where it is known as dialling from the use of a large compass mounted on a tripod.

suspension bridge a bridge with a roadway suspended from cables or chains slung between tall towers either side of the span, or from an elastic arch. Suspension bridges are of lightweight construction and permit wide spans. Cables or chains hang in a natural catenary curve between the tops of tall towers built at each end of the span, and are anchored to the ground behind the towers; vertical hangers of suitable lengths are spaced out across the cables or chains to support the road deck below. All members of the bridge are in tension except for the decking, which experiences local bending between support points.

Suspension bridge design was developed in France. The first successful large span suspension bridge erected in Britain was the Menai Bridge in Wales. Built by Thomas Telford (1757–1834) between 1819 and 1825, it carries the London to Holyhead (A5) road across a 579 ft span. The catenaries were originally made from the flat, wrought-iron, eyebar-and-pin chain links, invented by Samuel Brown (1774–1852, patent no. 4137, 1817). Brown's chains were extensively used on other, later suspension bridges. The wrought-iron links were replaced on the Menai Bridge by steel ones in 1939.

Suspension bridges using cables or chains were not considered safe for railways because of their flexing, but the alternative, more rigid, elastic arch suspension bridge has been used. An elastic arch is a curved lattice type girder spanning the gap, with the road or rail deck suspended from it by hangers.

suspension wheel a WATERWHEEL of all-metal construction, in which the power take-off is by gearing at or near the rim of the wheel instead of from the central axle. Since the power applied at the rim of the wheel by the water is taken off at or near the same place, the spokes of the wheel do not have to transmit a torque, and in consequence need only be of slender cross-section like those of a bicycle wheel. For this reason the design is also called a tension wheel, the spokes being in tension only.

The suspension wheel is considerably lighter than the traditional wooden waterwheel. The design was introduced by Thomas Cheek Hewes (1768–1832) a Manchester engineer, about 1795, and enabled some very large diameter wheels to be constructed.

swallet (or swallow) a lead mining term for a natural underground channel or passage which drains water away.

swape a dialect word with the general meaning of some form of lever. It is applied to the simple device for lifting water out of a river, etc. which comprises a long pole supported on a fulcrum with a bucket at one end which can be dipped into the water, lifted up and swung round for emptying. A swape is also known as a shaduf or shadoof in Eastern countries, such as Egypt, where this ancient means of raising water is still practised.

swash plate a flat circular plate fixed obliquely on a shaft so that its faces are not perpendicular to the shaft axis. A round ended rod, lying parallel to the shaft at a distance from the axis of the shaft and pressing continuously against the face of the swash plate, receives a reciprocating motion as the plate rotates. It is pushed in as the inclination of the plate is towards it, and follows the plate outwards as the inclination is away from it. The amount it moves in and out depends on the angle of inclination of the swash plate and the distance it is from the axis of the shaft. The face of the swash plate acts as a CAM, and the rod as a follower.

The device is sometimes used to drive pistons instead of a conventional CRANK and connecting rod mechanism; it was known to James Watt (1736–1819), who called it an ecliptic. Watt patented the swash plate method of converting the reciprocating motion of a beam engine to rotary motion (patent no. 1306, 1781), although he never used it; it was the first of five alternative methods for converting reciprocating motion to rotary covered in that patent. A swash plate was often used to drive plunger pumps, and because of this is also known as a pumping plate. The term swash plate probably comes from aswash, meaning aslant.

sweatshop a workplace where goods are made under iniquitous working conditions; to sweat a person means to extract the maximum amount of labour for a minimum wage. The term dates back to the 1840s, when it referred to conditions in subcontractors' workplaces in the tailoring trade; it soon was applied to all trades where workers were forced to work in overcrowded, insanitary surroundings for unduly long hours for a bare living wage.

Swedish iron iron from the famous DANNEMORA mine, imported from Sweden in the 18th and 19th centuries and was held in high regard in Britain, being purer and of better quality than iron made from indigenous ores. Although import duties were charged, Swedish iron was nevertheless still cheaper than British iron until BESSEMER perfected his process for cheap steel, which soon replaced iron as the principal ferrous metal. Around 1750, Sweden was the world's chief producer of iron, making about one-third of the world's total: it was the preferred iron for making steel by the CEMENTATION PROCESS because of its superior quality.

sweep **1.** term for the sail of a windmill, used mostly in the south of England. **2.** the rotating arm of a circular BUDDLE.

sweep rod rod connecting the end of the beam of a ROTATIVE BEAM ENGINE to a CRANK.

swift **1.** the main rotating cylinder in a CARDING engine whose circumference is covered with CARD CLOTH. The swift works in conjunction with rollers or flats covered with similar card cloth, and arranged close to the upper half of the swift, to comb out the fibres of wool or cotton which is passed between them as a necessary preliminary to spinning the material into yarn (see Fig. 15). **2.** a lightweight, star-shaped rotating reel on which a skein of silk thread is placed so that it can be wound onto a bobbin ready for the next process. The swift has four or six arms made from an elastic wood such as West Indian lancewood. **3.** Scottish name for a fast, passenger-carrying canal boat (see FLYBOAT).

swing bridge a bridge which swings to one side on a pivot. There are several low-level swing bridges on canals, which can be moved out of the way of passing boats and barges. Some are moved manually by pushing a long arm, like opening a lock gate, the bridge turning on a pivot; others are turned by gearing, operated by winding a handle. Large swing bridges may be hydraulically operated. Two examples are the railway bridge at Queensferry, north Wales, spanning the river Dee, which is turned by hydraulic cylinders pulling a chain round; and the canal aqueduct at Barton, Lancs., over the Manchester Ship Canal.

swingle 1. the swinging part of a wooden hand flail, used for beating FLAX to remove the woody parts from the stem. Bundles of flax stalks were beaten against a board by the flail, the operation being known as swingling. Swingle comes from the German *schwingen*, meaning to swing. **2.** a crossbar suspended at its centre from the end of the arm of a HORSE WHIM or mill. Short lengths of chain hang from each end of the swingle, to which a horse can be harnessed to turn the arm to operate the whim.

swivel loom, *see* DUTCH LOOM

T

tabby a silk taffeta, originally striped. The name is an English corruption of the Arabic name *Attabiya* or *Atabi*, a quarter in Baghdad, where this type of cloth originated in the 12th century; the word taffeta probably comes from the same source. By rolling a heavy weight over the fabric, wavy lines are made which gives a watered appearance (moiré), and a fabric so treated is known as watered tabby; a tabby cat has the same wavy markings as watered silk.

table engine a compact steam engine of moderate power in which the steam cylinder was placed vertically on a 'table top' with the crosshead and guides mounted immediately above (*see* Fig. 67). The 'table' was supported on four columns from a baseplate. Two connecting rods, one either side of the cylinder, drove down to the crankshaft which was placed below the 'table' in bearings carried from the baseplate. It was thus a self-standing and self-contained engine, the first of this kind.

An engine of this design was first made by Sadler in 1797, and installed in the Royal Naval Dockyard, Portsmouth. Henry Maudslay patented a similar engine in 1807 (patent no. 3050), which became very popular for providing power for engineering and other types of workshops.

tackler a name used particularly in the Lancashire cotton industry, for the overlooker or man who maintains a POWER LOOM in working order, sets it up, and makes any necessary adjustments. He fits new warps and is generally responsible for the correct operation of the machines under his control. The weaver will call on the help of the overlooker should the loom go wrong, and the latter's skill is the main factor in maintaining a high percentage of time that a loom may continue weaving. Overlookers were usually regarded as a race apart by weavers and there was a humorous (and inaccurate) tradition that they were somewhat stupid; this gave rise to a series of 'tackler's tales' in the trade – fictitious accounts of some act of stupidity or credulous behaviour by overlookers.

The word clearly derives from the verb 'to tackle', i.e. to grapple with or endeavour to overcome a problem. In the Yorkshire woollen industry, a man with similar duties is generally known as a loom tuner.

taffeta (or taffety) a term applied to different materials at different times. Originally, it is believed that taffeta was a PLAIN WOVEN silk, but later, other yarns such as linen and cotton were added to the silk. Sometimes it was woven with a gold stripe, or in checks. Taffeta is used for ladies' dresses and shirtings. The word comes from the Persian *taftan*, meaning to twist.

tag a wooden piece fastened to the periphery of a RUNNER stone in a corn mill, which hangs vertically in the space between the stone and the surrounding tun. Its purpose is to sweep the ground meal towards the outlet chute as the runner stone revolves.

tag bail, *see* BOLE

tail box the compartment on the cap of a SMOCK or TOWER MILL that protects the winding gear which revolves the cap to keep the sails into the wind.

tailings the waste portion of an ore, usually small particles not worth working.

tail pole a strong projecting lever or arm leading to ground level, located diametrically opposite the sails on a POST MILL, by which the cap and sails could be manually turned into the wind when it changed direction.

tailrace a channel for conveying water away from a waterwheel or turbine for discharging downstream back into the source river.

taker-in the member of a team of glass blowers whose job it is to take the finished article from the team leader and place it in the ANNEALING furnace. The taker-in is the least experienced member, often an apprentice or boy in the 19th century. *See also* CHAIR (2).

take-up motion the mechanism on a loom for slowly winding woven cloth onto the front roller (often called the take-up roller) as weaving proceeds. This is done automatically by using the movement of the SLEY to activate a geared system which turns the roller a small amount at each PICK. Often this is done by a RATCHET and PAWL pair.

taking-in door (or piece door) a door giving access to a top storey LOOMSHOP, usually placed in the gable of the building and sometimes with outside stairs leading up to it. Its purpose was to enable raw materials, warp beams, and finished woven pieces to be taken into (and out of) the workspace without passing through the domestic living quarters below. In old weavers' cottages which have been modernized, a former taking-in door may have been converted into a window, or blocked off.

taking-in shop a building to which domestic weavers took their pieces of cloth to be gathered together before the CLOTHIER took or sent them to market. The taking-in shop was usually attached to or part of the premises lived in by the clothier.

tammie (or tammy) a fine, thin WORSTED cloth of good quality, often with a glazed finish, which was popular in the 17th and 18th centuries, but had died out by the mid-19th century. It was made in the Coventry area in the mid-17th century, and later Wakefield and Bradford became the centres for its manufacture. The name may be a corruption of the French *estame*, for worsted. Wakefield built its Tammy Hall in 1766 for the sale of worsted tammies, woven in surrounding districts from long wool brought from Lincolnshire and Leicestershire on the Calder Navigation. The glazed version of tammy cloth was used particularly for window blinds and curtains.

tandem compound a horizontal, stationary mill steam engine with two cylinders in line, one behind the other, the steam passing through each cylinder in turn. The cylinder farthest from the crank is usually the high pressure cylinder fed directly from the boiler, and the steam exhausting from it passes to the second, low pressure cylinder. There are two configurations for tandem compounding, single and twin (*see* Fig. 20).

In single tandem compounding, the two-cylinder engine drives one crank which is placed at one side of the flywheel (Fig. 20a). Only a narrow engine house is needed. Since the flywheel tends to be unbalanced with a crank on one side only, the flywheel width is normally kept narrow. Sometimes a mill was built with a wide engine house but only one tandem engine installed, the intention being that a second engine would be installed later. There are examples of mills where this doubling up was never carried out, the profits from the enterprise not being sufficient to warrant an extension.

In twin, or double tandem compounding, two identical tandems are placed side-by-side, each one driving a crank on either side of the flywheel, allowing much wider flywheels since it is balanced (Fig. 20c). In twin tandem installations there are four cylinders, two high pressure, and two low pressure. There are thus two parallel steam paths through the installation, the final exhaust steam meeting up in the condenser. The tandems are independent of each other, and it is possible to run one side only of the installation if required.

Large numbers of such engines were installed in 19th-century textile mills, some working well into the 20th century. A well-known large, twin tandem set is the preserved 3000 hp Ellenroad Mill engine at Milnrow, near Rochdale, Lancs., which occasionally is steamed. *See also* COMPOUNDING (1).

tanjib (or tanjeeb, tanzib) a fine muslin, made originally in north-east India, and brought to Britain by the East India Company in the early 18th century. The word is of Persian (Parsee) origin. A similar fabric woven in England was simply called a muslin.

tank bed engine a small, self-contained rotative BEAM STEAM ENGINE. The engine bed was in the form of an open topped tank containing the condenser, air pump, hotwell, boiler feed pump and cooling water pump for the condenser; the beam was carried either on A-frames or a six-column entablature above the tank. An outer crankshaft bearing was the only item not contained in the tank which also held the cooling water. Because of this, such engines were also known as wet bottom engines. They were mainly used to drive machinery in small factories, and date from around the mid-19th century.

tanning the conversion of animal hides and skins into leather by soaking them in a liquid containing tannin. Hides come from large animals such as cattle, and skins from smaller animals such as sheep and goats. Tanning has a long history, since leather has always had many uses. The old, traditional method is little used today since it was extremely slow, taking up to a year to produce the final product. Tanning was carried out in tan yards – open-sided buildings with many large pits in which the hides and skins were treated. After cleaning hair and wool etc. from them by soaking for about two weeks in milk of lime, called liming, the hides and skins were collectively called pelts. They were then treated by prolonged soaking in a solution containing tannin. Tannin is a vegetable material occurring naturally in birch, elm, hemlock, larch, oak, spruce and willow. Of these, oak is the best source, and the tannin comes from the bark of the tree. The trees were stripped of their bark in the spring (*see* BARK PEELERS) and ground to a powder in a bark mill, which was usually water-powered before the introduction of steam. The powdered bark was then soaked in water for some six to eight weeks to extract the tannic acid, a process known as leaching or leeching. To improve the strength of the tannin, ground-up unripe acorn cups from the Valonian oak were often added: the Valonian oak is particularly rich in tannin and the acorn cups were extensively imported from Asia Minor from the end of the 18th century.

The pelts were then soaked in large pits containing tannin of different strengths, known as layer pits or lay-away pits, the pelts being piled on top of each other with pieces of oak bark sandwiched between each pelt. They remained in the layer pits for up to ten months, being regularly lifted out of one pit to another, starting in a weak solution and finishing in the strongest. When the soaking was completed, the pelts, now leather, were hand scrubbed, and finally rolled with a weighted hand roller.

In the 19th century, wood-lined tanning drums were introduced in which the leathers were spun for three to four hours, a faster method than the laborious hand scrubbing. Quicker methods of tanning were introduced by the end of the 19th century using mineral solutions such as chromium to produce chrome leathers. Leather can be dyed, this being the work of a currier.

tape frame a machine for applying size to warp threads to strengthen them before they are fitted onto a loom. WARP, previously wound on a roller called a warp beam, is drawn through boiling size in a bath, then mangled between rollers to remove excess size and passed around large steam heated cylinders to dry. The individual warp threads are then separated into their correct spacing by being drawn through combs and finally wound onto the WEAVERS' BEAM.

Tape or warp sizing is so-called because the warp threads are wound onto the beam close together in the form of a wide tape; they are subsequently separated into their individual threads.

tapestry a textile fabric, dating from early times, in which the weft is stitched across the warp by hand to make up the design. The word comes from the French *tapisserie*. Tapestries were used as wall hangings, and for covering furniture. Russian tapestry is a strong linen or hemp fabric principally used for window blinds.

tap hole the small outlet hole in the base of a metallurgical furnace out of which the molten metal runs by gravity into moulds, etc. The tap hole is usually sealed by a clay plug whilst the metal is being melted and processed, and the plug broken out when the furnace is ready for tapping. A similar hole called the slag hole is sited higher above the tap hole, out of which unwanted slag floating on top of the molten metal is tapped before the metal is run off.

tappet loom, *see* WIPER LOOM

'tax on knowledge' name given to the excise duty on paper, first levied in 1712, halved in 1737, and not repealed until 1861. The tax was eliminated mainly thanks to the efforts of William Gladstone (1809–98), then Chancellor of the Exchequer, to give people cheap books and newspapers. The duty was collected by means of adhesive stamps affixed to newspapers ($\frac{1}{2}d$ per sheet in 1712). The duty made newspapers expensive for the ordinary person, and also applied to books.

teagle a northern dialect variation of the word 'tackle', used for a hoist or crane in a building such as a warehouse, for moving goods from floor to floor. The term is often used for the projecting crane situated above a LOADING SLOT, the openings on each floor being called teagle openings.

team a primitive storage bunker at a mine in which BOUSE was stored until it was dressed (*see* DRESSING OF ORE). Usually, teams were roughly built unroofed bunkers with stone walls, either rectangular or sometimes circular in plan, with an opening at the front through which the bouse was removed before it was hand sorted and broken up into small pieces by hammers.

teaser man who stoked the furnace in a GLASS CONE. It was also his task, when fresh supplies of glass were being melted down over the weekend, to take samples periodically and bring the melt to the correct temperature and condition ready for work to start on the Monday morning.

teazle (or teasel) the flower head of the plant

Dipsacus Fullonum which has a bristly surface, something like a thistle, and was used to raise the nap on cloth in GIG MILLS. Teazels were used to disentangle raw wool before CARD CLOTH was introduced, and they were cultivated in several parts of Britain to supply textile finishers; they were dried in brick buildings called handle houses with perforated walls to assist the drying. An old spelling is tassel.

teem to pour molten metal from a ladle into a mould. The word comes from an old English word meaning to empty.

telegraph system for conveying messages over long distances by means of visible signals and/or codes. Hilltop beacons were lit across England to warn of the approach of the Spanish Armada in 1588. Actual messages, not merely warnings, were sent by the semaphore invented in Britain in 1767 by Richard Edgeworth, and developed further in France by the end of the 18th century. The British Admiralty adopted the semaphore telegraph shortly after this, and erected two lines of semaphore towers about 10 miles apart between London and Portsmouth and London and Plymouth. At first, these towers supported six shutters or arms, arranged in two rotating circular frames which enabled some sixty different coded signals to be transmitted by opening and closing the arms in various ways. Aided by the use of telescopes, the speed of sending standard messages was remarkably quick: a signal could be sent from London to Portsmouth and an answer received back within 45 seconds. A number of these semaphore towers still exist. Although wasteful in terms of manpower, the system remained in use until 1847.

With the discovery of the relationship between electricity and magnetism, first demonstrated by Hans Christian Oersted of Copenhagen in 1819, the electric telegraph was developed. The first practical electric telegraph was, however, built by Francis Ronalds (1788–1873) in 1816, using static electricity to send charges down a single wire to a rotating dial driven by clockwork. The dial had letters and numbers marked on it, and the required letter or number was indicated by the movement of a pith ball, the sender having a similar dial synchronized to rotate at the same speed. Ronalds offered the system to the Admiralty, who promptly rejected it in favour of the visual semaphore they were then using. Some twenty years were to pass before further development took place, this time using current electricity, for which Charles Wheatstone (1802–75) and William Fothergill

Cooke (1806–79) took out a joint patent (no. 7390, 1837). Their first experiment was conducted along the London and North Western Railway line between Euston and Camden Town: their telegraph comprised five needles arranged on a diamond shaped board carrying the letters of the alphabet: the needles deflected in such a manner that they pointed out each letter of the message as it was sent. The success of the electric telegraph owed much to the timely invention of the Daniell cell (by John Fredrick Daniell, 1790–1854) in 1836 to provide a reliable electric current. Rapid developments were also taking place in the USA with electric telegraphs, an important one being the invention of the Morse code by Samuel S.B. Morse (1791–1872) and Alfred Vail (1807–59) in 1840, a code which was soon adopted worldwide. Within thirty years over 16,000 miles of electric telegraph lines were in use in Britain, originally operated by private companies, but taken over by the Post Office in 1870. Connection to other European countries via underwater cables soon followed, the first successful submarine cable being laid under the English Channel in 1851.

The old semaphore system still exists in simple form today in the signalling system used by railways, which were, in their early days, called telegraphs.

Fahie, J.J. *History of Electric Telegraphy*, 1884
Hubbard, G. *Cooke and Wheatstone and the Invention of the Electric Telegraph*, Routledge and Kegan Paul, 1965
Kieve, J. *The Electric Telegraph, a Social and Economic History*, David and Charles, 1973
Wilson, G. *The Old Telegraph*, Phillimore, 1976

temple (or template) the attachment on a loom which keeps the cloth as wide as the warp in the REED as weaving proceeds. This is necessary to stop the warp threads at the edges being pulled in or broken by the drag of the weft, thus narrowing the cloth. There are many types of temple, some in the form of a disk, and others a roller. Andrew Parkinson's temple patented in 1836 (patent no. 7051) comprised a disk with pins around its circumference. It was arranged horizontally near the cloth edges, and made to revolve with the action of the loom, the pins stretching the cloth out to its correct width. James Bullough and William Kenworthy, both of Blackburn, invented a spiked and fluted temple roller which did the same job in 1841 (patent no. 8790).

ten an old Tyneside measure for coal, once used for calculating rent or royalty. It was a large measure which varied over the years, reaching as much as 53 CHALDRONS. It was eventually superseded by the standard ton weight in the 19th century.

Ten Hours Act 1847 Act which reduced the hours of work of women and children in textile factories. It was forced through parliament by Richard Oastler (1789–1861) and John Fielden (1784–1849), and applied to the power-using textile industry only. Before 1847, young persons in textile factories were working up to 12 hours per day with a 69 hour week; even this was exceeded by unscrupulous employers who often worked protected persons in relays, making it difficult for factory inspectors to check that the law was not being broken. The Ten Hours Act reduced the hours of women and young persons to 11 per day with a 63 hour week; from 1 May 1848 a further reduction was made to 10 hours per day and a 58 hour week, with stops for breakfast and dinner. The Act did not apply to textile concerns not using power machinery, nor to calico printing or bleaching. It took some twenty years or so and several Acts for control over working hours to be extended to industry as a whole.

tension wheel, *see* SUSPENSION WHEEL

tenter 1. a person who minds or attends to the running of a machine such as a CARDING machine or DRAW FRAME in a spinning mill. In the case of a carding machine, for example, the tenter checks the correct working of the machine, repairs any SLIVERS which become broken, removes full sliver cans, and so on. The name is particularly used in the Lancashire textile industry, and is a variation of the noun 'attender', i.e. one who is in charge of machinery whilst it is working. The job name was reserved for persons (usually female) attending to those machines preparing cotton in successive stages before it was actually spun into yarn; the person (usually male) who runs the spinning machine was called the spinner. **2.** an alternative name for a STENTERING machine for stretching cloth.

tenter beam a horizontal beam pivoted at one end, supporting the RUNNER stone in a corn mill. Raising or lowering the tenter adjusts the gap between the working surfaces of the millstones. *See also* TENTERING.

tenter frame a framework, usually wooden, comprising two horizontal bars which could be set parallel to each other, with a row of small, sharp hooks spaced closely together in each bar. Woollen cloth after being fulled (*see* FULLING) was stretched on the frame by having each long edge attached to the rows of hooks to bring it to the required width, care being taken not to over-stretch it. The tenter frame was placed in a field

to air dry the cloth, and left so that the cloth was bleached by the action of prolonged sunlight. After it was set to width and length, the cloth would be removed from the tenter frame and bleaching continued with the cloth lying on the ground. It is from this practice that the expression 'to be on tenterhooks', i.e. to be in suspense, arose. The word tenter comes from the Latin *tentus*, meaning stretched.

In some Pennine areas, stone tenterposts can still be found standing in old tenter fields or tenter yards. Wooden frames were fastened to these, on which the cloth was stretched, dried and sun-bleached. Early Ordnance Survey maps marked tenter frames as rows of dots near woollen mills. Tenter frames were known as racks in some parts of the country, and hence a rack field is a tenter yard.

By the early 19th century indoor tentering in heated dryhouses was introduced, which speeded the drying and made it independent of inclement weather.

tenter ground, *see* TENTER FRAME

tentering adjustment of the grinding gap between a pair of millstones. The gap must be kept at the optimum distance as grinding proceeds, by adjustments while the mill is working: the size of gap depends on the type of grain, condition of the grinding surfaces, and speed of the RUNNER stone. Water mills run more or less at a constant speed, but the miller in a windmill has no control over the force and velocity of the wind, so variations in grinding speed can occur.

Fig. 74 shows one method of automatic tentering for a windmill, using a CENTRIFUGAL GOVERNOR for control. The governor is belt-driven from the stone spindle, and the grooved wheel at the governor base can slide up or down in response to speed changes. The forked end of a steelyard engages in the grooves, and pivots on a fulcrum to move a BRAYER up or down via a metal rod. The brayer supports a bridge tree which carries the cup bearing in which the stone spindle rotates. This compound lever system usually has a ratio of 200:1, so that a 1 in movement of the grooved wheel gives a 0.005 in change in the grinding gap. An increase in speed causes the runner to rise slightly, and the governor response lowers it to maintain a constant grinding gap. If the speed increase is great, because of high winds, the windmill sails have to be reefed in the usual way. In addition to automatic gap control, the miller can manually adjust the gap by turning the nut at the end of the screwed rod to suit the type of grain.

An alternative method for manually tentering a water mill is shown in Fig. 75. The bridge tree

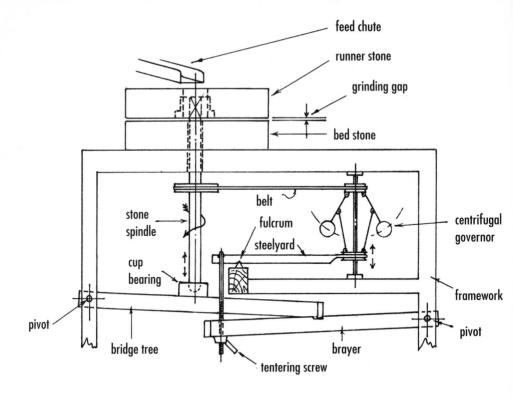

Fig. 74. Windmill tentering gear, with automatic speed control (the drive to the stones is omitted for clarity)

supporting the cup bearing is pivoted at one end, and can be raised or lowered a small amount by turning the nut at the other end. On more primitive mills the adjustment is made by tapping wedges farther in or out with a mallet, as shown.

terracotta a facing material used much in the 18th and 19th centuries on important buildings. Originating in Italy, and literally meaning 'baked clay' it was first produced in London about 1722, and is made from weathered clay and grog (either sand, or previously fired clay ground to a powder). It was frequently moulded into fancy shapes as decoration, particularly around doors and windows etc. The mixture was fired once for unglazed ware, or twice for glazed ware (called faience), the glaze being applied between firings. Available in two colours, a reddish-brown or a creamy-yellow, terracotta is a hard, long-lasting material, and is a cheap substitute for stone facings especially where decoration is required. It is also used for roofing tiles and items such as urns and statuettes. Terracotta making was usually a sideline to brick and sanitary pipe making. *See also* COADE STONE.

Stratton, Michael. 'The terracotta industry: its distribution, manufacturing processes and products', *Industrial Archaeology Review* VIII (1986), 194–214

terra poderosa, *see* WITHERITE

terry pile or velvet originally a cotton or linen cloth made with an uncut looped warp pile, dating from the mid-19th century. The loops are made by inserting a tag or wire instead of a weft PICK, with the wire secured by two or three normal picks, the sequence being repeated and the wires withdrawn as weaving progresses. The height of the warp loop so formed is dictated by the dimension of the wires used. The name terry is of obscure origin, but it has been suggested it may come from the French word *tiré*, meaning drawn, referring to the loops drawn from the warp threads.

textile industry an industry which grew from being cottage based, using indigenous wool and flax, to become Britain's leading industry in the Industrial Revolution, using imported raw materials, i.e. cotton and silk, to supplement home grown wool and flax. The industry was

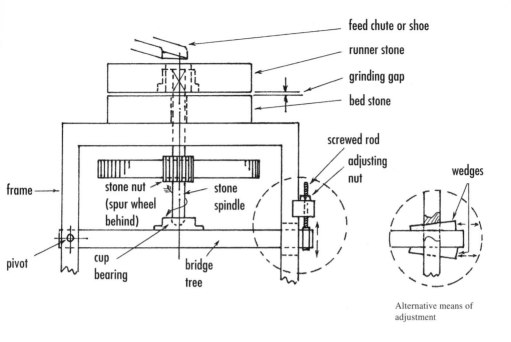

feed chute or shoe

runner stone

grinding gap

bed stone

screwed rod

adjusting nut

wedges

frame

stone nut (spur wheel behind)

stone spindle

pivot

cup bearing

bridge tree

Alternative means of adjustment

Fig. 75. Tentering arrangement for a watermill

the first to mechanize: spinning of yarn and weaving of cloth by hand methods moved from the cottage into the factory, with machinery powered first by waterwheel, then by steam engines, and finally by electricity.

The traditional sites of the early woollen industries were East Anglia and the West Country. By the early 18th century the woollen and worsted centre had moved to Yorkshire, and the importance of the southern centres declined. The cotton industry commenced in Lancashire in a small way in the early 17th century and developed to become one of great importance by the 19th century. Most of the inventions of spinning and weaving machinery were made in Lancashire during the 18th century. The silk industry originally had centres in Kent and London, but moved away to Derbyshire, Manchester, and Paisley in Scotland in the 18th century. Linen (from flax) became centred on Leeds, Yorks. The knitting industry was the pioneer in mechanization, when the hand worked STOCKING FRAME was invented by William Lee in 1589, near Nottingham, many years before the commencement of what is generally called the Industrial Revolution.

Specialization developed in each textile. The Lancashire cotton trade was traditionally a horizontal organization with four main sections: the spinning of yarn from raw cotton to specified COUNTS; manufacturing of cloth to merchants' specifications; finishing (bleaching, dyeing etc.) on commission, of cloth usually owned by merchants; and merchandizing by merchants who specify the type and finish of cloth, and sell it. Over the course of time, some vertical structuring took place: some firms spun and wove in the same mill; and mergers led to integration of spinners and weavers. Specialist firms serving the textile industry developed in the early days, such as doublers, warp sizers, and reed makers; textile engineers supplied machinery; they, or architects, designed mills. Similar arrangements occurred in the woollen industry. The British textile industry built up a large export market which peaked in the late Victorian years; the industry has declined ever since as other countries developed their own industries. Before the Industrial Revolution, indigenous wool had been the staple industry of the country, but cloth made from imported cotton became more important during the Industrial Revolution, both for home consumption and for export trade. An indication of the importance of cotton exports to Britain is shown by the following statistics:

Year	Value of cotton exports (£000s)	Cotton as a percentage of all UK exports
1775	221	–
1780	335	–
1785	865	–
1790	1,233	–
1795	2,089	–
1800	4,212	–
1825	16,900	47
1830	18,600	48
1840	23,800	46
1845	24,900	42
1850	30,500	36
1855	40,700	35

(1775–1800: figures not available)

Source: International Institute for Cotton.

See also BLEACHING, COTTON, DYEING, HOSIERY INDUSTRY, KNITTING, LINEN, SILK WEAVING, WOOL.

English, W. *The Textile Industry: An Account of the Early Inventions of Spinning, Weaving, and Knitting Machines*, Longmans, 1969
Hills, R.L. *Power in the Industrial Revolution*, Manchester University Press, 1970
Tippett, L.H.C. *A Portrait of the Lancashire Textile Industry*, Oxford University Press, 1969

textiles the general name given to cloths or fabrics which, before the introduction of synthetic materials, were made from yarns or threads of either vegetable or animal origin. It is probable that primitive coarse 'cloth' or matting, made by interlacing vegetable material, was made by early man; cotton cloth is known to date from some 5,000 years BC, and silk from a similar period.

The main textile materials of vegetable origin are COTTON, FLAX (LINEN), HEMP and JUTE; the individual natural fibres from the plants which grow them are spun into yarns from which their fabrics are constructed. Animal sources include ALPACA, MOHAIR, SILK and WOOL, which, with the exception of silk, give fibres which are spun into yarns in the same manner as vegetable fibres. Silk is produced by the silkworm in a continuous fine filament, unlike other textile materials, although several filaments have to be twisted together to make a workable yarn. The different kinds of textile materials have their own specific applications: for example, cotton, silk, and wool are mainly used for clothing and furnishings such as bedsheets, blankets, upholstery; hemp is used for ropes, sailcloth, and packaging such as sacks; and jute is also used for sacks and as backing for carpets, and in linoleum.

The word textile comes from the Latin *textilis* which means woven, but weaving is only one method of constructing a fabric, although the term is used to describe all types of fabric. There are in fact four constructions used to make a fabric: FELTING, KNITTING, LACE MAKING and WEAVING. All textile fabrics were originally made by hand methods – hand spinning of yarn, weaving on hand looms, etc., but as demand grew, mechanization of the various processes inevitably followed (*see* TEXTILE INDUSTRY).

thickset a strong, TWILLED cotton cloth with a short, very dense nap, used for hardwearing garments; its name is descriptive of the construction of the cloth. Thickset was being woven in north-west England in the 18th century.

Thomas process steel manufacture in a BASIC-lined BESSEMER converter. This process is named after Sidney Gilchrist Thomas (1850–85) who in 1878, with the help of his cousin Percy Gilchrist (1851–1935), discovered that by changing the lining of a Bessemer converter from acid to basic, phosphoric iron ores could be used for steel making. The process is also known as the Thomas–Gilchrist or basic process.

Thomson water turbine (or vortex wheel) an inward radial-flow REACTION TURBINE, developed by James Thomson (1822–92) in 1852. The water flows into the runner through pivoted curved guide vanes, sometimes called wicket gates, which are governor-controlled and which alter the inlet area to suit the volume flowing at part load. This maintains a high efficiency. A diagrammatic cross-section through a Thomson turbine is shown in Fig. 83.

thread a measure of length in cotton yarn of 54 in, the circumference of a warp reel.

three bar motion the first mechanism, used by James Watt (1736–1819) around 1780, to guide a piston rod in a straight line without the use of a CROSSHEAD. Newcomen and Watt's early BEAM ENGINES were single-acting only, with the power stroke acting downwards; the overhead beam was pulled down by a chain attached to the free end of the piston rod and the BEAM ARCH. When double-acting was introduced, a rigid connection between beam and piston rod was necessary so that an upwards thrust could be transmitted in addition to a downwards pull. Watt achieved this by a system of links which also guided the end of the piston rod in a straight line in the absence of a crosshead and guides. It was necessary that the piston rod moved in a straight line to prevent any straining at the stuffing box which would

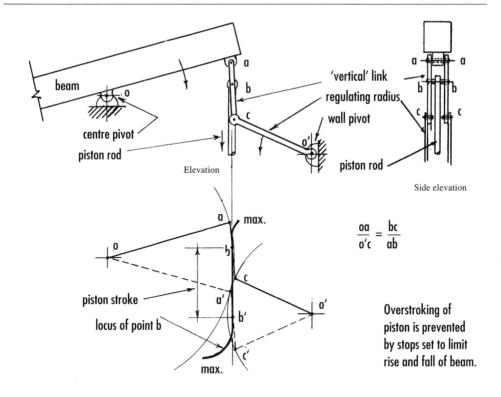

Elevation

Side elevation

'vertical' link

regulating radius

wall pivot

piston rod

beam

centre pivot

piston rod

max.

$$\frac{oa}{o'c} = \frac{bc}{ab}$$

piston stroke

locus of point b

max.

Overstroking of piston is prevented by stops set to limit rise and fall of beam.

Fig. 76. Watt three bar motion, 1785

result if any sideways movement or bending occurred. Three links were used: one pivoted off the engine house wall called the regulating radius (or from a stationary beam provided for the purpose); the second one joining it to the end of the rocking beam, called the 'vertical' link; and the beam itself making the third.

The system is shown in Fig. 76. The three links are the half beam *oa*, the vertical link *abc*, and the regulating radius *co'*. There are pivots at each of the points named. In practice, there are two links *abc*, one either side of the beam which act as one, and two links *co'* which also act as one. The piston rod terminates at *b* which lies between the two vertical links. If the linkages are moved to their extreme or maximum positions, an elongated S path or locus is described by point *b* as shown in the lower diagram. The central portion of the locus is a straight line and the lengths of the links are so arranged that the piston stroke *bb'* lies along this straight length; since the beam cannot rock farther than the stroke, the end *b* of the piston rod is guided in a straight line due to the

geometry of the system. Overstroking of the piston is prevented by stops set to limit the rise and fall of the beam.

A variation of the three bar motion, employing the same geometry, was used on the vertical rotative Durham-type beam winding engines, as shown in Fig. 78. Watt later devised another system using five links, known as the PARALLEL MOTION (Fig. 77).

threshing machine machine invented by Andrew Meikle (1719–1811) of East Linton, East Lothian, Scotland (patent no. 1645, 1788). Threshing (or thrashing) is the beating out or separation of grain from corn, etc.: before agriculture became mechanized, this was done by hand, usually just inside a barn with opposite doors wide open so that the wind blowing in helped the process.

throstle frame (or fly frame) an improved WATER FRAME spinning machine which differed from the water frame in mechanical details, being larger and operating at a much faster speed. It takes its name from the whistling noise made by the fast rotating flyers,

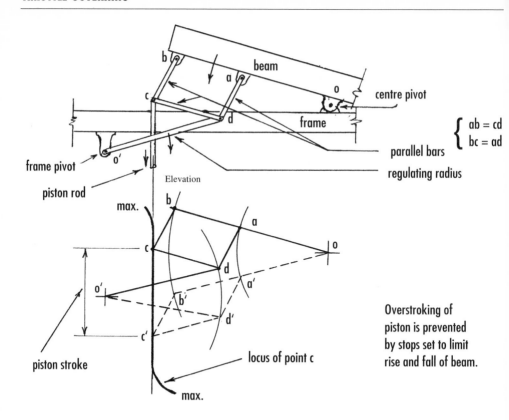

$$\begin{cases} ab = cd \\ bc = ad \end{cases}$$

Overstroking of
piston is prevented
by stops set to limit
rise and fall of beam.

Fig. 77. Watt parallel motion, 1796

throstle being a northern name for the song thrush.

Double sided machines with a central roving creel were made: the earliest ones had spindles driven from a single tin roller, with bobbins raised and lowered on a transverse rail, sliding up and down the spindles to give even winding on. The transverse rail was operated by a heart-shaped cam, and the yarn was wound onto bobbins as a cylindrical package, not in cop form as made on a MULE. Drawing, twisting, and winding on were continuous and simultaneous, producing a hard, strong, cotton yarn, sometimes known as water twist. Besides cotton, worsted was spun on throstles.

Throstles came into use after about 1815 and some development in the design took place during the first half of the 19th century. Charles Danforth (1797–1876) introduced some minor improvements in the USA c.1828, and Robert Montgomery's later improvements, also in the USA (British patent no. 8341, 1840), increased spindle speeds and production rates. The

biggest improvement was made in 1848 when Robert Shaw and Samuel Fletcher Cottam of Manchester introduced machines which had two tin rollers instead of one to drive the spindles. This allowed the driving belts to the spindles to be arranged almost horizontally, which was not possible with a single tin roller. A single tin roller meant that the machine had to be wide to reduce the angle of the belts at the spindle wharfs; by doubling the number of tin rollers the machine width could be substantially reduced, allowing more machines to be installed in a given space. Shaw and Cottam patented their invention in 1849 (patent no. 12441).

Throstle frames rivalled mules for many years, but by the 1880s had become obsolete. Their basic spinning principles led eventually to the RING SPINNING FRAME, which in turn began to replace mule spinning in Britain as early as the 1850s.

throstle governing a means of automatically controlling the speed of an engine relative to

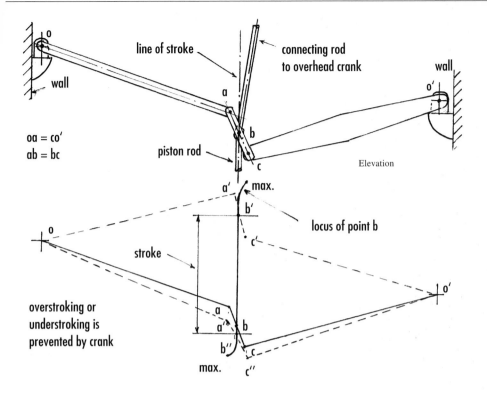

Fig. 78. Three bar parallel motion as used on Durham winders

the load on it by partially opening or closing the energy inlet valve under the action of a GOVERNOR. On steam engines, the governor varies the amount of opening of the steam inlet valve in this type of governing. On gas engines, throttle governing can operate on the gas supply valve alone, known as QUALITY GOVERNING, or on both the gas and air valves, when it is called QUANTITY GOVERNING.

throttling, *see* WIREDRAWING (1)

throw 1. (*vb.*) to shape clay on a potter's wheel into some circular form. **2.** (*vb.*) to twist or spin silk into a thread (*see* THROWING MILL). **3.** (*n.*) the vertical displacement of strata at a geological fault, also known as a heave. **4.** (*n.*) the diameter of the circular path described by a crankpin, or that of the centre of an eccentric sheave. It is equivalent to the stroke of, for example, a reciprocating pump. A three throw pump means a pump with three pistons or rams driven off a common crankshaft.

throwing machine a machine used in the SILK industry for applying the final twist to silk

threads to make them suitable for weaving into a fabric. The earliest throwing machine used in Britain was the Piedmontese machine patented in 1718 by Thomas Lombe (1685–1739) of London (patent no. 422) and installed in a Derby silk mill in 1721; it was also known as the Italian machine. It enabled high-twist ORGANZINE silk thread to be made for use as warps; before this date, organzine had to be imported from Italy. Silk intended for weft, known as TRAM, was not given as much twist. The Piedmontese machine was large and cumbersome, measuring some 18–19 ft high and 12–15 ft in diameter. It comprised a water-powered wooden inner cage, which was rotated on a vertical shaft, inside an outer stationary cage which contained the spindles. The rotating inner cage caused the spindles on the outer cage to revolve.

By the early 19th century more compact and faster machines with metal frames, not unlike THROSTLES in general appearance, had been invented for use in factories, and small hand-operated machines were available for use in the domestic silk industry. *See also* THROWING MILL.

throwing mill a factory where raw SILK is made into a yarn suitable for weaving. It is the silk industry's equivalent to the cotton spinning mill, although WASTE SILK can be spun in a similar manner to cotton.

In this instance throwing means twisting (coming from the Old English *thrawan*, meaning to twist or turn), just as a potter throws clay on a revolving wheel. A throwing mill houses a number of processes through which the raw silk passes before it becomes yarn. The silk thread, in a continuous length wound in skeins, is imported from the country where SERICULTURE is practised, and after being graded, is washed and dried. The skeins are then placed on lightweight reels called SWIFTS, mounted on winding machines and wound onto bobbins. In the early days of throwing mills this work was carried out by women and children. The thread is rewound onto another bobbin in a cleaning operation, passing through a narrow gap which removes any dirt still adhering and also any knots or snags. Broken threads are rejoined after the knot has been removed by hand, this work again being done originally by children.

Several individual threads are then twisted together to form a stronger, thicker thread, and then DOUBLED; finally, the doubled threads are twisted again in a THROWING MACHINE, which twists the doubled threads in the opposite direction to the previous twist, to make a silk yarn. The yarn may then be dyed, and despatched to weaving establishments or to the weaving shed if the mill possesses one.

throwster one who throws (twists) silk, i.e. a silk spinner. Early hand throwing frames comprised a stationary outer frame and a vertically rotating inner frame. The rotation of the inner frame caused the reels and spindles on the outer frame to rotate also, the reels slowly, the spindles rapidly, twisting the silk filaments as they were drawn from the spindles onto the reels. For silk weaving, several raw silk filaments are DOUBLED or twisted together (called throwing in the silk industry) to form a new stronger thread. A throwster is equivalent to a spinner in the cotton industry.

ticketing a 19th-century Cornish method of bidding for copper and tin ores. Smelters wrote their secret bids for loads of ore on slips of paper or tickets, which were then compared by the seller; the ore went to the highest bidder.

tickler a hand-held tool or instrument used by a stockinger working at a STOCKING FRAME, for slipping loops off one needle onto another in order to increase or decrease the width of the knitted fabric. It comprised four small points on the end of a stick. Later, the tickler was mechanized and could be made to imitate point-net lace on lace-making frames, where it causes certain loops in the fabric to be missed, enabling a series of holes to be formed in a pattern.

tide mill a water mill situated on the coast or a river estuary where it obtains its water supply from the ebbing and flowing of the sea. The mill operates on stored water from a large pond or existing creek, which might be several acres in area. A dam is built to hold the water, and a sluice or gate in it is opened when the tide comes in so that the pond or creek is filled. At high tide the sluice is closed and the mill commences working by allowing the water to drive its waterwheel once the level of the receding tide outside the sluice has fallen sufficiently to permit unrestricted discharge back into the sea. Since the head of water is low, tide mill wheels are usually UNDERSHOT, or low breast at best. Thus the mill is idle whilst the tide is filling the pond, and works during the period of low tide on water previously trapped. Working is therefore intermittent, and since there are two tides per day, but on about a 12.5 hour cycle, work starts about 50 minutes later each day. The miller therefore works irregular hours, sometimes by day, sometimes by night, according to the tide timetable. The number of hours a tide mill can work depends on the size of the pond or creek, but at least, unlike inland water mills, its source of water is regular and never dries up in a drought or freezes over.

Tide mills date from early times. The earliest recorded one in Britain was at Woodbridge in Suffolk in 1170. The Eling flour tide mill on Eling toll bridge causeway, Totton, near Southampton, is the oldest working tide mill in Britain, dating from the mid-18th century.

Weaver, M.A. *The Tide Mill, Woodbridge*, Woodbridge, 1973

tied house a house owned by a mining company, or similar concern, in which its workers were housed. Sometimes the tenancy included an obligation that other workers at the mine be taken in as lodgers, if their homes were too far away to travel to and from each day. Such arrangements usually applied where the mine was in a remote area, and the lodgers would return home at weekends.

tiffany (or tiphany, tiffney) a kind of gauze silk or muslin fabric, once popular for ladies' dresses for wearing on Twelfth Night (5 January) revels. Its name is possibly a shortening of Epiphany, having the sense of resplendent; the Feast of Epiphany (6 January) follows Twelfth Night. The name dates from c.1600.

tilt hammer (or trip hammer, helve hammer) a large, power driven forging hammer, used for beating out the impurities from a hot wrought iron BLOOM, an operation known as SHINGLING, and for shaping metal in a forge. Tilt hammers were also used for stamping ores.

Tilt hammers were introduced into Britain c.1500, and remained an important part of a forge for well over two centuries. The general design of a tilt hammer probably came from that of FULLING STOCKS, which it resembles in appearance and method of drive. It comprised a heavy cast-iron hammer head attached to a strong wooden arm or helve, usually made of ash, which was pivoted either at the end remote from the head or from some point along the length of the helve. The helve could be tilted about its pivot by a set of cams, trips or nogs, attached to the periphery of a large diameter revolving shaft or axletree, which raised the helve as they rotated until it was released as they slid clear. As the helve was raised, it pressed against a springy wooden board called a RABBET, and when released by the cam the hammer head fell onto an iron anvil by gravity, assisted by the elastic recovery of the rabbet to increase the impact of the blow. The work to be hammered was held on the anvil, and received rapidly repeated blows as the driving shaft revolved. Tilt hammers are of massive construction to withstand the shocks from the hammering.

There were different types of tilt hammers depending on where the lifting trips acted on the helve. If they acted on a short helve extension beyond the end pivot, they were known as a tail helve; if they acted on the helve between the hammer head and the pivots, they were known as a belly helve; and if lifting the helve at the hammer head end, a nose helve. Nose helves were favoured for shingling.

The earliest tilt hammers were water-powered, and constructed from massive timbers, except for the hammer, anvil and pivots which were of iron. By the 18th century cast iron frames were being used, and in addition to continued use of water power, steam engines were sometimes installed to drive the hammer through gearing. There were disadvantages to tilt hammers. The blow that could be given was constant in magnitude, and only from the gravity descent of the hammer assisted by the action of the rabbet. Further, the space between hammer and anvil was rather restricted, and large forgings 'gagged' the hammer, reducing the height of free fall and hence the effect of the blow. After the introduction of the vertical STEAM HAMMER in 1839, with its controllable blow, tilt hammers became obsolete.

It has been said that the expression 'full tilt', meaning full speed or with full force, comes from the days when tilt hammers were in use, and referred to running a hammer at maximum speed. However, it is more likely to date from earlier days, and refers to the martial exercise of tilting (charging) at a quintain, with a lance, as practised by mounted knights in a tiltyard.

timber wood cut from trees, humankind's earliest material for construction and fuel. Timber is an organic material, renewable by tree planting, and may be divided into softwoods and hardwoods, each having its own particular use. Early textile mills, warehouses, watermills and windmills all used timber extensively, having wooden beams, floors, and roof frames. Waterwheels were made of wood; Brunel (1806–59) built timber bridges and viaducts for the Great Western Railway; stocking frames, hand looms, spinning wheels, etc. were all made from wood, with a few metal parts for highly stressed areas. Newcomen atmospheric engines had massive timbers. Carts, canal boats and ships were all wooden at one time; the word carpenter comes from the Latin carpentum, meaning a waggon or cart. It has been estimated that 90 per cent of the world's merchant shipping was still wooden in 1840. Foreign woods such as mahogany began to be imported for the furniture trade from the West Indies in the early 18th century.

Some chemicals were originally wood based, such as oak bark for tanning leather, and oak galls, used as mordants in the dyeing industry. Many dyes themselves came from woods or bushes, such as logwood from central America, and yellow dye from broom and gorse. Charcoal was the only fuel for iron-making blast furnaces, and even after coke was successfully tried out at Coalbrookdale in 1709, charcoal continued in use elsewhere for many years. The great deforestation of trees for blast and glass-making furnaces caused sufficient alarm in the 16th century for Acts to be passed restricting the cutting down of oaks in case there would be insufficient for defence by the 'wooden walls of England'.

Trees were originally felled by hand tools, and logs sawn up at hand-worked SAW PITS. Many ingenious methods of joining timbers were devised using hardwood pegs. Woodworking machinery began to be used by the 19th century, at about the time when wrought and cast iron began replacing timber for many applications. However, the skills of the carriage builder, wheelwright and furniture maker have continued to this day.

tin a silvery-white, malleable non-ferrous metal whose chief ore is CASSITERITE. Its chemical symbol, Sn, is an abbreviation of *stannum*, the Latin for tin, but the word tin is old Anglo-Saxon; its discovery dates back to prehistoric times. Tin was mined in Cornwall and Devon for over 2,000 years, which was Europe's main source of the metal until Malayan tin began to supersede it *c.*1860. Tin has a low melting point of 232°C and possesses a high resistance to corrosion. It was used extensively to make PEWTER, alloyed with lead (80 per cent tin, 20 per cent lead); in solder, TINPLATE (sheet iron dipped in molten tin); alloyed with copper to make bronze (in a ratio of about 8:1); and also used in bearing metals.

Tin is mostly found in veins which lie almost vertical. The ore is crushed under STAMPS, roasted to remove arsenic (which is frequently found in association), and sulphur, and finally smelted in reverberatory furnaces. The deep mines in Cornwall are mostly abandoned today, and are characterized by the scattered ruined stone houses and chimneys which once contained steam engines driving dewatering pumps. It was the provision of steam engines for this duty that prompted the development of the first BEAM ENGINES. Tin may also be found in alluvial deposits in certain streams in Devon and Cornwall, from which it is removed by STREAMING. It may also be found in the same vein as copper, but at a greater depth. *See also* STANNERY.

Atkinson, R.L. *Tin and Tin Mining*, Shire Publications, Album No. 139, 1985
Barton, D.B. *A History of Tin Mining and Smelting in Cornwall*, Barton, Truro, 1967
Greeves, T. *The Mines and Miners of Dartmoor*, Devon Books, 1986
Hedger, E.S. *Tin in Social and Economic History*, Arnold, 1964

tin cylinder or roller the horizontal drum which spans the width of a spinning JENNY from which the spindles are driven by means of individual bands or ropes (*see* Fig. 41). The tin cylinder itself is rotated by a driving band from the large handwheel. It was added to Hargreaves' jenny by Haley, of Hoghton, near Blackburn, Lancs.

tinplate sheet steel (formerly iron) coated with an extremely thin layer of tin to provide a corrosion resistant surface. Its main use is in the manufacture of cans for preserving foodstuffs. Originally a German process, the method of tinning iron sheets was brought to Britain in 1665, but manufacture did not commence until 1720 when a small works was set up in Pontypool, south Wales; tinplate manufacture also spread to Wolverhampton soon after. Tin was brought from Cornwall, and local coal fired the metal melting furnaces. Water-powered ROLLING MILLS and shears were manually operated to reduce heated iron bars down to the required thickness, before they were dipped in molten tin. The process was very labour intensive, and became an important industry in south Wales around Swansea; for many years it was almost a British monopoly, and by the 1850s this area had the largest tinplate works in the world. The USA was the largest customer, needing tinplate for its developing canning industry, but in 1890 the MCKINLEY TARIFF brought a sudden collapse in demand. Many skilled workers emigrated to the USA from the Swansea area, and helped build up the American tinplate industry.

The tinplate manufacturing process of the 1830s onwards involved rolling iron bars (and later steel after the invention of the Bessemer process) down to a certain thickness, then doubling them over until there were eight layers, which were rolled down to a final single sheet not exceeding 0.01 in total thickness. The sheets were slowly annealed to remove hardness induced by rolling, and pickled in dilute acid to remove scale and oxide. They were dipped twice in a molten tin bath, and cold rolled to remove any irregularities in thickness. The tin coating was less than 0.005 in thick.

Little remains today of the old manufacturing plant, but some buildings still stand, which have been converted to other uses. Tinplate manufacture today is a fully automatic industry, with tin applied by electrolytic means.

Brooks, E.H. *Chronology of the Tinplate Works of Great Britain*, 1944
Minchinton, W.E. *The British Tinplate Industry: a History*, Oxford, 1947

tirl (or turle) the vertical wooden shaft of a NORSE MILL which supported the upper rotating grindstone at its top end and had wooden vanes projecting from its lower portion, onto one side of which the water was directed to rotate it. The word is a variant of twirl.

tirring a Scottish term for removing waste and worthless material or tirr before the extraction of granite can commence. Often this type of preliminary work was contracted out by the granite quarrying company to a labouring force.

toadstone (or blackstone) an old Derbyshire mining term for several types of worthless basaltic rock of volcanic origin found in lead bearing veins. The word may be an Anglicized version of the German *Todstein*, meaning dead stone, or it may be descriptive of the surface appearance of the rock, which resembles the skin of a toad. The rock also weathers into toad-like shapes. *See also* CHANNEL.

tobacco industry industry based around the dried leaves of several narcotic plants of the genus *nicotiana*, which originated in America but is also grown in Malaysia, the Balkans, Africa and India. It may be smoked, chewed, or sniffed in the form of snuff. Its introduction into England is attributed to Walter Raleigh in Elizabethan times. Expensive at first, it cheapened rapidly in the 17th century because of increased imports from the American plantations. At first, tobacco was smoked in pipes: white clay pipes were manufactured from the early 17th century by many small-scale family-run workshops, and often carried their maker's mark stamped on them. Clay pipes have been catalogued and intensively studied – discarded, broken pipes are useful dating aids when discovered on archaeological sites. Briar pipes were introduced at the end of the 19th century. Cigars were first imported around 1800, whilst cigarettes were being made in Britain by 1856.

To make tobacco, bundles of dried tobacco leaves are moistened and the mid ribs stripped out. The mid ribs and stalks are ground up in snuff mills, whilst the leaves chopped up to make either pipe tobacco or cigarettes. Snuff was popular from about 1700 to about 1850, when its use declined. There was a tobacco industry around the Lincolnshire ports in the 19th century, and at other bigger ports such as Glasgow and Bristol; Glasgow's 18th-century prosperity was built on tobacco from the Maryland and Virginia plantations. Most tobacco imported into Britain was exported onto the Continent, although the American War of Independence destroyed much of this trade.

Oswald, A. 'The archaeology and economic history of English clay tobacco pipes', *Journal of the British Archaeological Association* 23 (1960), 40–102

Walker, I.C. 'Statistical methods for dating clay pipe fragments', *Post-Medieval Archaeology* 1 (1967), 90–101

tobine (or tabine) a strong twilled silk fabric.

tod an old measure for weighing wool, equal to 28 lb.

toilonet (or toilinette) fine woollen cloths, popular in the first half of the 19th century for men's waistcoats.

toll a fee charged for the use of a facility such as a turnpike or canal. Users of turnpike roads were charged a toll, collected at a toll house, according to a scale of charges displayed on the toll house wall. The charges depended on the type of traffic, for instance, according to the weight carried in a cart, the width of its wheels (narrow wheels damaged the road), and the number of horses pulling it; driven animals, such as cattle and sheep, were charged per head or by the score; and stagecoaches, according to the number of passengers or the number of horses. Toll charges were not standard throughout the country, and were sometimes changed locally. Excessive tolls were the cause of resentment (*see* REBECCA RIOTS). A traveller making a through journey on turnpikes had to pay a toll about every 7 miles, and the money collected financed the upkeep of the road; any surplus was profit for the TURNPIKE TRUST. Road tolls were abandoned in the late 19th century when road upkeep was taken over by public authorities.

Canal tolls were based on the earlier turnpike system, users of the canal paying a toll based on goods carried and distance covered. Up until 1845, tolls were the only income for canal companies, since they were not permitted to act as carriers until that date. Fare-paying passengers were carried on railways' own rolling stock from the earliest days, but goods were carried in private trucks on payment of a toll to cover use of the track and cost of haulage. Tolls were paid at railway companies' offices. Whereas the right to charge tolls on turnpikes was limited to the duration of each Turnpike Act (usually twenty-one years) and had to be renewed, the power to charge tolls on canals and railways was perpetual.

In medieval days a toll known as a pontage had to be paid to cross some bridges.

Tolpuddle Martyrs six agricultural labourers who formed a trade union to oppose wage cuts, and were transported to Australia in 1834. The six men formed the Friendly Society of Agricultural Labourers in Tolpuddle, near Dorchester, Dorset, in an attempt to resist wage cuts by the combined action of local farmers. The initiation ceremony on joining the Society included the swearing of an oath, and it was under an old Unlawful Oaths Act of 1797, made during the French wars, that the alarmed authorities prosecuted the men. They were sentenced on 19 March 1834 to seven years' transportation, and sent to Tasmania, Australia. Such harsh treatment created a great public outcry, and their sentence was eventually commuted in 1837. They returned to England, and were granted tenancies of farms in Greensted, near Chipping Ongar, Essex, but eventually emigrated to Canada.

Marlow, J. *The Tolpuddle Martyrs*, History Book Club, 1971

tommy shop nickname given to a shop owned by an employer where his employees had to exchange vouchers or tokens, given instead of money as wages, for goods. This was known as the TRUCK SYSTEM. The word tommy was a slang word for bread, food, etc. A tommy tin was a tin box in which a collier carried his food underground.

'Tom Pudding' nickname for an iron compartment barge or boat, almost square in area and about 8 ft deep, used for shipping coal from South Yorkshire mines along the Aire and Calder Canal. Such barges were towed by tugs, in trains of up to thirty at a time, to the port of Goole where the coal could be transferred into coastal and sea-going ships. Specially long, quick-acting locks were built to accommodate them, and hydraulic lifting and tipping machinery was installed at Goole. Each barge held 35 tons of coal. The system was patented by William Bartholomew in 1862, and was in use until 1986. It is believed that the unusual name for these iron 'tubs' comes from the action of tipping them over when emptying the coal into a ship's hold, it being likened to turning a pudding out onto a plate.

top 1. a long length of combed wool without any twist, in ball form. Tops are produced by a wool comber and comprise long fibres only, short fibres or NOILS having been combed out. Tops are the raw material from which WORSTED yarn is made by spinning; a top maker is someone which specializes in making tops for the worsted industry. The short fibres which have been removed from the finished top are sold to woollen spinners. **2.** a circular, hand-held hardwood block, used in ROPE MAKING.

torpedo the undersea missile developed by Robert Whitehead (1823–1905) in his Fiume works, Italy, in 1866, based on an earlier design, the *Küsterbrander* (coastal fireship) of Giovanni de Luppis. The original torpedo had a body made from iron boiler plates. In 1873, John Ericsson (1803–89) introduced a wire-controlled torpedo.

Gray, Edwyn. *The Devil's Device*, Purnell Books, 1975

torrefying, *see* CHARKING

tow the short fibres of flax removed by SCUTCHING and HACKLING the stalks. Up to about one-third of the total flax can be tow, which makes a coarser linen yarn than that made from the long fibres or line.

tower mill a windmill, constructed with a stationary tower of brick etc. which houses the machinery, and a rotatable top cap, usually of timber, containing the sails. Only the top cap rotates to keep the sails in the wind. Tower mills date from the 14th century in Britain. In

The last surviving tower mill with eight sails, at Heckington, Lincs.

simple early mills the cap was turned by hand, the miller pushing a long tail pole which reached from the cap to ground level. More advanced designs incorporated a geared device which could be operated from an elevated gallery running round the tower, and cap turning was eventually made automatic by a FANTAIL.

town gas the common name for coal gas, made by the destructive distillation of low-ash bituminous coal in externally fired RETORTS. Coal gas was first used to light a few textile mills, replacing candles, but it soon became a public utility, lighting town and city streets, public buildings and domestic houses – hence the word town in its name. Later, its heating value was used in domestic cookers, water heaters, radiant fires, and industrial furnaces. It was also used for a number of years as fuel for GAS ENGINES for power production, until electric power became widespread.

After the gas has been drawn off the coal in the retort, the residue coke is removed, itself a useful fuel which has other uses. The crude gas from the retort requires purification before it can be consumed, and during this process tar and other valuable by-products are extracted. The cooled, clean gas is stored in large GASHOLDERS, and distributed through underground pipelines to consumers. The constituents of coal gas vary somewhat according to the type of coal used in its manufacture, but an approximate analysis is 55 per cent hydrogen, 30 per cent methane and 10 per cent carbon monoxide, with the balance made up of small amounts of other gases.

By the second decade of the 19th century joint stock gas companies were supplying gas from central stations to the public, municipalities and industrial users; by the middle of the century almost every town of any size in Britain, had its own gas manufacturing company, and private gas plants tended to die out. In 1859 there were over 900 independent gas companies, some large, some small, supplying gas to their immediate neighbourhood; in some cases rival companies operated in the same town. By 1870, electric lighting began to compete with gas lighting, and gradually gas disappeared from the lighting scene, but continued to supply domestic cooking and space heating needs, industrial furnaces, etc. *See also* GAS MANUFACTURE.

Steward, E.C. *Town Gas*, Science Museum, 1958

towpath a path alongside a canal on which the horse pulling a barge can walk. Normally there is only one towpath alongside a canal; where it is necessary for the towpath to change sides, a ROVING BRIDGE is often provided. The earliest recorded towpath was actually constructed alongside the river Severn in 1581, and was used by gangs of men hauling becalmed trows (sailing barges). A toll had to be paid for using this towpath.

When canal boats travelling in opposite directions met, the towrope of the boat farthest from the towpath was lifted over the boat nearest the towpath to enable the boats to pass each other. Towpaths were not popular with some landowners, who maintained that they gave poachers and unscrupulous boatmen access to their adjoining land. It was because of this objection that towpaths sometimes changed sides for no apparent topographical reason. Besides providing a path for towing, a towpath was the means for access to the canal for maintenance purposes. Alder trees, which tolerate damp conditions well, were sometimes planted alongside a towpath by the canal builders, so that their spreading roots would help to bind the base of the path and prevent collapse.

The side of the canal opposite the towpath is known as the off side.

track boat Scottish name for a canal PACKET BOAT.

traction engine officially known as a road locomotive, a vehicle with large road wheels, gear driven from a steam engine mounted on top of a horizontal boiler. Traction engines developed from STEAM CARRIAGES. Originally they were not self-propelling but were pulled by horses in agricultural areas from site to site, where they drove equipment such as steam ploughs and threshing machines. A power take-off pulley was driven by the steam engine from which belts drove the various other machines. By about 1850, traction engines were made self-propelling, but legislation restricted their speed on the roads to 4 mph. They were used for towing heavy loads, or hauling via a rope drum. The steam roller is a specialized version of a traction engine. Two well-known makers of traction engines were John Fowler (1826–64) of Woolston, Lincs., who was making engines for steam ploughing in 1854, and Thomas Aveling who made his first in 1858.

Beaumont, A. *Traction Engines Past and Present*, David and Charles, 1974
Hughes, W.J. *A Century of Traction Engines*, David and Charles, 1970

tractive effort the power of a steam locomotive, as measured by the force exerted at the rim of the driving wheels, which depends on the force produced by the pistons and the diameter of the driving wheels. The term HORSEPOWER is not suitable for steam locomotives, there being too many factors affecting its power output. The ability of a locomotive to grip the smooth rails without slipping is an important factor affecting its tractive effort, as is the weight carried by the wheels. The effect of climbing a gradient is also important. When locomotives were first being designed it was thought that gradients of 1 in 50 were the maximum that could be climbed; however, John Hawkshaw (1811–91) demonstrated that steeper gradients could be climbed, although 1 in 19 was the steepest on the British rail system. Another term for tractive effort is draw-bar pull, this being the pulling force in pounds available for hauling a train.

Tractive effort is usually measured at 85 per cent of the boiler working pressure to allow for inherent losses within the engine itself. As locomotive engineering progressed and higher steam pressures were used, the tractive effort improved. For example, the tractive effort of the *Rocket* in 1829 was a mere 825 lb; by 1838 the *Lion* had a tractive effort of 2,160 lb; and in 1846 *Coppernob* produced 7,718 lb. By the 1860s over 10,000 lb draw-bar pull had been reached. For a typical double-acting two-cylinder locomotive, the tractive effort in pounds, for each pound of effective steam pressure per square inch acting on the pistons, is given by the product of the square of the piston diameter and its stroke divided by the diameter of the driving wheels (in inches).

See also ADHESIVE FORCE.

trade marks symbols and distinguishing marks or letters which a company puts on its goods and products to denote their origin. Such marks have a long history, but it was not until the Trade Marks Registration Act of 1875, which came into operation on 1 January 1876, that legal entitlement became enforceable. Some 10,000 applications were filed in the first year. Trade mark no. 1 is the red triangle of Bass the brewers. There are thirty-four classes of goods in the system.

trade tokens metal 'coins' introduced in the late 18th century by some employers, because of a shortage of coins of the realm at that time. They were paid as wages and could be spent locally in return for goods: the shopkeepers returned the tokens to the issuing employer who exchanged them for real money. The system was open to abuse, and when there was an increase in the number of real coins in circulation, tokens were made illegal by the Act of Suppression 1818. John Wilkinson (1728–1808), the ironmaster, 'minted' tokens in the 1780s and 1790s.

In Cumberland, coal owners issued brass or bronze tokens to carriers who carted their coal from the pits to the harbours. The carters, often local farmers, exchanged the tokens for cash at the coal owner's agent in payment for their services. Such tokens had the name of the colliery on one side, and usually a picture of a horse whim, a chaldron, or steam locomotive on the other. Similar arrangements existed in other parts of the country. In addition to metal tokens, paper shop-notes were used by some employers, such as Samuel Oldknow (1756–1828), to pay wages. These would only be accepted by local shopkeepers on the understanding the issuer would convert them later into real money. Sometimes shopkeepers would only accept shop-notes at a discount.

Trade tokens are collectors' items today.

Trade Tokens, Shire Publications, Album No. 79
Whiting, J.R.S. *Trade Tokens*, David and Charles, 1971

trade union association of workers in a particular trade or industry formed for protecting their wages, working conditions and rights by collective bargaining. Many unions also acted as friendly societies.

Trade unionism developed out of the Industrial Revolution, and the historical documents of unions record one aspect of the social side of industry. As the factory system gradually replaced domestic working in the 18th century, it brought men and women together in mills and workshops for the first time, and gave the opportunity for combined action with regard to working conditions. Early attempts at combination in the last decade of the 18th century were suppressed by the authorities who feared revolutionary action similar to what was happening in France at that time. The COMBINATION LAWS of 1799 and 1800 made organized trade unions illegal, although many small unions were formed in secret.

In 1824 some relaxation of the laws allowed combinations for the purpose of negotiating wage rates and hours of work by collective bargaining, but organized strikes still fell within the common law of conspiracy. The swearing of oaths of secrecy was also forbidden, and this law was used against the Dorchester agricultural labourers in 1834 (*see* TOLPUDDLE MARTYRS). Unions continued to be formed, largely among skilled workers in various industries, but they were small and local. In 1834 an attempt was made to amalgamate local unions into a national one to increase bargaining power, and the National Consolidated Trade Union was formed with a membership of over 0.5 million. But it collapsed soon after formation, and many of its militant members began supporting the People's Charter which had been published by the London Working Men's Association in 1838 (*see* CHARTISTS).

After the failure of Chartism, several unions in the engineering industry combined to form the Amalgamated Society of Engineers in 1851. By fixing members' subscriptions at a substantial level, the union became wealthy enough to employ its own officials, pay sickness and unemployment benefits and strike pay, and provide legal assistance when required.

Some acts of violence against blackleg labour in Sheffield, and the embezzlement of union funds by a treasurer in Bradford in the 1860s, resulted in the setting up of a Royal Commission in 1867 to enquire into the conduct of unions. Its Report led to the Trades Union Act of 1871, which allowed unions to act in restraint of trade, and stipulated that a union should join the Register of Friendly Societies, and that its funds were protected, provided its Rules did not contain restrictive clauses. In 1875 peaceful picketing during an official strike was legalized.

During the 1870s, many new unions were formed modelled on the Engineer's Union, including some for unskilled workers; however, a downturn in the country's economy soon afterwards caused a number to disappear, including that for agricultural labourers, founded in 1872. The General Federation of Trade Unions was set up in 1889 to strengthen the movement.

Cole, G.D.M. *Short History of the British Working Class Movement*, 1927; revised edition printed by Macmillan, 1948
Pelling, H. *A History of British Trade Unionism*, Penguin, 1971
Webb, S. and B. *A History of Trade Unionism*, 1894; revised edition printed by Longman, 1920

trail barrow a kind of sledge for transporting slate. In the early days of slate quarrying in the Lake District, large blocks of freshly quarried slate were brought down the steep sided fells and screes, on these wooden sledges, which had two shafts at the front like a horse cart. A quarryman ran in front of the heavy load between the shafts, guiding the trail barrow. This was a highly dangerous practice which was later replaced by SELF-ACTING INCLINES and tramways.

training wall an embankment built to canalize a river estuary, by controlling the direction of flow of the water to prevent flooding and provide a definite channel. Some training walls are of great age and were formerly called dykes or levees. Training straightened the river channel and increased the speed of the current, so that the scouring effect on the river bed kept the channel open for the passage of boats.

train shed that part of a large railway station, usually a terminus, which comprises a large roof over platforms and tracks to give passengers and carriages cover from the weather. From the earliest days of railways, termini were roofed over: large roofs were constructed from iron frames and columns, while small ones were often of timber. Some very large spans were built over multi-platform stations, the largest in Britain being that at St Pancras, London, where an iron and glass span of 240 ft, designed by William Henry Barlow (1812–1902), was opened in 1868. Another large span train shed is the former Manchester Central Station, now the G-Mex exhibition hall. It has wrought iron arches of 210 ft span, and was opened in 1880.

Betjeman, J. *London's Historic Railway Stations*, Murray, 1972
Biddle, G. *Victorian Stations*, David and Charles, 1973
Fitzgerald, R.S. *Liverpool Road Station, Manchester – an Historical and Architectural Survey*, Manchester University Press, 1980

tram 1. in the 18th century, a small, wheeled trolley used for conveying ore or coal in mines along a primitive tramway or track. The word probably comes from the old German word *Traam*, associated with early mining practice when coal trucks ran along timber baulks which acted as rails. There is a popular misconception that the word tram came from the surname of Benjamin Outram, who ran vehicles on stone rails at Little Eaton, Derbys., in 1800, but the German derivation of the word is more likely.

2. (or tramcar, car) horse-drawn, rail-guided vehicle for public transport, introduced in the streets of British towns and cities, when tramways were built in the mid-19th century. In 1861, a tramway comprised lines of plates fixed in the roadway, with a central groove in which a guide wheel ran to keep the outer wheels of the tram on the iron plateway; the first horse-drawn tramways of this kind were in Manchester and in Birkenhead, near Liverpool. The Tramways Act of 1870 enabled local authorities to construct tramways within their own areas, but not to operate them themselves; this was altered in 1896, when they were permitted to run the system. By this date, the outer wheels of the trams ran in grooved rails with no central guiding system. Steam driven trams, compressed air driven trams, and cable haulage by fixed engines, were all tried in different towns until eventually electric traction superseded all other means of supplying power. The first electric tramway in Britain opened in Leeds in 1891.

Bett, W.H. and Gillham, J.C. *Great British Tramway Networks*, Light Railway Transport League, 1962
Klapper, C. *The Golden Age of Tramways*, Routledge, 1961

3. a silk thread intended for WEFT. It is not twisted as tightly as ORGANZINE warp in the THROWING process. The word comes from the Italian *trama*, meaning weft.

tramroad (or plateway) a primitive track laid to ease the movement of heavy weights, believed to have originated in German metal mines in the 16th century. The earliest known tramroad in Britain was in Brecon, south Wales, in 1798. Some early tramroads were laid out initially for horse-drawn, wheel-less sledges, and rails for wheeled trucks added later; but some tramroads had rails from the beginning.

Baxter, B. *Stone Blocks and Iron Rails*, David and Charles, 1966
Lewis, M.J.T. *Early Wooden Railways*, Routledge, 1970

transmission of power Power may be transmitted in several ways from a prime mover to drive machinery. Early textile mills used toothed gearwheels and vertical shafts to drive LINESHAFTS on each floor from a ground level waterwheel or steam engine. The final power drives to individual machines were by flat belts running over pulleys spaced out along the lineshafting. Speed changes between prime mover and machines were created by the ratio between gearwheels, and by pulley diameters. Around the 1860s, hemp or cotton rope drives from engine flywheel up to floor lineshafts began superseding geared systems in mills: on a six-storey spinning mill, the distance between flywheel and top floor pulley could be 100 ft, with the ropes running at speeds up to 7,000 ft per minute.

Wire ropes have been used to transmit power over long distances. In 1874, the Swiss were reported to be transmitting 540 hp to a factory 3,300 ft away by 0.75 in diameter wire ropes, running at 4,660 ft per minute. Chains are another means of transmitting power, but over shorter distances.

Wooden and iron bars have been used for long distances, with reciprocating motion. Underground water pumps up to 1,700 ft below the surface have been operated by beam engines at Cornish mines working vertical PUMP RODS. In a similar manner, mining equipment has been worked in remote areas by horizontal FLAT RODS stretching across open country, supported by rollers on top of a line of posts. A typical arrangement was a waterwheel driving flat rods to rock a bell crank positioned over a distant mine shaft. A mine near Tavistock, Devon, was still transmitting power in this manner over nearly 3 miles in the 1880s.

Power transmission by hydraulics is another method. In the last quarter of the 19th century, many British cities had quite extensive networks of pipelines distributing high pressure HYDRAULIC POWER to operate lifts, cranes, etc. from centralized pumping stations. Large dock gates were similarly opened and closed by hydraulics. The maximum economical distance for hydraulic power transmission is about 15 miles.

Transmission of power by mechanical means was, of course, superseded by the convenience of cable-fed electric motors at the turn of the century.

Fairbairn, W. *Treatise on Mills and Millwork*, 2 vols, 1861–3

transporter bridge a suspended moving platform or section of road crossing a river. The transporter bridge is an ingenious solution for bridging a navigable river in flat low-lying country which avoids the need to construct high sloping approach roads. The invention is attributed to a M. Arnodin of France. A high-level horizontal truss-type girder, supported on tall towers, spans the river, set high enough to allow shipping to pass underneath. A short length of roadway or platform is suspended on cables from a powered trolley which runs along rails on the girder. The platform is at road level on the river banks, and when positioned at one bank, a limited number of vehicles and pedestrians can pass onto it. It then transports them across to the other side of the river, providing a kind of short aerial extension to the road. A shuttle service across the river in either direction is thus provided, only interrupted whilst a vessel passes.

This type of bridge enjoyed a short popularity in the early 20th century: seventeen were built altogether, the first one in 1893. Four were built between 1905 and 1916 in England, three of which were for public use and one private. Two of the public bridges are still in operation – one in Middlesbrough, Yorks. (now Cleveland), over the river Tees, and the other over the river Usk at Newport, Mon. The world's largest was at Widnes in Lancashire, crossing the river Mersey and Manchester Ship Canal by a 1,000 ft span; built in 1905, it was demolished in 1961. The fourth (private) transporter also crosses the Mersey at Warrington, joining two sites of a chemical and soap works lying on opposite sides of the river. The drawback to transporter bridges is their intermittent operation which can hinder the flow of road traffic. The Widnes transporter was replaced by a high level bridge.

Redman, N. 'Crossings for the highly strung: history of the transporter bridge', *Country Life*, 11 April 1985

trapper a child working underground in a coal mine in the mid-19th century whose job was to open and close 'doors' as coal trucks passed through; the 'doors' were normally kept closed to direct the ventilation in the workings. Children as young as four years of age are recorded as trappers, working alone, often in the pitch dark for long hours.

traveller 1. a small, C-shaped component made of spring steel, which travels round the inner circumference of the RING which surrounds the spindle of a RING SPINNING FRAME. The yarn is passed through the 'eye' of the traveller on its way to the spindle tube; as the spindle rotates at speed, the traveller is dragged round the ring at a slightly slower speed, the spindle therefore winding yarn onto itself. The rotation of the traveller about the spindle imparts twist in the yarn, the traveller being equivalent to the eye or heck of a FLYER. The weight of the traveller is important: it controls the tension applied to the yarn, and a range of travellers of different weights is kept and used according to the COUNT of yarn being spun. Heavy travellers are used for low counts, and light ones for high counts. **2.** a weighted trolley carrying a frame with a hook which is free to rotate, used in a ropewalk (*see* ROPE MAKING).

traverse rail a mechanical device first used by Coniah Wood (patent no. 1018, 1772) on his spinning frame to dispense with HECKS on the FLYERS and wind yarn onto bobbins in even layers. This was soon improved by Richard Arkwright (1732–92), who made the motion automatic by introducing a heart-shaped CAM to control the movement of the bobbins up and down the spindle as winding on proceeded.

treadmill (or treadwheel) a wide, large wheel, often made of timber, which is rotated by a man or men treading it round, and used to power some device. Some treadmills were constructed so that the man or men walked on a continuous 'pathway' built on the inner side of the circumference; the man or men stood inside the wheel itself. Other treadmills had their periphery constructed in the form of a continuous 'staircase' around the outside. The wheel was then turned by the unbalanced weight on one side of the men treading the 'stairs' but never rising, as they were pressed downwards at each step made.

Treadmills have a long history as a form of animal or human power, long before PRIME MOVERS were invented. The Romans had treadmill cranes, and in the 16th century they had application in foundries and warehouses. Small treadmills, operated by dogs in what were known as dog-drums, were used to rotate roasting spits on the domestic scene. William Cubitt (1785–1861) is said to have invented a treadmill for use in prisons in 1817: such a treadmill was installed in the New Bailey prison in Manchester in 1824 to power a LOGWOOD grinder. Other prison treadmills ground corn. The prison treadmill was used as a form of hard labour for hardened criminals: prisoners had to spend so many hours a day treading the mill, in a line alongside each other, holding onto a fixed horizontal handrail across the width of the wheel which had 'stairs' or treads on its outer circumference.

Smaller treadmills, usually worked as needed by one man only, were installed in early warehouses to operate primitive cranes or hoists for lifting goods onto the various floors of the building. Carisbrooke Castle on the Isle of Wight has a treadmill once worked by prisoners in the 16th century, and now operated by a donkey as a tourist attraction. The wheel raises water from a 161 ft deep well, and dates from 1587.

tree suffix or prefix indicating that the item it describes is, or was originally, made from timber. Examples of such items which form a component of a structure or a machine are an axle-tree (a timber axle of a windmill or watermill); a plug-tree (a wooden rod which operated the valves or plugs on a NEWCOMEN ATMOSPHERIC ENGINE); a bridge-tree (part of the compound lever system in a windmill or watermill, which adjusted the grinding gap between the millstones); pump trees (hollowed out tree trunks joined together to make delivery pipes for Newcomen atmospheric engines dewatering mines); and trenail or treenail, a hardwood peg or dowel used to pin joints in timber framed buildings.

tree wool, *see* COTTON WOOL

trevette (or trevat, trivet) a small sharp-bladed knife, used for making the pile on VELVET and Wilton carpet in the days when they were hand woven. A short length of fabric would be woven with loops in the warps made over narrow bars or wires which had been inserted across the loom; the bars were called velour rods and each had a fine groove running along its edge. The weaver ran his trevette along the groove, which guided it straight while it cut the loops to make the warp pile. A further short length of looped fabric would then be woven and the cutting process repeated, the velour rods being used over and over again as the work progressed. The loops could also be cut off the loom.

Since the trevette had to be kept in a sharp condition to cut the loops cleanly, it is thought that the expression 'as right as a trevette' arose to describe something in peak condition. (An alternative source of the saying may refer to a three-legged stool or stand, which by virtue of its three legs will stand without rocking on an uneven floor.)

trewerne an old Welsh name for a mine truck. The word probably comes from the German *Truhen*, meaning large boxes, and was adapted from German miners working in early Welsh mines. In German mines, Truhen were large, ore-carrying boxes, moved at first on wheelbarrows before wheels were added to them to turn them into trucks. *See also* LEITNAGEL HUND.

triangular trade 18th-century shipping trade between Britain, Africa and North America. Woollen and iron goods were taken from Britain to Africa; Negro slaves from Africa to the North American colonies; and cotton, sugar and tobacco brought back to Britain. Liverpool in particular grew out of the cotton trade, and Glasgow largely out of the tobacco trade. *See also* SLAVE TRADE.

tributer a self-employed Cornish tin miner, who worked for a percentage of the value of ore he extracted, and received a payment called the tribute. The same arrangement applied in lead mining.

Trick valve (or Allen valve) a steam engine SLIDE VALVE designed to increase admission steam. Ordinary slide valves tend to throttle the steam flow by slow opening and closing of the ports; the Trick valve, invented in Germany by Joseph Trick around 1849, has an internal passageway in the valve block which increases the steam flow, particularly at small CUT-OFFS. A cross-section of a Trick valve is shown in Fig. 63d for an outside admission slide valve; a similar version exists for piston valves.

trip hammer, *see* TILT HAMMER

triple expansion engine   a design of steam engine in which either three cylinders, in the case of vertical engines, or four cylinders on horizontal engines, permit steam to be expanded three times as it passes through the installation.

In vertical engines, three cylinders of increasing diameter are arranged side-by-side, each driving its own crank onto a common crankshaft. The smallest cylinder is the high pressure one, taking steam direct from the boiler and exhausting it into a larger cylinder, the intermediate pressure cylinder. This in turn exhausts into the largest cylinder, the low pressure cylinder. Vertical engines are of the inverted design, are compact, and operate at higher speeds than the massive horizontal designs.

Triple expansion horizontal engines, such as those used to drive textile mills, normally have four cylinders (*see* Fig. 20d). In plan, they appear similar to twin TANDEM COMPOUND engines, in as much as there are two cylinders in line either side of a centrally placed flywheel. There is a high pressure cylinder, an intermediate pressure cylinder, and two low pressure cylinders. The latter are in effect equivalent to one low pressure cylinder, but to provide balance they each have piston areas half that of one low pressure cylinder. On one side of the flywheel the high pressure cylinder is in line with one of the low pressure cylinders, with a common piston rod driving onto one crank; on the other side, the intermediate pressure cylinder and the other low pressure cylinder are in line with a common piston rod driving the other crank. Steam from the boiler first enters the high pressure cylinder and exhausts across into the intermediate pressure cylinder, it then splits to feed each low pressure cylinder before rejoining to leave the installation via the condenser. There are thus three expansions in four cylinders. Variations to this configuration were made for triple expansion, such as the triple tandem – three horizontal cylinders in line – and another design had the high pressure and intermediate pressure cylinders in line driving one side of the flywheel, and one large low pressure cylinder

driving the other. Triple expansion became necessary when high steam pressures were introduced.

It is believed that triple expansion was first patented in France by Benjamin Normand in 1871. Triple expansion engines were soon installed in ships: A.C. Kirk (*fl.*1870s) installed an inverted vertical design in a British steamship in 1874. *See also* COMPOUNDING (1).

trommel   a rotating horizontal cylindrical sieve or mechanical BUDDLE used for washing and sizing crushed ores or stone. *Trommel* is the German word for a drum.

trompe   (or trombe) a primitive method, dating from the 16th century, of producing a low pressure air supply. This was obtained by arranging for a stream of water to run down a pipe or chute, sucking in air at the top: the entrained air left the base of the channel through a hole, and was led away to where it was wanted, the water running to a drain. The device was used for providing an air blast to primitive furnaces, and also to provide ventilation air in early mines. Is also called a water blast, water bellows, and Catalan forge or furnace, and was even described in old 18th-century documents as 'philosophical bellows'!

trow   a large, flat-bottomed sailing barge once used on the river Severn. Trows plied between Welshpool and Bristol, and were towed by men or horses when there was no wind; they carried goods on the Severn for several hundred years until the coming of the railways killed the river trade. The word is a dialect variation of 'trough', indicative of the general shape of the barge; a trowman was the master or captain of a trow.

truck system   the system of paying the wages of employees wholly or in part by goods, or by vouchers or tokens, which could only be exchanged for goods in a TOMMY SHOP. The tommy shop was almost invariably owned and run by the employer, or if not, was rented out by him to the shopkeeper.

The system mainly existed in the early days of the FACTORY SYSTEM, when factories and mills and their surrounding workers' houses were frequently sited a long way from towns and shops. The employer would build and run a shop selling food and other necessities for the convenience of his workers. Unfortunately, the system was abused by some employers who provided inferior goods or charged high prices to his captive customers. To some extent the system was also encouraged by the chronic shortage of coins in the early 18th century, the employer's tokens acting as money substitutes.

The unsatisfactory state of affairs brought about the 1701 Truck Act, which forbade the payment of wages in clothes, victuals or commodities in the textile and iron industries. This was later extended to other trades by the General Truck Act of 1831, and other Acts of 1881 and 1896 which forbade employers from forcing conditions on their employees as to where they should spend their wages. These Acts laid down that wages should be paid in coin of the realm, and that workers were free to dispose of their wages as they wished. Trade unions fought against truck, and the presence of a tommy shop often made recruitment of labour difficult due to dislike of the system.

Associated with the truck system were the practices known as poundage and arrestment. Poundage was when an employer deducted a shilling or two in the £1 when paying an advance on wages (known as a 'sub', short for subsidy) to employees who could not manage their financial affairs. Arrestment was when a shopkeeper obtained payment for an employee's debt from his employer, who in turn stopped (i.e. arrested) the sum from the employee's next wages.

The truck system was responsible for the saying 'have no truck with him', meaning to have no dealings with a person.

Hilton, G.W. *The Truck System, Including a History of the British Truck Act, 1465–1960*, Heffer, 1960

trunk steam engine a steam engine in which the pistons are long relative to their diameters, and there are no piston rods and crossheads. Such pistons are called trunk pistons, and being longer than normal pistons they can take the oblique thrust of the connecting rod against the side walls of the cylinder. Their extended length guides them along the cylinder bore.

James Watt (1736–1819) patented such pistons (no. 1432, 1784) and they were later developed for marine use, particularly by John Penn (1805–78) in the 1840s. A problem to be overcome in those days was to reduce the overall height (or length) of ships' engines. This was solved by designing large bore, short stroke, trunk engines, which because of the elimination of piston rod and crosshead, made compact units. Many trunk engines were single-acting, but a double-acting design was patented by Francis Humphrys in 1835 (patent no. 6801). This design was intended for Brunel's *Great Britain*, but was in fact never installed. It involved a hollow extension (the trunk) to the piston which passed through the cylinder cover in a stuffing box, forming an annular space on one side of the piston into which high pressure steam was admitted. The steam was exhausted into the other side of the piston at a lower pressure (*see* Fig. 48). Single-acting trunk pistons are used today in most internal combustion engines.

trunnions (or stools) a pair of protruding JOURNALS, one either side of a vessel, cannon, overhead beam of a beam engine, etc., which are supported in bearings to form a pivot on which the item may rock or tilt. Sometimes trunnions are hollow, permitting the passage of a fluid into the vessel. The word trunnion comes from the French *trognon*, meaning a stump or core.

truss (or roof brace) a load-carrying open framework comprising a number of straight bars joined together at their extremities and all lying in the same vertical plane (*see* Figs 12 and 57). A truss is so designed that ideally its members are only in pure tension or pure compression, with no bending stresses. The joints between members, called nodes, are either pegged with hardwood pegs or trenails in the case of timber trusses, or riveted or bolted together with plate cleats in the case of iron or steel frames. A member carrying a compressive stress is called a strut, and one carrying a tensile stress a tie.

The Italian architect Andrea Palladio (1518–90) is credited with the first known truss design, c.1570. Trusses are used to support roof coverings and tie the supporting walls together, and for bridge work. In the case of ROOF TRUSSES, the loads are static and the stresses in the members are constant; however, for BRIDGE GIRDERS, loading is variable and moving, and some members may experience a reversal of stress. They may therefore have to act as struts or ties depending on where the load is, and must be designed accordingly.

tubbing a wall lining a mine shaft to prevent ingress of water, or inward collapse of poor surrounding soil or rock. Early mine shafts were usually timber lined, sometimes called cribbing, and it is possibly from the impression of being inside a tub or barrel that the name tubbing arose. The term was later applied to shaft linings of any materials, including metal. *See also* GINGING.

tub boat canal a canal which was dug to carry short boats of limited carrying capacity. Usually such canals were only short in length, and were private canals for transporting coal, lime, etc. They originated in the Coalbrookdale area in the mid-1760s. Tub boats were usually towed in trains. The Hay rail incline at Ironbridge, Salop., built in 1792–3, raised and lowered tub boats on wheeled carriages between the two levels of the Shropshire Canal and Coalport basin.

tube mill an ore grinder, comprising a large diameter, long perforated cylinder of iron or steel, slightly inclined to the horizontal, which rotates about its long axis. It is partly filled with a mixture of broken pieces of metallic ore and heavy iron balls or rods. As rotation proceeds, the ore is crushed by the tumbling action of the iron balls or rods, and small pieces fall through the perforations, the size of which control the fineness of the grinding. After leaving the tube mill, the metallics are separated from the waste rock on CONCENTRATING TABLES. Tube mills were introduced in the 19th century to facilitate the preparation of ores prior to smelting.

tubular bridge a bridge constructed from metal tubes, either where the tubes form structural components, or where the whole bridge itself is in the form of a large tube. The tubes may be rectangular, square, round, or oval in cross-section. Two large span tubular bridges comprising large rectangular tubes, through which a railway passes as if in a tunnel, were built in the mid-19th century – the Conwy Bridge and the Britannia Bridge, both in north Wales, the former carrying the railway across the river Conwy, the latter carrying the same railway across the Menai Straits to Anglesey. The Conwy Bridge consists of two tubes of 400 ft span, side-by-side, carrying the up line in one tube and the down line in the other, and was completed in 1849. It was the prototype for the larger Britannia Bridge, which had four spans – two of 460 ft and two of 230 ft – and opened in 1850. The Conwy Bridge is still in use, but the Britannia Bridge was destroyed by fire on 23 May 1970. Both bridges were the result of several years of co-operation between Robert Stephenson (1803–59), William Fairbairn (1789–1874) and Eaton Hodgkinson (1789–1861), designing and testing models before the full-sized bridges were constructed. The tubes were floated out on barges, and lifted into position; they were made from riveted wrought-iron plates, suitably stiffened, and a patent (no. 11401, 1846) was taken out in Fairbairn's name for a 'hollow iron beam bridge'. However, bridges of this design weighed too much and few were built afterwards, being replaced by LATTICE GIRDER bridges which were more economical of material.

Another type of tubular bridge is represented by bridges designed by Isambard Kingdom Brunel (1806–59), who used large tubes as top compression members, traffic passing on a decking hung from the tube. The Royal Albert railway bridge over the Tamar, Saltash, Devon, opened in 1859, comprises two 465 ft spans of lenticular arched trusses 16 ft 9 in wide by 12 ft 3 in deep in wrought iron, and is still in use today.

Clark, Edwin. *The Britannia and Conwy Tubular Bridges*, 1850
Tyson, S. 'Notes on the history, development and use of tubes in the construction of bridges', *Industrial Archaeology Review* II (1978), 143–53

tuckers' clay, *see* FULLER'S EARTH

tucking mill, *see* FULLING

tulle a fine silk bobbin-net type of fabric used for women's dresses, veils, hats, etc. The name comes from the town of Tulle, mid-France, where this kind of fabric was once made

tumbler needle, *see* LATCH NEEDLE

tumming a northern dialect word for the action of CARDING wool.

tun the casing enclosing the grindstones in a corn mill to keep in the ground material. An outlet in the side of the tun leads to a chute down which the ground material flows into a sack.

tuner, *see* TACKLER

tungsten, *see* WOLFRAM

tunnel an underground large diameter tube or passageway, which is horizontal or nearly so, to convey a road, railway or canal under a river or through a hill. The construction of a tunnel depends on the nature of the soil or rock to be removed. Some tunnels require an outer lining to prevent the surrounding soil falling in, whilst tunnels bored through solid rock often do not need walls if the rock is self supporting. The nature of the ground in which a tunnel is to be built is determined by trial boring or vertical shafts. Long tunnels are often constructed by working outwards from a number of shafts sunk along its line until all the short tunnels join up. The shafts then act as ventilators, and in the case of railways as exit routes for smoke.

Most tunnels in Britain are railway tunnels, built to avoid the circuitous routes necessary to keep within the RULING GRADIENT when traversing hilly country. Tunnels under rivers usually dip down to their lowest point under the centre of the river, whilst road tunnels are usually level, and canal tunnels have to be level. Spoil heaps frequently surround tunnel exits and entrances and ventilation shafts, formed by dumping the material excavated during construction, although in some cases it is carted away to make embankments. Tunnelling was dangerous work in the 19th century, and many casualties and deaths occurred. An unusual memorial to the navvies killed digging the Bramhope railway tunnel in 1845–9 at Otley, Yorks., is in the form of a replica of the tunnel entrance.

James Brindley (1716–72) built the first canal tunnel in the 1770s on the Trent and Mersey Canal under a ridge at Harecastle, near Tunstall, Staffs. It was only 9 ft wide, and narrow boats had to be propelled through the 2,880 yd length by LEGGING, since there was no TOWPATH. The first public underwater tunnel was built by Marc Isambard Brunel (1769–1849) at Rotherhithe, London, under the Thames. It was begun in 1825 but not completed and officially opened until 1843, because of great constructional difficulties and lack of finance. It was 1,506 ft long, of horseshoe cross-section 23 by 37 ft, and was restricted to pedestrians only until it was extended by the East London Railway and became a railway tunnel. An early 'railway' tunnel is that at Chapel Milton on the Peak Forest Tramway, Derbys., which was opened in 1800 as a PLATEWAY tunnel. One of the earliest road tunnels is in the centre of Reigate, Surrey, built in 1823–4: it still exists, but is only for pedestrian use today. A well-known railway tunnel is the Severn, completed in 1886.

A tunnel under the English Channel was first proposed by the French mining engineer, Albert Mathieu-Favier in 1802. It was to be a twin bore tunnel, for horse-drawn vehicles. A modified scheme was suggested at a Paris Exhibition in 1867 and was favoured by Queen Victoria and Napoleon III, but nothing came of it. A Channel Tunnel Bill was rejected by Parliament in 1882 on defence grounds.

Clements, P. *Marc Isambard Brunel*, Longman, 1970
Walker, T.A. *The Severn Tunnel*, 1888; reprinted by Kingsmead, 1969

turbine a rotary PRIME MOVER, of which there are two types – the IMPULSE TURBINE and the REACTION TURBINE. Turbines may be steam, water or gas operated. The word turbine is said to have been first used in print by the Frenchman Claude Burdin (1790–1873) in 1824 in connection with his work on waterwheels; it comes from the Latin *turboinis*, meaning a spinning top or whirlwind. *See also* GAS TURBINE, STEAM TURBINE, WATER TURBINE.

Turkey red (or Adrianople red, Levant red) a brilliant red dyestuff, essentially a MADDER and oil dye used with an alum MORDANT. It was first introduced into Britain c.1788 in the Glasgow area. Ox blood was sometimes added during its preparation. The use of Turkey red declined when the synthetic dye alizarin was introduced in the 1860s.

turmeric (or Indian safflower) a natural dye made from the root of an Asian plant related to the ginger species. MORDANTed with alum, it produced an orange-yellow colour, and with

iron a brownish-black. It was used to dye cotton, silk and wool, had medicinal uses, and is also used to colour certain foods such as curry. It should not be confused with SAFFRON.

turn (or sump) a Derbyshire miners' old name for an underground shaft or WINZE connecting levels together.

turning pound, *see* WINDING HOLE

turn-out 1. a passing place on a single line railway where the track is doubled for a distance a little longer than the length of the longest train expected to operate the system. Such turn-outs were common on early railways until twin tracks were laid. The idea is also used on inclined planes and rack railways to save the cost of twin tracks running the full distance. **2.** a term used in the mid-19th century for an industrial strike.

turnover bridge, *see* ROVING BRIDGE

turnpike trusts bodies of trustees administering turnpike roads on which users had to pay a TOLL before a spiked bar (the pike) placed across the road, was opened. Before the 18th century roads in Britain were notoriously bad, and goods were transported by PACKHORSE or on navigable rivers where available. Improvement to a road was effected by an association (mostly of local landowners) forming a trust, and obtaining an Act of Parliament empowering them to charge a toll for use of the road they had repaired or built. The Act usually lasted twenty-one years and included the right to apply for a renewal Act if desired. The trust paid the wages of the toll keeper, and maintained the road out of the tolls collected.

The first turnpike, an isolated occurrence, was in 1663 at Wadesmill, Herts. Further turnpiking did not take place for some forty years, when a growing population and agricultural expansion, resulting in an increase in the movement of goods, necessitated urgent improvements to roads. By 1750, some 400 turnpike trusts had been set up, which eventually formed the network of major roads in the country. In the mid-1830s the peak was reached with some 22,000 miles controlled by some 4,000 trusts. Transportation costs were reduced, journey times cut, all-year round travel became possible, and rural isolation was broken down. The use of packhorses declined as wheeled traffic could now carry heavier goods more easily.

Turnpikes were unpopular with most people (*see* REBECCA RIOTS) and most trusts ran at a loss, so few renewal Acts were applied for. The building of the canal system slowed down the applications for new trusts; and within ten years of the arrival of railways nearly every trust was bankrupt, with road maintenance falling on local authorities. By 1871 only 854 trusts were left, and in 1890 there were only two. There are many relics left of turnpike roads: toll houses, most converted into private residences, and milestones, a statutory obligation under each Act. Although turnpikes were an improvement on earlier roads, the conditions for their use imposed by trusts were designed more to make the traffic fit the road than to provide a road suitable for the traffic.

Albert, W. *The Turnpike Road System in England, 1663–1840*, Cambridge University Press, 1972
Pawson, E. *The Turnpike Roads of 18th Century Britain*, 1977
Searle, M. *Turnpikes and Toll Bars*, 1930

turn tree, *see* STOW

tussah silk (or tuss, tasar) a coarse, brown wild silk imported from India and China from the tussah moth or worm. Yarn from this source is generally spun, as most tussah cocoons cannot be reeled (*see* REELING). The word *tussah* is Hindi and Urdu for shuttle.

tutwork work performed by men under a contract for sinking shafts and driving levels through valueless rock in tin or lead mines, etc. A West Country word, it has a similar meaning to piecework; it was also known as a driving bargain.

tuyère (or twyer, tweer, twire, tuiron) the nozzle through which the air blast is forced into the charge in a BLAST FURNACE. Several tuyères are spaced round the combustion zone of the furnace, and when hot blast was introduced in the early 19th century it became necessary to cool tuyères by surrounding them with an annular space, through which cold water is circulated. The invention of the water-cooled tuyère is attributed to John Condie. The name is of French origin. The nozzles in the base of a BESSEMER converter are also called tuyères.

tweed a twilled woollen, or wool and cotton, fabric with an unfinished surface, usually made with two or more colours combined in the yarn. Wool intended for tweed manufacture is dyed before CARDING, so that several colours may be blended together.

Tweed is a speciality of Scotland, and its name came about by accident. In 1826, a consignment of cloth was sent to James Locke, the London agent for a Scottish manufacturer, and the word tweel, the Scottish form of twill, was misread on the invoice as tweed. This name seemed at the time to be confirmed as correct, since the cloth had been made close to the river Tweed, and from that time on tweed was adopted as the name for that type of cloth.

Tweed is made in other parts of Scotland, and today is a particular hand craft industry of the island of Harris.

twill a form of woven cloth in which diagonal ridges or ribs are made on the surface, known as twill lines. This effect is obtained by arranging for weft threads to pass alternately over one warp thread, and then under two or more warps; successive wefts are staggered sideways relative to the warps they cross (*see* Fig. 50). A common twill weave is when each weft passes successively over two warps, under two, and then repeats with the warp doing the same. This construction is called a 2 × 2 weave, or four ends (end is another name for a warp). A 2 × 1 twill is called a PRUNELLA or three ends.

Apart from producing a more interesting appearance than a plain weave, a twill cloth is softer and more flexible because there are fewer intersections between warp and weft. Fancy twill such as herringbone and diamond patterns may be woven: the type of pattern is determined by the SHEDDING arrangement of the loom. This method of weaving can be applied to any sort of material.

The word twill was originally reserved for the common 2 × 2 weave. Twill comes from the Latin *bilicium*, *bi* meaning two and *licium* thread; the *bi* was changed in English to 'twi', again meaning two or double. The alternative spellings tweel or twilly are used in Scotland and northern England.

twist the turns imposed on a yarn to combine the individual fibres from which it is made to give it strength. Twist is usually denoted by the number of turns per linear inch: fine yarns have more twist than coarse, and the purpose for which a yarn is to be used will determine the amount of twist given to it. Woollen yarns for the KNITTING INDUSTRY will be soft twisted (fewer turns per inch); yarn intended as WEFT is medium twisted; and WARP is hard twisted. Twist is normally applied by clockwise rotation of the spindles on which the yarn is wound, giving an angle of incline from left to right, known as right twist. Too much twist causes snarling, which causes the yarn to curl back when the tension on it is released.

Twist is also loosely used as another name for warp.

twister, *see* LOOMER

twist hand the operator of a lace-net making machine. Twist net means an open mesh.

twizzle a dialect word for the eye or small hole in a FLYER. It can also mean to twist.

two-stroke cycle the working cycle of an INTERNAL COMBUSTION ENGINE, invented by Dugald Clerk (1854–1932) in 1880. It has one power stroke in each revolution of the engine, with a blower or pump to force an air–gas mixture into the cylinder at the beginning of the compression stroke. The spent gases are exhausted by the piston uncovering ports in the cylinder wall at the end of the return stroke. Thus, inlet and compression take place on the first stroke, expansion and exhaust on the second.

Another pioneer working on the two-stroke engine contemporary with Clerk was Joseph Day of Bath (1855–1946), who perfected his design in 1892.

Clerk, D. *The Gas, Petrol, and Oil Engine*, 2 vols, Longmans Green, 1916
Torrens, H.S. *Joseph Day, 1855–1946*, Bath Industrial Heritage Trust, 1992

tye (or gounce) a sloping trough with water flowing down it, used for washing away light gravels and leaving behind heavier tin particles. It was the simple forerunner of the BRUNTON BUDDLE. Used in tin streaming.

tymp (or timp) the arched opening above the tapping hole of a BLAST FURNACE, the word is a shortening of tympanum, an arch. Sometimes the stone or brickwork of the arch is protected from the molten iron by a cast-iron plate called the tymp plate.

Tyrian purple, *see* MUREX

U

U-leather a ring of soft leather with a U-shaped cross-section, used to pack glands on HYDRAULIC PRESSES etc. to prevent leakage of the operating fluid. The U-leather is fitted into a recess in the cylinder with the open end of the U facing the pressure side. The water or oil enters the U and expands its sides against the ram or plunger and the cylinder, sealing against leakage past it, yet allowing the ram or plunger to slide as required.

There is controversy as to whether it was Joseph Bramah (1749–1814), inventor of the hydraulic press in 1795, or Henry Maudslay (1771–1831) who was working for Bramah at that time, who invented the U-leather.

ulnager, *see* ALNAGER

underdrift the drive to the grinding stones of a corn mill which comes from below. Watermills are almost invariably of the underdrift kind. If the drive comes from above, as in a windmill, it is called OVERDRIFT.

underpick loom, *see* AUTOMATIC LOOM

undershot wheel (or Vitruvian wheel) a WATERWHEEL where the inflow of water strikes the paddles or FLOATBOARDS well below the axis of the wheel, i.e. the water more or less passes under it (*see* Fig. 84a). Such wheels are used where there is only a low head of water available. At least 3 ft head is usually needed to turn the wheel, with the TAILRACE clear of the lowest part of the wheel. Only low power is obtained from an undershot wheel, which is very inefficient, the turning action being mainly obtained from the current of the water flow. Undershot wheels could be stopped by backwater when the level of the river or tailrace rose above the bottom of the wheel in times of flooding. Jean-Victor Poncelet (1788–1867) of France made improvements to undershot wheel design by introducing curved paddles, which reduced the impact of the water and raised the efficiency of the wheel.

undertaker 1. an early name for a railway contractor. **2.** a middleman between a silk weaver and a master. The master gave the undertaker the prepared silk yarn, and he would undertake to return it woven into cloth by a certain date. The undertaker distributed the yarn to domestic workers, and bargained a price with them. Often the undertaker owned the looms, and sometimes the house as well, which he rented out to the weaver, for whom he found work. In a similar manner, an undertaker in the hosiery trade was one who contracted with a hosier to produce a certain amount of knitted goods for a given price. The undertaker gave the work to hand-frame knitters, paying them a lesser figure to make a profit for himself. **3.** man who financed the improvement of navigable rivers, or was a commissioner of a canal company.

undulating line a railway built with gradients at strategic places. In the early days, from about 1831 to 1846, it was thought that railway tracks should be built with up gradients either side of a station, to assist in starting and stopping. George Stephenson (1781–1846) was opposed to the concept, but the Central London Underground Railway revived the principle in 1900.

uniflow steam engine (or central exhaust engine) a steam engine in which steam flows in one direction only at each stroke, as opposed to the more common CONTRA-FLOW ENGINES. Professor Johann Stumpf of Germany is credited with the first successful steam engine working on the unidirectional flow principle, but he could not patent the basic idea because of previous work by Leonard Jennett Todd in 1885. Stumpf did take out several British patents, including no. 8371, 1908, and uniflows (short for uniform flow) were made in Britain under licence until Stumpf's patents ran out.

A uniflow engine is DOUBLE-ACTING, and has a long cylinder with steam admission valves at each end, and a row of exhaust ports in the cylinder walls at the centre. The piston is long too, and uncovers the central exhausts at the end of each stroke. Steam is admitted with an early CUT-OFF, and is exhausted when the piston reaches the end of its stroke. The steam therefore flows in one direction only at each stroke. The main advantage of the uniflow is that temperatures are kept uniform at each end of the cylinder. Low temperature exhaust steam does not reach the high temperature inlets, so condensation losses are minimized, which raises the thermal efficiency. Many uniflows were built with one cylinder only, but for large engines compounds were made with a conventional contra-flow high pressure cylinder using superheated steam, in tandem with a uniflow low pressure cylinder.

The uniflow was more or less the last major development in steam engine technology, but it had a comparatively short period of popularity since it soon could not compete in initial cost with STEAM TURBINES and diesel engines.

Allen, T. *Uniflow, Back-pressure, and Steam Extraction Engines*, Pitman, 1931
Hills, R.L. 'The uniflow engine, a re-appraisal', *Newcomen Society Transactions* 57 (1985–6), 59–77
Stumpf, J. *The Una-flow Steam Engine*, Constable, 1922

union cloth a woven fabric made from two or more different materials, for example linen and cotton. The description came into use in the 18th century.

United Society of Mines Royal and Mineral and Battery Works, *see* MINES ROYAL
universal joint, *see* HOOKE'S JOINT
upcast shaft (or uptake) the shaft up which vitiated air from a mine is exhausted to the atmosphere, fresh incoming air being brought in via the DOWNCAST SHAFT. In the early days of coal mining, a fire was maintained at the base of the upcast shaft so that the chimney effect of the hot gases rising up the shaft sucked in fresh air at the downcast shaft and through the underground workings, to provide ventilation for the miners. The air, by then vitiated, rose up the upcast shaft with the hot gases. (*See also* VENTILATION FURNACE.) By the late 19th century, mechanical fans were being placed on top of the upcast shaft to draw fresh air through the workings from the downcast shaft, replacing the use of fires.

Upland cotton the bulk of North American cotton. It is a good quality, white cotton with a 0.75–1.25 in STAPLE LENGTH, grown mostly in California, Arizona and New Mexico, i.e. on land higher than the coastal areas, hence its name. It is of the *Gossypium hirsutum* variety.
urine, *see* LANT

V

vacuum engine an alternative name for an ATMOSPHERIC ENGINE as opposed to a high pressure engine. The operating principle of a vacuum engine was that low pressure steam was condensed below the piston in an open-topped vertical cylinder to produce a partial vacuum, so that the weight of the atmosphere forced the piston down. Newcomen's and early Watt steam engines were vacuum engines.

valonia acorn cups from the Turkish oak *Quercus aegilops*, which are rich in tannin and used in the tanning of leather, and in dyeing and ink making. The prickly, unripe acorn cups have been imported into Britain since the end of the 18th century by tanners, and ground to a powder to add to indigenous oak bark powder to increase the tannin content.

valve mechanical device for controlling the flow of a fluid, e.g. water, steam or gas. It can be automatic in action, or operated by an outside force. Valve comes from the Latin *valva*, meaning the leaf of a folding door. Many designs of valves have been developed for specific purposes. There are valves to stop the flow, regulate it, or prevent a reverse flow. A SAFETY VALVE is a valve designed to open at a pre-arranged pressure to allow steam (as an example) to escape to atmosphere and prevent an explosion or damage to the equipment it protects due to an excessive internal pressure build-up.

Valves act by a moving part housed within a fluid-tight enclosure, covering or uncovering a through route, opening or PORT available to the fluid it is designed to control. There are four main movements used in valve design: (i) rotation (full or partial), used in the cock or plug valve, and the CORLISS VALVE; (ii) sliding (reciprocating), used in the D-VALVE or SLIDE VALVE, and the piston valve; (iii) rise and fall,

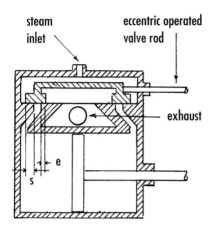

D-slide valve (outside admission)

s steam lap
e exhaust lap

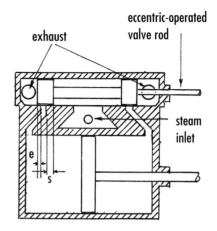

Piston valve (inside admission)

s steam lap
e exhaust lap

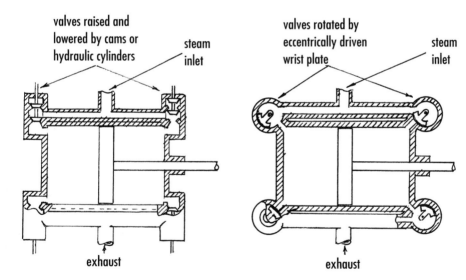

Equilibrium drop valves

Corliss valves

Fig. 79. Four different designs of valve for double-acting steam engines

used in the DROP VALVE, POPPET VALVE, and some types of CLACK VALVE; and (iv) hinged (swinging), used in some types of clack or check valve.

Fig. 79 shows four different types of valve used on double-acting steam engines. These include sliding valves, rise and fall valves, and rotating valves. The motion given to the moving parts is controlled by VALVE GEAR. Hinged valves on water PUMPS are shown in Figs 53b and 53d. These valves operate automatically, responding to the pressure generated inside the pump body.

valve gear a mechanism controlling the motion of valves in a steam engine or a locomotive which enables the steam expansion ratio or steam CUT-OFF point to be varied, and/or the direction of rotation or travel to be reversed. The correct and economical working of a steam engine or a locomotive depends on the operation of its valve gear. Some valve gears are known as link motions. Several designs have been invented: the principal ones are described under ALLAN STRAIGHT LINK MOTION; GAB VALVE GEAR; GOOCH LINK MOTION; HACKWORTH RADIAL VALVE GEAR; JOY VALVE GEAR; LOOSE ECCENTRIC VALVE GEAR; MEYER VARIABLE EXPANSION VALVE; STEPHENSON LINK MOTION; and WALSCHAERT VALVE GEAR.

Burgh, N.P. *Link Motion and Expansion Gear Practically Considered*, 1872

Hurst, C. *Valves and Valve-Gearing: A Practical Textbook*, 8th edition, 1919

valve trip gear a mechanism on a STATIONARY STEAM ENGINE which allows the valves to close rapidly. CORLISS and DROP VALVES are designed to be closed rapidly by a spring or some other method: Fig. 21 shows the mechanism for governor controlled Corliss valves. Other patented trip gears include the Inglis-Spencer, the Dobson, etc. Some trip gears are adjusted by hand, and not automatically by governors.

vanning testing the quality, or making a rough assay of an ore by spreading it out on a shovel and gently washing it in water. For example, tin concentrate was gently swirled on a vanning shovel, and the tin content could be estimated by a practised and experienced eye. The word in its mining sense dates from the 17th century, and was probably borrowed from the tossing of corn when winnowing, which is known by the same name.

vapour engine, *see* LOCOMOTIVE

vatman the man who makes a sheet of paper by dipping the mould and DECKLE into the vat containing the warm paper pulp solution, before passing it on to his assistant, the COUCHER. Great skill was needed to ensure an even thickness and constant weight for each paper sheet made by this hand method. *See also* PAPER MAKING.

vein a metallic mineral deposit occurring in a fissure or fault in rock. Veins are usually comparatively narrow in thickness and lie almost vertically, but can have considerable width. *See also* LODE (1).

velocity compounding lowering the inlet velocity of high pressure steam in a succession of controlled stages before it leaves a turbine at low pressure. Examples of velocity compounded turbines are a De Laval machine, which has more than one stage, and the Rateau machine; both are IMPULSE TURBINES.

velveret (or velverette) a variety of FUSTIAN with a velvet surface, first introduced c.1769 and used for men's clothing in Victorian days.

velvet originally a silk fabric with a short, dense smooth pile on its surface. The pile was made by leaving the warp threads with small loops which were subsequently cut to make the pile on one side; the word comes from the Latin *villus*, meaning shaggy hair. Cotton velvet, it is claimed, was first made by Jeremiah Clarke (1715–72) of Bolton, Lancs., in 1756, and VELVET CUTTING became a skilled domestic industry in south Lancashire. Similar materials are described as velour (made from wool) and velure, and are used extensively in HAT MAKING.

velvet cutting a domestic industry, particularly in south Lancashire, where the manufacture of velvet originated. VELVET cloth was woven with loops left in the warp threads on one surface and these had to be cut by hand to form the pile. The work was very skilled and was not mechanized until modern times. Velvet cutters worked at home, usually in workrooms on an upper storey with large windows to give good lighting. Merchants would bring uncut velvet pieces to the home worker, who spread the cloth out on a table between two rollers to stretch it whilst the rows of loops were cut with a very sharp knife called a TREVETTE run along the width. A finely woven velvet could have over 1,000 loops of warp in its width, and great care was needed as well as good eyesight.

velveteen an imitation of VELVET, but made in cotton whereas true velvet is made from silk. Velveteen has a short, dense, and smooth pile on one side, and is said to have been first introduced by John Wilson of Ainsworth, Lancs., in the late 18th century. It was popular in the 19th century for ladies' dresses, men's waistcoats and trousers.

ventilated buckets a design of metal bucket for a waterwheel introduced by William Fairbairn (1789–1874). Each bucket incorporated an open-ended passageway at its rear which allowed air to escape as the bucket filled with water (*see* Fig. 84h). This enabled the bucket to hold more water when filled, and increased the power obtained from the wheel. Another advantage was that in the event of the lower part of the wheel becoming immersed in the tailrace water, the buckets drained more readily via the ventilation slots as they rose out of the water.

ventilation furnace (or furnace pit) a fire maintained at the bottom of a mine shaft to improve underground air flow through the workings. As coal mines became deeper and the workings more extensive, provision of fresh air to the coalface became a problem. Before mechanically driven fans were introduced, fires were maintained at the bottom of an UPCAST SHAFT, using the poor quality coal not suitable for sale. The ascending hot gases created a draught through the workings, drawing down fresh air via the DOWNCAST SHAFT, any short circuiting being prevented by strategically placed traps (heavy full length 'curtains' hung across the roadways). This method persisted until the 1890s in some mines, with isolated examples still in use up till the 1940s. In gassy pits, the furnace drew its own air supply from the surface via an independent shaft or tunnel, to avoid the risk of fire. *See also* FANS AND BLOWERS.

vertical boiler a cylindrical, shell-type steam boiler, which stands upright with an internal firebox in its base (*see* Fig. 61e). It is compact and requires no brick setting. Various designs have been developed, the main purpose of each being to increase the thermal efficiency by arranging for a larger heating surface within the boiler. This was often achieved by including tubes either in the combustion chamber or in the steam space. A well-known design is that introduced by Edward Crompton and J.T. Cochran in 1878 (patent no. 770) which had horizontal firetubes above the firebox. Vertical boilers were for modest steam outputs, and were popular where there was a premium on floor space. Small verticals were more or less self-contained with the feedwater pump attached to one side. They were used on steam launches in Victorian times, and fire engines. Cochran boilers were made up to about 9 ft in diameter and 19 ft high.

vertical steam engine an engine in which the cylinder (or cylinders) lies in a vertical plane on a baseplate, with the crosshead and crankshaft positioned immediately above it supported in a substantial framework. Vertical engines have the advantage of occupying much less floor space than horizontal engines of equal power, although a greater headroom is required. They were often chosen to replace 18th- and 19th-century BEAM ENGINES when prime movers were being modernized or up-rated, since they fitted better into existing tall engine houses with their more limited floor space.

If the crankshaft is positioned below the cylinders in the vertical plane, the engine is known as an INVERTED VERTICAL STEAM ENGINE.

viaduct a structure carrying a road or railway across a valley. It is in effect a number of connected short span bridges, often in the form of a series of arches. The name comes from the Latin *via*, meaning a way or road, and *ductus*, meaning to lead. There are road viaducts, but it is the railways that were responsible for most viaducts standing today, built to maintain a level track across a valley or dip in the ground. In general, viaducts were cheaper to build than EMBANKMENTS.

The most common railway viaduct is a series of brick, sometimes masonry, arches. Timber viaducts, or trestle bridges, were built by I.K. Brunel (1806–59) in Devon and Cornwall on the Great Western Railway (replaced with steel in 1908), and WARREN GIRDER wrought-iron viaducts have been made. Some viaducts are very long. London's first railway, the London and Greenwich, was carried into the city in 1836 on a long viaduct of almost 3.75 miles, comprising 878 brick arches, which is still standing in parts. Many railways were brought into towns and cities on viaducts to elevated stations, in order to keep demolition of property to a minimum. A series of arches also presented less of a barrier in the town than a ground level track: streets could pass through the arches, and the spaces under them not occupied by streets could be let off as small workshops, warehouses, etc., to provide an income.

Binding, J. *Brunel's Cornish Viaducts*, Pendragon, 1993

vicuna (or vicugna, becunia) a fine silky woollen fabric made from the wool of the South American animal of the same name which inhabits the Andes; the name is the Spanish version of the local name. Vicuna was first imported in the 1830s and was shown at the Great Exhibition of 1851. It was used for ladies' dresses and for hat making.

viewer Tyneside name for a colliery or mining engineer.

vitriol, *see* SULPHURIC ACID

Vitruvian wheel another name for an UNDERSHOT WATERWHEEL, so named after Marcus Vitruvius Pollio (*fl.* 46 BC), an architect and engineer who first described such waterwheels in Roman times.

vortex wheel, *see* THOMSON WATER TURBINE

vug (or vugh, lough) a lead mining term for a naturally occurring cavity found in a VEIN which is lined with lead ore.

vulcanization the physical change induced by heating a mixture of masticated RUBBER with sulphur and other minor ingredients, which convert it from a soft plastic mass into a tough elastic material. Vulcanization of rubber was accidently discovered by Charles Goodyear (1800–60) of Philadelphia, USA, in 1839. The main ingredient effecting the change is sulphur, which prevented former rubber articles from softening and becoming sticky when warmed, and hardening when cold. Since the process removed these unwanted characteristics, it was at first known as 'curing' rubber; the name vulcanization originated later in England. Goodyear's process was not patented in the USA until 1844. Thomas Hancock (1786–1865) 're-invented' vulcanization in England more or less at the same time, having obtained a clue to the secret of the process from a sample of Goodyear's rubber.

In practice, a warm plastic rubber mix is first calendered, extruded or moulded into its final shape and more heat applied until it is vulcanized and permanently takes up the shape into which it has been forced. The degree of vulcanization can be controlled by the amount of sulphur mixed in to give end products of desired softness and elasticity, right up to hard, rigid ebonite or vulcanite. There is also a cold vulcanization process, discovered by Alexander Parkes (1813–90) of Birmingham, England, in 1846. This involved dipping a naphtha solution of raw rubber in liquid sulphur chloride. However, only thin sheets of rubber can be so processed.

The vulcanization process was speeded up by the discovery in 1906 that certain coal tar derivatives shortened the time taken for the process to complete itself. These additives are called accelerators.

W

wad 1. a Derbyshire mining term for impure manganese ore, a mixture of oxides of manganese and iron. **2.** (or wadd) a Lake District name for GRAPHITE. The term is of obscure origin, but dates back to the 17th century. Graphite is used for blacklead pencils, a Lakeland industry, and for making crucibles for metal melting.

Waddle fan, *see* FANS AND BLOWERS

Wade roads roads and bridges built in the Highlands of Scotland by the government under the direction of General George Wade (1673–1748) to facilitate military movement and help to curb Jacobite activity, following the rebellion of 1715. He began them in 1725 and by 1740 had completed about 250 miles when he was posted elsewhere. Major William Caulfield continued extending the network and by 1767 had built a further 800 miles. Many of the roads are disused today.

Salmond, J.B. *Wade in Scotland*, Moray Press, 1934
Taylor, William. *The Military Roads in Scotland*, David and Charles, 1976

wadmol (or wadmal, wedmole) a rough, thick woollen cloth, which was being woven in Wales and the Orkneys in the 17th century and was still being made in Victorian times. A similar material was made in Scandinavia, and known as vadmal in Old Norse, so it is probable that the English name comes from this. It was used for saddle cloths, lining horse collars, heavy curtains, and waistcoats.

waggon boiler a low pressure steam boiler having the shape of a covered waggon (*see* Fig. 61b). It had an arched top and sides which curved inwards to give them strength. James Watt (1736–1819) patented such a boiler in 1785 (patent no. 1485) although it was based on earlier designs. Some waggon boilers were fired from below; later designs had internal firetubes. Both types were set in brickwork.

waggonway a track of wooden rails on which waggons were pulled by horses. The term waggonway is usually reserved for twin tracks of wooden rails pegged onto wooden sleepers, along which waggons or CHALDRONS were drawn by horses. By about 1790, wooden waggonways began to be replaced by iron rails fastened to stone blocks.

Most waggonways were owned by coal mines, and were short in mileage, and dedicated to the company's own business, without any interconnection with other nearby waggonways. They usually ran from a pit to STAITHES on a river bank. Some waggonways were connected with iron foundries and carried ironstone as well as coal. The track for loaded waggons was called the main way, and the other, for returning empties, the bye way. There was no standard gauge – anything from 2 ft up to 4 or 5 ft were in use, as each company had its own. The coalfields of Tyneside and Shropshire were the birthplaces of waggonways.

Waggons or chaldrons were drawn singly by a horse under the control of a waggonman or boy who walked alongside guiding the horse. Connected trains of waggons were virtually unknown. Where a waggon could descend by gravity down a graded slope, called a run, the horse was hitched on behind, and the man or boy rode on the waggon controlling its speed by a simple brake lever called a convoy. A waggon normally had a hinged bottom for easy discharge.

An indication of the growth in waggonways is shown in the following table:

Mileage of waggonways in Britain

area	1650	1700	1750	1800
Tyneside	1	37	94	146
elsewhere	2	4	39	146
totals	3	41	133	292

Source: Lewis (1970)

The steam locomotive replaced horse drawn waggonways, and iron rails the wooden ones. Little remains of the old waggonways apart from traces of their routes, indicated by overgrown embankments, cuttings, and inclines. In some places stone blocks embedded in the ground may be found. An alternative name for a waggonway is Newcastle road.

Baxter, B. *Stone Blocks and Iron Rails*, David and Charles, 1966
Lewis, M.J.T. *Early Wooden Railways*, Routledge and Kegan Paul, 1970
Warn, C.R. *Waggonways and Early Railways of Northumberland*, Frank Graham, 1976

wale a vertical column of loops, ridges or stitches running down the length of a knitted fabric, which may be regarded as equivalent to the warp in a woven fabric. The term wale comes from an Old English word *walu*, meaning stripe or ridge. The opposite to the wale is the COURSE.

Walker fan, *see* FANS AND BLOWERS

walking, *see* FULLING

walking wheel, *see* GREAT WHEEL

walkmill (or waulkmill) an old name for a FULLING mill in which woollen cloth was thickened. The name comes from the earlier method of thickening cloth before the process was mechanized, when the cloth was 'walked' under the bare feet in a trough of water and FULLER'S EARTH, a process similar to treading grapes. The old Flemish word *walche* for a fulling mill is the probable origin of the English word. Men whose job it was to 'walk' the cloth were known as walkers, and this is the origin of the common surname today.

wall box an iron casting, rectangular in shape, which is built into a wall to support a pedestal bearing for a shaft, such as a LINESHAFT in a mill or workshop. The box distributes the weight of the bearing and shaft onto the wall, supports the wall above the opening, and provides access to the bearing. Wall boxes may be blind for use where the shaft does not pass through the wall, or open when it does.

Walloon process the manufacturing process for producing bar iron by use of two separate hearths. The first hearth or FINERY was for melting down cast-iron pigs and refining them into a malleable iron; the second hearth or CHAFERY was for re-heating and hammering the iron into bars. The name of the process comes from the district near Liège in Belgium, which stretched also into the north of France, where this method of wrought-iron production probably originated.

wallower the first driven gearwheel in a corn mill, which meshes with the BRAKE WHEEL in a windmill or with the PIT WHEEL in a watermill. The word has the general sense of 'to roll', and comes from the Old English *wielwan* which had that meaning. A wallower is also known as a crown wheel.

walnut a source of brown vegetable dye, made from the juice from the green husks or peel of the fruit of the plant *Juglans nigra*, and frequently used to colour linen cloth. It was replaced in the 19th century by synthetic dyes.

Walschaert valve gear a mechanism for reversing locomotives and varying the expansion ratio by altering the point of steam CUT-OFF. First invented in 1844 by Egide Walschaert (1820–1901) of the Belgian State Railway, it uses the movement of the engine CROSSHEAD in combination with that of a single ECCENTRIC or a RETURN CRANK to control the valve travel. Walschaert improved his original design in 1848 but was not allowed by Belgian bureaucracy to register a patent under his own name and it was filed under the name of Fischer. For many years the gear was known as the Fischer gear because of this. The basic design underwent several modifications by later engineers and became the most commonly used locomotive valve gear.

Its principal parts are shown in Fig. 68e. A single eccentric is keyed onto the engine crankshaft, and set at an angle to the crank of slightly over 90°. The eccentric rod *ab* oscillates a curved EXPANSION LINK *bcd* about its mid-point *e*, and a block *f* can slide in the slot in the expansion link. Block *f* is one end of a radius arm *fh*, which can be raised or lowered by the lifting link *gl* via the reversing rod and bell crank *lmn*. A combination lever *jh* receives motion from the crosshead via a union link *kj*, and at *i*, the valve rod is pivoted from the combination lever. The lengths of the various links and positions of connections *g* and *i* are carefully worked out to give the required valve travel; generally, when the sliding block *f* is in the lower half of the expansion link *bcd*, the locomotive travels forward, and in reverse when *f* is in the top half. As with other valve gears, when block *f* is in the mid-position of the expansion link, minimum valve travel occurs, and no steam is admitted to the cylinders so the locomotive remains stationary, or coasts if already moving, i.e. as with neutral gear on an automobile. At other positions of *f*, the valve travel is changed and the cut-off point and hence the expansion ratio are different. Constant LEAD (2) at all cut-offs is achieved.

The Walschaert valve gear is lightweight, compact and performed efficiently. It was not introduced into Britain, however, until *c*.1878, the STEPHENSON LINK MOTION being preferred in general until then. When used on outside cylinders, return cranks are used to drive the gear, but eccentrics are used for inside cylinders.

A German engineer, Edmund Heusinger von Waldegg, also invented independently in 1848 a very similar valve gear to the Walschaert, and this caused more confusion in the name(s) given to this type of valve gear. *See also* REVERSING GEARS.

want, *see* WASH OUT (2)

warehouse a large building for storing goods or raw materials, and fitted with cranes and hoists for handling heavy loads. There are two types of warehouse. Carriers' warehouses, such as those of canal and railway companies are warehouses in which goods in transit are temporarily stored awaiting collection or transferral to other forms of transport. Usually sited at canal or railway terminii or interchange points, these warehouses are often austerely built with security in mind, having small windows, high surrounding walls, and so on. They are usually fitted with loading slots to facilitate taking in and removing goods from the various floors, a hoist or CAT HEAD projecting above the top floor. Cranes are usually installed inside. Canal warehouses often have SHIPPING HOLES to enable canal boats to enter the building and be loaded or unloaded under cover.

The other type of warehouse is the merchant's warehouse. This is usually sited in the city or town centre and often built to impress prospective customers. The front facade is often ornamental, with well-appointed first floor offices where sales and business are transacted. In the case of textile warehouses, samples are frequently on display on a well lit top floor, and packing for despatch is carried out on the ground floor or in a basement. Some internal cranes or hoists are provided, and there may be loading slots at the rear of the building.

There are bonded warehouses which are under the control of customs and excise men, for storing goods subject to import tax etc.

The study of warehouse construction and their goods lifting arrangements is of interest to the industrial archaeologist. Construction usually mirrors that of contemporary mills, with cast-iron pillars, fire resistant flooring, etc. Lifting devices might be powered by water or by hydraulic JIGGERS. Besides canal and railside warehouses, there are many in docks, often specializing in handling a particular commodity.

Jones, Edgar. *Industrial Architecture in Britain: 1750–1939*, Batsford, 1985 (covers the external architecture of many warehouses)

warp that thread or yarn which runs longitudinally in a piece of woven cloth. Warps are crossed from side to side by the WEFT, and together they form the web or body of the cloth. In a loom, warp threads are wound round the warp BEAM ROLLER parallel to each other across the width of the fabric to be woven, and pass through the eyes of the HEALDS to meet that part of the cloth already woven by the interlacing of the weft. The interlacing is achieved by upwards and downwards movement of the healds prior to each pass of the shuttle carrying the weft; this movement of the healds raises and lowers the warp threads in accordance with the pattern of cloth being woven. Warp threads are kept under tension in the loom.

Warps need to be stronger than wefts since they are subjected to much rubbing action in the loom during weaving. As well as being twisted tighter to give the extra strength needed, warps are sized before weaving to give added stiffness and protection (*see* WARP SIZING). Early cotton spinning machines could not produce a yarn strong enough for warps, and linen thread was used for this purpose, as in FUSTIAN cloth. Richard Arkwright's WATER FRAME of 1769 was the first cotton spinning machine that made hard-twisted yarn suitable for warps in the coarser types of cloth.

The word warp is somewhat loosely used because it can mean an individual thread running lengthwise in a cloth, or collectively mean the whole assembly of such threads.

Alternative words sometimes used for warp are chain, twist, hard yarn, and end. Warp costs more than weft of the same COUNT. In the silk industry, warp threads are called organzine, and in the old vertical looms, the warp was called a stammin. The word warp is an ancient one, and dates back to the 8th century.

warp beam, *see* BEAM ROLLER

warping mill equipment for assembling loom WARPS, laid parallel, in sufficient number and of equal length, to make the required width and length of the cloth to be woven. In the early days of weaving, warps were made by hand on pegs protruding from a wall, set at the required distance apart. The warper took a number of balls of yarn, placed them in a box, and having attached the end of each yarn to the first wall peg, walked to the far peg slipping the yarns through his fingers, passing them under and over two intermediate pegs to form a LEASE. Having reached the far peg, he passed the yarns round it and returned to the first peg, and repeated the process until the required number of threads had been built up.

This monotonous procedure was speeded up when the warping mill was invented *c*.1760. It comprised a vertical wooden CREEL containing rows of bobbins, and a large skeleton wooden drum which could be rotated on a vertical spindle held in a stationary frame positioned near the creel. A metal comb was arranged to slide up and down a vertical rod close to the drum by a cord which was wound round a top extension of the drum spindle, and brought over a pulley at the top of the rod down to the comb. To operate, threads from the creel were passed through the comb and their ends fastened to the drum. The drum was then slowly rotated and the threads wound off the bobbins onto the drum, the comb rising or falling on the vertical rod to guide the threads onto the drum in a gentle spiral. When the comb reached either the top or the bottom of the rod, the direction of rotation of the drum was reversed until the number of threads required to make the width of the cloth had been reached. The threads were then disconnected from the creel, and the completed warp drawn off the drum carefully and formed into a ball by hand. This was known as ball warping. The earliest warping mills were turned by hand, but later, improved and larger machines were water or steam driven.

warp knitting the construction of a knitted fabric in which each stitch in a row is made by a different warp yarn or thread; there are as many warps as stitches in the width of the fabric. Each warp thread loops right and left in successive rows to form stitches with adjacent

warps, as shown in the diagram in Fig. 71. It is believed that the first warp knitting frames were made in 1775 by J. Crane and James Tarrett of Nottingham independently of each other; but the first patented warp knitter was by John Morris (patent no. 1282, 1781).

warp sizing protecting warp yarns against the rubbing action they receive by coating them with a starch size before weaving. The process has also been known as tape or slasher sizing. In the days of handloom weavers, size was applied by brush and allowed to dry before weaving commenced. As weaving became mechanized, the sizing process was also speeded up, the warps on the warper's beam (*see* BEAM ROLLER) being drawn through a vat of boiling size, mangled to remove excess size, and passed round steam-heated cylinders to dry, before being wound onto the weaver's beam. The amount of size put onto the warp thread is important; if there is too much the yarn becomes stiff and harsh, and gives trouble during weaving, and if insufficient is applied, the yarn is inadequately protected, again giving trouble at the weaving stage. Sizes are usually starch-based, but particularly in the early days of weaving, sundry secret mixtures were favoured by individual weavers, the process of sizing approaching that of a 'black art' in some cases. The size has to be removed from the cloth in a later finishing stage.

Sizing is usually done in the weaving shed, but there have been independent warp sizers working on a commission basis for larger weaving concerns. The cotton warp sizer, also known as a dressing frame, was invented by Thomas Johnson in 1803 (patent no. 2684).

Warren girder a lattice girder or truss frequently used in bridge construction (*see* Fig. 12). Its top and bottom horizontal members are joined at regular intervals by inclined members, sloping alternately in opposite directions to form equilateral triangles. The design was patented in 1848 by James Warren and Willoughby Theobald Monzani (patent no. 12242).

wash kiln, *see* BUDDLE

wash out 1. a short side tunnel leading from an underground water conduit or tunnel into a nearby river, etc. and controlled by a gate or sluice. Its purpose is for emptying the main tunnel for inspection or repair. **2.** (or want) a coal seam which disappears as a result of local erosion. Usually the material above the seam fills the space where the coal should be.

waste silk substandard silk, not suitable as the raw material for throwing (*see* THROW (2)) but still a valuable commodity, used in the silk industry for making a cheaper variety. Waste silk may originate in a country where SERICULTURE is practised, being a residue from the reeling process, or it can be a product of the various stages through which raw silk passes in the THROWING MILL, which creates a high proportion of waste. Another source is waste from a weaving shed. Waste silk was being used in Britain from the earliest days of the silk industry, and it is processed in a similar manner to cotton, being spun, not thrown, to make a yarn. After arrival in the silk spinning factory, it is SCUTCHED to remove foreign matter. This involves passing it through rotating iron blades which chop the waste into small pieces; dirt and dust are sucked away by a fan. The short staple lengths are CARDED and spun into a continuous thread, on THROSTLES in the early days, and later on MULES. A final process was to pass the silk across a gas jet which singed off any protruding hairs and improved the lustre. Spinning of waste silk was sometimes carried out in the same factory that produced thrown raw silk.

Besides being used on its own for the cheaper grades of silk, spun waste silk was used in mixed fabrics such as silk and alpaca, and silk and mohair. It was also used in the manufacture of plush and velvet.

waste spinning, *see* CONDENSER SPINNING

waste weir a side exit from a water channel or leat feeding a waterwheel, usually controlled by an adjustable gate for discharging surplus water back into the source river or stream.

watchmaking a handcraft or domestic industry which grew out of CLOCKMAKING as small tools with greater precision became available. Watchmaking was largely concentrated in south-west Lancashire, especially around Prescot in the 18th century as a cottage industry. Specialization often took place, with workers making only certain parts such as springs, balances, wheels, etc. Accurate small machine tools such as lathes, gear cutters, etc. were developed: machine-cut wheels were available as early as 1675. Watch parts were sent to London and Coventry for assembly, and some export abroad also took place. The industry was supported locally by the development of small hand-file manufacture in the nearby Warrington area. The houses in which the industry was carried on were similar in appearance to handloom weavers' cottages, with workshops either on upper storeys, well lit by multiple windows, or in rear extensions. The industry died out in Lancashire when competition from Switzerland and North America in the late 19th century became too

strong, but was carried on in London and the Midlands on a reduced scale.

Bailey, F.A. and Barker, T.C. *The 17th Century Origins of Watchmaking in South-West Lancashire*

water-balance engine a device for raising loads or operating pumps using water as a balancing medium. Fig. 80 shows the main features of a water-balance engine arranged for raising loads from a mine shaft. A headgear positioned over the mine shaft supported two winding drums of different diameters, fastened on a common axle. A lifting rope wound round the larger drum hung down the mine shaft, ending in a KIBBLE or load container. Another rope wound round the smaller drum hung down an adjoining, shallower, balance shaft or pit, and was attached to a large water bucket which had an emptying valve in its base. A drainage ADIT ran from the bottom of the balance shaft to a conveniently sited stream. The emptying VALVE in the bucket could be opened from ground level by a chain. The difference in drum diameters was in the same ratio as the difference in depths of the mine shaft and balance pit, and the weight of the empty kibble was greater than that of the empty bucket. A brake controlled the turning speed of the drums. To operate, waste water was run into the bucket until its weight exceeded that of the loaded kibble, which then ascended the mine shaft. At the surface, the system was held stationary by the brake while the kibble was emptied, and the bucket emptied of water. The empty kibble then descended the mine shaft because of its greater weight, raising the bucket so that the cycle could be repeated.

The advantage of a water-balance engine was that no prime mover was needed, so it was very suitable for remote mining areas where water could usually be brought from a nearby source. The application of this device in Britain is attributed to M. Menzies (d. 1766) in 1761. Water-balance engines have also been used to raise spoil from tunnelling operations, and to operate underground pumps for dewatering mines; in this case they resembled a BEAM ENGINE with a water bucket at one end of the beam, and vertical pump rods at the other. These pumps were known as flop-jacks in Cornwall, and bobbing Johns in Scotland. Water-balance engines are also known as water-bucket engines or pumps.

Downs-Rose, G. and Harvey, W.S. 'Water-bucket pumps and the Wanlockhead Engine', *Industrial Archaeology* 10 (1973), 129

water bellows, *see* TROMPE

water blast, *see* TROMPE

water frame a water-powered cotton spinning machine, patented by Richard Arkwright in

$$\frac{D}{d} = \frac{H}{h}$$

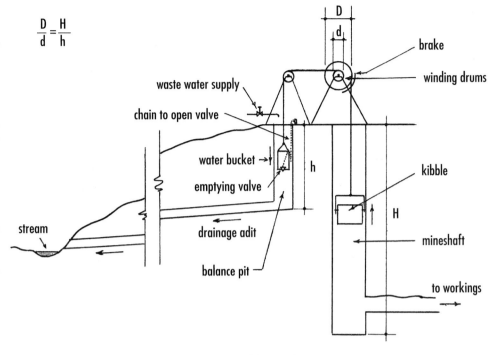

Fig. 80. Water-balance engine

1769 (no. 931). Originally horse driven, by 1771 the machine was being driven by water power at Cromford, Derbys., where Arkwright (1732–92) had his cotton mill. The water frame incorporated the principles of the SPINDLE and FLYER of the SAXONY WHEEL with the drafting rollers developed from Paul and Wyatt's earlier attempts (*see* DRAFTING). The machine is regarded as the first true factory-operated spinning machine, where it was supervised by women and children. The first model produced four yarns at once, suitable for both WARP and WEFT, enabling all-cotton fabrics to be woven.

Fig. 81 shows the main features of a 1769 machine. Draft was achieved by passing ROVINGS through four pairs of equal diameter rollers, each pair turning faster than the previous pair, to draw out the cotton fibres. The top, leather-covered rollers were weighted to press on the driven, fluted bottom rollers. The drive is omitted from the diagram for clarity. Twist, and winding on, were done by the flyers and bobbins, a light string brake slowing the bobbins to create the necessary speed differential. Improvements to the 1769 machine soon followed, such as a CAM mechanism to

raise and lower the bobbins to give continuous working and even winding. Early machines had to be stopped every so often to move a yarn onto a fresh HECK on the flyer. Later developments led to the THROSTLE FRAME. The action of the water frame was too robust for spinning wool, but by about 1784 it was spinning worsted.

water gas (or blue water gas) a mixture of carbon monoxide and hydrogen obtained by passing steam over red-hot coke in a retort, and sometimes further enriched by adding gas oil. It was used as a fuel in GAS ENGINES and mixed with coal gas to form TOWN GAS.

water gate 1. another name for a FLASH LOCK. **2.** a SOUGH for draining a mine.

water level gauge a device enabling a boiler operator to see the level of water inside the boiler, so that the level is not allowed to fall dangerously low. The glass water level gauge was introduced by John Urpeth Rastrick (1780–1856) of Stourbridge, Worcs., in 1829 on a locomotive, but it soon became standard equipment on all types of steam boilers. Before the glass gauge was invented, two small cocks, one above the normal water level, the other

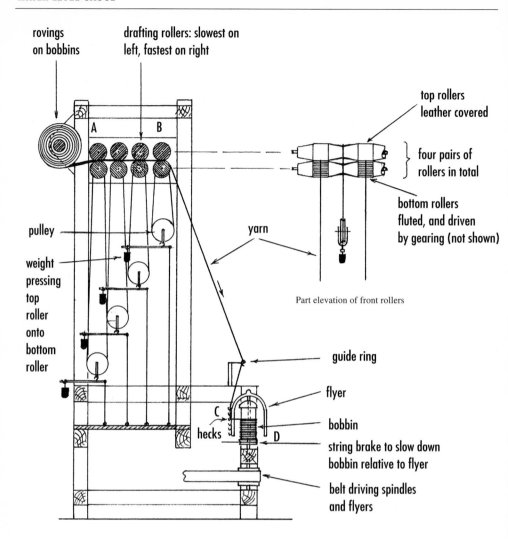

rovings
on bobbins

drafting rollers: slowest on
left, fastest on right

A   B

top rollers
leather covered

} four pairs of
  rollers in total

bottom rollers
fluted, and driven
by gearing (not shown)

pulley

yarn

weight
pressing
top
roller
onto
bottom
roller

Part elevation of front rollers

guide ring

flyer

C

hecks   D

bobbin

string brake to slow down
bobbin relative to flyer

belt driving spindles
and flyers

Action of machine
A–B drafting of roving
B–C twisting of yarn
C–D winding onto bobbin

Fig. 81. Side view of 1769 water frame

below it, were usually fitted to boilers. By opening the cocks in turn, and noting whether steam or water was discharged, the correct water level could be maintained within limits.

watermark the faint mark in the form of lettering, a symbol, or a portrait, etc. which appears in some paper when it is held up to the light. It is added during the manufacture of the paper as a trademark or for security reasons, such as on banknotes.

Watermarks were used from the early days of hand-made PAPER MAKING, originating in Italy, and made by sewing onto the base 'sieve' the required pattern in fine wire, bent to the required shape. The pattern caused a slight thinning of the paper which becomes visible when the paper is held up to the light. The use of fine wire resulted in watermark lines of constant depth and width, but by the 1850s a technique had been developed to give a shadow effect which improved portrait watermarks. When machine-made paper was introduced at the beginning of the 19th century there were no watermarks until the DANDY ROLL was invented in 1825, which added the watermark as the wet paper passed under it.

watermill a corn grinding mill driven by water power. The watermill was one of the first machines to harness a natural power source, since it uses the potential and kinetic energy of flowing water to turn a wheel to rotate grindstones. Corn mills may be divided into two types depending on whether the wheel lies in a horizontal or a vertical plane. Grindstones driven by the former are known as NORSE WHEELS, and are primitive mills with the grindstones mounted directly above the wheel on the same axle; they are low powered and inefficient. More important are vertical wheels, which are known as VITRUVIAN WHEELS. Of over 5,600 watermills listed in the Domesday Book (1080–6) in Britain, most had Vitruvian wheels. In the Middle Ages, watermills were normally owned by the lord of the manor, and all his tenants had to have their own corn ground at his mill.

A watermill is entirely dependent on its water supply, and is vulnerable to droughts and flooding (*see* BACKWATERING). RESERVOIRS or mill ponds provide a reserve against drought. River water is fed onto the mill wheel from upstream or from the mill pond, via a headrace which incorporates a sluice to control the flow, and leaves the wheel via a tailrace back into the river, downstream. The power developed by a waterwheel depends on its diameter, width, and point of entry of the water onto the wheel circumference. In flat country, to work a large

wheel, a weir is built across the river well upstream on a higher contour, and water is led from above the weir along a long LEAT or channel into the mill pond or onto the wheel. This gives a higher point of entry onto the wheel than would have been the case if water were taken at the mill site. In hilly country, long leats are unnecessary, and mills were often sited at nip points on a river to give a useful fall of water.

Most watermills have a grain drying kiln attached consisting of a ventilated room with a floor of perforated cast-iron plates on which the grain is spread about 4 in deep. A firegrate below the floor provided the heat, and waste husks from the grinding process were often used to supplement the fuel.

The importation of foreign grain in the 19th century, and cheap flour from steam driven ROLLER MILLS sited at ports, made the traditional watermill obsolete.

Bennett, C.E. 'The watermills of Kent, east of the Medway', *Industrial Archaeology Review* I (1977), 205–35

Reynolds, J. *Windmills and Watermills*, Hugh Evelyn, 1970

Syson, L. *British Watermills*, Batsford, 1965

water power mechanical power derived from water turning a wheel, or some type of impeller (*see* Figs 83 and 84). WATERWHEELS have provided power from ancient times: mechanical power is obtained from rotation of a vertical wheel by water either striking FLOATBOARDS or filling buckets spaced round the wheel circumference. A waterwheel is dependent on its river water supply, and reservoirs or ponds provide a reserve against drought. Waterwheels were prime movers for factories, mills, etc. for at least a century. Even long after steam engines were being built, waterwheels were still in use. In 1834, it was estimated that about one-third of all cotton mills in Britain were water-powered, and at the Great Exhibition of 1851, waterwheels were still being exhibited and sold. The main advantages of waterwheels are their simplicity, low maintenance cost, and almost free energy source. Their disadvantages are that a factory or mill is tied to a river site, the power they could develop was limited, and reliance on water supply.

Other forms of water power were later developed. WATER TURBINES of various designs date from 1826, mostly developed by French engineers. Water turbines are more efficient than waterwheels, occupy less space, and can work at low heads; some waterwheels were replaced by turbines. Modern water turbines can generate thousands of horsepower in hydroelectric schemes. In about 1870, the PELTON WHEEL was invented, which converts a jet of high pressure water into high speed rotation. Pelton wheels are normally used in mountainous country where a high head of water from an elevated reservoir can be arranged. The high speed of the wheel has to be reduced by gearing to a more convenient one to drive machinery.

All the methods described here for generating mechanical power use the kinetic energy of moving water; the energy of water under high pressure is used in hydraulic systems (*see* HYDRAULIC POWER). *See also* TIDE MILL.

Shaw, J. *Water Power in Scotland, 1550–1870*, John Donald, 1984

Tucker, D.G. 'Hydro-electricity for public supply in Britain, 1881–94', *Industrial Archaeology Review* I (1977), 126–63

Weaver, M.A. *The Tide Mill, Woodbridge*, Woodbridge, 1973

Wilson, P.N. 'Early water turbines in the UK', *Newcomen Society Transactions* 31 (1957–9), 285ff.

Main developments in water-powered prime movers

*c.*46 BC	Vitruvius describes undershot waterwheels
7th–8th centuries	Norse-type vertical axle waterwheels
1170	Wheel operated by tides at Woodbridge, Suffolk
*c.*1500	Tilt hammers operated by wheels
1759	Wheel design improved by Smeaton
*c.*1760	Borda reaction water turbine
*c.*1795	Suspension design waterwheels by Hewes
1820s	Poncelet curved vanes undershot waterwheel
1826	Poncelet inward flow water turbine
1827	Fourneyron outward flow water turbine
1840	Francis mixed flow water turbine
1843	Jonval axial flow water turbine
*c.*1850	Ventilated buckets added to waterwheels by Fairbairn
1852	Thomson inward flow water turbine
1850s–60s	Waterwheels being replaced by water turbines
*c.*1870	Pelton impulse wheel

water pressure engine, *see* HYDRAULIC ENGINE

water-returning engine (or re-circulating engine) a steam engine, often used in the 18th century, which drove a pump to return water back to a WATERWHEEL so that it could be used over and over again. Such engines were usually early non-rotative beam engines, and their purpose was twofold: first, the engine was added to an already existing waterwheel installation driving a textile mill so that the mill could continue to run in times of drought and to conserve water; and secondly, it was a means of obtaining rotation from a reciprocating beam engine before rotative engine designs became available. In fact, it ensured a more steady speed of rotation from the wheel (necessary to drive spinning machines) than could be obtained from the first rotative engines, which could be somewhat irregular in operation. When smoother-running rotational steam engines became available waterwheels were gradually replaced, and engines took over driving machinery directly.

Another use of water-returning was to pump lock water up from lower levels of canals to higher levels, or the summit in cases, where the water supply was poor.

Andrew, J. 'Canal Pumping Engines', *Industrial Archaeology Review* XV (1993), 140–59

watershot masonry the shallow zig-zag or rippled surface effect created on the walls of some old stone buildings. This is often characteristic of the solid walls of 18th and early 19th-century weavers' and other cottages in Lancashire and surrounding districts, and is designed to prevent or reduce damp and rain penetration. Most stone cottages in these areas are built from millstone grit or sandstone blocks, and these materials are layered sedimentary rocks, not impervious to water seepage. The stone blocks are laid with their outer faces tipping slightly forward, so that the inherent layers and the mortar joints are inclined slightly towards the outside, thus encouraging any moisture which may have entered to run out. Corner quoins are of necessity laid horizontally. Since some older cottages did not originally have roof gutters, rain running down the wall face would also tend to be thrown clear by the ledges formed at each course of stone blocks. Watershot walls give a distinctive and attractive surface texture, especially when viewed in oblique sunlight.

water supply, *see* PUBLIC UTILITIES

watertube boiler a steam-raising boiler which includes a number of inclined tubes through which water circulates, picking up heat from the hot gases which surround the watertubes. The tubes provide a large heating surface enabling steam to be raised quickly, and watertube boilers can operate at much higher pressures than the older SHELL BOILERS.

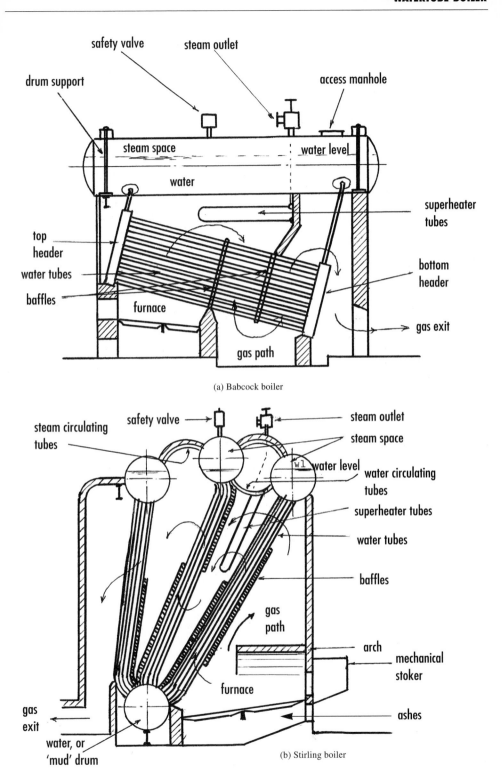

(a) Babcock boiler

(b) Stirling boiler

Fig. 82. Watertube steam boilers

Many types of watertube boilers have been designed over the years, known by their designer's name. Their ability to generate steam at a higher pressure than shell boilers is a result of the small diameter of the tubes (compared with the containing body of a shell boiler) being able to withstand considerably higher bursting pressures; the top collecting drum (or drums) holding the steam is also out of reach of the fierce heat from the fire and is much smaller than the body of a shell boiler. Watertube designs were introduced as higher steam pressures were required above the safe limit of shell boilers (around 200 psi). An early design was that first proposed by Arthur Woolf (1776–1837) in 1803 which had the beginnings of later designs and comprised two large 'tubes' slung beneath a steam drum (see Fig. 10). This design became popular in textile mills around 1830–50, and was known as the ELEPHANT BOILER.

A well-known watertube boiler is the Babcock (see Fig. 82a), designed by George Herman Babcock (1832–93) and Stephen Wilcox (1830–93) in the USA in 1867. It comprised a large number of watertubes, each about 4 in bore, inclined at an angle towards the front and expanded at each end into vertical header tubes. The headers fed into a top horizontal drum, the lower half containing water, the upper being a steam space. There was a firegrate at the front below the nest of tubes, and the hot gases passed between the tubes within a brick combustion chamber. The water descended via the back headers, rose through the inclined tubes and returned to the top drum via the front headers, steam being collected in the steam space of the top drum. A good circulation of water resulted with a good heat exchange. Other variations on the basic design of the Babcock boiler were introduced, such as the Yarrow boiler (1894) and the Stirling boiler (Fig. 82b); there were many others, each claiming a particular advantage over its competitors.

Robertson, L.S. *Watertube Boilers*, 1901

water turbine a PRIME MOVER in which a central wheel with curved vanes, enclosed in a chamber, receives water directed onto the curved vanes by a ring of fixed guide vanes, causing the wheel to rotate about its axis. Water turbines are a natural development from the simple WATERWHEELS and inventions of various designs commenced in the second decade of the 19th century, particularly in France. There are various designs, some of the reaction type, others of the impulse type, the former being the most common; there are also inward radial flow turbines, outward flow turbines, and parallel or axial flow machines (see Fig. 83). The principal use of large water turbines today is for hydroelectric schemes, but in the early 19th century smaller machines were often used for industrial drives where there was a suitable water supply. Many textile mills replaced waterwheels with water turbines after c.1850. See also AMERICAN WATER TURBINE; FOURNEYRON WATER TURBINE; FRANCIS WATER TURBINE; IMPULSE TURBINE; JONVAL WATER TURBINE; PELTON WHEEL; PONCELET WATER TURBINE; REACTION TURBINE; THOMSON WATER TURBINE.

water twist (or hard twist) name given to yarn which is well twisted and intended for use as WARP, in the days of the WATER FRAME.

waterwheel a wheel rotated by water to generate mechanical power. Waterwheels have played an important part in providing power to drive machinery, from medieval corn and fulling mills to the time of the Industrial Revolution. Waterwheels are of two fundamental types: primitive, low power, horizontal wheels known as NORSE WHEELS, and the common vertical wheels, of which there are several designs, as shown in Fig. 84. The simplest vertical wheel is the UNDERSHOT or VITRUVIAN WHEEL (Fig. 84a), which comprises a wooden wheel with protruding flat FLOATBOARDS (Fig. 84e) which dip into flowing water. The wheel is turned by impulse action arising from kinetic energy as the water strikes the floatboards. Later designs substituted buckets (Fig. 84g) for floatboards: water is arranged to fill the buckets on one side of the wheel to produce an out-of-balance, which rotates the wheel by gravity. Thus, the potential energy of the height the water falls whilst in the buckets is used. Depending on where the water enters the wheel, each design has its own name. If the water enters below the top of the wheel, it is called a BREAST WHEEL – high breast if above the axle, low breast if below (Fig. 84b). If entry is at the top of the wheel, it is called an OVERSHOT WHEEL if the wheel rotates in the same direction as the entering water (Fig. 84c), or a PITCHBACK if the wheel rotates backwards (Fig. 84d). Overshot wheels use a combination of the kinetic and potential energy of the water.

Early waterwheels were designed empirically, but as the need for greater power arose, their design was approached scientifically. Jean Victor Poncelet (1788–1867) of France substituted curved sheet-metal iron paddles for flat floatboards on undershot wheels, giving a smoother action which raised the wheel efficiency considerably (Fig. 84f).

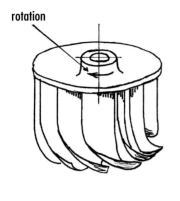

American mixed-flow reaction turbine runner

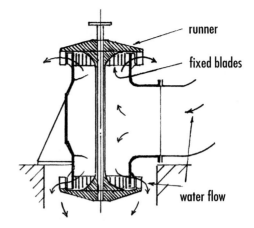

Cross-section through Fourneyron reaction turbine

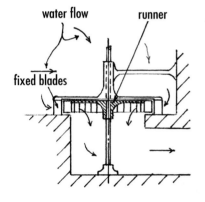

Cross-section through Francis reaction turbine

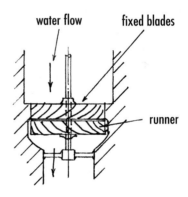

Cross-section through Jonval reaction turbine

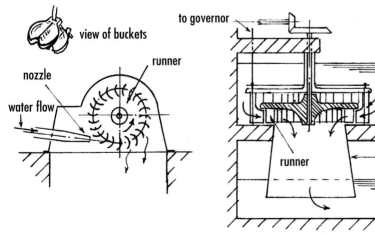

Cross-section through impulse Pelton wheel

Cross-section through low head Thomson reaction turbine

Fig. 83. Water turbines

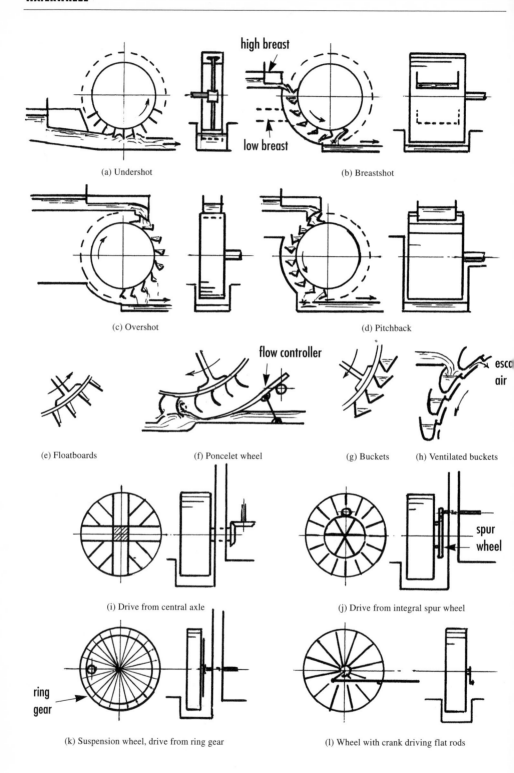

Fig. 84. Waterwheels

William Fairbairn (1789–1874) introduced VENTILATED BUCKETS which allowed buckets to hold more water (Fig. 84h) and thus give greater power.

A waterwheel installation has to be engineered to suit its location. Since the power a wheel can develop depends on factors such as its diameter, width, and velocity of the water, all these have to be matched to the height the water can be made to fall. Undershot wheels give only low power: greater power comes from breast, overshot and pitchback wheels. Long LEATS may be necessary to give the fall required by the latter.

At first, waterwheels were of massive all-wood construction, of compass or clasp arm design (*see* Fig. 85). Compass arms were fastened to the axle tree by mortice and tenon, which weakened the wheel at the point where strength was most needed; clasp arm design made a stronger wheel, as the arms formed a square clasping the axle tree without weakening it. By about 1770, cast-iron axles were introduced, and by the early 19th century wrought-iron rims, spokes and buckets were common. A lightweight design, known as the SUSPENSION or tension wheel (Fig. 84k) was invented by Thomas Cheek Hewes (1768–1832) which had a ring gear and power take-off via a pinion. This relieved the central axle and spokes of transmitting the torque, and also gave a faster, more suitable take-off speed.

Strings of textile mills spread out along river valleys, each mill drawing water for its wheel, and returning it for use by the next mill downstream. Water velocity was important, as the power a wheel can develop varies with the square of water velocity. Fast moving 'infant' streams could therefore generate the same power with less water than slow moving 'mature' rivers. Besides powering factories and mills, waterwheels have been used for many other duties such as driving pumps and raising ores. Steam power made the traditional waterwheel obsolete, as steam engines made the siting of an enterprise independent of a river, permitted all year operation, and generated greater power. *See also* TIDE MILL, WATER POWER.

Syson, L. *The Watermills of Britain*, Batsford, 1980
Vince, J. *Discovering Watermills*, Shire Publications, 1987
Wenham, P. *Watermills*, Hales, 1989

Watt governor, *see* CENTRIFUGAL GOVERNOR

wayleave the annual payment to a landowner made by a railway or canal company, for the right to run their traffic across the land. Wayleaves still apply today.

waymarker, *see* STOOP (1)

wayshaft a rocking shaft for working the SLIDE VALVES from an ECCENTRIC on a steam engine.

Wealden iron iron made during the 16th to 18th centuries on the Weald of Kent, Surrey, and Sussex. The Weald, once heavily wooded, was an early centre of iron making in England. Iron ore was dug locally from BELL PITS (1), and simple, charcoal-fired BLAST FURNACES and foundries made cast-iron articles such as cannons, cannonballs, firebacks, domestic pots, and even iron 'gravestone' slabs. Water-powered forges converted cast iron into wrought iron for blacksmithing work, and traces may be found of small ponds which once supplied water for bellows and trip hammers. Sites are remembered in place names which include the words 'hammer' or 'forge', such as Abinger Hammer and Huggetts Furnace in Surrey. *See also* HAMMER POND.

Straker, E. *Wealden Iron*, David and Charles, 1970

weather the slight longitudinal twist given to windmill sails, designed to help them catch the wind better.

weaver's alley the passageway between rows of looms in a weaving shed from which the weavers service the machines. The looms are arranged so that the front take-up rollers face each other across the alley, thus enabling a weaver to attend to either row merely by turning round.

weaver's beam, *see* BEAM ROLLER

weavers' windows rows of mullioned windows in stone cottages for admitting plenty of daylight into LOOMSHOPS. In woollen districts, such windows would be on the top storey where the handlooms were placed; in cotton districts they would be either on the ground floor, to one side or at the rear of the living quarters, or arranged to light a cellar. Cotton weaving was carried out on the ground floor or in cellars because damp conditions helped the weaving, and sometimes the floor would be kept wet to create the condition. Weavers' windows are also known as weavers' lights or longlight windows, and are characteristic features of buildings which were once the homes of domestic hand weavers. After the house had been converted into a normal dwelling, frequently some of the long windows were blocked off to give separated windows, and this alteration can usually be detected by the presence of a long lintel which once spanned the original window. The houses of domestic STOCKING FRAME knitters had similar windows to give plenty of daylight.

Timmins, J.G. *Handloom Weavers' Cottages in Central Lancashire*, Occasional Paper No. 3, University of Lancaster, 1977

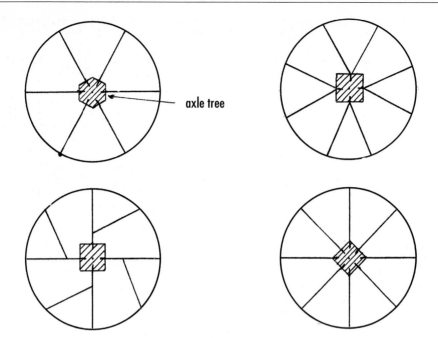

(a) Compass arm wheels

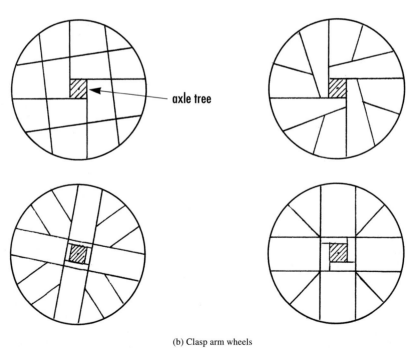

(b) Clasp arm wheels

Fig. 85. Construction of wooden waterwheels

Handloom weavers' factory, Delph, Greater Manchester

weaving the manufacturing of a cloth from threads which are interlaced at right angles to each other in a LOOM. Weaving dates from ancient times, probably pre-dating the spinning of threads: for example, the making of matting from untwisted natural fibres or grasses, and intertwining twigs to make hurdles for simple walls and fencing, are both primitive forms of weaving. When the spinning into threads of natural fibres such as flax, wool, cotton, was developed, primitive vertical looms were devised on which elementary cloths were woven. From these times, improvements both in spinning of thread and the weaving of cloth were made. At first, hand methods were used, and then simple machines invented and developed, culminating in power driven machinery by the late 18th century.

The simplest form of weaving, known as PLAIN WEAVE, is when the threads cross over and under adjacent threads alternately. Other forms of weaving are done to make different types of cloth, and the manner in which the longitudinal threads are raised before the cross threads pass under them is known as shedding (*see* SHED). Cloth is made up from longitudinal threads called WARPS or ends, and cross threads called picks or WEFT; the action of passing weft across the warps from either side is called

PICKING. The warp, which has previously been prepared off the loom, is fitted onto the loom with each thread passing through a HEALD, while the weft is wound onto small bobbins held in a SHUTTLE which is passed across the loom from side to side, trailing a length of weft behind it. Each succeeding pass lies alongside the previous pass to build up the cloth: a REED pushes each pick in turn up against the previous pick to consolidate the cloth as weaving proceeds. *See also* WEAVING PROCESSES.

The type of cloth that is woven depends on factors such as the shedding pattern, the diameter of the thread used, known as its COUNT, the spacing of the warps and wefts, etc. A cotton handkerchief might have around 80 threads per inch in each direction, giving 6,400 intersections per square inch. Weaving is known as conversion in the textile trade.

weaving processes the processes involved in the manufacture of cloth. A cotton weaving shed will be laid out to accommodate all the preparatory work and the actual weaving with the minimum handling of material; a typical plan is shown in Fig. 86. The main weaving processes are as follows. Yarn is purchased from a spinning company (or received from the spinning section if the weaving shed is part of an integrated company) and stored in the YARN

425

STORE until required. It is usually received in COP or HANK form, and samples are tested to check that it conforms to the quality and standard ordered. The yarn intended for WARPS needs some preparatory processes, whereas WEFT yarn does not. Warp yarn passes to the *winding section* where it is wound onto bobbins. It then goes to the *beaming section* where the correct number of bobbins are placed on a CREEL and wound onto a warp beam to form the warp of parallel threads of the required dimensions, a process also known as warping. It then is sized in a *sizing machine* to strengthen it and bind any loose fibres. After drying, it is ready to be prepared for the loom. This involves a process known as *drawing-in* (*see* DRAWING AND REACHING) in which individual threads are drawn through a set of HEALDS in a certain order so as to produce the type of cloth intended. The warp is then fitted into the loom in the *weaving shed*, the healds connected up as appropriate. The weft yarn is wound into PIRNS, from the package form received, in the winding section and taken to the weaving shed for supplying the shuttles. The actual weaving of the cloth then takes place, and after manufacture, the finished cloth is taken into the *cloth warehouse*, where it is examined for faults which are rectified, if necessary, and stored awaiting purchase.

The above description applies to a weaving shed fitted with POWER LOOMS. In the days of the HANDLOOM WEAVER, the weaver received yarn from a CLOTHIER and made up the warp and fitted it into his loom himself. He sized the warp on the loom, a short section at a time as weaving proceeded. He then delivered the finished PIECE to the clothier, receiving payment for his work and a fresh supply of yarn for weaving the next piece.

The power requirements of a weaving shed are lower than for an equivalent spinning mill. Weaving sheds are almost always a single storey, since looms work better on a solid ground floor. Good lighting is essential, and the single storey shed readily gives this; it is usually obtained by use of NORTH LIGHT roofs. Weaving sheds are noisy and a fair amount of loose fibres and dust from the warp size floats about in the air. Whereas handloom weaving was a man's job, power looms are almost always attended to by women. The looms are arranged in rows, back to back, with a passageway between their fronts, so that the weaver can walk between two rows and attend to each row merely by turning round.

Marsden, R. *Cotton Weaving: Its Development, Principles, and Practice*, Bell, 1895

web (or awebb, oweb) an old name for the body of a piece of woven fabric or cloth comprising the interlaced WARP and WEFT.

wedge and groove an old method of splitting rocks in quarries and mines so that they could be extracted. A line of grooves about 5–6 in long, and some 3 in deep with around 2 in space in between, was cut into the rock, and wooden wedges driven into the slots. The wedges were then soaked with water, and the resulting expansion was usually sufficient to split the rock along the line. The PLUG AND FEATHERS method superseded the wedge and groove in the early 19th century.

weft (or woof, owef, shoot) the threads which pass across the width of woven cloth. Weft threads cross over and under the longitudinal warp threads or ends at right angles according to the pattern being woven, this being determined by the SHEDDING arrangement. Weft is also known as filling, since it 'fills out' the substance of the cloth. Weft yarns do not need to be as tightly twisted as warp yarns. The old name woof today only has a literary or poetic use.

weft fork a device for detecting the presence or absence of a WEFT thread during weaving on an automatic POWER LOOM. It immediately stops the machine when the weft is missing to prevent weaving faulty cloth (*see* BROKEN-WEFT STOPPING MOTION).

weft knitting construction of a knitted fabric in which one continuous length of yarn or thread passes in loops or stitches across the width, from left to right and vice versa, looping into the previously made row of similar stitches (*see* Fig. 71). This is the type of knitting made by hand using two needles, and by a knitting or STOCKING FRAME in machine knitting; it is the oldest form of knitting. The plain stitch is called a knit or stocking stitch, and a reversed stitch, which forms a raised rib on the surface, is called a purl stitch (from a Scottish word 'pirl', meaning to twist or turn). Weft knitting is also known as filling knitting, because each course of stitches across the width 'fills' the fabric.

weighbridge a platform weighing machine placed in a pit so that vehicles etc. can be driven onto it from the roadway without needing to be lifted. A platform weighbridge for carts was invented by John Wyatt (1700–66) of Birmingham in about 1740, using a compound lever system. The need for weighbridges arose out of the Turnpike Act of 1741 which authorized toll collectors to weigh carts etc. to calculate tolls, although most toll houses were equipped with crane-type 'weighing engines'.

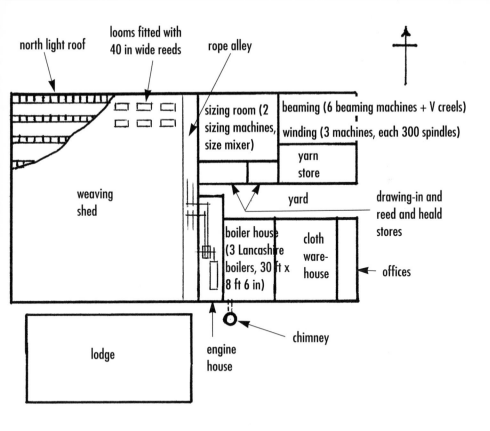

north light roof

looms fitted with 40 in wide reeds

rope alley

sizing room (2 sizing machines, size mixer)

beaming (6 beaming machines + V creels)

winding (3 machines, each 300 spindles)

yarn store

weaving shed

yard

drawing-in and reed and heald stores

boiler house (3 Lancashire boilers, 30 ft x 8 ft 6 in)

cloth ware-house

offices

lodge

engine house

chimney

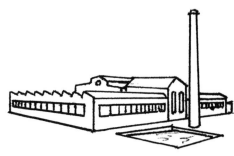

Fig. 86. Layout of a typical weaving shed for 500 power looms and preparation equipment, *c.* 1870s. Source: Marsden, R. *Cotton Weaving*, 1895

weir a low wall or barrier built across a river to raise the water level upstream, or to control the flow. Weirs date from the Middle Ages, when they were made to conserve water in dry seasons for water-powered corn and fulling mills. On navigable rivers, FLASH LOCKS were made in weirs to permit passage of boats. Water is taken from a river just above a weir by a LEAT to give a sufficient fall at a WATERWHEEL sited some distance downstream. Most weirs were built of stone, although timber weirs were sometimes built across small streams. Stepped weirs, like a shallow staircase, and sloping weirs prevent water turbulence from undermining the foundation of a high weir, by reducing the impact of the fall. Simple weirs run across a river at right angles to the water flow; large weirs are built curved, like an arch lying on its side with the arch crown facing upstream, so that water pressure consolidates the construction. Long weirs placed diagonally across a river reduce the rise in water level at a leat entrance in times of river spate. Canals have side weirs to control their water level by allowing excess to run off to a lower level, and prevent flooding; weirs or spillways at the sides of reservoir dams serve the same purpose. Some weirs have fish passes built into them, while others may include a water measuring notch. Circular weirs direct water down a central hole or swallow into an underground culvert. In Scotland, a weir is called a caul or cauld.

weld 1. (or dyers' weed, woold) an old dyestuff dating from the 16th century, made from the leaves, seeds and stems of the plant *Reseda Luteola*, which gave a yellow dye. Weld was frequently used with INDIGO or WOAD to make a green dye. The weld plant was once cultivated in England and other parts of Europe to supply textile dyers. 2. in Yorkshire dialect, to sort and card wool for knitting.

wem an old Cornish word for a windlass for winding tubs in a mine shaft; it is probably a variation of WHIM.

West of England cloth a general name for the woollen cloth made in the counties of Gloucestershire, Wiltshire and Somerset from the 14th to the 19th centuries. These counties became one of the principal woollen cloth-making centres in Britain before the industry began to move to the West Riding of Yorkshire at the beginning of the 19th century. From about the 14th to the end of the 16th century woollen cloth woven by hand methods flourished in the West Country, particularly around Bristol and in the valleys around Stroud. When the factory system developed, many water-powered woollen mills and cloth finishing establishments were built in the area. Later, these mills changed to steam power, and by about the 1830s the West of England industry was probably at its peak. As the industry moved north, mills became redundant and were occupied by other industries, as many are today.

Most cloth woven was medium quality, PLAIN WEAVE woollen broadcloth, with some narrow ossets. Various names were given to the types of cloth, such as Stroudwaters, which were normally dyed red, and Spanish cloths, an imprecise, confusing name since it was not necessarily woven from Spanish merino wool, but from local wool from the large numbers of sheep reared in the area. Much of the cloth was exported to Europe, either white or dyed blue, but this trade declined in the 18th century. Cloth is still produced in the area, but in nowhere near the same quantity as it was formerly.

Mann, J. de Lacy. *The Cloth Industry in the West of England 1640–1880*, 1971; reprinted by Alan Sutton, 1987
Ponting, K.G. *A History of the West of England Cloth Industry*, Macdonald, 1957
Smith, B.S. and Lewis, R.A. *The Cloth Industry in Gloucestershire, 1700–1840*, 1976
Tann, J. *Gloucestershire Woollen Mills*, 1967

wet bottom engine, *see* TANK BED ENGINE

wet puddling (or pig boiling) a method of making wrought iron from cast pig iron, patented by Joseph Hall (1789–1862) of Tipton, Staffs., under a patent (no. 7778, 1838) shared with Richard Bradley and William Barrows. Hall's process replaced the older DRY PUDDLING method of Henry Cort and comprised the use of a reactive lining in the bath of the puddling furnace, called fettling, in place of Cort's siliceous sand bath. It became the standard way for making wrought iron (*see also* PUDDLING FURNACE).

wet spinning a method of spinning flax in which the ROVING is first passed through a trough of hot water positioned above the spinning frame to soften the inherent gum in the flax. The process enables finer COUNTS of linen to be spun. A wet spinning machine was invented by Matthew Murray (1765–1826) and James Kay in 1825 (patent no. 5226); the idea originated from France in 1814.

wey an old Cornish measure for coal. There was a long wey of 72 BUSHELS and a short wey of 64 bushels.

wharf 1. (or wharve) an old name for the small pulleys attached to the FLYER and SPINDLE of a spinning wheel, which rotated them by being driven by a cord from the large wheel. Another name for these pulleys was whorl, or more rarely wharl(e), both being variants of the word whirl. **2.** a loading and unloading place on a canal or dock. A typical canal wharf would have warehouses, a WEIGHBRIDGE, crane(s), some hard standing for storing certain commodities outside (such as coal), a nearby bridge to facilitate reaching both sides of the canal, and places where canal boats could tie up. It might also have lime kilns, stables for horses, a boat repair yard, a GAUGING DOCK and a pub. A large wharf would have a house for the manager, who was called a wharfinger. Access to the road system was essential, and some wharfs were connected to nearby collieries by TRAMROADS.

wheal a Cornish name for a tin mine. The word comes from the Cornish 'huel' meaning a mine; it is added as a prefix to the name of a mine, such as Wheal Prosper.

wheel draught a brick flue surrounding a steam boiler, melting pot, etc. The flue leads the hot gases from the fire or furnace around the outside of the boiler, etc., so that more heat can be extracted before the gases leave for the chimney. The old HAYSTACK BOILERS had wheel draught.

wheelgate, *see* JENNYGATE

wheel pit the rectangular pit in which the lower part of a WATERWHEEL revolves. A wheel pit is often the only remaining evidence of a former waterwheel installation. Examination of its dimensions can normally give some indication of the probable size of the wheel, and from this, the possible power it developed. It may not be clear, however, whether the wheel was breastshot, overshot, or pitchback, unless there is also evidence of how the water reached it. The pit may be shaped to conform to the periphery of the wheel to trap the water in the buckets as long as possible. Undershot wheels will have a channel leading water into the pit, and all pits will have a TAILRACE. The width of pits for undershot wheels is normally only very slightly wider than the wheel, to reduce losses by water passing either side of the FLOATBOARDS; there is usually more side clearance for other types of wheel. Sometimes there is evidence of the position of the axle bearings, which helps in determining the wheel diameter.

wheel shuttle, *see* FLYING SHUTTLE

whee-wah local name given to an 18th-century needle polishing device in the Redditch area of Worcestershire. It comprised a heavy flat board, which was mounted on a table and could be moved backwards and forwards across the table surface by a pivoted lever and linkage. Needles requiring polishing were laid alongside each other on a leather or strong cloth, covered with a fine abrasive powder and oil, and rolled up and tied into a tight 'swiss roll'. A number of these rolls were placed between the board and table surface, and rolled to and fro for a considerable time until it was judged the needles were sufficiently polished by the scouring action. Whee-wahs were manually worked at first, often by children. Later, HORSE GINS were used to operate several larger units simultaneously. The unusual name is obviously onomatopoeic.

wherry a rowing boat used for carrying passengers. Wherries were once operated on rivers as water taxis; such a service was operated regularly on the river Severn from Shrewsbury to Worcester in the 18th century. Canal boats were also called wherries in Norfolk. Although the word was in use in the 16th century, its origin is unknown.

whim (or whimsey) terms loosely used in the 18th and 19th centuries for a mine winding or pumping engine. An 18th-century HORSE WHIM, also known as a gin, is shown in Fig. 28. Such machines were used for raising ore, coal, and water in buckets, from shallow mines, by a horse (or horses) walking round in a circle driving primitive winding gear. In the 19th century, horses were replaced by steam driven beam engines, either turning a winding drum, or working underground water pumps, as shown in Fig. 22; these machines were also called whims or gins.

The alternative name whimsey comes from the obsolete name for a fairground roundabout which a horse whim resembles. Unfortunately, the word whimsey was often used in old documents to describe steam driven as well as horse driven whims, making it difficult to determine which was meant.

whip 1. the wooden backbone of a windmill sail to which the vanes or shutters etc. are attached. The whip is in effect an extension to the stocks which are fastened to the protruding end of the WINDSHAFT. **2.** (or whip and derry, whipsiderry) a simple hoisting device comprising a rope passing over an overhead pulley and attached to a horse, which raised a load attached to the other end of the rope by walking away from it. A whip gin is a similar lifting arrangement, with the hoisting rope divided into several ends, so that a gang of men could raise a heavy load acting together. COAL WHIPPERS in docks used whip gins.

Whipple-Murphy truss a lattice type bridge truss invented in the UK by Squire Whipple (1804–88) and John W. Murphy (1828–74) in 1847. It comprises upper and lower horizontal STRINGERS joined together at regular intervals by vertical members; inclined members slope downwards from the joint of each vertical with the top stringer to the bottom joint of the next but one vertical, in each half of the truss (*see* Fig. 12).

whipsiderry, *see* WHIP (2)

'whirling engine' Richard Trevithick's (1771–1833) abortive attempt in 1815 at making a STEAM TURBINE.

'whirling regulator' James Watt's (1736–1819) name for the CENTRIFUGAL GOVERNOR which he applied to a steam engine c.1788 to regulate its speed.

whisky manufacture the making of an alcoholic drink by a distillation process. The name whisky is derived from the Gaelic *uisge beatha*, meaning 'water of life', and the spirit is also known as Scotch. It is principally made in Scotland, and in Ireland where it is spelt whiskey. The earliest mention of whisky in Britain occurs in the 16th century, but its manufacture in quantity only commenced at the beginning of the 18th century. There are three kinds of whisky: pure malt whisky distilled from malted barley; grain whisky made from maize or unmalted barley; and blended whisky made by a mixture of the other two.

A typical distillery for making malt whisky will have a barley store; a malting floor where the barley is soaked and left to germinate; a tall drying kiln fired by peat which gives flavour to the end product; malt processing equipment (milling and mashing); a fermentation room; and heated copper pot stills and condensers, where the alcohol is recovered by distilling and cooling the boiling liquid. A bulk spirit store and a bottling plant complete the equipment. Malt whisky is matured in oak casks, which often once held sherry, for a minimum of three years (age improves the quality) during which it acquires its colour. Distilleries have a distinctive external appearance which has altered little over the years. An outstanding feature is the tall pagoda-like top to the kiln. Grain whisky is made in a similar manner, using patent stills. Blending of the two whiskies dates from the 1860s to produce a cheaper and milder tasting spirit.

In Scotland malt distilleries are small and number over 100 today: they are mostly scattered in the glens of the Highlands and Western Isles, close to springs and streams whose waters, it is claimed, give each whisky its own unique taste. Grain distilleries are large units, mostly concentrated in the Edinburgh–Glasgow area. The distilling of whisky has been under strict government control since the 19th century, and the spirit is highly taxed. Whisky today is exported in large quantities.

Butt, J. *The Industrial Archaeology of Scotland*, David and Charles, 1967, 46–53

white cloth woollen cloth woven from undyed wool, and left in the undyed condition. White cloth was frequently exported onto the Continent between the 16th and 18th centuries in the early days of the hand weavers; the West Country in particular built up a big trade with the Low Countries.

white coal (or cordwood, chopwood) small wood stripped of its bark which has been dried on an ELLING HEARTH and which was a popular fuel for ORE HEARTHS in the 18th century, particularly for lead smelting.

white lead, *see* CERUSSITE

white metal, *see* BABBIT METAL

white walnut, *see* BUTTERNUT

whitster another name for a bleacher, i.e. one who makes cloth white.

whorl, *see* WHARF (1)

wild-fire, *see* FIREDAMP

Willans centre valve steam engine a high-speed, single-acting compound steam engine with centrally placed piston valves controlling the distribution of steam. Invented by Peter William Willans (1851–92) of Rugby, this novel design engine was made in a series of sizes up to 2,500 hp in inverted vertical configuration. Its principal use was driving generating equipment in the early electrical power stations until it was superseded by STEAM TURBINES at the turn of the century. Some Willans engines were used in textile mills.

Fig. 87 shows a cross-section through a twin, double-expansion Willans engine. High-pressure steam enters the top cylinder via admission ports in the wall of the hollow cast-iron piston rod or trunk when it is at the top of its stroke. A line of piston valves inside the trunk is driven from an ECCENTRIC on the crank pin, and moves up and down covering and uncovering various PORTS to admit steam into the cylinders and exhaust it from the upper to the lower side of each piston via the annular spaces in the trunk. A space below each piston is a receiver, and after expanding and doing work in the top high pressure cylinder, the steam enters the receiver below at a lower pressure. The low pressure cylinder draws its steam from this receiver and after further expansion the steam enters the bottom receiver and finally exhausts out to atmosphere or a condenser. The engine is thus single-acting only, the working stroke being downwards. Air trapped in a chamber below the low-pressure cylinder is compressed during the return upwards stroke to prevent any upward pull on the bearings due to inertia of the moving parts. The long piston and cylinder walls of the air unit act as crosshead and guide for the two in-line steam cylinders above.

Willans engines were economical in steam consumption and had a high thermal efficiency. They were made single-acting only with short stroke pistons in double, triple and quadruple expansion form, and with more than one set of cylinders arranged side-by-side in one frame, all driving one crank. Since they were single-acting they were larger than double-acting engines of equivalent power, but nevertheless occupied a small floor area, although tall.
'Peter William Willans, 1851–1892', *Newcomen Society Transactions* XXVII (1951–2)

willey or willy, *see* WILLOW

willow a machine for cleaning dirt out of raw cotton, wool, and similar materials. In the early days of cotton spinning, the preliminary opening up and cleaning of the cotton mass was known as willowing. This was a manual operation: the cotton was spread out on an inclined frame having a fine network of wire or some other material, and when it was beaten with willow switches, the dirt etc. fell through. To assist the dust removal, an air current was added later by means of a fan. Later still, the process was mechanized, and since an air stream is an important aid to the removal of dust, etc. the room in which this preliminary cleansing of the cotton was done became known as the BLOWING ROOM, a name which is still in use today.

The mechanized version of willowing is known as a willow, and was particularly used in the Oldham area of Lancashire, mainly to deal with waste cotton. In its simple form, a willow comprises a cylindrical chamber with rows of fixed spikes protruding inwards. A revolving drum with similar spikes projecting outwards is inside the chamber, and a quantity of cotton is introduced into the annular space between drum and chamber, to be dashed against the spikes. After a few seconds, the cotton is removed. Whilst in the willow it has been opened out, and the matted fibres loosened; any foreign matter will have fallen out through a grid in the base, and dust drawn away by an exhaust fan attached to the machine.

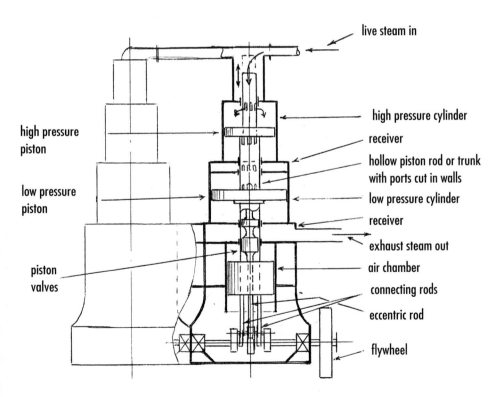

Fig. 87. Cross-section through a twin, double-expansion Willans centre valve steam engine

live steam in

high pressure cylinder

receiver

hollow piston rod or trunk with ports cut in walls

low pressure cylinder

receiver

exhaust steam out

air chamber

connecting rods

eccentric rod

flywheel

high pressure piston

low pressure piston

piston valves

A willow is also called a willey or willy, particularly in the woollen trade which also used such machines for cleaning wool. Before efficient exhaust fans were developed, operating willows was a particularly dirty and unhealthy job with dust and loose fibres floating about in the air. It was probably because of this that willows earned another name of 'devil'. A similar machine is used in the paper industry for removing dirt from rags, etc.

wince a winch for winding cloth through a dye vat.

winceyette a lightly napped fabric made from soft 'woolly' yarns such as that produced by CONDENSER COTTON SPINNING; the name is possibly a corruption of LINSEY-WOOLSEY. A kind of FLANNELETTE, winceyette is popular for making into nightclothes.

winch, *see* CRANES AND HOISTS

wind engine a simple wind driven water pump, also known as a windpump. These names are used to differentiate from conventional windmills. Wind engines once dotted the rural countryside of Britain, pumping water to farms and nearby domestic users. Some generated 12V electricity which was stored in batteries with a suitable cut-off device.

A wind engine comprised a latticework tower of light angle-iron (similar to a modern electricity pylon) with annular sails mounted on top which could rotate through 360° to face the wind as required. The blades of the sails were made from sheet metal, and usually numbered from 12 to 24 according to size. There were two designs. The simpler one had a flat FANTAIL projecting behind the sails whose function was to keep the sails facing into the wind: if the wind speed increased, the sails were turned away from facing it directly so that wind pressure on the blades was reduced, to prevent overspeeding. The other design had the fantail protruding to one side of the sails at approximately 90° to the sail shaft, and pivoted to the sail turntable; a brake acted on the sail shaft which was connected to the fantail. When the wind pressure on the fantail rose above a certain value, the fantail pivoted slightly and applied the brake to the sail shaft, releasing the brake when the wind returned to normal. The sail shaft drove a reciprocating pump via a vertical pump rod running down the centre of the tower, which delivered water from a well, spring, etc. into a storage tank.

Such devices were popular in remote or rural areas *c.*1850–1960, raising water for local use, and running for long periods unattended using free energy from the wind when it blew sufficiently strongly. When small petrol and

diesel engines became available they were often fitted so that water could be constantly pumped, and the gradual spread of public water and electricity supplies to rural districts brought about the demise of wind engines. Very few are left today.

Douglas, G. and Oglethorpe, M. 'A survey of Scottish windpumps', *Industrial Archaeology Review* VII (1984), 74–84
Major, K.J. 'The Rolt Memorial Lecture, 1990: Wind engines', *Industrial Archaeology Review* XIV (1991), 55–63

winding drum a large diameter drum around which a rope for raising coal etc. from deep mines is wound. The drum is rotated by the WINDING ENGINE, and since the latter has to start against the dead weight of the load to be lifted, plus the weight of the long rope, every time winding commences, specially shaped drums were devised to ease the starting effort.

As early as in Watt's day, double-spiral balancing drums were in use to compensate for the weight of the rope when winding from deep mines. On a conical drum the rope is wound first onto the small diameter so that minimum torque is needed to commence the wind. The rope climbs up a spiral groove which assists the acceleration of the cage up the shaft until the large diameter is reached, onto which the remaining rope is wound. At some mines two cages were wound up from one shaft, with timber conductors running down the shaft centre to guide each cage. Two drums were then necessary, and if of conical shape they were arranged side-by-side with the small diameters together at the centre. Such configurations were known as diabolo drums, a name taken from the child's spinning toy popular in late Victorian times, and also as equalizer cones. BI-CYLINDRO-CONICAL DRUMS were also made, as well as stepped drums where one engine wound from two adjacent shafts but of different depths, the larger drum winding from the deeper pit. In each case a brake operated on the periphery of the drum, to control speed and to hold the drum stationary during loading and unloading of the mine cage or kibble. In Cornish mines, a winding drum was known as a cage.

Flat wire ropes, invented by John Curr of Sheffield (patent nos. 2270, 1798 and 3711, 1813), were popular for a while: they were wound up upon themselves like a clock spring, with radial arms on the drum to act as guides keeping the coils of rope in their correct position as winding proceeded. This method of winding also assisted the winding engine, since at the start of the lift the rope wound onto the small diameter, and minimum torque was needed.

winding engine engines for directly winding up coal, etc. from deep mines, which made their first appearance in the late 18th century. The first steam driven winding engine was at Walker colliery, Tyneside in 1784, and a particular type of engine was developed in this area, known as the DURHAM WINDER. Before the introduction of direct winding, BEAM ENGINES pumping water onto waterwheels to produce rotation of a rope drum had been used at some sites. As engine design improved and mines got deeper, special types of engine driving WINDING DRUMS were developed. The duty is severe: a winding engine has to start against the dead weight of the mine cage and its contents, plus the not inconsiderable weight of the long rope itself; rapid acceleration to reduce winding time to a minimum, together with a slow landing speed and accurate positioning, are essential. Steam-operated brakes are usually fitted, and the engine is continually reversing and must be completely reliable.

Up until the mid-19th century some coal winding engines in Lancashire operated an endless iron chain through a clutch, the loaded coal tubs being hooked on one ascending loop of the chain, and empties lowered to the shaft bottom on the descending side. In this case the engine ran continuously in the same direction. However, once shaft depths became greater than *c.*120–150 yd, the chains tended to break under the combined weight of the loaded tubs and their own weight, and were abandoned in favour of metal ropes. Some mines had two upcast shafts side-by-side, and the winding engine operated two ropes, one rope winding up as the other went down the other shaft. This tended to balance the load on the engine to some extent, and speeded up the winding operation.

Many winding engines were twin-cylinder using high pressure steam in both cylinders, with cranks set at right angles to avoid DEAD CENTRES. Compound engines (*see* COMPOUNDING (1)) were also used, and winders of considerable power were built, some over 3,000 hp.

Hill, A. *Single Cylinder Vertical Lever Type Winding Engines as Used in the North of England*, De Archaeologische Pers., 1986

winding hole a turning point on a canal for full-length boats. It may take the form of a short side branch off the canal, opposite the towpath, into which the boat can be led and backed out to face the other way, i.e. similar to a reversing bay on a road. An alternative name is a turning pound, which may be a local widening of a canal pound sufficient to enable a boat to turn.

winding on the action in spinning when yarn is wound onto a bobbin to form a COP. In hand spinning, this is achieved by the spinner holding the yarn at right angles to the axis of the revolving spindle. In machine spun yarn, winding on is carried out automatically as spinning proceeds, even layers being wound on either by arranging for the bobbin to move up and down the spindle, or by leading the yarn up and down the revolving bobbin which stays in the same position.

winding rope, *see* WINDING DRUM, WINDING ENGINE

windle 1. (or winnel) a dialect word for a basket used as a measure, usually holding about 3 BUSHELS, and used for transporting grain, limestone, etc. The word comes from the Old English 'windel'. 2. an old dialect word for a yarn spindle.

windmill a mill driven by wind power for grinding corn or working machinery. Windmills date from early times and were among the first machines to use a natural source of power. They are sited in places where there is normally a wind blowing to turn their SAILS, which in the case of corn mills drive grindstones through a system of gears. Because the wind does not always blow from the same direction, the sails have to be turned round to face into it when there is a change. A wind speed of about 6 mph is usually enough to move the sails, but there are periods when a windmill cannot work because of insufficient wind. On the other hand, the sails have to be prevented from racing round in high winds and gales, and damaging the machinery and the mill itself. Most mills have four sails rotating anticlockwise when viewed from outside the mill, but mills with up to eight sails have been built. There are three types of windmill: the POST MILL, TOWER MILL, and SMOCK MILL. Turning the sails into the wind was done manually at first, but was made automatic by the invention of the FANTAIL in 1745. The speed of the sails was controlled by a number of inventions, all based on automatically reducing their surface area as wind strength increased: *see* SPRING SAIL, REEFING SAIL, and PATENT SAIL.

Windmills were still numerous until the commencement of the First World War, when, as with WATERMILLS, steam driven ROLLER MILLING made them obsolete.

Freese, S. *Windmills and Millwrighting*, Cambridge University Press, 1957

Major, J.K. and Watts, M. *Victorian and Edwardian Windmills and Watermills*, Batsford, 1977

Reynolds, J. *Windmills and Watermills*, Hugh Evelyn, 1970

Wailes, R. *The English Windmill*, Routledge and Kegan Paul, 1954

windpump, *see* WIND ENGINE

windrow (or winrow) a stack of peat or wood intended for converting into CHARCOAL, laid out for drying by the action of the wind.

windshaft the main shaft in a WINDMILL which carries the sails and the brake wheel and transmits the drive to the mill machinery. Windshafts were made from timber before cast iron became available, and restricted the number of sails to four since a greater number weakened it too much; cast-iron windshafts permitted windmills to be made with multi-sails. Windshafts were usually inclined about 10° from the horizontal so that the sweep of the sails could clear the tapering mill body.

winze a shaft underground in a mine, connecting two or more different levels of working, and sunk for access, ventilation, or to prospect for or prove a vein, etc. A winze does not come out to the surface. It is an alternative to the words wind or winds, or may be a variation of winch, and is of Cornish origin. Other names are drop shaft and staple shaft, the latter being a north-east mining term.

wiper, *see* CAM

wiper loom (or tappet loom) an early POWER LOOM in which the shedding actions of the machine were controlled by tappets or 'wipers', which received their motion from a rotating cam shaft positioned at one side of the loom. Introduced in 1796 by Robert Miller of Glasgow (patent no. 2122), the early models could only weave fairly plain cloths. William Horrocks of Stockport improved wiper looms by adding a separate cam shaft to operate the SLEY movement.

wire a flexible rod or strand of metal. Manufacturing wire from several metals such as iron, copper, brass, etc. has a long history. The two main methods of making wire are either by drawing rods through dies to reduce the diameter, or by passing rods through grooves in rolls, with each successive groove reducing the cross-sectional area.

Chain mail armour was made from wire in the Middle Ages. A water-powered wire works was set up at Tintern, Mon., in 1566–7 where small iron bars were first 'strained' (made thinner and longer by rolling), drawn through WORTLES or draw plates down to the required diameter, and finally annealed. The MINERAL AND BATTERY WORKS also made copper wire in the 16th century. Early uses of wire included PIN AND NEEDLE MANUFACTURE, and the making of CARD CLOTH for wool. Drawn pinion wire in brass and steel, with longitudinal ridges or channels which formed gear wheels when the wire was cut into disks or short pieces, was used in early clock and watch manufacture; this specialized form of shaped wire originated in the Prescot and Liverpool areas in the 18th century where WATCHMAKING was concentrated. Smooth round wire had, and still has, many uses, particularly for machine-made nails. Wire was also drawn to a triangular cross-section for specialized applications.

The making of wire ropes for mine shaft winding and for suspension bridges was a 19th-century development. A wire suspension road bridge was first built by Marc Seguin in France in 1825. What became known as the Belgian train was developed by George Bedson (1820–84) in 1862 for producing wire by the rolling process. This comprised a sequence of horizontal and vertical grooved rolls, which gradually reduced square sectioned bars into circular wire in a continuous process as the material passed through each pair of rolls. High tensile steel wire was made by J. Horsfall in 1854 in a process involving passing a wire through a heating furnace, a quenching bath, and a tempering bath of molten lead, in a continuous sequence.

The demand for copper wire increased with the introduction of the TELEGRAPH from 1860, and greatly again for electrical work from the 1880s.

wiredrawing 1. reducing pressure in a fluid by passing it through a small opening. This is also called throttling, and the method is used to control a steam engine by a GOVERNOR throttling the steam pressure at the inlet valve by partial closure. **2.** manufacturing WIRE from rod by pulling it through small holes in a die block made of harder material. Each hole drawn through is slightly smaller than the previous one, until the final diameter of the wire is reached. Iron wire was made in the 17th century by being drawn through hardened steel WORTLES using a water-powered crank to exert the pulling effort. Pincers, attached to the crank by a long rod, took a fresh grip on the wire at each revolution of the crank, pulling the wire through in a series of short pulls. Wire may be drawn cold or hot, and annealed afterwards if required.

wisket an old Derbyshire lead mining term for a strongly made wooden box with a carrying handle, used for carrying lead ore.

witch an old name for a DOBBY, probably so named because the action of the device in producing figured cloth was likened to sorcery or witchcraft. A witch loom was a hand loom fitted with a simple dobby.

witherite a form of barium carbonate, originally called *terra poderosa*, discovered about 1784 by a Dr Withering in the Anglezarke lead mines, near Bolton, Lancs. It is usually associated with galena, the lead ore, and is also found in the lead deposits on Alston Moor, Cumberland. Witherite took its name from its discoverer, and was used by Josiah Wedgwood (1730–95) for glazing pottery. It was also exported to Germany and used in the German pottery industry.

woad (or pastel) a blue dyestuff obtained from the root and leaves of the plant *Isatis tinctoria*. Woad is a substantive dye needing no mordant, and was used in Britain from ancient times. The plant was cultivated for this purpose, but after the 14th century supplies were augmented by imports from France where it was grown around Toulouse. By about the late 16th century, woad was being replaced by imported INDIGO which has a greater colouring power. Woad was used with MADDER to make black, or with WELD to make various shades of green.

wobbler a kind of universal joint interposed between the drive and the rolls in a metal ROLLING MILL, to allow the rolls to rise or fall as the metal being rolled passes between them.

wolfram (or wolframite, wolframium) a steely, grey-to-white, heavy, brittle metallic ore, with a high melting point. It is usually associated with tin stone, and is difficult to separate from it since it has a similar specific gravity. A ferrous tungstate, it is the main source of tungsten metal, which is obtained by boiling wolfram with hydrochloric acid, followed by intensive heating with carbon. Deposits are found in Cornwall. Tungsten is used for hardening steel, and for electric lamp filaments. *See also* OXLAND PROCESS.

wood ash, *see* POTASH PITS

wood faller, *see* FULLING STOCKS

woodworking machinery tools which use power for shaping wood introduced in the 18th century. The earliest 'machines' for shaping wood, such as the pole and treadle lathe and the bow drill, were worked by hand and foot. A water-powered circular saw was invented by Walter Taylor some time before 1780. Samuel Bentham (1757–1831) invented machines for planing, rebating, and mortising window sashes in 1793 (patent no. 1951), and the first rotary wood planer was invented by Joseph Bramah (1749–1814) in 1802 (patent no. 2652). The classic example of early power driven woodworking machinery was for the mass production of ships' blocks, from the tough woods elm and vignum vitae, at the naval dockyard, Portsmouth. Forty-four different machines were designed by Marc Isambard Brunel (1796–1849), made by Henry Maudslay

(1771–1831) and installed between 1801 and 1808. Output of blocks was greatly increased with a much reduced labour force. Tongue and grooved wooden floorboards were being mass produced by the 1830s, and the mass production of furniture commenced about this time. In many respects, the development of woodworking machinery mirrored that of metal MACHINE TOOLS, which were similar in design.

Cooper, Carolyn. 'The production line at Portsmouth Block Mill', *Industrial Archaeology Review* VI (1981), 28–44

Gilbert, K.R. *The Portsmouth Block-making Machinery*, HMSO, 1965

Goodman, W.L. *The History of Woodworking Tools*, Bell, 1964

Sims, W.L. *Two Hundred Years of History and Evolution of Woodworking Machinery*, Walders Press, 1986

woof an old name for WEFT, the thread thrown from side to side by the shuttle in the weaving process. Early spellings are owef, and wooft. The word woof was used more in poetry and literature than in the textile industry, as in Thomas Gray's poem *The Bard* (1757):

> Weave the warp, and weave the woof,
> The winding sheet of Edward's race:
> Give ample room and verge enough
> The characters of hell to trace.

wool the soft, hairy covering which grows on sheep, alpaca and similar animals, from which cloth is manufactured. The manufacture of woollen cloth from the fleeces of sheep was Britain's main industry long before the arrival of cotton. To supplement indigenous wool, more was imported from foreign sources, and later, from the old Colonies. Foreign wools were mainly Spanish and German, and colonial wool came from Australia (from 1810), South Africa (1816), and the East Indies (1834). The table shows wool imports in the 18th and 19th centuries.

	Wool imports (in 1,000 lb)	
Year	*Foreign sources*	*Colonial sources*
1766	1,926	–
1790	2,582	–
1820	9,653	122
1850	26,102	48,224
1857	44,522	82,868

Source: Baines (1875)

Wool grows in curly locks of varying lengths, called its staple, and the fibres of which it is made are elastic. When spun into a yarn, the fibres are stretched, and their curly nature helps to lock them together. When wet, the fibres tend to shrink back to their original length, and

Belvedere woollen mill and pond, Chalford, Glos.

FELTING takes place when pressure is applied, the fibres becoming looped and entangled. This property is exploited in the FULLING of woollen cloth to consolidate it and close up the weave. Wool is classified by its staple length: short fibres are CARDED for woollen cloth, and long fibres are COMBED for worsted.

The woollen industry was once carried on in Norfolk, the West Country, south Scotland, and the West Riding of Yorkshire, but gradually it became centred in Yorkshire, particularly around Bradford. Spinning and weaving of wool was once a domestic industry, working on the DOMESTIC SYSTEM. Mechanization of the processes in factories spread only slowly: not only was it technically difficult to adapt cotton machinery to handle woollen fibres, but also most woollen industrialists were stubbornly conservative. For example, POWER LOOMS were not in general use in woollen mills until after the 1850s, long after they were in use in the cotton industry.

Baines, E. *An Account of the Woollen Manufacture of England*, 1875; reprinted by David and Charles, 1970
Bischoff, J.A. *A Comprehensive History of the Woollen and Worstead Manufacture*, 1842; reprinted by Cass, 1968
Giles, C. and Goodall, I.R. *Yorkshire Textile Mills, 1770–1930*, HMSO, 1993
Jenkins, D.T. and Ponting, K.G. *The British Wool Textile Industry, 1770–1914*, 1982
Jenkins, D.T. *The West Riding Wool Textile Industry, 1770–1835*, Pasold Research Fund, 1975
Jenkins, J.G. (ed.) *The Wool Textile Industry in Great Britain*, Routledge and Kegan Paul, 1972
Power, Eileen. *The Medieval English Wool Trade*, 1941

wool combing, *see* COMBING

wooldriver (or wool stapler) a small scale Yorkshire wool merchant, who provided wool to users in the early days of the DOMESTIC SYSTEM. He bought wool from a sheep farmer to sell, either in a market, or direct to handloom spinners and weavers.

Woolf compound steam engine a BEAM STEAM ENGINE, reciprocating or rotative, which is powered by two steam cylinders side by side, i.e. compounded. The cylinders comprise a high pressure cylinder which takes steam from the boiler, and a larger low pressure cylinder which takes the exhaust steam from the high pressure cylinder. Both cylinders lie to one side of the central rocking point of the overhead beam, the reciprocating motion or the rotating crank lying on the opposite side. The high pressure cylinder is placed closest to the centre and therefore has a shorter stroke than the low pressure cylinder, since the arc swept by the beam is less at that point. This type of compounding was patented by Arthur Woolf (1766–1837) in 1804 (patent no. 2772). Woolf compound engines were built in large numbers, even as late as 1902; they were particularly suitable as pumping engines at waterworks on account of their slow speed and reliability.

Harris, T.R. *Arthur Woolf, The Cornish Engineer, 1766–1837*, Bradford Barton, 1966

woolmark a woollen merchant's personal identification seal or badge, marked on the cloth to show ownership.

wool stapler, *see* WOOLDRIVER

wool wall a dry stone wall, usually built with a south facing sloping side, on which raw wool or yarn could be spread out for natural drying in the sun. Used in the days of HANDLOOM WEAVERS in country areas.

work a measure of output sometimes used in 18th-century collieries. A work usually equalled 3 tons.

workers' houses, *see* BACK-TO-BACK HOUSES, INDUSTRIAL SETTLEMENTS

working class in a class-conscious society, that stratum of wage-earners, usually of low status, who provide the manual effort in a country's economy. At the commencement of the Industrial Revolution, the term was unknown, and the working population, who made up the bulk of the population, were called the 'labouring poor', or just the 'poor'. Although Frederick Engels' classic 1845 study was entitled *The Conditions of the Working Class in England*, he called wage-earners the 'proletariat'. In Victorian times, ordinary workmen and artisans were usually referred to as the 'manufacturing or operative classes' or the 'lower orders'.

Morris, R.J. *Class and Class Consciousness in the Industrial Revolution, 1780–1850*, Macmillan, 1979
Thompson, E.P. *The Making of the English Working Class*, Penguin, 1968

working tun, *see* SQUARE

'Workshop of the World' allusion to Britain made by Benjamin Disraeli (1804–81) in a speech he delivered to the House of Commons on 15 March 1838, when he said: 'The Continent will not suffer England to be the workshop of the world.' He was referring to the fact that the INDUSTRIAL REVOLUTION had made Britain the principal manufacturing nation in the then developed world. His phrase was quickly taken up, and is still widely quoted today.

Disraeli's statement was prophetic: Britain's industrious example was soon copied by other nations, particularly by Germany and the USA, both of which had their own industrial revolutions some three decades later than Britain's. The GREAT EXHIBITION OF 1851 acted as a spur to several countries to improve their own manufacturing industries and make them less reliant on British imports.

worm and wormwheel a pair of toothed gears which give a high reduction ratio between the input driving shaft and the output driven shaft, in a compact space. To achieve this, the shafts have to be at right angles to each other but not intersecting. The mating pair of gears comprises a smaller diameter gear – the worm – which has spiral teeth like a screw, which meshes with a larger diameter gear – the wormwheel – which has helical teeth, usually concave to increase the arc of contact with the worm. The worm usually drives the wormwheel; because of the friction involved between them, the reverse is not normally possible. This non-reversibility can be an advantage, since the wormwheel will remain stationary holding a load when the worm has ceased turning, and will not drive the worm in the opposite direction. This property is often used on winches and CRANES, lifting and lowering being done via a worm.

Worm gearing in a crude form dates from Roman times. It is used on machines where a high reduction ratio is required, combined with compactness. To obtain the same reduction by ordinary spur gearing, one wheel would have to be of considerable diameter, or compound gearing used. Worm gearing is also known as screw or spiral gearing.

worsted a well-twisted woollen yarn made from long STAPLE wool, which has been COMBED to lay the long fibres parallel (as opposed to carding, which is used on shorter fibred wool). Worsted yarn therefore has a compact construction and a smooth surface; woollen yarn, being made from shorter fibres, has a rougher, more hairy surface.

Worsted is particularly appropriate for suits and other garments. The name comes from that of the town near Norwich where Flemish settlers started up a weaving industry in the 12th century. (An old spelling of worsted is wolsted.) The industry eventually centred in the West Riding of Yorkshire, particularly in Bradford, which became the worsted capital of the world – earning itself the name 'Worstedopolis'. The name of the yarn gradually came to be given to the cloth from which it was made. Worsted cloth does not require FULLING, and although it is thinner than woollen cloth, it is just as warm. The pattern of the weave is much more visible than in woollen cloth because of its smoothness, and worsted has good draping properties, making it more suitable for clothing.

The revolution in worsted manufacture occurred about thirty years later than that of cotton. This was mainly the result of both a shortage of hand combers, which restricted cloth output, and the fact that worsted cloth was more expensive than wool, so that demand for it rose more slowly. Successful combing machines were not invented until the 1840s and 1850s. However, by the 1830s sufficient machine-combed TOPS were available to effect an increase in worsted output, and around this time POWER LOOMS were being introduced for weaving worsted cloth.

Bischoff, J.A. *A Comprehensive History of the Woollen and Worstead Manufacture*, 1842; reprinted by Cass, 1968
Jenkins, D.T. *The West Riding Wool Textile Industry, 1770–1835*, Pasold Research Fund, 1975

Worsted Committee an association formed about 1775 in Yorkshire to safeguard the interests of WORSTED masters by attempting to prevent fraudulent practices by domestic workers, such as embezzlement of material. The organization obtained parliamentary backing in the Worsted Act of 1777 for enforcing its measures, which comprised the appointment of inspectors of domestic workshops (paid for out of a drawback on soap duty); the setting of maximum times for the completion of work by employees; and the prohibition of the export of wool and woollen machinery.

The Committee also encouraged, by financial awards, inventors of machinery and processes which might improve the worsted industry, in exchange for complete knowledge of the invention. For example, the sum of £100 given to James Hartley of Gisburn, Yorks., in 1785 for an improved method of washing wool after he had revealed his process to them. The main income of the Committee was cut off when soap duty was abolished in 1853, but later, firms began annual subscriptions for the Committee to continue; however, by then worsted production was becoming factory-based, and most of the aims of the organization had changed.

wort the sweet, unfermented liquid made in a MASH TUN as an intermediate stage in the production of beer or whisky.

wortle a hard metal draw plate with a set of small holes of diminishing bore, through which iron WIRE is drawn in successive passes to reduce its diameter. Wortle plates date back to the days when chain armour was made, the iron wire from which it was built up being made with the aid of these plates. Wortle plates are also used in the manufacture of lead pipe. Two old spelling are wirtil and wurdle, the origin being obscure.

wright a suffix meaning workman, where the prefix indicates the trade involved, e.g. millwright, shipwright, wheelwright. 'Wright' comes from an old English word 'wryhta', a variation of the word work.

Millwrights were the first craftsmen 'engineers', the trade dating from the Middle Ages when millwrights constructed water and windmills. They were used to working in both timber and iron, being both carpenter and blacksmith. They designed structures and mechanisms based on empirical knowledge of the strength of materials and mechanics. A seven-year apprenticeship was normally served under a master millwright, and millwrights played an important role in the pioneer days of steam engines, textile mills, etc. In the days when corn was ground between millstones, the periodical recutting of the stones was frequently undertaken by millwrights. A Society of Millwrights was founded in London in 1805. Today there are few millwrights, and their work is mainly confined to the repair and restoration of windmills etc.

The wheelwright was a skilled craftsman who made wooden spoked wheels for coaches, carts and waggons, supplying coach builders with wheels correctly designed for the duty to be performed by the vehicle. Many early railway locomotives, such as Stephenson's *Rocket*, had oak spoked driving wheels. A wheelwright usually worked with a blacksmith, who supplied and shrunk on the iron tyres.

Examples of the millwright's skill may be examined in preserved water and windmills, and that of the wheelwright in old horse-drawn vehicles; some museums house a wheelwright's workshop complete with the special tools of his trade.

wrist plate that component on the mechanism controlling the action of CORLISS VALVES on steam engines. It rocks about its central pivot through limited arcs in a similar manner to the human wrist, and receives its motion from an ECCENTRIC keyed on the engine crankshaft.

wrought iron a malleable, almost pure iron obtained from pig iron by the puddling process from the 17th century onwards. Wrought iron (abbreviated to wrot iron or WI) literally means worked iron, and was known from ancient times, being the first form of iron made. Strong and tough, it has high tensile and good compressive strengths. It can easily be shaped when hot by blacksmithing methods, but cannot be hardened or tempered.

Wrought iron was first made by the direct method in a BLOOMERY, but after the introduction of BLAST FURNACES in the early 17th century the indirect method became the normal way. Cast-iron pigs from a blast furnace were melted in a PUDDLING FURNACE until almost all the carbon was burned off. The hot, pasty iron lump was removed and hammered into a BLOOM under a SHINGLING HAMMER; it then contained 1–3 per cent of ferrous silicate slag particles intimately mixed with the iron particles.

The bloom was then reheated and passed through a ROLLING MILL which elongated the slag particles in one direction only, giving the iron its characteristic 'grain'. Different grades of iron were made according to the amount of working it then received. One rolling produced the common grade known as Crown or merchant bar. By cutting up Crown bars, piling several lengths together (known as faggotting) and rolling them when hot to make one bar again, a better grade called Best iron or B iron was made. This operation was repeated with B iron pieces to give Best-Best iron (BB or Double Best), and repeating the operation yet again gave the finest and most expensive grade BBB or Treble Best. Each reheating and re-rolling improved the ductility and tensile strength of the iron.

The iron was finally rolled into bar iron, with round or square cross-sections, etc., or into flat plates, angle iron, etc., for use by blacksmiths, the engineering and structural industries, and other users of iron. The sizes of bars, plates, etc. were limited to the size of the blooms made in the puddling furnace. Larger pieces had to be made by riveting or welding smaller pieces together. Wrought iron was the principal construction material until the 19th century when mass-produced steel began replacing it, after which its use steadily declined. No wrought iron is made in Britain on a commercial scale today; the last firm working puddling furnaces closed down in 1986.

wuzzing hole a hole in a wall or gatepost, usually a stone wall, into which one end of a short pole was placed; a basket containing wet washed yarn was hung from the free end of the pole. This end was swung round and round with a quick motion to expel water from the contents of the basket by centrifugal action; in other words, this was a primitive spin drier. Wuzzing was carried out outside, before weaving the yarn into cloth. The word is probably of Yorkshire origin, and must be a variant of 'whizzing'. Examples of wuzzing holes cut into stone walls dating from the 16th century may still be found in areas of former domestic weaving.

Y

yard of tin the long post horn carried by guards on horse-drawn stage and mail coaches. This was blown at intervals to warn other travellers of the approach of the vehicle, and to warn ostlers to have a change of horses ready at the next staging inn. The horn was also blown to warn TURNPIKE keepers to open the turnpike gates in advance of a mail coach, which, by law, was not to be delayed unnecessarily.

yarn a general name for a filament of twisted fibres of various materials such as wool or cotton, or any thread-like structure which has been spun. Yarns differ in diameter and construction: their size is measured in COUNTS which is generally the number of units of length in a standard weight, different units being used for different materials. Yarn is sometimes known as thread; an archaic 17th-century word for yarn was clew, which had poetic use.

Yarn may be twisted with either a right-hand twist, known as a right twist or Z-TWIST, or with a left-hand twist, known as a left twist or S-TWIST. It may also be soft spun, which means there are fewer twists per inch length of yarn, or hard spun, meaning a greater number of twists per inch. Hard spun yarn is stronger than soft spun. WARP yarns are harder twisted than WEFT yarns. To make stronger yarns, two or more individual yarns may be twisted together in the operation known as DOUBLING: such yarns are known as MANIFOLD YARNS, and are made in a subsequent spinning process on doubling machines.

yeddle a northern dialect name for a hand-operated chain bucket pump (*see* CHAIN PUMP).

Yellow brazilwood, *see* FUSTIC

Z

zephyr a fine, lightweight cotton fabric, similar to a GINGHAM, with colours woven in, and used in Victorian times for ladies' dresses. It is also known as Berlin wool, and was supposed to have originated in Germany.

zinc a brittle metallic element which occurs naturally as zinc sulphide (or blende), zinc carbonate (or calamine), and zinc ferrite. Pure zinc was first produced in England by William Champion (1709–89) in Bristol, and he patented his process in 1738 (patent no. 564). Before this, zinc's existence passed unnoticed because of its low boiling point (906°C); when heated in wood fires, zinc ore simply boiled away. Zinc ore was known as 'counterfeit' at one time because it transformed copper into a golden coloured alloy. Since it is fairly stable in air, it has been used since the mid-19th century for protecting (or GALVANIZING) iron from rust, by dipping the iron into molten zinc. Zinc is also used as an ingredient in several alloys and in dry cells and batteries. It is poisonous, although it has medical uses in small quantities.
Cocks, E.J. and Walters, B. *A History of the Zinc Smelting Industry in Britain*, Harrap, 1968

Zollverein a 19th-century customs union between German states, led by Prussia in 1829. The removal of internal customs barriers between the many independent states and small principalities that made up Germany at that time heralded the start of the German industrial revolution. By 1871, a unified Germany had become a significant competitor to Britain in world markets, particularly in iron and steel, machinery, and heavy chemicals.

Z-twist right-hand or clockwise twist given to a yarn. When yarn is twisted or DOUBLED, it can be twisted either to the right or to the left: these directions are taken relative to the direction of rotation of the spindle or FLYER, being either clockwise or anticlockwise. In a simple spinning wheel, when the spindle turns clockwise viewed from its free end, the yarn twists into a spiral from left to right towards the spindle. This is called Z-twist, after the direction of the slope of the central portion of the letter Z. The reverse twist is known as S-TWIST. Z-twist is used for weak, crimpy wool as it tends to strengthen it.

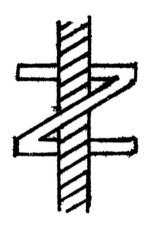

Z-twist

INDEXES TO SELECTED INDUSTRIES

The following pages comprise quick reference lists or indexes, arranged in alphabetical order, to the headwords of the most important industries or themes covered in this dictionary.

BLEACHING

atmospheric bleaching
Berthollet process
bleach croft
bleaching
bowk
bowking
buck (2) and (3)
bucking
buttermilk
chemick
chlorine
cliff
croft breaking
crofter
dashwheel
dephlogisticated marine acid
dephlogistic system
discharge bleaching
Eau de Javelle
grassing
grey cloth
grey room
hooking
hydrochloric acid
kier
lant
muriatic acid
oxymuriatic acid
pearl ash
plaiting
souring
sulphur house
tenter frame
whitster

BREWING

ale
back
brewing industry
couching
grist
hop
malthouse
malt mill
mash tun
oast house
racking
sparging
steeping
whisky manufacture
wort

CANALS AND CANAL BOATS

accommodation bridge
aqueduct
balance arm
basin
boat lift
bye-wash
canal
canal boat
canal mania
contour canal
cut (1)
distance posts
dry hurry
Duke's canal
flats (2)
flight of locks
flyboat
gabart
gauging dock
guillotine gate
horse pull-out
inclined plane
inverted syphon
knobstick (2)
legging
lengthman
lock
navigation
packet

CLOTH NAMES

mockado
mohair
moiré
moleskin
mousseline
mull
mungo
muslin
nankeen
new draperies
noyal
orleans cloth
paduasoy
penistone
perpetuana
pilot-cloth
plush
poplin
prunella
quilting
ramie
rash
raven-duck
romal
russel
Russell cord
russet
sagathy
sateen
satin
say
seersucker
serge
shalloon
shantung
shoddy
stammet
stammin
tabby
taffeta
tammie
tanjib
tapestry
terry pile
thickset
tiffany
tobine
toilonet
tulle
tweed
twill
union cloth
velveret
velvet
velveteen
vicuna
voile
wadmol

winceyette
zephyr

COAL MINING

adit
agent
air shaft
banksman
basset
bell pit (1)
bi-cylindro-conical drum
bituminous coal
black damp
brattice
chartermaster
Clanny lamp
coal
coal bearer
coal measures
corf
dataller
Davy lamp
day pit
day's eye
dialing
dip
dog belt
downcast shaft
drawer (1)
drift mine
Durham winder
firedamp
fireman
flint mill (2)
footrid
Freeminer
furnace pit
gallery
'Geordie' lamp
gin (1)
goaf
goffan
grieve
gripper truck
hade
headgear
heapstead
hurry (2)
ladder pit
leitnagel Hund
level (1)
longwall
mine
mine cage
mine haulage steam engine
mine safety hook
mine shaft

CORN MILLING (Watermills, Windmills and Roller Mills)

DYES AND DYEING

copperas
corkir
cudbear
cutch
dyes and dyeing
dye-woods
fustic
gall nuts
green vitriol
henna
indigo
kermes
logwood
madder
mordant
murex
Persian berries
picric acid
quercitron
safflower
saffron
sanderswood
sapan wood
sorrel
sumac
Turkey red
turmeric
valonia
walnut
weld (1)
wince
woad

GLASS MAKING

annealing
barilla
bit-gatherer
calcar
chair (2)
crown glass
cullet
cylinder glass
footmaker
foundry
frit
gaffer
glass
glass cone
glasswort
glory hole
kinney
lehr
lunette
marmre
parison
plate glass
pontil

servitor
taker-in
teaser

HYDRAULICS

accumulator (1)
cup leather
hat leather
head
hydraulic engine
hydraulic power
hydraulic press
hydraulic ram
intensifier
jigger (1)
ram
U-leather

INDUSTRIAL ARCHAEOLOGY

Association for Industrial Archaeology
CADW
English Heritage
fieldwork in industrial archaeology
grid reference
Historic Scotland
industrial archaeology
information sources
IRIS
listed building
Monuments Protection Programme
National Archaeological Record
National Buildings Record
National Monuments Record
National Record of Industrial Monuments
Royal Commissions on Historical Monuments
Sites and Monuments Record

IRON AND STEEL MANUFACTURE

acid lining
acid steel
after blow
ancony
annealing
ball
ball furnace
bar iron
bar mill
basic lining
basic steel
Bessemer steel
billet
blast furnace
blast pipe (2)
blister steel
bloom (1) and (2)

KNITTING

bagman (2)
bearded needle
course
Derby rib frame
framework knitting
fully fashioned
hosiery
jack (2)
knitting
latch needle
presser
rack rent
sinker (1)
slurcock
slurgall
stockinger
stocking frame
tickler
wale
warp knitting
weft knitting

LACE MAKING

bobbin (2) and (3)
bobbin lace
lace
lace making
lace runner
Luddites
mechlin lace
needlepoint lace
net
'Old Loughborough'
pusher lace
secondhand mistress
tickler
twist hand

LEGISLATION

Acts of Parliament
Althorp's Act
Anti-Corn Law League
apprentice
Artificers, Statute of
burial in wool
child labour
coal and wine tax posts
Combination Laws
Corn Laws
enclosure of land
Factory Act 1833
Factory Acts
Factory Law Amendment Association
General Enclosure Act
Iron Act
Locomotive and Highways Act 1865

Manchester Act 1736
mine shaft
Navigation Acts
patent
Settlement, Law of
Six Acts of 1819
'Tax on knowledge'
Ten Hours Act 1847
trade unions

LOCOMOTIVES

adhesive force
Allan straight link motion
angle of advance
anti-priming pipe
Belpaire firebox
blast pipe (1)
boiler
Bourdon gauge
coupling rod
cut-off (1)
drag link
D valve
eccentric
expansion link
expansive working
gab valve gear
Gooch link motion
Hackworth radial valve gear
hammer blow
injector
Joy valve gear
lap (1)
lead (2)
locomotive
loose eccentric valve gear
Meyer variable expansion valve
notching up
piston valve
radial valve gear
Rainhill trials
regulator valve
return crank
reversing gear
roundhouse (2)
safety valve
slide valve
steam
Stephenson link motion
stuffing box
tractive effort
valve gear
Walschaert valve gear
water level gauge

MACHINE TOOLS

band saw
block
boring machine
circular saw
clapper box
drilling machine
engineering industry
gear cutting machine
grinding machine
headstock (2)
hydraulic press
jim crow
lathe (1)
machine tools
Men of Maudslay's
milling machine
planing machine
quick return mechanism
shaping machine
shingling hammer
slotting machine
steam hammer
woodworking machinery

NON-FERROUS METALS MINING
(*see also* Ore Dressing)

adit
adventurer
bal
balance bob
bargain
Barmaster
Barmote
basset
bellanding
bell pit (1)
bent
bing (1)
bouse
brakesman
brazen dish
bunning
captain
coe
copper (1)
'Copper King'
costeaning
'Cousin Jack'
dip
drum house
dyke (1)
freeing dish
gad (2)
gale
gangue
gin (1)
ginging

goffan
groove
groove ore
gugg
hade
halvans (1) and (2)
hillocking
hoppit
huel
'in fork'
jack roller
lead (1)
liberty
lime blasting
lode (1)
London Lead Company
man engine
meer
Mineral and Battery Works, Company of
Mines Royal
mining industry
nicking
old man workings
ore
outcrop
pipe
pitwork
plug and feathers
plug rod
pump rods
rake (1)
rider (2)
safety fuse
scrin
self-open
sett (1)
shammelling
sollar (1) and (2)
sough
stannary
stockwork
stope
stope and feather
stow
streaming
strike
stulls
swallet
tin
toadstone
trewerne
tributer
turn
tutwork
tye
vein
vug
wem

bevel gears
cam
clutch
cog
cog and rung gin
cone pulley drive
countershaft
coupling
crossed belt
crown wheel (2)
dog clutch
dolly wheel
eccentric
epicyclic gear
fast and loose pulleys
flat rods
footstep bearing
gearing
helical gears
Hooke's joint
idler
jockey pulley
journal
lantern gear
lineshafting
mitre wheel
mortice wheel
Oldham coupling
open belt
pinion (1)
plummer block
ratchet
roller chain
rope driving
rope race
second motion shaft
shaft (1)
sheave (1)
slack belt drive
speed cone
sprocket
spur wheel
strap (1)
swash plate
transmission of power
wall box
wayshaft
worm and wormwheel

PRIME MOVERS (*see also* Steam Engine Plant, Water Power)

animal power
Barker's mill
Carnot cycle
common engine
compression ignition engine
Diesel engine

disk engine
donkey engine
engine
four stroke cycle
gas engine
gas turbine
horse mill
horsepower
hot air engine
hydraulic engine
internal combustion engine
locomotive
oil engine
Otto cycle
petrol engine
steam engine
steam turbine
stroke
turbine
two stroke cycle
water-balance engine
water turbine
waterwheel
windmill
wind engine

RAILWAYS (*see also* Locomotives)

adhesive force
amalgamation of railways
atmospheric railway
bogie
chair (1)
cog railway
cut-off (2)
deposited plans
edge rails
fish plate
fixed engine
frog
gauge
gauntlet track
granite railway
hammer blow
hybrid railway
inclined plane
line
mineral line
monorail
narrow gauge railway
parliamentary fare
parliamentary fence
permanent way
plateway
Quakers' line
railcar
rail coach
rails

railway
railway clearing house
'Railway King'
railway mania
'Railways, Father of English'
railway time
Rainhill trials
ruling gradient
sleeper (1)
stone block sleepers
train shed
turn-out (1)
undertaker (1)
undulating line
waggonway

ROADS AND ROAD USERS

badger
bagman (1)
causeway
causey stones
cock horses
'Colossus of Roads'
drag (1) and (2)
drovers' roads
Gal
higgler
huckster
jagging
mail coach
packhorse
packway
parish road
posting
post road
raker
Rebecca Riots
roads
ruling gradient
scotchman
sett (2) and (3)
shillibeer
stagecoach
steam carriage
steamer
stoop (1)
toll
traction engine
tram (2)
turnpike trusts
Wade roads
yard of tin

SOCIAL MATTERS (*see also* Legislation)

Althorp's Act

Anti-Corn Law League
apprentice
apprentice houses
back-to-back houses
Blanketeers
burial in wool
Chartist
child labour
club houses
Combination Laws
Corn Laws
Cotton Famine
'Cousin Jack'
'Dark Satanic Mills'
domestic system
enclosure of land
Factory Act 1833
Factory Acts
'Factory King'
factory system
Freehold Land Society
Guilds
half-timer
hands
Hungry Forties
Industrial Revolution
industrial settlements
journeyman
kebbing
knobstick (1)
laithe house
'Little Ireland'
loomshop
Luddites
Mechanics' Institutes
mill time
oakum
Peterloo
Plug riots
rack rent
Rebecca Riots
Rochdale pioneers
room and power
Settlement, Law of
Six Acts of 1819
slave trade
Speenhamland System
sweatshop
'tax on knowledge'
Ten Hours Act 1847
Tolpuddle Martyrs
Tommy shop
trade tokens
trade union
triangular trade
truck system
turn-out (2)
working class

STEAM BOILERS

anti-priming pipe
boiler
Bourdon gauge
bridge (2)
chimney
condensate
Cornish boiler
damper
economizer
'elephant' boiler
Fairbairn–Beeley boiler
Field boiler
firetube boiler
flash boiler
fusible plug
Galloway tube
haystack boiler
hotwell
injector
Lancashire boiler
lodge
mechanical stoker
multi-tubular boiler
pressure
priming (1)
safety valve
Scotch boiler
shell boiler
steam
superheat
vertical boiler
waggon boiler
water level gauge
watertube boiler

STEAM ENGINE PLANT

A-frame steam engine
air pump
angle of advance
assistant cylinder
atmospheric engine
back pressure
barring engine
beam (1)
beam arch
beam loft
beam steam engine
bedplate
bob wall
Bull engine
buoy controller
cataract controller
catchwing
centrifugal governor
clearance

'come into the house'
common engine
compensating motion
compounding (1)
condenser (1)
condensing steam engine
connecting rod
contra-flow steam engine
Corliss valve
Cornish engine
Cornish valve
coupling rod
crank
cross compound
crosshead
cushioning
cut-off (1)
cut-off governing
cylinder (1)
dead centre
direct-acting engine
double-acting
driving floor
drop valve
duty
D valve
eduction pipe
engine indicator
'Engine Reporter'
entablature
equal beam
equilibrium ring
equilibrium valve
expansive working
extraction engine
fire engine
flywheel
grasshopper engine
Heslop steam engine
horizontal steam engine
horsepower
house built
hydraulic lock
hypocycloid steam engine
indicator diagram
inverted vertical steam engine
jacketing
jet condenser
junk ring
lap (2)
lead (2)
lever wall
locomobile steam engine
Manhatten engine
McNaughting
medium piston
Meyer variable expansion valve
'Miners' Friend'

STRUCTURES

TEXTILE FINISHING PROCESSES

TEXTILE PREPARATION

WATER POWER (Waterwheels, Water Turbines, etc.)

WEAVING

WOODLAND INDUSTRIES

YARN PRODUCTION

GENERAL BIBLIOGRAPHY

1. OVERVIEWS OF INDUSTRIAL ARCHAEOLOGY

Ashton, T.S. *The Industrial Revolution 1760–1830*, Oxford University Press, 1948
Bracegirdle, B. *The Archaeology of the Industrial Revolution*, Heinemann, 1973
Briggs, Asa. *Ironbridge to Crystal Palace*, Thames and Hudson, 1979
Buchanan, R.A. *Industrial Archaeology in Britain*, Penguin, 1972 and 1982
Butt, J. and Donnachie, I. *Industrial Archaeology in the British Isles*, Paul Elek, 1979
Chapman, S.D. *The Early Factory Masters*, David and Charles, 1967
Cossons, N. *The BP Book of Industrial Archaeology*, 3rd edn, David and Charles, 1993
Hudson, K. *Exploring our Industrial Past*, Hodder and Stoughton, 1975
——. *Industrial Archaeology: An Introduction*, John Baker, 1963
Major, K.J. *Fieldwork in Industrial Archaeology*, Batsford, 1975
Mantoux, P. *The Industrial Revolution of the Eighteenth Century*, tr. M. Vernon, Methuen, 1961
Pannell, J.P.M. *The Techniques of Industrial Archaeology*, David and Charles, 1966
Raistrick, A. *Industrial Archaeology*, Granada/Paladin, 1973
Trinder, B. *The Making of the Industrial Landscape*, Dent, 1982

2. REGIONAL STUDIES

There are many regional studies of industrial archaeology in Britain. In particular, David and Charles have published a series entitled *The Industrial Archaeology of the British Isles*, edited by E.R.R. Green, which include gazetteers; and the Association for Industrial Archaeology (AIA) has published several regional gazetteer booklets in association with its annual conferences.

Alderton, D. and Booker, J. *The Batsford Guide to the Industrial Archaeology of East Anglia*, Batsford, 1980
Ashmore, O. *The Industrial Archaeology of Lancashire*, David and Charles, 1969
Austin, B., Cox, D., and Upton, J. (eds). *Sussex Industrial Archaeology: A Field Guide*, Phillimore, 1985
Bennett, John and Jan (eds). *A Guide to the Industrial Archaeology of Cumbria*, AIA, 1993
Booker, F. *The Industrial Archaeology of the Tamar Valley*, David and Charles, 1967
Briggs, C.S. (ed.), *Welsh Industrial Heritage: A Review*, CBA Research Report 79, 1992
Buchanan, R.A. and Cossons, N. *The Industrial Archaeology of the Bristol Region*, David and Charles, 1969
Butt, J. *The Industrial Archaeology of Scotland*, David and Charles, 1967
Crocket, Glenys (ed.), *A Guide to the Industrial Archaeology of Surrey*, AIA, 1993
Crompton, J. (ed.), *A Guide to the Industrial Archaeology of the West Midland Iron District*, AIA, 1991
Curnow, W.H. *The Industrial Archaeology of Cornwall*, Tor Mark Press, 1969
Davies, K. and Williams, C.J. *The Greenfield Valley*, 2nd edn, Holywell Council, 1986
Davies-Shiel, M. and Marshall, J.D. *The Industrial Archaeology of the Lake Counties*, David and Charles, 1969
Dodd, A.H. *The Industrial Revolution in North Wales*, University of Wales, 1950
Harris, Helen. *The Industrial Archaeology of Dartmoor*, David and Charles, 1968

——. *The Industrial Archaeology of the Peak District*, David and Charles, 1971
Hatcher, Jane. *The Industrial Archaeology of Yorkshire*, Phillimore, 1985
Hudson, K. *The Industrial Archaeology of Southern England*, David and Charles, 1965
Hughes, S. and Reynolds, P. (eds). *A Guide to the Industrial Archaeology of the Swansea Region*, AIA, 1988
Johnson, W.B. *The Industrial Archaeology of Hertfordshire*, David and Charles, 1970
Laws, P. *Industrial Archaeology in Bedfordshire*, Bedfordshire County Council, 1967
McCutcheon, W.A. *The Industrial Archaeology of Northern Ireland*, HMSO, 1981
Mills, S. *et al.* (eds). *A Guide to the Industrial Archaeology of Gloucestershire*, AIA, 1992
Minchinton, W.E. *Industrial Archaeology in Devon*, Dartington Trust, 1968
Moore, Pam. *The Industrial Heritage of Hampshire and the Isle of Wight*, Phillimore, 1988
Nixon, F. *The Industrial Archaeology of Derbyshire*, David and Charles, 1969
Palmer, Marilyn and Neaverson, P. *Industrial Landscapes of the East Midlands*, Phillimore, 1992
——. *Industry in the Landscape 1700–1900*, Routledge, 1994
Rees, D.M. *The Industrial Archaeology of South Wales*, David and Charles, 1975
——. *Mines, Mills and Furnaces: Industrial Archaeology in Wales*, National Museum of Wales, 1969
Riley, R. (ed.), *A Short Guide to the Industrial Archaeology of Hampshire*, AIA, 1994
Scottish Industrial Heritage Society, *Sixty Industrial Archaeological Sites in Scotland*, AIA, 1985
Sherlock, R. *The Industrial Archaeology of Staffordshire*, David and Charles, 1976
Singleton, F. *Industrial Revolution in Yorkshire*, Dalesman, 1970
Smith, D.M. *The Industrial Archaeology of the East Midlands*, David and Charles, 1965
Starmer, G. *Industrial Archaeology of Northamptonshire*, Northants Museum, 1970
Tann, Jennifer. *Industrial Archaeology: Gloucestershire Woollen Mills*, David and Charles, 1967
Thompson, W.J. (general ed.). *A Brief Guide to the Industrial Heritage of West Yorkshire*, AIA, 1989
Trinder, B. *The Industrial Revolution in Shropshire*, Phillimore, 1981
Wilson, A. *London's Industrial History*, David and Charles, 1967

3. INDUSTRIAL ARCHAEOLOGY OVERSEAS

Bruchey, S. *The Roots of American Growth, 1607–1861*, Hutchinson, 1965
Derry, T.K. *The Industrial Revolution in Scandinavia*, Allen and Unwin, 1979
Dunham, A.L. *The Industrial Revolution in France, 1815–48*, 1955
Habakkuk, H.J. *American and British Technology in the Nineteenth Century*, Cambridge University Press, 1962
Henderson, W.O. *Britain and Industrial Europe: 1750–1870*, Leicester University Press, 1954
——. *The Industrial Revolution on the Continent*, Cass, 1967
Hudson, K. *The Archaeology of Industry*, Bodley Head, 1976
——. *World Industrial Archaeology*, Cambridge University Press, 1979
Kirkby, R.S. *et al. Engineering in History: Industrial Archaeology in the USA*, McGraw-Hill, 1956
Landes, D.S. *The Unbound Prometheus: Technological Change in Western Europe from 1759*, David and Charles, 1969
Trinder, B. (ed.). *The Blackwell Encyclopedia of Industrial Archaeology*, Blackwell, 1993. (Entries from 31 countries in Europe, Australasia and English speaking areas of the New World.)

4. TRANSPORT

A series entitled *The Canals of the British Isles*, published by David and Charles under the editorship of Charles Hadfield, covers the major canals in Britain. A series called *The Forgotten Railways*, edited by J.A. Patmore, was published by David Thomas.

Anderson, P.H. *Forgotten Railways of the East Midlands*, David Thomas, 1973
Bird, A. *Roads and Vehicles*, Arrow Books, 1973
Boyes, J. and Russell, R. *Canals of Eastern England*, David and Charles, 1977
Christiansen, R. *Forgotten Railways of North and Mid Wales*, David Thomas, 1984
——. *Forgotten Railways of the West Midlands*, David Thomas, 1985

Clew, K.R. *Kennet and Avon Canal*, David and Charles, 1968
——. *The Somersetshire Coal Canal and Railway*, David and Charles, 1970
Compton, H. *The Oxford Canal*, David and Charles
Copeland, J. *Roads and their Traffic 1750–1850*, David and Charles, 1968
Davies, R. & Grant, M.D. *Forgotten Railways of the Chilterns and Cotswolds*, David Thomas, 1975
Delaney, Ruth. *The Grand Canal of Ireland*, David and Charles, 1973
Gagg, J. *Canals*, Bloomsbury Books, 1988
Hadfield, C. *British Canals: An Illustrated History*, Readers Union, 1952
——. *Canals of the East Midlands including part of London*, David and Charles, 1966
——. *Canals of South and South-East England*, David and Charles, 1969
——. *Canals of South-West England*, David and Charles, 1967
——. *Canals of South Wales and the Border*, David and Charles, 1967
——. *Canals of the West Midlands*, David and Charles, 1969
——. *Canals of Yorkshire and North-East England*, 2 vols, David and Charles, 1972 and 1973
—— and Biddle, G. *Canals of North-West England*, 2 vols, David and Charles, 1970
—— and Norris, J. *Waterways to Stratford*, David and Charles, 1968
Hoole, K. *Forgotten Railways of North-East England*, David Thomas, 1973
Houshold, H. *The Thames and Severn Canal*, David and Charles, 1969
Jackson, A.A. *The Railway Dictionary: An A–Z of Railway Terminology*, Alan Sutton Publishing, 1992
Joby, R.S. *Forgotten Railways of East Anglia*, David Thomas, 1977
Lewis, M.J.T. *Early Wooden Railways*, Routledge and Kegan Paul, 1970
Lindsay, Jean. *Canals of Scotland*, David and Charles, 1968
Marshall, J. *Forgotten Railways of North-West England*, David Thomas, 1981
——. *The Guinness Book of Rail Facts and Feats*, Guinness Superlatives, 1975
McCutcheon, W.A. *Canals of the North of Ireland*, David and Charles, 1965
MacDermot, E.T. *History of the Great Western Railway*, revised by C.R. Clinker, Ian Allen, 1964
Page, J. *Forgotten Railways of South Wales*, David Thomas, 1979
Pawson, C.E. *Transport and Economy: Turnpike Roads of the Eighteenth Century*, Academic Press, 1977
Ransom, P.J.G. *The Archaeology of the Transport Revolution 1750–1850*, World's Work, 1984
——. *The Victorian Railway, and How it Evolved*, Heinemann, 1990
Stretton, C.E. *The Development of the Locomotive: A Popular History 1803–1896*, 1896; reprinted by Bracken Books, 1989
Thomas, J. *Forgotten Railways of Scotland*, David Thomas, 1976
Tomlinson, W.W. *Tomlinson's North Eastern Railway: its Rise and Development*, 1914; reprinted by David and Charles, 1967
Vine, P.A.L. *London's Lost Route to the Sea*, David and Charles, 1965
White, H.P. *The Forgotten Railways of Britain*, David Thomas, 1986
——. *Forgotten Railways of South-East England*, David Thomas, 1976
Willan, T.S. *River Navigation in England, 1600–1750*, Cass, 1964

5. BIOGRAPHIES

Boyson, Rhodes. *The Ashworth Cotton Enterprise: 1818–1890*, Clarendon Press, 1990
Dickinson, H.W. *Matthew Boulton*, Cambridge University Press, 1936
Fairbairn, W. *The Life of Sir William Fairbairn, Bart.* 1877; reprinted by David and Charles, 1970
Harris, T.R. *Arthur Woolf: The Cornish Engineer 1766–1837*, Barton Books, 1966
Marshall, J. *A Biographical Dictionary of Railway Engineers*, David and Charles, 1978
Raistrick, A. *Dynasty of Ironfounders: The Darbys and Coalbrookdale*, 1953; reprinted by David and Charles, 1970
Reader, W.J. *Macadam: The McAdam Family and the Turnpike Roads 1798–1861*, Heinemann, 1980
Rimmer, W.G. *Marshalls of Leeds: Flax Spinners 1788–1886*, Cambridge University Press, 1960
Rolt, L.T.C. *Isambard Kingdom Brunel: A Biography*, Penguin, 1970
——. *James Watt*, Batsford, 1962
Skeat, W.O. *George Stephenson: The Engineer and his Letters*, Institution of Mechanical Engineers, 1973